Gilmanton
New Hampshire

Vital Records
1887-2001

Richard P. Roberts

HERITAGE BOOKS
2011

HERITAGE BOOKS
AN IMPRINT OF HERITAGE BOOKS, INC.

Books, CDs, and more—Worldwide

For our listing of thousands of titles see our website
at
www.HeritageBooks.com

Published 2011 by
HERITAGE BOOKS, INC.
Publishing Division
100 Railroad Ave. #104
Westminster, Maryland 21157

Copyright © 2002 Richard P. Roberts

All rights reserved. No part of this book may be reproduced or transmitted in any form or by any means, electronic or mechanical, including photocopying, recording or by any information storage and retrieval system without written permission from the author, except for the inclusion of brief quotations in a review.

International Standard Book Numbers
Paperbound: 978-0-7884-2161-7
Clothbound: 978-0-7884-8864-1

CONTENTS

Introduction	1
Births	4
Marriages	144
Bride's Names	314
Deaths	349

INTRODUCTION

Early vital records of many New Hampshire towns can be located either through the State's Vital Records Department or on microfilms made available through LDS Family History Centers. Some, however, have been lost or are inaccessible for various reasons. A valuable, but time-consuming, source of information for events occurring after 1886 is the vital statistics which are provided in a section of the Annual Town Reports of many New Hampshire towns. Many of these town reports have been collected at the New Hampshire State Library in Concord, as well as more local repositories.

The amount of information published in these Annual Town Reports varies tremendously over time. Early records are far more detailed and comprehensive. Recent records are rather cursory, but issues of confidentiality and sensitivity to the privacy of those residents still living offsets the lack of information of genealogical value.

While the information provided is often very helpful, one must remember that it is not fool-proof or universally accurate, nor is it the primary source or the actual vital record itself. The fact that much of the data is self-reported suggests that it is reliable. However, errors in transcription, spelling (particularly with respect to French-Canadian and European families), and printing often are obvious. In addition, there may be, for example, two children listed as the third child of a particular couple, or the mother's maiden name, age or place of birth differs or is inconsistent from one entry to another. It is also important to note that a birth, marriage or death may have been reported in another town although the subject resided in Gilmanton, or the entry may not have been made in the first place.

Despite these shortcomings, the information contained in the Annual Town Reports can be a valuable tool for the genealogist. Marriage and death records from the late 1800's often identify parents who were married nearly a century before. Finally, those families that have remained in Gilmanton or adjacent towns for several generations can be traced and connected to the present.

Births - To the extent the information is available, the entries in the list of births are given as follows: child's name; date of birth; place of birth (Gilmanton, unless otherwise indicated); the number of children in the family; father's name, place of birth, age and occupation; and the mother's maiden name, age and place of birth. As noted above, the amount of information in earlier records is substantially greater than in more recent years.

At times, the given names of many children are missing from the early reports. In this case, the sex of the child is given and they are listed chronologically at the beginning of the surname heading. On occasion, the child's name can be determined from marriage or death records, as well as secondary sources. These names are shown in brackets where available.

Marriages - To the extent the information is available, the entries in the list of marriages follow this format: groom's name; groom's residence; bride's name; brides residence; date of marriage; place of marriage (Gilmanton, unless otherwise indicated, although no place of marriage is given in recent years); H, signifying husband's information, and W, signifying wife's information, each in the following order - age, occupation, number of the marriage (if other than first), father's name, father's place of birth, father's occupation, mother's name, mother's place of birth, and mother's occupation. The name of the official conducting the marriage has been omitted but is generally provided in the original document. A separate listing of brides in alphabetical order follows this section in order to allow for cross-referencing.

Deaths - To the extent available, the entries in the list of deaths contain the following information: name of decedent; place of death; date of death; age at death; cause of death; marital status; birthplace; father's name; father's place of birth; mother's name; and mother's place of birth. Most of the entries listing a cause of death are self-explanatory.

Those entries marked with a "*" indicate that the person was brought to Gilmanton for burial. Those entries which are marked with "**" indicate that the dates of birth are taken from the Social Security Death Benefit Index.

In addition to general sources of local and regional history, additional information can be obtained from Daniel Lancaster's history of the town which covers the period through 1845 (available in reprint from Heritage Books), and William Badger's supplement to Lancaster's book, which covers the next thirty years.

BIRTHS

ACHORN,
Christopher William, b. 7/11/1984 in Rochester; Christopher B. Achorn and Tammy P. Fisher
Heidi Joan, b. 1/4/1987 in Rochester; Christopher B. Achorn and Tammy P. Fisher
Tyler John, b. 5/20/1989 in Rochester; Christopher B. Achorn and Tammy P. Fisher

ADEL,
Alexis Kathryn, b. 11/15/1987 in Gilmanton; Daniel J. A. Adel and Teri L. Bigelow
Connor William, b. 8/17/2000 in Gilmanton; Daniel Adel and Teri Adel
Daniel J. A., IV, b. 8/26/1980 in Gilmanton; Daniel J. A. Adel, III and Teri Lee Bigelow
Nicholas Ian, b. 1/15/1985 in Gilmanton; Daniel J. A. Adel, III and Teri Lee Bigelow
Raelyn Mary, b. 4/26/1972 in Laconia; Jack I. Adel (NH) and Mary E. Stockwell (NH)
Raquel Jackie, b. 2/27/1974 in Laconia; Jack I. Adel (NH) and Mary E. Stockwell (NH)

AINSWORTH,
Amanda Rose, b. 5/28/1986 in Laconia; Herbie R. Ainsworth and Betty M. Pike

ALEXANDER,
Joseph Howard, Jr., b. 11/28/1994 in Laconia; Joseph Howard Alexander, Sr. and Donna Marie Giguere
Michael Douglas, b. 5/30/1996 in Laconia; Joseph Howard Alexander, Sr. and Donna Marie Giguere

ALTON,
Winter Lee-Campbell, b. 3/8/2001 in Laconia; Guy Alton and Shawn Alton

AMELL,
Darrell L., Jr., b. 12/2/1955; first; Darrell L. Amell (shipper, VT) and Lois E. Sansouci (NJ)

AMIRAULT,
Alicia Dawn, b. 9/27/1983 in Laconia; Frank E. Amirault, Jr. and
  Patricia A. Inman
Deric Allen, b. 3/23/1987 in Laconia; Frank E. Amirault, Jr. and
  Patricia A. Inman
John Paul, b. 8/8/1985 in Laconia; Frank E. Amirault, Jr. and
  Patricia A. Inman
Shana Ann, b. 5/5/1981 in Laconia; Frank E. Amirault, Jr. and
  Patricia A. Inman

AMOUR,
David Milton, b. 6/9/1973 in Laconia; Milton Richard Amour (MA)
  and Vivian Clara Richard (RI)

ANDERSON,
Carly Elizabeth, b. 11/7/1995 in Concord; Carl E. Anderson and
  Krista A. Hast
Catherine Mary, b. 10/25/1991 in Concord; Carl E. Anderson and
  Krista A. Hast

ANDERSON-FERRE,
Aidan Christopher, b. 8/7/1990 in Concord; Daniel M. Anderson-
  Ferre and Katharine M. Ferre

ASHCROFT,
Mira Alice, b. 6/11/1930; first; William P. Ashcroft (farmer, Malden,
  MA) and Rosie DeSell (Canada)

AUBUT,
Aimee Elisabeth, b. 10/16/2000 in Laconia; Tracy Aubut and
  Michelle Aubut

AUSTIN,
Gerald Leonard, 3rd, b. 1/30/1962 in Laconia; first; Gerald Leonard
  Austin, Jr. (dyer, NH) and Rita Ann Morin (NH)
Mark Wilfred, b. 11/3/1967 in Laconia; second; William Charles
  Austin, Sr. (dyer, NH) and Carol Elizabeth Brown (NH)
Michael James, b. 6/23/1970 in Laconia; Gerald Leonard Austin
  and Rita Ann Morin (NH)
Morgan Leigh, b. 5/17/1997 in Laconia; William Charles Austin, Jr.
  and Rebecca Joan Caldon

Peter Francis, b. 6/29/1963 in Laconia; second; Gerald Leonard Austin, Jr. (dyer, NH) and Rita Ann Morin (NH)
Scott Allen, b. 7/21/1973 in Laconia; Gerald L. Austin (NH) and Rita Ann Morin (NH)
Tammy Alberta, b. 2/13/1969 in Laconia; William Charles Austin (NH) and Carol E. Brown (NH)
William Charles, Jr., b. 2/2/1966 in Laconia; first; William Charles Austin, Sr. (bleacher, NH) and Carol Elizabeth Brown (NH)

AVERY,
daughter [Mabel H.], b. 5/18/1913; second; George Avery (farmer, Strafford) and Carrie E. Paige (Laconia)
stillborn daughter, b. 9/2/1915; third; George H. Avery (farmer, Strafford) and Carrie Belle Paige (Laconia)
Annika June, b. 9/16/1996 in Dover; Richard John Avery, Jr. and Kerry Jean Fortier
Curtis Michael, b. 2/14/1988 in Concord; Donald R. Avery and Donna E. Dupont
Kyle Robert, b. 9/6/1985 in Concord; Donald R. Avery and Donna E. DuPont
Taylor Scott, b. 6/7/1989 in Concord; Spencer L. Avery and Cindy A. Spaulding

AVIZA,
John Alphonse, b. 1/13/1919; third; Joseph J. Aviza (farmer, Russia) and Bessie Skidlancky (Russia)

AYLES,
Kenard Franklin, Jr., b. 3/3/1941; second; Kenard F. Ayles (rancher, Sheridan, WY) and Kathryn L. Felix (Alvira, PA)
Virginia R., b. 2/17/1935 in Pittsfield; first; Kenard F. Ayles (instructor, Sheridan, WY) and Kathryn L. Felix (Alvira, PA)

BABCOCK,
Frank K., b. 5/13/1982 in Concord; Frank E. Babcock, Jr. and Debra A. Ransom
Kathleen Rebecca, b. 7/15/1985 in Concord; Frank E. Babcock and Debra A. Ransom

BADGER,
James R., b. 6/10/1892; first; John C. Badger (machinist, Belmont) and Addie A. Jones (Gilmanton)

BAER,
Courtney Elise, b. 5/21/2001 in Concord; Richard Baer and Karen Baer

BAGLEY,
Ronald Everett, b. 12/16/1952; third; Earl E. Bagley (lumber, NH) and Margaret V. Joyce (NH)

BAILEY,
Arthur Joseph, b. 10/27/1950; first; Lloyd Eldred Bailey (truck driver, NH) and Rose Ann Goupil (NH)
Holly Ann, b. 1/9/1991 in Laconia; Paul L. Bailey and Janet T. Scalesse

BAIOCCHETTI,
Ashley Marie, b. 12/11/1992 in Laconia; Vincent A. Baiocchetti and Tammy L. Taylor

BAKER,
daughter [Elsie G.], b. 12/12/1895; first; Fred L. Baker (laborer, NS) and Mary A. P. Greene (Gilmanton)
daughter, b. 3/29/1902; fourth; Fred L. Baker (laborer, Barrington, NS) and Mary A. P. Green (Gilmanton)
Abigail Sharon, b. 8/8/1983 in Concord; Douglas A. Baker and Karen D. Moore
Adriel Frederick, b. 6/15/1904; fifth; Frederick L. Baker (farmer, NS) and Mary A. P. Greene (Gilmanton)
Elsie Leslie, b. 1/1/1898; second; Fred L. Baker (laborer, Bear Point, NS) and Mary A. P. Green (Gilmanton)
Olive Louise, b. 5/29/1901; stillborn; third; Fred L. Baker (laborer, Barrington) and Mary A. P. Greene (Gilmanton)

BALDWIN,
Finn Aurelius, b. 11/22/2000 in Concord; Robert Baldwin and Lori Baldwin
William Reed, b. 1/20/1999 in Concord; Robert Baldwin and Lori Baldwin

BALLARD,
son, b. 7/22/1912; fourth; C. P. Ballard (physician, Concord) and Maude E. Gilman (Gilmanton)
Edna Viola, b. 1/23/1909; first; Clarence P. Ballard (physician, Concord) and Maude E. Gilman (Gilmanton)
Henry Clarence, b. 6/17/1911; third; Clarence P. Ballard (physician, Concord) and Maude E. Gilman (Gilmanton)
Horace Charles, b. 8/22/1914; fifth; Clarence P. Ballard (physician, Concord) and Maude E. Gilman (Gilmanton)
Robert Gilman, b. 4/11/1910; second; Clarence P. Ballard (physician, Concord) and Maude E. Gilman (Gilmanton)

BALLOU,
Joshua M., b. 2/18/1980 in Laconia; Richard E. Ballou and Wendy L. Maxwell

BANKS,
Christopher J., b. 7/21/1982 in Concord; Jeffrey N. Banks and Norma J. Jordan
Jessica L., b. 10/22/1980 in Laconia; Jeffrey N. Banks and Norma J. Jordan

BANNISTER,
Jessalyn Rae, b. 1/19/1996 in Laconia; Raymond Henry Bannister and Marcia Joan Tibbals

BARKER,
Kenneth Arnold, b. 9/15/1909; first; Ellsworth B. Barker (mill hand, Torringford, CT) and Lillian C. Barker (Burlington, CT)

BARNES,
son, b. 6/25/1916; second; Burton C. Barnes (farmer, NS) and Susie A. Pease (Gilmanton)
Cecil Maida, b. 7/7/1915; first; Burton Barnes (laborer, NS) and Susie Pease (Gilmanton)

BARON,
Matthew Graham, b. 10/16/1981 in Concord; Jay S. Baron and Eleanor A. Mullaney

BARR,
Audrey Susan, b. 9/20/1984 in Concord; Richard O. Barr and Susan M. Roberts
Benjamin Otis, b. 5/2/1981 in Concord; Richard O. Barr and Susan M. Roberts

BARRON,
daughter, b. 6/20/1897; first; Leonard B. Barron (farmer, Gilmanton) and Nettie P. Marston (Boscawen)

BARTASKA,
Steve, b. 4/17/1915; first; Justin Bartaska (laborer, Russia) and Mary Mezis (Russia)

BARTLETT,
Brooke, b. 10/15/1981 in Laconia; Stephen Charles Bartlett and Sheila M. Gammon
Kristen Jennings, b. 6/26/1990 in Concord; David J. Bartlett and Sue E. Erickson
Kurtis David, b. 11/19/1989 in Concord; Timothy E. Bartlett and Cynthia W. Weller
Lydia, b. 9/5/1991 in Laconia; Andrew J. Bartlett and Anne Marie Mailloux
Nicholas Reginald, b. 10/30/1998 in Laconia; Reginald Bartlett and Sheila Bartlett
Samantha Eleanor, b. 10/17/1991 in Concord; Timothy E. Bartlett and Cynthia J. Weller
Stephanie, b. 12/27/1978 in Laconia; Stephen Charles Bartlett (NH) and Sheila May Gammon (NH)
Stephen Tyler, b. 9/18/1989 in Laconia; Andrew J. Bartlett and Anne M. Mailloux

BARTON,
Irvin Roland, Jr., b. 11/6/1948; third; Irvin R. Barton (molder, Franklin) and Helen J. Bowman (Littleton)

BATCHELDER,
daughter [Hazel B.], b. 5/10/1895; second; Charles M. Batchelder (farmer, Loudon) and Dora Staples
Abaigeal Elizabeth, b. 9/16/1994 in Gilmanton; Daniel Bruce Batchelder and Catherine Aileen Boyd

Aidan Leathers, b. 11/18/2001 in Gilmanton; Daniel Batchelder and Catherine Batchelder
Fiona Aislinn, b. 1/24/1999 in Gilmanton; Daniel Batchelder and Catherine Batchelder
Keavy Blaithe, b. 9/20/1996 in Gilmanton; Daniel B. Batchelder and Catherine Aileen Boyd
Molly Letitia, b. 8/6/1991 in Gilmanton; Daniel B. Batchelder and Catherine Boyd

BATES,
Colleen Christian, b. 12/28/1983 in Concord; Mark C. Bates and Cynthia E. Volk

BATSTONE,
Adam Craig, b. 5/25/1986 in Laconia; Gary W. Batstone and Susan J. Adams
Erin L., b. 5/18/1982 in Laconia; Gary O. Batstone and Susan J. Adams

BAUMEISTER,
Jenna Margaret, b. 11/6/1999 in Concord; Chris Baumeister and Deborah Baumeister

BAYER,
Timothy Daniel, b. 9/2/1981 in Laconia; Bruce H. Bayer and Anne Marie Ott

BEANE,
Kyle Douglas, b. 10/11/2001 in Laconia; Jason Beane and Bridget Beane

BEASLEY,
Jeanne, b. 11/21/1919; second; John E. Beasley (farmer, Kansas City) and Isabel Starrett (White Sul. Sp., MT)

BECK,
child, b. 11/–/1899; first; Charles H. Beck (farmer, Gilmanton) and Hulda Beck (Dover)
Alan Ernest, b. 10/22/1960 in Laconia; first; Wendell Ernest Beck (poultry farmer, NH) and Nancy Carol Gooch (MA)

Duane Adelbert, b. 10/27/1963 in Concord; second; Wendell Ernest Beck (poultryman, NH) and Nancy Carol Gooch (MA)
Ernest Wendall, b. 5/2/1938 in Wolfeboro; first; Ernest Smith Beck (electrician, Charlestown, MA) and Alice E. Rollins (Gilmanton); residence - Gilmanton I. W.
Nicholas August, b. 8/14/1981 in Laconia; James N. Beck, Jr. and Carol Norell
Wendy Mae, b. 1/28/1971 in Laconia; Wendell Ernest Beck (NH) and Sandra Jean Denault (NH)

BECKMAN,
daughter, b. 11/27/1907; seventh; Sadie Beckman (N. Bridgewater, VT)

BEDARD,
Drew Robert, b. 5/13/1986 in Concord; Stephen P. Bedard and Elizabeth A. Johnson
Kate, b. 5/13/1986 in Concord; Stephen P. Bedard and Elizabeth A. Johnson
Letty, b. 10/18/1982 in Concord; Stephen P. Bedard and Elizabeth A. Johnson

BEDFORD,
Kate Marie, b. 12/1/1981 in Laconia; Daniel R. Bedford and Cynthia A. Eisenhauer
Lisa Ann, b. 1/25/1984 in Laconia; Daniel R. Bedford and Cynthia A. Eisenhauer

BELANGER,
Benjamin Giles, b. 7/5/1990 in Concord; Kenneth A. Belanger and Laurie G. Giles

BENNETT,
Dawnadee Elizabeth, b. 5/21/1968 in Laconia; Norman Edwin Bennett (MA) and Carole Margaret Kelley (MA)
Elizabeth Ann, b. 8/29/1989 in Laconia; Dean M. Bennett and Ann M. Ingraham
Jadrien Galadriel, b. 4/15/1998 in Wolfeboro; Shawn Alton Bennett and Shay Ellen Beaulieu
Mary Ada, b. 4/26/1924; second; Marvin S. Bennett (farmer, Clinton, NY) and Velena Vinal (Jefferson, ME)

BENSON,
Devon Mary, b. 7/31/1981 in Derry; Daniel W. Benson, Jr. and Janie L. Schott
Lauren Schott, b. 4/7/1986 in Laconia; Daniel W. Benson, Jr. and Janie L. Schott

BERNDT,
Jennifer, b. 2/17/1981 in Concord; David F. Berndt and Katanya Taggart

BERRY,
son, b. 7/20/1897; first; Lyman E. Berry (farmer, New Durham) and Ella Page (Gilmanton)
daughter, b. 10/9/1904; second; Lyman E. Berry (farmer, New Durham) and Lulie M. Foss (Danvers, MA)

BERTRAND,
Jamie Ann, b. 6/7/1981 in Concord; James M. Bertrand and Sandra A. Seaman

BERUBE,
Pamela Lynne, b. 5/12/1965 in Laconia; first; Paul Roger Berube (laborer, MA) and Theresa Delvina Lang (MA)

BEST,
Alyssa Barbara, b. 4/24/1984 in Concord; Barry C. Best and Janice R. Elliott
Christopher James, b. 12/27/1985 in Laconia; Barry C. Best and Janice R. Elliott
Jessica R., b. 8/25/1981 in Concord; Barry C. Best and Janice R. Elliott

BICKFORD,
son [Herbert S.], b. 6/3/1907; first; Arthur R. Bickford (farmer, Franklin) and Ida M. Brewster (Barnstead)
son [David M.], b. 4/18/1913; fourth; Arthur Bickford (farmer, Franklin) and Ida Brewster (Barnstead)
Clarence Harry, b. 4/9/1909; second; Arthur R. Bickford (farmer, Franklin) and Ida M. Brewster (Barnstead)
David Arthur, Jr., b. 6/19/1973 in Laconia; David Arthur Bickford (NH) and Linda Jean Sanborn (NH)

Evelyn Mabel, b. 4/1/1934; first; David M. Bickford (farmer, Gilmanton) and Lizzie E. Twombly (Gilmanton)
George Albert, b. 2/10/1920; fifth; Arthur R. Bickford (farmer, Franklin) and Ida M. Brewster (Barnstead)
Georgie Annie, b. 11/5/1910; third; Arthur R. Bickford (carpenter, Franklin) and Ida M. Brewster (Barnstead)
Mina Julia, b. 12/14/1891; first; Frederick A. Bickford (mechanic, Meredith) and Henrietta Downing (Woodstock); residence - Weirs

BIGELOW,
Craig A., b. 12/8/1987 in Gilmanton; Michael S. Bigelow and Cherly M. Mudgett

BISHOP,
Nathan Gregory, b. 10/30/1999 in Concord; Dana Bishop and Karen Bishop
Taylor Joan, b. 10/19/2001 in Concord; Dana Bishop and Karen Bishop

BLACKSTONE,
daughter, b. 7/30/1897; third; Sumner E. Blackstone (lawyer, Groton) and Lillia I. Welcome (Hill)
son, b. 3/5/1902; fifth; Sumner E. Blackstone (lawyer, N. Groton) and Lillian Welcome (Concord)

BLAIS,
Albert George, II, b. 3/27/1963 in Laconia; first; Albert George Blais (postmaster, NH) and Joanne Doris Auclair (NH)
Benjamen Goodwin, b. 5/13/1968 in Laconia; Albert George Blais (NH) and Joanne Doris Auclair (NH)
Joan Auclair, b. 7/12/1966 in Laconia; second; Albert George Blais (postmaster, NH) and Joanne Doris Auclair (NH)
Karen Elaine, b. 12/14/1946; third; Albert G. Blais (carpenter, Laconia) and Marguerite L. Carty (New York, NY)

BLAKE,
son, b. 3/10/1893; second; Laurel A. Blake (farmer, Peacham, VT) and Lizzie M. Page (Gilmanton)
daughter, b. 1/2/1896; third; Laural A. Blake (farmer, Peacham, VT) and Lizzie M. Page (Gilmanton)

Amy Kathryn, b. 6/14/1985 in Laconia; Alan J. Blake and Kathleen M. Colburn
Eric Noel, b. 1/5/1983 in Laconia; Paul F. Blake and Debra J. Stendor
Mabel, d. 4/7/1897; fourth; Laural A. Blake (farmer, Peacham, VT) and Lizzie M. Page (Gilmanton)
Nicholas Paul, b. 12/5/1993 in Concord; Paul L. Blake and Cheryl A. Amabile
Sadie May, b. 7/16/1890; first; Laural A. Blake (farmer, Peacham, VT) and Lizzie M. Page (Gilmanton)
Zachary John, b. 7/18/1991 in Concord; Paul L. Blake and Cheryl A. Amabile

BLANCHARD,
Barbara Ann, b. 9/1/1941; fourth; Charles E. Blanchard (farmer, Greenfield) and Ruth A. Tibbetts (Northfield)

BLANCHETTE,
Eric Matthew, b. 2/19/1972 in Laconia; Philip J. Blanchette, Jr. (NH) and Julijone D. Rudzinski (NH)

BLIXT,
Barry Crane, II, b. 7/31/1986 in Laconia; Barry C. Blixt, I and Debbie J. Bousquet

BLOOD,
Elizabeth Hope, b. 12/12/1909; second; William A. Blood (farmer, Chichester) and Augusta May Clifford (Chichester); residence - Chichester

BLOOM,
Anthony Albert, b. 9/12/1958 in Laconia; third; Edward D. Bloom (moulder, MI) and Cora E. Green (VT)

BODWELL,
Ian Leavitt, b. 8/18/1976 in Laconia; Kimberly L. Bodwell (ME) and Kathleen Noel Henry (CT)

BOHL,
Brandon Douglass, b. 11/21/1971 in Laconia; Karl Frederick Bohl (NH) and Barbara Vea Lincks (CT)

BOLDUC,
Jeffrey Donat, b. 2/8/1972 in Laconia; Anthony M. Bolduc (NH) and
   Barbara E. Trefethen (NJ)

BOLTON,
James Dana, b. 3/1/2001 in Laconia; James Bolton and Sarah
   Bolton

BONACCORSI,
David Joseph, b. 7/29/1991 in Concord; Thomas J. Bonaccorsi and
   Dolores J. Mefford

BOND,
child, b. 9/11/1922; Noys F. Bond and Susie M. Brown
Iris Norrine, b. 4/2/1927; fourth; Noyes F. Bond (machinist,
   Henniker) and Susie M. Brown (Tilton); residence - Portsmouth

BORDEAU,
Margaret Rosilla, b. 2/10/1931; fourth; Jason J. Bordeau (chauffeur,
   St. Albans, VT) and Florence Edgerly (Gilmanton)

BOSIAK,
Ann Aurore, b. 11/30/1965 in Concord; second; Frank Charles
   Bosiak, Sr. (farmer, NH) and Jacqueline Muriel Boisvert (NH)
Catherine Yadwiga, b. 4/1/1976 in Concord; Frank C. Bosiak (NH)
   and Jacqueline M. Boisvert (NH)
Frank Charles, Jr., b. 5/3/1964 in Concord; first; Frank Charles
   Bosiak (farmer, NH) and Jacqueline Muriel Boisvert (NH)
John, b. 9/4/1972 in Concord; Frank C. Bosiak (NH) and Jacqueline
   M. Boisvert (NH)
Patricia Ann, b. 7/12/1969 in Concord; Joseph Bosiak (CT) and
   Olive May Thorne (NH)
Steven Philip, b. 10/12/1970 in Concord; Frank Charles Bosiak
   (NH) and Jacqueline Marie Boisvert (NH)
William Joseph, b. 11/24/1952; third; Peter P. Bosiak (farmer, NH)
   and Evelyn I. Vogel (OH)

BOUCHER,
Joseph Arthur, b. 5/30/1970 in Okinawa; Dennis J. Boucher (NH)
   and Mary L. Emond (Washington, DC)

Scott Joel, b. 5/30/1970 in Okinawa; Dennis J. Boucher (NH) and Mary L. Emond (Washington, DC)

BOULANGER,
Christopher Robert, b. 6/18/1986 in Laconia; Paul R. Boulanger and Deborah J. Thornton
Silas Paul, b. 4/26/2001 in Concord; Ronald Boulanger and Celina Boulanger

BOURGOINE,
Melissa Jeanne, b. 8/6/1984 in Concord; Bruce Bourgoine and Barbara J. Devito

BOURQUE,
Felicia J., b. 6/14/1982 in Laconia; Michael R. Bourque and Wilma L. Sanville
Sarah Lee, b. 6/4/1978 in Laconia; Michael Roy Bourque (NH) and Wilma Lee Sanville (NH)

BOUWENS,
Kenneth F., b. 6/13/1982 in Laconia; Kenneth R. Bouwens and Darlene L. Hyslop

BOWLES,
Kenneth J., b. 4/13/1982 in Concord; Dan J. Bowles and Patricia S. Daine

BOYCE,
Michael George, b. 4/20/1984 in Gilmanton; Kenneth G. Boyce and Denise V. Gagnon

BOYD,
Jennifer Louise, b. 7/8/1989 in Laconia; Gilbert D. Boyd, Jr. and Anne A. Abbott
Richard Abbott, b. 10/27/1994 in Laconia; Gilbert Dixon Boyd and Anne Louise Abbott

BOYNTON,
Jeffrey Alan, b. 9/29/1983 in Laconia; Russell A. Boynton and Diane L. Martel

BRADFORD,
Gary Guy, Jr., b. 11/30/1989 in Laconia; Gary G. Bradford, Sr. and Michelle S. McCann

BRAGG,
daughter [Georgie E.], b. 12/4/1907; first; George E. Bragg (farmer, ME) and Edith G. Brown (Gilmanton)
daughter, b. 10/27/1908; second; George E. Bragg (farmer, ME) and Edith G. Brown (Gilmanton)

BREAU,
Gregory C., b. 11/3/1982 in Concord; Patrick H. Breau and Brenda L. Heffner
Heidi Lorraine, b. 3/16/1984 in Concord; Patrick H. Breau and Brenda L. Heffner

BRECKNEY,
Gladis Betsy, b. 9/17/1919; second; Edward Breckney (needleshop, Northfield) and Ruth Altha Mathews (Northfield); residence - Tilton

BRESSE,
Nicholas Scott, b. 5/8/1985 in Laconia; John A. Bresse, Jr. and Hope E. Ballou

BRETON,
Ross Benjamin, b. 5/5/1995 in Concord; Normand G. Breton and Janet A. Potter

BREWER,
Holly Elizabeth, b. 12/13/1978 in Concord; Jerome Donald Brewer (CT) and Sara Beth McIntyre (NY)

BRIGGS,
Daniel George, Jr., b. 10/2/1968 in Concord; Daniel George Briggs, Sr. (NH) and Nancy Lee Littlefield (NH)

BROBST,
Caleb Kenneth, b. 9/9/1999 in Concord; Kenneth Brobst and Krystal Brobst

Kelly Arlene, b. 11/2/2000 in Concord; Kenneth Brobst and Krystal Brobst

BROCHU,
Joseph Walter, b. 10/4/1994 in Concord; Jason Michael Brochu and Michelle Marie Laro
Madison Laura, b. 6/23/1996 in Concord; Jason Michael Brochu and Michelle Marie Laro
Molly Beth, b. 2/25/1998 in Concord; Jason Michael Brochu and Michelle Marie Laro
Victoria Elizabeth, b. 3/26/1993 in Concord; Jason M. Brochu and Michelle M. Laro

BROCK,
son, b. 10/4/1896; second; Erwin C. Brock (laborer, Pittsfield) and Carrie L. Dowst (Epsom)
daughter, b. 8/16/1898; third; Erving C. Brock (laborer, Pittsfield) and Carrie L. Dowst (Epsom)
son, b. 8/14/1900; fourth; Ervin C. Brock (laborer, Pittsfield) and Carrie L. Dowst (Epsom)
stillborn daughter, b. 8/6/1903; tenth; Irving C. Brock (farmer, Pittsfield) and Caroline Dowst (Epsom)
daughter, b. 11/17/1904; eleventh; Irving C. Brock (laborer, Pittsfield) and Caroline Dowst (Epsom)
daughter, b. 6/9/1906; second; Inez M. Brock (Pittsfield)
daughter, b. 3/31/1907; twelfth; Irving C. Brock (farmer, Pittsfield) and Carrie L. Dowst (Epsom)
stillborn daughter, b. 3/31/1907; thirteenth; Irving C. Brock (farmer, Pittsfield) and Carrie L. Dowst (Epsom)
Spencer Chase, b. 4/24/1913; fifteenth; Irving Brock (laborer, Pittsfield) and Caroline Dowst (Epsom)
Vivian Izalee, b. 10/12/1909; fourteenth; Irving C. Brock (farmer, Pittsfield) and Carrie L. Dowst (Epsom)

BRONSON,
Callum Paul, b. 6/24/1998 in Laconia; James Paul Bronson and Cynthia Ann Haas

BROOKS,
Clarence E., b. 3/27/1913; fifth; William F. Brooks (farm laborer, Boston, MA) and Lizzie M. York (Farmington)

BROWN,
son, b. 10/20/1887; first; Charlemagne Brown (merchant, Gilmanton) and Annie Griffin
child [George C.], b. 7/6/1894; first; George H. Brown (physician, Haverhill, MA) and Lizzie H. Orange (Lowell, MA)
daughter, b. 7/23/1898; second; Alfred M. Brown (farmer) and Edna Marsh (Gilmanton)
son, b. 12/14/1898; fifth; Charlemagne Brown (shoemaker, Gilmanton) and Annie Griffin (Gilmanton); residence - Pittsfield
daughter [Edna Myrtle], b. 5/2/1900; third; Alfred M. Brown (farmer, Epsom) and Edna Marsh (Gilmanton)
daughter, b. 6/25/1900; first; Edwin S. Brown (laborer, Gilmanton) and Mary E. Walsh (NS)
son [Richard I.], b. 6/18/1902; fourth; Alfred M. Brown (farmer) and Edna Marsh (Gilmanton)
daughter, b. 5/7/1904; second; George H. Brown (physician, Haverhill, MA) and Lizzie H. Orange (Lowell, MA)
stillborn son, b. 10/25/1908; fifth; Alfred M. Brown (farmer, Epsom) and Edna M. Marsh (Gilmanton)
Alberta Rae, b. 1/9/1951; third; Raymond A. Brown (lumberman, NH) and Bernice Mabel Willard (NH)
Amanda Sue, b. 9/20/1983 in Laconia; Raymond A. Brown and Linda D. Blake
Carissa Lyn, b. 5/26/1991 in Laconia; Timothy S. Brown and Kimberly S. Butman
Carol Elizabeth, b. 3/27/1948; second; Raymond A. Brown (logger-lumber, Portsmouth) and Bernice M. Willard (Gilmanton)
David W., b. 6/9/1956 in Laconia; third; Junior L. Brown (hiway maint., Columbus, OH) and Doris M. Conners (Peabody, MA)
Herbert J., b. 11/10/1955; fourth; Herbert J. Brown (lumber sawyer, Portsmouth) and Bernice M. Willard (Belmont)
Holly Ann, b. 12/21/1957; first; Robert A. Brown (tractor maintenance, NH) and Carolyn A. Blanchard (NH)
J. Everett, b. 3/28/1909; first; Ethel M. Brown (Gilmanton)
James M., b. 5/29/1954; second; Junior L. Brown (bus driver, OH) and Doris M. Conners (MA)
Jamie Karyl, b. 10/16/1977 in Laconia; Raymond A. Brown (NH) and Linda D. Blake (NH)
Kathryn Lee, b. 12/3/1959 in Laconia; fifth; Junior Lee Brown (refinishing furniture, OH) and Doris Marie Conners (MA)

Morse, b. 7/15/1895; first; John Wheeler Brown (farmer, Gilmanton) and Lizzie Batchelder Lane (Meredith)
Nancy Jean, b. 7/21/1958 in Laconia; fourth; Junior Lee Brown (farmer, OH) and Doris Marie Conners (MA)
Raymond Arthur, b. 5/5/1970 in Laconia; Raymond Arthur Brown (NH) and Linda Doris Blake (NH)
Robert Alfred, b. 4/17/1932; first; Richard I. Brown (farmer, Gilmanton) and Sadie P. Twombly (Hampton)
Virginia May, b. 9/25/1922; Morse E. Brown and Rebecca Dolliff

BRUNELLE,
Elsie Marie, b. 6/6/1990 in Concord; Dale R. Brunelle and Lynne M. Rogalsky
Renae Elena, b. 2/1/1994 in Laconia; Dale Raymond Brunelle and Lynne Marie Rogalsky
Scott Joseph, b. 9/15/1991 in Concord; Dale R. Brunelle and Lynne M. Rogalsky

BRUNT,
Aaron Robert, b. 2/14/1988 in Concord; Robert P. Brunt and Gail M. Aubertin
Aimee Clare, b. 7/9/1999 in New London; Robert Brunt and Gail Brunt
Alex Joshua, b. 5/27/1990 in Concord; Robert P. Brunt and Gail M. Aubertin
Anna Rose, b. 8/21/1992 in Concord; Robert P. Brunt and Gail M. Aubertin
Katherine Anne, b. 5/24/1997 in New London; Robert Paul Brunt and Gail Marie Aubertin
Sophie Marie, b. 2/14/1995 in Gilmanton; Robert P. Brunt and Gail M. Aubertin

BRYANT,
Jacob Thomas, b. 10/20/1992 in Concord; Richard A. Bryant and Mary M. Fogg
Tyler Scott, b. 12/2/1990 in Concord; Richard A. Bryant and Mary M. Fogg

BUNKER,
Lura May, b. 5/28/1921; fourth; Daniel Bunker (laborer, Barnstead) and Florence L. Hilliard (Loudon)

Muriel Lura, b. 3/2/1916; third; Daniel Bunker (laborer, Barnstead) and Florence Hilliard (Loudon)

BUONOPANE,
Anthony Paul, b. 3/7/1992 in Laconia; Paul C. Buonopane and Nancy J. Cerone
Vincent Joseph, b. 5/5/1994 in Laconia; Paul Carmen Buonopane and Nancy Jane Cerone

BURBANK,
Alonzo Calvin, b. 12/13/1912; second; Alonzo P. Burbank (laborer, Gilmanton) and Sadie L. Gault (Bridgewater)
George David, b. 6/21/1961 in Concord; first; Neil Stuart Burbank (pressman, NH) and Esther Joyce Edgerly (NH)
Hilda Lucia, b. 6/22/1911; first; Alonzo P. Burbank (laborer, Gilmanton) and Sadie L. Gault (Bridgewater)
Jessica Summer, b. 4/6/1996 in Laconia; George David Burbank and Sandra June Conrad
John Stuart, b. 5/31/1966 in Concord; second; Neil Stuart Burbank (pressman, NH) and Esther Joyce Edgerly (NH)
Whitney Page, b. 5/19/1992 in Laconia; George D. Burbank and Sandra J. Conrad

BURCHARD,
Hannah Grace, b. 8/26/1986 in Concord; Joseph E. Burchard and Paula G. Martin

BURLINGAME,
Matthew Billings, b. 12/6/1985 in Laconia; Roger G. Burlingame and Teresa L. Lopez

BURNHAM,
Rose Josephine, b. 11/8/1909; first; Abraham Burnham (laborer, Manchester) and Rose Surprenent (Sutton, Canada)

BURRES,
daughter [Gladys M.], b. 9/8/1912; first; Orman L. Burres (farmer, Gilmanton) and Eva Mabel Jones (Gilmanton)
daughter, b. 12/6/1914; second; Orman Burres (farmer, Gilmanton) and Eva M. Jones (Gilmanton)

daughter, b. 12/19/1924; fifth; Orman L. Burres (laborer, Gilmanton) and Eva M. Jones (Gilmanton)
Ed. Leslie, b. 12/28/1919; fourth; Orman Burres (teamster, Gilmanton) and Eva M. Jones (Gilmanton)
Olive Eva, b. 4/15/1918; third; Orman L. Burres (farmer, Gilmanton) and Eva M. Jones (Gilmanton)

BUSHNELL,
Barbara Jeannette, b. 6/18/1960 in Laconia; sixth; Richard Barrett Bushnell (machinist, VT) and Charlotte Marie Barneetz (VT)
Brenda May, b. 10/31/1961 in Laconia; seventh; Richard Barrett Bushnell (lumberman, VT) and Charlotte Marie Barneetz (VT)
Carol Marie, b. 6/2/1954; fifth; Richard B. Bushnell (lumberman, VT) and Charlotte Barneetz (VT)
Miranda Marion, b. 11/17/1997 in Laconia; Richard Eugene Bushnell and Michele Marion Mudgett
Peter James, b. 8/17/1950; fourth; Richard Barrett Bushnell (farmer, VT) and Charlotte Marie Barneetz (VT)

CADY,
Jessica L., b. 10/10/1974 in Laconia; Richard M. Cady (VT) and Donna M. Young (NY)

CAFIERO,
Grace Jo, b. 11/13/2001 in Concord; Joseph Cafiero and Kristy Cafiero

CALDON,
Amanda Lee, b. 12/9/1987 in Concord; Jeffrey S. Caldon and Michelle R. Gaudet
Brett Michael, b. 7/23/1972 in Concord; Thomas W. Caldon (NH) and Suzann J. Barr (NH)
Douglas Kevin, b. 8/29/1948; third; Winston D. Caldon (carpenter, Campton) and Loise Gallagher (Fitchburg, MA)
Jessica Lynn, b. 3/28/1989 in Concord; Jeffrey S. Caldon and Michelle R. Gaudet
Joan Rachel, b. 2/25/1953; fourth; Winston D. Caldon (carpenter, NH) and Loise Gallagher (MA)
Melissa Sue, b. 10/14/1977 in Hanover; Thomas W. Caldon (NH) and Suzann J. Barr (NH)

Thomas Justin, b. 8/4/1971 in Concord; Thomas Winston Caldon (NH) and Suzann Joy Barr (NH)

CAMIRE,
Abigail, b. 10/3/2000 in Laconia; Jonathan Camire and Polly Camire

CAMPBELL,
Ashley Emily, b. 6/26/1986 in Laconia; Timothy K. Campbell and Nancy L. Burbank
Mariam Esther, b. 8/8/1924; first; George Campbell (woodchopper, ME) and Myrtle Brock (Gilmanton); residence - Dover, ME

CANNEY,
stillborn daughter, b. 4/1/1928; third; Forrest S. Canney (laborer, Gilmanton) and Lura Davis (Pittsfield)

CANNON,
Eric Vaughn, b. 3/16/1990 in Concord; Kenneth W. Cannon and Marcia K. McPahil

CANTO,
Sisily Bree, b. 6/21/1978 in Laconia; Richard Paul Canto (MA) and Elaine Christine Hupprich (MA)

CANTOR,
Rebecca Elizabeth, b. 7/21/1985 in Concord; Alan M. Cantor and Patricia A. Rogers

CARBONE,
Austin Joseph, b. 11/28/1998 in Concord; David Carbone and Ann Carbone

CARLSON,
Charles Kenneth, b. 2/17/1947; fifth; Fred H. Carlson (farmer, Cranbury, NJ) and Marion Brill (Paughquag, NY)

CARMODY,
Alex, b. 3/29/1998 in Laconia; Walter James Carmody and Jody Fosburgh

Townsend Marie, b. 12/19/1993 in Laconia; Walter J. Carmody and Jody M. Fosburgh

CARROLL,
stillborn son, b. 2/26/1893; fourth; Henry Carroll (clerk, Albany, NY) and Sarah E. Cook (S. Boston, MA)

CARTIER,
Cohen L., b. 11/30/1979 in Laconia; Gary A. Cartier and Linda D. Rudzinski

CARUFEL,
Doris Therase, b. 10/13/1932; seventh; Simon S. Carufel (farmer, Pawtucket, RI) and Eva F. Surprenant (Pawtucket, RI)

CASEY,
Corina Lee, b. 6/9/1987 in Concord; Francis J. Casey, Jr. and Tammy E. Berger
Seth Jaquith, b. 9/29/1973 in Kittery, ME; Peter Jaquith Casey (MA) and Sylvia Patricia Garcia (AZ)
Shannon Renee, b. 5/9/1984 in Concord; Francis J. Casey, Jr. and Tammy E. Berger

CASSAVAUGH,
Heidi Lee, b. 1/16/1967 in Laconia; first; Terry Lawrence Cassavaugh (router, NH) and Beatrice Berta Adel (NH)
Tanya Lynn, b. 8/30/1976 in Concord; Terry L. Cassavaugh (NH) and Beatrice B. Abel (NH)

CATE,
daughter, b. 2/22/1896; third; Richard B. Cate (laborer, Barrington) and Kate M. Murphy (MA)

CATER,
daughter, b. 3/5/1903; seventh; Richard D. Cater (farmer, Barrington) and Kate Murphy (MA)
Arthur W., b. 8/22/1899; fifth; Richard Cater (laborer, Barrington) and Kate M. Murphy (Cotoville, MA)

CHAMBERL[A]IN,
son, b. 7/1/1904; fifth; Charles H. Chamberlain (lumber dealer, Boston, MA) and Bertha Emerson (Barnstead)
Amy Bertha, b. 10/19/1910; first; Harry I. Chamberlain (farmer, Barnstead) and Ella M. Jones (Gilmanton)
E. T. Harvey, b. 4/26/1911; sixth; Charles Chamberlain (farmer, Boston, MA) and Bertha Emerson (Barnstead)
Ida Helen, b. 5/13/1915; second; Harry I. Chamberlain (farmer, Gilmanton) and Ela Maud Jones (Gilmanton)
Jason Leroy, b. 6/7/1967 in Laconia; seventh; Robert Wesley Chamberlain (truck driver, ME) and Marjorie May Seavey (NH)
Leon Chester, b. 10/3/1899; fourth; Charles H. Chamberlin (farmer, Boston, MA) and Addie B. Emerson (Barnstead)
Randy Lee, b. 8/14/1964 in Laconia; sixth; Robert Wesley Chamberlain (truck driver, ME) and Marjorie Mary Seavy (NH)
Stanley Robert, II, b. 3/29/1967 in Laconia; first; Stanley Robert Chamberlain (molder, NH) and Virginia Catherine Dunn (NY)
Wanda Ruth, b. 10/6/1946 in Laconia; fourth; Woodbury T. Chamberlain (lumberman, Colebrook) and Helen R. Greer (Colebrook)
William James, b. 4/4/1950; fifth; Robert Wesley Chamberlain (truck driver, ME) and Marjorie May Seavey (NH)

CHANCE,
Robert Edward Lee, III, b. 3/22/1963 in Concord; second; Robert Edward Lee Chance, II (serviceman, FL) and Alice Louise Adel (NH)

CHAPMAN,
stillborn son, b. 6/26/1945 in Laconia; fifth; Herbert D. Chapman (machinist, Westerly, RI) and Marie M. Deans (Phippsburg, ME)
Stella May, b. 10/5/1914; second; Frank Chapman (teamster, Gilmanton I. W.) and Cecilia McPherson (PEI)

CHASE,
son, b. 6/27/1895; first; Daniel J. Chase (farmer, Gilford) and Addie Fogg (Loudon)
Elizabeth Emmeline, b. 5/11/1910; first; Royal E. Chase (farmer, Brockton, MA) and Lere Benton (Concord)

Lena Emma, b. 7/20/1908; first; Bernard L. Chase (clergyman, Sheffield, VT) and Mabelle Sargent (Sharon, VT)
Nicholas Adam, b. 2/4/1985 in Laconia; George R. Chase and Tina Helen Young

CHENEY-WELCH,
Kaely Erin, b. 7/28/1996 in Laconia; Daniel Rupert Cheney and Deborah Ellen Welch

CHEVALIER,
Kevin W., b. 10/15/1975 in Concord; William J. Chevalier (MA) and Virginia M. Jette (MA)
Timothy William, b. 10/18/1974 in Concord; William J. Chevalier (MA) and Virginia M. Jette (MA)

CHMIELECKI,
David Edward, b. 5/27/1976 in Laconia; Francis M. Chmielecki (MA) and Jean E. Hoey (MD)
Mark Francis, b. 10/13/1974 in Laconia; Francis M. Chmielecki (MA) and Jean E. Hoey (MD)
Steven John, b. 5/14/1978 in Laconia; Francis M. Chmoelecki (sic) (MA) and Jean Ellen Hoey (MD)

CILLEY,
Christian Colin, b. 9/23/1992 in Laconia; Dexter G. Cilley and Karen L. Craig

CLAIRMONT [see Claremont],
son, b. 12/18/1903; first; Olive Clairmont (mill operative, Sherbrooke, PQ) and Celina Roberts (Eastman, PQ); residence - Belmont
Christopher Marc, b. 3/24/1974 in Laconia; David P. Clairmont (NH) and Cheryl M. Ellsworth (NH)
Cindy Lee, b. 1/14/1972 in Laconia; Lynn R. Clairmont (NH) and Phyllis Louise Jewell (NH)
Danielle Dawn, b. 5/20/1999 in Laconia; David Clairmont and Lynn Clairmont
David Patrick, b. 8/26/1953; fifth; Joseph L. Clairmont (lumberman, NH) and Katherine A. Bouchard (NH)
Delmer Joseph, b. 5/17/1981 in Concord; David P. Clairmont and Caroline J. Woodard

Eric Raymond, b. 3/1/1973 in Wolfeboro; Wesley Wayne Clairmont (NH) and Betty Ann Blad (NH)
Gina Kay, b. 8/3/1983 in Concord; Omar Leo Clairmont and Cynthia S. McCarthy
Levi F., b. 12/12/1980 in Concord; Omar L. Clairmont and Cynthia S. McCarthy
Nancy Lynne, b. 5/22/1967 in Laconia; first; Lynn Robert Clairmont (student, NH) and Phyllis Louise Jewell (NH)
Omar L., b. 10/10/1955; sixth; Joseph L. Clairmont (lumberman, Belmont) and Katherine Bouchard (Belmont)
Timothy David, b. 2/22/1991 in Laconia; David A. Clairmont and Lynne A. Ouellette

CLAREMONT [see Clairmont],
Mary Eveline, b. 7/27/1905; second; Levi Claremont (laborer, Sherbrooke, PQ) and Celina Roberts (Sherbrooke, PQ)

CLARK,
Bernice Maud, b. 4/21/1891; first; Leslie D. Clark (farmer) and Minnie M. Clark
Brady Bickford, b. 5/3/2000 in Laconia; Roger Clark and Jamie Clark
Colby Scott, b. 9/8/1994 in Laconia; Roger Scott Clark and Jamie Lynn Hancock
Laura Jean, b. 6/17/1961 in Laconia; first; Richard Albert Clark (water control man, MA) and Joyce Lorraine Brown (NM)
Taylar Michelle, b. 10/28/1992 in Laconia; Roger S. Clark and Jamie L. Hancock

CLARKE,
Bethany Mariah, b. 8/2/1992 in Laconia; Donald J. Clarke and Jean E. Mortimer

CLEVELAND,
Mackenzie Charles, b. 5/4/1995 in Concord; Charles H. Cleveland and Kelly M. Shaw
Mariah Chase, b. 6/24/1993 in Concord; Charles H. Cleveland and Kelly M. Shaw

CLEWLEY,
Bryan Augustus, b. 2/22/1987 in Laconia; Scott A. Clewley and
   Patricia E. LeBlanc
Joseph S., b. 3/28/1982 in Laconia; Scott A. Clewley and Patricia E.
   LeBlanc

CLIFFORD,
daughter, b. 5/22/1889; fourth; John L. Clifford (farmer, Gilmanton)
   and Jennie N. Leavitt (Loudon)
son [Earl Clinton], b. 1/22/1893; sixth; John L. Clifford (farmer,
   Gilford) and Jennie N. Leavitt (Loudon)
daughter, b. 8/28/1899; seventh; John L. Clifford (farmer, Gilford)
   and Jennie N. Leavitt (Loudon)
Everette Earle, b. 3/22/1920; third; Earl C. Clifford (laborer,
   Gilmanton) and Nellie M. Ellsworth (Gilmanton)
Lois May, b. 5/21/1915; first; Earle C. Clifford (farmer, Gilmanton)
   and Nellie M. Ellsworth (Gilmanton)
Melba Jean, b. 5/12/1930; fifth; Earl C. Clifford (laborer, Gilmanton)
   and Nellie M. Ellsworth (Gilmanton)
Nellie Evelyn, b. 5/2/1927; fourth; Earle C. Clifford (farmer,
   Gilmanton) and Nellie M. Ellsworth (Gilmanton)
Ruth Arlene, b. 3/8/1918; second; Earle C. Clifford (farmer,
   Gilmanton) and Nellie N. Ellsworth (Gilmanton)
Shannon Gale, b. 12/21/1998 in Wolfeboro; Fred Clifford and Karen
   Clifford

CLINTON,
Michael Paul, b. 8/15/1971 in Concord; Paul Douglas Clinton (KS)
   and Darlene Lee Hyslop (NH)

CLOUGH,
stillborn son, b. 10/31/1891; seventh; Elbridge G. Clough (farmer
   and butcher, Gilmanton) and Emma Clough
son, b. 1/21/1892; third; Oscar Clough (farmer, Alton) and Clara I.
   Ross (Gilmanton)
Alexandra Jaymes, b. 7/1/1993 in Concord; James A. Clough and
   Jessica G. Pierce
Carl G., b. 6/12/1895; Elbridge G. Clough (farmer, Gilmanton)
Christopher Pierce, b. 1/1/1992 in Lebanon; James A. Clough and
   Jessica G. Pierce
John Henry, b. 5/27/1922; John P. Clough and Grace Blaisdell

COBB,
Nicholas Carey-Wayne, b. 3/27/1993 in Laconia; Douglas A. Cobb
 and Mary Alice Manning

COGAN,
William Joseph, b. 4/6/1987 in Concord; William E. Cogan and
 Susan M. Gallaher

COLE,
Amy Ella, b. 4/16/1977 in Concord; Robert L. Cole (MA) and Elayne
 L. Nelson (NH)

COLLINS,
daughter, b. 12/10/1890; first; Frank T. Collins (farmer, Alton) and
 Charlotte J. Lewis (Allenstown)

COLSON,
Samantha Rose, b. 2/26/1978 in Laconia; George Samuel Colson
 (NH) and Susan Jane Weeks (NH)

COMPTON,
Angela Denee, b. 1/8/1983 in Laconia; Douglas J. Compton and
 Karen A. Ouellette
Dathon James Bickford, b. 8/17/1981 in Laconia; Douglas J.
 Compton and Karen A. Ouellette

CONNER,
Kathleen Eloise, b. 8/21/1948; third; Elmer W. Conner (marking
 lumber, Northfield) and Arlene T. Dion (Franklin)
Sandra Anne, b. 11/4/1952; second; Clarence E. Conner
 (contractor, NH) and Sarah E. McClary (CT)

CONNOLLY,
Christina Elizabeth, b. 2/8/1989 in Concord; Kevin M. Connolly and
 Tracey A. Heap
Matthew Kevin, b. 5/10/1991 in Concord; Kevin Michael Connolly
 and Tracey A. Heap

CONNOR,
Clarence Edwin, b. 7/20/1939 in Laconia; first; Clarence E. Connor (mason tender, Hanover) and Sarah E. McClary (Abington, CT)

CONSTANT,
Kenneth Lloyd, b. 9/23/1984 in Laconia; Thomas L. Constant and Betty L. Dorman
Sara Louise, b. 9/23/1984 in Laconia; Thomas L. Constant and Betty L. Dorman

CONVERSE,
stillborn son, b. 10/11/1895; first; Frank A. Converse (blacksmith) and Hattie Jones (Gilmanton)

COOK,
Gwendolyn, b. 5/31/1988 in Laconia; Jon Douglas Cook and Margaret S. Champagne
Joseph Robert, b. 3/7/1986 in Laconia; Jon Douglas Cook and Margaret S. Champagne

COPP,
Josie Bowles, b. 3/23/1927; third; George S. Copp (teamster, Concord) and Lucy M. Bowles (Bascom)

CORRIVEAU,
Benjamin Allan, b. 12/7/1993 in Laconia; Allan W. Corriveau and Nancy W. Childress
Nannette Burleigh, b. 4/3/1987 in Laconia; Allan W. Corriveau and Nancy W. Childress

COTA,
Louis Leslie, b. 2/17/1932; first; Leslie H. Cota (ski factory, Sanbornton) and Ethel L. White (Henniker)
Louise Alice, b. 2/1/1947; second; Leslie H. Cota (machine operator, Sanbornton) and Ethel L. White (Henniker)

COTTON,
Joseph Henry, IV, b. 6/22/1987 in Laconia; Joseph H. Cotton, III and Belinda A. Gilbert

COURNOYER,
Natalie A., b. 3/8/1979 in Laconia; Denis R. Cournoyer and Linda A. Newton
Nicholas R., b. 9/10/1980 in Concord; Denis R. Cournoyer and Linda A. Newton

COUSINS,
Grace Ann, b. 10/5/1940; first; William C. Cousins (farmer, NY) and Eleanor Andreotta (Passaic, NJ)
Janet, b. 9/20/1944 in Laconia; second; William E. Cousins (state hi-way, Jersey City, NJ) and Eleanor Andriotta (Passaic, NJ)

COUTURE,
Cameron Spencer, b. 2/4/1998 in Laconia; Mark Gerard Couture and Autumn Caisse
Karen Elizabeth, b. 2/21/1962 in Laconia; second; Roger Arthur Couture (supervisor, NH) and Marjorie Mae Munsey (NH)
Kevin Matthew, b. 3/10/1961 in Laconia; first; Roger Arthur Couture (tech., NH) and Marjorie Mae Munsey (NH)
Robert Alphonse, b. 10/4/1963 in Laconia; third; Roger Arthur Couture (supervisor, NH) and Marjorie Mae Munsey (NH)
Sara Marie, b. 1/26/1983 in Laconia; Kevin M. Couture and Sandra L. Austin

COX,
Leslie Raymond, b. 6/26/1929 in Belmont; first; Arthur L. Cox (mechanic, Concord) and Arlene Springer (Nashua)

CRAIG,
Peter Alden, b. 2/8/1950; fifth; Dana Henderson Craig (woodsman, WV) and Doris Evelyn Libby (MA)

CRESBY,
son, b. 2/14/1913; first; Clinton Cresby (druggist, PA) and Edith G. Batchelder (Gilmanton); residence - Tilton

CROCKETT,
Cassandra Lee, b. 10/18/1991 in Laconia; Brian D. Crockett and Heidi L. Rath
Chad Brian, b. 5/31/1989 in Laconia; Brian D. Crockett and Heidi L. Rath

Chelsea Mae, b. 1/12/1993 in Laconia; Brian D. Crockett and Heidi L. Rath

CROSBY,
Susan Hale, b. 7/1/1963 in Laconia; second; Robert Shackford Crosby, Jr. (farmer, NH) and Phyllis Lucille Cutting (ME)

CULLEN,
Rebekka L., b. 6/28/1980 in Concord; Matthew G. Cullen and Krista V. Carlson

CURRAN,
Rachel Annette, b. 11/29/1977 in Laconia; Donald C. Curran (NY) and Muriel A. MacDonald (NH)

CURRIER,
Geoffrey Laurence, b. 9/20/1947; second; Cyrus R. Currier (stock clerk, S. Orange, NJ) and Dorothy M. Nash (Jersey City, NJ)
Matthew Brett, b. 5/25/1983 in Concord; Brett A. Currier and Brenda L. McClary
Rebekah Lynn, b. 1/5/1988 in Concord; John K. Currier, Jr. and Deborah G. Goupille
Sarah Rae, b. 7/26/1986 in Concord; John K. Currier and Deborah J. Goupille
Tricia Lynne, b. 6/16/1987 in Concord; Brett A. Currier and Brenda L. McClary

CUSHING,
Sandra Lee, b. 10/31/1945 in Laconia; first; Russell W. Cushing (US Navy, Belmont) and Ethel M. Page (Gilmanton); residence - Belmont

DAGGETT,
Alexander D., b. 4/14/1982 in Concord; Kenneth E. Daggett and Susan E. Salls
Danielle A., b. 2/19/1980 in Concord; Kenneth E. Daggett and Susan E. Salls

DAIGLE,
Allison Paige, b. 6/27/1994 in Laconia; Robert Joseph Daigle and Melissa Wingate Stevens

Hugh Callahan, b. 2/7/1981 in Concord; Steven A. Daigle and Edith F. Callahan
Matthew Travis, b. 11/11/1991 in Lebanon; Robert J. Daigle and Melissa W. Stevens

DAIGNEAU,
Eliza Jane, b. 6/8/1953; fifth; Arthur H. Daigneau (farmer, NH) and Daura N. Cass (VT)
Mackenzie Lorraine, b. 7/14/2000; Jason Daigneau and Kim Daigneau
Nicole Elizabeth, b. 1/5/1993 in Laconia; Jason R. Daigneau and Kim L. Stone
Priscilla Jean, b. 5/28/1957 in Laconia; sixth; Arthur H. Daigneau (farmer, NH) and Daura Nena Case (VT)

DAILEY,
James Allan, b. 2/28/1950; second; Merle Harry Dailey (woodsman, VT) and Elizabeth Rose Conner (NH)

DAME,
daughter, b. 6/22/1912; third; Perley C. Dame (laborer, New Durham) and Eva W. Straw (Pittsfield)
Herman Perley, b. 4/10/1910; second; Perley C. Dame (laborer, New Durham) and Eva M. Straw (Pittsfield)

DAMI,
Matthew Steven, b. 12/9/1998 in Laconia; Steven Todd Dami and Tammy Lee Hatch
Tyler Steven, b. 9/8/1993 in Laconia; Steven T. Dami and Tammy L. Hatch

DANDENEAU,
Kristyn Ashley, b. 1/12/1987 in Laconia; Joseph B. Dandeneau and Janet M. Payne

DANIELS,
Kenneth Ivan, b. 9/18/1944 in Laconia; second; Kenneth I. Daniels (farmer, Meredith) and Viola J. Miller (Meredith)

DANIS,
Tina Marie, b. 10/27/1960 in Concord; first; Robert Edmund Danis (ass't. sulphiter, NH) and Sandra Jean Denault (MD)

DARBYSHIRE,
Zachary Gallien, b. 3/22/1978 in Laconia; Paul Michael Darbyshire (MA) and Carol Ann Gallien (NH)

DAVIES,
Elizabeth Jael, b. 5/17/1996 in Rochester; William Henry Davies and Valerie Ann Patterson
Melody Ann, b. 3/18/2000 in Rochester; William Davies and Valerie Davies
Ruth Moriah, b. 5/12/1998 in Rochester; William Davies and Valerie Davies

DAVIS,
daughter, b. 5/2/1931; third; Edna Davis (Laconia)
Beatrice Ann, b. 6/7/1947; second; Ellen M. Davis (Gilmanton)
Blanche Irene, b. 8/15/1935; sixth; G. Ernest Davis (laborer, Dover) and Irene Page (Gilmanton)
Danielle Nicole, b. 4/15/1993 in Laconia; Jeffrey P. Davis and Pamela K. Swanson
David Ernest, b. 3/31/1927; second; George E. Davis (marine engineer, Dover) and Irene M. Page (Gilmanton)
Donna Rachel, b. 9/15/1945 in Wolfeboro; first; Ellen M. Davis (Gilmanton)
Ellen M., b. 11/9/1928; third; George E. Davis (laborer, Dover) and Irene M. Page (Gilmanton)
Freida Alice, b. 3/9/1937 in Wolfeboro; seventh; George E. Davis (laborer, Dover) and Irene Page (Gilmanton)
George Henry, b. 6/23/1922; Ephriam H. Davis and Louise Deselle
Grace Emma, b. 3/30/1934 in Wolfeboro; fifth; George E. Davis (laborer, Dover) and Irene May Page (Gilmanton)
Jacquelyn Gail, b. 5/11/1936 in Laconia; fifth; William J. Davis (real estate, Dorchester, MA) and Beatrice E. Lowell (Saco, ME); residence - Gilmanton I. W.
Jaime Lauren, b. 1/5/1984 in Laconia; Douglas W. Davis and Diane I. Graves
Kaileigh Ruth, b. 3/9/1998 in Concord; Andrew Lloyd Davis and Heather Leigh Flint

Kelsea Rose, b. 7/26/1999 in Concord; Andrew Davis and Heather
  Davis
Lester Charles, b. 6/9/1931; fourth; G. Ernest Davis (laborer,
  Dover) and Irene Page (Gilmanton)
Lester Ernest, b. 10/2/1954; third; Lester C. Davis (woodsman, NH)
  and Helen M. Joy (NH)
Lisa Marie, b. 5/25/1987 in Laconia; Richard E. Davis and Dorothy
  L. Hiltz
Matthew Whitney, b. 6/3/1988 in Laconia; Douglas W. Davis and
  Diane I. Graves
Nathan Dudly, b. 1/16/1997 in Concord; Richard Dudly Davis and
  Colleen Leigh Genest
Rachel Li, b. 7/12/1995 in Concord; Richard D. Davis and Colleen
  Leigh Genest
Robert L., b. 9/2/1927; fifth; Henry Davis (laborer, Wentworth) and
  Louise Laselle (Lynn, MA)
William Charles, b. 5/18/1924; third; Henry Davis (farmer,
  Wentworth) and Louise Derrelle (Lynn, MA)

DAWSON,
James Rexford, b. 12/31/1965 in Concord; third; Robert William
  Dawson (farmer, NH) and Lee Edna Wheet (NH)
Kari-Lee Ann, b. 8/15/1977 in Laconia; David B. Dawson (CA) and
  Renee E. Morrill (NH)
Kenneth Chester, b. 9/7/1964 in Concord; second; Robert William
  Dawson (farmer, NH) and Lee Edna Wheet (NH)
Robert Lee, b. 6/6/1963 in Concord; first; Robert William Dawson
  (farmer, NH) and Lee Edna Wheet (NH)

DAY,
Michael J., b. 1/19/1979 in Laconia; William F. Day and Lucille T.
  Labonte
Peter Travis, b. 4/8/1977 in Laconia; William F. Day (NH) and
  Lucille T. Labonte (NH)
Stephen Scott, b. 4/22/1983 in Laconia; William F. Day and Lucille
  T. Labonte

DEAN,
Lauren Elizabeth, b. 1/20/2000 in Concord; John Dean and Karen
  Dean

DEANE,
Joshua E., b. 6/13/1982 in Concord; Lonnie A. Deane and Lynn R. Cheney

DEARBORN,
Vanessa Marie, b. 5/14/1999 in Laconia; Peter Dearborn and Stacey Dearborn

DECOSTER,
Caitlin Jeanne, b. 1/19/1989 in Concord; David A. Decoster and Maureen S. Ballester

DENNIS,
child, b. 9/13/1922; Gerald W. Dennis and Lillian W. Cooper
son, b. 10/26/1926; seventh; Gerald W. Dennis (farmer, St. Andrews, Can.) and Lillian Cooper (Montreal, Can.)
Bessie, b. 5/12/1919; second; Gerald W. Dennis (farmer, Canada) and Lillian M. Cooper (Canada)
Gerald Edward, b. 5/9/1924; fifth; Gerald W. Dennis (farmer, Canada) and Lillian M. Cooper (Montreal, Can.)
John William, b. 5/16/1920; third; Gerald W. Dennis (farmer, Canada) and Lillian M. Cooper (Canada)

DEVOID,
Ernest Louis, b. 2/17/1915; sixth; Frank Devoid (laborer, Stocksboro) and Hattie LaRose (Sherburn, VT)

DEWARE,
William Robert, b. 2/5/1950; first; Robert William Deware, Jr. (mechanic, MA) and Leona Josephine Durette (NH)

DEXTER,
daughter, b. 8/12/1888; second; Caleb Dexter (gen'l laborer, Strafford) and Hattie Gault (Gilmanton)
Etta F., b. 1/26/1890; second; Caleb Dexter (laborer, NS) and Hattie Gault (Gilmanton)

DICKERSON,
daughter, b. 4/10/1921; second; Paul Dickerson (baker, Mobile, AL) and Sarah E. McWilliams (Fall River, MA); residence - Fall River, MA

DICKEY,
Jeffrey Allen, b. 5/19/1976 in Laconia; John Lewis Dickey (PA) and Carolyn M. Wheeler (MA)
Jonathan L., b. 5/2/1979 in Laconia; John L. Dickey and Carolyn M. Wheeler
Melissa M., b. 12/1/1980 in Laconia; John L. Dickey and Carolyn M. Wheeler

DICKINSON,
Christina Rayel, b. 9/3/1988 in Laconia; Theodore A. Dickinson and Cynthia M. Devaney

DIMOND,
Alice Florence, b. 1/10/1924; first; Chester Dimond (shoeworker, Detroit, MI) and Florence Gilman (Gilmanton)
Ernestine B., b. 3/24/1928; second; Chester L. Dimond (laborer, Detroit, MI) and Florence B. Gilman (Gilmanton)
Ralph Eric, b. 10/16/1930; third; Chester L. Dimond (laborer, MI) and Florence Gilman (Gilmanton)

DION,
Jessica Maria, b. 2/1/2000 in Laconia; Rudolphe Dion and Michelle Dion
Katie Marie, b. 7/15/1992 in Gilmanton; Paul M. Dion and Mellissa A. Gauthier
Quentin Michael, b. 12/12/2001 in Laconia; Rudolphe Dion and Michelle Dion
Rudolphe Louis, Jr., b. 7/27/1997 in Laconia; Rudolphe Louis Dion, Sr. and Michelle Leigh Page

DIVERS,
Andrew S., Jr., b. 11/3/1982 in Laconia; Andrew S. Divers and Rachel R. Hyslop

DOBENS,
Kate Ellen, b. 10/15/1990 in Laconia; David J. Dobens and Carol D. Anderson

DOHERTY,
Joshua Daniel, b. 6/29/1997 in Laconia; Gary Ralph Doherty and Karen Edla Nordquist

DONOVAN,
Deborah L., b. 7/23/1975 in Concord; Michael A. Donovan (NH) and Janet L. Thompson (NH)

DORSEY,
Matthew Nicholas, b. 7/5/1986 in Concord; David M. Dorsey and Orba J. Hodges
Robin Brianna, b. 2/14/1984 in Concord; David M. Dorsey and Jeannie Hodges

DOUGLAS,
Clyde Edgar, b. 11/24/1911; first; George L. Douglas (office clerk, Concord, MA) and Mildred N. Place (Gilmanton)
Grace Loretta, b. 3/20/1917; third; George L. Douglas (clerk, Concord, MA) and Mildred N. Place (Gilmanton); residence - Boston, MA
Lawrence Malcolm, b. 9/3/1915; second; George Louis Douglas (clerk, Concord, MA) and Mildred N. Place (Gilmanton); residence - MA

DOW,
Amanda Lynn, b. 6/22/1987 in Laconia; Robert B. Dow and Linda A. Perry
Oscar Everett, b. 4/15/1904; first; Oscar C. Dow (teacher, Gilmanton) and Zilla N. Pease (Gilmanton)

DOWES,
son, b. 4/20/1908; second; Arthur E. Dowes (laborer, Bradford, VT) and Maud A. Haskell (Pittsfield)
Arthur Albert, b. 6/24/1905; first; Arthur Dowes (laborer, Bradford, VT) and Maud Haskell (Pittsfield)

DOWNING,
Kimberly Jean, b. 10/14/1974 in Wolfeboro; Gregory M. Downing (MA) and Pauline E. Price (NH)

DREW,
Alice May, b. 8/23/1913; first; David Drew (farmer, Boscawen) and Edith Adams (Mason)
Camryn Anndrea, b. 5/2/2000 in Concord; Jason Drew and Christine Drew

Clarence David, b. 11/15/1917; third; David J. Drew (farmer,
   Boscawen) and Edith Abbie Adams (Mason)
Jordan Elizabeth, b. 10/25/1997 in Concord; Jason Fearing Drew
   and Christine Ann Janes
Vera Mildred, b. 4/23/1914; seventh; Carl F. Drew (laborer, Loudon)
   and Flora A. Cate (Loudon)
Walter James, b. 1/31/1916; second; David J. Drew (farmer,
   Boscawen) and Edith Adams (Mason)

DUANE,
Natalie, b. 1/24/1986 in Concord; Richard D. Duane, Jr. and Carole
   J. Ham
Samantha, b. 1/24/1986 in Concord; Richard D. Duane, Jr. and
   Carole J. Ham

DUBE,
Jaime Majel, b. 8/31/1977 in Wolfeboro; Yves A. Dube (Canada)
   and Sophie G. Hawes (NH)

DUBIA,
daughter, b. 7/17/1907; fourth; John H. Dubia (laborer, VT) and
   Josephine J. Clairmont (Sherbrooke, PQ)
Joseph Omer Levi, b. 4/2/1906; third; John H. Dubia (teamster,
   Newport, VT) and Josie Julia Claremont (Canada)
Naulbert John, b. 4/2/1906; second; John H. Dubia (teamster,
   Newport, VT) and Josie Julia Claremont (Canada)

DUBUC,
Forrest Wentworth, b. 11/29/1988 in Hanover; Russell T. Dubuc
   and Dereth W. French

DUCA,
Eric Michael, b. 6/11/1993 in Concord; William H. Duca, Jr. and Jill
   H. Joki
Kyle William, b. 9/12/1991 in Concord; William H. Duca, Jr. and Jill
   H. Joki

DUDLEY,
Barbara J., b. 1/20/1955; sixth; Irving D. Dudley, Jr. (livestock
   dealer, Concord) and Dorothy A. Hurlbutt (Groveton)

Beatrice Ellen, b. 3/17/1953; seventh; Irving D. Dudley, Jr. (cattle dealer, Concord) and Dorothy A. Hurlbutt (Groveton)
Daniel Dean, b. 2/12/1960 in Laconia; ninth; Irving Dean Dudley, Jr. (storekeeper, NH) and Dorothy Arlene Hurlbutt (NH)
David Irving, b. 10/1/1961 in Concord; eighth; Irving Dean Dudley, Jr. (self-emp. farmer, NH) and Dorothy Arlene Hurlbutt (NH)
Helen Elizabeth, b. 10/28/1950; sixth; I. Dean Dudley (cattle dealer, Concord) and Dorothy Hurlbutt (Groveton)

DUNNE,
Daniel Joseph, b. 2/22/1969 in Concord; John James Dunne (NY) and Judith Anne Coucci (NY)
Jennifer Anne, b. 8/1/1971 in Concord; John James Dunne (NY) and Judith Anne Coucci (NY)
John James, Jr., b. 12/8/1967 in Concord; first; John James Dunne, Sr. (welder, NY) and Judith Anne Coucci (NY)
Margaret Mary, b. 3/27/1970 in Concord; John James Dunne (NY) and Judith Anne Coucci (NY)

DUSSAULT,
Alexander Samuel, b. 12/18/1995 in Laconia; Maurice R. Dussault and Tammy Ann Larkin

DUTTON,
Douglas Everette, b. 6/4/1966 in Laconia; eighth; Mark Erastus Dutton (unemployed, NH) and Catherine Elaine Hinshaw (CA)
Katherine Alice, b. 11/8/1933; second; Carroll F. Dutton (farmer, Morgan, VT) and Dorothy F. Edgerly (Gilmanton); residence - Morgan, VT
Mark Erastus, b. 5/16/1935; third; C. Fred Dutton (laborer, Morgan, VT) and Dorothy Edgerly (Gilmanton)

DWYER,
Jonathan Michael, b. 7/1/1991 in Concord; Michael J. Dwyer and Amelia E. Sears

DYER,
Curtis Alan, b. 6/15/1994 in Laconia; Jason Alan Dyer and Dianne Marie LaPlante
Emily Erin, b. 10/21/2000 in Concord; Brandon Dyer and Kelly Dyer

Ralph Edgar, b. 3/9/1921; second; Joseph N. Dyer (laborer, Chesterville, ME) and Lillian A. Groton (Washington, ME)
Sasha Lynn, b. 10/18/1991 in Laconia; Jason A. Dyer and Dianne M. LaPlante

EASTMAN,
Brian Glenwood, b. 1/18/1993 in Concord; Douglas R. Eastman and Linda A. Joyce
Judith Lynne, b. 10/25/1939 in Wolfeboro; second; Ralph W. Eastman (garage prop., Swampscott, MA) and Beatrice Carpenter (Houlton, ME)
Rebecca Mae, b. 6/2/1989 in Concord; Douglas R. Eastman and Linda A. Joyce

EATON,
Catherine, b. 5/10/1909; third; Theodore H. Eaton (teacher, St. Louis, MO) and Theodora West (Brookville, MA)
Julia, b. 11/14/1910; fourth; Theodore F. Eaton (farmer, St. Louis, MO) and Theodora West (Brookline, MA)

EDGERLY,
Albert David, b. 1/23/1915; second; Frank A. Edgerly (teacher, Gilmanton) and Mary Morgan (Mois River, PQ)
Charles George Morgan, b. 11/29/1918; third; Frank A. Edgerly (rec'r U.S. Ser., Nashville, TN) and Mary R. Morgan (Moes River, PQ)
Dorothy Zoa, b. 7/6/1909; first; Frank A. Edgerly (farmer, Nashville, TN) and Mary A. Morgan (Moer River, PQ)
Esther Joyce, b. 6/10/1938 in Wolfeboro; first; George David Edgerly (heel laster, Gilmanton) and Lavinia E. Gooch (Alton); residence - Gilmanton I. W.
Florence C., b. 10/26/1897; second; Walter J. Edgerly (merchant, Gilmanton) and Anna C. Cogswell (Gilmanton)
George David, b. 9/25/1914; first; Roy C. Edgerly (farmer, Gilmanton) and Minnie F. McLean (Barre, VT)
Margaret Constance, b. 4/26/1921; fourth; Frank A. Edgerly (farmer, Nashville, TN) and Mary A. Morgan (Mors River, PQ)
Phyllis, b. 4/29/1916; first; Florence C. Edgerly (Gilmanton)
Ruth, b. 2/14/1901; third; Walter J. Edgerly (teamster, Gilmanton) and Anna M. Cogswell (Gilmanton)

EDMUNDS,
Michael Robert, b. 8/23/1995 in Laconia; Michael J. Edmunds and Tamara J. Dow

EDWARDS,
Donald John, Jr., b. 3/4/1965 in Laconia; third; Donald John Edwards (field ret., PA) and Mary Jane White (PA)
Patricia Ann, b. 12/30/1940; second; Glenn Edwards (mill owner, Shandaken, NY) and Mildred E. E. Hayes (New Durham)
Sandra Jean, b. 12/20/1962 in Laconia; second; Donald J. Edwards (field repre., PA) and Mary Jane White (PA)
Shirley Mae, b. 2/10/1939 in Wolfeboro; first; Glenn Edwards (truck driver, Shandaken, NY) and Mildred E. Hayes (New Durham); residence - Gilmanton I. W.

EISENHAUER,
Charles Earl, b. 11/14/1984 in Concord; John D. Eisenhauer and Anita B. Goupil
Sara Patricia, b. 6/1/1981 in Laconia; John D. Eisenhauer and Anita B. Goupil

EISENMANN,
Michael John, b. 5/24/2001 in Concord; Phillip Eisenmann and Danielle Eisenmann

ELKINS,
daughter, b. 7/19/1891; first; John T. Elkins (farmer, Gilmanton) and Cora Bell Ham (Gilmanton)
daughter, b. 10/5/1895; eighth; Frank J. Elkins (carpenter, Gilmanton) and Mary E. Dunbar (Quincy, MA)
daughter, b. 3/2/1901; twelfth; Frank J. Elkins (farmer, Gilmanton) and Mary E. Dunbar (Quincy, MA)
stillborn daughter, b. 3/27/1902; thirteenth; Frank J. Elkins (farmer, Gilmanton) and Mary E. Dunbar (Quincy, MA)
son, b. 7/7/1904; fourteenth; Frank J. Elkins (carpenter, Gilmanton) and Mary E. Dunbar (Quincy, MA)
Bessie Watson, b. 12/4/1899; eleventh; Frank J. Elkins (farmer, Gilmanton) and Mary E. Dunbar (Quincy, MA)
Emma L., b. 6/25/1894; seventh; Frank J. Elkins (carpenter, Gilmanton) and Mary E. Dunbar (Quincy, MA)

ELLINGER,
Uriah Richard, b. 9/8/1992 in Concord; Richard L. Ellinger and
    Patricia A. Hickey

ELLIOTT,
daughter, b. 4/6/1905; fifth; D. William Elliott (teamster, Rumney)
    and Bertha C. Plummer
Caleb Bradley, b. 1/16/1996 in Lebanon; Larry Ernest Elliott and
    Tara Lee Buchholz

ELLIS,
son, b. 1/6/1890; third; Horace Ellis (farmer, Alton) and Ella Page
    (Gilmanton)
Roger Michael, b. 12/16/1947; second; Horace D. Ellis (mill
    operator, Sanbornville) and Audrey M. Dowst (Laconia)

ELLSWORTH,
child, b. 12/10/1892; fifth; Alfred P. Ellsworth (farmer, Gilmanton)
    and Hannah Birmingham (England)
daughter, b. 12/14/1892; sixth; Euraldo P. Ellsworth (farmer,
    Gilmanton) and Mary Allen (NY)
child, b. 3/1/1894; Alden Ellsworth (farmer)
daughter, b. 12/2/1900; second; Lester F. Ellsworth (farmer,
    Gilmanton) and Alice A. Gilman (Lakeport)
daughter, b. 12/25/1901; third; Lester H. Ellsworth (farmer,
    Gilmanton) and Alice A. Gilman (Gilmanton)
son, b. 8/18/1905; sixth; Lester H. Ellsworth (farmer, Gilmanton)
    and Alice A. Gilman (Lakeport)
daughter, b. 7/22/1907; sixth; Lester H. Ellsworth (farmer,
    Gilmanton) and Alice A. Gilman (Gilford)
daughter, b. 3/3/1909; seventh; Lester Ellsworth (farmer,
    Gilmanton) and Alice Gilman (Lakeport)
daughter, b. 4/1/1910; eighth; Lester Ellsworth (farmer, Gilmanton)
    and Alice Gilman (Lakeport)
son, b. 1/3/1913; first; Earl M. Ellsworth (farmer, Gilmanton) and
    Blanche E. Pease (Belmont); residence - Belmont
son [Clyde W.], b. 1/3/1913; second; Earl M. Ellsworth (farmer,
    Gilmanton) and Blanche E. Pease (Belmont); residence -
    Belmont
daughter, b. 6/21/1914; tenth; Lester H. Ellsworth (farmer,
    Gilmanton) and Alice A. Gilman (Lakeport)

son, b. 10/17/1916; tenth; Lester H. Ellsworth (farmer, Gilmanton) and Alice A. Gilman (Lakeport)
Frances, b. 10/12/1920; twelfth; Lester Ellsworth (farmer, Gilmanton) and Alice Gilman (Lakeport)
Leon Everard, b. 2/18/1904; fifth; Elmer (sic) H. Ellsworth (farmer, Gilmanton) and Alice A. Gilman
Lionel Edward, b. 2/18/1904; fourth; Lester H. Ellsworth (farmer, Gilmanton) and Alice A. Gilman
Nellie, b. 11/4/1889; fifth; Euraldo P. Ellsworth (farmer, Gilmanton) and Mary E. Ellen (NY)
Steven Franklin, b. 12/16/1978 in Laconia; Leon Lester Ellsworth, Jr. (NH) and Suzanne Marie Jacques (NH)

EMERSON,
son, b. 6/28/1901; fifth; Samuel H. Emerson (teamster, Canada) and Carrie L. Smith (Shelbyville, KY)
son, b. 7/11/1903; sixth; Samuel Emerson (teamster, Brookfield) and Carrie L. Smith (Shelbyville, KY)
daughter, b. 4/18/1905; first; Loren H. Emerson (teamster, Danville, Canada) and Lena D. Tardy (Quebec, Canada)
Grace Bernice, b. 3/18/1893; first; Ansel Emerson (blacksmith, Barnstead) and Alice J. Page (Gilmanton)

ENGLISH,
son, b. 4/2/1910; fourth; Edward T. English (cigarmaker, Webster, MA) and Abbie M. McCarthy (Pittsfield)

ERWIN,
Richard M., b. 7/21/1940; second; Richard H. Erwin (teacher, New Britain, CT) and Margaret I. Marston (Brockton, MA)

ESTY,
Allan Hugelman, b. 10/30/1989 in Laconia; Edward I. Esty and Roxanne H. Hugelman
Kathryn Marie, b. 10/8/1991 in Plymouth; Edward I. Esty and Roxanne H. Hugelman

EVANS,
James Wong, b. 8/23/1934 in Pittsfield; first; George W. Evans (laborer, Canada) and Elsie L. Wong (Vineland, NJ)

Phillip, b. 10/4/1953; fourth; Victor F. J. Evans (welder - carp., MA) and Jeannette Pennington (NH)
Robert Monroe, b. 9/12/1936; fourth; Chester D. Evans (farmer, Weymouth, MA) and Rena H. Johnson (Rochester, VT)
Virginia Anne, b. 9/18/1943; third; George W. Evans (grinder, NS) and Elsie Li Wong (Vineland, NJ)

EVANS-BROWN,
Ellis Charles, b. 5/9/1983 in Concord; Hammond F. Brown and Anne E. Evans
Samuel Tyler, b. 2/17/1986 in Gilmanton; Hammond F. Brown and Anne Eliza Evans

FABIAN,
Derek Paul, b. 12/17/1993 in Concord; Thomas S. Fabian and Janet S. Desrosiers

FALARDEAU,
Laura B., b. 2/5/1979 in Laconia; James J. Falardeau and Barbara A. Beaulieu

FANNING,
Amy Lee, b. 8/28/1976 in Laconia; John R. Fanning (DE) and Lynn Carey (DE)
Michael James, b. 1/26/1972 in Laconia; John Robert Fanning (DE) and Lynn Carey (DE)

FELLOWS,
Rachel Adele, b. 5/25/1934 in Laconia; second; Harry B. Fellows (farmer, W. Stewartstown) and Effie B. Johnson (Laconia)

FERNANDEZ,
Kevin B., b. 11/8/1979 in Concord; Brian Fernandez and Michele M. Gallien

FIELD,
Charles Philip, b. 10/26/1932; first; Walter A. Field (gardener, Putnam, CT) and Juanita Gorman (Killingly, CT)

FIELDERS,
James Alan, b. 7/1/1970 in Laconia; Eugene Arthur Fielders (NH) and Louise Margaret Bennett (NH)
Pamela Susan, b. 6/19/1965 in Laconia; third; Eugene Arthur Fielders (Sulloway Mills, NH) and Louise Margaret Bennett (NH)
Scott Jay, b. 12/11/1968 in Laconia; Eugene Arthur Fielders (NH) and Louise Margaret Bennett (NH)

FILLION,
Abigael Elizabeth, b. 5/25/2001 in Laconia; Jeffrie Fillion and Cindy Fillion
Brid Elizabeth, b. 12/26/1995 in Concord; William A. Fillion and Kathleen M. Carr
David Christopher, b. 8/11/1967 in Laconia; first; David Allen Fillion (teacher, NY) and Rosalie Ellen Karzeniewski (NY)
Margaret Katherine, b. 5/16/1997 in Laconia; Jeffrie Scott Fillion and Cindy Lee Clairmont
Mitchell Scott, b. 3/1/1995 in Laconia; Jeffrie Scott Fillion and Cindy Lee Clairmont
Sarah Carr, b. 7/29/2000 in Laconia; William Fillion and Kathleen Fillion
William Arthur, b. 4/30/1963 in Laconia; first; William Eugene Fillion (restaurant opr., VT) and Constance Madonna Landroche (NH)
William Arthur, Jr., b. 11/18/1992 in Concord; William A. Fillion and Kathleen M. Carr

FISCHER,
Jessica, b. 4/29/1975 in Laconia; Joseph A. Fischer (NY) and Christine T. Monfre (NY)

FISH,
Katie Elizabeth, b. 5/14/1978 in Concord; Stanley Allen Fish (MA) and Karen Elizabeth Moore (NH)
Timothy M., b. 12/12/1979 in Concord; Stanley A. Fish and Karen E. Moore

FLANDERS,
Elsie Virginia, b. 3/12/1925; first; Victor C. Flanders (laborer, Gilmanton) and Elsie Purcell (Westford, MA)

Jane Ann, b. 7/25/1957 in Concord; third; Robert J. Flanders (plumber, NH) and Grace E. Davis (NH)
Jay Alan, b. 7/22/1956 in Concord; first; Robert J. Flanders (plumber, Loudon) and Grace E. Davis (Wolfeboro)
Jean Ann, b. 7/25/1957 in Concord; second; Robert J. Flanders (plumber, NH) and Grace E. Davis (NH)
Verlie Merle, b. 10/21/1922; Harry L. Flanders and Edith L. Thatcher
Victor Asahel, b. 8/14/1926; second; Victor C. Flanders (laborer, Gilmanton) and Elsie B. Purcell (Westford, MA)
Victor Converse, b. 5/10/1899; first; Rufus L. Flanders (sawyer, Gilmanton) and Alice G. Converse (Monson, MA)

FOGG,
son, b. 9/4/1905; second; Albion Fogg (laborer, Gilmanton) and Jennie La Foo (Lakeport)
daughter, b. 4/29/1906; second; Jason Fogg (laborer, Gilmanton) and Myrtie Jones (Gilmanton)
son, b. 12/3/1908; third; Jason Fogg (laborer, Gilmanton) and Myrtie E. Jones (Gilmanton)
daughter, b. 12/4/1925; second; Clifton W. Fogg (farmer, Lakeport) and Bessie Bean (Gilford)
daughter, b. 5/20/1932; first; Mary R. Fogg (Gilmanton)
Emily M., b. 4/10/1913; fifth; Jason Fogg (laborer, Gilmanton) and Myrtle Jones (Gilmanton)
Jessie Rebecca, b. 10/13/1992 in Laconia; Michael B. Fogg and Stephanie Stevens
Leon Cleveland, b. 9/9/1910; fourth; Jason Fogg (farmer, Gilmanton) and Myrtie Jones (Gilmanton)
Martha Ann, b. 9/30/1927; third; Clifton W. Fogg (laborer, Lakeport) and Bessie M. Bean (Gilford)
Nellie Adeline, b. 6/10/1915; sixth; Jason Fogg (laborer, Gilmanton) and Myrtie E. Jones (Gilmanton)

FORD,
Jeanette Lou, b. 10/18/1933 in Laconia; first; Herbert Ford (mechanic, New Warner) and Lucille Stickney (Lisbon)

FORST,
Barry John, b. 6/19/1971 in Concord; Kenneth Melvin Forst (NH) and Elaine Carol Saturley (NH)

Brian Allen, b. 6/17/1966 in Concord; first; Kenneth Melvin Forst (dairy farmer, NH) and Elaine Carol Saturley (NH)
Heidi Lynn, b. 5/28/1973 in Concord; Kenneth Melvin Forst (NH) and Elaine Carol Saturley (NH)
John Allen, b. 2/26/1994 in Concord; Brian Allen Forst and Donna Marie Smith
Laure Ruth, b. 9/3/1977 in Concord; Kenneth M. Forst (NH) and Elaine C. Saturley (NH)

FORSYTH[E],
Amanda Jane, b. 9/14/1976 in Wolfeboro; Ralph G. Forsyth (NH) and Leslie A. Brown (MA)
Bernice Ruth, b. 2/18/1939 in Wolfeboro; ninth; Harvey A. Forsyth (WPA worker, Canada) and Marion L. Jordan (Piermont)
Florence, b. 2/20/1937; eighth; Harvey A. Forsyth (farmer, Ontario, Can.) and Marion Jordan (Piermont)
George Scott, b. 5/5/1945 in Wolfeboro; second; Harry G. Forsyth (truck driver, Chatham, Canada) and Evelyn C. Rollins (Dalton)
George Scott, II, b. 9/3/1966 in Wolfeboro; first; George Scott Forsyth (Army, NH) and Mary Ann Price (NH)
Jennifer Sue, b. 9/17/1969 in Wolfeboro; George Scott Forsyth (NH) and Maryann Price (NH)
Malcolm Eugene, b. 1/12/1947; first; George N. Forsyth (shoe cementer, Ontario, Canada) and Mary D. Gilliam (Olive Hill, KY)
Michael Stanley, b. 4/13/1947; third; Harry G. Forsyth (truck driver, Chatham, Canada) and Evelyn O. Rollins (Dalton)
Ralph Gordon, b. 6/21/1942; first; Harry G. Forsythe (truckman, Ontario, Can.) and Evelyn Rollins (Dalton)
Sarah Elizabeth, b. 12/9/1977 in Wolfeboro; Ralph G. Forsyth (NH) and Leslie A. Brown (MA)
Steven H., b. 11/8/1956 in Wolfeboro; fourth; Harry G. Forsyth (road agent, Ontario, Canada) and Evelyn O. Rollins (Dalton)

FOSS,
daughter, b. 8/18/1899; first; Carroll E. Foss (farmer, Gilmanton) and Bessie M. Peaslee (Gilmanton)
stillborn daughter, b. 4/17/1901; first; Frank W. Foss (farmer, Gilmanton) and Nettie Peaslee (Gilmanton)

daughter, b. 10/30/1903; second; Carroll E. Foss (farmer,
    Gilmanton) and Bessie M. Peaslee (Gilmanton)
Ivan Frank, b. 4/6/1916; first; Frank W. Foss (farmer, Gilmanton)
    and Florence A. Foss (Strafford)
Shirley May, b. 9/11/1932 in Pittsfield; third; John H. Foss (farmer,
    Haverhill, MA) and Nina M. Higgins (Fairlee, VT)

FOSTER,
Alec L., b. 12/6/1979 in Concord; William L. Foster and Elizabeth A.
    Mitchel
Catherine Anne, b. 8/15/1985 in Concord; William L. Foster and
    Elizabeth A. Mitchell

FOUNTAIN,
Christopher Harrison, b. 5/6/1998 in Concord; Timothy Francis
    Fountain and Susan Marie Fitzpatrick
Kimberly Rose, b. 3/1/2000 in Concord; Timothy Fountain and
    Susan Fountain

FRANZ,
Pauline Elizabeth, b. 2/8/1917; third; Alfred August Franz (farmer,
    S. Boston, MA) and Margaret E. Smith (S. Boston, MA)

FREEMAN,
Jerry Robert, II, b. 10/26/1968 in Laconia; Jerry Robert Freeman
    (NH) and Gwendolyn Agnes Taylor (NH)

FREESE,
Elliott William, b. 2/19/1988 in Concord; Timothy S. Freese and
    Linda M. Finnegan
Lindsay Marie, b. 2/12/1986 in Concord; Timothy S. Freese and
    Linda M. Finnegan

FRENCH,
son, b. 6/17/1895; fifth; Jeremiah S. French (farmer, Gilmanton)
    and Ida B. Locke
daughter, b. 5/24/1901; sixth; Jeremiah S. French (farmer,
    Gilmanton) and Ida B. Locke (Loudon)
stillborn son, b. 2/2/1903; third; Fred S. French (farmer, Gilmanton)
    and Mary Latuche (Canada)

son, b. 5/3/1904; first; John S. French (farmer, Gilmanton) and
   Mary L. Pearl (Loudon)
son [Ivo P.], b. 10/15/1905; second; John S. French (farmer,
   Gilmanton) and Mary L. Bell (Loudon)
son [Wesley E.], b. 1/14/1908; first; Will A. French (farmer,
   Gilmanton) and Annie M. Carr (Gilmanton)
Althea June, b. 10/13/1934; first; Ivo P. French (farmer, Gilmanton)
   and Althea M. Fulton (Boston, MA)
Barbara Jean, b. 6/10/1938; third; Ivo P. French (farmer,
   Gilmanton) and Althea M. Fulton (Boston, MA)
Buzzie Bill, b. 10/24/1956 in Laconia; second; William C. S. French,
   Jr. (mechanic, Chichester) and Laura E. Page (Gilmanton)
Carl, b. 4/11/1889; fourth; Jeremiah S. French (farmer, Gilmanton)
   and Ida B. Lock (Gilmanton)
Jeremy Alan, b. 1/15/1988 in Laconia; Timothy M. French and
   Donna A. Sasko
Louise A., b. 6/23/1930 in Concord; first; Charles C. French
   (farmer, Loudon) and Grace E. Andrews (Corinna, ME)
Marjorie Pearl, b. 1/21/1949; fourth; Ivo P. French (farmer,
   Gilmanton) and Althea M. Fulton (Boston, MA)
Martha Pauline, b. 5/5/1919; fourth; John S. French (farmer,
   Gilmanton) and Mary L. Pearl (Loudon)
Penny Hope, b. 11/27/1962 in Laconia; third; William C. S. French
   (mechanic, NH) and Laura Ella Page (NH)
Sylvia Joyce, b. 1/13/1937; second; Ivo P. French (farmer,
   Gilmanton) and Altha M. Fulton (Boston, MA)

FREYMUTH,
Kelli D., b. 4/19/1982 in Laconia; Fred H. Freymuth and Gail J.
   Gustafson

FRICK,
Kelley Holland, b. 6/24/1990 in Laconia; John L. Frick and Sharon
   A. Arena

FRIZZLE,
Bruce Arthur, b. 1/6/1948; fourth; Charles D. Frizzle (lumber jack,
   Concord, MA) and Shirley M. Richardson (Chester)

FROST,
daughter, b. 4/4/1899; third; William L. Frost (blacksmith, Rowley, MA) and Carrie B. Smith (Kingston)
son [Philip M.], b. 8/17/1908; third; Harry M. Frost (shoemaker, Portland, ME) and Ida A. Cuthbertson (Charleston, MA); residence - Winthrop
Cassandra Lynn, b. 1/1/1974 in Concord; Maurice A. Frost (NH) and Jean L. McClary (NH)
Daniel George, b. 4/23/1971 in Concord; Maurice Arthur Frost (NH) and Jean Louise McClary (NH)

FULK,
Ethan Carl, b. 2/1/1992 in Concord; Stephen R. Fulk and Gayle J. Sanborn
Jonathan Stephen, b. 10/2/1989 in Concord; Stephen R. Fulk and Gayle J. Sanborn
Julia Gayle, b. 1/21/1994 in Concord; Stephen Robert Fulk and Gayle Jean Sanborn
Kylie Joy, b. 8/9/1998 in Concord; Stephen Fulk and Gayle Fulk

FULLER,
Colin P., b. 11/7/1979 in Laconia; Paul J. Fuller and Donna M. Caldrain

GAGNE,
Madeline Alyssa, b. 10/5/1988 in Laconia; Jon E. Gagne and Sara E. Wing
Seth Michael, b. 2/14/1985 in Laconia; Gary R. Gagne and Paula M. Gagne

GAGNON,
Garrett Harold, b. 6/13/1974 in Concord; Harold Alphee Gagnon (NH) and Myra L. Little (MA)
Jason Phillip, b. 1/22/2001 in Laconia; Mark Gagnon and Jean Gagnon
Margaret Jean, b. 11/12/1932; first; Eugene W. Gagnon (farmer, Thetford, PQ) and Dorothy Hislop (Berwick, ME)

GALLANT,
Bailee Jae, b. 8/8/2001 in Concord; Michael Gallant and Victoria Gallant

GAMACHE,
Katiana Morgan, b. 10/10/2001 in Laconia; Christopher Gamache and Kristina Toth
Sandor Joseph, b. 12/22/1999 in Lebanon; Christopher Gamache and Kristina Toth

GARDNER,
Amy E., b. 7/3/1975 in Laconia; Leslie A. Gardner (NY) and Jacqueline F. Geddes (NH)
Erin R., b. 7/6/1979 in Laconia; Leslie A. Gardner and Jacqueline F. Geddes
Ian Buchanan, b. 4/22/1999 in Lebanon; Dana Gardner and Sherry McInroy-Gardner

GASSETT,
Angela Roseann, b. 8/3/1967 in Concord; first; Ronald Kenneth Gassett (laborer, NH) and Linda Ann Littlefield (NH)

GAULT,
stillborn son, b. 3/7/1892; Charles W. Gault (merchant, Gilmanton) and Ida L. Varney (Rochester)
son, b. 6/11/1895; third; Charles W. Gault (merchant, Gilmanton) and Ida L. Varney (Rochester)
son, b. 1/24/1897; fourth; Charles W. Gault (merchant, Gilmanton) and Ida L. Varney
daughter, b. 6/11/1902; third; John Gault (laborer) and Malvina Battis (Gilmanton)
Augustus S., b. 6/7/1905; sixth; John C. Gault (laborer, Bridgewater) and Malvina Battis (Gilmanton)
Charles William, b. 8/30/1910; eleventh; John C. Gault (carpenter, Bridgewater) and Melvina Battis (Gilmanton)
Dorothy Frances, b. 1/31/1909; tenth; John C. Gault (laborer, Bridgewater) and Melvina Battis (Gilmanton)
Edna Elvira, b. 3/9/1907; ninth; John C. Gault (laborer, Bridgewater) and Melvina Battis (Gilmanton)

GEDDES,
daughter, b. 7/9/1924; second; Walter R. Geddes (farmer, Ontario, Can.) and Glemia Anair (Stowe, VT)
Christina A., b. 11/10/1975 in Laconia; Duncan J. Geddes (NH) and Barbara A. Tasker (NH)

David Douglas, b. 4/28/1987 in Laconia; David W. Geddes, Jr. and
    Diane L. Gray
David Walter, Jr., b. 3/7/1958 in Concord; fifth; David W. Geddes,
    Sr. (skilled carpenter, NH) and Ann A. Hogan (NH)
Duncan J., b. 6/14/1956 in Concord; fourth; David W. Geddes
    (lumberman, Gilford) and Anna A. Hogan (Farmington)
Duncan J., Jr., b. 6/6/1981 in Laconia; Duncan J. Geddes, Sr. and
    Barbara A. Tasker
Jacqueline F., b. 6/25/1955; third; David W. Geddes (lumberman,
    NH) and Anna A. Hogan (NH)
John Donald, b. 10/17/1988 in Laconia; David W. Geddes, Jr. and
    Diane L. Gray
Mary Florence, b. 4/9/1923; John A. Geddes and Florence A.
    Edgerly
Stephanie Anne, b. 1/30/1954; first; David W. Geddes (lumberman,
    Gilford) and Anna Alice Hogan (Farmington)
Trisha Lynn, b. 6/18/1978 in Laconia; Duncan John Geddes (NH)
    and Barbara Ann Tasker (NH)
Virginia May, b. 6/22/1927; first; Kenneth D. Geddes (laborer,
    Ontario, Can.) and Edna M. Davis (Gilmanton)

GENTILE,
Anthony James, b. 6/28/2000 in Laconia; James Gentile and
    Pamela Gentile
Hailey Alexandra, b. 2/13/1994 in Laconia; Thomas Richard Gentile
    and Stacie Nicole Buiak
Nicole Elizabeth, b. 3/19/1992 in Laconia; Thomas R. Gentile and
    Stacie N. Buiak

GERSHUN-HALF,
Emma Sarah, b. 10/21/1989 in Gilmanton; William H. Half and
    Ellen C. Gershun
Isaac Morgan, b. 2/1/1994 in Gilmanton; William Howard Half and
    Ellen Carol Gershun
Maya Rebecca, b. 6/26/1997 in Gilmanton; William Howard Half
    and Ellen Carol Gershun

GILBERT,
Adam Lawrence, b. 10/9/1978 in Concord; Joseph Albert Gilbert
    (NH) and Jo-Anne Clairmont (NH)

GILL,
Justin Robert, b. 11/26/1976 in Concord; Robert A. Gill (MA) and
  Eileen Mary Jantomaso (MA)

GILLANT,
Jason Scott, b. 8/3/1971 in Laconia; John Francis Gillant (NH) and
  Dorothy Mae Judd (NH)

GILLE,
Amber, b. 4/16/1985 in Laconia; Paul W. Gille and Cynthia R.
  Currier

GILMAN,
daughter, b. 8/30/1905; second; Ira Gilman (farmer, Gilmanton) and
  Cora York (Pittsfield)
Charon A., b. 7/20/1956 in Laconia; fourth; Paul E. Gilman
  (mechanic, NH) and Lucile A. Hawkins (NH)
Charles A., b. 7/20/1956 in Laconia; fifth; Paul E. Gilman
  (mechanic, NH) and Lucile A. Hawkins (NH)
Helen Mary, b. 5/8/1920; third; Ira Gilman (farmer, Gilmanton) and
  Cora B. York (Pittsfield)
Kathleen H., b. 8/9/1956 in Laconia; second; Murray L. Gilman
  (stock chaser, Woodstock) and Jean E. Godreault (New York,
  NY)
Lewis Melvin, b. 2/10/1903; first; Ira Gilman (farmer, Gilmanton)
  and Cora B. York (Pittsfield)
Michael Allen, b. 12/13/1958 in Laconia; third; Murray Lewis Gilman
  (stock clerk, NH) and Jean Elizabeth Gadreault (NY)
Mildred E., b. 11/2/1896; first; Arthur L. Gilman (farmer, Gilmanton)
  and Emma J. Marsh (Gilmanton)
Robert Alan, b. 9/26/1950; second; Paul Edwin Gilman (truck
  driver, NH) and Lucille Ann Hawkins (NH)
Sheila Eileen, b. 9/1/1954; third; Paul E. Gilman (salesman, NH)
  and Lucile A. Hawkins (NH)

GLIDDEN,
stillborn child, b. 10/–/1894; Charles H. Glidden (editor, Gilmanton)
  and Mary G. Orange (Lowell, MA); residence - Boston, MA
Carl Henry, b. 9/21/1916; third; A. Mooney Glidden (farmer, Alton)
  and Florence M. Tibbetts (Alton)

Charles T., b. 10/31/1913; first; Mooney Glidden (farmer, Alton) and Florence Tibbetts (Alton)
Frank Benjamin, b. 1/7/1915; second; A. Mooney Glidden (farmer, Alton) and Florence M. Tibbetts (Alton)
Suzanne, b. 8/11/1947; second; Carl H. Glidden (veteran, Gilmanton) and Dorothy K. Boudreau (Springfield, MA)

GLINES,
Eva Maud, b. 7/8/1890; second; Albert H. Glines (farmer, Boston, MA) and Lucinda C. Jones (Loudon)

GOLDEN,
Brian Alfred, b. 8/21/1960 in Wolfeboro; fourth; Alfred Kenneth Golden (N.E. Tel. & Tel., NH) and Thelma May Rollins (NH)
Colleen Ann, b. 4/11/1970 in Laconia; Alfred Kenneth Golden (NH) and Thelma Mae Rollins (NH)
Debra L., b., 8/21/1955; second; Alfred K. Golden (N.E. Tel. & Tel., NH) and Thelma M. Rollins (NH)
Kathleen A., b. 7/19/1957 in Wolfeboro; stillborn; third; Alfred K. Golden (laborer, NH) and Thelma Rollins (NH)
Patrick Michael, b. 5/25/1953; first; Alfred K. Golden (laborer, NH) and Thelma M. Rollins (NH)
Paula Ann, b. 2/18/1950; first; Paul Anthony Golden (cable splices, NH) and Leona Christine Parker (SC)

GOODWIN,
Byron C., b. 10/10/1922; Clifton Goodwin and Ethel Dame
Edward L., b. 3/7/1911; second; Clifton Goodwin (farmer, Gilmanton) and Ethel Dame (New Durham)
Harold, b. 12/10/1915; third; Clifton Goodwin (farmer, Gilmanton) and Ethel Dame (New Durham)
Jacob John, b. 5/18/1981 in Laconia; Ernest E. Goodwin and Joan M. Mont
Olive June, b. 12/15/1938; first; Ralph L. Goodwin (truck driver, Gilmanton) and Roberta T. Hayes (New Durham)
Paula Hayes, b. 6/27/1944 in Wolfeboro; third; Ralph L. Goodwin (US Navy, Gilmanton) and Roberta F. Hayes (New Durham)
Ralph Leslie, b. 2/11/1916; first; Ernest H. Goodwin (merchant, Pittsfield) and Florence A. Watson (Pittsfield)
Ralph Leslie, Jr., b. 6/20/1949; second; Ralph Leslie Goodwin (sexton, Gilmanton) and Cliftine A. Goodfield (Pittsfield)

Sylvester Harold, b. 11/20/1907; first; Clifton Goodwin (farmer, Gilmanton) and Ethel Dame (New Durham)

GORDON,
Amanda M., b. 9/23/1982 in Laconia; Harry W. Gordon, Jr. and Charlene D. Noyes
Harry Wesley, III, b. 2/14/1981 in Laconia; Harry W. Gordon, Jr. and Charlene D. Noyes
Lillian Devoid, b. 7/28/1913; first; Clarence Gordon (laborer, VT) and Lillian Devoid (Canada)

GRAASKAMP,
Cameron William Girard, b. 7/27/1993 in Concord; Garrett W. Graaskamp and Nancy L. Girard
Kelsey Elaine Girard, b. 5/23/1990 in Concord; Garrett W. Graaskamp and Nancy L. Girard

GRAF,
Josiah Daniel, b. 10/20/1991 in Concord; Timothy P. Graf and Kimberly Jo Currier
Marissa Elaine, b. 1/6/1993 in Concord; Timothy P. Graf and Kimberly J. Currier
Philip Allen, b. 5/22/1988 in Concord; Timothy P. Graf and Kimberly J. Currier

GRAVES,
Douglas Edward, b. 4/17/1972 in Concord; William A. Graves (MA) and Rena G. George (MA)
William Alfred, Jr., b. 4/30/1968 in Concord; William Alfred Graves, Sr. (MA) and Linda Ellen DiBartolomeo (MA)

GRAY,
son [Emanuel], b. 3/28/1888; tenth; Orrin W. Gray (sawyer, Barrington) and Carrie O. Cater (Dover)
daughter, b. 3/28/1888; eleventh; Orrin W. Gray (sawyer, Barrington) and Carrie O. Cater (Dover)
Jesse Thomas, b. 1/16/1981 in Wolfeboro; George H. Gray, Jr. and Mary E. Glum
Karen Jean, b. 11/12/1962 in Concord; fifth; George Henry Gray, Sr. (carpenter, NH) and Mary Ella Beede (NH)

Kevin Douglas, b. 8/18/1961 in Concord; fourth; George Henry
  Gray, Sr. (carpenter, NH) and Mary Ella Beede (NH)
Seth E., b. 11/12/1982 in Concord; George H. Gray, Jr. and Mary E.
  Glum
Troy Andrew, b. 8/30/1966 in Laconia; first; William Irving Gray
  (mechanic, NH) and Jane Eva Maheux

GREEN [see Greene],
son [Archie W.], b. 5/1/1898; first; Walter L. Green (farmer) and ----
  Sargent
son [Jay H.], b. 1/2/1904; fourth; Elmer L. Green (farmer,
  Gilmanton) and Antonia Kratzert (Germany)
Donald Maurice, II, b. 2/8/1976 in Concord; Donald M. Green (NH)
  and Fay E. Minery (NH)
Elmer Raymond, b. 10/1/1926; first; Jay H. Green (farmer,
  Gilmanton) and Beulah Willard (Gilmanton)
Frederick Lawrence, b. 5/5/1934 in Pittsfield; first; Lawrence K.
  Green (forestry, Pittsfield) and Ruth E. Stockman (Pittsfield)
Jay Daniel, b, 5/12/1935 in Pittsfield; third; Jay H. Green (farmer,
  Gilmanton) and Beulah Willard (Gilmanton)
Maurice Garden, b. 4/25/1929; second; Jay H. Green (farmer,
  Gilmanton) and Beulah E. Willard (Gilmanton)
Roland W., b. 4/16/1892; second; Elmer L. Green (farmer,
  Gilmanton) and Antonia Kratzert (Germany)
Shirley Ann, b. 6/22/1938; fourth; Jay H. Green (truck driver,
  Gilmanton) and Beulah E. Willard (Gilmanton)

GREENE [see Green],
daughter, b. 3/17/1895; third; Elmer L. Greene (farmer, Gilmanton)
  and Antonia Kratzert (Germany)
Norman David, b. 6/3/1931; first; Roland W. Greene (farmer,
  Gilmanton) and Edna A. Paige (Gilmanton)

GREENFIELD,
Briann Gail, b. 5/31/1970 in Laconia; Harry Greenfield (MA) and
  Edna Sandra Sadzewicz (NH)

GREENOUGH,
daughter, b. 2/25/1888; fourth; Thomas M. Greenough (farmer,
  Concord) and Etta F. Robinson (West Rumney)

GREENWOOD,
Diane M., b. 4/10/1956 in Laconia; second; Eugene F. Greenwood (laborer, VT) and Prudella J. Sherman (NY)
Raymond D., b. 4/10/1956 in Laconia; third; Eugene F. Greenwood (laborer, VT) and Prudella J. Sherman (NY)

GRENIER,
Monique Leana, b. 10/28/1989 in Laconia; Thomas G. Grenier and Laura A. Skopek

GRIFFIN,
daughter, b. 12/18/1903; first; Nathan D. Griffin (farmer, Gilmanton) and Eva D. Osborne (Gilmanton)
son, b. 2/3/1908; second; Nathan D. Griffin (farmer, Gilmanton) and Eva G. Osborne (Gilmanton)
Lorraine, b. 8/7/1936 in Laconia; second; Harold W. Griffin (farmer, Gilmanton) and Doris Davis (Enfield)
Robert Davis, b. 9/9/1934 in Laconia; first; Harold W. Griffin (salesman, Gilmanton) and Doris Davis (Enfield)

GRITZ,
Pauline, b. 10/30/1916; first; Frank J. Gritz (piano key finisher, Russia) and Lucy M. Martin (Russia); residence - MA

GROVER,
Reta Ann, b. 9/15/1912; sixth; Joseph Grover (laborer, Loudon) and Cora Mansfield (N. Berwick, ME)
Willie Joseph, b. 9/23/1904; fourth; Joseph B. Grover (laborer, MA) and Cora A. Mansfield (ME)

GUARINO,
Dustin James, b. 9/22/1988 in Concord; Donald J. Guarino and Sandra S. Stevens
Megan Angela, b. 3/3/1993 in Laconia; Donald J. Guarino and Sandra Stevens

GUDBOIS,
Arthur, b. 9/10/1905; eleventh; Sammy Gudbois (saw mill hand, Canada) and Josephine Oswald (Canada)

GULLAGE,
Dannie Arthur, b. 1/29/1968 in Laconia; Donnie Carl Gullage (NH) and Linda I. Willard (NH)
Jody L., b. 2/25/1975 in Laconia; Dannie C. Gullage (NH) and Linda Ilene Willard (NH)

GUYER,
Megan Elizabeth, b. 1/24/1984 in Laconia; Peter S. Guyer and Cynthia H. Adams

HACKLEY,
Caledonia Elizabeth, b. 10/10/1998 in Concord; Patrick Hackley and April Hackley

HADDOCK,
Amanda Rose, b. 4/6/1992 in Wolfeboro; George B. Haddock and Kathleen M. Thorpe

HAGER,
Annie Elizabeth, b. 7/9/1969 in Concord; Dennis Sterling Hager (MA) and Elizabeth Hess Sears (DC)

HAIGH,
Justin Sampson, b. 12/2/1974 in Wolfeboro; George F. Haigh, III (CA) and Ann E. Sampson (MA)

HALEY,
Jessalynn, b. 8/29/1979 in Concord; James L. Haley and Janet N. Nagel

HALL,
child, b. 4/2/1894; Harvey Hall (farmer)
Francis Norman, b. 9/27/1922; Harold C. Hall and Flora H. Parsons
Susannah Jane, b. 2/14/1989 in Laconia; Jonathan J. Hall and Deborah J. Jenkins
Victoria Leigh, b. 8/24/1986 in Laconia; Jonathan J. Hall and Deborah L. Jenkins

HAMBLETT,
Jennifer A., b. 11/23/1980 in Concord; Robert B. Hamblett and Catherine L. Moon

HAMILTON,
Winter, b. 8/6/1984 in Concord; David E. Hamilton and Joyce A. Halter

HANCOCK,
Jennifer Nicole, b. 9/7/1999 in Laconia; Dean Hancock and Kimberly Hancock
Zachery Bennett, b. 10/2/1996 in Laconia; Dean Allan Hancock and Kimberly Anne Bennett

HARDWICK,
Heidi Sue, b. 8/7/1974 in Laconia; Philip F. Hardwick (MA) and Dianne S. Hyslop (NH)

HARPER,
Jacob Thomas, b. 5/28/1992 in Concord; Eric T. Harper and Linda L. Haskell
Molly Hannah, b. 5/3/1990 in Concord; Eric T. Harper and Linda L. Haskell

HARRIS,
Dorothy Louise, b. 7/11/1927 in Laconia; second; Walter C. Harris (knitter, Somerville, MA) and Lula Blake (Gilmanton)
Laural Blake, b. 11/8/1929; fourth; Walter C. Harris (mail carrier, Somerville, MA) and Lulu Blake (Gilmanton)
Melvin Franklin, b. 1/16/1934 in Concord; second; Ora W. Harris (laborer, Canaan) and Jessie McClary (Bridgeport, CT)
Patrick Robert, b. 9/5/1989 in Laconia; Robert E. Harris and Mary Beth Balukonis
Wendell Richard, b. 4/21/1932; first; Ora W. Harris (laborer, Canaan) and Jessie B. McClary (Bridgeport, CT)

HART,
M. Wentworth, b. 3/4/1891; first; M. A. H. Hart (physician, Milton) and Estella L. Hart (Fair Haven, VT)

HARTFORD,
Anthony E., b. 9/19/1955; third; Arlington Hartford (seller, NH) and Olive D. Young (NS)
Bonnie Kendra, b. 9/1/1944 in Laconia; second; Arlington Hartford (machinist, Belmont) and Olive D. Young (NS)

Hilary Faye, b. 4/3/1985 in Laconia; Anthony E. Hartford and Faye
 D. Anders
Tony Anders, b. 4/21/1983 in Laconia; Anthony E. Hartford and
 Faye D. Anders

HARVEY,
Brandon Thomas, b. 2/23/1977 in Laconia; Steven C. Harvey (RI)
 and Geraldine Manchester (RI)
Kathryn E., b. 1/17/1979 in Laconia; Steven C. Harvey and
 Geraldine D. Manchester

HASKELL,
son, b. 12/11/1901; sixth; George F. Haskell (laborer, Canterbury)
 and Emma E. Battis (Northfield)
Tracie Lee, b. 8/31/1972 in Laconia; Walter A. Haskell (NH) and
 June A. Cota (NH)

HATAB,
Jeffrey Blaine, b. 3/14/1990 in Concord; John C. Hatab and
 Maryann H. Newell

HATCH,
David D., b. 12/30/1982 in Laconia; Daniel D. Hatch and Karol A.
 Jenkins

HAWKINS,
daughter, b. 10/6/1914; first; Shurldin A. Hawkins (farmer, Boston,
 MA) and Amy D. Osborne (Gilmanton)
Carl Rolland, b. 3/22/1959 in Concord; first; Rolland Carl Hawkins
 (mechanic, NH) and Margaret June Gagnon (NH)
Carleena M., b. 3/11/1980 in Concord; Carl Rolland Hawkins and
 Debra Lisa Wessely
Charles Allen, b. 4/20/1916; second; Shurldin A. Hawkins (farmer,
 Boston, MA) and Amy Osborne (Gilmanton)
Eugene R., b. 4/26/1982 in Concord; Carl R. Hawkins and Debra L.
 Wessely
Geraldine Eleanor, b. 5/7/1921; third; Shurldin Hawkins (farmer,
 Boston, MA) and Amy Osborne (Gilmanton)
Jeffrey Arden, b. 9/22/1965 in Concord; second; Rolland Carl
 Hawkins (mechanic, NH) and Helen Doreen Eldridge (NS)

Lucille Ann, b. 4/24/1923; Shurldin A. Hawkins and Amy D. Osborne
Rolland C., b. 8/29/1928; fifth; Shurldin Hawkins (farmer, Boston, MA) and Amy D. Osborne (Gilmanton)
Sherry Lee, b. 7/3/1973 in Laconia; Garey Lee Hawkins (NH) and Lois Louise Lake (MA)
Shurldon W., b. 4/26/1982 in Concord; Carl R. Hawkins and Debra L. Wessely

HAYES,
James Connor, b. 5/7/1999 in Laconia; Sean Hayes and Kim Hayes

HAYNES,
daughter, b. 12/30/1896; first; Horace F. Haynes (laborer, Loudon) and Carrie B. Howard (Barrington)

HEALY,
Matthew Corey, b. 12/18/1985 in Laconia; Margaret R. Healy

HEATH,
Carter Eldon, b. 5/12/1972 in Concord; Roger Eldon Heath (NH) and Janet Leigh Aycock (MA)
Nathan Taylor, b. 10/8/1974 in Laconia; Roger E. Heath (NH) and Janet L. Aycock (MA)

HEBERT,
Sarah M., b. 3/8/1982 in Franklin; Paul G. Hebert and Linda J. Patten

HEMLIN,
Mitchell David, b. 6/21/1995 in Laconia; Theodore D. Hemlin and Lori Ann Dumais

HEMPEL,
Corrie Anne, b. 4/6/1985 in Laconia; Paul J. Hempel, III and Robin M. White
Meghann Alice, b. 10/6/1988 in Laconia; Paul J. Hempel, III and Robin W. White
Paul Jordan, IV, b. 1/9/1992 in Laconia; Paul J. Hempel, III and Robin W. White

HENDRYX,
Katelyn Elisabeth, b. 5/6/1985 in Concord; Mark K. Hendryx and Wendy J. Glassner

HERLIHY,
Jeremy P., b. 8/20/1979 in Concord; Robert P. Herlihy and Enid B. Porter
Kethleen A., b. 11/18/1980 in Laconia; Robert P. Herlihy and Enid B. Porter

HEUBER [see Hueber],
Sheery Ann, b. 8/22/1971 in Concord; Roland Albert Heuber (NH) and Jean Harriett Stockbridge (NH)

HEWETT,
Daniel Malcolm, b. 8/16/1991 in Concord; Jay M. Hewett and Mary Ellen McMahon

HEYWOOD,
Patricia Jane, b. 3/15/1934 in Wolfeboro; second; William C. Heywood (shoe cutter, Pittsfield) and Una M. Geddes (Canada)
Richard Frederick, b. 5/30/1932; first; William C. Heywood (shoe cutter, Pittsfield) and Una Geddes (BC)

HILL,
daughter, b. 9/4/1903; second; Elwood H. Hill (farmer, Gilmanton) and Ceda M. Dame (New Durham)
Flossie, b. 4/27/1900; first; Elwood Hill (pedler, Gilmanton) and Ceda May Dame (Middleton)
Kara Anne, b. 7/12/1965 in Concord; third; Joseph Philip Hill, Jr. (planer, NH) and Patricia Marie Sirrell (NH)
Kelly Jo, b. 12/4/1966 in Laconia; fourth; Joseph Philip Hill, Jr. (self-employed, NH) and Patricia Marie Sirrell (NH)

HILLIARD,
son, b. 3/17/1895; first; Leander A. Hilliard (farmer, Gilmanton) and Lillian E. Marston (Sutton)
child, b. 12/1/1897; second; Fred Hilliard (laborer)
son, b. 4/18/1900; fourth; Leander Hilliard (farmer, Gilmanton) and Lillian Marston (Sutton Mills)

daughter, b. 7/27/1908; seventh; Leander A. Hillard (sic) (laborer, Gilmanton) and Lillian E. Marston

HILLSGROVE,
Connor James, b. 6/29/1993 in Concord; Richard G. Hillsgrove and Sarah B. Stapleton
Jackson Henry, b. 3/17/1995 in Concord; Richard G. Hillsgrove and Sarah Beth Stapleton
Leon Joseph, b. 9/8/1952; first; Joseph H. Hillsgrove (sawmill worker, NH) and Lois S. Partridge (NH)
Randy Wade, b. 1/2/1971 in Wolfeboro; Richard Allen Hillsgrove (NH) and Viola Margueritte Polhamus (VA)
Roland Alfred, b. 6/5/1947; second; Merl W. Hillsgrove (farmer, Barnstead) and Frances L. Prescott (Gilmanton)

HILTZ,
Allen Frederic, b. 1/26/1971 in Laconia; Donald Frederic Hiltz (NH) and Hilda Anne Danforth (NH)
Angus Blenum, b. 8/28/1940; third; Fred L. Hiltz (farmer, Leominster, MA) and Cynthia I. Hiltz (Canada)
Angus Leslie, b. 8/7/1970 in Laconia; Angus Blenum Hiltz (NH) and Virginia Dawn Banfill (NH)
Donald Frederick, b. 1/27/1942; fourth; Fred L. Hiltz (farmer, Leominster, MA) and Cynthia T. Hiltz (NS)
Dorothy Louise, b. 5/9/1968 in Laconia; Angus Blenum Hiltz (NH) and Virginia Dawn Banfill (NH)
Dorothy Pauline, b. 2/27/1939 in Wolfeboro; second; Fred L. Hiltz (farmer, Leominster, MA) and Cynthia I. Hiltz (NS); residence - Gilmanton I. W.
Ruthanne Blanche, b. 1/6/1972 in Laconia; Donald F. Hiltz (NH) and Hilda A. Danforth (NH)

HINDS,
Raymond C., b. 4/20/1933 in Laconia; first; Raymond C. Hinds (sign painter, Charlestown, MA) and Evelyn R. Melanson (Littleton)

HISLOP [see Hyslop],
Cory David, b. 11/27/1978 in Laconia; David William Hislop (NH) and Cindy Brockett (NY)

David William, b. 5/26/1960 in Concord; third; Donald Lewis Hislop, Jr. (machinist, NH) and Ruth Irene McAuley (ME)
Joan Ellen, b. 9/28/1936 in Laconia; first; Robert E. Hislop (truck driver, Merrimac, MA) and Dorothy Hinds (Allston, MA)
Michael James, b. 11/28/1958 in Concord; second; Donald W. Hislop, Jr. (machinist, NH) and Ruth I. McAuley (ME)
Nicholas Michael, b. 2/5/1990 in Concord; Michael J. Hislop and Louise I. Noel
Richard Walter, b. 8/25/1923; R. Willis Hislop and Bertha M. Ellis
Richard Walter, Jr., b. 3/19/1948; first; Richard W. Hislop (student, Gilmanton) and June R. E. Manning (Miami, FL)
Sandra Lee, b. 4/26/1949; second; Richard W. Hislop (student, NH) and June R. E. Manning (FL)
Susan Margaret, b. 5/23/1969 in Concord; Donald Willis Hislop, Jr. (NH) and Ruth Irene McAuley (ME)

HOAG,
Edwina Covert, b. 9/24/1948; stillborn; fourth; Paul F. Hoag (autograph dealer, Brooklyn, NY) and Dorothy M. Smith (Freeport, NY)

HOFFMAN,
Jonathan Edward, b. 10/18/1987 in Laconia; Kenneth P. Hoffman and Amy J. V. Weglarz
Joseph Michael, b. 9/1/1985 in Laconia; Kenneth P. Hoffman and Amy J. V. Weglarz
Sarah Elizabeth, b. 5/16/1973 in Wolfeboro; William Warner Hoffman (NY) and Elizabeth Jane Stimson (MA)

HOLIDAY,
Jane Diane, b. 5/18/2001 in Laconia; Christopher Holiday and Lisa Holiday

HOODLET,
Christopher James, b. 7/23/1987 in Wolfeboro; Kenneth M. Hoodlet and Susan E. Purcell
Keith Mathew, b. 11/5/1985 in Wolfeboro; Kenneth M. Hoodlet and Susan E. Purcell
Melissa Sue, b. 12/31/1983 in Wolfeboro; Kenneth M. Hoodlet and Susan E. Purcell

HOOPER,
Todd Garrett, b. 1/24/1970 in Concord; Bartlett Dawson Hooper, Jr. (NH) and Sandra Marie Hall (NH)
Tricia Suzanne, b. 11/30/1971 in Concord; Bartlett Dawson Hooper, Jr. (NH) and Sandra Marie Hall (NH)

HOSFORD,
Harold Buck, b. 4/7/1898; first; C. J. Hosford (buttermaker, Nashua) and Mattie Buck (Haverhill)

HOWE,
son, b. 11/25/1906; first; Carl D. Howe (lumber operator, Grantham) and Grace E. Foss (Gilmanton)
Peter Attean, b. 5/2/1996 in Concord; Thomas Atkinson Howe and Sarah Chase Thorne
Phoebe Thorne, b. 12/16/1993 in Concord; Thomas A. Howe and Sarah C. Thorne

HUARD,
Alfred Victor, b. 6/22/1936 in Laconia; sixth; Stephen A. Huard (farmer, Manchester) and Flora McDonnell (Manchester); residence - Gilmanton I. W.
Francis J., b. 3/26/1935 in Laconia; fifth; Stephen A. Huard (farmer, Manchester) and Flora MacDonnell (Manchester)

HUEBER [see Heuber],
Carrie Lynn, b. 7/23/1974 in Concord; Roland A. Hueber (NH) and Jean H. Stockbridge (NH)
Jeannie Marie, b. 12/23/1985 in Concord; Roland A. Hueber and Jean H. Stockbridge
Jimmy Roland, b. 9/12/1976 in Concord; Roland A. Hueber (NH) and Jean H. Stockbridge (NH)

HUFSCHMID,
Christine Maria, b. 4/22/1972 in Concord; Erich Hufschmid (NY) and Maria Hofpointner (Austria)
Erich Michael, b. 7/24/1974 in Concord; Erich Hufschmid (NY) and Maria Hofpointner (Austria)

HUGHES,
Bridget Elizabeth, b. 3/22/1989 in Concord; Charles E. Hughes and
  Winifred M. McGuire
Emily Ann, b. 7/5/1983 in Concord; John F. R. Hughes and
  Elizabeth A. Hislop
Joshua Richard, b. 12/6/1981 in Concord; John F. R. Hughes and
  Elizabeth A. Hislop

HURST,
Taylor Nicole, b. 10/13/2001 in Concord; James Hurst and Maranda
  Hurst

HUTCHINSON,
Janaye Marie, b. 11/7/1997 in Manchester; William James
  Hutchinson and Kellie Marie Reynolds

HYSLOP [see Hislop],
Carlene Ann, b. 9/21/1951; seventh; Donald W. Hyslop (machinist,
  MA) and Rachel A. Straw (NH)
Darlene Lee, b. 9/21/1951; sixth; Donald W. Hyslop (machinist, MA)
  and Rachel A. Straw (NH)
Dianne S., b. 6/15/1955; tenth; Donald W. Hyslop (machinist, MA)
  and Rachel A. Straw (NH)
Donna Marie, b. 12/25/1976 in Laconia; Willis Edmund Hyslop (NH)
  and Sandra J. Moulton (NH)
Douglas W., b. 4/11/1954; ninth; Donald W. Hyslop (machinist, MA)
  and Rachel A. Straw (NH)
Ericka Frances, b. 11/27/1973 in Laconia; Glen G. Hyslop (NH) and
  Frances Marie Tilton (NH)
Gerald Brian, b. 12/18/1952; eighth; Donald W. Hyslop (machinist,
  MA) and Rachel A. Straw (NH)
Glen Gale, b. 12/18/1949; fifth; Donald Willis Hyslop (road agent,
  Merrimack, MA) and Rachel Anna Straw (Tilton)
James Allen, b. 12/11/1962 in Concord; fourteenth; Donald Willis
  Hyslop, Sr. (machinist, MA) and Rachel Anna Straw (NH)
Jane Emma, b. 12/11/1981 in Laconia; Gerald B. Hyslop and Ruth
  E. Boyd
John Thomas, b. 5/10/1945; third; Donald W. Hyslop (farmer,
  Merrimac, MA) and Rachel A. Straw (Tilton)
Kenneth R., b. 10/13/1975 in Laconia; Robert G. Hyslop (NH) and
  Barbara J. Dimock (VA)

Kimberly A., b. 8/31/1980 in Concord; Douglas W. Hyslop and
    Constance L. Roberts
Luther, b. 6/4/1983 in Concord; Glen F. Hyslop and Frances M.
    Tilton
Nancy Lou, b. 12/20/1957; eleventh; Donald Willis Hyslop
    (machinist, MA) and Rachel Anna Straw (NH)
Priscilla G., b. 1/17/1982 in Laconia; Robert G. Hyslop and Barbara
    J. Dimock
Rachel Rebecca, b. 12/18/1960 in Laconia; thirteenth; Donald Willis
    Hyslop, Sr. (prop. machine shop, MA) and Rachel Anna Straw
    (NH)
Rebecca Thelma, b. 1/5/1972 in Concord; Willis Edmund Hyslop
    (NH) and Sandra J. Moulton (NH)
Richard T., b. 6/2/1980 in Rochester; Gerald B. Hyslop and Ruth E.
    Boyd
Robert Raddin, b. 10/24/1970 in Laconia; Robert Grant Hyslop (NH)
    and Barbara Jayne Dimock (VA)
Sally Jane, b. 4/11/1959 in Laconia; twelfth; Donald Willis Hyslop
    (machinist, MA) and Rachel Ann Straw (NH)
Willis Edmund, b. 9/21/1946; fourth; Donald W. Hyslop (farmer,
    Merrimac, MA) and Rachel A. Straw (Tilton)

IDE,
Neil David, b. 5/23/1978 in Laconia; Raymond B. Ide (MA) and
    Susan B. Nash (NH)

INGOLDSBY,
Drew James, b. 4/30/1997 in Rochester; Karl Joseph Ingoldsby and
    Judith Ann Varney
Hudson Robert, b. 5/5/1999 in Rochester; Karl Ingoldsby and Judith
    Ingoldsby

JACKSON,
Rosalie, b. 9/2/1946 in Pittsfield; second; Benjamin Jackson (US
    Navy, Philippines) and Myrtle P. Cronin (Randolph)

JAKUBENS,
Alexis Serra, b. 9/25/1998 in Concord; John Jakubens and Sandra
    Jakubens

JANSURY,
Catherine Rose, b. 6/18/1997 in Laconia; Edward Joseph Jansury, Jr. and Pamela Jean Smith
Sarah Allison, b. 3/3/2001 in Concord; Edward Jansury and Pamela Jansury

JEMERY,
son, b. 9/28/1917; fourth; Alexander Jemery (laborer, Boscawen) and Violet Boynton (Nashua); residence - Canterbury

JENNESS,
Kristine Louise, b. 10/18/1969 in Laconia; Steven Michael Jenness (NH) and Beverly Ann Sanville (NH)
Steven Michael, Jr., b. 1/9/1971 in Laconia; Steven Michael Jenness (NH) and Beverly Ann Sanville (NH)

JENOT,
Charles Harrison, b. 10/11/1994 in Laconia; John Fitzgerald Jenot and Mary Rose Durocher

JOHANSSON,
Emily Amelia, b. 1/3/1993 in Laconia; Michael S. Johansson and Jennifer L. Hempel
Samuel Michael, b. 7/2/1994 in Laconia; Michael Stephen Johansson and Jennifer Lund Hempel

JOHNSON,
daughter, b. 1/–/1888; first; Charles Johnson (farmer, Strafford) and Mamie Goodwin (Gilmanton)
daughter, b. 9/26/1895; third; Charles A. Johnson (farmer, Strafford) and Mary E. Young (Gilmanton)

JONES,
daughter, b. 7/–/1888; second; Joseph Jones (farmer, Gilmanton)
daughter, b. 5/23/1889; first; Otis W. Jones and Cora Brown (Gilmanton)
child, b. 7/22/1894; George A. Jones (farmer, Gilmanton) and Olive Speare (Canterbury)
daughter, b. 1/3/1897; sixth; George A. Jones (laborer, Gilmanton) and Olive E. Moody

daughter, b. 11/2/1898; seventh; George A. Jones (laborer, Gilmanton) and Olive E. Moody
son [Karl E.], b. 8/26/1902; third; Allie C. Jones (farmer, Gilmanton) and Lillian E. Brown (Belmont)
Allie John, b. 5/25/1926; first; Karl E. Jones (farmer, Gilmanton) and Mary K. Canney (E. Concord)
Carlton E., b. 7/31/1927 in Laconia; second; Karl E. Jones (farmer, Gilmanton) and Mary C. Canney (Concord)
Carrie E., b. 5/5/1900; first; Allie C. Jones (farmer, Gilmanton) and Lillian E. Brown (Belmont)
Doris Mabel, b. 5/31/1914; first; Mr. Willy (Boston, MA) and Ethel Louise Jones (Gilmanton)
Ella S., b. 5/17/1901; second; Allie C. Jones (farmer, Gilmanton) and Lillian E. Brown (Belmont)
Eva Maybell, b. 11/7/1895; fifth; George A. Jones (laborer, Gilmanton) and Olive E. Moody (Canterbury)
Evelyn Blanche, b. 4/21/1947; first; Ralph A. Jones (farmer, Gilmanton) and Marjorie B. Stearns (Wilmot)
George Henry, b. 3/17/1900; eighth; George A. Jones (laborer, Gilmanton) and Olive E. Speare (Canterbury)
Katherine Ann, b. 8/20/1967 in Concord; third; Lawrence Charles Jones (carpenter, CT) and Wilma Josephine Foss (ME)
Lindsay, b. 10/3/1976 in Laconia; Jack H. Jones (NH) and Carol F. Shaw (NH)
Mertie Estelle, b. 5/13/1888; first; George A. Jones (laborer, Gilmanton) and Olive E. Moody (Canterbury)
Pauline K., b. 11/4/1928; third; Karl E. Jones (farmer, Gilmanton) and Mary C. Canney (E. Concord)
Robert J., b. 10/6/1913; second; Morrill Jones (laborer, Gilmanton) and Mary Gowling (Manchester)
Steven Lawrence, b. 11/25/1965 in Concord; second; Lawrence Charles Jones (carpenter, CT) and Wilma Josephine Foss (ME)

JORDAN,
daughter [Jenet], b. 10/19/1939 in Wolfeboro; seventh; Harold V. Jordan (farmer, Hyde Park, MA) and Irene M. Wettre
Amy Elizabeth, b. 1/7/1978 in Wolfeboro; Eric Ellis Jordan (NY) and Gail Joyce Chrisenton (MA)
Jay Gardner, b. 4/26/1984 in Hanover; James B. Jordan and Kathy Gingras

Jayson Emery, b. 12/10/1987 in Laconia; Jay E. Jordan and Rebecca A. Clough

JOSLYN,
son, b. 9/17/1908; third; Edwin A. Joslyn (farmer, Greenfield) and Augusta M. Foss (Alton)
Belle Augusta, b. 12/1/1912; fifth; Edwin A. Joslyn (farmer, Greenfield) and Augusta M. Foss (Alton Bay)
Dolly Josephine, b. 7/3/1917; seventh; Edwin A. Joslyn (farmer, Greenfield) and Augusta M. Foss (Alton Bay)
Ethel Louise, b. 9/4/1915; sixth; Edwin A. Joslin (sic) (farmer, Greenfield) and Augusta M. Foss (Alton Bay)
Harry Waldo, b. 11/15/1910; fourth; Edwin A. Joslyn (laborer, Greenfield) and Augusta M. Foss (Alton Bay)

JOYCE,
Cecil Edward, b. 3/3/1958 in Concord; third; Frank T. Joyce (painter, NH) and Myrtle P. Cronan (NH)
Darryl Wayne, b. 7/8/1965 in Laconia; fourth; Wesley Delanor Joyce (machinist, NH) and Jennie Elizabeth Jane Hill (NH)
Eileen Germaine, b. 5/15/1945 in Laconia; eighth; Frank T. Joyce (US Navy, Northfield) and Eileen G. Sullivan (Boston, MA)
Glenn Charles, b. 10/15/1961 in Winchester, MA; third; Norman Lewis Joyce (advance salesman, MA) and Doris Anne Miller (MA)
Ricky James, b. 10/16/1964 in Concord; fourth; Bernard David Joyce, Sr. (constr. worker, NH) and Sandra Jean Denault (MD)

JUDKINS,
Jenny Lynn, b. 12/6/1976 in Concord; Richard A. Judkins (NH) and Alice M. Mansfield (MA)

JUNEAU,
Mitchell Thomas, b. 11/1/1999 in Concord; James Juneau and Cynthia Juneau

KAAR,
Michael Patrick, b. 1/26/1988 in Laconia; Mark D. Kaar and Annie V. McCarthy

KAPPES,
Brianna Joy, b. 12/26/2000 in Franklin; Anthony Kappes and Sonja Kappes

KARDINAL,
Joanna Lynn, b. 2/6/1972 in Concord; Herman H. Kardinal, Jr. (NH) and Beverly C. Brazelton (CA)
Kathryn Charlotte, b. 11/3/1974 in Concord; Herman H. Kardinal, Jr. (NH) and Beverly C. Brazelton (CA)

KEAN,
Amy Beth, b. 12/8/1986 in Laconia; John C. Kean and Beth A. McNutt

KEANE,
Matthew Evan, b. 7/23/1989 in Laconia; Stephen P. Keane and Delores A. Matos
Nicholas Logan, b. 8/29/1992 in Laconia; Stephen P. Keane and Delores A. Matos

KEEFE,
Mary-Ellen, b. 6/25/1989 in Laconia; Daniel W. Keefe and Joanne Pridham

KEENE,
Benjamin Orin, b. 4/20/1996 in Laconia; Gregory Scott Keene and Ann Morgyn Morrell

KELLEY,
son, b. 5/24/1902; seventh; George F. Kelley (farmer, Gilmanton) and Delia C. Janes (Alton)
Ann Marie, b. 4/9/1953; first; Celon E. Kelley (shoe cutter, VT) and Anita T. Twombly (NH)
Charlotte Adelia, b. 5/17/1924; fourth; Charles G. Kelley (farmer, Gilmanton) and Hattie B. Page (Utica, NY)
Cindy Jean, b. 3/28/1958 in Laconia; fifth; Celon E. Kelley (shoe cutter, VT) and Anita T. Twombly (NH)
Donald Page, b. 3/29/1922; Charles G. Kelley and Hattie B. Page
George Francis, b. 12/24/1920; first; Charles G. Kelley (farmer, Gilmanton) and Hattie B. Page (Utica, NY)

Harriett Elizabeth, b. 3/28/1923; Charles G. Kelley and Hattie B. Page
Heather Anne, b. 6/3/1984 in Laconia; Richard J. Kelley, Jr. and Carole A. Rogers
John Sherburne, b. 8/7/1925; fifth; Charles G. Kelley (farmer, Gilmanton) and Hatty B. Page (Utica, NY)
Keith James, b. 7/6/1978 in Laconia; John David Kelley (NH) and Nancy Lee MacMartin (NH)
Linda Elaine, b. 5/25/1964 in Laconia; seventh; Celon Edward Kelley (Laconia Shoe Co., VT) and Anita Theresa Twombly (NH)
Mary G., b. 8/1/1928; sixth; Charles G. Kelley (farmer, Gilmanton) and Hattie B. Page (Utica, NY)
Melvin Edward, b. 11/12/1960 in Laconia; fourth; Celon Edward Kelley (shoe cutter, NY) and Anita Theresa Twombly (NH)
Ruth W., b. 7/11/1897; sixth; George F. Kelley (farmer, Gilmanton) and Adelia C. Jones (Alton)
Susan Gail, b. 2/7/1956 in Laconia; fourth; Celon E. Kelley (cutter, VT) and Anita T. Twombly (NH)
Thomas William, b. 12/18/1990 in Laconia; John D. Kelley and Tina Marie Danis

KELSON,
Martha Jean, b. 12/11/1948; third; Robert B. Kelson (bottle gas man, Somerville, MA) and Ruth M. Bund (Malden, MA)
Pamela Val, b. 12/11/1948; second; Robert B. Kelson (bottle gas man, Somerville, MA) and Ruth M. Bund (Malden, MA)

KETCHUM,
Conor A., b. 6/4/1979 in Concord; Allen R. Ketchum and Suzanne Stevens
Ross L., b. 5/16/1982 in Concord; Allen R. Ketchum and Suzanne Stevens

KIMBALL,
David Wayne, Jr., b. 4/7/1970 in Laconia; David Wayne Kimball (NH) and Alberta Rae Brown (NH)
Ethan Priscott, b. 5/26/1977 in Laconia; Wilfred R. Kimball (NH) and Marylee E. Reed (NH)
Jason Andrew, b. 1/9/1974 in Laconia; David W. Kimball (NH) and Alberta R. Brown (NH)

Jeffrey James, b. 3/19/1972 in Laconia; David W. Kimball, Sr. (NH) and Alberta R. Brown (NH)

Keith Adam, b. 3/13/1977 in Laconia; David W. Kimball (NH) and Alberta R. Brown (NH)

KING,
Andrew Raymond, b. 7/7/1985 in Laconia; David Thena King and Debra A. Ransom

KINGSBURY,
Allan Alonzo George, b. 12/14/1984 in Laconia; Allan A. Kingsbury and Bonnie L. Bombard

KLEFOS,
Susan Amelia, b. 6/30/1961 in Rochester; sixth; Brede Syver Klefos (printing plant owner, Norway) and Constance Hopkins Snow (NH)

KNOWLES,
Courtney Elizabeth, b. 5/23/1991 in Concord; Russell Knowles III and Karen E. Dupont

Samantha Read, b. 6/13/2000 in Concord; Russell Knowles and Karen Knowles

KOCH,
Allan Paul, b. 1/12/1978 in Laconia; Allan Bruce Koch (NH) and Patricia Ann Judkins (NH)

KORDAS,
Mayghan Raye, b. 4/2/1999 in Concord; William Kordas and Sharon Kordas

KORHONEN,
Brian Douglas, b. 2/18/1988 in Concord; Dale T. Korhonen and Darlene K. Jameson

KRAMER,
Christina K., b. 3/30/1979 in Exeter; John M. Kramer and Gloria J. Ward

James Paul, b. 11/17/1981 in Laconia; John M. Kramer, Jr. and Gloria J. Ward

KUCHINSKY,
Abby Lynn, b. 9/6/1983 in Laconia; George N. Kuchinsky and Carol
A. Rose
Amanda L., b. 8/28/1982 in Laconia; George N. Kuchinsky and
Carol A. Rose

KUNKEL,
Henry Jacob, b. 10/22/1922; Henry J. Kunkel and Mary W. Lynch

LABELLE,
Edward Ernest, b. 5/14/1914; fourth; Benjamin Labelle (farmer,
Canada) and Marguerite Rayno (Boscawen)
Ida Ruth, b. 2/15/1913; third; Benjamin LaBelle (laborer, Canada)
and Marguerite Rayns (Boscawen)
Philip Rayno, b. 6/1/1909; second; Benjamin LaBelle (laborer,
Stanstead Plain, PQ) and Margaret Rayno (Boscawen)

LACLAIR,
Michaelle J. M., b. 6/16/1979 in Concord; James M. LaClair and
Cynthia D. Splett
Patrick Andrew M., b. 3/12/1983 in Concord; Dennis P. LaClair and
Sharyn K. Splett
Paul Vincent Stephen, b. 11/24/1977 in Concord; Dennis P. LaClair
(NH) and Sharyn Kelly Splett (PA)
Philip B., b. 8/15/1979 in Concord; Dennis P. LaClair and Sharyn K.
Splett

LACOSTE,
Jordan Lee, b. 5/14/1993 in Laconia; Norman P. Lacoste and Janet
M. Strybuc
Tyler Paul, b. 7/28/1991 in Laconia; Norman P. Lacoste and Janet
M. Strybuc

LACROIX,
Katherine Noelle, b. 3/7/1993 in Concord; Charles L. Lacroix and
Wanda R. Lawton
Nancy Anne, b. 12/5/1954; first; Joseph L. LaCroix (woodsman, VT)
and Ola V. Thompson (VT)

LAFRANCE,
son [Lucian C.], b. 8/2/1904; fourth; Joseph H. LaFrance (laborer, Canada) and Bertha Burbank (Gilmanton)
daughter [Hilda M.], b. 7/15/1906; fifth; Joseph LaFrance (laborer, Canada) and Bertha A. Burbank (Gilmanton, black)
Heather Mae, b. 6/25/1972 in Concord; Philip C. LaFrance (NH) and Nancy I. Shields (VT)
Irene Marion, b. 10/25/1910; sixth; Joseph Lafrance (laborer, Canada) and Bertha Burbank (Gilmanton)
Joseph, b. 9/13/1914; seventh; Joseph LaFrance (laborer, Canada) and Bertha Burbank (Gilmanton)

LAHEY,
Griffin J., b. 5/14/1980 in Laconia; Timothy J. Lahey and Virginia L. Ferland

LAMPER,
Herbert, b. 3/5/1920; first; Herbert D. Lamper (laborer, Alton) and Edith M. Jones (Gilmanton); residence - Alton

LAMPREY,
Ann M., b. 4/23/1887; first; Willie C. Lamprey (blacksmith, Laconia) and Etta M. Hodge (Salisbury)

LANGEVIN,
Sandra Louise, b. 3/19/1944 in Laconia; fifth; Oliver N. Langevin (logger, Pittsfield) and Mary J. Maltais (Concord)

LANGLEY,
child, b. 6/13/1894; first; Rufus H. Langley (clerk, 23, Cambridgeport, MA) and Alice E. Abbott (22, Belmont)
stillborn son, b. 11/5/1934 in Pittsfield; fourth; Howard G. Langley (farmer, Gilmanton) and Laura Nelson (Perth Amboy, NJ)
Gary Nelson, b. 1/18/1945 in Laconia; first; Henry N. Langley (US Navy, Metuchen, NJ) and Grace A. McClary (Gilmanton)
Gerald Allan, b. 11/23/1946 in Laconia; second; Henry N. Langley (elec. engineer, Metuchen, NJ) and Grace A. McClary (Gilmanton)
Kathleen Anne, b. 11/1/1950; fourth; Donald Chan Langley (Army Air Corps, NH) and Dorothy Mae Milnne (MA)

Matthew Paul, b. 2/19/1974 in Wolfeboro; Paul N. Langley (MA) and Elaine Marie Thompson (NH)
Paul Nelson, b. 5/10/1954; fifth; Donald C. Langley (USAF, NH) and Dorothy M. Milne (MA)

LANIER,
Florence May, b. 1/2/1948; Raymond Lanier (mechanic, Richmond, VA) and Murilla E. Partridge (Gilmanton); residence - Norfolk, VA

LANK,
Aaron David, b. 7/4/1970 in Concord; Stephen David Lank (NH) and Margie Ann Morse (NH)
Carol June, b. 8/21/1947; first; Howard J. Lank (plumber, Providence, RI) and Hazel I. Parker (Detroit, MI)
Clinton L., b. 11/24/1955; fourth; Howard J. Lank (plumber, Providence, RI) and Hazel I. Parker (Detroit, MI)
Gail Nancy, b. 10/26/1949; second; Howard John Lank (plumber) and Hazel Isabelle Parker (Detroit, MI)
Howard Robert, b. 10/16/1950; third; Howard John Lank (plumber, Providence, RI) and Hazel Isabelle Parker (Detroit, MI)

LAROCHE,
Michael Alfred, b. 2/21/1961 in Laconia; second; Alfred Ephraim Laroche, Jr. (machinist, NH) and Melba Jean Clifford (NH)
Stephen Earle, b. 7/3/1964 in Laconia; third; Alfred Ephrem LaRoche, Jr. (Scott & Williams, NH) and Melba Jean Clifford (NH)

LATICI,
Margot Stewart, b. 8/23/1983 in Laconia; Steven M. Latici and Laura J. Howland

LAUBI,
Amy Kristine, b. 12/13/1967 in Concord; fourth; Paul Klingbeil Laubi (manager, MA) and Anne Martin Winthrow (RI)

LAVALLEE,
Garrett Jean, b. 5/13/1981 in Concord; Gary K. Lavallee and Mary E. Collins

Vanessa Eva, b. 1/27/1985 in Concord; Gary K. Lavallee and Mary E. Collins

LAVINE,
Lena Rose, b. 4/6/1935; third; Victor Lavine (laborer, Canada) and Rosa DeSelle (Canada)

LAWR[E]Y,
son, b. 3/19/1903; first; Annie M. Lawrey (Gilmanton)
son, b. 1/27/1907; second; Annie M. Lawry (Gilmanton)

LAWSON,
Robert R., b. 2/10/1955; second; Lester A. Lawson (laborer, farmer, MA) and Marie L. Jacques (MA)

LEAVITT,
daughter, b. 6/13/1887; fifth; Dixi S. Leavitt (farmer, Gilmanton) and Myra O. Ordway

LECLERC,
Ryan Kelley, b. 7/14/1988 in Concord; Ronald M. LeClerc and Susan K. Kelley

LEE,
Timothy M., b. 5/14/1979 in Laconia; George M. Lee and Carolynn A. Cushman

LEIGHTON,
child, b. 5/25/1893; seventh; John F. Leighton (farmer) and Katharine Bean (Lempster)

LESSARD,
Justin Paul, b. 2/4/1976 in Laconia; Raymond P. Lessard (NH) and Karen O. Ouellette (NH)

LEVINE,
Irene Gertrude, b. 3/26/1933; second; Victor Levine (laborer, Canada) and Rosiana Decelle (Canada)

LEWIS,
Caddie L., b. 12/20/1979 in Laconia; Alan L. Lewis and Nancy A. Kendall
Joshua Kendall, b. 12/16/1981 in Laconia; Alan Lewis and Nancy Ann Kendall

LIBARDI,
Christopher Paul, b. 9/28/1983 in Laconia; Carl F. Libardi and Karen M. Prouty
Eric Carl, b. 4/13/1981 in Laconia; Carl F. Libardi and Karen M. Prouty

LIMOGE,
Eric John, b. 2/27/1992 in Concord; John E. Limoge and Louise P. Chouinard

LINCOLN,
Katrina Marie, b. 12/28/1992 in Laconia; John C. Lincoln and Jennie L. Peschel

LINDBLOOM,
Anna Virginia Aurilla, b. 1/29/2001 in Laconia; Eric Lindbloom and Janice Lindbloom

LINES,
Abigail Iris, b. 4/11/1996 in Laconia; John Alan Lines and Jodi Lynn Hilton
Christopher Paul, b. 6/22/1988 in Laconia; Paul Lines and Catherine C. Colby
Derek, b. 10/23/1973 in Concord; Paul Lines (NH) and Nance Evelyn Strout (NY)
Gregory Evan, b. 8/25/1990 in Laconia; John A. Lines and Jodi L. Hilton
Heather A., b. 7/10/1975 in Concord; Gary Lines (MA) and Betty L. Graeme (NH)
Heidi Lynn, b. 5/21/1977 in Concord; Gary Lines (MA) and Betty L. Graeme (NH)
Paul, b. 1/26/1955; fourth; John W. Lines (machinist, MA) and Iris S. Austin (MA)
Shaun Ryan, b. 10/7/1987 in Laconia; Paul Lines and Catherine E. Colby

LINGQUIST,
Valerie A., b. 5/23/1980 in Concord; Paul W. Lingquist and Janice R. Holloway

LINQUATA,
Tyler Joseph, b. 9/19/1994 in Concord; Joseph Patrick Linquata and Erin Elizabeth Shaw

LINSCOTT,
daughter, b. 10/13/1894; Sidney W. Linscott (farmer, Newfield, ME) and Emma F. Hall (Barrington)

LITTLE,
stillborn child, b. 7/21/1894; Romie Little
daughter, b. 1/28/1903; fifth; Romie Little (farmer, Montcello, MA) and Lula M. Beaman (Laconia)
daughter, b. 7/13/1908; eighth; Romie Little (farmer, Mississippi) and Lula M. Beaman (Laconia)
daughter, b. 1/2/1913; ninth; Romie Little (farmer, Mt. Silo, MS) and Lora M. Barnum (Laconia)
Betsey Anne, b. 10/21/1949; third; Charles Porter Little (farmer, NH) and Rena Frances Marsh (NH)
Elva C., b. 8/28/1900; fourth; Romie Little (farmer, Montecello, MA) and Lula M. Beaman (Laconia)

LITTLEFIELD,
George Ernest, Jr., b. 3/19/1952; third; George E. Littlefield (mechanic, NH) and Ramona E. Bagley (NH)
Marie E., b. 1/12/1954; fourth; George E. Littlefield (mechanic, Rumney) and Ramona E. Bagley (Campton)
Nancy Lee, b. 7/15/1950; second; George Ernest Littlefield (mechanic, NH) and Romona Earline Bagley (NH)

LIVERNOIS,
Amanda Marie, b. 12/21/1995 in Concord; Gregory S. Livernois and Mona J. Cross
Christina Leigh, b. 8/28/1993 in Laconia; Michael A. Livernois and Tresa L. Boire
Patrick Kimball, b. 8/30/1997 in Concord; Gregory Stuart Livernois and Mona Jean Cross

LORD,
Hannah Christina, b. 11/25/2001 in Concord; Sean Lord and Martina Lord

LORDEN,
Michael Allen, b. 4/29/1970 in Laconia; James Dennis Lorden (NH) and Germaine Ada Wolfenden (NH)

LOSO,
Jeremy Steven, b. 11/13/1972 in Concord; Steven M. Loso (NH) and Roxanne B. Bickford (NH)

LOTHROP,
Eliot Hays, b. 9/2/1978 in Concord; William Wallace Lothrop (IN) and Kate Hays Spindell (NY)

LOUGEE,
daughter, b. 8/30/1887; fourth; Reuben P. Lougee (farmer, Gilmanton) and Ella M. Lougee (Gilmanton)
son [Cecil R.], b. 8/30/1887; fifth; Reuben P. Lougee (farmer, Gilmanton) and Ella M. Lougee (Gilmanton)

LUMSDEN,
Elizabeth May, b. 4/10/1987 in Laconia; William H. Lumsden and Carol A. Vance
Eric William, b. 7/19/1989 in Laconia; William H. Lumsden and Carol A. Vance

LUND,
stillborn son, b. 9/8/1902; first; Leon C. Lund (farmer, Chicago, IL) and Ina F. Crowell (Gilmanton)
stillborn daughter, b. 8/3/1903; second; Leon C. Lund (laborer, Chicago, IL) and Ina F. Connell (Gilmanton)

LUNDY,
Eleanor Arlene, b. 9/9/1925; fourth; Robert C. Lundy (laborer, Boothbay Harbor, ME) and Ruth Varney (Portland, ME)
Elsie Ruth, b. 5/10/1927; fifth; Robert C. Lundy (laborer, Southport, ME) and Ruth Varney (Windham, ME)

LUTKUS,
Laura Brianna, b. 7/20/1990 in Laconia; David V. Lutkus and Linda J. Bjorkman

LYFORD,
son, b. 5/18/1890; first; John Lyford (farmer, Gilmanton) and Addie Lyford (Canterbury); residence - Belmont

LYSTER,
son, b. 12/6/1900; first; Herbert L. Lyster (butter maker, Canada) and Jennie B. Lyster (Waterford, VT)

LYTTEL,
Hattie, b. 8/23/1904; first; Peter Lyttel (laborer, St. Regis Falls, NY) and Annie Bouchard (Canada); residence - MA

MACKENZIE,
Jessie Idell, b. 2/17/1911; third; N. Y. B. MacKenzie (physician, Ellsworth, ME) and Addie Trask (Salisbury)
Katherine M., b. 3/24/1913; fourth; N. Y. B. MacKenzie (physician, Ellsworth, ME) and Addie P. Trask (Stockholm, NY)
Kim, b. 6/8/1950; fourth; Morton Holden MacKenzie (lumbering, MA) and Mildred Leona St. Cyr (NH)
Margaret Holden, b. 6/1/1948; third; Morton H. MacKenzie (lumber man, Swampscott, MA) and Mildred L. St. Cyr (Laconia)
Stewart Bradford, b. 7/5/1915; fifth; Nicholas Y. Mackenzie (physician, Ellsworth, ME) and Addie P. Trask (Stockholm, NY)

MACKES,
Nicholas William, b. 4/20/1999 in Concord; Brian Mackes and Irene Mackes
Samantha Jordan, b. 5/14/1996 in Laconia; Brian Kevin Mackes and Irene Marie Craig

MACNEILL,
David William, b. 4/5/1986 in Laconia; Charles W. MacNeill and Cheryl R. Smith
Douglas Charles, b. 4/5/1986 in Laconia; Charles W. MacNeill and Cheryl R. Smith

MACPEEK,
Steven Douglas, b. 1/21/1973 in Laconia; Douglas Russell MacPeek (NY) and Stephanie Anne Geddes (NH)

MADDEN,
Jeanne Patricia, b. 2/18/1931; third; John Henry Madden (laborer, Boston, MA) and Martha Patricia Lloyd (Liverpool, England)

MAGWOOD,
daughter, b. 8/14/1898; first; William Magwood (minister, Leeds, PQ) and Nellie E. Girdlen (Dalton)
daughter, b. 12/30/1899; second; William Magwood (minister, Canada) and Nellie E. Girdler (Dalton)

MAHAN,
Philip Ray, b. 4/5/1923; ----- and Irene May Page

MAHEUX,
Jane Eva, b. 10/7/1946 in Laconia; third; William R. Maheux (laborer, Laconia) and Ruth M. Willard (Gilmanton)

MALLORY,
Anna Curtis, b. 6/1/1981 in Rochester; Bruce L. Mallory and Susan R. Curtis
Dylan Sumner, b. 8/10/1986 in Concord; Mark L. Mallory and Nancy L. Ball
Kirsten Gilmore, b. 2/23/1993 in Concord; Mark L. Mallory and Nancy L. Ball

MALSBURY,
Job Alonzo, b. 2/22/1910; second; William A. Malsbury (laborer, Gilmanton) and Minnie E. Bickford (Wolfeboro)

MALTAIS,
Hannah Irene E., b. 9/7/1989 in Laconia; Danny R. Maltais, Sr. and Anne E. Drouin
Jason Eli, b. 4/25/1973 in Laconia; Danny Roy Maltais (CT) and Linda Ruth Davis (NH)
Laura Kristen, b. 5/22/1997 in Laconia; Jason Eli Maltais and Ashley Meredith Haselton

Leah J., b. 7/27/1979 in Laconia; Danny R. Maltais and Anne E. Drouin
Seth J., b. 1/17/1982 in Laconia; Danny R. Maltais, Sr. and Anne E. Drouin
Wendy Michelle, b. 6/25/1967 in Laconia; first; John E. Maltais, Jr. (molder, CT) and Norma Jean Garland (TN)

MANCINI,
Russell James, b. 1/30/1993 in Concord; Donald J. Mancini and Carol M. Cassady

MANN,
Jordan Kendall, b. 2/5/1990 in Gilmanton; Charles W. Mann and Deborah K. Bigelow

MANNING,
Brianne Eleanor, b. 8/11/1992 in Laconia; John W. Manning and Deborah E. Rieck

MANSFIELD,
child, b. 7/6/1898; third; William Mansfield (laborer, Wells, ME) and Cora Tilton (Gilmanton)
son, b. 11/12/1904; fifth; William I. Mansfield (laborer, Wells, ME) and Cora A. Tilton (Gilmanton)
Archie Ollie, b. 8/4/1917; tenth; William Mansfield (laborer, Wells, ME) and Cora Tilton (Gilmanton)
Florence E., b. 6/3/1894; first; William Ira Mansfield (farmer, 22, Wells, ME) and Cora M. Tilton (19, Gilmanton)
George Edward, b. 12/24/1906; sixth; William I. Maxfield (sic) (laborer, Wells, ME) and Cora M. Tilton (Gilmanton)
Janie Illa, b. 12/5/1913; ninth; William I. Mansfield (laborer, Wells, ME) and Cora M. Tilton (Gilmanton)
Roswell Frances, b. 4/27/1912; eighth; William Mansfield (laborer, Wells, ME) and Cora M. Tilton (Wentworth)
Wilson Sylvester, b. 9/22/1909; seventh; W. I. Mansfield (farmer, Wells, ME) and Cora Tilton (Gilmanton)

MARDEN [see Mardin],
Marie Martha, b. 1/6/1926; second; George H. Marden (laborer, Jefferson) and Mabel Hilliard

Willard Clement, Jr., b. 7/8/1936; sixth; Willard C. Marden (farmer, Littleton) and Addie M. Davis (Northwood)

MARDIN [see Marden],

Barbara Adeline, b. 2/20/1932; fourth; Willard C. Mardin (laborer, Littleton) and Addie M. Davis (Northwood)

Robert Irving, b. 4/28/1933; fifth; Willard C. Mardin (laborer, Littleton) and Addie M. Davis (Northwood)

MARGESON,

child [Edward M., Jr.], b. 8/3/1923; Edward M. Margeson and Edith M. Bruce

son [Ramon W.], b. 5/19/1925; second; Manning Margeson (clerk, NS) and Edith E. Bruce (Canada)

Austin D., b. 12/23/1928; fifth; Edward M. Margeson (farmer, Grafton, Can.) and Edith M. Bruce (Plodden, Can.)

Betty Jane, b. 3/8/1932; sixth; Edward M. Margeson (farmer, NS) and Edith E. Bruce (Canada)

Nelson, b. 11/30/1926; third; Edw. M. Margeson (farmer, Grafton, NS) and Edith Bruce (P. I., Can.)

Norris, b. 11/30/1926; fourth; Edw. M. Margeson (farmer, Grafton, NS) and Edith Bruce (P. I., Can.)

MARSH,

son [Ralph Davis], b. 5/2/1904; second; Erskine H. Marsh (laborer, Gilmanton) and Jennie B. Davis (Alton)

son, b. 7/7/1906; first; Joseph H. L. Marsh (farmer, Manchester) and Alice C. Page (S. Boston, MA)

son, b. 9/19/1907; second; Joseph H. L. Marsh (farmer, E. Manchester) and Alice C. Page (S. Boston, MA)

Fred E., b. 8/11/1896; first; Erskine H. Marsh (merchant, Gilmanton) and Jennie B. Davis (Gilmanton)

Irad Herbert, b. 1/28/1909; third; Joseph H. L. Marsh (farmer, Manchester) and Alice C. Page (S. Boston, MA)

Rhena Frances, b. 12/7/1912; fourth; Joseph H. L. Marsh (farmer, E. Manchester) and Alice C. Page (S. Boston, MA)

Shirley May, b. 11/25/1924; fifth; Joseph H. L. Marsh (farmer, Manchester) and Alice C. Page (S. Boston, MA)

MARSTON,
Taylor Russell, b. 2/18/1993 in Laconia; Rodney L. Marston and
Holly H. Hughes

MARTEL,
Heather Rebecca, b. 9/26/1991 in Laconia; Glenn K. Martel and
Rebecca L. Rowe

MARTIN,
Louis[e] Margaret, b. 10/29/1906; third; Arthur C. Martin (farmer,
VT) and Elizabeth Monty (NJ)
Ronald Wayne, b. 12/26/1949; first; Paul Donald Martin (lumber
sticker, ME) and Frances May Wells (NH)

MAXFIELD,
son, b. –/–/1887; first; Walter N. Maxfield (farmer, Gilmanton) and
L. A. Scales (Plymouth)
daughter, b. 2/11/1889; fifth; Charles H. Maxfield (farmer,
Gilmanton) and Maniah S. Pierce

MAYHEW,
Albert Paul, b. 5/27/1950; second; Eldon Burgess Mayhew (kitchen
assistant, NH) and Georgie Annie Bickford (NH)

McALLEN,
Charles Herbert, b. 9/26/1907; fifth; Charles H. McAllen
(shoemaker, St. Johns, NB) and Ellen M. Carigier (Lynn, MA)

McARDLE,
Jennifer C., b. 11/5/1982 in Concord; Harold O. McArdle and
Lorraine C. Golankiewicz
Stephanie M., b. 4/10/1980 in Concord; Harold O. McArdle and
Lorraine C. Golankiewicz

McAVENIA,
Bailey Anne, b. 8/13/1986 in Laconia; Richard C. McAvenia, Jr. and
Nancy L. Clairmont

McCARTHY,
Hannah Kirsten, b. 1/25/1996 in Laconia; Joseph Carl McCarthy
and Paula Jean Pinnataro

McCLARY,
son [Frank L.], b. 5/27/1903; first; J. Frank McClary (farmer,
   Gilmanton) and Ephema A. Battis
daughter [Helen], b. 7/9/1903; second; Horace E. McClary (laborer,
   Gilmanton) and Clara J. Butcher (Dover)
daughter, b. 9/21/1903; second; Willard G. McClary (laborer,
   Bristol) and Dorothy J. Butcher (Dover)
daughter [Stella May], b. 1/2/1905; fourth; Horace E. McClary
   (farmer, Gilmanton) and Clara J. Butcher (Dover)
son, b. 3/10/1935 in Laconia; first; Bertrude McClary (laborer,
   Pomfret, CT) and Lois M. Clifford (Gilmanton)
Andrea Renee, b. 5/27/1983 in Concord; Frank J. McClary and
   Christine A. Leonard
Brenda Lee, b. 4/20/1959 in Laconia; first; Frank Leslie McClary, Jr.
   (oiler, NH) and Betty May Deware (MA)
Donald W., b. 1/21/1925; third; Arthur E. McClary (laborer,
   Gilmanton) and Clara Bean (Gilford)
Estella Ann, b. 2/1/1906; third; William G. McClary (laborer, Bristol)
   and Dorothy Butcher (Dover)
Frances Jane, b. 10/31/1931; sixth; Arthur McClary (farmer,
   Gilmanton) and Clara Bean (Gilford)
Frank J., b. 4/9/1962 in Laconia; second; Frank Leslie McClary
   (road agent, NH) and Betty May Deware (MA)
Frank L., b. 11/30/1928; fourth; Frank L. McClary (laborer,
   Gilmanton) and Lena M. Nutter (Parsonsfield, ME)
George Frank A., b. 10/29/1921; first; Frank L. McClary (laborer,
   Gilmanton) and Lena M. Nutter (Parsonfield, ME)
Grace Amy, b. 7/5/1921; fifth; Horace E. McClary (farmer,
   Gilmanton) and Hatty Amy Alberty (Charlestown, MA)
Gregory Frank, b. 11/8/1986 in Concord; Frank J. McClary and
   Christine A. Leonard
Guy Bradford, b. 7/16/1934 in Laconia; seventh; Arthur E. McClary
   (laborer, Gilmanton) and Clara I. Bean (Gilmanton)
Jean Louise, b. 8/12/1947; first; George McClary (woodsman,
   Gilmanton) and Lura M. Bunker (Gilmanton)
Jo-Ann Betty, b. 8/24/1957 in Concord; second; George F. A.
   McClary (bulldozer operator, NH) and Lura M. Bunker (NH)
Marion Myrtle, b. 8/29/1927; third; Frank L. McClary (laborer,
   Gilmanton) and Lena M. Nutter (Parsonsfield, ME)
Phyllis Evelyn, b. 1/13/1927; fourth; Arthur E. McClary (laborer,
   Gilmanton) and Clara Bean (Gilford)

Robert Noel, b. 7/9/1929 in Laconia; fifth; Arthur E. McClary (farmer, Gilmanton) and Clara Bean (Gilford)
Walter Everett, b. 11/5/1922; Arthur E. McClary and Clara I. Bean

McCLINTOCK,
Aren Jesse, b. 6/15/2000 in Gilmanton I.W.; Liam Cornell McClintock and Sheryl Anne McClintock

McCOWN,
Erin J., b. 7/21/1979 in Laconia; Gordon McCown, Jr. and Sylinda M. Brabant
Kelly Ann, b. 7/22/1983 in Laconia; Gordon McCown, Jr. and Sylinda M. Brabant

McCRADY,
Corey David, b. 8/22/1986 in Laconia; Douglas B. McCrady and Doris L. Lagasse

McDONALD,
Bryan Keith, b. 11/16/1990 in Gilmanton; Matthew P. McDonald and Donna Lee Gilmore
Sally Rose, b. 7/29/1998 in Concord; David McDonald and Linda McDonald

McELROY,
Ian P., b. 8/6/1979 in Concord; James W. McElroy and Lynn M. Miner

McEVOY,
Faith April, b. 5/28/1996 in Laconia; Brian Patrick McEvoy and Melissa Elaine Mickler

McKEAN,
Marguerite Louise, b. 3/8/1976 in Laconia; Edgar D. McKean, III (IL) and Louise G. M. Dempsey (Canada)
Matthew Dempsey, b. 6/5/1978 in Laconia; Edgar Doty McKean, III (PA) and Louise Dempsey (Canada)

McKINNA,
Catherine Ann, b. 6/25/1960 in Laconia; third; David Douglas McKinna (lineman, NY) and Ann Catherine Geiger (NY)

Kenneth David, b. 10/3/1953; first; David D. McKenna (machinist, NY) and Ann C. Geiger (NY)
Robert John, b. 8/24/1954; second; David D. McKinna (lineman, NY) and Ann C. Geiger (NY)

McLEAN,
Megan Frances, b. 8/8/1985 in Laconia; William J. McLean, III and Gertrude M. Dempsey
William J., IV, b. 4/15/1979 in Concord; William J. McLean, III and Heather Mudgett

McNAYR,
son, b. 12/22/1902; fifth; Richard McNayr (farmer, NS) and Sarah Nason (Salem, MA)
stillborn son, b. 12/22/1902; sixth; Richard McNayr (farmer, NS) and Sarah Nason (Salem, MA)

McQUADE,
Alexander Joseph, b. 11/14/1990 in Concord; Michael J. McQuade and Stephanie C. Sardella
Cameron Stephen, b. 6/7/1994 in Concord; Michael Joseph McQuade and Stephanie Camille Sardella

McQUILLEN,
Emily Kate, b. 4/18/1995 in Laconia; Michael A. McQuillen and Deborah C. Miller

McWHINNIE,
Christopher Robert, b. 5/14/1984 in Laconia; Robert C. McWhinnie, Jr. and Teresa C. Ross
Nicole Danielle, b. 6/8/1984 in Laconia; Thomas J. McWhinnie and Denise M. Lavoie

MEADER,
daughter, b. 10/8/1936 in Laconia; first; George Meader (laborer) and Dorothy Stone (Gilmanton)

MEEKINS,
James Clyde, b. 7/2/1947; first; Roth M. Meekins (Exeter)

MERCIER,
Robert Norman, III, b. 3/24/1981 in Laconia; Robert N. Mercier, Jr. and Sally M. Bach

MERRILL,
daughter, b. 6/25/1897; first; Charles L. Merrill (farmer, Gilmanton) and Mary E. Weeks (Gilmanton)
stillborn son, b. 3/16/1902; third; Charles L. Merrill (farmer, Gilmanton) and Mary E. Weeks (Gilmanton)
Corenna, b. 6/16/1965 in Concord; first; Robert Mack Merrill, III (attendant, NH) and Beverly Joyce Coursey (NH)
Richard David, b. 11/4/1977 in Concord; Richard H. Merrill (NH) and Jeanne D. Hueber (NH)
Richard Gordon, Jr., b. 4/11/1958 in Laconia; second; Richard G. Merrill (US Air Force, NH) and Rita R. M. Maltais (NH)

MESERVE,
Alice N., b. 12/19/1928; sixth; Frank C. Meserve (laborer, Freedom) and Marguerite Emerson (Barnstead)
Lydia Lynne, b. 7/20/2000 in Concord; Steven Meserve and Sarah Meserve

MEZROLL,
Lena May, b. 11/19/1901; first; Sylvester S. Mezroll (carpenter, NB) and Margaretta Currier (NB); residence - NB

MICHAUD,
Gregory Russell, b. 3/5/1985 in Laconia; Peter A. Michaud and Robin R. Cook

MICK,
David Stetson, b. 8/10/1949; first; Clarence S. Mick (student, MA) and Caroline Taylor Small (NY)

MIDDLETON,
Michael Joseph, b. 4/18/1991 in Manchester; Dana J. Middleton and Pamela J. Chadwick

MILLER,
Mark John, b. 10/9/1957; first; John D. Miller (US Air Force, OH) and Donna M. Gard (NH)

MILLIKEN,
Dustin Robert, b. 1/15/1984 in Laconia; Richard D. Milliken and Gail M. Wiggin

MILLS,
Summer Rene, b. 8/15/1999 in Laconia; Shawn Mills and Kathy Mills

MILMORE,
James Clifford, b. 2/11/1984 in Laconia; Dennis F. Milmore and Mary A. Fisher

MINER,
child, b. 10/5/1898; third; Fred Miner (laborer)
Allyssa Ramey, b. 10/19/1998 in Concord; Leonard Miner and Lea Miner
Jacob Frederick, b. 8/21/2001 in Concord; Leonard Miner and Lea Miner

MITCHELL,
child, b. 4/8/1922; Edwin W. Mitchell and Marie A. Ellsworth
Benton Jacob, b. 3/15/1993 in Concord; Walter L. Mitchell and Carol E. Nash

MOLLOY,
Delaney Kendra, b. 7/31/1992 in Concord; Dennis J. Molloy and Ellen M. Osborne
Regan Mackenzie, b. 4/22/1994 in Concord; Dennis Joseph Molloy and Ellen Margaret Osborne

MOODY,
Keith Nathaniel, b. 3/5/1918; first; Clarence N. Moody (mill operative, Loudon) and Nannie Pease (Gilmanton)

MOORE,
Hunter Robert, b. 4/2/1998 in Laconia; Dana Moore and Kerry Moore
Laura Charlene, b. 4/28/1962 in Concord; third; Karl Richard Moore (self-employed, NH) and Elaine Seavey Gordon (NH)
Michael Richard, b. 4/25/1965 in Concord; fourth; Karl Richard Moore (dairy farmer, NH) and Elaine Seavey Gordon (NH)

MOOREHEAD,
Abby, b. 8/15/1980 in Concord; Rickey E. Moorehead and Doreen D. Thompson
Adam Alexander, b. 2/16/1983 in Laconia; Shane A. Moorehead and Kathleen A. Langley
Alex Oland, b. 5/24/1991 in Laconia; Shane A. Moorehead and Kathleen A. Langley
Carl Eldon, b. 5/24/1964 in Laconia; fourth; Carl Ellison Moorehead (machinist, MI) and Jeanine Louise Segole (VT)
Cassie, b. 2/28/1979 in Concord; Rickey E. Moorehead and Doreen D. Thompson
Grace Ellen, b. 5/9/1959 in Laconia; third; Carl Ellison Moorehead (machinist, MI) and Jeanine Louise Segole (VT)
Nicholas Shane, b. 8/21/1981 in Laconia; Shane A. Moorehead and Kathleen A. Langley
Rickey E., b. 3/22/1956 in Laconia; second; Carl E. Moorehead (machinist, MI) and Jeanine L. Segale (VT)
Shane Alan, b. 9/23/1953; first; Carl E. Moorehead (US Navy, MI) and Jeanine L. Segalini (VT)

MORGAN,
Mackenzie Rose, b. 3/28/2000 in Concord; Charlie Morgan and Tiffany Morgan

MORIN,
Andrew Steven, b. 4/21/1989 in Laconia; Steven F. Morin and Patricia N. Neal
Rachel Marie, b. 3/18/1985 in Concord; Thomas R. Morin and Carla A. Frisbee
Rose Marie, b. 12/20/1951; ninth; Joseph A. Morin (laborer, NH) and Arlene E. Patten (NH)

MORRIS,
Kassidy Connor, b. 5/30/1999 in Concord; David Morris and Robin Morris
Zakaria Ellen, b. 7/19/1997 in Concord; David Edward Morris and Robin Lynn Stock

MORSE,
Donald Branhall, b. 9/5/1959 in Concord; third; Howard Branhall Morse (laborer, ME) and Mary Florence Geddes (NH)

Donna Lee, b. 5/22/1963 in Concord; fourth; Howard Branhall
Morse (laborer, ME) and Mary Florence Geddes (NH)
John Howard, b. 6/5/1958 in Concord; second; Howard B. Morse
(sander, ME) and Mary F. Geddes (NH)

MOSHER,
Erika Olivia, b. 9/23/2000 in Concord; Michael Mosher and Claudia
Mosher
Juliet Christian, b. 2/2/1998 in Laconia; Scott Douglas Mosher and
Debra Ann Riley

MOULTON,
son, b. 12/18/1914; second; Carroll Moulton (farmer, Gilmanton)
and Edna Tibbetts (Alton)
Albert Henry, b. 2/14/1918; fourth; Carroll H. Moulton (farmer,
Gilmanton) and Edna J. Tibbetts (Alton)
Elsie Catherine, b. 10/7/1920; sixth; Carroll H. Moulton (farmer,
Gilmanton) and Edna J. Tibbetts (Alton)
Verna Belle, b. 7/3/1919; fifth; Carroll H. Moulton (farmer,
Gilmanton) and Edna J. Tibbetts (Alton)

MULCAHY,
Mick Edward, b. 10/8/2001 in Concord; Francis Mulcahy and Betsy
Mulcahy

MULLIGAN,
Devon M., b. 1/28/1987 in Laconia; Sean D. Mulligan and Diane J.
Cooper

MUNDELL,
Dawn Marie, b. 3/22/1962 in Laconia; second; Harold William
Mundell (plant engineer, MA) and Yvonne Lois Dargie (NH)

MUNSEY,
daughter [Martha A.], b. 2/4/1887; second; Jay R. Munsey (farmer,
Concord) and Jos. May Osborne (Gilmanton)
daughter, b. 10/16/1932 in Laconia; seventh; John J. Munsey (tel.
foreman, Gilmanton) and Julia Bruce (Canada)
Arletta Harriett, b. 11/15/1916; second; John J. Munsey (farmer,
Gilmanton) and Julia Bruce (Flodden, PQ)

Glenna Jean, b. 1/13/1959 in Laconia; third; John J. Munsey, Jr. (machine operator, NH) and Jane Hoag (NY)

Glenna M., b. 7/22/1928; fifth; John J. Munsey (tel. foreman) and Julia Bruce (Canada)

Herbert Earl, b. 5/15/1920; third; John J. Munsey (farmer, Gilmanton) and Julia F. Bruce (Flodden, PQ)

Herbert Earl, Jr., b. 11/24/1943; second; Herbert E. Munsey (US Army, Gilmanton) and Ruth M. Willard (Gilmanton)

James Jay, b. 5/2/1958 in Laconia; third; Maurice E. Munsey (truck driver, NH) and Gloria I. Roberts (ME)

John J., Jr., b. 3/5/1930 in Pittsfield; sixth; John J. Munsey (laborer, Gilmanton) and Julia F. Bruce (Montreal, Can.)

John Jay, b. 3/1/1893; third; Jay R. Munsey (farmer, Concord) and Josephine Osborn (Gilmanton)

Linda Gail, b. 2/9/1962 in Laconia; fourth; John Jay Munsey, Jr. (machinist, NH) and June Hoag (NY)

Mabel Osborne, b. 6/18/1913; first; John Jay Munsey (farmer, Gilmanton) and Julia Florence Bruce (Flodden, PQ)

Martha Jean, b. 5/27/1962 in Concord; third; Herbert Earl Munsey, Sr. (weaver, NH) and Evelyn Elizabeth Corson (NH)

Maxine Hilary, b. 1/11/1986 in Gilmanton; James J. Munsey and Jean M. Munsey

Megin Ellyn, b. 3/10/1978 in Laconia; Thomas Allen Munsey (VT) and Jean Frances Douphinett (NH)

Morris Eugene, b. 6/6/1926; fourth; John J. Munsey (laborer, Gilmanton) and Julia F. Bruce (Flodden, P.I.)

Norton James, b. 10/10/1984 in Laconia; James Jay Munsey and Jean M. Moreau

Paul Lawrence, b. 7/1/1952; first; John J. Munsey (US Navy, NH) and Jane Hoag (NY)

Steven Alan, b. 9/4/1958 in Concord; third; Herbert E. Munsey, Sr. (weaver, NH) and Evelyn E. Corson (NH)

Susan Elizabeth, b. 9/5/1951; first; Maurice E. Munsey (time keeper, NH) and Gloria I. Roberts (ME)

Thomas J., b. 10/22/1979 in Laconia; Thomas A. Munsey and Jean F. Douphinett

MURPHY,

Maura Breckan, b. 2/27/1973 in Laconia; Michael C. Murphy (NH) and Joanne Vorel (MA)

NELSON,
son, b. 12/3/1889; first; Edwin F. Nelson (farmer, Gilmanton) and Nellie Nelson (Warner)
daughter [Marion G.], b. 8/29/1898; third; Edwin F. Nelson (farmer, Gilmanton) and Nellie A. Nelson (Warner)
son, b. 10/31/1902; fifth; Edwin F. Nelson (farmer, Rochester) and Helen A. Nelson (Plymouth)
Elaine Linda, b. 10/8/1949; fifth; George Martin Nelson (garage proprietor, NH) and Eleanor Hislop (MA)
George J., b. 6/23/1979 in Concord; Wayne D. Nelson and Judith D. Ehlen
George Martin, b. 2/28/1942; second; George M. Nelson (mechanic, Moultonboro) and Eleanor M. Hislop (Merrimac, MA)
Marguerite, b. 7/7/1893; second; Edwin F. Nelson (farmer, Gilmanton) and Nellie A. Nelson
Maurice J., b. 8/4/1895; third; Edwin F. Nelson (farmer, Gilmanton) and Nellie A. Nelson
Meghan Beth, b. 9/5/1970 in Concord; George Martin Nelson, II (NH) and Sharon Ann Fournier (NY)
Timothy James, b. 9/7/1966 in Concord; first; George Martin Nelson, 2nd (teacher, NH) and Sharon Ann Fornier (NY)
Wayne D., b. 3/5/1982 in Concord; Wayne D. Nelson and Judith D. Ehlen
Wayne Dana, b. 10/8/1949; fourth; George Martin Nelson (garage proprietor, NH) and Eleanor Hislop (MA)

NICHOLSON,
Brian David, b. 11/7/1978 in Laconia; David William Nicholson (MA) and Kathleen Ann Harrison (MA)
Christina Marie, b. 1/23/1981 in Gilmanton I. W.; George N. Nicholson and Suzanne L. Nageli
Jill Kathleen, b. 5/28/1981 in Laconia; David W. Nicholson and Kathleen A. Harrison

NIEUWEJAAR,
Kiersten Rene, b. 3/25/1972 in Laconia; Claus E. Nieuwejaar (Norway) and Nirvana T. Ronning (TX)
Sonja Ingrid, b. 9/15/1974 in Laconia; Claus Erik Nieuwejaar (Norway) and Nirvana T. Ronning (TX)

NILGES,
Amanda Lee, b. 2/27/1986 in Concord; Karl L. Nilges, Jr. and Ann M. Roy
Nicole Elizabeth, b. 2/27/1986 in Concord; Karl Lawson Nilges, Jr. and Ann M. Roy

NOFTLE,
Janelle Erin, b. 3/10/1989 in Laconia; Edward J. Noftle, Jr. and Michel A. Gordon

NOLIN,
Dustin P., b. 6/28/1979 in Concord; Dennis A. Nolin and Kathy E. Foster
Gena Lyn, b. 9/8/1977 in Concord; Dennis A. Nolin (NH) and Kathy E. Foster (NH)

NORELL,
Karen, b. 2/28/1962 in Laconia; third; William Charles Norell (carpenter, NY) and Ursula Mueller (Germany)
Robert Kurt, b. 7/16/1960 in Laconia; second; William Charles Norell (carpenter, NY) and Ursula Mueller (Germany)

NOVAK,
Michael Joseph, b. 9/9/1978 in Concord; Frank Chester Novak, Jr. (NJ) and Susan Ellen Logdahl (NH)

NOYES,
son, b. 5/8/1904; first; Forrest Noyes (laborer, Deerfield) and Pheobe Butcher (Dover); residence - Northwood
Stella Mae, b. 5/6/1958 in Laconia; fifth; Donald H. Noyes (machinist, NH) and Elizabeth L. Hoadley (VT)

NUTTER,
stillborn son, b. 2/27/1929 in Belmont; third; Clyde E. Nutter (mechanic, Maplewood, ME) and Doris I. Springer (Lawrence, MA)
Steven B., b. 3/2/1954; third; Kenneth N. Nutter (lumberman, NH) and Ethelyn G. Jones (ME)
William Kenneth, b. 8/2/1952; second; Kenneth N. Nutter (lumbering, NH) and Ethelyn G. Jones (ME)

NYE,
Jennifer Rose, b. 10/22/1977 in Laconia; Marshall E. Nye (MA) and
 Diane C. Hanson (MA)

O'CONNOR,
Meghan Erin, b. 3/22/1988 in Laconia; Charles B. O'Connor and
 Betsy-Jean McBride

O'SHEA,
John Dennis, III, b. 5/3/1976 in Laconia; John D. O'Shea, Jr. (MA)
 and Elizabeth J. Barrett (MA)

OETINGER,
Thomas Joseph, Jr., b. 1/20/1990 in Concord; Thomas J. Oetinger,
 Sr. and Michelle C. Silvestri

OLSON,
Adam S., b. 7/10/1979 in Concord; Kirke H. Olson and Deborah S.
 French

ONION,
Joshua C., b. 8/22/1979 in Laconia; Perry W. Onion and Anne W.
 Harris
Rebecca Stiles, b. 9/25/1977 in Laconia; Perry W. Onion (CO) and
 Anne W. Harris (NY)

OSBORN[E],
son, b. 11/27/1896; fifth; Charles A. Osborn (laborer, Gilmanton)
 and Grace A. True (Pittsfield)
daughter, b. 12/17/1906; first; John G. Osborne (blacksmith,
 Haverhill, MA) and Tessie O. Emerson (Wentworth)
Ann Elizabeth, b. 4/29/1951; third; Donald L. Osborn (ministry, MN)
 and Rachel D. Rowden (NH)
Asa Thomas, b. 10/13/2001 in Concord; Thomas Osborne and
 Heather Osborne
Robert Donald, b. 10/9/1952; fourth; Donald L. Osborn (clergyman,
 MN) and Rachel D. Rowden (NH)
Samuel Philip, b. 1/3/2000 in Concord; Thomas Osborne and
 Heather Osborn (sic)

OSGOOD,
Caroline Elaine, b. 8/4/1962 in Laconia; fifth; Newell Clifton Osgood (DAV, NH) and Rita Rosemarie Maltais (NH)
Newall Clifton, Jr., b. 3/18/1961 in Laconia; fourth; Newell Clifton Osgood (unemployed, NH) and Rita Rose-Marie Maltais (NH)

OSMAN,
Ari Penn, b. 11/26/1981 in Concord; David S. Osman and Fredda J. Chertok

OSMER,
Jason James, b. 11/22/1984 in Laconia; Steven D. Osmer and Sandra L. Bresse
Steven D., Jr., b. 3/31/1980 in Concord; Steven D. Osmer and Sandra L. Bresse

PAGE,
son [Roy T.], b. 5/27/1888; sixth; Royal Page (farmer, Gilmanton) and Annie ----- (Gilmanton)
stillborn child [Minnie Frances], b. 11/12/1894; Walter Page
daughter, b. 10/8/1895; second; Walter E. Page (laborer) and Mabel McClary
daughter, b. 10/18/1896; third; Walter E. Page (laborer, Gilmanton) and Mabelle McClary (Gilmanton); residence - Loudon
son [Ralph G.], b. 5/23/1897; fourth; George E. Page (farmer, Gilmanton) and Ella Jones
son [Andrew Tasker], b. 5/4/1901; second; Henry S. Page (farmer, Gilmanton) and Emma A. Tasker (Northwood)
son [Ernest C.], b. 8/17/1902; third; Henry S. Page (farmer, Gilmanton) and Emma A. Tasker (Northwood)
daughter, b. 3/21/1905; third; Henry E. Page (farmer, Gilmanton) and Ida A. Pendergast (Barnstead)
son, b. 10/10/1929; sixth; Frank J. Page (farmer, Franklin) and Helen Otis Wyatt (Tilton)
Albert E., b. 3/19/1900; first; Henry E. Page (farmer, Gilmanton) and Ida A. Pendergast (Barnstead)
Alvin George, b. 6/30/1934; first; Andrew T. Page (farmer, Gilmanton) and Mabel Avery (Gilmanton)
Carl Gale, b. 1/22/1952; first; Edward G. Page (laborer, NH) and Louise E. Sortor (MA)

Edna, b. 4/27/1900; second; William E. Page (laborer, Gilmanton) and Cora E. Couch (Sutton Mills)

Edward Gale, b. 2/12/1927 in Laconia; first; Harold G. Page (farmer, Plymouth, MA) and Etta Day (Plymouth)

Elise Lucile, b. 6/11/1902; second; Henry E. Page (farmer, Gilmanton) and Ida A. Pendergast (Barnstead)

Ethel May, b. 6/5/1921; second; Frank J. Page (farmer, Franklin) and Helen Wyatt (Tilton)

Evelyn Alice, b. 6/27/1920; first; Frank J. Page (farmer, Franklin) and Helen Otis Wyatt (Tilton)

Henry Vincent, b. 3/22/1936 in Wolfeboro; second; Andrew T. Page (laborer, Gilmanton) and Mabel H. Avery (Gilmanton)

Ida J., b. 1/15/1892; first; William S. Page (laborer, Gilmanton) and Cora E. Couch (Sutton)

Jeanette P., b. 9/6/1930; first; Ray B. Page (laborer, Gilmanton) and Lorna Stockbridge (Gilmanton)

John S., b. 12/13/1955; George O. Page (student, Gilmanton) and Ruth F. Berry (Boston, MA)

John Sidney, b. 2/7/1925; fourth; Frank J. Page (farmer, Franklin) and Helen Wyatt (Tilton)

Joshua Connor, b. 10/23/1987 in Laconia; Kevin C. Page and Sheila J. Twombly

Laura Ella, b. 12/6/1922; Frank J. Page and Helen O. Wyatt

Leo Henry, b. 4/2/1936; fourth; Ray B. Page (laborer, Gilmanton) and Lorna Stockbridge (Gilmanton)

Marlene May, b. 3/29/1934; third; Ray B. Page (laborer, Gilmanton) and Lorna Stockbridge (Gilmanton)

Ray Ballard, b. 6/5/1909; eighth; William A. Page (merchant, Gilmanton) and Sadie Buckman (N. Bridgewater, VT)

Richard Allen, b. 9/27/1964 in Laconia; second; Henry Vincent Page (carpenter, NH) and Olive Darlene Headley (PA)

Robert Ray, b. 12/20/1932; second; Ray B. Page (laborer, Gilmanton) and Lorna Stockbridge (Gilmanton)

PAIGE,

Allyson McGuire, b. 10/7/1998 in Laconia; Carroll Monroe Paige and Lynn Aaron Sawyer

John Ham, b. 10/29/1892; first; Charles Franklin Paige (shoemaker, Pittsfield) and Vona Ham (Gilmanton); residence - Pittsfield

PALLADINO,
Kirk Douglas, Jr., b. 9/18/1997 in Nashua; Kirk Douglas Palladino, Sr. and Renee Marie Boilard

PALMER,
son [Charles E.], b. 12/27/1896; first; George L. Palmer (carpenter, Dover) and Daisy Smith (Gilmanton)
daughter [Edna Estella], b. 9/1/1898; second; George L. Palmer (carpenter, Dover) and Daisy M. Smith (Gilmanton)
daughter [Florence J.], b. 9/24/1905; fourth; George L. Parmer (sic) (carpenter, Deerfield) and Daisy M. Smith (Gilmanton)
Leon L., b. 10/18/1902; third; George L. Palmer (carpenter, Dover) and Daisy M. Smith (Gilmanton)

PAQUETTE,
Joseph Henry, b. 8/19/1977 in Laconia; Donald R. Paquette (NH) and Merralee A. Thompson (MA)

PARENT,
Kristi Lee, b. 8/31/1989 in Laconia; Leon W. Parent and Wendy S. Willard
Zachary Israel, b. 7/30/1987 in Laconia; Leon W. Parent and Wendy S. Willard

PARKER,
Sandra Louise, b. 8/21/1946 in Wolfeboro; first; Albert R. Parker, Jr. (carpenter, Fall River, MA) and Jean P. Haight (Philadelphia, PA)

PARRINGTON,
Kelly Jean, b. 4/2/1981 in Laconia; Dennis J. Parrington and Cindy J. Kelley

PARSONS,
daughter [Flora H.], b. 6/12/1889; first; Usher S. Parsons (farmer, Gilmanton) and Ada Hill (Gilmanton)
daughter, b. 6/5/1892; second; Usher S. Parsons (farmer, Gilmanton) and Addie Hill (Gilmanton)
son, b. 5/8/1894; third; Usher S. Parsons (farmer, Gilmanton) and Addie Hill (Gilmanton)

Barbara Louise, b. 2/10/1936 in Wolfeboro; third; Frank W. Parsons (laborer, Gilmanton) and Gladys M. Burres (Gilmanton)
George Rufus, b. 8/26/1934; second; Frank W. Parsons (laborer, Gilmanton) and Gladys Burres (Gilmanton)
Hazel, b. 11/28/1898; fourth; Usher S. Parsons (farmer, Gilmanton) and Addie M. Hill (Gilmanton)

PARTRIDGE,
daughter [Daisy M.], b. 12/24/1934; eighth; Horace F. Partridge (farmer, Blackstone, MA) and Florence J. Palmer (Gilmanton)
Edwin L., b. 12/15/1935; ninth; Horace Partridge (farmer, Blackstone, MA) and Florence Palmer (Gilmanton)
Florence E., b. 4/2/1944; fourteenth; Horace F. Partridge (farmer, Blackstone, MA) and Florence J. Palmer (Gilmanton)
Frederick Horace, b. 5/16/1945; fourteenth; Horace F. Partridge (farming, Blackstone, MA) and Florence J. Partridge (Gilmanton)
George Arthur, b. 4/28/1932; sixth; Horace F. Partridge (farmer, Blackstone, MA) and Florence J. Palmer (Gilmanton)
Horace Woods, b. 12/24/1925; second; Horace F. Partridge (farmer, Blackstone, MA) and Florence Palmer (Gilmanton)
Kenneth Palmer, b. 3/28/1942; twelfth; Horace F. Partridge (farming, Blackstone, MA) and Florence Palmer (Gilmanton)
Leon Everett, b. 12/7/1926; third; Horace F. Partridge (farmer, Blackstone, MA) and Florence J. Palmer (Gilmanton)
Lois F., b. 4/24/1933; seventh; Horace F. Partridge (farmer, Blackstone, MA) and Florence Palmer (Gilmanton)
Marilla, b. 11/17/1928; fourth; Horace F. Partridge (farmer, Blackstone, MA) and Florence J. Palmer (Gilmanton)
May Edna, b. 10/21/1924; first; Horace F. Partridge (farmer, Blackstone, MA) and Florence Palmer (Gilmanton)
Olive B., b. 3/22/1930; fifth; Horace F. Partridge (farmer, Blackstone, MA) and Florence J. Palmer (Gilmanton)
Patricia Arlene, b. 6/4/1937; tenth; Horace F. Partridge (farmer, Blackstone, MA) and Florence Palmer (Gilmanton)

PATCH,
Garrett Bradley, b. 10/18/2000 in Laconia; Dan Patch and Shelley Patch
Haleigh Frances, b. 7/10/1998 in Laconia; Dan Steven Patch and Shelley Marie Jameson

PATTEN,
Claude Burton, Jr., b. 4/15/1942; third; Claude B. Patten (carpenter, Webster) and Barbara E. Dow (Belmont)
Dolen Joseph, b. 8/17/1998 in Laconia; Roland Leo Patten, Jr. and Naomi Rae Baron

PAUL,
Harriet, b. 6/14/1907; second; colored; John M. Paul (laborer, Sanbornton) and Almena M. Haskell (Belmont)

PAULEY,
Richard James, III, b. 8/28/1995 in Laconia; Richard J. Pauley, Jr. and Robyn Louise Sawyer

PEARL,
Brett Daniel, b. 5/29/1983 in Laconia; Bruce A. Pearl and Diane J. Moore
Brian Michael, b. 8/21/1984 in Laconia; Bruce A. Pearl and Diane J. Moore

PEASE,
daughter, b. 10/16/1889; second; John L. Pease (laborer, Loudon) and Nancy Greenough (Loudon)
son, b. 6/21/1897; fourth; John L. Pease (laborer, Loudon) and Nancy Greenough

PELISSIER,
Emily Marie, b. 6/23/1986 in Laconia; George A. Pelissier and Elizabeth R. Helbling

PELTON,
Elizabeth Collins, b. 4/10/1964 in Concord; second; Bruce Ingalls Pelton (guidance counselor, NY) and Margaret Lois Surdy (NH)
Kathryn Laura, b. 10/1/1961 in Concord; second; Bruce Ingalls Pelton (teacher, NY) and Margaret Lois Surdy (NY)

PENNOCK,
John Duncan, b. 11/8/1946 in Laconia; fourth; James G. Pennock (control clerk, Woodsville) and Florence V. Pennock (Somerville, MA)

Joy Leslie, b. 11/3/1941; second; James G. Pennock (orchardist, Woodsville) and Florence V. Pennock (Somerville, MA)

Winnie Louise, b. 6/24/1938 in Wolfeboro; first; James G. Pennock (farm hand, Woodsville) and Florence Pennock (Somerville, MA)

PERKINS,

daughter, b. 6/29/1920; fifth; Walter C. Perkins (farmer, Gilmanton) and Eva Glines (Gilmanton)

Alice May, b. 8/16/1913; second; Walter Perkins (farmer, Gilmanton) and Eva Glines (Gilmanton)

Christopher Joshua, b. 9/13/1989 in Laconia; Daniel W. Perkins and Sara L. Stanley

Clarence Lewis, b. 1/29/1911; first; Walter C. Perkins (farmer, Gilmanton) and Eva M. Glines (Gilmanton)

Daniel Walter, b. 11/27/1962 in Concord; third; Harold Chester Perkins (lumbering, NH) and Rachel Teresa Goupil (NH)

Doris, b. 12/18/1915; third; Walter Charles Perkins (farmer, Gilmanton) and Eva Maud Glines (Gilmanton); residence - Gilmanton I. W.

Ethel, b. 6/5/1902; first; Lorenzo H. Perkins (farmer, Gilmanton) and Helen A. Wyatt (Farmington)

Harold C., b. 1/5/1930; sixth; Walter C. Perkins (farmer, Gilmanton) and Eva Maude Glinn (Gilmanton)

Harold J. N., b. 2/12/1954; second; Harold C. Perkins (lumbering, NH) and Rachel T. Goupil (NH)

Leon Walter, b. 10/9/1917; fourth; Walter C. Perkins (farmer, Gilmanton) and Eva M. Glines (Gilmanton)

Mary Isobel, b. 2/4/1918; third; Fred G. Perkins (carpenter, builder, Canada) and Nellie M. Kirby (Rome, PQ)

Monica Jean, b. 10/30/1988 in Laconia; Paul H. Perkins and Ellen J. Emberley

Patrick Joseph, b. 1/24/1989 in Concord; Harold J. Perkins and Julie I. Butman

Paul Henry, b. 8/18/1964 in Concord; fourth; Harold C. Perkins (truck driver, NH) and Rachel T. Goupil (NH)

Roseanna Eva, b. 4/13/1951; first; Harold C. Perkins (truck driver, NH) and Rachel T. Goupil (NH)

Stephen Paul, b. 12/20/1995 in Laconia; Paul Henry Perkins and Ellen Jean Emberley

Tara Lee, b. 3/24/1987 in Concord; Harold J. N. Perkins and Julie I. Butman

PERLEY,
Allan Russell, b. 7/11/1987 in Laconia; Robert A. Perley and Lida Katris

PETHEWAY,
daughter, b. 11/27/1905; first; Stephen Petheway (laborer, Russia) and Lillian Preo (Chichester)

PHILIPPS,
Daniel Albert, b. 8/28/1978 in Concord; Albert Edward Philipps (NY) and Phyllis Evelyn Barnes (NH)

PHILLIPS,
Sarah Emily, b. 8/24/1977 in Laconia; Charles R. Phillips (MA) and Renee L. Chenez (MA)

PHILPOT,
Natalie Conant Van Blarcom, b. 4/19/1981 in Laconia; William Philpot, Jr. and Karen C. Harris

PICARD,
Tiffany Marion, b. 7/10/1984 in Laconia; Lynwood S. Picard and Laura M. Lelievre

PICKERING,
daughter, b. 5/15/1888; second; Fred Pickering (storekeeper, Barnstead) and Clara -----

PICKOWICZ,
Anne R., b. 10/4/1982 in Concord; Michael P. Pickowicz and Rachel M. Frechette
Katherine Anna, b. 4/29/1981 in Laconia; George J. Pickowicz, Jr. and Eleanor J. Ingaharro
Laura Beth, b. 10/5/1985 in Concord; Michael P. Pickowicz and Rachel M. Frechette
Nathan M., b. 8/4/1979 in Laconia; Michael P. Pickowicz and Rachel M. Frechette

PIDGEON,
Dalton James, b. 5/7/1995 in Laconia; Gilbert L. Pidgeon and Maureen S. Ballester

PIERCE,
daughter, b. 12/31/1897; Augustus E. Pierce (farmer)
Wilbert Maurice, II, b. 11/27/1970 in Concord; Wilbert Maurice Pierce, Sr. (NH) and Doris Adelaide Boyd (NH)

PILLING,
Kathryn Anne, b. 5/26/1995 in Laconia; Richard J. Pilling and Jennifer L. Forbes

PINNATARO,
Augustino John, b. 9/8/1972 in Laconia; Augustino J. Pinnataro (NY) and Cena Ann Lamy (MA)

PIRO,
Nicole Anastasia, b. 3/16/1983 in Rochester; Victor S. Piro and Stephanie Hammerling

PLACE,
son, b. 9/23/1890; second; Jesse Place (laborer) and Grace Page (Gilmanton)
Josephine Sibyl, b. 11/27/1892; third; Jesse F. Place (mill hand, Alton) and Grace Paige (Gilmanton)

PLEETER,
Megan Rachel, b. 3/26/1994 in Laconia; Daniel Pleeter and Wendy Anne Kidder

PLOURDE,
Jason Michael, b. 9/8/1971 in Laconia; Gary Wayne Plourde (NH) and Valerie Ann Begin (TX)
Jeremy Scott, b. 10/10/1974 in Laconia; Gary W. Plourde (NH) and Valerie A. Begin (TX)

POLITO,
Jessica Marie, b. 2/19/1989 in Laconia; James M. Polito and Patricia F. Barnes

POROSKY,
Abby E., b. 6/30/1980 in Concord; Roger B. Porosky and Nancy E. Hunt
Timothy Daniel, b. 4/7/1984 in Concord; Roger B. Porosky and Nancy E. Hunt

PORTER,
Melissa Jean, b. 3/22/194 in Concord; Stephen M. Porter and Marianne P. Gaydos

POTTER,
son [George D.], b. 5/15/1890; first; Charles F. Potter (farmer, Gilmanton) and Ardena Maria Diamond (Loudon)
daughter, b. 4/13/1892; second; Charles Fred Potter (farmer, Gilmanton) and Ardena M. Diamond (Loudon)
child, b. 2/26/1900; third; C. Fred Potter (farmer, Gilmanton) and Andena M. Diamond (London)
son, b. 1/23/1903; fourth; Charles F. Potter (farmer, Gilmanton) and Ardena M. Dimond (Loudon)
Bernice C., b. 1/27/1928; fourth; George D. Potter (farmer, Gilmanton) and Mildred E. Page (Dorchester, MA)
Carl Robert, b. 10/30/1992 in Concord; Robert L. Potter, Jr. and Melissa A. Aikins
Carlton Wesley, b. 3/30/1939; first; S. Earl Potter (farmer, Gilmanton) and Julia F. Smith (Hill)
Dorothy Winona, b. 6/26/1923; George D. Potter and Mildred E. Page
Eric George, b. 6/19/1998 in Concord; Robert L. Potter, Jr. and Melissa Ann Aikins
Florence A., b. 4/13/1926; third; George D. Potter (farmer, Gilmanton) and Mildred E. Page (Dorchester, MA)
Janet Ann, b. 1/8/1964 in Concord; second; Robert Leo Potter (farmer, NH) and Nancy Jane Sanborn (NH)
Katherine Lyn, b. 4/29/1991 in Concord; Robert L. Potter, Jr. and Melissa A. Aikins
Richard George, b. 11/15/1971 in Concord; Robert Leo Potter (NH) and Nancy Jane Sanborn (NH)
Robert Leo, b. 3/7/1931; sixth; George D. Potter (farmer, Gilmanton) and Mildred E. Page (Dorchester, MA)
Robert Leo, Jr., b. 9/29/1969 in Concord; Robert Leo Potter, Sr. (NH) and Nancy Jane Sanborn (NH)

Ruth Eleanor, b. 11/23/1924; second; George D. Potter (farmer, Gilmanton) and Mildred E. Page (Dorchester, MA)
Samuel James, b. 10/22/1996 in Concord; Robert Leo Potter, Jr. and Melissa Ann Aikins
Virginia M., b. 9/22/1929; fifth; George D. Potter (farmer, Gilmanton) and Mildred E. Page (Dorchester, MA)

POULIN,
Aiyana Calandra Kendra, b. 11/26/1996 in Laconia; Robert George Poulin and Kimberly Anne Moore
Dagan Vaughn Dryden, b. 10/15/1999 in Laconia; Robert Poulin and Kimberley Poulin

POWELL,
Abe Walton, b. 4/25/1984 in Concord; Luke Peyton Powell and Donna Elaine Rounds
Abigail Elizabeth, b. 12/17/1991 in Rochester; Luke P. Powell and Donna E. Rounds
Jonathan Robert, b. 2/16/1987 in Rochester; Luke P. Powell and Donna E. Rounds

PREVOST,
Sophia Lisa, b. 2/10/1998 in Concord; Richard Fernand Prevost and Gina Marie Cavagnavo

PRICE,
daughter, b. 9/4/1887; second; Charles A. Price (farmer, Gilmanton) and Anna E. Price (Barnstead)
daughter [Elizabeth M.], b. 10/7/1892; third; Charles A. Price (farmer, Gilmanton) and Ora Emerson (Pittsfield)
Angelique Renee, b. 3/23/1972 in Laconia; Charles A. Price (NH) and Judy B. Hough (NH)
Caleb Walter, b. 2/23/1998 in Laconia; Jonathan Charles Price and Jolene Marie Barton
Charles Amos, b. 1/28/1950; fourth; Amos Richard Price (farmer, Manchester) and Paulien Marjorie Richards (Haverhill, MA)
Doris, b. 11/12/1910; second; Amos R. Price (farmer, Gilmanton) and Emma F. Wight (Gilmanton)
Elizabeth Mary, b. 7/30/1908; first; Amos R. Price (farmer, Gilmanton) and Emma F. Wight (Gilmanton)

Jonathan Charles, b. 7/14/1973 in Laconia; Charles Amos Price (NH) and Judith Beth Hough (NH)

Mary Ann, b. 5/24/1948; third; Amos R. Price (farmer, Manchester) and Pauline M. Richards (Haverhill, MA)

Natalie Jean, b. 4/6/1939 in Wolfeboro; first; Amos R. Price (poultryman, Manchester) and Pauline M. Richards (Haverhill, MA); residence - Gilmanton I. W.

Pauline E., b. 6/15/1955; fifth; Amos R. Price (farmer, Manchester) and Pauline M. Richards (Haverhill, MA)

Richard Charles, b. 9/5/1983 in Wolfeboro; Richard E. Price and Pamela A. Fell

Richard Ernest, b. 7/1/1957 in Concord; sixth; Amos Richard Price (farmer, NH) and Pauline M. Richards (MA)

William Richard, b. 3/27/1947; second; Richard A. Price (farmer, Manchester) and Pauline M. Richards (Haverhill, MA)

William Richard, II, b. 4/30/1971 in Wolfeboro; William Richard Price (NH) and Ena May Stockwell (NH)

PRINDLE,

Elizabeth Rodman, b. 1/25/1949; fourth; William E. Prindle, Jr. (student, New Haven, CT) and Myra C. Kitchen (Great Neck, NY)

Michael Harrison, b. 7/19/1947; William E. Prindle, Jr. (pilot, New Haven, CT) and Myra C. Kitchen (Great Neck, NY)

William Rodman, b. 4/24/1950; sixth; William Edwin Prindle, Jr. (student, CT) and Myra Constant Kitchen (NY)

PROCTOR,

son, b. 4/11/1956; second; Charles A. Proctor (agent 4-H Club, New York, NY) and Betty-Anne Stephenson (Boston, MA)

Carole, b. 11/20/1958 in Gilmanton; third; Charles A. Proctor (ins. agent, NY) and Betty-Anne Y. Stephenson (MA)

Lynn, b. 2/24/1954; first; Charles A. Proctor (4H Ext. Sec., NY) and Betty Stephenson (MA)

PROVENCAL,

George Alden, b. 9/1/1973 in Concord; Frank John Provencal (NH) and Jane Arlene Witham (MA)

William John, b. 10/9/1969 in Concord; Frank John Provencal (NH) and Jane Arlene Witham (MA)

PROWN,
Bill, b. 12/3/1934; sixth; colored; Bill Prown (laborer, East Tilton) and Emma Paul (Franklin)

PUBLICOVER,
Charles Joseph, b. 3/16/1949; third; Robert G. Publicover (unemployed, NS) and Annie Mary Shlaitas (Gilmanton)
John Michael, b. 10/8/1954; sixth; Robert G. Publicover (NS) and Annie M. Shlaitas (NH)
Kenneth George, b. 10/26/1950; fourth; Robert George Publicover (US Army, NS) and Annie Mary Shlaitas (NH)
Robert William, b. 12/8/1947; second; Robert G. Publicover (miller, Truro, Canada) and Annie M. Shlaitas (Gilmanton)
Sandra Jean, b. 9/16/1946 in Concord; first; Robert G. Publicover (soldier, Truro, NS) and Annie M. Shlaitas (Gilmanton)
Teresa Ann, b. 3/25/1952; fifth; Robert G. Publicover (radio repairman, NS) and Annie M. Shlaitas (NH)

PURTELL,
Diana Lynn, b. 2/5/1961 in Concord; first; Stanley Philip Purtell (machine operator, NH) and Barbara June Parker (NH)
Michael Leon, b. 3/21/1967 in Laconia; third; Stanley Philip Purtell (bed laster, NH) and Barbara June Parker (NH)
Stanley Philip, Jr., b. 2/2/1962 in Concord; second; Stanley Philip Purtell, Sr. (lathe operator, NH) and Barbara June Parker (NH)

RAFFERTY,
Jessica Lin, b. 6/2/1986 in Concord; Patrick K. Rafferty and Vicki Ann Bladecki
Joseph Edward, b. 6/2/1986 in Concord; Patrick K. Rafferty and Vicki Ann Bladecki

RALLS,
Michael Austin, b. 3/11/1969 in Laconia; Arthur Joseph Ralls (MA) and Theresa Delvina Berube (MA)

RALYS,
Alexander Joel, b. 9/14/1987 in Concord; William C. Ralys and Linda S. Dirth
Matthew Ward, b. 2/13/1985 in Concord; William C. Ralys, Sr. and Linda S. Dirth

REED,
Carrie A., b. 5/11/1980 in Laconia; Thomas Robertson Reed and Charlotte A. Monroe
Tyler Monroe, b. 1/31/1986 in Concord; Thomas R. Reed and Charlotte A. Monroe

REINHOLZ,
Lance K., b. 7/11/1980 in Laconia; Lance K. Reinholz and Dianne S. Hyslop

RELF,
David Thomas, b. 1/12/1976 in Concord; George D. Relf (MA) and Lola M. Kenney (ME)

RENAUD,
Anthony Mark, b. 10/24/1992 in Manchester; Mark A. Renaud and Patricia C. Peterson

RENDALL,
Benjamin Ellis, b. 11/10/1988 in Concord; Geoffrey U. Rendall and Nancy B. Beckwith
Katherine Anne, b. 9/27/1991 in Concord; Geoffrey U. Rendall and Nancy J. Beckwith
Thomas Upham, b. 1/26/1986 in Concord; Geoffrey U. Rendall and Nancy J. Beckwith

RHODES,
Megan Erica, b. 8/22/1981 in Concord; Barry Rhodes and Joanne Chow

RICE,
Timothy Herbert, b. 12/17/1997 in Plymouth; Herbert Edward Rice and Patricia Ann O'Connor

RICHARDS,
Lilium Grace, b. 5/27/1989 in Concord; Robert E. Richards and Susannah G. Nichols

RICHARDSON,
Leon Howard, b. 12/24/1926 in Concord; second; Leon Richardson (farmer) and Georgianna St. Onge (Georgiaville, RI)

Royal Lincoln, b. 6/30/1926; sixth; Leslie A. Richardson (laborer, McGalaway, ME) and Jennie W. Denyalt'n (Cumberland, ME)

RIEL,
Karen Lee, b. 1/6/1965 in Concord; first; Thomas Alden Riel (laborer, NH) and Frances Irene Tarbox (NH)
Linda Elizabeth, b. 5/11/1943; second; Alden L. Riel (laborer, Pittsfield) and M. Pauline French (Gilmanton)
Thomas Alden, b. 4/19/1944; third; Alden L. Riel (lumberman, Pittsfield) and M. Pauline French (Gilmanton)
Vicki Lynn, b. 12/2/1967 in Concord; second; Thomas Alden Riel (laborer, NH) and Frances Irene Tarbox (NH)

RIGMONT,
Emily Shayna, b. 6/26/1977 in Gilmanton; Jeffrey B. Rigmont (MA) and Judy L. Cool (MA)

RING,
Mary Elizabeth, b. 8/26/1909; first; Charles E. Ring (farmer, Loudon) and Vinna Sleeper (Grafton)

ROBERGE,
Stacey Lynn, b. 11/16/1984 in Concord; Ronald R. Roberge and Sharon G. Fletcher

ROBERTS,
Abigail E., b. 12/30/1975 in Concord; George B. Roberts, Jr. (MA) and Margaret F. Edmunds (NH)
Erin Sue, b. 6/17/1981 in Concord; Neil Richard Roberts and Susan E. Munsey
Ian N., b. 2/13/1979 in Concord; Neil R. Roberts and Susan E. Munsey
Jessica Swift, b. 11/28/1977 in Concord; George B. Roberts, Jr. (MA) and Margaret F. Edmunds (NH)
Marie E., b. 4/6/1930; second; Ernest W. Roberts (farmer, England) and Louise F. Baynham (England)
William J., b. 7/6/1928; first; Ernest W. Roberts (farmer, England) and Louie F. Baynham (England)

ROBERTSON,
son, b. 1/12/1901; third; John Robertson (teamster, NB) and Mary Mezroll (NB)
daughter, b. 8/20/1902; fourth; John Robertson (teamster, NB) and Mary Mezroll (NB)
Alfred Worcester, b. 6/29/1889; first; Samuel W. Robertson (teacher, Tullahassee Mission, Indian Terr.) and Grace Knight (Franconia)

ROBICHAND,
daughter, b. 11/26/1902; fourth; Placide Robichand (sawyer, Rogersville, NB) and Sarah E. Jendreau (Lowell, MA)

ROBILLARD,
Olivia Lauren, b. 8/5/2000 in Concord; Robert Robillard and Elizabeth Robillard

ROBINETTE,
Curran David, b. 9/2/1986 in Concord; Michael J. Robinette and Muriel A. Steenstra
Morgan Leigh, b. 11/1/1993 in Concord; Michael J. Robinette and Muriel A. Steenstra

ROBINSON,
son, b. 8/14/1897; seventh; Etta I. Robinson
Christian Michael, b. 1/26/1994 in Concord; Brian James Robinson and Susan Jean Smith
Janie Emma, b. 2/23/1917; first; Thomas I. Robinson (farm hand, NB) and Gladys A. Hilliard (Canterbury); residence - Lynn, MA
Robert Irving, b. 4/26/1918; first; Tom Robinson (electric, NB) and May Reid (NB)

ROCHE,
Meghan Mae, b. 2/9/1985 in Concord; Kevin B. Roche and Lisa Mae Kohut

ROGER,
Harry William, III, b. 7/18/1965 in Laconia; first; Harry William Rogers, Jr. (ass't manager, NH) and Janet Irene Seaholm (NY)

ROGERS,
Ivy, b. 8/20/1907; first; John I. Rogers (jeweler, Watertown, MA) and Bessie A. Doane (Providence, RI)

ROLLINS,
daughter [Alice E.], b. 6/7/1901; fourth; Seldon B. Rollins (farmer, Gilmanton) and Alma L. Ellis (Gilmanton)
daughter [Doris M.], b. 2/9/1907; third; Seldon B. Rollins (farmer, Gilmanton) and Alma L. Ellis (Alton)
son [Everett B.], b. 9/29/1909; fourth; Seldon B. Rollins (farmer, Gilmanton) and Alma L. Ellis (Alton)
daughter [Jeanette], b. 1/4/1928; sixth; Selden B. Rollins (laborer, Gilmanton) and Eva Jones (Gilmanton)
daughter, b. 5/11/1933; sixth; Arthur Rollins (laborer, Oxford) and Marion Jordan (Piermont); residence - Concord
Gertrude, b. 4/1/1904; second; Seldon B. Rollins (farmer, Gilmanton) and Alma Ellis (Alton)
Harvey James, b. 12/2/1934; seventh; Arthur Rollins (farm hand, Orford) and Marion Jordan (Piermont)
Ian Patrick, b. 7/19/1998 in Concord; Patrick Rollins and Patricia Rollins
Leon Selden, b. 3/26/1950; first; Selden Bartlett Rollins (shoe worker, NH) and Belle Joan Parker (MI)
Louise Frances, b. 12/6/1913; fifth; S. B. Rollins (teamster, Gilmanton) and Alma L. Ellis (Alton)
Selden B., Jr., b. 9/29/1929; seventh; Selden B. Rollins (laborer, Gilmanton) and Eva Jones (Gilmanton)
Thelma May, b. 7/3/1931; eighth; Selden B. Rollins (laborer, Gilmanton) and Eva Jones (Gilmanton)
Walter Everett, b. 3/6/1934; ninth; Selden B. Rollins (laborer, Gilmanton) and Eva Jones (Gilmanton)

ROSS,
Zra Aslan, b. 7/8/1974 in Wolfeboro; Lawrence G. Ross (NY) and Shana Winer (NH)

ROTH,
Charles Thomas, b. 2/4/1947; first; Theodore F. Roth (cabinet maker, Boston, MA) and Cora B. Whitehouse (Peabody, MA)
David Frank, b. 6/12/1948; second; Theodore F. Roth (cabinet maker, Boston, MA) and Cora B. Whitehouse (Peabody, MA)

ROWE,
daughter, b. 10/2/1916; first; Gertrude Rowe (Gilmanton)

ROWLEY,
Hunter Christian, b. 9/23/1992 in Laconia; Eric C. Rowley and Nancy B. Hunter
Seth Jared, b. 5/30/1996 in Laconia; Eric Christian Rowley and Nancy Beth Hunter

RUCHTI,
Dana Catherine, b. 7/11/1998 in Concord; Jon Ruchti and Norma Ruchti
Samuel Peter, b. 4/11/2001 in Concord; Jon Ruchti and Norma Ruchti

RUSSELL,
Amy, b. 9/18/1977 in Wolfeboro; Sven E. Russell (NH) and Dawn M. Henry (CT)
Andrea Rosinski, b. 8/30/1981 in Concord; Gordon W. Russell and Jane L. Rosinski
Carl Rosinski, b. 4/3/1984 in Concord; Gordon W. Russell and Jane L. Rosinski
Charlotte Lorraine, b. 9/30/1951; second; Kenneth P. Russell (grinder (foundry), VT) and Blanche D. Martin (ME)
David Allen, b. 8/30/1953; third; Kenneth P. Russell (grinder, VT) and Blanche D. Martin (ME)
Erin Dee, b. 3/3/1963 in Concord; fourth; Sven Charles Russell (attendant, CA) and Beatrice Ann Thompson (MA)
Karel Andrea, b. 3/13/1966 in Concord; fifth; Sven Charles Russell (stone mason, CA) and Beatrice Ann Thompson (MA)
Rhonda Rose, b. 2/22/1959 in Laconia; third; Charles Sven Russell (drill operator, CA) and Beatrice Ann Thompson (MA)
Roger Alvin, b. 7/16/1950; first; Kenneth Perle Russell (lumberman, VT) and Blanche Doris Martin (ME)
Ryan, b. 11/7/1979 in Wolfeboro; Sven E. Russell and Dawn M. Henry
Shaunee Sioux, b. 2/29/1968 in Concord; Sven Charles Russell (CA) and Beatrice Ann Thompson (MA)
Sven Erich, b. 7/23/1954; second; Charles S. Russell (lumberman, CA) and Beatrice Thompson (MA)

RYAN,
child, b. 10/25/1987 in Concord; Michael S. Ryan and Donna J. Fredette

SALMON,
Andrew Bradford, b. 2/8/1983 in Laconia; Maurice R. Salmon, II and Marsha A. Bemis
Melissa A., b. 11/21/1980 in Laconia; Maurice R. Salmon, II and Marsha A. Bemis

SANBORN,
stillborn son, b. 8/14/1902; first; Harry W. Sanborn (farmer, Gilmanton) and Gertrude M. Brown (Chichester)
son, b. 7/14/1903; fifth; James H. Sanborn (laborer, Sandwich) and Maria Sherman (Bethlehem)
Audrey Jane, b. 7/29/1915; first; Carl J. Sanborn (farmer, Columbus, MI) and Evelyn M. Sanborn (Pittsfield)
Hunter Augustus, b. 5/4/1998 in Manchester; Chad Patrick Sanborn and Laurie Jane Paquette
Karly Marcel, b. 5/2/2001 in Manchester; Chad Sanborn and Laurie Sanborn
Marguerite, b. 12/5/1908; second; Harry W. Sanborn (poultryman, Gilmanton) and Gertrude M. Brown (Chichester)
Nathaniel C., b. 10/5/1902; first; Nathaniel M. Sanborn (painter, Alzaniz) and Clara Desmaras (Raston Fall, Ca.)
Wayne Wilson, b. 1/26/1918; second; Carl J. Sanborn (farmer, Columbia, MO) and Evelyn M. Sanborn (Pittsfield)

SANVILLE,
Emily Ann, b. 3/21/1985 in Laconia; Joseph L. Sanville, III and Sheryl A. Goode
Robert John, b. 11/30/1957; seventh; William Henry Sanville (fireman, NH) and Florence W. Bresseau (NH)
Vicki Ann, b. 3/9/1974 in Laconia; Wilfred L. Sanville (NH) and Brenda G. Glidden (NH)
Wilfred Lee, Jr., b. 7/22/1972 in Laconia; Wilfred L. Sanville (NH) and Brenda G. Glidden (NH)

SARGENT,
child, b. 5/11/1894; W. I. Sargent

son, b. 9/16/1898; first; Charles P. Sargent (farmer, Gilmanton) and ----- Dow
daughter, b. 2/5/1901; second; Charles P. Sargent (farmer, Gilmanton) and Alace A. Dow (Hill)
daughter, b. 9/8/1903; third; Charles P. Sargent (farmer, Gilmanton) and Alice A. Dow (Hill)
Blanche M., b. 6/14/1892; second; William Sargent (shoemaker, Pittsfield) and Minnie E. Bickford (Eden, VT); residence - Haverhill, MA
Caleb Alden, b. 8/23/1996 in Laconia; Wesley Ethan Sargent and Valerie Ann Brown
Elinor Marie, b. 10/21/1918; second; Clarence L. Sargent (mechanic, Gilmanton) and Rena Prescott (Alton)
Horace D., b. 9/--/1893; first; Herbert Sargent (farmer, Gilmanton) and Carrie Ellis (Alton)
Mary Estella, b. 3/1/1935 in Alton; second; Horace Sargent (farmer, Gilmanton) and Edna Palmer (Gilmanton)
Mason Prescott, b. 12/21/1993 in Laconia; Wesley E. Sargent and Valerie A. Brown
Prescott Nathan, b. 1/8/1938 in Laconia; first; Clarence L. Sargent (farmer, Laconia) and Frances E. Stone (Laconia)

SASKO,
Meredith Christina, b. 9/18/1988 in Laconia; Douglas A. Sasko and Robin L. York

SAUNDERS,
Charles William, b. 7/4/1927; second; Lester A. Saunders (farmer, Medford, MA) and Nellie S. Salls (Clarenceville, Can.)

SAWICKI,
Thomas Edward, b. 7/4/1987 in Laconia; James S. Sawicki and Marlene M. Batiste

SAWYER,
John David, b. 3/30/1911; second; David Sawyer (farmer, Gilmanton) and Betsey M. Knowles (Gilmanton)
Lynn A., b. 8/25/1975 in Laconia; Mark A. Sawyer (NH) and Louise A. Barnett (NH)
Matthew Ryan, b. 5/28/1973 in Laconia; Charles Franklin Sawyer (CT) and Janice Louise Strople (NH)

Robyn Louise, b. 5/18/1972 in Laconia; Mark A. Sawyer (NH) and Louise Arlene Barnett (NH)

Theodore Howard, b. 3/28/1909; stillborn; first; David Sawyer (farmer, Gilmanton) and Betsey M. Knowles (Gilmanton)

SCANLAN,
Francis J., Jr., b. 7/1/1940; first; Francis J. Scanlan (tariff exam., Boston, MA) and Mina R. Wells (Gilmanton)

SCHAEFFER,
daughter, b. 8/8/1910; first; George J. Schaeffer (laborer, Boston, MA) and Mertie E. Bell (Whitefield, RI)

SCHAFFNIT,
Brion S., b. 10/10/1979 in Laconia; Leonard J. Schaffnit and Andrea J. Sayles

SCHMIDT,
Danielle Elizabeth, b. 7/16/1992 in Laconia; John D. Schmidt and Darlene E. Drouin

SCHNEIDER,
Scott Alan, b. 7/31/1990 in Concord; Mark K. Schneider and Jeanne M. Lawrence

SCHREMPF,
Heidi A., b. 7/3/1980 in Laconia; Stephen M. Schrempf and Mary A. White

SCHULZE,
Hans W., b. 7/25/1979 in Laconia; Robert Schulze and Louise A. Couture

SCOTT,
Joseph Gray, Jr., b. 5/13/1986 in Laconia; Joseph Gray Scott, Sr. and Corella Anderson

SCOVILL,
Judson Laurence, b. 11/26/1943; first; Laurence S. Scovill (farmer, Clinton, MA) and Virginia Prescott (Barnstead)

Kent Christopher, b. 12/22/1986 in Rochester; Paul K. Scovill and Karen E. Wozmak

Mildred Virginia, b. 1/30/1945 in Wolfeboro; second; Laurence S. Scovill (farmer, Clinton, MA) and Virginia A. Prescott (Barnstead)

Paul K., b. 4/17/1956 in Concord; fourth; Lawrence S. Scovill (poultry farmer, Clinton, MA) and Virginia A. Prescott (Barnstead)

Sara Elizabeth, b. 7/28/1983 in Rochester; Paul K. Scovill and Karen E. Wozmak

Winifred May, b. 9/9/1949; third; Lawrence S. Scovill (farmer, Clinton, MA) and Virginia A. Prescott (Barnstead)

SEARLE,

Malcolm Miller, b. 1/6/1920; stillborn; third; Carl N. Searle (farmer, Baldwinsville, MA) and Martha Miller (Buffalo, NY)

SEARS,

son, b. 1/23/1892; first; Joseph Sears (shoemaker, Canada) and Carrie Giles (Chichester)

SEAVEY,

Inez, b. 8/11/1891; first; Joseph E. Seavey (farmer, Alexandria) and Nellie S. Jones (Gilmanton); residence - Farmington

SECORD,

Eleanor Doris, b. 9/1/1918; first; Harold B. Secord (farmer, Jamaica Plains, MA) and Gertrude M. McNayr (Beverly, MA)

SEGALINI,

Andrew Shane, b. 12/23/1969 in Laconia; Recardo Louie Segalini (NH) and Gloria Jean Hunkins (NH)

Anthony John, b. 5/29/1981 in Concord; Recardo L. Segalini and Elizabeth A. Coulson

Mitchel James, b. 12/26/1995 in Laconia; Recardo L. Segalini, Jr. and Heidi Ann Smith

Recardo Louie, Jr., b. 7/13/1966 in Laconia; first; Recardo Louie Segalini (mechanic, NH) and Gloria Jean Hunkins (NH)

SELVEY,
Catherine, b. 8/18/1916; second; John J. Selvey (laborer, Boston, MA) and Edna H. Hill (Loudon)

SENIOR,
Joanne May, b. 6/9/1954; fifth; Walter Senior, Jr. (toolmaker, MA) and Eileen M. Lumsden (NY)
Ronald Smith, b. 6/9/1954; fourth; Walter Senior, Jr. (toolmaker, MA) and Eileen M. Lumsden (NY)

SEVEY,
Megan Elizabeth, b. 9/4/1986 in Laconia; Stewart L. Sevey and Cherylene L. Smith

SHANNON,
Maurice Cook, b. 8/27/1910; first; Winfield S. Shannon (clerk, Gilmanton) and Bertha L. Cook (Gilmanton)

SHATTUCK,
Amy Elizabeth, b. 3/30/1984 in Concord; Steven J. Shattuck and Jo-Ann B. McClary
Steven James, b. 3/31/1987 in Concord; Steven J. Shattuck and Jo-Ann B. McClary

SHAW,
Lillian Margaret, b. 7/11/1946 in Pittsfield; ninth; Francis A. Shaw (laborer, Franklin) and Marguerite Denish (Franklin)

SHEPARD,
Fred Everett, b. 10/18/1940; fourth; Wendell E. Shepard (laborer, Laconia) and Virginia H. Twombly (Exeter, NJ)
Noah Benjamin P., b. 7/19/1973 in Concord; Peter Ransome Shepard (CT) and Judi Anne Draper (CT)

SHERIDAN,
Melissa Mae, b. 3/24/1991 in Concord; Thomas J. Sheridan and Kathryn A. Waite

SHIELDS,
Patricia Mae, b. 8/18/1936 in Wolfeboro; first; Hartley J. Shields (clerk, Lewiston, ME) and Louise A. Gilman (Alton); residence - Gilmanton I. W.

SHLAITAS,
Alice Lucy, b. 6/23/1917; second; Konstant Shlaytis (sic) (farmer, Russia) and Marie Wayshein (Russia)
Annie Mary, b. 9/8/1922; Konstant Shlaitas and Mary A. Wayshnor
Wanda Aguilska, b. 1/28/1919; third; Koustail Shlaitas (farmer, Russia) and Mary Annie Wayshrier (Russia)

SHUMWAY,
Joshua William, b. 8/14/1999 in Laconia; Aaron Shumway and Shelli Shumway

SHUTE,
Kevin Ernest, b. 12/3/1977 in Laconia; Henry M. Shute, Jr. (NH) and Sharon B. Heath (NH)

SIDLAUSKAS,
Stephen Brian, b. 3/13/1948; third; John J. Sidlauskas (time study, Detroit, MI) and Wanda A. Shlaitas (Gilmanton)

SIDOR,
Anna L., b. 2/14/1975 in Concord; Reinhard Sidor (Germany) and Ellen Y. Sutherland (MA)

SIMMONS,
Earl Hanson, b. 12/30/1917; first; James Earl Simmons (laster, Gardiner, ME) and Ruth Altha Matthews (Northfield); residence - Gardiner, ME

SIMONDS,
Richard Eugene, Jr., b. 10/31/1960 in Wolfeboro; fourth; Richard Eugene Simonds (laborer, NH) and Olive May Wells (NH)

SIMPSON,
Patrice May, b. 10/7/1946 in Wolfeboro; first; Allan E. Simpson (shoemaker, New York, NY) and Patrice M. Gooch (Brockton MA)

Rebecca Louise Pearl, b. 3/1/1997 in Lebanon; Mark Wayne Simpson and Karen Lee Riel

SISTI,
Grace Louise, b. 1/8/1989 in Concord; Mark L. Sisti and Jane E. Mitchell
Salvatore John, b. 3/7/1990 in Concord; Mark L. Sisti and Jane E. Mitchell
Vincenzo Lyman, b. 9/8/1994 in Concord; Mark Leonard Sisti and Jane Elizabeth Mitchell

SKANTZE,
Donald Eric, b. 8/20/1958 in Laconia; first; Walter H. Skantze (student, NJ) and Florence A. Roberts (MA)
William Eversen, b. 6/13/1989 in Concord; Norman W. Skantze and Terri L. Nichols

SKRAJEWSKI,
Dominic Raymond, b. 2/24/1991 in Laconia; Dennis J. Skrajewski and Debra A. Fortin

SLOCUM,
Richard Paul, b. 5/10/1970 in Laconia; David Paul Slocum (PA) and Marilyn Myrna Morse (NH)

SMALL,
Margaret, b. 12/6/1903; second; James D. Small (carpenter, NB) and Nina E. Walker (NS)

SMITH,
child, b. 9/19/1897; first; Warren M. Smith (farmer, Gilmanton) and Ann M. Haines (Loudon)
daughter, b. 11/13/1898; second; Wilbur Smith (farmer)
son, b. 8/21/1915; second; Ida Smith (Lowell, MA)
Arica Lynn, b. 6/6/1989 in Laconia; William H. Smith and Jill E. Smith
Barbara Louise, b. 9/27/1921; first; Florence W. Smith (Wolfeboro); residence - Wolfeboro
Carl Thompson, b. 8/12/1891; first; George E. Smith (hotel keeper, Gilmanton) and Etta McAlpine

Carlton Osborne, b. 6/15/1910; first; Edwin W. Smith (farmer, Plymouth) and Gladys E. Plummer (Farmington)

Charles L., b. 2/2/1906; fourth; J. Wilbur Smith (R.D. carrier, Gilmanton) and Edith L. Hannaford (Manchester)

Edith Gertrude, b. 1/18/1933; third; Charles L. Smith (laborer, Gilmanton) and Hattie Stockbridge (Gilmanton)

Elaine G., b. 2/26/1954; sixth; George L. Smith (truck driver, NH) and Ellen M. Davis (NH)

Eugene L., b. 3/25/1955; seventh; George L. Smith (truck driver, NH) and Ellen M. Davis (NH)

Eva Gertrude, b. 12/21/1900; first; J. Wilbur Smith (farmer, Gilmanton) and Edith L. Hannaford (Manchester)

George Ernest, b. 10/16/1948; stillborn; third; George L. Smith (laborer, Gilmanton) and Ellen M. Davis (Gilmanton)

George Lyndell, b. 1/6/1927; first; Charles L. Smith (farmer, Gilmanton) and Hattie Stockbridge (Gilmanton)

Helen Louise, b. 6/16/1902; second; J. Wilbur Smith (farmer, Gilmanton) and Edith L. Hannaford (Manchester)

Louisa May, b. 10/29/1930; second; Charles L. Smith (laborer, Gilmanton) and Hattie M. Stockbridge (Gilmanton)

Malinda Lea, b. 1/25/1973 in Laconia; Nathan Ralph Smith (NH) and Martha Linda Hamel (NH)

Mary Lee, b. 1/3/1951; fourth; George L. Smith (truck driver, Gilmanton) and Ellen M. Davis (Gilmanton)

Michael Charles, b. 1/6/1950; fourth; George Lyndall Smith (woodsman, NH) and Ellen May Davis (NH)

Muriel Edith, b. 3/3/1904; third; J. Wilbur Smith (mail carrier, Gilmanton) and Edith L. Hannaford (Manchester)

Nancy Ann, b. 9/23/1952; fifth; George L. Smith (truck driver, NH) and Ellen M. Davis (NH)

Natalie Jean, b. 8/13/1971 in Laconia; Nathan Ralph Smith (NH) and Martha Linda Hamel (NH)

Raymond H., b. 4/6/1925; first; Arthur E. Smith (farmer, Lynn, MA) and Anna McCormack (St. Johns, NB)

Ruth Eleanor, b. 5/5/1935 in Wolfeboro; fourth; Charles L. Smith (laborer, Gilmanton) and Hattie Stockbridge (Gilmanton)

Ryan James, b. 3/28/1988 in Laconia; William H. Smith and Jill E. Smith

Sarah Mae, b. 3/13/1987 in Franklin; Edward F. Smith and Melody A. Tibbetts

Sheena Rae, b. 6/29/1990 in Concord; Stephen R. Smith and Debra A. Cushing

SMITHERS,
Nichole Rae, b. 6/21/1978 in Laconia; Thomas William Smithers, IV (MA) and Dodie June Brown (NH)
Tamsen Lyndsay, b. 7/23/1981 in Laconia; Timothy J. Smithers and Ronilee R. Smith
Terrance, b. 4/28/1958 in Laconia; third; Thomas W. Smithers (hoisting engineer, MA) and Elizabeth R. Belcastro (MA)
Thomas William, V, b. 10/9/1981 in Laconia; Thomas W. Smithers, IV and Dodie J. Brown
Tracy Jean, b. 7/8/1963 in Laconia; fourth; Thomas William Smithers (MA) and Elizabeth Rachel Belcastro (MA)

SNOW,
Jaclyn Elizabeth, b. 2/23/1991 in Laconia Steve R. Snow and Roya R. Reinholz
Thomas Jonathan, b. 5/26/1989 in Laconia; Steve R. Snow and Roya R. Reinholz
Zachary Thomas, b. 3/6/1994 in Laconia; Craig Thomas Snow and Deborah Marie Wonoski

SPAULDING,
Matthew P., b. 2/27/1980 in Laconia; Gerald J. Spaulding and Elena Glove

SPENCER,
Justin Abraham, b. 4/7/1977 in Laconia; Michael P. Spencer (NH) and Janice E. Wilder (MA)

STEELE,
May Louise, b. 8/2/1948; first; Robert E. Steele (laborer, Gilford) and Louise M. Smith (Gilmanton)

STEENSTRA,
Muriel Ann, b. 4/13/1952; third; Walter H. Steenstra (engineer, MA) and Ruth E. Miner (ME)

STEIN,
Matthew K., b. 2/2/1980 in Concord; Robert A. Stein and Babette E. Lipsitz

STENDOR,
Debra Joyce, b. 6/22/1958 in Laconia; fourth; Noel B. Stendor (state hwy. dept., MA) and Eva G. Gagnon (NH)

STETSON,
Gerald Ellsworth, b. 4/7/1921; second; Ralph E. Stetson (farmer, Groveland, MA) and Florence A. Gerald (Concord)
Glendon George, b. 2/15/1924; third; Ralph E. Steston (farmer, Groveland, MA) and Florence A. Gerald (Concord)

STEVENS,
Grace Ina, b. 4/6/1969 in Concord; Sherman Alfred Stevens (ME) and Mildred Arlene Ross (ME)
Hunter Richard, b. 4/29/1998 in Manchester; Richard Hudson Stevens, Jr. and Lorraine Mary Murray
Kathryn, b. 6/14/1983 in Laconia; Richard H. Stevens, Sr. and Eleanor J. Williams
Lori Lyn, b. 12/17/1973 in Concord; Sherman Alfred Stevens (ME) and Mildred Arlene Ross (ME)
Nathan Reed, b. 9/7/1971 in Concord; Sherman Alfred Stevens (ME) and Mildred Arlene Ross (ME)
Sherman Luke, b. 4/13/1970 in Concord; Sherman Alfred Stevens (ME) and Mildred Arlene Ross (ME)
Wayne Erroll, b. 12/3/1972 in Concord; Sherman A. Stevens (ME) and Mildred A. Ross (ME)

STOCKBRIDGE,
daughter, b. 9/12/1907; third; George S. Stockbridge (farmer, Gilmanton) and Inez M. Roby (Pittsfield)
son [Joseph S.], b. 9/12/1908; fourth; George S. Stockbridge (farmer, Gilmanton) and Ina M. Roby (Pittsfield)
Carl Louis, b. 7/25/1921; eighth; George S. Stockbridge (farmer, Gilmanton) and Ina M. Roby (Pittsfield)
Carla M., b. 10/7/1982 in Laconia; Michael J. Stockbridge and Crystal M. McLeod
Eugene Samuel, b. 4/3/1927; ninth; George S. Stockbridge (farmer, Gilmanton) and Irene M. Roby (Pittsfield)

Harry Eugene, b. 8/7/1911; sixth; George S. Stockbridge (farmer, Gilmanton) and Ina M. Roby (Pittsfield)
Izall Maud, b. 4/18/1910; fifth; George S. Stockbridge (farmer, Gilmanton) and Ina M. Roby (Pittsfield)
Lorna Leigh, b. 7/14/1914; seventh; George S. Stockbridge (farmer, Gilmanton) and Ina M. Roby (Pittsfield)
Matthew Richard, b. 12/23/1964 in Concord; eleventh; Carl Lewis Stockbridge (laborer, NH) and Ruby Pamela Head (MA)
Michael James, b. 12/5/1963 in Concord; tenth; Carl Lewis Stockbridge (laborer, NH) and Ruby Pamela Head (MA)
Steven Michael, b. 11/26/1984 in Laconia; Michael J. Stockbridge and Crystal M. McLeod

STOCKWELL,
Andrew Donald, b. 12/20/1970 in Concord; Clifford Harmon Stockwell (NH) and Frances Lorraine Hyslop (NH)
Ashley Rae, b. 12/10/1994 in Plymouth; Daniel Clifford Stockwell and Ginger Rae Willard
Benjamin Andrew, b. 6/19/1990 in Concord; Andrew D. Stockwell and Arlene T. Green
Caleb Clifford, b. 9/12/1991 in Concord; Andrew D. Stockwell and Arlene T. Green
Clifford Harmon, b. 10/1/1941; first; Leonard A. Stockwell (stock clerk, Chelmsford, MA) and Ruth A. Clifford (Gilmanton)
David Thomas, b. 10/24/1963 in Laconia; first; John H. Stockwell (engineer, NH) and Sanae Yamaji (Japan)
Douglas Everton, b. 5/24/1997 in Laconia; Daniel Clifford Stockwell and Ginger Rae Willard
Edith Joy, b. 12/12/1934 in Laconia; seventh; Harmon Stockwell (farmer, Charleston, ME) and Roxey E. Mitchell (NB)
Eli Oliver, b. 11/15/1993 in Concord; Andrew D. Stockwell and Arlene T. Green
Ena May, b. 4/3/1949; fourth; Leonard A. Stockwell (mechanic, MA) and Ruth Arlene Clifford (Gilmanton)
Jillian C., b. 6/28/1982 in Laconia; Daniel C. Stockwell and Katharine Colby
Leonard Alfred, Jr., b. 1/25/1961 in Laconia; fifth; Leonard A. Stockwell (mechanic, MA) and Ruth Arlene Clifford (NH)
Mary Elizabeth, b. 2/17/1947; third; Leonard A. Stockwell (mechanic, Chelmsford, MA) and Ruth A. Clifford (Gilmanton)

Nancy Jane, b. 1/7/1945 in Laconia; second; Leonard A. Stockwell (machinist, Chelmsford, MA) and Ruth A. Clifford (Gilmanton)
Ramona, b. 9/29/1967 in Laconia; third; John Harmon Stockwell (engineer, NH) and Sanae Yamaji (Japan)
Roxanne Rae, b. 9/21/1985 in Laconia; Daniel C. Stockwell and Ginger R. Willard

STOLTE,
Alexander David, b. 9/13/1990 in Hanover; William C. Stolte and Eileen N. Blaney

STONE,
son [Charles L.], b. 2/27/1907; fourth; Fred L. Stone (farmer, Franklin) and Mamie Hilliard (Weirs)
daughter, b. 5/21/1908; fifth; Fred L. Stone (farmer, Franklin) and Mary S. Hilliard (Laconia)
son [Edward G.], b. 4/1/1910; sixth; Fred L. Stone (farmer, Franklin) and Mamie Hilliard (Laconia)
son [Kenneth R.], b. 6/25/1912; first; Fred L. Stone (farmer, Franklin) and Bertha Avery (Winona)
son [Earl L.], b. 5/2/1914; ninth; Fred L. Stone (farmer, Franklin) and Mamie Hilliard (Weirs)
Anna Emily, b. 6/26/1992 in Concord; Andrew W. Stone and Amanda J. Lindley
Dorothy Ilene, b. 9/3/1912; eighth; Fred Stone (farmer, Franklin) and Mamie Hilliard (Weirs)
Elsie Ruth, b. 8/31/1911; seventh; Fred L. Stone (farmer, Franklin) and Mamie Hilliard (Weirs)
Jason Laurent, b. 4/29/1978 in Laconia; Gary Ernest Stone (NH) and Norma Jean Laurent (NH)
Jessica Susan, b. 3/27/1994 in Concord; Andrew William Stone and Amanda Jane Lindley
Villa Belle, b. 3/8/1917; tenth; Fred L. Stone (farmer, Franklin) and Mary S. Hilliard (Weirs)

STORY,
daughter, b. 10/16/1894; first; Fred S. Story (laborer, ME) and Celia A. Miller (NS)
son, b. 11/11/1895; second; Fred Smith Story (farmer, Vienna, ME) and Celia Ann Miller (Oxford, NS)

daughter, b. 2/3/1897; third; Fred S. Story (farmer, Vienna, ME) and
    Celia A. Miller (Oxford, NS)
child, b. 9/18/1898; third; Fred S. Story (laborer, Vienna, ME) and
    Celia A. Miller (Oxford, NS)

STRAIGHT,
Jesse Oliver, b. 1/7/1981 in Concord; Dennis H. Straight and Judy
    M. Chambers

STROMSOE,
Frederick A., b. 11/23/1913; first; Albert F. Stromsoe (laborer,
    Denver, CO) and Mary A. Munsey (Pittsfield); residence -
    Pittsfield

STRZEPEK,
Andrew Frank, b. 3/26/2000 in Concord; Gary Strzepek and Sandra
    Strzepek
Gary James, b. 7/28/1998 in Concord; Gary Strzepek and Sandra
    Strzepek

STURGEON,
Carey Nelson, b. 6/29/1974 in Concord; Richard N. Sturgeon (NH)
    and Pamela M. Simpson (IN)
Crystal Mae, b. 5/2/1976 in Laconia; Richard N. Sturgeon (NH) and
    Pamela M. Simpson (IN)

SWETT,
son [Fred H.], b. 6/14/1899; first; Herbert W. Swett (shoe cutter, E.
    Kingston) and Carrie B. Page (Laconia)
Nikole Synne, b. 11/9/2000 in Concord; Mark Swett and Sherry
    Swett
Stanley Fred, b. 9/20/1929; third; Fred Swett (farmer, Gilmanton)
    and Stella Patten (Bristol)
Virginia Ella, b. 1/16/1927; second; Fred H. Swett (laborer,
    Gilmanton) and Stella Patten (Bristol)

SWORMSTEDT,
Eric Scott, b. 3/7/1985 in Laconia; Scott C. Swormstedt and Cathy
    L. Holcomb

SYKES,
Heidi Lynn, b. 8/21/1997 in Concord; Robert Gordon Sykes, Jr. and Vicki Lynne Riel
Molly Autumn, b. 3/19/1994 in Concord; Robert Gordon Sykes, Jr. and Vicki Lynne Riel
Robert Samuel, b. 11/5/1995 in Concord; Robert G. Sykes and Vicki L. Riel

SYKIE,
David Wayne, Jr., b. 9/15/1995 in Laconia; David Wayne Sykie and Sally Ann Fournier

TARDIFF,
Lucille Florence, b. 9/2/1925; fifth; Joseph D. Tardiff (lumberman, Canada) and Carrie E. Grace (Tamworth)

TAYLOR,
Allie Mariah, b. 2/15/1995 in Concord; Brian M. Taylor and Susan Lois Walker
Josie Adrienne, b. 7/26/1997 in Concord; Brian Malcolm Taylor and Susan Lois Walker

TEDOUCUSK,
Eddie, b. 4/24/1916; Joseph Tedoucusk (laborer, Poland) and R. Dumcyk (Poland)

TENNEY,
Kassandra Lynn, b. 3/20/1991 in Concord; Mark A. Tenney and Tammy L. Johnson
Rebecca Jacqueline, b. 11/18/1993 in Concord; Mark A. Tenney and Tammy L. Johnson

TERRELL,
son, b. 1/31/1906; fourth; Fred W. Terrell (butcher, Nashua) and Annie B. Patten (Strafford)

TETREAULT,
Isabel Margaret, b. 12/8/1993 in Laconia; William D. Tetreault and Mary M. Fitch

TEUNESSEN,
James Francis, b. 9/23/2001 in Lebanon; Michael Teunessen and Kelley Teunessen

THIBODEAU,
Breanna Morgan, b. 5/26/1998 in Concord; Todd Jeffrey Thibodeau and Jane Marie Cotto
Tyler James, b. 8/2/1999 in Concord; Todd Thibodeau and Jane Thibodeau

THOMPSON,
Alex Martin, b. 5/8/1986 in Laconia; Dayne F. Thompson and Mary B. Hansen
Antoinette, b. 5/21/1926; second; Maro B. Thompson (clerk, N. Wilmington, MA) and Cordelia Carpenter (Fall River, MA)
Avery Hansen, b. 3/23/1984 in Laconia; Dayne F. Thompson and Mary B. Hansen
Cynthia Jean, b. 2/15/1960 in Concord; sixth; Edward Carpenter Thompson (carpenter, MA) and Angela Dolores Delafano (MA)
Deborah Ann, b. 3/18/1953; third; Edward C. Thompson (lumberman, Fall River, MA) and Angela D. Delafano (Revere, MA)
Doreen Diane, b. 3/16/1950; first; Edward Carpenter Thompson (lumber jack, MA) and Angela Dolores Delafano (MA)
Elaine Marie, b. 12/27/1951; second; Edward C. Thompson (lumberjack, MA) and Angela D. Delafano (MA)
Elizabeth Helen, b. 6/17/1943; fifth; Harry F. Thompson (state forestry, Ashburnham, MA) and Beulah E. Horne (Alton)
Geneva Maxine, b. 7/20/1941; fourth; Henry S. Thompson (carigrapher, Ashburnham, MA) and Beulah E. Horne (Alton)
Gordon Spencer, b. 5/16/1945 in Pittsfield; sixth; Henry S. Thompson (state forestry, Ashburnham, MA) and Beulah E. Horne (Alton)
Janet L., b. 5/22/1956 in Concord; fifth; Edward C. Thompson (carpenter, Fall River, MA) and Angela D. Delafano (Revere, MA)
Joyce Susan, b. 6/12/1961 in Concord; seventh; Edward Carpenter Thompson (carpenter, MA) and Angela Delores Delafano
Linda Eileen, b. 3/18/1965 in Concord; eighth; Edward Carpenter Thompson (carpenter, MA) and Angela Delores Delafano (MA)

Marie C., b. 9/10/1975 in Laconia; Clement A. Thompson (NH) and
 Claire S. Desmarais (NH)
Warren Whitehill, b. 6/27/1996 in Concord; Dayne Frederick
 Thompson and Renee Kathryn Pickard

THOROUGHGOOD,
Graig Dennis, b. 3/20/1978 in Concord; Richard J. Thoroughgood
 (NH) and Diana Lynn Purtell (NH)
Todd M., b. 3/18/1980 in Concord; Richard J. Thoroughgood and
 Diana L. Purtell

THURBER-WELLS,
Maizie Inez, b. 3/28/2001 in Concord; John Wells and Karen
 Thurber

TIBBETTS,
Elaine Roberta, b. 5/13/1971 in Laconia; Robert Carson Tibbetts
 (MA) and Bernadette Claire LaTulippe (MA)
Robert Francis, b. 2/12/1924; first; Henry Tibbetts (farmer, Alton)
 and Doris Rollins (Gilmanton); residence - Alton
Robert Oliver, b. 6/23/1947; first; Robert F. Tibbetts (truck driver,
 Gilmanton) and Olive B. Partridge (Gilmanton)

TILTON,
John Walter, b. 12/3/1911; fifth; Amos A. Tilton (teamster,
 Gilmanton) and Maude F. Bubier (Boston, MA)

TONG,
daughter, b. 11/17/1940; fifth; Frank Tong (painter, Northfield) and
 Eileen G. Sullivan (Boston, MA)

TOWLE,
Michael Andrew, b. 11/17/1950; fourteenth; Robert Levi Towle
 (farmer, NH) and Mary Grace French (NH)

TRASK,
Michael Thomas Elias, b. 8/22/1983 in Laconia; Michael Thomas
 Trask and Dorothy E. Dutton

TREMBLAY,
Brian Henry, b. 3/12/2001 in Concord; Brian Tremblay and Diane Tremblay

TRINIDADE,
Olivia Rose, b. 1/11/2000 in Concord; Neil Trinidade and Karen Trinidade
Owen Daniel, b. 3/5/1997 in Laconia; Neil Roger Trinidade and Karen Anne Audette

TUCKER,
Ashlie Morgan, b. 6/19/1996 in Laconia; Gary Richard Tucker and Janet Lee Hodgdon
Kasie Lee, b. 1/6/1994 in Laconia; Gary Richard Tucker and Janet Lee Hodgdon

TURGEON,
Natalie Elizabeth, b. 10/1/1987 in Concord; Henry A. Turgeon, Jr. and Judith Lynne Ford

TURNER,
Joel J., b. 8/26/1977 in Laconia; Jere James Turner (NJ) and Joyce A. Halter (NJ)
Tyler Whittier, b. 11/6/1973 in Wolfeboro; Norman Whittier Turner, Jr. (MA) and Alexis Ann Corric (OH)

TWOMBLY,
son, b. 7/26/1888; second; Frank M. Twombly (farmer, Gilmanton) and Florence A. Sanborn (Gilmanton)
son, b. 12/3/1890; third; Frank M. Twombly (druggist and farmer, Gilmanton) and Florence A. Sanborn (Gilmanton)
son [Everett T.], b. 8/17/1908; eighth; Dixia C. Twombly (carpenter, Meredith) and Emma M. Batchelder (Meredith)
daughter, b. 8/17/1908; ninth; Dixia C. Twombly (carpenter, Meredith) and Emma M. Batchelder (Meredith)
Cathy Ann, b. 11/26/1958 in Laconia; first; Charles A. Twombly (truck driver, NH) and Edith G. Smith (NH)
Charles A., b. 1/1/1928; third; Benjamin K. Twombly (carpenter, Gilmanton) and Margaret E. O'Brian (Chatham)
Charles Alvin, Jr., b. 10/14/1961 in Laconia; second; Charles Alvin Trombly (sic), Sr. (laborer, NH) and Edith Gertrude Smith (NH)

Clarence Everett, b. 7/28/1916; first; C. Herbert Twombly (farmer, Belmont) and Hazel Pease (Gilmanton)
James Richard, b. 10/29/1941; seventh; Benjamin K. Twombly (carpenter, Belmont) and Margaret E. O'Brien (Stratham)
Jean, b. 10/16/1925; fourth; Clarence Twombly (carpenter, Belmont) and Hazel A. Pease (Salem, MA)
Pauline E., b. 8/4/1937; sixth; Benjamin K. Twombly (laborer, Belmont) and Margaret O'Brien (Stratham)
Phyllis A., b. 1/12/1931; fifth; Benjamin K. Twombly (laborer, Belmont) and Margaret E. O'Brien (Stratham)
Rosatis Faye, b. 9/9/1934 in Wolfeboro; first; Everett T. Twombly (laborer, Gilmanton) and Ina Emerson (Pittsfield)
Sandra Lee, b. 6/15/1942; first; Fred W. Twombly (carpenter, Hampton) and Gertrude A. Rollins (Gilmanton)
Walter Edward, b. 3/26/1929 in Pittsfield; fourth; Benjamin K. Twombly (farmer, Gilmanton) and Margaret O'Brien (Stratham)

URQUHART,
Heather Anne, b. 12/5/1984 in Concord; Glen A. Urquhart and Laurie A. Smith

VACHON,
Kathleen Ruth, b. 8/9/1952; first; Francis L. Vachon (shipping clerk, NH) and Gloria M. Clark (NH)

VALAS,
Kristopher Mark, b. 1/12/1994 in Lebanon; Mark Randall Valas and Christine Marie Miller

VALLEE,
Molly Rose, b. 5/22/2000 in Concord; Norman Vallee and Cherie Vallee

VARNEY,
daughter, b. 11/8/1887; fourth; Edwin Varney (farmer, Gilmanton) and Julia F. Butt (Wareham, MA)

VOLPE,
Carrie J., b. 8/26/1980 in Concord; Dennis Volpe and Jane M. Elkins

Victoria Margaret, b. 7/27/1978 in Concord; Dennis Richard Volpe (NH) and Jane Margaret Elkins (NH)

WADE,
daughter, b. 3/12/1905; second; Edward D. Wade (laborer, Center Harbor) and Clara Desmarais (Brocton Falls)
Ernest Henry, b. 9/6/1909; sixth; Edward D. Wade (farmer, Sandwich) and Clara Desmarias (Paris, France)

WAITE,
Andrew Seth, b. 8/7/1994 in Laconia; Nicholas Seth Waite and Chrissy-Ann Sweezey
Benjamin Garrett, b. 6/29/1996 in Laconia; Nicholas Seth Waite and Chrissy-Ann Sweezey
Hannah Gabriell Rose, b. 8/14/2001 in Laconia; Nicholas Waite and Chrissy-Ann Waite
Matthew James, b. 5/27/1998 in Laconia; Nicholas Seth Waite and Chrissy-Ann Sweezey

WALLACE,
Isaac Robert, b. 5/3/2001 in Concord; Keith Wallace and Jessica Wallace
Leora Kathryn, b. 12/9/1981 in Concord; Gary S. Wallace and Murdeel K. Odman

WALTERS,
Jeannette Marie, b. 1/14/1932; first; John E. Walters (laborer, Concord) and Irene V. Marin (Franklin)

WALTON,
Dianna Rowena, b. 6/19/2000 in Laconia; Jonathan Walton and Karen Walton
Ian Kenneth, b. 2/10/1998 in Laconia; Jonathan Henry Walton and Karen Dianne Schricker
Jonathan Henry, b. 12/3/1958 in Laconia; second; Kenneth Ingraham Walton (oil burner ser., CT) and Gainor Romona Small (CT)

WANG,
Brendan Mark, b. 7/20/1990 in Hanover; Guojiang Wang and Margaret M. Considine

WARBURTON,
Gail Margaret, b. 10/7/1960 in Concord; third; John Frederick
   Warburton (farmer, NH) and Muriel Ruth Emerson (NH)
John Frederick, b. 1/27/1926; second; John H. Warburton (farmer,
   Liverpool, England) and Clara Elkins (Gilmanton)
Leanne, b. 8/28/1968 in Concord; John Frederick Warburton (NH)
   and Muriel Ruth Emerson (NH)
Margaret Ham, b. 9/2/1923; John H. Warburton and Clara H. Elkins
Sheri Lynne, b. 6/10/1957 in Laconia; first; John F. Warburton
   (farmer, NH) and Muriel R. Emerson (NH)
Valarie Jean, b. 3/24/1959 in Laconia; second; John Frederick
   Warburton (farmer, NH) and Muriel Ruth Emerson (NH)

WARING,
Ryan Andrew, b. 3/5/2000 in Concord; Glen Waring and Jody
   Waring

WATERMAN,
Timothy William, b. 7/3/1985 in Laconia; William R. Waterman and
   Maryann Price

WATERS,
Joseph Mark, b. 8/25/1972 in Laconia; Warren J. Waters (NE) and
   Beatrice M. Paplow (MA)

WATKINS,
Nicholas Peter, b. 12/30/1986 in Concord; Richard A. Watkins and
   Suzan M. Biocca

WATSON,
son, b. 11/30/1887; third; Selvin Watson (farmer, Gilmanton) and
   Ada S. Watson (Gilmanton)
Ernest Arthur, Jr., b. 3/26/1946 in Concord; third; Ernest A. Watson
   (lumber operator, Northwood) and Alice W. French (Plant City,
   FL)
Eunice Annette, b. 11/6/1948; fourth; Ernest A. Watson (lumber
   dealer, Northwood) and Alice W. French (Plant City, FL)
Everett Alexander, b. 10/27/1951; fifth; Ernest A. Watson
   (executive box I. co., NH) and Alice W. French (FL)

WEAR[E],
Kenneth, b. 9/20/1908; tenth; Frank Wear (farmer, Ingersoll, ON) and Mary C. Frimily (Windsor, ON)
Virginia E., b. 10/10/1912; eleventh; Frank Weare (farmer, Ontario)

WEATHERBEE,
Amber Anne, b. 6/25/1992 in Concord; Philip Weatherbee and Sandra A. Simpson

WEBER,
Kyia Ashlee, b. 9/13/1990 in Laconia; Henry A. Weber and Traci E. Drew

WEBSTER,
son, b. 1/25/1888; first; Benjamin F. Webster (farmer, Gilmanton) and Elizabeth Smith
Eleanor E., b. 10/15/1931; second; William C. Webster (farmer, Gilmanton) and Marjorie E. Pitman (Alexandria)
Elizabeth Ann, b. 10/15/1959 in Laconia; third; Roger Byron Webster (merchant, NH) and Patricia Ann Hickel (NJ)
Mark Byron, b. 9/29/1960 in Laconia; fourth; Roger Byron Webster (store owner, NH) and Patricia Ann Hikel (NJ)
Pamela J., b. 3/7/1956 in Laconia; first; Roger B. Webster (merchant, NH) and Patricia A. Hikel (NJ)
Peter Anthony, b. 6/18/1962 in Concord; fifth; Roger Byron Webster (merchant, NH) and Patricia Ann Hikel (NJ)
Susan Marie, b. 2/17/1957 in Laconia; second; Roger B. Webster (merchant, NH) and Patricia A. Hikel (NJ)
William Howard, b. 1/10/1919; second; Otis L. Webster (teamster) and Pearl M. Whittemore (Goffstown)

WEEKS,
son, b. 5/9/1902; third; James Weeks (lumber dealer, Gilmanton) and Nellie Pease (Loudon)
son, b. 6/14/1902; second; Ivo F. Weeks (farmer, Gilmanton) and Addie Flanders
son, b. 4/19/1906; third; Herbert N. Weeks (farmer, Gilmanton) and Lilla A. M. Durgin (Gilmanton)
Caroline Eugeni, b. 10/17/1950; first; Carroll Richard Weeks (painter, NH) and Genevieve Louise Sullivan (CT)

Christopher Marin, b. 12/10/1993 in Rochester; Francis M. Weeks
and Candace S. Sargent
Dorothy Laurinda, b. 3/10/1911; fifth; Stephen L. Weeks (farmer,
Gilmanton) and Bertha Batchelder (Loudon)
Ernest Elwin Mark, b. 6/7/1910; third; Ivo F. Weeks (farmer,
Belmont) and Addie A. Flanders (Gilmanton)
John Fremont, b. 6/24/1903; third; Stephen L. Weeks (farmer,
Gilmanton) and Bertha E. Batchelder (Loudon)
Maitland B., b. 1/15/1898; first; Stephen Weeks (farmer, Gilmanton)
and Bertha Batchelder (Loudon)
Margery Lois, b. 2/12/1901; second; Stephen L. Weeks (farmer,
Gilmanton) and Bertha E. Batchelder (Loudon)
Stephen Norman, b. 9/14/1905; fourth; Stephen L. Weeks (farmer,
Gilmanton) and Bertha Batchelder (Loudon)
William Silsby, b. 11/15/1900; first; Lorrain E. Weeks (farmer,
Gilmanton) and Charlotte E. Mace (Lynn, MA)

WEEMAN,
Joel David, b. 8/29/1978 in Concord; Peter Anthony Weeman (ME)
and Paula Ann Golden (NH)
Matthew Paul, b. 1/28/1981 in Concord; Peter A. Weeman and
Paula A. Golden

WEISBERG,
Trevor M., b. 12/29/1986 in Laconia; Michael Weisberg and Janice
A. Graustein

WELCH,
Jette Danielle, b. 4/14/1990 in Concord; Donald D. Welch, II and
Sharon K. Freese
Lexie Mariah, b. 10/29/1991 in Concord; Donald D. Welch, II and
Sharon K. Freese
Moira Elizabeth, b. 8/29/1983 in Concord; Kenneth J. Welch and
Elizabeth A. Ferguson
Sierra Gabrielle, b. 5/9/1996 in Concord; Donald David Welch, II
and Sharon Kay Freese

WELLS,
son [E. Russell], b. 7/21/1903; first; Ernest L. Wells (laborer) and
Laura G. Jones (Gilmanton)

son [Fred R.], b. 3/4/1905; second; Ernest L. Wells (laborer, Alton) and Laura G. Jones (Gilmanton)

son, b. 2/12/1906; third; Ernest L. Wells (teamster, Alton) and Laura G. Jones (Gilmanton)

stillborn son, b. 2/3/1932; fourth; E. Russell Wells (farmer, Gilmanton) and Laura Hanson (Malden, MA)

Arnold Leslie, b. 9/30/1937; sixth; E. Russell Wells (laborer, Gilmanton) and Laura Hanson (Malden, MA)

Barbara K., b. 4/18/1930 in Strafford; third; E. Russell Wells (farmer, Gilmanton) and Laura Hanson (Malden, MA)

Beulah Rosina, b. 5/12/1909; fifth; Ernest L. Wells (teamster, Alton) and Laura G. Jones (Gilmanton)

Daniel James, b. 9/15/1913; eighth; Ernest Wells (teamster, Alton) and Laura Jones (Gilmanton)

Ernest Russell, Jr., b. 4/17/1929; second; E. Russell Wells (farmer, Gilmanton) and Laura Hanson (Malden, MA)

Fred Harry, b. 7/30/1941; third; Fred R. Wells (farmer, Gilmanton) and Dorothy B. Lucia (MA)

Gertrude Laura, b. 8/6/1947; fourth; Fred R. Wells (farmer, Gilmanton) and Dorothea B. Lucia (Bellingham, MA)

Maurice H., b. 12/21/1933; fifth; Ernest R. Wells (farmer, Gilmanton) and Laura Hanson (Malden, MA)

Mina Violet, b. 11/25/1911; seventh; Ernest L. Wells (teamster, Alton) and Laura G. Jones (Gilmanton)

Olive May, b. 3/18/1939 in Wolfeboro; second; Fred R. Wells (farmer, Gilmanton) and Dorothea B. Lucia (Bellingham, MA); residence - Gilmanton I. W.

Rena Evelyn, b. 5/15/1910; sixth; Ernest L. Wells (teamster, Alton) and Laura G. Jones (Gilmanton)

Sybil Katherine, b. 2/11/1920; ninth; Ernest L. Wells (farmer, Alton) and Laura Jones (Gilmanton)

WENDELL,
Joshua Spencer, b. 7/31/1988 in Laconia; Warren K. Wendell and Kristen H. Head

WENTWORTH,
Barbara Jean, b. 3/2/1938 in Rochester; first; Lawrence Wentworth (shoe worker, Middleton) and Marguerite Carty (New York, NY); residence - Gilmanton I. W.

WEST,
Camrin Alexander, b. 5/25/2001 in Laconia; Corey West and Karen West
Lori Ruth, b. 3/21/1989 in Concord; George M. West and Nancy L. Knee

WHELAN,
John Joseph, IV, b. 12/15/1968 in Laconia; John Joseph Whelan, III (MA) and Bonnie Kendra Hartford (NH)

WHITCHER,
daughter, b. 2/7/1892; second; Edwin W. Whitcher (farmer, Dorchester) and Cora Richardson (Manchester)

WHITEHOUSE,
Jason David, b. 6/7/1984 in Laconia; David L. Whitehouse and Laurie A. Greenleaf
Justin Richard, b. 6/7/1984 in Laconia; David L. Whitehouse and Laurie A. Greenleaf

WHITING,
daughter, b. 12/31/1896; third; Henry B. Whiting (laborer, S. Tamworth) and Minnie E. Marston (Salisbury)

WIGGINS,
Laura Rose, b. 4/19/1983 in Laconia; Stephen A. Wiggins and Linda D. Romig
Robert Raymond, Jr., b. 11/11/1974 in Laconia; Robert R. Wiggins (NH) and Linda A. Doring (NY)

WIGHT,
son, b. 7/25/1903; second; Nahum Wight (butter-maker, Gilmanton) and Florence E. Leland (Ryegate, VT)
Marion Marguerite, b. 12/4/1904; third; Nahum Wight (button maker, Gilmanton) and Florence E. Leland (Ryegate, VT)
Nahum, Jr., b. 12/30/1901; first; Nahum Wight (butter maker, Gilmanton) and Florence Ethel Leland (Ryegate, VT)

WILKENS,
David M. J., b. 4/21/1989 in Laconia; John R. P. Wilkens and Deborah L. Vaughn

Johanna Beth, b. 3/25/1971 in Concord; John Robert-Paul Wilkens (NH) and Janis Elizabeth Beth (IL)
John Robert Paul, b. 6/6/1949; fourth; William B. Wilkens (electrical eng., NY) and Laurose Schulze-Berge (NY)
Megan Elizabeth, b. 9/17/1993 in Manchester; John R. P. Wilkens and Claire M. Pinard
Summer Laurie, b. 5/19/1987 in Laconia; John R. P. Wilkens and Deborah L. Vaughn

WILKINS,
Ernest P., b. 11/5/1902; third; John H. Wilkins (clergyman, Stockport, England) and Laura McLean (St. George, NB)

WILLARD,
child, b. 7/21/1894; Daniel Willard (farmer, Belmont) and Amorette Thompson (Belmont)
Alberta Sadie, b. 5/20/1917; first; Raymond C. Willard (farmer, Alton) and Hazel B. Batchelder (Gilmanton)
Angela M., b. 6/14/1980 in Laconia; Edward L. Willard and Priscilla J. Daigneau
Arthur Everton, Jr., b. 8/18/1937 in Laconia; first; Arthur E. Willard (saw-mill, Belmont) and Mary C. Heinis (Cambridge, MA)
Beatrice Estella, b. 8/3/1911; second; Israel R. Willard (laborer, Gilmanton) and Georgie F. McClary (Gilmanton)
Bernice, b. 9/23/1913; third; Israel Williard (sic) (laborer, Gilmanton) and Georgia McClary (Gilmanton)
Beulah Ethelyn, b. 8/7/1909; first; Israel R. Willard (laborer, Gilmanton) and Georgie F. McClary (Gilmanton)
Dian Florence, b. 10/6/1942; third; Arthur E. Willard (roller in, Belmont) and Mary C. Heinis (Cambridge, MA)
Edward Louis, b. 8/12/1950; sixth; Arthur Everton Willard (sawyer, NH) and Mary Christine Heinis (MA)
Israel Raymond, b. 2/11/1889; fourth; Daniel Willard (farmer, Belmont) and Amoretta Thompson Willard (Belmont)
Israel Raymond, b. 12/12/1944 in Pittsfield; fourth; Arthur E. Willard (saw mill, Belmont) and Mary C. Heinis (Cambridge, MA)
Israel Raymond, Jr., b. 10/17/1969 in Laconia; Israel Raymond Willard (NH) and Candace Rae Franzen (NH)
Linda Ilene, b. 9/28/1948; fifth; Arthur E. Willard (roller, saw mill, Belmont) and Mary C. Heinis (Cambridge, MA)

Linda Lee, b. 8/4/1965 in Laconia; third; John Richard Willard
(plantman, NH) and Mary Rose Brown (MA)
Marilyn Elizabeth, b. 2/26/1963 in Laconia; second; John Richard
Willard (attendant, NH) and Mary Rose Brown (MA)
Ruth Marion, b. 9/28/1922; Israel R. Willard and Georgia A.
McClary
Shawn Edward, b. 2/3/1971 in Laconia; Edward Louis Willard (NH)
and Rose Mary Hamel (NH)
Tina Rose, b. 10/28/1967 in Laconia; fourth; John Richard Willard
(NH H'way Dept., NH) and Mary Rose Brown (MA)

WILLIAMS,
son, b. 6/11/1887; first; Henry Williams (Bellows Falls, VT) and
Nellie M. Burbank (Hopkinton); residence - Gilford
Kristina Carroll, b. 7/11/1986 in N. Conway; Kenneth C. Williams
and Lynn E. Shattuck

WILSON,
son, b. 1/27/1908; first; Charles E. Wilson (farmer, Boston, MA) and
Alexandra Hagstrom (Gottenberg, Sweden)
Anton O., b. 10/29/1980 in Concord; David G. Wilson and Rachel
M. Goulet
Charles Axell, b. 10/23/1909; second; Charles E. Wilson (farmer, E.
Boston, MA) and Alexandra Hagstrom (Gottenberg, Sweden)
Emily Myra, b. 12/29/1987 in Laconia; Woodrow S. Wilson and
Judith T. Prindle
Florence May, b. 9/20/1911; third; Charles E. Wilson (carpenter, E.
Boston, MA) and Sandra Hagstrom (Gottenburg, Sweden)
Kathryn Louise, b. 7/12/1984 in Laconia; Woodrow S. Wilson and
Judith T. Prindle
Tanner Jacob, b. 5/23/1991 in Manchester; Scott L. Wilson and
Sandra J. Williams

WING,
Douglas Stephen, b. 1/16/1964 in Laconia; second; Ormond Leo
Wing (mechanic, ME) and Honora Marie MacLellan (MA)
Karen Leigh, b. 12/20/1964 in Laconia; second; Ormond Leo Wing
(mechanic, ME) and Honora Marie MacLellan (MA)
Kimberly Jo, b. 12/20/1964 in Laconia; third; Ormond Leo Wing
(mechanic, ME) and Honora Marie MacLellan (MA)

WITHAM,
Alden Wilfred, Jr., b. 5/6/1951; sixth; Alden W. Witham (carpenter, ME) and Dorothy I. Thomas (MA)
Allen J., b. 9/27/1975 in Concord; Allen G. Witham (MA) and Maureen E. Dame (NH)
Alma Helen, b. 4/16/1944 in Concord; fifth; George W. Witham (farmer, Cabot, VT) and Helen M. Gilman (Gilmanton)
Cindy Lou, b. 12/4/1958 in Laconia; eighth; Alden Wilfred Witham (carpenter, ME) and Dorothy Irene Thomas (MA)
Diane Bess, b. 11/30/1971 in Concord; Allen George Witham (MA) and Maureen Eleanor Dame (NH)
Hope Amelia, b. 6/8/1977 in Wolfeboro; Kenneth T. Witham (MA) and Elizabeth H. Glum (NY)
Jacqueline E., b. 2/14/1980 in Wolfeboro; Kenneth T. Witham and Elizabeth H. Glum
Jason J., b. 9/6/1975 in Concord; John A. Witham (NH) and Mary L. Geddes (NH)
Jennifer Marie, b. 6/2/1974 in Concord; John A. Witham (NH) and Mary L. Geddes (NH)
Jo Ann, b. 6/20/1954; seventh; Alden W. Witham (carpenter, ME) and Dorothy I. Thomas (MA)
Michele Lee, b. 7/16/1970 in Concord; Allen George Witham (MA) and Maureen Eleanor Dame (NH)
Peter Timothy, b. 7/14/1964 in Laconia; ninth; Alden Wilfred Witham (foreman - constr., ME) and Dorothy Irene Thomas (MA)

WITHINGTON,
Andrea Jessie, b. 2/23/1998 in Concord; Timothy Mark Withington and Tina Marie Lebel
Elizabeth Theres, b. 4/12/1999 in Concord; Timothy Withington and Tina Withington

WOOD,
Olivia Ann, b. 7/3/1987 in Winchester, MA; James L. Wood and Cynthia M. Chambers

WOODBURY,
David A., b. 3/20/1893; third; David A. Woodbury (blacksmith, Bangore, NY) and Etta Frances Emery (Manchester)

WOODWARD,
Evelyn, b. 11/2/1908; fourth; Frank B. Woodward (merchant, Parsonsfield, ME) and Ethel R. Clay (Hiram, ME)

YEATON,
daughter, b. 11/6/1947; second; Perley G. Yeaton (farmer, Northwood) and Grace J. Magoon (E. Corinth, VT)
Bruce Wendell, b. 7/25/1941; second; Bernard J. Yeaton (laborer, Raymond) and Esther M. Sanborn (Loudon)

YORK,
daughter, b. 11/22/1896; eighth; Fred Albert York (farming, Gilmanton) and Anna Frances Jones (Pittsfield)
Clarence Ray, b. 6/6/1919; second; Raymond York (fireman, Belmont) and Caroline E. Jones (Gilmanton)

YOUNG,
Brittany Mae, b. 1/16/1992 in Concord; Brooks E. Young and Jayne M. Stanley
Bruce Anthony, b. 8/14/1966 in Laconia; sixth; Howard Young, Jr. (heavy equip., NH) and Elnora Fay Lane (NH)
Caroline M., b. 10/9/1892; first; Joseph S. Young (farmer, Portland, ME) and Elizabeth A. Morrill (Gilmanton)
Porter William, b. 11/22/1989 in Concord; Brooks E. Young and Jayne M. Stanley

ZANES,
Clarice J., b. 5/6/1912; first; William B. Zanes (machinist, Gilmanton) and Martha A. Munsey (Gilmanton); residence - Laconia
June Karen, b. 2/17/1960 in Laconia; first; James Edgerly Zanes (expeditor, NH) and Johanna Adriana diBruin (Indonesia)

ZAVOROTNY,
Nicholas Peter, b. 11/19/1996 in Concord; Alan Dana Zavorotny, II and Sharon Marie Gray

ZELA,
Nathaniel Miles, b. 7/1/1991 in Laconia; Peter M. Zela and Barbara J. West

ZNACS,
John Florian, b. 5/4/1917; third; Joseph Znacs (wheelwright, Vienna, Austria) and Pauline Znacs (Vienna, Austria)

MARRIAGES

ADAMS,
Brice R. of Bloomington, IN m. Susan R. **McIntyre** of Gilmanton 8/23/1986
Edward Cass of Durham m. Mina Catherine **Edgerly** of Gilmanton 1/1/1918; H - 24, farmer, b. Durham, s/o Edward H. Adams (Epping) and Fannie Harvey (Epping); W - 24, at home, b. Wesson, MS, d/o Albert T. Edgerly (Sanbornton) and Catherine Elmina Keyes (Sycamore, IL)

ADAMSON,
Patrick E. of Laconia m. Wendi L. **Gray** of Gilmanton 10/24/1987

ADEL,
Jack I. of Gilmanton m. Dorieann **Dockham** of Gilmanton 10/14/1983
Jack Israel of Gilmanton m. Mary Elizabeth **Stockwell** of Gilmanton 5/28/1966; H - 22, machinist, b. NH, s/o Daniel J. Adel (Germany) and Beatrice W. Willard (NH); W - 19, secretary, b. NH, d/o Leonard Alfred Stockwell (MA) and Ruth Arlene Clifford (NH)

AINSWORTH,
Jason W. of Worcester, MA m. Etta C. **Smith** of Gilmanton 12/31/1899; H - 59, retired, 2nd, b. Randolph, VT, s/o Laban Ainsworth (Randolph, VT) and Martha F. Keith (Randolph, VT); W - 37, housewife, 2nd, b. Warner, d/o Christopher McAlpine (Warner) and Anna H. Osgood (Warner)

ALBERT,
Robert A. of Gilmanton m. Cheryl L. **Thompson** of Gilmanton 10/9/1976 in Laconia; H - b. 1/6/1946 in NH, s/o Walter Albert (NH) and Cecile Simoneau (NH); W - b. 2/3/1955 in MA, d/o Edward Thompson (MA) and Ann Delafano (MA)

ALDRICH,
David Hartford of Gilmanton m. Tammy Alberta **Austin** of Gilmanton 8/7/1988
Robert Bruce of Penacook m. Denise **Hartford** of Gilmanton 8/18/1962; H - 30, auto mech., b. NY, s/o Ralph E. Aldrich

(VT) and Pearl Marquis (NH); W - 24, recep., b. MA, s/o
Arlington E. Hartford (NH) and Olive Young (NS)

ALLEN,
David W. of Gilmanton m. Carol M. **Bowes** of E. Sandwich, MA
10/10/1987

ALLEY,
Robert M. of Gilmanton m. Judith L. **Seifert** of Gilmanton 7/28/1979

ALTON,
Guy William of Gilmanton m. Shawn Lee **Shalek** of Gilmanton
5/6/2000

AMADON,
Roger William of Concord m. Eliza Jane **Daigneau** of Gilmanton
12/1/1973 in Concord; H - b. 1/7/1949 in NH, s/o William
Amadon (NH) and Cecilia Grenier (MA); W - b. 6/8/1953 in
NH, d/o Arthur Daigneau (CT) and Daura Cass (VT)

AMARAL,
Michael G. of Gilmanton m. Teresa **Ferrara** of Gilmanton
12/14/1985

AMBELAS,
Gary George of Gilmanton m. Denise Elaine **Georgopoulos** of
Basking Ridge, NJ 10/16/1999

AMELL,
Darrel L. of Thompsonville, CT m. Lois E. **Sansouci** of Gilmanton
6/12/1954 in Alton; H - 22, Navy, b. VT, s/o Joseph Amell (NY)
and Eliza LaFlower (MA); W - 17, at home, b. NJ, d/o Henry
M. Sansouci (NH) and Christine M. Vincent (NJ)

AMES,
Michael E. of Concord m. Renee **Jacques** of Gilmanton 9/1/1990

AMIRAULT,
Frank, Jr. of Gilmanton m. Patricia A. **Inman** of Gilmanton 9/25/1980

ANAIR,
Lloyd Robert of Gilmanton m. Hazel Maud **Tilley** of Laconia 4/28/1951 in Laconia; H - 19, Navy, b. VT, s/o Leonard A. Anair (VT) and Gracie M. Astbury (Canada); W - 17, clerk, b. England, d/o Samuel J. Tilley (England) and Florence M. Harwood (England)

ANDERSEN,
Arvid, Jr. of Lynn, MA m. Elizabeth **Manley** of Arlington, MA 10/3/1958 in Gilmanton I. W.; H - 42, machinist, b. MA, s/o Arvid E. Anderson (Sweden) and Emma K. Bengston (Sweden); W - 21, key punch operator, b. NH, d/o Leroy A. Manley (MA) and Dorothy E. Huckins (NH)

ANDREWS,
Albert L. of Keene m. Edna Lois **Key** of Gilmanton 11/14/1941 in Keene; H - 22, chauffeur, b. Montgomery, AL, s/o Joseph E. Andrews (Providence, RI, painter) and Mary E. Rainy (Columbus, GA, housewife); W - 22, at home, b. Columbus, GA, d/o Cecil D. Key (Troy, AL, carpenter) and Ella M. Smith (Pratville, AL, housewife)

ANNETTI,
Anthony Domenick of Stoneham, MA m. Claire Lucille **Boulanger** of Gilmanton 12/30/1995

ARCHIBALD,
Christopher S. of Gilmanton m. Carla M. **Mann** of Gilmanton 8/24/2001

ARSENAULT,
George E. of Gilmanton m. Carol F. **Haskell** of Gilmanton 7/11/1992

ARVANITIS,
James of Manchester m. Chrystine **Gardner** of NY 8/21/1971; H -
b. 4/2/1948 in NH, s/o George D. Arvanitis (NH) and Alice M.
Kremedes (NH); W - b. 1/26/1951 in NY, d/o A. Harvey
Gardner (MA) and Barbara Collins (MA)

ASHCROFT,
Herbert W. of Gilmanton m. Etta E. **Walsh** of Loudon 5/3/1902; H -
20, farmer, b. Lynn, MA, s/o William P. Ashcroft (Worcester,
MA, farmer) and Abbie E. Rogers (Pittsfield, housewife); W -
17, housemaid, b. Loudon, d/o John Walsh (teamster) and
Sarah Finnegan (housewife)

ASHTON,
Jonathan of Concord m. Cheryl **Stevens** of Gilmanton 5/20/1977; H
- b. 11/19/1950 in NY, s/o Richard V. Ashton (MA) and Julia
Dietrich (NJ); W - b. 7/12/1955 in MA, d/o Richard H. Stevens
(MA) and Nancy Wilson (MA)

AUBUT,
Tracy E. of Gilmanton m. Michelle C. **Beaudry** of Gilmanton
6/3/1995

AUSTIN,
Bruce L. of Middlesex, MA m. Barbara J. **Dudley** of Gilmanton
6/25/1977; H - b. 9/1/1954 in NH, s/o Robert S. Austin, Sr.
(NH) and Joan N. Blair (NH); W - b. 1/20/1955 in NH, d/o I.
Jean Dudley (NH) and Dorothy Hurlbett (CA)
Gerald, Jr. of Gilmanton m. Rita Anne **Morin** of Gilmanton
7/22/1961 in Laconia; H - 19, grinder, b. NH, s/o Gerald L.
Austin and Florence Brassaw (NH); W - 17, at home, b. NH,
d/o Joseph Morin (NH) and Arlene E. Patten (NH)
Gerald Leonard, III of Gilmanton m. Laurie Jeanne **Barlow** of
Gilmanton 10/23/1998
William C. of Gilmanton m. Carol E. **Brown** of Gilmanton
4/10/1965; H - 22, bleacher, b. NH, s/o Gerald Austin
(unknown) and Florence Russell (NH); W - 17, looper, b. NH,
d/o Raymond A. Brown (NH) and Bernice Willard (NH)
William C. of Gilmanton m. Linda **Blake** of Gilmanton 8/1/1992

AVERY,
Donald R. of Gilmanton m. Donna E. **DuPont** of Concord 5/29/1985
George Hawley of Gilmanton m. Blanche Lyle **Manson** of Gilmanton 1/14/1950 in Chichester; H - 67, retired, b. NH, s/o John W. Avery (NH) and Hannah Libby (NH); W - 63, at home, b. NH, d/o James H. Beck (NH) and Martha J. Leighton (NH)

AYER,
Walter H. of Gilmanton m. Blanche L. **Sawyer** of Gilmanton 6/1/1899; H - 27, farmer, b. Gilmanton, s/o Daniel S. Ayer (Gilmanton, farmer) and Nancy C. Canney (Farmington); W - 21, housemaid, b. Gilmanton, d/o John R. Sawyer (Belmont, farmer) and Mary Marsh (Gilmanton, housewife)

AYLWARD,
Dana A. of Middleton, MA m. Carol L. **Downing** of Gilmanton 6/26/1976 in Alton; H - b. 3/14/1956 in MA, s/o Donald A. Aylward (MA) and Mildred Humphreys (MA); W - b. 8/23/1957 in MA, d/o Paul J. Downing (MA) and Margaret Leonard (MA)
Dana A. of Gilmanton m. Lynn **Carey** of Gilmanton 12/10/1983
Dana Alden of Gilmanton m. Belinda Joy **Broek** of Belmont 8/16/1997

AZOTEA,
Beinvenido, Jr. of Gilmanton m. Esther Ann **Vachon** of Laconia 5/26/1962; H - 22, farmer, b. NH, s/o Beinvenido Azotea (P.Is.) and Myrtle P. Crounin (NH); W - 19, at home, b. NH, d/o Paul W. Bristow (OK) and Mildred Schueneman (WI)
Beinvenido, Jr. of Gilmanton m. Judith Ellen **Dixey** of Laconia 5/22/1964 in Belmont; H - 24, painter, b. NH, s/o Beinvenido Azptea (P.I.) and Myrtle P. Cronin (NH); W - 20, attendant, b. ME, d/o Arthur B. Clairmont (NH) and Edith M. Corriveau (NH)

BACON,
John M. of Gilford m. Jane C. **Barlow** of Gilmanton 8/8/1954; H - 20, Navy, b. NH, s/o Milo F. Bacon (NH) and Minnie M. Page (NH); W - 19, nurse, b. NH, d/o Austin C. Barlow (MA) and Phoebe P. Hinckley (ME)

BAER,
Richard Adolf of Gilmanton m. Karen Ann **Fournier** of Gilmanton 9/13/1997

BAGLEY,
Earl Everett of Plymouth m. Margaret Virginia **Brake** of Gilmanton 6/7/1952 in Rumney; H - 25, Army, b. NH, s/o Charles W. Bagley (NH) and Elizabeth G. Romprey (NH); W - 25, housekeeper, b. NH, d/o James H. Joyce (NH) and Velma I. Quint (NH)

Robert E. of Gilmanton m. Blanche I. **Davis** of Gilmanton 5/28/1954 in Manchester; H - 22, asst. shipper, b. NH, s/o Charles W. Bagley (NH) and Elizabeth G. Romprey (NH); W - 18, at home, b. NH, d/o George E. Davis (NH) and Irene M. Page (NH)

BAILLIE,
Paul Sheldon of Belmont m. Judith Ellen **McIntire** of Gilmanton 3/16/1974 in Belmont; H - b. 4/12/1944 in MA, s/o Richard Baillie (OH) and Marion Eldridge (MA); W - b. 1/19/1943 in MA, d/o Harold Cunliffe (England) and Ellen Preston (MA)

BAIOCCHETTI,
Vincent Anthony, III of Gilmanton m. Tammy Lee **Taylor** of Gilmanton 9/23/1989

BAKER,
Donald Keeler of Gilmanton m. Laura Anne **Bowman** of Reading, MA 7/29/1995

Douglas A. of Gilmanton m. Karen D. **Moore** of Pembroke 9/10/1977 in Laconia; H - b. 2/16/1951 in NH, s/o William Baker (MA) and Jean Houghton (OH); W - b. 4/24/1955 in NY, d/o William Moore (NY) and Helena Hochadel (OH)

Fred L. of Gilmanton m. Mary A. **Greene** of Gilmanton 6/1/1895; H - 30, farmer, b. NS, s/o John Baker (farmer) and Jedada Mathews (housewife); W - 29, school teacher, b. Gilmanton, d/o Adrial H. Greene (farmer) and Olive J. Greene

Lewis Vernon of Gilmanton m. Debra Allyson **King** of Gilmanton 8/19/1971 in Belmont; H - b. 5/21/1948 in VT, s/o Arthur Tifft

(VT) and Minnie Philips (VT); W - b. 2/26/1955 in NJ, d/o Frank King (NJ) and Alice Craig (NJ)
Sylvester E. of Pomfret, CT m. Mary A. **Barron** of Orange, NJ 9/15/1920 in Tilton; H - 44, carpenter, 2nd, b. Pomfret, CT, s/o Warren S. Baker (Brooklyn, CT) and Susan I. Burdick (Stonington, CT); W - 42, housework, b. Orange, NJ, d/o John Barron (Ireland) and Mary Callahan (Ireland)

BALDWIN,
David G. of Lake Forest, IL m. Sara E. **Patscott** of Lake Forest, IL 8/11/1979
Robert Henry of Gilmanton m. Laurie Jean **Glum** of Concord 6/26/1993

BALLARD,
Clarence P. of Gilmanton m. Maud E. **Gilman** of Gilmanton 10/30/1907; H - 30, physician, b. Concord, s/o Charles E. Ballard (Concord, farmer) and Cynthia Dunlap (Andover, ME, housewife); W - 31, teacher, b. Gilmanton, d/o Horace T. Gilman (Gilmanton, farmer) and Etta M. Edgerly (Gilmanton, housewife)

BARNES,
Oliver Willard of Alton m. Shirley MacNeil **Vorel** of Gilmanton 10/9/1971 in Alton; H - b. 10/11/1909 in NH, s/o Albert E. Barnes (MA) and Flora Sudsbury (Canada); W - b. 2/2/1916 in MA, d/o Albert W. MacNeil (MA) and Jessie Benway (Canada)
William J. of Gilmanton m. Helena G. **Murphy** of Gilmanton 3/16/1990

BARNETT,
Brian A. of Gilmanton m. Ellen J. **Harrison** of Gilmanton 10/13/1974; H - b. 12/23/1937 in MN, s/o Charles W. Barnett (KS) and Ruth Thompson (WI); W - b. 10/8/1947 in NY, d/o Stanley Harrison (NY) and Merriam Ferber (NY)

BARON,
Jay S. of Gilmanton m. Eleanor A. **Mullaney** of Gilmanton 10/24/1980

BARRON,
Edwin S. of Gilmanton m. Mary E. **Walsh** of Gilmanton 5/21/1900; H - 31, farmer, b. Belmont, s/o George Barron; W - 20, housekeeper, b. NS, d/o Smith Walsh

BARTLETT,
Andrew J. of Gilmanton m. Carol A. **Needham** of Dover 6/4/1977 in Dover; H - b. 8/30/1954 in NH, s/o John Bartlett (MA) and Charlotte Noddin (ME); W - b. 8/31/1955 in NH, d/o Edward Needham (MA) and Hazel Allen (MA)
Andrew John of Gilmanton m. Anne Marie Annis **Mailloux** of Gilmanton 9/15/1989
Timothy E. of Gilmanton m. Cynthia J. **Weller** of Gilmanton 6/6/1986

BASCUAS,
Joseph W. of Alpharetta, GA m. Ardith A. **Peters** of Atlanta, GA 8/1/1994

BATCHELDER,
Albert W. of Gilmanton m. Blanche E. **Hill** of Gilmanton 4/3/1965 in Loudon; H - 38, woodsman, b. NH, s/o Willey H. Batchelder (NH) and Florence Emerson (NH); W - 42, housewife, b. NH, d/o Edwin E. Morse (NH) and Elizabeth E. Martin (NH)
Charles M. of Gilmanton m. Dora **Staples** of Gilmanton 11/5/1892 in Meredith; H - 31, farmer, b. Loudon, s/o Nathan C. Batchelder (Loudon, farmer) and Susan Moulton (housewife); W - 20, operative, d/o Nelson Staples (farmer)
Isaac Walker of Pembroke m. Ruth Eleanor **Potter** of Gilmanton 10/4/1959; H - 47, clerk, b. NH, s/o James R. Batchelder (KS) and Florence J. Walker (NH); W - 34, at home, b. NH, d/o George D. Potter (NH) and Mildred E. Page (NH)
Josiah A. of Gilmanton m. Nellie F. **Marshall** of Alton 4/28/1888 in Pittsfield; H - 44, farmer, b. Nottingham, s/o Gideon Batchelder (Vershire, VT, farmer) and Ruth M. Hill (Lee, housewife); W - 32, housewife, b. Alton, d/o Noah Glidden (Alton, clergyman) and Susan Glidden (Alton, housewife)
William N. of New York City m. Helen F. **Ayer** of Gilmanton 10/8/1890; H - 42, merchant, 2nd, b. Loudon, s/o William Batchelder (farmer) and Mary Batchelder (housewife); W - 27,

housewife, b. Gilmanton, d/o Daniel S. Ayer (farmer) and Nancy C. Ayer (Farmington, housewife)

BATTIS,
Harry J. of Gilmanton m. Ida **Clement** of Belmont 9/29/1897; H - 20, black, teaming, b. Gilmanton, s/o John F. Battis (Canterbury, farmer) and Lydia A. Battis (housewife); W - 17, housemaid, b. Laconia, d/o Samuel Clement (farmer) and Ida Clement (housewife)

John H. of Gilmanton m. Sadie E. **Veasey** of N. Hampton 9/15/1895 in N. Hampton; H - 22, farmer, b. Gilmanton, s/o John F. Battis (Northfield, farmer); W - 18, housekeeper, b. Meredith, d/o Hoza Veasey (farmer)

BAXTER,
William Frederick of Holliston, MA m. Beverly **Stone** of Marlboro, MA 6/1/1993

BEAL,
Stephen W. of Roslindale, MA m. Christina M. **Raither** of Brockton, MA 5/18/1984

BEAN,
Dennis E. of Wolfeboro m. Sandra L. **Twombly** of Gilmanton 10/1/1966; H - 24, bookkeeper, b. NH, s/o Lester E. Bean (NH) and Evelyn W. York (NH); W - 24, bookkeeper, b. NH, d/o Fred W. Twombly (NH) and Gertrude A. Rollins (NH)

BEANE,
Jason D. of Gilmanton m. Bridget D. **Gault** of Gilmanton 8/26/2000

BEAUCHESNE,
Donald H. of Laconia m. Rosalie E. **Joyce** of Gilmanton 9/4/1965 in Pittsfield; H - 22, ass't manager, b. VT, s/o Harvey T. Beauchesne (VT) and Theresa Guillette (VT); W - 18, file clerk, b. NH, d/o Frank Joyce (unknown) and Myrtle Cronin (NH)

BEAVERS,
Scott Allen of Gilmanton m. Patricia Mary **Mulroy** of Gilmanton 10/5/1996

BEBO,
Nelson W. of Ctr. Barnstead m. Dorothy E. **Wilson** of Gilmanton 11/21/1932; H - 23, clerk, b. Ctr. Barnstead, s/o John F. Bebo (Canada, laborer) and Harriett C. Gray (Chichester, housework); W - 21, at home, b. Rockland, MA, d/o Clarence W. Wilson (Arbarden, ND, clergyman) and Ada E. Chadborne (Augusta, ME, housework)

BECK,
Charles W. of Gilmanton m. Hulda A. **Beck** of Gilmanton 7/17/1898; H - 19, farmer, b. Gilmanton, s/o J. H. Beck (Gilmanton, farmer) and Marie Sanderson (Gilmanton); W - 18, housekeeper, b. Dover, d/o Wesley Beck (Effingham, engineer)

Ernest S. of Gilmanton m. Alice E. **Rollins** of Gilmanton 9/28/1932 in Laconia; H - 33, electrician, b. Charleston, MA, s/o Smith C. Beck (Gilmanton, mechanic) and Lucy J. Allen (Canada, housework); W - 31, housework, b. Gilmanton, d/o Selden B. Rollins (Gilmanton, laborer) and Alma Ellis (Alton, housework)

James Nicholas, Jr. of Gilmanton I. W. m. Carol **Norell** of Gilmanton 1/22/1978; H - b. 1/4/1941 in MD, s/o James N. Beck, Sr. (DC) and Katherine Cotter (MD); W - b. 7/31/1958 in Germany, d/o William C. Norell (NY) and Ursula Mueller (Germany)

Smith C. of Gilmanton m. Lucy J. **Allen** of Stanstead, Quebec 4/18/1895 in Dover, VT; H - 29, farmer, b. Gilmanton, s/o John S. Beck (farmer) and Julia M. Hill (Barnston, Can., housewife); W - 16, housekeeper, b. Canada, d/o George Allen (tinsmith)

Wendell E. of Gilmanton m. Sandra Denault **Joyce** of Gilmanton 4/1/1969; H - b. 5/2/1938 in NH, s/o Ernest Beck (MA) and Alice Rollins (NH); W - b. 12/24/1942 in MD, d/o Eugene Denault (MA) and Daisy Furris (MA)

Wendell Ernest of Gilmanton m. Nancy Carol **Gooch** of Nottingham 4/16/1960 in Nottingham; H - 21, truck driver, b. NH, s/o Ernest Smith Beck (MA) and Alice Elizabeth Rollins (NH); W - 18, attendant, b. MA, d/o Adelbert Oscar Gooch, Jr. (MA) and Natalie Fickett (MA)

BECKLEY,
Bruce Hallam of Gilmanton m. Ann-Marie **Anderson** of Manchester 6/2/1962 in Manchester; H - 23, electron. insp., b. CT, s/o Lewis Fred. Buckley (NH) and Lillian Jameson (SD); W - 20, beautician, b. NH, d/o Herbert W. Anderson (NH) and Joanne Morreels (NH)

BEDFORD,
Daniel R. of Gilmanton m. Cynthia A. **Eisenhauer** of Gilmanton 9/27/1980

BEEDE,
Herbert of Gilmanton m. Celia H. **Marsh** of Gilmanton 12/11/1895; H - 39, farmer, b. Gilmanton, s/o David Beede (Sandwich, farmer) and Elizabeth Varney (Dover, housewife); W - 46, housekeeper, b. Gilmanton, d/o Henry E. Marsh (farmer) and Hannah Marsh

BELANGER,
Kenneth A. of Gilmanton m. Laurie J. **Giles** of Gilmanton 7/26/1986

BELCASTRO,
Jerome T. of Ayer, MA m. Janice M. **Lowrey** of Ayer, MA 11/30/1985

BENITEZ,
Frank H. of Gilmanton m. Lilla M. **Durgin** of Gilmanton 5/4/1892 in Laconia; H - 35, carpenter, 3rd, b. Middleton, MA, s/o Francisco R. Benitez (Cadiz, Spain, farmer) and Hannah R. Benitez (Holderness, housewife); W - 20, housekeeper, b. Gilmanton, d/o Anna P. Durgin (housewife)

BENNETT,
Adellman S. of Gilmanton m. Yvette J. **Hamelin** of Manchester 2/7/1948 in Nashua; H - 31, civil service, b. Jefferson, ME, s/o Marvin S. Bennett (Bainbridge, NY, rural carrier) and Velina V. Vinal (Washington, ME, housewife); W - 20, stenographer, b. Manchester, d/o Wilfred P. Hamelin (New Bedford, MA) and Aline M. Maher (Canada, housewife)

BERGEVIN,
William J. of Suncook m. Gladys Ella **Nason** of Freedom 11/16/1929 in Gilmanton I. W.; H - 21, laborer, b. Suncook, s/o Odilon Bergevin (Canada, laborer) and Mary Petrin (Canada, housework); W - 19, housework, b. Freedom, d/o Jason Nason (Standish, ME, truckman) and Bertha Beck (Ctr. Effingham, housework)

BERLIND,
Allan of MA m. Wendy Ann **Prindle** of Gilmanton 8/18/1968; H - b. 12/24/1942 in NY, s/o Morris Berlind (Russia) and Ruth Fischer (NY); W - b. 4/14/1944 in NC, s/o William C. Prindle (CT) and Myra Kitchen (NY)

BERNDT,
David F. of Gilmanton m. Kimberly A. **Longver** of Gilmanton 5/16/1992

BERRY,
Lyman E. of Gilmanton m. Lulu M. **Foss** of Gilmanton 4/3/1900; H - 36, farmer, 3rd, b. New Durham, s/o Eben E. Berry (New Durham, farmer) and Lucy M. Chesley (New Durham, housewife); W - 22, housemaid, b. Danvers, MA, d/o John C. Foss (Gilmanton, shoemaker) and Ella M. Watson (Alton, housewife)

Robert L. of OH m. Sandra B. Twiford **Bice** of OH 2/26/1978; H - b. 5/20/1939 in MA, s/o Lewis H. Berry (MA) and Virginia Crocker (MA); W - b. 11/28/1946 in OH, d/o Richard W. Bice (OH) and Nellie Currence (WV)

BESSEY,
Burton Marks of E. Derry m. Marion G. **Nelson** of Gilmanton 4/29/1917 in Manchester; H - 24, shoemaker, b. Lynn, MA, s/o Arthur M. Bessey (Gardner, MA) and Gertrude Worth (Deerfield); W - 18, school teacher, b. Gilmanton, d/o Edwin F. Nelson (Rochester) and Helen A. Nelson (Plymouth)

BEST,
Barry C. of Brunswick, ME m. Beverly J. **Bibber** of Harpswell, ME 11/9/1974; H - b. 8/30/1947 in NH, s/o George A. Best (NY)

and Barbara M. Chick (ME); W - b. 3/11/1953 in ME, d/o
Charles A. Bibber (ME) and Beverly Baker (ME)
Barry C. of Gilmanton m. Janice Ruth **Elliott** of Gilmanton
7/15/1978; H - b. 8/30/1947 in NH, s/o George A. Best (NY)
and Barbara Chick (ME); W - b. 10/12/1951 in RI, d/o Franklin
J. Elliott (RI) and Ruth Donnelly (RI)

BICKFORD,
Arthur R. of Gilmanton m. Ida M. **Brewster** of Barnstead 5/13/1906
in S. Barnstead; H - 32, farmer, b. Franklin, s/o David Bickford
(Rochester, farmer) and Weltha A. C. Smith (Loudon,
housewife); W - 22, housekeeper, b. Barnstead, d/o Mark W.
Brewster (Barnstead, farmer) and Annie Merrill (Barnstead,
housewife)
Clarence H. of Gilmanton m. Vera **Hill** of Pittsfield 6/11/1932 in
Pittsfield; H - 25, truck driver, b. Gilmanton, s/o Arthur R.
Bickford (Franklin, farmer) and Ida R. Brewster (Barnstead,
housework); W - 28, forelady, b. Gilmanton, d/o Elwood H. Hill
(Alton, merchant) and Mercedes H. Dame (Middleton, stitcher)
David M. of Gilmanton m. Lizzie E. **Twombly** of Gilmanton
8/6/1933; H - 20, laborer, b. Gilmanton, s/o Arthur Bickford
(Franklin, farmer) and Ida M. Brewster (Barnstead,
housework); W - 24, at home, b. Gilmanton, d/o Dixie
Twombly (Gilmanton, carpenter) and Emma Batchelder
(Meredith, housework)
George A. of Gilmanton m. Ruth M. **Holt** of Franklin 8/20/1942 in
Farmington; H - 22, farmer, b. Gilmanton, s/o Arthur R.
Bickford (Franklin, farmer) and Ida M. Brewster (Barnstead,
housewife); W - 18, housework, b. Ashland, d/o Ernest Holt
(mill worker) and Grace Nichols (mill worker)
Herbert S. of Gilmanton m. Lillian M. **Smith** of Rochester 1/3/1934
in Rochester; H - 26, laborer, b. Gilmanton, s/o Arthur R.
Bickford (Franklin, farmer) and Ida M. Brewster (Barnstead,
housework); W - 24, at home, b. Rochester, d/o Harry A. Smith
(Boston, MA, laborer) and Hazel L. Hussey (Rochester,
housework)

BISHOP,
Dana A. of Gilmanton m. Karen Lynn **Louis** of Gilmanton 5/4/1996
Lewis Marshall of Worcester, MA m. Mary Edith **Valpey** of
Gilmanton 7/12/1915; H - 42, physician, b. Cooleyville, MA, s/o

Simson N. Bishop (Readsboro, VT, farmer) and Almina B.
Bishop (Readsboro, VT, physician); W - 42, teacher, b. Lynn,
MA, d/o Henry R. Valpey (Lynn, MA, retired) and Nancy H.
Newhall (Lynn, MA)

Wallace Putnam, Jr. of Groton, MA m. Coral Diane **Alund** of
Gilmanton 10/6/1963 in Laconia; H - 20, student, b. MA, s/o
Wallace P. Bishop and Miriam D. Mulligan; W - 18, student, b.
NY, d/o Edward J. Alund and Gladys M. Berling

BLAIS,

Clifford Edward of Gilmanton m. Darlene Marjorie **Mitchell** of
Gilmanton 5/28/1988

BLAKE,

Alan J. of Gilmanton m. Kathleen M. **Colburn** of Laconia 9/6/1975
in Loudon; H - b. 4/7/1949 in NH, s/o Victor Blake (NH) and
Loretta Lecour (NH); W - b. 4/4/1955 in NJ, d/o David M.
Colburn (NJ) and Marilyn Pilkington (NJ)

Jeremiah I. of Gilmanton m. Lucy Charity **Bailey** of Alexandria
6/1/1914 in Bristol; H - 31, farmer, b. Loudon, s/o Warren
Blake (Loudon, farmer) and Caroline Ingals (Walpole, MA,
housekeeper); W - 28, housekeeper, b. Alexandria, d/o Joseph
Peter Bailey (Alexandria, farmer) and Lovina Gore
(Alexandria, housekeeper)

Laural A. of Whitman m. Lizzie M. **Page** of Gilmanton 11/26/1887;
H - 30, laborer, b. Peacham, VT, s/o Daniel W. Blake and
Marietta Z. Blake; W - 24, b. Gilmanton, d/o John S. Page and
Sarah Page

BLANCHETTE,

Gene R. of Barnstead m. Valerie S. **Anderson** of Gilmanton
2/14/1976; H - b. 9/9/1951 in NH, s/o Roland Blanchette (NH)
and Leatrice DeRosia (NH); W - b. 2/13/1954 in MA, d/o
Howard Anderson (MA) and Dorothy Spaulding (MA)

BLODGETT,

Thomas J. of Gilmanton I. W. m. Donna L. **Morgan** of Gilmanton I.
W. 5/6/1978 in Sunapee; H - b. 2/3/1949 in NH, s/o Ralph W.
Blodgett (NH) and Pauline Kelly (NH); W - b,. 8/30/1948 in NH,
d/o Theodore L. Morgan (NH) and Virginia Nichols (NH)

BLOOM,
Edward D. of Gilmanton m. Cora E. **Green** of Northfield 10/18/1957 in Franklin; H - 29, HiWay opt., b. MI, s/o Eskil Bloom (MI) and Edith Ditty (MI); W - 20, leather shop, b. VT, d/o Charles B. Green (VT) and Ethel M. Donaghy (VT)

BODDY,
Christopher of MA m. Judy **Hunt** of MA 8/15/1967; H - 22, truck driver, b. CA, s/o Lee Boddy (WA) and Jeannette C. Jones (CA); W - 18, at home, b. MA, d/o Egar C. Hunt (NH) and Margaret H. McLatchy (MA)

BOISVERT,
James Garrett of Gilmanton m. Bonnie Lee **Runnals** of Laconia 11/23/1974 in Laconia; H - b. 11/19/1955 in MA, s/o Paul Boisvert (MA) and Lillian Desjardins (NH); W - b. 9/3/1953 in NH, d/o Noel Runnals (NH) and Dorothy Smith (NH)

BOOTH,
William R. of Gilmanton m. Amy E. **Gardner** of Gilmanton 6/30/2001

BORDEAU,
Jason of Gilmanton m. Florence C. **Edgerly** of Gilmanton 1/19/1918 in Laconia; H - 26, laborer, b. St. Albans, VT, s/o Frank Bordeau and Julia -----; W - 20, at home, b. Gilmanton, d/o Walter J. Edgerly (Gilmanton) and Anna Cogswell (Gilmanton)

Paul C. of Gilmanton m. Carolyn A. **Prybylo** of Gilmanton 7/4/1981

Philip P. of Gilmanton m. Elizabeth D. **Hayes** of Laconia 8/12/1946 in Laconia; H - 24, bookkeeper, b. Laconia, s/o Jason J. Bordeau (St. Albans, VT, road agent) and Florence C. Edgerly (Gilmanton, housewife); W - 21, assembler, b. Wolfeboro, d/o Frederick Hayes (Alton) and Ruth P. Duncan (Beverly, MA, mach. oper.)

Robert E. of Gilmanton m. Barbara **Bushey** of Laconia 2/17/1940 in Rochester; H - 20, laborer, b. Laconia, s/o Jason J. Bordeau (St. Albans, VT, laborer) and Florence Edgerly (Gilmanton, housewife); W - 19, at home, b. Laconia, d/o Edwin Dockham (laborer) and Norma Bushey (Laconia, housewife)

BOSIAK,
Frank Charles of Gilmanton m. Jacqueline Muriel **Boisvert** of Somersworth 4/27/1963 in Somersworth; H - 30, farmer, b. NH, s/o Stephen Bosiak (Poland) and Yadwiga Dutka (Poland); W - 24, office worker, b. NH, d/o Phillipe A. Boisvert (Canada) and Aurore Binette (Canada)

Joseph of Gilmanton m. Olive May **Thorne** of Concord 9/17/1960 in Concord; H - 41, farmer, b. CT, s/o Stephen Bosiak (Poland) and Hadwaig Ducke (Poland); W - 32, hospital attendant, b. NH, d/o Alfred W. Thorne (NH) and Iona E. Chase (NH)

BOUCHER,
Dennis Joseph of Laconia m. Mary Louise **Emond** of Gilmanton 12/14/1968 in Laconia; H - b. 7/26/1948 in NH, s/o Lucien J. Boucher (NH) and Thelma G. Wakefield (NH); W - b. 2/8/1950 in DC, d/o Wilfred A. Emond (MA) and Bobby-Jean Williams (AL)

BOUDREAU,
Michael of Gilmanton m. Rebecca **Stanley** of Gilmanton 10/19/1979

Robert T. of Haverhill, MA m. Phyllis A. **Twombly** of Gilmanton 11/24/1947; H - 20, truck driver, b. Bradford, MA, s/o Philip L. Boudreau (NS, leather worker) and Martha V. McDonald (Harrisville, housewife); W - 16, at home, b. Gilmanton, d/o Benjamin K. Twombly (Belmont, mill worker) and Margaret A. O'Brien (Stratham, housewife)

BOUGHTON,
Michael Grant of Gilmanton m. Norma Jean **Durette** of Gilmanton 8/14/1993

BOURGOINE,
Bruce of Gilmanton m. Barbara J. **Devito** of Gilford 5/23/1981

BOWDOIN,
Harry L. of Gilmanton m. Doris I. **Nutter** of Gilmanton 6/15/1946 in Chichester; H - 38, laborer, 2nd, b. Ripley, ME, s/o Charles A. Bowdoin (Dexter, ME, retired) and Ruth W. Bubier (Orneville,

ME, housewife); W - 42, postmaster, 2nd, b. Lawrence, MA, s/o Sanford R. Springer and Edith Horsman (England, postmaster)

BOWLES,
John R. of Gilmanton m. Dorothy A. **Edson** of Concord 7/29/1976 in Loudon; H - b. 7/29/1931 in NH, s/o Leonard Bowles (Canada) and Evelyn ----- (NH); W - b. 2/23/1947 in NH, d/o Elbridge Edson and Dorothy Frost (NH)

BOYAJIAN,
Bryan R. of Gilmanton m. Heather L. **Ervin** of Gilmanton 10/7/2000

BOYD,
Gregory R. of MA m. Mary A. **Crowley** of MA 2/8/1975; H - b. 1/26/1950 in MA, s/o David P. Boyd (MA) and Harriet A. Rathbun (MA); W - b. 7/21/1950 in MA, d/o Roger E. Crowley (MA) and Margaret M. Entwistle (MA)
Robert O. of Gilmanton m. Lynn L. **Clarke** of Gilmanton 2/28/1986

BOYDEN,
Joy W. of Gilmanton m. Sharon J. **Willette** of Gilmanton 8/12/2000

BRAGG,
Dellie of Hartland, ME m. Hazel **Nevins** of Hartland, ME 1/5/1908; H - 19, mill hand, b. Pittsfield, s/o Will Bragg (Dixmont, ME, farmer) and Annie Batchelder (Troy, ME, housewife); W - 18, housemaid, b. Hartland, ME, d/o David Nevins (farmer)
George E. of Gilmanton m. Edith G. **Brown** of Gilmanton 4/14/1907 in Loudon; H - 26, harness maker, b. Troy, ME, s/o W. P. Bragg (Dixmont, ME, farmer) and Annie S. Batchelder (Troy, ME, housewife); W - 27, housekeeper, b. Gilmanton, d/o Joseph Brown (Loudon, farmer) and Anna M. Rollins (Gilmanton, housewife)

BRAUN,
Carl L. of Gilmanton m. Vicki L. **Nadeau** of Laconia 5/20/2000

BRAWLEY,
Harry E., III of Gilmanton m. Gail M. **Lawrence** of Merrimack 8/8/1986

BRENNAN,
Casey B. of Laconia m. Tracy E. **Whitehouse** of Gilmanton
9/30/2001

BRESSE,
John A., Jr. of Gilmanton m. Carol A. **Rose** of Gilmanton 6/20/1992

BRETON,
Normand G. of Gilmanton m. Janet A. **Potter** of Gilmanton
8/11/1990

BRIGGS,
Daniel George of Pittsfield m. Nancy Lee **Littlefield** of Gilmanton
4/20/1968 in Alton; H - b. 1/16/1946 in NH, s/o Gordon Briggs
(USA) and Mary Jane Pauquette (Canada); W - b. 7/15/1950 in
NH, d/o George Littlefield (NH) and Romona Bagley (NH)
Edward Herbert of Clearwater, FL m. Veronica Myrtle **Diehl** of
Shirley, ME 11/4/1961; H - 59, retired, b. NY, s/o Charles E.
Briggs and Laura Brown; W - 52, housewife, b. MA, d/o
Charles McGee and Elizabeth Griffin

BRITTON,
Jonathan D. of Gilmanton m. Rita E. **West** of Loudon 10/11/1975 in
Loudon; H - b. 1/6/1954 in CA, s/o Albert J. Britton (MA) and
Eleanor F. Sterline (ME); W - b. 3/11/1953 in NH, d/o Charles
E. West (NH) and Lois A. Jones (NH)

BROCK,
Charles T. of Gilmanton m. Carrie L. **Roby** of Gilmanton 6/13/1900
in Barnstead; H - 31, farmer, b. Pittsfield, s/o John B. Brock; W
- 31, housekeeper, 2nd, b. Epsom, d/o Orrin Dowst and Martha
Griffin

BRONSON,
James Paul of Gilmanton m. Cynthia Ann **Haas** of Gilmanton
8/16/1997

BROUGH,
Kelly Steven of Gilmanton m. Joy Marie **Young** of Gilmanton
9/13/1998

BROWN,
Arthur Robert of Gilmanton m. Annette **Huxford** of Gilmanton 6/30/1991

Carl Strachan of Strafford m. JoAnn **Casey** of Gilmanton 11/28/1964; H - 20, farmer, b. NH, s/o Lawrence W. Brown (NH) and Ethel F. Rudd (MA); W - 21, hostess, b. MA, d/o Joseph J. Casey (MA) and Grace A. Barton (MA)

Daniel David of Gilmanton m. Trudy Lee **Poire** of Gilmanton 8/21/1993

Earl D. of Gilmanton m. Cynthia L. **Pennock** of Laconia 1/5/1933; H - 40, violin maker, b. Loudon, s/o John Brown (Loudon, farmer) and Florence P. Day (Bradford, MA, housework); W - 42, hosiery worker, 2nd, b. Franconia, d/o Elwin C. Nelson (Concord, VT, farmer) and Elizabeth Brooks (Franconia, housework)

George Clinton of Gilmanton m. Lois May **Brock** of Bristol 12/31/1919 in Bristol; H - 25, carpenter, b. Gilmanton, s/o Dr. George H. Brown and Lizzie H. Orange (Lowell, MA); W - 27, at home, b. Bristol, d/o Joseph H. Brock and Nellie May Jones

George H. of Gilmanton m. Lizzie H. **Orange** of Gilmanton 12/31/1889; H - 36, physician, b. Haverhill, MA, s/o Velaria Clark (Tilton, housewife); W - 27, housewife, b. Lowell, MA, d/o Henry S. Orange (Milton, retired merchant) and Elizabeth A. Orange (Somersworth, housewife)

John Wheeler of Gilmanton m. Lizzie Batchelder **Lane** of Gilmanton 1/14/1894; H - 21, farmer, b. Gilmanton, s/o Joseph Brown (storekeeper) and Anna M. Rollins (Gilmanton, housekeeper); W - 19, dressmaker, d/o Thomas B. Lane (farmer) and Maria Williams (housekeeper)

Morse E. of Gilmanton m. Kathryn **Thistle** of Gilmanton 10/6/1968; H - b. 7/15/1895 in NH, s/o John Wheeler Brown (NH) and Lizzie Batchelder (NH); W - b. 12/8/1901 in NJ, d/o Clerhiew R. Treat (NJ) and Evelyn Conover (NJ)

Morse Everett of Gilmanton m. Rebecca Roberts **Dolliff** of Biddeford, ME 7/15/1915 in Laconia; H - 19, farmer, b. Gilmanton, s/o John W. Brown (Gilmanton, farmer) and Lizzie B. Lane (Gilmanton, housewife); W - 19, teacher, b. Biddeford, ME, d/o J. Byron Dolliff (Kennebunk, ME, farmer) and Ida Roberts (Biddeford, ME, housewife)

Ralph Drisko of Belmont m. Diana Eliot **Bartholomew** of Gilmanton 5/5/1962 in Laconia; H - 28, sales manager, b. ME, s/o Russell F. Brown (ME) and Merial B. Brophy (ME); W - 25, at home, b. NY, d/o Eliot K. Bartholomew (MA) and Margaret A. Martin (MA)

Raymond A. of Gilmanton m. Bernice M. **Willard** of Gilmanton 12/10/1934 in Enosburg Falls, VT; H - 21, truck driver, b. Portsmouth, s/o Percy R. Brown (Belmont, laborer) and Mildred Rogers (Loudon, housewife); W - 21, at home, b. Gilmanton, d/o Israel Willard (Gilmanton, laborer) and Georgia McClary (Gilmanton, housewife)

Raymond Arthur of Gilmanton m. Linda Doris **Blake** of Laconia 7/15/1967; H - 31, core maker, b. NH, s/o Raymond A. Brown (NH) and Bernice M. Willard (NH); W - 19, at home, b. NH, d/o Clyde D. Blake (NH) and Gladys E. Grant (NH)

Richard I. of Gilmanton m. Sadie P. **Twombly** of Gilmanton 6/16/1928; H - 25, farmer, b. Gilmanton, s/o Alfred Brown (Epsom, farmer) and Edna Marsh (Gilmanton, housework); W - 24, housekeeper, b. Hampden, d/o Dixie Twombly (Gilmanton, carpenter) and Emma Batchelder (Meredith, housework)

Robert A. of Gilmanton m. Carolyn **Blanchard** of Loudon 1/28/1956 in Loudon; H - 23, lumber worker, b. NH, s/o Richard I. Brown (NH) and Sadie P. Twombly (NH); W - 19, nurse's aide, b. NH, d/o Walter R. Blanchard (NH) and Phyllis C. Mullaney (VT)

BRUNK,
Michael D. of Barnstead m. Cynthia J. **Martin** of Gilmanton 7/22/1980

BRUNS,
Frederick L. of Jamaica Plain, MA m. Nina J. **Linscott** of Jefferson, ME 9/7/1925 in Gilmanton I. W.; H - 42, creditman, b. Boston, MA, s/o Anton Bruns (Bremen, Germany, painter) and Lucy Holmes (Manomet, MA, housework); W - 38, teacher, b. Jefferson, ME, d/o Roscoe G. Linscott (Jefferson, ME, farmer) and Augusta ----- (Washington, ME, housework)

BRYANS,
Robert L. of Monson, MA m. Mariam **Perkins** of Hampden, MA 6/22/1933; H - 23, clerk, b. Monson, MA, s/o Robert Bryans (Scotland, mill worker) and Mary Gates (Scotland, housework); W - 23, school teacher, b. Lowell, MA, d/o Fred Perkins

(Lowell, MA, school jan.) and Elizabeth Wilkinson (Lawrence, MA, housework)

BRYANT,
Clyde C., Jr. of Bradenton, FL m. Carol J. **Conrad** of Bradenton, FL 12/29/1990

George H. of Gilmanton m. Rebecca **Ludeman** of Chicago, IL 6/28/1929 in Bridgeport, CT; H - 41, writer, 2nd, b. Bombay, India, s/o Charles H. Bryant and Idella M. French; W - 38, teacher, b. Butler Co., IA, d/o George Ludeman and Catherine Muller

John A. of Gilmanton m. Rachel A. **Goodwin** of Gilmanton 10/20/1983

BRYSON,
Jon Lindsay of Gilmanton m. Betty Ann **Morin** of Gilmanton 6/25/1961 in Belmont; H - 24, truck driver, b. NH, s/o Louis A. Bryson (NH) and Florence Jordan (NH); W - 19, at home, b. NH, s/o Joseph Morin (NH) and Arlene E. Patten (NH)

BUCCIARELLI,
Robert H. of Gilmanton m. Arlene M. **Morancy** of E. Hartford, CT 10/9/1965 in E. Hartford, CT; H - 18, factory work, b. CT, s/o Fred Bucciarelli and Mary V. Geezen; W - 18, at home, b. NH, d/o Reginald Morancy and Alfreda St. Arnaud

BUMPUS,
Charles H., Sr. of Gilford m. Dorrice T. Gardner **Tenney** of Gilmanton 11/7/1975; H - b. 7/31/1899 in MA, s/o William Bumpus (ME) and Susan J. Dale (NB); W - b. 8/16/1896 in MA, d/o Frank E. Tenney (MA) and Isabelle Evans (MA)

BUNKER,
Merton E. of Gilmanton m. Anna M. **Gobis** of Manchester 11/10/1945 in Manchester; H - 31, mechanic, b. Pittsfield, s/o Daniel Bunker (Barnstead, farmer) and Florence Hilliard (Loudon, housewife); W - 32, teacher, b. Manchester, d/o Gabriel Gobis (Lithuania, storekeeper) and Elizabeth Sincarage (Lithuania, housekeeper)

BUNNELL,
Robert E. of Concord m. Carolyn E. **Nelson** of Gilmanton 4/23/1966; H - 28, carpenter, b. NH, s/o Paul Webster Bunnell (NH) and Florence Mary Johnson (NH); W - 22, teacher, b. NH, d/o George Martin Nelson (NH) and Eleanor Margarite Hyslop (MA)

BURBANK,
Alonzo P. of Gilmanton m. Sadie L. **Gault** of Gilmanton 10/29/1910; H - 20, laborer, b. Gilmanton, s/o Alonzo Burbank (Hopkinton, farmer) and Lucia A. Dustin (Haverhill, housekeeper); W - 15, b. Bridgewater, d/o John C. Gault (Bridgewater, carpenter) and Melvina A. Battis (Gilmanton, housewife)

George David of Gilmanton m. Sandra June **Conrad** of Gilmanton 10/10/1988

Neil Stuart of Pittsfield m. Esther Joyce **Edgerly** of Gilmanton 9/10/1960; H - 24, ass't pressman, b. NH, s/o Kenneth A. Burbank (Canada) and Ruth M. Pickering (NH); W - 22, secretary, b. NH, d/o George D. Edgerly (NH) and Lavina E. Gooch (NH)

BURDETT,
David of Framingham, MA m. Jolene **Salisbury** of Framingham, MA 7/29/1978; H - b. 9/20/1954 in CT, s/o Leonard Burdett (MA) and Dorothy Louise (MI); W - b. 1/30/1957 in UT, d/o John Salisbury (UT) and Leah Engle (PA)

BURDITT,
Anrthony D. of Gilmanton m. Kathy J. **Moulton** of Gilmanton 9/27/1986

BURGESS,
Paul M. of N. Kingstown, MA m. Beatrice B. **Cassanaugh** of Gilmanton

BURLINGAME,
Roger G. of Gilmanton m. Teresa L. **Harrison** of Gilmanton 10/14/1984

BURROUGHS,
Orman L. of Gilmanton m. Eva M. **Jones** of Gilmanton 6/6/1912; H - 25, farmer, b. Potter Place, s/o George W. Burroughs (laborer) and Flora B. Marsh (Gilmanton, housewife); W - 16, housemaid, b. Gilmanton, d/o George A. Jones (Gilmanton, laborer) and Olive Moody (Canterbury, housewife)

BUSSEY,
Charles Bernard of Revere, MA m. Cherylle Anne **Mullen** of Revere, MA 5/10/1997
Robert D. of Gilmanton m. Elaine K. **Davis** of Newburyport, MA 8/19/2000

BUTT,
Earl A. of Belmont, MA m. Florence G. **Whitney** of Everett, MA 9/15/1933 in Nashua; H - 28, accountant, b. Chelsea, MA, s/o John Butt (Newfoundland, contractor) and Effie M. Oates (Newfoundland, housework); W - 19, waitress, b. Bangor, ME, d/o Roy C. Whitney (Brownville, ME, carpenter) and Fanny E. Donaldson (Brownville, ME, housework)

BYERS,
Robert Allen of Monroe, NY m. Dorothy Winona **Potter** of Gilmanton 4/11/1962; H - 39, mechanic, b. NS, s/o Walter D. Byers (NS) and Maude K. Chute (MA); W - 38, at home, b. NH, d/o George D. Potter (NH) and Mildred E. Page (MA)

CALDON,
Brett M. of Gilmanton m. Jessica R. **Ballinger** of Gilmanton 6/9/2001
Jeffrey S. of Gilmanton m. Michelle R. **Gaudet** of Gilmanton 12/8/1987
Thomas W. of Belmont m. Suzann Joy **Barr** of Gilmanton 8/29/1970; H - b. 4/8/1947 in NH, s/o Winston Caldon (NH) and Louise Gallagher (MA); W - b. 2/9/1949 in NH, d/o Otis D. Barr (Canada) and Julia Terris (NH)

CAMUSO,
Peter J. of Norwood, MA m. Diane L. **Haley** of Norwood, MA 12/31/1985

CANFIELD,
Stanley P. of Pittsfield m. Oiive **Burres** of Gilmanton 1/20/1935 in Pittsfield; H - 25, clerk, b. Lunenburg, VT, s/o Archie Canfield (Lunenburg, VT, weaver) and Florence Pierce (Manchester, waitress); W - 18, at home, b. Gilmanton, d/o Orman Burres (Franklin, laborer) and Eva J. Rollins (Belmont, housewife)

CANNEY,
Forrest S. of Gilmanton m. Lura A. **Pratt** of Gilmanton 1/16/1926; H - 26, laborer, b. Gilmanton, s/o John W. Canney (Tuftonboro, carpenter) and Laura J. Smith (E. Concord, housework); W - 28, housework, 2nd, b. Pittsfield, d/o John E. Davis (Barnstead, laborer) and Marian A. Rogers (Bedford, housework)
John W. of Gilmanton m. Laura J. **Smith** of E. Concord 9/7/1898 in Concord; H - 22, farmer, b. Tuftonboro, s/o Lafayette Canney (Melvin Village, farmer) and Mary E. Tibbetts (Wolfeboro, housekeeper); W - 20, housekeeper, b. E. Concord, d/o Thomas H. Smith (Ireland, currier) and Caroline Lysle (PEI, housewife)

CAPRARIO,
Ronald David of Gilmanton m. Joanne Elaine **Hickey** of Gilmanton 5/6/1989
Ronald David of Gilmanton m. Marie Ruth **Ashcraft** of Gilmanton 4/22/1995

CAREY,
Jeremiah S. of Gilmanton m. Helen L. **Mulhern** of Taunton, MA 1/5/1914 in Pittsfield; H - 36, salesman, b. Chelsea, MA, s/o John Carey (Ireland, jobber) and Mary Harrigan (Chelsea, MA, housewife); W - 25, housemaid, b. Taunton, MA, d/o Peter Mulhern (Ireland, moulder) and Mary McDonald (NS, housewife)

CARMODY,
Walter J. of Gilmanton m. Jody M. **Fosburgh** of Gilmanton 6/13/1992

CARPENTER,
Al. S. of Gilmanton m. Ethel G. **Thompson** of Gilmanton 3/15/1974; H - b. 2/21/1938 in RI, s/o Leonard J. Carpenter (RI) and Mildred Wainwright (RI); W - b. 9/16/1945 in NH, d/o Daniel Adel, Sr. (Germany) and Beatrice Willard (NH)

CARROLL,
Eugene E. m. Roxey E. **Mitchell** 2/17/1922 in Concord

CASALE,
John Dennis of Newton, MA m. Sharyl Lee **Boudreau** of Gilmanton 4/20/1968 in Newton, MA; H - 27, b. MA, s/o Joseph J. Casale and Gladys Agnes Dennis; W - 21, b. MA, d/o Wibster J. Boudreau and Olga Cranton

CASAZZA,
Joseph A. of Arlington, MA m. Linda J. **Clark** of Concord, MA 9/6/1980

CHAMBERLAIN,
Dennis A. of Gilmanton m. Donna Jene **Chase** of Gilmanton 5/27/1989

Dennis A. of Gilmanton m. Sylvia A. **Sims** of Gilmanton 6/3/1995

Eve. H. of Gilmanton m. Vera Elizabeth **Mitchell** of Concord 12/24/1914 in Concord; H - 22, iceman, b. Barnstead, s/o Charles Chamberlain (Loudon, farmer) and Bert. M. Emerson (Barnstead, housewife); W - 19, at home, b. NB, d/o Walter Mitchell (NB) and Elizabeth Heywood (NB)

Harry I. of Gilmanton m. Ella M. **Jones** of Gilmanton 2/14/1910 in Belmont; H - 22, sawmill hand, b. Barnstead, s/o Charles H. Chamberlain (Loudon, farmer) and Bertha A. Emerson (Barnstead, housewife); W - 22, housework, b. Gilmanton, d/o Joseph I. Jones (Loudon, farmer) and Ida Glidden (Williamstown, VT, housewife)

LeRoy of Belmont m. Florence E. **Redman** of Gilmanton 2/20/1938 in Center Harbor; H - 40, marine engineer, 2nd, b. Ft. Fairfield, ME, s/o William Chamberlain (ME, mechanic) and Lillian Wentworth (ME, housewife); W - 24, at home, 2nd, b. Warren, d/o Leslie W. Ford (Saranac, NY, farmer) and Nellie C. Chase (Soldier Valley, IA, housewife)

Randy L. of Gilmanton m. Joyce L. **Hodge** of Gilmanton 6/10/1984
Robert W. of Belmont m. Marjorie **Seavey** of Gilmanton 12/23/1939 in Fryeburg, ME; H - 18, laborer, b. Lewiston, ME, s/o I. W. Chamberlain (Ft. Fairfield, ME, engineer) and Josephine Jayne (Hibernia, NJ, housewife); W - 17, student, b. No. Conway, d/o Edward Seavey (Conway, chef) and Annie Winrow (Fleetwood, England, housewife)
Stanley R. of Gilmanton m. Virginia C. **Dunn** of Gilmanton 12/18/1965; H - 22, molder, b. NH, s/o Robert W. Chamberlain (ME) and Marjorie M. Seavey (NH); W - 18, seamer, b. NY, d/o Robert G. Dunn (OH) and Virginia M. Vineyard (NY)
Stephen Edward of Gilmanton m. Marlene May **Carignan** of Laconia 7/29/1967 in Laconia; H - 22, boarder, b. NH, s/o Robert W. Chamberlain (ME) and Marjorie Sevey (MA); W - 19, clerk, b. NH, d/o Ernest J. Carignan (NH) and Marie Prince (Canada)

CHARCALIS,
Harry G. of Gilmanton m. Kimberly C. **Fish** of Gilmanton 4/23/2000

CHASE,
Arthur F. of Gilmanton m. Daisy E. **Weinmann** of Gilmanton 12/3/1928; H - 45, lumber dealer, 2nd, b. Douglas, MA, s/o Frank A. Chase (Douglas, MA, retired) and Mary Tappan (Sandwich, housework); W - 43, housework, 3rd, b. Detroit, MI, d/o Fred E. Wood (Hampstead, illustrator) and Margaret Habbin (Dundas, Can., housework)
Gary A. of Gilmanton I.W. m. Sheri A. **Rivard** of Gilmanton I.W. 8/19/2000

CHENEY,
James M., Sr. of Gilmanton m. Robin L. **Pearson** of Gilmanton 8/17/1990

CHRISTIE,
John S. of FL m. Nancy E. **Steenstra** of Gilmanton 8/10/1968; H - b. 11/17/1937 in FL, s/o William J. Christie (NC) and Sybil Rousseau (FL); W - b. 1/11/1944 in VA, d/o Walter H. Steenstra (MA) and Ruth E. Miner (ME)

CHRISTOFORE,
Richard W. of New Durham m. Elizabeth F. Burleigh **Perkins** of Farmington 8/9/1975; H - b. 6/23/1947 in MA, s/o William Christofore (MA) and Esther Bergquist (MA); W - b. 10/1/1941 in NH, d/o George H. Perkins (NH) and Thirza Elliott (NH)

CLAIRMONT,
David P. of Gilmanton m. Cheryl Mae **Ellsworth** of Belmont 8/7/1971 in Belmont; H - b. 8/26/1953 in NH, s/o Joseph L. Clairmont (NH) and Katherine Bouchard (NH); W - b. 11/8/1955 in NH, d/o Wendell L. Ellsworth (NH) and Helen Stone (NH)
Kerry Joseph of Gilmanton m. Linda Sue **Canney** of Laconia 8/26/1967 in Laconia; H - 19, student, b. NH, s/o Joseph L. Clairmont (NH) and Katherine A. Bouchard (NH); W - 18, cashier, b. NH, d/o Harold Roy Canney (NH) and Eva Rosemarie Chabot (NH)
Lynn R. of Gilmanton m. Barbara C. **Gray** of Gilmanton 9/27/1998
Lynn Robert of Gilmanton m. Phyllis Louise **Jewell** of Belmont 11/12/1966 in Belmont; H - 20, student, b. NH, s/o Joseph L. Clairmont (NH) and Katherine A. Bouchard (NH); W - 18, bookkeeper, b. NH, d/o Joseph D. Jewell (NH) and Clara E. Elwell (ME)
Omar Leo of Gilmanton m. Cynthia Susan **McCarthy** of Concord 11/20/1976; H - b. 10/10/1955 in NH, s/o Joseph L. Clairmont (NH) and Katherine Bouchard (NH); W - b. 10/8/1953 in VT, d/o Leon J. McCarthy and Frances E. Stone (NH)

CLAREMONT,
David A. of Gilmanton m. Lynne A. **Ouellette** of Gilmanton 12/15/1990

CLARK,
Carroll Percy m. Viola Muriel **Stockbridge** 9/4/1923
Eugene F. of Barnstead m. Marion Elizabeth **Ham** of Gilmanton 5/23/1925 in Pittsfield; H - 19, farmer, b. Barnstead, s/o Jonathan Clark (Barnstead, farmer) and Ida ----- (Barnstead, housework); W - 15, at home, b. Shrewsbury, MA, d/o Henry Ham (Barnstead, farmer) and Gertrude Davis (Worcester, MA, housework)

CLIFFORD,
Earl C. of Gilmanton m. Nellie M. **Ellsworth** of Gilmanton 10/20/1914 in Belmont; H - 21, farmer, b. Gilmanton, s/o John L. Clifford (Gilmanton, farmer) and Jennie Leavitt (Loudon, housewife); W - 24, teacher, b. Gilmanton, d/o Euraldo Ellsworth (Gilmanton, farmer) and Mary Allen (NY, housewife)

Everett E. of Gilmanton m. Cecile R. **Morin** of Laconia 8/25/1945 in Laconia; H - 25, asst. foreman, b. Gilmanton, s/o Earle C. Clifford (Gilmanton, road agent) and Nellie A. Ellsworth (Gilmanton, at home); W - 24, hairdresser, b. Laconia, d/o Aime H. Morin (Quebec, at home) and Generia Fillion (Quebec, at home)

Forrest H. of Northfield m. Laura Ella **Page** of Gilmanton 12/25/1944; H - 28, tool grinder, b. Belmont, s/o George W. Clifford (Walden, VT, painter) and Rose E. Plant (Tamworth, housewife); W - 22, at home, b. Gilmanton, d/o Frank J. Page (Franklin, road agent) and Helen O. Wyatt (Tilton, teacher)

CLIFTON,
Peter R. of Gilmanton m. Cindy J. **Vincent** of Gilmanton I. W. 11/19/1977; H - b. 4/29/1956 in NH, s/o Robert O. Houle (NH) and Marie Landry (NH); W - b. 8/25/1961 in NH, d/o Gilbert Cheney (NH) and Sandra Ridlon (NH)

CLINTON,
Paul Douglas of Gilmanton m. Darlene Lee **Hyslop** of Gilmanton 8/27/1969 in Belmont; H - b. 7/24/1950 in KS, s/o Dale L. Clinton (USA) and Dorothy Israel (AL); W - b. 9/21/1951 in NH, d/o Donald Hyslop (MA) and Rachael Straw (NH)

CLOUGH,
Clarence F. of Gilmanton m. Ethel C. **Tarr** of Manchester 4/18/1914 in Gilmanton I. W.; H - 24, farmer, b. Gilmanton, s/o Elbridge G. Clough (Gilmanton, farmer) and Emma Sargent (Lowell, MA, housewife); W - 22, housemaid, b. Rochester, d/o Charles M. Tarr (Pacific City, IA, carpenter) and Nettie B. Twombly (Dover, housewife)

Irving A. of Gilmanton m. Florence P. **Brown** of Pittsfield 9/30/1909 in Pittsfield; H - 49, poultryman, b. Loudon, s/o Myron S. Clough (Alton, farmer) and Elizabeth H. Prescott (Alton, housewife); W - 47, housemaid, 2nd, b. Bradford, MA, d/o

William F. Day (Bradford, MA, shoe mfr.) and Sarah W. Perley (Haverhill, MA, housewife)
James Allan of Gilmanton m. Jessica Gertrude **Pierce** of Gilmanton 7/19/1991
John Page of Gilmanton m. Grace Gertrude B. **Hight** of Alton 10/16/1920 in Alton; H - 44, farmer, b. Manchester, s/o Elbridge G. Clough (Gilmanton) and Emma S. Sargent (Lowell, MA); W - 34, shoemaker, 2nd, b. Alton, d/o Benjamin L. Blaisdell (Boston, MA) and Abbie B. Horne (Farmington)
Nahum O. of Ortonville, MN m. Gertrude M. **Kimball** of Gilmanton 4/3/1906; H - 51, b. Gilmanton, s/o John P. Clough (Gilmanton, farmer) and Tamson H. Whitney (Strafford, housewife); W - 44, housekeeper, b. Gilmanton, d/o Josiah L. Kimball (Gilmanton, laborer) and Ann P. Kimball (Gilmanton, housewife)

CLOW,

Barry L. of Gilmanton m. Margaret N. **Timko** of Gilmanton 2/12/1977; H - b. 7/7/1940 in NH, s/o Phil H. Clow (NH) and Marjorie Clifford (NH); W - b. 1/11/1956 in ME, d/o Bart Timko (Czechoslovakia) and Barbara Narchwicz (Poland)

COCHRAN,

Guy Eugene of Gilmanton m. Jane Pauline **Vallee** of Laconia 2/25/1950 in Laconia; H - 23, mechanic, b. NH, s/o Joseph E. Cochran (NH) and Mildred C. Athaern (NH); W - 17, housework, b. NH, d/o Paul H. Vallee (Canada) and Elizabeth M. Boucher (Canada)

COCHRANE,

Ryan V. of Rutland, VT m. Jaime M. **Dube** of Gilmanton I.W. 8/18/2001

COGSWELL,

Thomas of Gilmanton m. Caroline M. **Jones** of Gilmanton 10/6/1902; H - 61, lawyer, 2nd, b. Gilmanton, s/o Thomas Cogswell (Atkinson, farmer) and Mary Noyes (Plaistow, housewife); W - 38, teacher, b. Gilmanton, d/o Richard Jones (Gilmanton, millwright) and Martha A. Gale (Gilmanton, housewife)

COLBY,
Travis J. of Gilmanton m. Shari A. **Aubut** of Belmont 5/27/2000

COLE,
Daniel A. of Gilford m. Brenda L. **McClary** of Gilmanton 11/19/1977; H - b. 11/29/1958 in FL, s/o William D. Cole (NY) and Nelda Roberts (FL); W - b. 4/20/1959 in NH, d/o Frank L. McClary (NH) and Betty M. Deware (MA)
Robert L. of Alton m. Elayne L. **Nelson** of Gilmanton 7/12/1976; H - b. 1/28/1944 in MA, s/o Leland B. Cole (ME) and Beatrice Hapgood (MA); W - b. 10/9/1949 in NH, d/o George M. Nelson (NH) and Eleanor Hyslop (MA)

COLIN,
Dennis P. of Gilmanton m. Rita **Santin** of Gilmanton 7/1/1997

COLLIER,
Alfred Joseph of Gilmanton m. Barbara Ann **Blackey** of Belmont 5/5/1966 in Laconia; H - 42, state trooper, b. MA, s/o Leo Joseph Collier (NH) and Elmire Theresa Balis (NH); W - 25, attend. at state school, b. NH, d/o Albert J. Akerstrom, Jr. (MA) and Arlene Mary Bosselait (NH)

COLUMB,
Ronald M. of Gilmanton m. Bethany L. **Provencal** of Lakeport 2/8/1986

CONNELL,
Daniel of Gilmanton m. Elizabeth A. **Tebbetts** of Gilmanton 7/2/1912; H - 68, storekeeper, 2nd, b. Strafford, s/o Eben Connell (Strafford, carpenter) and Catherine Connell (Strafford, housewife); W - 56, housemaid, b. Gilmanton, d/o Dearborn Tebbetts and Martha J. Tebbetts (Gilmanton, housewife)

CONNELLY,
Timothy S. of Gilford m. Ronda **Lines** of Gilmanton 10/31/1985

CONNER,
Clarence A. of Tilton m. Sarah E. **McClary** of Gilmanton 2/10/1929 in Northfield; H - 20, carpenter, b. Hanover, s/o Clarence Conner (Worcester, VT, mail carrier) and Jennie M. Chase (Springfield, housework); W - 19, clerk, b. Abington, CT, d/o Horace E. McClary (Gilmanton, farmer) and Amy H. Alberty (Charleston, MA, housework)

CONVERSE,
Frank A. of Gilmanton m. Harriet F. **Jones** of Gilmanton 11/10/1894; H - 22, machinist, b. Stafford, CT, s/o D. L. Converse (Chicopee, MA, farmer) and Mary Ledoyt (Stafford, CT, housewife); W - 20, housekeeper, b. Gilmanton, d/o James A. Jones (Gilmanton, miller) and Mary Lock (Gilmanton, housewife)

COOK,
Jon D. of Gilmanton m. Margaret S. **Malcolm** of Gilmanton 6/24/1983

CORRIVEAU,
Allan W. of Gilmanton m. Nancy W. **Childress** of Gilmanton 8/30/1986

COTTON,
Fred S. of Gilmanton m. Laura A. **Gilman** of Gilmanton 9/15/1925; H - 51, farmer, b. Gilmanton, s/o Joseph T. Cotton (Gilmanton, farmer) and Sarah Varney (Gilmanton, housework); W - 54, housekeeper, 4th, b. Strafford, VT, d/o Stephen E. Norton (Chelsea, VT, farmer) and Clara J. Viellard (Sharon, VT, housework)

Joseph H., III of Gilmanton m. Belinda A. **Gilbert** of Belmont 2/5/1983

COUPAL,
Armand of Canterbury m. Harriett W. **Thompson** of Gilmanton 7/17/1965; H - 51, farm manager, b. NH, s/o Napoleon Coupal (Canada) and Mary DeRoche (MA); W - 35, music teacher, b. CT, d/o Homer B. Waller (IA) and Helen J. Keeler (CT)

COUTURE,
Lucien P. of Northfield m. Margaret L. **Downing** of Gilmanton 4/14/1984

Roger Arthur of Laconia m. Marjorie Mae **Munsey** of Gilmanton 5/14/1960 in Pittsfield; H - 20, technician, b. NH, s/o Alphonse Couture (MA) and Antoinette Lebrecque (Canada); W - 18, technician, b. NH, d/o Herbert E. Munsey (NH) and Ruth M. Willard (NH)

COX,
Arthur A. of Concord m. Arlene H. **Springer** of Gilmanton 7/22/1928; H - 24, mechanic, b. Concord, s/o George H. Cox (Meredith, truckman) and Elizabeth Baker (Concord, housework); W - 19, asst. postmaster, b. Nashua, d/o Sanford Springer (Trenton, ME, store mgr.) and Edith Horsman (Bradford, Eng., postmaster)

CRANDELL,
William E. of Boston, MA m. Marie **Penta** of Boston, MA 8/24/1942 in Alton; H - 31, chef, b. Kiev, Russia, s/o Emil Kacharonsky (Russia, Army colonel) and Olga Kournosova (Russia, housewife); W - 29, waitress, b. Roxbury, MA, d/o Guisseppe Penta (Italy, shoe stitcher) and Lillian Murray (Boston, MA, housewife)

CULLEN,
John William, Jr. of Gilmanton m. Sandra Elaine **McCarthy** of Gilmanton 9/11/1993

CUMMINGS,
Brian of Gilmanton m. Judy **Henchey** of Gilmanton 1/16/1977; H - b. 9/16/1952 in NH, s/o Winfred Cummings (NH) and Doris Tucker (NH); W - b. 5/8/1952 in NH, d/o Roland A. Stokes (NH) and Ruth Sanson (ME)

CURRIER,
Brett A. of Rumney m. Brenda L. **Cole** of Gilmanton 11/14/1982

CURTIN,
Daniel J. of Gilmanton m. Margaret T. **Dwyer** of Boston, MA 10/14/1908 in Laconia; H - 25, hatter, 2nd, b. Troy, NY, s/o Dennis P. Curtin (Boston, MA, picturemaker) and Catherine Allen (Troy, NY, housewife); W - 24, bookkeeper, b. Hyde Park, MA, d/o Patrick J. Dwyer (grocer) and Ellen Gilmarten (housewife)

CUSHING,
Russell W. of Belmont m. Ethel M. **Page** of Gilmanton 6/14/1942; H - 22, welder, b. Belmont, s/o Russell Cushing (Belmont, laborer) and Carrie L. Wyatt (Tilton, housewife); W - 20, teacher, b. Gilmanton, d/o Frank J. Page (Franklin, road agent) and Helen O. Wyatt (Tilton, housewife)

DAGGETT,
Kenneth E. of Gilmanton m. Susan E. **Salls** of Gilmanton 6/16/1979

DAIGLE,
Raymond M. of Laconia m. Candace J. **LaRoche** of Gilmanton 8/4/1973; H - b. 1/1/1953 in NH, s/o Raymond J. Daigle (NH) and Lorraine Dupont (NH); W - b. 1/25/1953 in NH, d/o Alfred LaRoche (NH) and Melba Clifford (NH)
Robert J. of Gilmanton m. Melissa W. **Stevens** of Gilmanton 4/28/1990

DAIGNEAU,
Jason R. of Gilmanton m. Kim L. **Stone** of Gilmanton 4/4/1992
Robert A. of Gilmanton m. Carol A. Bilodeau **Leroux** of Laconia 1/23/1981
Robert Arthur of Gilmanton m. Wendy Orrie **Rand** of Warner 12/23/1967 in Warner; H - 21, Marine Corps, b. NH, s/o Arthur Howard Daigneau (VT) and Daura Nina Cass (VT); W - 19, office worker, b. NH, d/o Wesley Frand Rand (NH) and Pearl L. Swain (NH)

DAME,
Perley C. of Gilmanton m. Eva M. **Straw** of Gilmanton 7/2/1905 in Loudon; H - 22, farmer, b. New Durham, s/o Alonzo H. Dame

(Barrington, farmer) and Etta French (Farmington, housewife); W - 18, housemaid, b. Pittsfield, d/o George E. Straw (Pittsfield, farmer) and Eva M. Emerson (Northwood, housewife)

DANBY,
Craig James of Gilmanton m. Pamela Louise **Kelley** of Wells, ME 5/4/1991

Scott Raymond of Gilmanton m. Holly Beth **Keyser** of Sanbornton 10/15/1994

DANDENEAU,
Joseph B. of Gilmanton m. Janet M. **MacIn** of Gilmanton 11/29/1986

DANIS,
Robert Edumond of Pittsfield m. Sandra Jean **Denault** of Gilmanton 2/22/1960 in Pittsfield; H - 21, shoeworker, b. NH, s/o Gilbert J. Danis (NH) and Rose E. Labbie (NH); W - 17, at home, b. MD, d/o Eugene Denault (MA) and Daisy M. Burris (MA)

DARBYSHIRE,
Paul Michael of Gilmanton m. Carol **Gallien** of Gilmanton 11/5/1991

DAVIES,
David Penchoen of Ft. Collins, CO m. Ruth Ann **de la Garza** of Ft. Collins, CO 8/4/1999

DAVIS,
Duane M. of Tucson, AZ m. Tracy J. **Smithers** of Tucson, AZ 7/19/1992

Elmer G. of Gilmanton m. Lena M. **Ellsworth** of Gilmanton 3/10/1910 in Belmont; H - 23, farmer, b. Lowell, MA, s/o Edward A. Davis (Webster, MA, farmer) and Celia L. Gay (Lowell, MA, housewife); W - 20, housemaid, b. Gilmanton, d/o Alfred P. Ellsworth (Gilmanton, farmer) and Hannah P. B'rningham (England, housewife)

Elwin W. of Gilmanton m. Grace M. **Rowe** of Gilmanton 6/25/1910 in Laconia; H - 30, laborer, b. Island Pond, VT, s/o William Davis (Island Pond, VT, farmer) and Helen C. Worthley (Island Pond, VT, housewife); W - 16, housemaid, b. Belmont, d/o Fred E. Rowe (Belmont, teamster) and Minnie L. White (Windsor, VT, dressmaker)

Frank A. of Boston, MA m. Anna Belle **Dimick** of Gilmanton 10/27/1891; H - 25, observer in U.S. weather inst., b. Lee, s/o Albert W. Davis (Lee, farmer) and Sarah E. Randall (Milton, housewife); W - 23, student, b. Gilmanton, d/o William Dimick and Anna M. Folsom (Gilmanton, housewife)

Frederick Alvah of Pittsfield m. Josephine Sybil **Place** of Gilmanton 6/12/1915 in Pittsfield; H - 21, shoemaker, b. Northwood, s/o John E. Davis (Barnstead, shoemaker) and Mary E. Rogers (Bedford, housewife); W - 22, housekeeper, 2nd, b. Gilmanton I. W., d/o Jesse F. Place (Alton, wood work) and Grace W. Page (Gilmanton I. W., housewife)

George E. of Gilmanton m. Irene M. **Page** of Gilmanton 7/3/1926; H - 37, marine engineer, 2nd, b. Dover, s/o Reuben Davis (Dover, surveyor) and Flora B. Wiley (Barrington, housework); W - 18, housework, b. Gilmanton, d/o William A. Page (Gilmanton, farmer) and Sarah Buckman (Bridgewater, VT, housework)

Lester Charles of Gilmanton m. Helen May **Joy** of Pittsfield 11/10/1951 in Pittsfield; H - 21, woodsman, b. NH, s/o George E. Davis (NH) and Irene Page (NH); W - 18, at home, b. NH, d/o Calvin Joy (NH) and Gladys Fifield (NH)

Richard Poole of Laconia m. Gayle Taylor **Aycock** of Gilmanton 6/16/1962; H - 31, engineer, b. NH, s/o Philip C. Davis (VT) and Gertrude Collins (NH); W - 20, student, b. MA, d/o Thomas W. Aycock (GA) and Shirley Ruth MacNeil (MA)

Robert Bruce of Gilmanton m. G. Marie **Bousquet** of Gilmanton 6/30/1998

Seldon J. of Gilmanton m. Myra E. **Jones** of Gilmanton 1/4/1888 in Tilton; H - 24, stage driver, b. Springfield, s/o Samuel L. Davis (Springfield, stage driver) and Edna A. Pillsbury (Springfield, housewife); W - 21, dressmaker, b. Gilmanton, d/o James A. Jones (Gilmanton, miller) and Mary E. Locke (Gilmanton, housewife)

DAWSON,

Robert William of Gilmanton m. Lee Edna **Wheet** of Barnstead 5/12/1962; H - 28, farming, b. NH, s/o Joseph C. Dawson (MA) and Mary C. Fantom (MA); W - 26, at home, b. NH, d/o Rexford E. Wheet (NH) and Bessie W. McDuffee (NH)

DAY,

Larry V., Sr. of Gilmanton m. Carol A. **McLeod** of Gilmanton 5/18/1986

William F. of Gilmanton m. Lucille Therese **Labonte** of Gilmanton I. W. 6/28/1975 in Manchester; H - b. 1/9/1953 in NH, s/o Charles Day (NH) and Rose Engberg (MS); W - b. 1/18/1954 in NH, d/o Andre Labonte (NH) and Theresa Hardy (NH)

DEAN,

John K. of Gilmanton m. Karen E. **Miller** of Gilmanton 12/19/1998 (see following entry)

John Kelly of Gilmanton m. Karen Elizabeth **Miller** of Gilmanton 10/19/1998 (see preceding entry)

DEBOW,

Ronald D. of Sanbornville m. Tina M. **Phillips** of Gilmanton 6/5/1982

DECORMIER,

Robert Armand of Laconia m. Janis Louise **Chamberlain** of Gilmanton 1/15/1968; H - b. 9/25/1946 in NH, s/o Armand Decormier (Canada) and Gabrielle Paquette (NH); W - b. 1/14/1947 in NH, d/o Robert Chamberlain (ME) and Marjorie Seavey (MA)

DEES,

Jesse W. of Cambridge, MA m. Francis **Sherwood** of Cambridge, MA 5/26/1913; H - 32, clergyman, b. Vergennes, IL, s/o Byron Dees (Dugnom, IL, farmer) and Naomi Riggs (Waltonville, IL, housewife); W - 26, housemaid, b. Cambridge, MA, d/o Frank Sherwood (Harrison, NY, salesman) and Martha Reed (Philadelphia, housewife)

DEFLUMERO,
Lawrence of Walpole, MA m. Mabel D. Moreau **Maltais** of Wrentham, MA 7/4/1964; H - 50, carpenter, b. MA, s/o Nicola DeFlumero (Italy) and Angelina Losco (Italy); W - 56, machine op., b. Canada, d/o Elzear E. Moreau (Canada) and Mary J. Billeau (Canada)

DEMERIT,
Nelson L. of Gilmanton m. Marion **Bloom** of Concord 1/18/1932 in Saxton's River, VT; H - 27, laborer, b. Barrington, s/o Samuel Demerit (Barrington) and Elizabeth Locke (Dover); W - 18, b. Randolph, MA, d/o Edgerton Bloom (Canada) and Florence McDonald (Cambridge, MA)

DERBY,
Wayne A. of Bethlehem m. Suzanne B. **Schott** of Bethlehem 10/4/1980

DESILETS,
Douglas H. of Gilmanton m. Coreen K. **Zela** of Gilmanton 8/30/1997

DESMARIS,
Michael F. of Concord m. Ethel-Marie **Giuliano** of Gilmanton 6/26/1976 in Laconia; H - b. 9/10/1952 in NH, s/o George Desmaris (NH) and Irene Brochu (NH); W - b. 7/23/1952 in MA, d/o Domenic Giuliano (MA) and Helen Crowder (MA)

DESROCHERS,
Aleck of Gilmanton m. Luella B. **Ackerman** of Gilmanton 10/5/1919 in Loudon Ridge; H - 40, laborer, 2nd, b. Canada, s/o Joseph Desrochers (Canada) and Saphrena Desrochers (Canada); W - 37, housework, 2nd, b. Gilmanton, d/o Alonzo C. Burbank (Hopkinton) and Lucia Dustin (Haverhill, MA)

DEWARE,
Robert W., Jr. of Gilmanton m. Leona J. **Durette** of Laconia 5/29/1948 in Gilford; H - 20, US Navy, b. MA, s/o Robert W. Deware (Pike, machinist) and Mary Brown (Laconia, cashier); W - 18, Gilbert Clock Co., b. Gilford, d/o Lorenzo Durette

(Canada, bldg. construction) and Josephine Marchand (Concord, at home)

DICKINSON,
Thomas J. of Johnsonburg, PA m. Susan M. **Aiello** of Johnsonburg, PA 7/6/1988

DIMOCK,
Ronald V., Jr. of Gilmanton m. Joyce E. **Gale** of Gilmanton 12/18/1966; H - 23, student, b. MA, s/o Ronald V. Dimock (MA) and Barbara Louise Raddin (MA); W - 22, reg. nurse, b. NY, d/o Robert S. Gale (MA) and Julia K. Korodin (PA)

DIMOND,
Chester L. of Gilmanton m. Hazel G. **Bunker** of Newport 11/25/1937 in Winchester; H - 31, mill hand, 2nd, b. Detroit, MI, s/o Harry Dimond and Clara Saunders (NS); W - 37, mill worker, 2nd, b. Wolcott, VT, d/o William S. Carpenter (Danville, VT) and Avis Richardson (Lowell, VT, project work)
Chester Lacy m. Florence Bell **Gilman** 7/14/1923

DION,
Rodney Donat of Gilmanton I. W. m. Betty A. Riddinger **Javery** of Gilmanton I. W. 12/12/1978; H - b. 4/24/1957 in VT, s/o Donat Diuon (Quebec) and Laurette Bouchard (ME); W - b. 2/2/1957 in FL, d/o George K. Riddinger (MI) and Mary L. Javery (CT)
Rudolphe Louis of Gilmanton m. Michelle Leigh **Paige** of Gilmanton 8/17/1996

DIVERS,
Andrew S. of Laconia m. Rachel R. **Hyslop** of Gilmanton 5/1/1982
David M. of Laconia m. Sally J. **Hyslop** of Gilmanton 10/10/1980
John E. of Laconia m. Mary G. **Moore** of Gilmanton 6/9/2001

DODGE,
Paul T., Jr. of Gilmanton m. Beverly L. **Tippett** of Gilmanton 12/15/1984

DOE,
Frederick E. of Gilmanton m. Jane A. **Morse** of Gilmanton 6/28/1980

Frederick Earl of Gilmanton m. Patricia Louise **Hill** of Gilmanton 5/28/1964 in Loudon; H - 26, Air Force, b. NH, s/o Claude A. Doe (NH) and Florence A. Emerson (NH); W - 16, at home, b. NH, d/o Joseph P. Hill (NH) and Blanche E. Morse (NH)

Melvin B. of Gilmanton m. Patricia L. Doe **Hill** of Gilmanton 9/22/1978 in Loudon; H - b. 8/6/1934 in NH, s/o Claude A. Doe (NH) and Florence Emerson (NH); W - b. 2/27/1948 in NH, d/o Joseph P. Hill (NH) and Blanche E. Batchelder (NH)

DOHERTY,
Brad S. of Lawrence, MA m. Sandra A. **Weatherbee** of Gilmanton 8/21/1999

DONAGHY,
Barry M. of Gilmanton m. Silvia L. **Malcolm** of Gilmanton 7/4/1980

DONOVAN,
Michael A. of Laconia m. Janet L. **Thompson** of Gilmanton I. W. 4/5/1975 in Lakeport; H - b. 2/17/1955 in NH, s/o John L. Donovan (NH) and Constance P. Piuma (NH); W - b. 5/22/1956 in NH, d/o Edward Thompson (MA) and Angela Delafano (MA)

DORE,
Alan Michael of Gilmanton m. Cynthia Jane **Quimby** of Somersworth 6/10/1972; H - b. 10/20/1950 in NH, s/o Myron Dore (NH) and Elizabeth Dunbar (NH); W - b. 4/24/1950 in NH, d/o William Quimby (NH) and Nellie Perrin (VT)

Brian K. of Gilmanton m. Linda Lou Miller **Hunter** of Salem 7/6/1974; H - b. 6/19/1948 in NH, s/o Myron Dore (NH) and Elizabeth Dunbar (NH); W - b. 1/26/1941 in IN, d/o Robert Hunter (KY) and Inez Adkins (IN)

Steven Brent of Gilmanton m. Linda Lea **Locke** of Hanover 3/21/1970 in Concord; H - b. 7/16/1949 in NH, s/o Myron Winslow Dore (NH) and Elizabeth B. Dunbar (NH); W - b.

12/17/1948 in CA, d/o Arthur J. Locke (NH) and Lorraine Cochrane (NH)

DORLEY,
Robert E. of Gilmanton m. Candice J. **Marcoux** of Gilmanton 12/31/2001

DOSTER,
Douglas S. of Franklin m. Orry R. Matulonis **Gibbs** of Gilmanton 12/20/1978 in Gilford; H - b. 11/22/1946 in MD, s/o Howard E. Doster (MD) and Rose W. Eder (Germany); W - b. 2/2/1951 in MA, d/o Edward Gibbs (MA) and Violet Orry Arnold (MA)

DOUCETTE.,
Robert C. of Gilmanton m. Elaine A. Monfette **Fillion** of Gilmanton 5/17/1981
Robert G. of Gilmanton m. Lucille L. Crews **Lievens** of Manchester 9/22/1978 in Manchester; H - b. 11/22/1930 in MA, s/o Arthur Doucette (MA) and Mary Palladino (MA); W - b. 5/21/1948 in NH, d/o Robert Lievens (NH) and Beatrice Brunelle (NH)

DOW,
Oscar C. of Gilmanton m. Zilla N. **Pease** of Gilmanton 7/2/1903; H - 21, teacher, b. Gilmanton, s/o Daniel Dow (Madbury, farmer) and Olive A. Chase (Gilmanton); W - 18, housemaid, b. Gilmanton, d/o Fred V. Pease (Gilmanton, carpenter) and Annie L. Pierce (Loudon)
William E. L. of Gilmanton m. Beulah A. **Flynn** of Lancaster 8/11/1909; H - 22, painter, b. Graniteville, MA, s/o James M. Dow (Laconia, carpenter) and Maria E. Fennell (NB, housewife); W - 18, dressmaker, b. Guildhall, VT, d/o John B. Flynn (Guildhall, VT, drover) and Annie M. Reed (Concord, dressmaker)

DOWNING,
Gregory Michael of Gilmanton m. Pauline Elizabeth **Price** of Gilmanton 7/13/1974; H - b. 12/12/1955 in MA, s/o Paul Downing (MA) and Lois Leonard (MA); W - b. 6/15/1955 in NH, d/o A. Richard Price (NH) and Pauline Richards (MA)

Herbert W. of Gilmanton m. Margaret A. **McLeod** of Loudon 7/3/1900 in Loudon; H - 25, farmer, b. Gilmanton, s/o L. W. Downing (farmer) and Martha Webber (Gilmanton); W - 24, dressmaker, b. PEI, d/o James McLeod and Mary McLaughlin

Ned W. of Weston m. Carol L. **Burdett** of Brighton 9/6/1972; H - b. 7/29/1946 in ME, s/o Harold L. Downing (ME) and Agatha Smith (ME); W - b. 8/26/1948 in CT, d/o Leonard Dean Burdett (MA) and Dorothy Nesbitt (OH)

DOWNS,
James A. of Derry m. Leann **Warburton** of Gilmanton 9/9/1990
John E. m. Ethel May **Leavitt** 4/8/1923

DOYLE,
James F. of Gilmanton m. Lydia C. **Riley** of Gilmanton 3/3/1979

DREW,
David J. of Loudon m. Edith A. **Adams** of Gilmanton 5/19/1913 in Gilmanton I. W.; H - 21, farmer, b. Boscawen, s/o William Drew (farmer) and Lucinda Drew (housewife); W - 20, housemaid, b. Mason, d/o Henry Adams (Mason) and Jennie Brooks (Brooklyn)

DROWN,
Bradford G. of Gilmanton m. Isidore **Kamilis** of Gilmanton 12/16/2000

DUANE,
Richard Daniel, Jr. of Gilmanton m. Tamara Jane **Lynch** of Gilmanton 5/25/1996

DUBUC,
Russell T. of Gilmanton m. Dereth W. **French** of Deerfield 7/4/1986

DUCA,
William H., Jr. of Gilmanton m. Jill H. **Joki** of Gilmanton 8/11/1990

DUDMAN,
Gary S. of Gilmanton m. Karen L. **Buckley** of Gilmanton 7/7/1984

DUGAL,
Drew L. of Gilmanton m. Adrienne G. **Martin** of Gilmanton
    10/5/1985

DULUDE,
Douglas D. of Dunbarton m. Marcia L. **Barnard** of Gilmanton
    12/26/1963 in Dunbarton; H - 20, store, b. NH, s/o Octave J.
    Dulude (NH) and Gertrude E. Putnam (NH); W - 18, at home,
    b. NH, d/o Beverly G. Eastman (NH) and Ethel W. Dawes
    (ME)

DUNBAR,
Raleigh E., Jr. of Laconia m. Donna Lee **Blajda** of Gilmanton
    7/9/1983

DUNHAM,
Richard M., Jr. of Gilmanton m. Margaret Lynne **Ward** of Gilmanton
    7/1/1978; H - b. 3/30/1949 in MA, s/o Richard M. Dunham, Sr.
    (MA) and Jean Crowell (MA); W - b. 8/11/1948 in IL, d/o
    Jackson F. Ward (IL) and Frances J. Fry (IL)

DUNN,
Robert B. of Peabody, MA m. Mabel M. **Reid** of Peabody, MA
    2/7/1918; H - 20, machinist, b. NB, s/o John Dunn (NB) and
    Emma Oulton (NB); W - 19, house maid, b. NB, d/o John Reid
    (NB) and Catherine McLean (NB)
Robert G. of Gilmanton m. Lucille **Aldrich** of Gilmanton 1/23/1982

DUPUIS,
Edward Paul of Gilmanton m. Marsha Joan **Metalious** of Gilmanton
    9/10/1961; H - 23, construction, b. MA, s/o Norman Dupuis and
    Dorothy LaPierre; W - 18, at home, b. NH, d/o George
    Metalious and Grace M. deRepentigny

DURGIN,
Arthur Leyland of Gilmanton m. Florence Belle **Merrill** of Gilmanton
    8/1/1915 in E. Rochester; H - 35, farmer, b. New Durham, s/o
    Nehemiah Durgin (New Durham, farmer) and Ida Belle
    McKean (Sweden, ME, housewife); W - 31, teacher, b.

Gilmanton, d/o Frank N. Merrill (Stoneham, MA, farmer) and Clara Page (Barnstead, housewife)

DUSO,
W. N. of Warner m. Mary E. **Page** of Gilmanton 3/1/1910 in Gilmanton I. W.; H - 34, farmer, b. Warner, s/o Joseph Duso (Canada, farmer) and Melinda Ewins (Warner, housewife); W - 27, housework, b. Gilmanton, d/o Albert R. Page (Gilmanton, farmer) and Addie C. Clement (Alton, housewife)

DUTTON,
Douglas E. of Laconia m. Charity E. **Dow** of Gilmanton 5/8/1987

DYER,
Joseph N. of Gilmanton m. Athalee L. **Groton** of Gilmanton 7/27/1916 in Gilmanton I. W.; H - 50, chopper, 2nd, b. Chesterville, ME, s/o Charles Dyer (Lisbon, ME, blacksmith) and Vilette Crockett (Wilton, ME, housework); W - 20, housekeeper, b. Washington, ME, d/o George W. Groton (ME, farmer) and Lila A. Bragg (Washington, ME, housewife)
Roland of Gilmanton m. Myra **Houston** of Gilmanton 12/2/1916 in Gilmanton I. W.; H - 19, fireman, b. New Vineyard, ME, s/o Joseph Dyer (Lisbon, ME, chopper) and Mary Billman (housewife); W - 20, housework, b. Washington, ME, d/o George Groton (Aroostic Co., ME, farmer) and Lillian Bragg (Washington, ME, housework)

DYMOND,
George Charles of Gloucester, MA m. Laura May **Jones** of Gloucester, MA 8/22/1962; H - 20, cook, b. MA, s/o Charles Andrew Dymond (MA) and Vencenzina Lentine (MA); W - 18, baby sitter, b. MA, d/o Clarence William Jones (MA) and Evelyn Moore (MA)

EAGLES,
Charles Malcolmson of Gilmanton m. Diane I. **Todd** of Gilmanton 8/12/1988

EASTMAN,
Albert N. of Gilmanton m. Suzanne M. **Lewis** of Concord 6/19/1992

Clifford C. of Laconia m. Antoinette **Thompson** of Gilmanton 3/10/1945; H - 24, Marine Corps, b. Berlin, s/o Richard Eastman (Paris, ME, retired) and Edith Seavey (Elgin, IL, housewife); W - 18, at home, b. Gilmanton, d/o Maro B. Thompson (Wilmington, MA, lumberman) and Cordelia Carpenter (Fall River, housewife)

Douglas R. of Gilmanton m. Linda A. **Joyce** of Gilmanton 3/22/1986

Gordon Merle of Gilmanton m. Debra Ellen **Graffam** of Kittery, ME 12/2/1972 in Portsmouth; H - b. 9/28/1943 in CT, s/o Beverly G. Eastman (NH) and Ethel L. Dawes (ME); W - b. 1/8/1953 in ME, d/o Walter D. Graffam (ME) and Ruth G. Trian (ME)

EATON,

Frank G. of Gilmanton m. Edith L. **Wyatt** of Barnstead 12/8/1901; H - 25, laborer, b. Loudon, s/o William Eaton (Barnstead, laborer) and Rachel Allen (Laconia, housewife); W - 18, housekeeper, b. Farmington, d/o Asa Wyatt (farmer) and Belle Wyatt (housewife)

EDDY,

Dean E. of Gilmanton m. Catherine A. **Hardy** of Tilton 6/6/1987

EDGERLY,

Carlton J. of Gilmanton m. Sadie P. **Ross** of Gilmanton 11/2/1892; H - 21, farmer, b. Gilmanton, s/o Ida Edgerly (Gilmanton, housewife); W - 15, housekeeper, b. Gilmanton, d/o Clara I. Ross (Gilmanton, housewife)

Frank A. of Gilmanton m. Mary R. **Morgan** of Gilmanton 9/5/1906; H - 20, teacher, b. Nashville, s/o Albert T. Edgerly (Sanbornton, salesman) and Katherine Keyes (Sycamore, IL, housewife); W - 23, teacher, b. Quebec, d/o David M. Morgan (Thornton, farmer) and Alice A. Metcalf (Cookshire, Que., housewife)

George D. of Gilmanton m. Lavinnia E. **Gooch** of Alton 10/16/1937 in Wolfeboro; H - 23, shoemaker, b. Gilmanton I. W., s/o Roy Edgerly (Gilmanton I. W., farmer) and Minnie McLean (Barre, VT, housewife); W - 16, student, b. Alton, d/o Wilbur F. Gooch (Alton, foreman) and Bertha Elkins (Melrose, MA, housekeeper)

Roy C. of Gilmanton m. Minnie F. **McLean** of Hardwick, VT 2/19/1902; H - 24, farmer, b. Gilmanton, s/o David E. Edgerly (Gilmanton, farmer) and Hannah T. Hussey (Barnstead, housewife); W - 20, milliner, b. Barre, VT, d/o George B. McLean (St. George, NB, stone polisher) and Amy H. Lee (St. George, NB, housewife)

Walter J. of Gilmanton m. Anna M. **Cogswell** of Gilmanton 10/31/1894; H - 26, merchant, b. Gilmanton, s/o George W. Edgerly (Gilmanton, farmer) and Angeline V. Smith (Gilmanton, housekeeper); W - 20, b. Gilmanton, d/o Thomas Cogswell (Gilmanton, lawyer) and Florence M. Mooers (Manchester)

EISENHAUER,

John D. of Gilmanton m. Anita B. **Goupil** of Laconia 2/19/1977 in Laconia; H - b. 1/2/1958 in MA, s/o Earl A. Eisenhauer (MA) and Beverly Miller (MA); W - b. 5/15/1957 in NH, d/o Leonce J. Goupil (NH) and Eva Jarvis (NH)

EKLUND,

H. William of Norwood, MA m. Diana Carnegie **Sears** of Cambridge, MA 5/26/1962; H - 36, technician, b. MA, s/o Oscar R. Eklund (Sweden) and Elna C. Carlson (Sweden); W - 25, secretary, b. MA, d/o Keith C. Steele (MA) and Jane B. Smith (MA)

ELKINS,

John T. of Gilmanton m. Cora B. **Ham** of Gilmanton 11/20/1887 in Pittsfield; H - 26, farmer, b. Gilmanton, s/o Daniel H. Elkins (Gilmanton, farmer) and Liberty W. Ham (Farmington, housewife); W - 25, housewife, b. Gilmanton, d/o John W. Ham (Gilmanton, farmer) and Abbie Y. Varney (Augusta, ME, housewife)

ELLINGSON,

William Roger of Laconia m. Evelyn Mabel **Fosie** of Gilmanton 6/16/1963; H - 30, pressman, b. WI, s/o William C. Ellingson (WI) and Melva V. Johns (WI); W - 29, bookkeeper, b. NH, d/o David M. Bickford (NH) and Lizzie E. Twombly (NH)

ELLIOTT,
Anthony C. of Gilmanton I.W. m. Kristen A. **Goodreau** of Gilmanton I.W. 11/16/2001
Robert A. of Gilmanton m. Andrea S. **Hammond** of Gilmanton 9/4/1982

ELLIS,
Herbert A. of Gilmanton m. Blanche L. **Beck** of Gilmanton 7/27/1904; H - 40, farmer, b. Alton, s/o Moses A. Ellis (Alton, farmer) and Sally Lougee; W - 18, housemaid, b. Gilmanton, d/o James H. Beck (farmer) and Martha J. Leighton
Horace D. of Gilmanton m. Audrey M. **Fatello** of Gilmanton 7/7/1945 in Chichester; H - 26, mill worker, b. Sanbornville, s/o Henry P. Ellis (Gilmanton, carpenter) and Lelia I. Patch (Shapleigh, ME, housewife); W - 24, at home, b. Laconia, d/o Frank O. Dowst (Pittsfield, police officer) and Lillian Bies (Lynn, MA, waitress)
John Maurice of Gilmanton m. Christine Ann **Lockwood** of Gilmanton 6/12/1999
Oscar Alfred of Gilmanton m. Gladys B. **Ellis** of Alton 6/15/1920 in Norwich, VT; H - 30, farmer, b. Gilmanton, s/o Horace D. Ellis (Alton) and Ella Page (Gilmanton); W - 31, housekeeping, b. Alton, d/o Elbridge Ellis (Alton) and Elizabeth Hayes (Alton)

ELLSWORTH,
Alfred P. of Gilmanton m. Hannah B. **Ellsworth** of Gilmanton 2/2/1888; H - 29, farmer, b. Gilmanton, s/o John Ellsworth (Gilmanton, farmer) and Calista B. Ellsworth (Gilmanton, housewife); W - 34, housewife, b. Norwich, England
Earle M. of Gilmanton m. Blanche E. **Greenleaf** of Gilmanton 2/4/1912 in Belmont; H - 19, farmer, b. Gilmanton, s/o Alfred P. Ellsworth (Gilmanton, farmer) and Hannah Burnin'han (Norwich, England, housewife); W - 26, 2nd, b. Gilmanton, d/o John Pease (Gilmanton, farmer) and Nancy Greenough (housewife)
Leon E. of Gilmanton m. Bertha **Zilichovsky** of Vienna, Austria 9/19/1909 in Laconia; H - 30, farmer, b. Gilmanton, s/o Euraldo P. Ellsworth (Gilmanton, farmer) and Mary E. Allen (NY, housewife); W - 26, cook, b. Vienna, Austria, d/o John

Zilichovsky (Vienna, landlord) and Susana Fherban (Vienna, housewife)

Lester H. of Gilmanton m. Alice May **Gilman** of Belmont 6/13/1899; H - 19, farmer, b. Gilmanton, s/o E. P. Ellsworth (Gilmanton, farmer) and Mary Allen (NY, housewife); W - 17, housemaid, b. Gilford, d/o Ed Gilman (NY, painter) and Lizzie Leavitt (Gilford, housewife)

EMBERLEY,
Kevin T. of Gilmanton I. W. m. Patrice M. **Beaver** of Gilmanton I. W. 5/30/1975 in Seabrook; H - b. 5/2/1956 in MA, s/o George I. Emberley (MA) and Mary Buchanan (MA); W - b. 3/21/1956 in MA, d/o John W. Beaver (MA) and Edna Connolly (MA)

EMERSON,
Ansel of Barnstead m. Alice J. **Page** of Gilmanton 8/24/1892; H - 23, blacksmith, b. Barnstead, s/o Charles F. Emerson (Barnstead, farmer) and Emily J. Hall (Barnstead, housewife); W - 23, housekeeper, b. Gilmanton, d/o Harlan Paige (sic) (Gilmanton, shoemaker) and Lydia Sleeper (Alton, housewife)

Loren H. of Gilmanton m. Lena D. **Tardy** of Alton 11/26/1903 in E. Concord; H - 19, teamster, b. Canada, s/o Samuel Emerson (Brookfield, teamster) and Carrie L. Smith (Shelbyville, KY); W - 17, housemaid, d/o John Tardy (farmer)

EMERY,
Alden Chester of Gilmanton m. Jennie **Wallingford** of Rochester 11/9/1921 in Lebanon; H - 29, farmer, 2nd, b. Morrisville, VT, s/o Nathan Emery (Littleton) and Sarah Rich (Belvidere, VT); W - 18, stenographer, b. Rochester, d/o Charles Wallingford (New Durham) and Carribel Kendall (New Durham)

EVANS,
Benjamin Isaac of N. Clymer, NY m. Ruth May **Meekins** of Gilmanton 11/20/1951 in Gilmanton I. W.; H - 48, lumbering, b. NH, s/o Benjamin I. Evans (NH) and Nellie Mabel Rogers (MA); W - 24, shoeworker, b. NH, d/o Roy A. Meekins (Canada) and Addie M. Mardin (NH)

EVELETH,
Clarence M. of Gilmanton m. Lizzie M. **May** of Barton, VT 4/5/1887 in Tilton; H - 23, carpenter, b. Gilmanton, s/o Samuel E. Eveleth (Gilmanton, farmer) and Jennie H. Brown (Concord, housewife); W - 20, housewife, b. Barton, d/o Sanford May (farmer) and Sarah ----- (housewife)
Edwin Everett of Gilmanton m. Alice Moulton **Swift** of Boston, MA 4/23/1917; H - 44, farmer, b. Gilmanton, s/o Samuel E. Eveleth (Gilmanton) and Hannah J. Brown (Concord); W - 39, bookkeeper, b. Taunton, MA, d/o Albert B. Swift (Wilmington, VT) and Helen A. Moulton (Macon, GA)

EVERETT,
Adelbert T. of Gilmanton m. Elsie M. **Glidden** of Alton 1/26/1910 in Gonic; H - 32, clergyman, b. Waggoner, NS, s/o Jeremiah S. Everett (Plympton, NS, farmer) and Metilda Thibbetts (Plympton, NS); W - 24, teacher, b. Alton, d/o Fred E. Glidden (Wolfeboro, farmer) and Mary L. Jones (Alton, housewife)
Allen T. of Edmonds, WA m. Suzanne **Slater** of Gilmanton I.W. 10/26/2000

FABIAN,
Thomas Stephen of Gilmanton m. Janet Susan **Desrosiers** of Gilmanton 7/16/1993

FANCY,
Albert S. of Laconia m. Florence M. **Glidden** of Gilmanton 9/26/1926 in Laconia; H - 37, chauffeur, 2nd, b. NS, s/o Arthur Fancy (NS, blacksmith) and Bessie Patterson (NS, housework); W - 32, farming, 2nd, b. Gilmanton, d/o Charles Tibbetts (Gilmanton, farmer) and Ida M. Perkins (Gilmanton, housework)

FANNING,
John R. of Gilmanton m. Charmein L. **Blais** of Gilmanton 9/5/1987
Michael James of Gilmanton m. Jody Lee **Gullage** of Gilmanton 9/6/1998

FAULKNER,
William J. of Londonderry m. Robin **Seaman** of Hudson 9/30/1978; H - b. 10/1/1955 in CT, s/o Robert J. Faulkner, Sr. (CT) and Alma M. McConnell (CT); W - b. 11/3/1957 in NH, d/o William R. Seaman (NH) and Joann Gove (NH)

FEIGES,
Adam Joshua of Hinton, IA m. Alyssa Todd **McCulloch** of Hinton, IA 8/28/1993

FERNANDES,
Peter David of W. Wareham, MA m. Kathy Susan **Palladino** of W. Wareham, MA 6/2/2000

FILLION,
Jeffrie S. of Gilmanton m. Cindy L. **Clairmont** of Gilmanton 10/17/1992

FISH,
Stanley Allen of Loudon m. Karen E. **Moore** of Gilmanton 1/20/1978; H - b. 12/8/1960 in MA, s/o William L. Fish (VT) and Rachel Fillian (NH); W - b. 7/27/1959 in NH, d/o K. Richard Moore (NH) and Elaine Gordon (NH)

FITZ,
Spencer A. of Gilmanton m. Donna M. **Hawkes** of Gilmanton 9/12/1992

FITZGERALD,
Robert C. of Boston, MA m. Nancy A. **Cherry** of Boston, MA 7/29/1978; H - b. 6/6/1956 in MA, s/o Robert F. Fitzgerald (MA) and Virginia Carpenter (MA); W - b. 5/9/1955 in MA, d/o John A. Cherry (MA) and Eleanor Fisher (MA)

FLANDERS,
Lewis Rufus of Gilmanton m. Alice G. **Converse** of Gilmanton 11/27/1895; H - 19, sawyer, b. Gilmanton, s/o Asahel G. Flanders (Meredith, carpenter) and Lizzie E. Riggs (Gloucester, MA, housewife); W - 21, housekeeper, b.

Monson, MA, d/o Danforth L. Converse (Chicopee, MA, farmer) and Mary LeDoyt (Stafford, CT, housewife)

Robert J. of Pittsfield m. Grace E. **Davis** of Gilmanton 5/6/1956 in Chichester; H - 25, plumber, b. NH, s/o Rhuna N. Flanders (NH) and Fern M. Sargent (NH); W - 22, stitcher, b. NH, d/o George E. Davis (NH) and Irene M. Page (NH)

Victor C. m. Elsie V. **Purcell** 6/28/1922 in Loudon

FLYNN,

David of Gilmanton m. Kristine **Hoffman** of Gilmanton 4/19/1976; H - b. 6/11/1957 in NY, s/o Edgar A. Flynn (NY) and Allison Walsh (NY); W - b. 1/17/1961 in CT, d/o Edward Hoffman (NY) and Penelope Risley (CT)

FOGG,

Albion of Gilmanton m. Mary J. **Lafoe** of Gilmanton 4/–/1899; H - 24, laborer, b. Gilmanton, s/o David Fogg and Esther Fogg (Loudon, housewife); W - 18, housework, b. Lakeport, d/o Charles Lafoe (Canada, farmer) and Annie Lafoe (Lakeport, housewife)

Albion of Gilmanton m. Nellie R. **Dyer** of N. Sutton 11/28/1908; H - 32, farmer, 2nd, b. Gilmanton, s/o David S. Fogg (Gilmanton, blacksmith) and Esther Smith (Gilmanton, housewife); W - 18, housemaid, b. Danbury, d/o Joseph Dyer (Lewiston, ME, laborer) and Mary Billington (West Mills, ME, housewife)

Michael B. of Belmont m. Stephanie **Stevens** of Gilmanton 10/4/1986

Orlando of Gilmanton m. Annie M. **Ring** of Loudon 7/1/1897 in Belmont; H - 34, blacksmith, 2nd, b. Gilmanton, s/o David S. Fogg (Loudon, blacksmith) and Ester Fogg (Loudon, housewife); W - 29, housemaid, 2nd, b. Loudon, d/o Taylor Haines and Nancy Haines (Gilmanton, housewife)

FONTAINE,

Andrew J. of Belmont m. Evelyn M. **Richard** of Belmont 8/9/1965 in Littleton; H - 51, lathe operator, b. NH, s/o Charles E. Fontaine (Canada) and Maryrose Fortier (Canada); W - 44, nurse aide, b. NH, d/o Howard L. Reed (NH) and Mabel F. Hanaford (NH)

FORCIER,
Kenneth Paul of Gilmanton m. Charlene Elaine **Reynolds** of Gilmanton 11/27/1992

FORD,
Herbert F. of Gilmanton m. Lucille M. **Stickney** of Gilmanton 12/24/1932; H - 22, mechanic, b. Warner, s/o Leslie W. Ford (Saranac, NY, farmer) and Nellie Chase (Soldiers Valley, IA, housework); W - 18, at home, b. Lisbon, d/o Harold Stickney (Lyman, painter) and Salina Belware (Littleton, housework)

William A. of Nashua m. Muriel B. **Prescott** of Gilmanton 3/20/1954 in Hudson; H - 21, US Navy, b. NH, s/o Arthur Ford (NH) and Emma Glover (NH); W - 22, nurse, b. NH, d/o Harold F. Prescott (NH) and Caroline Eastman (MA)

FORST,
Brian Allen of Gilmanton m. Donna Marie **Smith** of Belmont 4/23/1988

FORSYTH,
George Scott of Gilmanton m. Mary Ann **Price** of Gilmanton 3/26/1966 in Pittsfield; H - 20, US Army, b. NH, s/o Harry G. Forsyth (Canada) and Evelyn G. Rollins (NH); W - 17, student, b. NH, d/o Amos Richard Price (NH) and Pauline M. Richardson (MA)

Harry G. of Gilmanton m. Syble O. **Jordan** of Northfield 8/27/1932 in Northfield; H - 22, farmer, b. Canada, s/o Harvey Forsyth (Canada, farmer) and Florence E. Knott (Canada, housework); W - 18, housework, b. Lancaster, d/o Herman E. Jordan (Colebrook, shop mgr.) and Jennie E. Smith (Groveton, housework)

Harvey A. of Gilmanton m. Mary Ann **Graeme** of Gilmanton 4/10/1930; H - 49, farmer, 2nd, b. Arthur, Can., s/o William A. Forsyth (Harrisburgh, Can., brickmason) and Sarah A. McKay (Canada, housework); W - 40, housework, 3rd, b. Rothesham, England, d/o James Woodhouse (miner) and Louisa Alderston (Norfolk, Eng., at home)

Harvey A. of Gilmanton m. Marion L. **Jordan** of Gilmanton 5/19/1936 in Gilmanton I. W.; H - 55, farmer, 3rd, b. Arthur, Canada, s/o William A. Forsyth (ON, mason) and Sarah

McKay (ON, housework); W - 35, housework, 2nd, b. Piermont, d/o Herman Jordan (Canada) and Jennie Smith (Groveton, housework)

Michael Stanley of Gilmanton m. Laurie Elizabeth **McDonough** of Manchester 9/12/1970 in Manchester; H - b. 4/13/1947 in NH, s/o Harry G. Forsyth (Canada) and Evelyn Rollins (NH); W - b. 8/10/1948 in NH, d/o William J. McDonough (NH) and Winifred Akey (NH)

Ralph Gordon of Gilmanton m. Leslie Ann **Brown** of Ctr. Barnstead 5/18/1974; H - b. 6/21/1942 in NH, s/o Harry G. Forsyth (Canada) and Evelyn Rollins (NH); W - b. 10/13/1946 in MA, d/o Charles Brown (NY) and Elizabeth Godfrey (MA)

FORTIN,

Paul Damase of Gilmanton m. Mary Frances **Herzing** of Gilmanton 4/14/1974 in Laconia; H - b. 7/27/1949 in PA, s/o Paul M. Fortin (PA) and Marian Pilarski (PA); W - b. 7/29/1954 in CA, d/o Arthur F. Herzing (PA) and Mary Tramack (PA)

FORTUNA,

Steven E. of Newburyport, MA m. Kimberly A. **Dockham** of Gilmanton I. W. 10/2/1999

FOSIE,

Richard Elton of Alton m. Evelyn Mabel **Bickford** of Gilmanton 9/14/1951 in Alton; H - 21, lineman, b. NH, s/o Alfred L. Fosie (NH) and Thelma V. Wright (NH); W - 17, at home, b. NH, d/o David M. Bickford (NH) and Lizzie E. Twombly (NH)

FOSS,

Carroll E. of Gilmanton m. Bessie **Peaslee** of Gilmanton 5/13/1899; H - 18, farmer, b. Gilmanton, s/o Charles W. Foss (Deerfield, farmer) and Lucy J. Marsh (Gilmanton, housewife); W - 18, housemaid, b. Gilmanton, d/o Caleb W. J. Peaslee (Gilmanton, farmer) and Luanna M. Abbott (Warner, housewife)

Frank E. of Gilmanton m. Myra L. **Moulton** of Belmont 7/8/1897; H - 52, farmer, 2nd, b. Gilmanton, s/o Alvah Foss (Gilmanton, farmer) and Miriam Foss (Barnstead, housewife); W - 51, housemaid, b. Belmont, d/o Eben Moulton

Frank W. of Gilmanton m. Nettie R. **Peaslee** of Gilmanton
9/1/1900; H - 24, farmer, b. Gilmanton, s/o Charles W. Foss
(Deerfield, farmer) and Lucy J. Marsh (Gilmanton, housewife);
W - 22, housekeeper, b. Gilmanton, d/o Caleb W. J. Peaslee
(Gilmanton, farmer) and Luanna M. Abbott (Warner,
housewife)

Frank W. of Gilmanton m. Nellie C. **Whitehouse** of Barnstead
1/9/1908 in Lowell, MA; H - 32, farmer, 2nd, b. Gilmanton, s/o
C. Warren Foss (Alton, farmer) and Lucy J. Marsh (Gilmanton,
housewife); W - 23, housekeeper, b. Canada, d/o Charles
Whitehouse (Canada, stonemason) and Lucy Fifield (VT,
housewife)

Frank W. of Gilmanton m. Florence A. **Foss** of Strafford 7/6/1913
in Ctr. Strafford; H - 37, farmer, 3rd, b. Gilmanton, s/o Charles
W. Foss (Alton, farmer) and Lucy J. Marsh (Gilmanton,
housewife); W - 24, teacher, b. Strafford, d/o Henry R. Foss
(Strafford, farmer) and Addie Tripp (Barnstead, housewife)

John Henry of Gilmanton m. Elizabeth N. **Davis** of Barnstead
2/27/1892 in Pittsfield; H - 31, shoemaker, 2nd, b. Gilmanton,
s/o John Foss (Alton, carpenter) and Emily Foss (Alton,
housewife); W - 40, housekeeper, 2nd, b., New York City, d/o
John Neville (iron worker)

John Henry of Gilmanton m. Nina M. **Higgins** of Barnstead
11/12/1921; H - 60, RR employee, 5th, b. Haverhill, MA, s/o
John Foss (Alton) and Emily A. Watson (Alton); W - 22,
housekeeper, b. Fairlee, VT, d/o Frank Higgins (VT) and Sadie
Porter (VT)

Richard C. of Gilmanton m. Lois R. **Towle** of Gilmanton 4/11/1987

FOSTER,

John Robert of Gilmanton m. Jennifer Ann **Goodall** of Gilmanton
10/17/1991

Robert B. of Laconia m. Lorraine **Griffin** of Gilmanton 6/15/1957; H
- 24, student, b. NH, s/o Charles S. Foster (ME) and Ruth A.
Atherton (NH); W - 20, student, b. NH, d/o Harold W. Griffin
(NH) and Doris Davis (NH)

FRARY,

Arthur Frederick of Gilmanton m. Frances Jane **Manning** of
Gilmanton 11/10/1964 in Alton; H - 68, retired, b. MA, s/o
Frederick A. Frary (MA) and Charlotte A. Dyke (Canada); W -

62, retired, b. MA, d/o Walter R. Clancy (MA) and Mary J. Kennedy (Canada)

FRASER,
William P. of Pittsfield m. Janique A. **Riel** of Gilmanton I. W. 11/11/1978 in Pittsfield; H - b. 10/10/1952 in MA, s/o Leo W. Fraser (MA) and Patricia A. Murray (MA); W - b. 8/27/1956 in NH, d/o Armand W. Riel (MA) and Nelda A. Elkins (NH)

FREEMAN,
Francis R. of Gilmanton m. Michele E. **Begin** of Laconia 10/18/1980
Jerry R., Sr. of Gilmanton m. Gwendolyn A. **Fournier** of Gilmanton 4/17/1980
Murray Sumner of Boston, MA m. Linda Joyce **Lerner** of Boston, MA 9/4/1999

FRENCH,
Arthur W. of Gilmanton m. Florence A. **Wight** of Gilmanton 12/25/1913; H - 31, teacher, b. Haverhill, MA, s/o Eben E. French (Nottingham, shoemaker) and Ada M. Savery (Dixfield, ME, housewife); W - 23, teacher, b. Gilmanton, d/o Albert R. Wight (Gilmanton, farmer) and Emma F. Jones (Gilmanton, housewife)
Buzzie Bill of Gilmanton I. W. m. Elizabeth Ann **Dutton** of Laconia 6/24/1978 in Gilmanton I. W.; H - b. 10/24/1956 in NH, s/o William French (NH) and Laura Page (NH); W - b. 9/5/1959 in CA, d/o Mark Dutton (NH) and Catherine Hinshaw (CA)
Buzzie Bill of Gilmanton m. Susan **Jackson** of Gilmanton 8/22/1992
Clifton S. of Gilmanton m. E. Hope **Blood** of Pittsfield 6/5/1932 in Alton; H - 25, laborer, b. Gilmanton, s/o John S. French (Gilmanton, farmer) and Mary L. Pearl (Loudon, housework); W - 28, weaving, 2nd, b. Gilmanton, d/o Adolphe Blood (Chichester, farmer) and Augusta Clifford (Loudon, housework)
Fred S. of Gilmanton m. Mary **Latouche** of Loudon 11/25/1899; H - 26, farmer, b. Gilmanton, s/o Charles H. French (Gilmanton, farmer) and Luanna Newton (Loudon, housewife); W - 17, housemaid, d/o John H. Latouche (coal dealer) and Mary H. ---

Guy Charles of Laconia m. Frieda **Prendergast** of Gilmanton 10/17/1970; H - b. 7/29/1900 in NH, s/o George W. French (VT) and Vitaline Garland (NH); W - b. 7/17/1899 in NY, d/o Joseph Dashner (Bulgaria) and Mary A. Campbell (Canada)

Ivo P. of Gilmanton m. Althea M. **Fulton** of Manchester 9/3/1933 in Penacook; H - 27, farmer, b. Gilmanton, s/o John S. French (Gilmanton, farmer) and Mary L. Pearl (Loudon, housework); W - 23, teacher, b. Boston, MA, d/o William L. Fulton (Bedford, advertising) and Bessie L. Marston (Boston, MA, housework)

Ivo Shepard of Gilmanton m. Patricia Ann **Toutaint** of Laconia 6/30/1973 in Laconia; H - b. 4/25/1954 in NC, s/o William French (NH) and Laura Page (NH); W - b. 6/2/1954 in NH, d/o Armand Toutaint (NH) and Charlotte Smith (NH)

Jeremiah S. of Gilmanton m. Alice M. **Rogers** of Loudon 6/6/1916 in Loudon; H - 57, farmer, 2nd, b. Gilmanton, s/o Sylvester F. French (Gilmanton, farmer) and Mercy Hayes (Strafford, housewife); W - 40, domestic, 2nd, b. E. Concord, d/o John Welsh (Canaan, stone mason) and Eliza Kimball (Canterbury, housewife)

John S. of Gilmanton m. Mary L. **Pearl** of Loudon 3/30/1902 in Loudon; H - 40, farmer, b. Gilmanton, s/o George S. French (Gilmanton, farmer) and Martha A. Holmes (Strafford, housewife); W - 22, housemaid, b. Loudon, d/o Leroy Pearl (Loudon, farmer) and Rhoda Peaslee (Loudon, housewife)

Will A. of Gilmanton m. Annie M. **Carr** of Pittsfield 11/30/1899; H - 24, farmer, b. Gilmanton, s/o Merwin E. French (Gilmanton, farmer) and Addie M. Gilman (Gilmanton, housewife); W - 18, housemaid, b. Gilmanton, d/o John H. Carr (Gilmanton) and Belle F. True (Pittsfield)

FROST,

Maurice Arthur of Barnstead m. Jean Louise **McClary** of Gilmanton 11/19/1966 in Chichester; H - 19, mechanic, b. NH, s/o Arthur L. Frost (NH) and Betty Jane Frenette (NH); W - 19, manager, b. NH, d/o George F. A. McClary (NH) and Lura May Bunker (NH)

FUNK,

Wilfred John of Gilmanton m. Deborah Fowkes **Chase** of Gilmanton 8/12/2000

GAGNON,
Eugene W. of Gilmanton m. Dorothy **Hislop** of Gilmanton
  6/17/1930 in Belmont; H - 29, auto mechanic, b. Thetford,
  Can., s/o Octave Gagnon (St. Nasbert, Can., carpenter) and
  Rosanna Blanchet (St. Christophe, Can., housework); W - 23,
  attendant, b. Berwick, ME, d/o R. Willis Hislop (Strafford,
  farmer) and Bertha M. Ellis (Gilmanton, housework)

GALE,
Robert S. of Gilmanton m. Arletta M. **Herson** of Acton, ME
  1/27/1968; H - b. 2/12/1910 in Canada, s/o Robert E. Gale
  (Canada) and Annie L. Strum (Canada); W - b. 11/15/1916 in
  NH, d/o John J. Munsey (NH) and Julia F. Bruce (Canada)

GALLANT,
Michael Paul of Gilmanton m. Victoria Ann **Baptistella** of
  Gilmanton 8/21/1999

GALLIEN,
Timothy N. of Gilmanton m. Beth S. **Fitzgerald** of Gilmanton
  12/24/1991

GAMACHE,
Christopher Joseph of Gilmanton m. Kristina Ann **Toth** of
  Gilmanton 10/13/1996

GARD,
Bruce of Gilmanton m. Bette **Polley** of Laconia 2/22/1968 in
  Laconia; H - b. 5/9/1940 in NH, s/o John H. Gard, Jr. (NH) and
  Margaret O. Munsey (NH); W - b. 1/23/1941 in NH, d/o George
  L. Cutting (NH) and Ruth E. Young (NH)
Bruce Munsey of Gilmanton m. Nancy Ann **Osgood** of Loudon
  3/28/1964 in Loudon; H - 23, laborer, b. NH, s/o John H. Gard,
  Jr. (NH) and Margaret O. Munsey (NH); W - 21, student, b.
  NH, d/o William M. Osgood (NH) and Alice May Ross (NH)

GARDNER,
Andrew H. of Gilmanton m. June T. **Bassemir** of Centerport, NY
  11/17/1990
Andrew H. of Gilmanton m. Mary K. **Kaucher** of Laconia 3/28/1992

Leslie A. of Gilmanton m. Jacqueline **Geddes** of Gilmanton
6/23/1973; H - b. 7/29/1952 in NY, s/o Andrew Gardner (MA)
and Barbara Collins (MA); W - b. 6/21/1955 in NH, d/o David
Geddes (NH) and Anna Hogan (NH)

William H. of MA m. Noreen A. **McManus** of MA 2/7/1982

GARNEAU,
John M. of Gilmanton m. Ellen F. **Welch** of Gilmanton 2/18/1977 in
Pittsfield; H - b. 10/5/1940 in NH, s/o Leon J. Garneau (NH)
and Gertrude Fortin (NH); W - b. 4/29/1946 in ME, d/o Thomas
E. Flagg (ME) and Mildred Coathup (MA)

GARON,
Richard K. of Gilmanton m. Kathryn E. **Knott** of Franklin 7/5/1980

GASSETT,
Ronald Kenneth of Alton m. Linda Ann **Littlefield** of Gilmanton
1/26/1967; H - 18, shoe worker, b. NH, s/o Kenneth Eugene
Gassett (NH) and Arline Maryann Roy (NH); W - 17, at home,
b. NH, d/o George Ernest Littlefield (NH) and Ramona Earline
Bagley (NH)

GATES,
Sidney C. of Gilmanton m. Patricia L. **Perkins** of Pittsfield 4/6/1955
in Durham; H - 17, student, b. MA, s/o Kenneth G. Gates (NS)
and Elizabeth C. Freeman (NH); W - 19, student, b. NH, d/o
Robert E. Perkins (NH) and Flora I. Ide (NH)

GAULT,
Charles W. of Gilmanton m. Ida L. **Varney** of Rochester 2/28/1890;
H - 32, merchant, 2nd, b. Gilmanton, s/o George W. Gault
(Concord, merchant); W - 20, housewife, b. Rochester, d/o
George W. Varney (Dover, farmer) and Nancy Smith
(Rochester, housewife)

GEDDES,
David W., Jr. of Gilmanton m. Diane L. **Gray** of Pittsfield 6/14/1980
David Walter of Gilmanton m. Anna Alice **Hogan** of Gonic
7/26/1952 in Rochester; H - 25, lumber work, b. NH, s/o John
A. Geddes (Canada) and Florence A. Edgerly (NH); W - 18, at

home, b. NH, d/o Joseph I. Hogan (NY) and Pauline H. Terrill (ME)

Douglas M. of OR m. Virginia Mary **Potter** of Gilmanton 1/2/1968; H - 62, b. Canada, s/o Duncan Geddes (Canada) and Ida Wilson (Canada); W - 38, b. NH, d/o George G. Potter (NH) and Mildred Eva Page (MA)

Duncan John of Gilmanton m. Barbara A. **Tasker** of Strafford 6/13/1975; H - b. 6/16/1956 in NH, s/o David Geddes (NH) and Anna Hogan (NH); W - b. 8/23/1956 in NH, d/o Francis Tasker (NH) and Evelyn Corliss (NH)

John A. m. Florence A. **Edgerly** 4/8/1922

Kenneth D. of Gilmanton m. Abbie I. **Watson** of Lebanon, ME 4/14/1934 in Gilmanton I. W.; H - 27, shoeworker, b. Ontario, Can., s/o Duncan Geddes (ON, farmer) and Ida Wilson (ON, housework); W - 18, housework, b. Franklin, d/o Selvin Watson (Meredith, shoemaker) and Ida Stevens (Alton, housework)

GENTILE,
James Leonard, Jr. of Gilmanton m. Pamela Lynn **Dauphin** of Gilmanton 9/20/1997

GEORGIUS,
Robert H. of Gilmanton m. Denise D. Georgius **Dorwin** of Gilmanton 1/25/1988

GIBEAU,
Joseph L. of Gilmanton m. Nancy E. **Ness** of Gilmanton 6/28/1997

GILBERT,
Anthony Joseph of Gilmanton m. Rebekah Elizabeth **Price** of Gilmanton 10/12/1996

GILES,
Fred S. of Gilmanton m. Flora **Howe** of Franklin 7/13/1895 in Franklin; H - 32, machinist, b. Laconia, s/o Reuben Giles (carpenter) and Abbie Staniels (Chichester, housekeeper); W - 33, b. Franklin, d/o John M. Howe (Methuen, MA, machinist) and Emily J. Evans (Salem, MA, housewife)

Oscar A. of Gilmanton m. Loleta E. **Hill** of Haverhill, MA 9/8/1899; H - 21, machinist, b. Gilmanton, s/o Reuben Giles (Sanbornton) and Abbie Staniels (Chichester, housework); W - 18, typewriter, b. Haverhill, MA, d/o John Hill (Deerfield, shoemaker) and Addie M. Ladd (Deerfield, housewife)

GILKES,
Cooper A., Jr. of Gilmanton m. Christine F. **Bowes** of N. Woodstock 12/7/1963 in N. Woodstock; H - 43, scout executive, b. MA, s/o Cooper A. Gilkes, Sr. (B.W.I.) and Elsie Schrimier (MA); W - 43, clerk, b. NH, d/o Lyman E. Cloud (NH) and Clara M. Paschal (NH)

GILL,
Robert Allen of Gilmanton m. Dawn Marie **Elliott** of Gilmanton 3/16/1991

GILLE,
Paul of Gilmanton m. Cynthia **Currier** of Belmont 9/6/1980

GILMAN,
Arthur L. of Gilmanton m. Emma J. **Marsh** of Gilmanton 5/15/1896 in Laconia; H - 22, farmer, b. Gilmanton, s/o John T. Gilman (Gilmanton, farmer) and Sarah L. Dame (housewife); W - 18, housekeeper, b. Gilmanton, d/o Andrew H. Marsh and Martha E. McCarthy

Caleb K. of Gilmanton m. Charlotte B. **Hill** of Gilmanton 10/29/1893; H - 70, farmer, 5th, b. Gilmanton, s/o Nathaniel Gilman (sea captain) and Eliza Haines; W - 65, housekeeper, 2nd, b. Alton, d/o Stephen Dudley

Charles F. of Gilmanton m. Clara J. **Norton** 7/21/1910 in Pittsfield; H - 59, farmer, 2nd, b. Gilmanton, s/o Ira D. Gilman (Gilmanton, farmer) and Sarah J. French (Great Falls, housewife); W - 58, housework, 2nd, b. Sharon, VT, d/o Daniel Builard (E. Brookfield, MA, farmer) and Clarissa J. Batchelder (housewife)

Haven F. of Gilmanton m. Laura A. **Kendall** of Gilmanton 10/19/1908; H - 39, farmer, b. Gilmanton, s/o Enos F. Gilman (Gilmanton, farmer) and Annie L. Hancock (Boscawen, housewife); W - 37, housekeeper, b. Strafford, VT, d/o

Stephen E. Norton (Strafford, VT, farmer) and Clara J. Bullard (Fayette, VT, housewife)

Ira of Gilmanton m. Cora B. **York** of Gilmanton 2/17/1901; H - 34, farmer, b. Gilmanton, s/o Ira D. Gilman (Gilmanton, farmer) and Martha A. French (Dover, housewife); W - 18, housekeeper, b. Pittsfield, d/o Fred York (Pittsfield, farmer) and Anna Jones (Chichester, housewife)

Paul E. of Woodstock m. Lucile A. **Hawkins** of Gilmanton 9/1/1947; H - 22, mechanic, b. Woodstock, s/o Fred S. Gilman (Woodstock, woods supt.) and Florence A. Russell (Chelsea, MA, housewife); W - 24, teacher, b. Gilmanton, d/o Shurldin A. Hawkins (Boston, MA, farmer) and Amy Osborne (Gilmanton, housewife)

GLASS,

Darrell Winston of Gilmanton m. Tina Mae **Foley** of Concord 8/27/1994

GLEASON,

Frederick E., Jr. of Manchester m. Judith Helen **Baldwin** of Gilmanton 5/25/1991

GLIDDEN,

Charles H. of Boston, MA m. Mary G. **Orange** of Gilmanton 11/20/1889; H - 32, editor, b. Gilmanton, s/o David L. Glidden (Alton, stonecutter) and Elvira M. Glidden (Gilmanton, housewife); W - 26, housewife, b. Lowell, MA, d/o Henry S. Orange (Milton, retired merchant) and Elizabeth A. Orange (Somersworth, housewife)

William Leslie of Gilmanton m. Beulah Estelle (Horne) **Thompson** of Gilmanton 8/19/1969; H - b. 11/26/1924 in NH, s/o William C. Glidden (NH) and Mary Maud (MA); W - b. 8/13/1910 in NH, d/o George W. Horne (NH) and Ellie May Meserve (ME)

GLUM,

Christopher E. of Gilmanton m. Cynthia D. **McClintock** of Pittsfield 6/5/1976 in Chichester; H - b. 2/5/1957 in NY, s/o Edward F. Glum (NY) and Hope M. Miller (CA); W - b. 5/10/1957 in MA, d/o William McClintock (MA) and Elsie Terp (MA)

Edward F. of Gilmanton m. Jean **Henderson** of Penacook 6/30/1979

GOLDEN,
Alfred Kenneth of Gilmanton m. Thelma May **Rollins** of Gilmanton 12/10/1949 in New Durham; H - 21, US Army, b. NH, s/o John E. Golden (NY) and Nellie B. Locke (NH); W - 18, at home, b. NH, d/o Selden B. Rollins (NH) and Eva M. Jones (NH)

Patrick Michael of Gilmanton m. Carol Ann **Sawyer** of Epsom 11/4/1972 in Epsom; H - b. 5/25/1953 in NH, s/o Alfred K. Golden (NH) and Thelma M. Rollins (NH); W - b. 3/6/1955 in NH, d/o John W. Sawyer (NH) and Ruth M. Quimby (NH)

GOOCH,
Wilbur A. of Alton m. Bertha F. **Elkins** of Gilmanton 9/28/1904; H - 27, foreman, b. Alton, s/o Page D. Gooch (Lee, farmer) and Emma J. Pinkham (New Durham); W - 16, housemaid, b. Melrose, MA, d/o Frank J. Elkins (Gilmanton, carpenter) and Mary E. Dunbar (Quincy, MA)

GOODWIN,
Clifton of Gilmanton m. Ethel **Dame** of New Durham 5/31/1906; H - 21, farmer, b. Gilmanton, s/o Sylvester Goodwin (Gilmanton, farmer) and Sarah Doe (Deerfield, housewife); W - 17, housemaid, b. New Durham, d/o Alonzo Dame (Barrington, farmer) and Etta French (Farmington, housewife)

Ernest H. of Gilmanton m. Florence A. **Watson** of Barnstead 9/28/1910 in Pittsfield; H - 35, merchant, b. Gilmanton, s/o Charles H. Goodwin (Gilmanton, farmer) and Irene A. Dorr (Ossipee, housewife); W - 26, teacher, b. Pittsfield, d/o Daniel Watson (Pittsfield, farmer) and Nancy A. Wheeler (Londonderry, housewife)

Ralph L. of Gilmanton I. W. m. Roberta T. **Hayes** of Farmington 4/23/1938 in Farmington; H - 22, truck driver, b. Gilmanton, s/o Ernest Goodwin (Gilmanton, store keeper) and Florence Watson (Pittsfield, postmaster); W - 18, shoe shop, b. New Durham, d/o Colo E. Hayes (New Durham, mechanic) and Bertha McCarlie (Farmington, ME, at home)

Ralph L. of Gilmanton m. Rachel A. **Hyslop** of Gilmanton 12/18/1968; H - b. 2/11/1916 in NH, s/o Ernest H. Goodwin

(NH) and Florence A. Watson (NH); W - b. 12/18/1919 in NH, d/o Frank A. Straw (NH) and Hallie Brown (NH)

Ralph Leslie of Gilmanton m. Cliftine A. **Goodfield** of Chichester 5/13/1949 in Chichester; H - 33, sexton, b. NH, s/o Ernest H. Goodwin (NH) and Florence A. Watson (NH); W - 19, at home, b. NH, d/o Clifton A. Emerson (NH) and Lucy J. Tuttle (NH)

GORDON,
Harry W. of Gilmanton m. Charlene D. **Noyes** of Alton 9/6/1980

GORMAN,
Richard W. of Gilmanton m. Crystal A. **Carter** of Gilmanton 10/25/1996

GOSS,
William H. m. Dorothy **Stevens** 9/23/1922 in Laconia

GOSSELIN,
Frederick P. of Gilmanton m. Lea M. **Morris** of Gilmanton 5/5/1911 in Laconia; H - 42, painter, b. Lawrence, MA, s/o Peter Gosselin (Burlington, VT, butcher) and Celina Byron (Canada, housewife); W - 41, laundress, 2nd, b. Shelbrook, Canada, d/o Charles Lacour (laborer) and Marie Lacour (Canada, housewife)

GOULD,
Jeffrey C. of Gilmanton m. Kimberly A. **Hawkins** of Gilmanton 6/8/1986

GOUPIL,
Gary G. of Belmont m. Erin D. **Russell** of Gilmanton 1/5/1985

GOVE,
Charles R. of Gilmanton m. Jane E. **Gray** of Gilmanton 1/11/1983

GOWEN,
Frank B. of Waterbury, CT m. Marie Agnes **Verzier** of Waterbury, CT 8/30/1941 in Gilmanton I. W.; H - 34, production clerk, b. St. Charles, MO, s/o Frank A. Gowen (St. Charles, MO, farmer) and Mary Fitzwater (Sullivan, MO, housekeeper); W -

34, clerk, b. Waterbury, CT, d/o Nicholas Verzier (Waterbury, CT, retired) and Kathrine A. Nolan (Hartford, CT, housewife)

GRADY,
James E. of Gilmanton m. Sandra S. **Alder** of Concord 1/23/1982

GRANT,
James Wallingford of Gilmanton m. Virginia Minerva **Stanley** of Gilmanton 10/10/1964; H - 29, super. in garage, b. VT, s/o Forrest F. Grant (NH) and Beatrice T. Bebeau (VT); W - 38, nurse, b. MA, d/o Herbert J. White (MA) and Bertha M. Pool (MA)

GRAVES,
William Alfred of Gilmanton m. Rena Grace **McMahon** of Gilmanton 12/30/1971; H - b. 9/19/1942 in MA, s/o Harold L. Graves (MA) and Belle Foss (NH); W - b. 4/11/1942 in MA, d/o James W. George (MA) and Hazel Ransom (VT)

GRAY,
Edwin M. of Gilmanton m. Carrie D. **Spiller** of Laconia 11/11/1901 in Laconia; H - 51, laborer, b. Great Falls, s/o Reuben M. Gray (Sheffield, VT, physician) and Elizabeth Carr (Morgan, VT, housewife); W - 54, housekeeper, 2nd, b. Sharon, VT, d/o William Flanders (farmer) and Isabelle A. Flanders (Lebanon, housewife)

George H., Jr. of Gilmanton I. W. m. Mary E. **Glum** of Gilmanton I. W. 9/30/1978 in Gilmanton I. W.; H - b. 6/12/1957 in NH, s/o George H. Gray, Sr. (NH) and Mary Beede (NH); W - b. 7/7/1960 in NY, d/o Edward F. Glum (NY) and Mary Miller (CA)

Wayne S. of Gilmanton m. Daren J. **Randlett** of Gilmanton 8/22/1981

William I. of Laconia m. Jane E. **Maheux** of Gilmanton 9/4/1965 in Laconia; H - 21, service attend., b. NH, s/o Richard I. Gray (NH) and Sylvia Burden (NH); W - 18, secretary, b. NH, d/o Robert W. Maheux (NH) and Ruth M. Willard (NH)

GREEN,
Archie Wyman of Gilmanton m. Rhoda Ellen **Pearl** of Loudon 11/24/1921; H - 23, farmer, b. Gilmanton, s/o Walter A. Green (Gilmanton) and Ada Sargent (Canterbury); W - 23, housekeeper, b. Loudon, d/o Leroy S. Pearl (Loudon) and Rhoda H. Peaslee (Loudon)

Elmer L. of Gilmanton m. Antonia **Kratzert** of Pittsfield 6/1/1889; H - 24, farmer, b. Gilmanton, s/o Oliver L. Green (Gilmanton, farmer) and Arvilla H. Fogg (Loudon, housewife); W - 24, housewife, b. Gilmanton, d/o Robert Kratzert

Elmer R. of Gilmanton m. Dorothy P. **Pickard** of Canterbury 3/29/1944 in Pittsfield; H - 17, farming, b. Gilmanton, s/o Jay H. Green (Gilmanton, farming) and Beulah E. Willard (Gilmanton, housewife); W - 19, at home, b. Canterbury, d/o Arthur E. Pickard (Canterbury, farming) and Jennie E. Sargent (Canterbury, housewife)

Jay H. of Gilmanton m. Beulah E. **Willard** of Gilmanton 10/18/1925; H - 21, farmer, b. Gilmanton, s/o Elmer L. Green (Gilmanton, farmer) and Antonia Krazet (Germany, housework); W - 16, housework, b. Gilmanton, d/o Israel Willard (Gilmanton, sawyer) and Georgia F. McClary (Gilmanton, housework)

Laurence K. of Gilmanton m. Ruth E. **Stockman** of Pittsfield 3/19/1934 in Pittsfield; H - 27, forestry, b. Pittsfield, s/o Harry C. Green (Chichester, ice business) and Bertha Purtell (Quebec, Can., housewife); W - 20, at home, b. Pittsfield, d/o Everett Stockman (Pittsfield, farmer) and Josephine Dennett (Pittsfield, housewife)

Ronald Walter of Gilmanton m. Edna Austin **Page** of Gilmanton 5/1/1918 in Loudon; H - 26, farmer, b. Gilmanton, s/o Elmer L. Green (Gilmanton) and Antonia Kratzert (Germany); W - 18, at home, b. Gilmanton, d/o William S. Paige (sic) (Gilmanton) and Cora Crouch (Sutton)

Walter S. of Gilmanton m. Ada **Sargent** of Gilmanton 12/11/1897; H - 31, farmer, b. Gilmanton, s/o Oliver L. Greene (sic) (Loudon, farmer) and Arvilla Fogg (Loudon, housewife); W - 15, housemaid, b. Canterbury, d/o William Sargent (Loudon, farmer) and Jennie Sanborn (Concord, housewife)

Walter S. of Gilmanton m. Mary A. **MacDonald** of Gilmanton 6/29/1903; H - 37, farmer, 2nd, b. Gilmanton, s/o Oliver L. Green (Loudon, farmer) and Arvilla H. Fogg; W - 35, housemaid, b. Sandwich, d/o Royal MacDonald (Moultonboro, clergyman) and Mary A. Bickford (Windham, ME)

GREENE,

Horace Daniel of Loudon m. Mabel Erdine **Joyce** of Gilmanton 8/18/1951 in Belmont; H - 28, farmer, b. NH, s/o Lester F. Greene (NH) and Gladys M. Tibbetts (NH); W - 19, seamer, b. NH, d/o James H. Joyce (NH) and Velma I. Quint (NH)

GREENOUGH,

George H. of Gilmanton m. Charlotte M. **McGilbary** of NS 6/23/1891 in Springfield, VT; H - 41, farmer, 2nd, b. Concord, s/o William C. Greenough (farmer) and Nancy K. Greenough (Concord, housewife); W - 37, housekeeper, 2nd, b. NS, d/o David McNair (farmer)

GREENWOOD,

Clayton of Gilmanton m. Cleo Rachel **Houle** of Laconia 2/15/1958 in Laconia; H - 26, machine operator, b. VT, s/o Clifford A. Greenwood (NH) and Mary J. Forrest (VT); W - 21, at home, b. NH, d/o Roland J. Houle (NH) and Clemence Caron (NH)

Leo M. of Gilmanton m. Beverly A. **Sevene** of Gilmanton 1/15/1957 in Laconia; H - 23, truck driver, b. NH, s/o Clifford A. Greenwood (NH) and Jeanette M. Forest (VT); W - 19, at home, b. MA, d/o Francis O. Sevene (NH) and Marjorie A. Baker (MA)

Raymond of Gilmanton m. Margaret **Milmore** of Center Harbor 6/11/1956 in Pittsfield; H - 20, state worker, b. NH, s/o Clifford A. Greenwood (NH) and Jeannette M. Forrest (VT); W - 19, clerk, b. MA, d/o Francis J. Milmore (NH) and Druzelle M. Scott (MA)

GRIFFIN,

Nathan D. of Gilmanton m. Eva G. **Osborne** of Gilmanton 8/18/1901; H - 34, farmer, b. Gilmanton, s/o Joseph T. Griffin (Gilmanton, farmer) and Mary O. Brown (housewife); W - 22, teacher, b. Gilmanton, d/o Charles A. Osborne (Gilmanton, farmer) and Grace A. True (housewife)

Robert D. of Gilmanton m. Sally E. **Wilkinson** of Wolfeboro 9/17/1954 in Seabrook; H - 20, student, b. NH, s/o Harold W.

Griffin (NH) and Doris Davis (NH); W - 19, student, b. NH, d/o F. Clifford Wilkinson (NH) and Ethelyn M. Hodgdon (NH)

Robert Davis of Gilmanton m. Nancy Elaine **Rankin** of Lincolnville, ME 12/24/1964; H - 30, food manager, b. NH, s/o Harold W. Griffin (NH) and Doris Davis (NH); W - 22, research asst., b. ME, d/o George E. Rankin (ME) and Lula M. Jones (ME)

Shirley Edward of Sanbornton m. Donna Marie **Kelley** of Gilmanton 6/5/1972 in Sanbornton; H - b. 5/25/1947 in NH, s/o Sherwood E. Griffin (NH) and Eunice Jondrow (NH); W - b. 10/26/1951 in NH, d/o Harvey S. Kelley (VT) and Mary Moulton (NH)

GROLEAU,
James P. of Gilmanton m. Devere D. **Hurst** of Ctr. Barnstead 6/30/1979

GRONDIN,
Richard Paul of Cumberland, ME m. Susan Jean **Burnham** of Gilmanton 10/26/1991

GUARINO,
Donald J. of Gilford m. Sandra **Stevens** of Gilmanton 8/21/1976 in Gilford; H - b. 12/4/1954 in HI, s/o Donald Guarino (MA) and Sally James (NH); W - b. 3/5/1957 in MA, d/o Richard Stevens (MA) and Nancy Wilson (MA)

GUERRIER,
Kevin Kenneth of Gilmanton m. Barbara Ann **Lockhart** of Gilmanton 8/22/1998

GUILBAULT,
Robert C. of Gilmanton m. Donna L. **Wessell** of Gilmanton 11/25/1982

GUILMETTE,
Randy C. of Gilmanton m. Angelique N. **Harty** of Gilmanton 8/19/1990

GULLAGE,
Dannie C. of Penacook m. Linda I. **Willard** of Gilmanton 7/29/1967; H - 20, welder, b. NH, s/o Thomas A. Gullage (Newfoundland)

and Faith Johnson (NH); W - 18, factory worker, b. NH, d/o Arthur E. Willard (NH) and Mary C. Heinis (MA)

HABERSTROH,
Joseph Kevin of Seattle, WA m. Elizabeth Kennedy **Moore** of Seattle, WA 8/10/1991

HACKETT,
Wayne L. N. of Gilmanton m. Elizabeth L. **Anish** of Gilmanton 12/3/1988

HAHN,
Thomas C. of MI m. Catherine B. **Eddy** of MI 10/14/1978; H - b. 12/20/1952 in NH, s/o Carsten Hahn (Canada) and Simone Fournier (NH); W - b. 6/24/93 (sic), d/o Edward Eddy (NY) and Mary Schurman (NY)

HAINES,
John H. of Gilmanton m. Bertha **Howard** of Gilmanton 7/12/1896; H - 26, blacksmith, b. Loudon, s/o Taylor Haines and Mary E. Doe (housekeeper); W - 20, housekeeper, b. Dover, d/o Emery Howard and Emma Howard

HALF,
William H. of Gilmanton m. Ellen C. **Gershun** of Gilmanton 9/23/1984

HALL,
Harold Chaperon of Gilmanton m. Flora H. **Parsons** of Gilmanton 4/25/1916 in Loudon Ridge; H - 22, farmer, b. Gilmanton, s/o Harvey James Hall (Gilmanton, farmer) and Julia A. Chaperon (Wotton, PQ, housewife); W - 26, housework, b. Gilmanton, d/o Usher S. Parsons (Gilmanton, farmer) and Addie Hill (Gilmanton, housewife)

HALTER,
Daniel J. of Gilmanton m. Heidi **Herzberger** of Gilmanton 9/21/2001

HAMILTON,
Edward Anderson of Seattle, WA m. Sarah Lynn **Bean** of Seattle, WA 4/1/1995

HAMLEY,
Thom M. of Gilmanton m. Nanette L. **Fort** of Gilmanton 10/10/1981

HAMMOND,
Anthony D. of Gilmanton m. Roberta E. **Doucette** of York, ME 11/23/1983

HANNA,
Morgan Randall of Warner m. Briann Gail **Greenfield** of Gilmanton 8/10/1996

HANSCOM,
Herman M. of Boston, MA m. Cora F. **Nutter** of Gilmanton 9/8/1892 in Pittsfield; H - 24, seaman, b. Gonic, s/o Micajah S. Hanscom (Center Harbor, carpenter) and Clara D. Gray (Strafford, housewife); W - 27, housewife, 2nd, b. Gilmanton, d/o Mirom S. Clough (Alton, farmer) and Elizabeth Prescott (Alton, housewife)

HANSEN,
Richard A. of Gilmanton m. Susan L. **Monier** of Gilmanton 9/9/1978 in Rindge; H - b. 10/9/1953 in NY, s/o John A. Hansen (NY) and Jennine Cashion (NY); W - b. 3/10/1948 in MA, d/o Edward A. Monier (MA) and Marjorie Stark (Canada)

HANSON,
Carl N. of Gilmanton m. Sarah E. **Nutter** of Barnstead 7/10/1930 in Barnstead; H - 24, farmer, b. Barnstead, s/o Sidney E. Hanson (Barnstead, farmer) and Laura M. Nutter (Gilmanton, housework); W - 24, housekeeper, b. Barnstead, d/o Carroll Nutter (Barnstead, farmer) and Iva Berry (Barnstead, housework)

HARDWICK,
Philip F. of Gilmanton m. Dianne Sue **Hyslop** of Gilmanton 12/30/1972; H - b. 11/4/1951 in MA, s/o William F. Hardwick

(MA) and Violet Crowder (NJ); W - b. 6/15/1955 in NH, d/o
Donald W. Hyslop (MA) and Rachel A. Straw (NH)

HARDY,
Forrest E. of Gilmanton m. Lois E. Amell **Sansouci** of Gilmanton
2/15/1978; H - b. 1/16/1929 in NH, s/o Earl Hardy (USA) and
Celia Dutton (USA); W - b. 5/27/1937 in NJ, d/o Henry
Sansouci (NJ) and Margaret Vincent (NJ)

HARPER,
David Graham of Gilmanton m. Vivian Eunice **Cutter** of Gilmanton
12/24/1996

HARRIMAN,
Paul Nathan of Gilmanton m. Marcey Maria **Blandini** of Gilmanton
10/16/1994

HARRIS,
David G., Jr. of Gilmanton m. Vycki M. **Sylvain** of Gilmanton
12/31/1994
James N. of Gilmanton m. Gladys **Wallace** of Gilmanton 10/5/1935
in Plymouth; H - 41, carpenter, b. Gilmanton, s/o James Harris
(Ashland, farmer) and Katherine Guy (Quebec); W - 38, nurse,
3rd, b. Hooksett, d/o Fred A. Locke (Loudon) and Loretto Foote
(Bow, housewife)
Ora Wendell of Belmont m. Jessie B. **McClary** of Gilmanton
11/26/1931 in Meredith; H - 21, laborer, b. Canaan, s/o George
R. Harris (Hopkinton, MA, shoe merchant) and Bertha I.
Hingman (Bear River, NS, housework); W - 18, housework, b.
Gilmanton, d/o Horace E. McClary (Gilmanton, farmer) and H.
Amy Allard (Charl'n City, MA, housework)

HARTFORD,
Anthony E. of Gilmanton m. Faye D. **Anders** of Gilmanton 9/6/1980

HARVEY,
Brandon Thomas of Gilmanton m. Nicole Marie **Evans** of
Gilmanton 12/31/1999

HATAB,
John Christopher of Gilmanton m. Maryann McKenna **Newell** of Gilmanton 12/2/1989

HATCH,
Michael James of Gilmanton m. Rachel Marie **Frechette** of Gilmanton 12/1/1996

HATEM,
Thomas D. of ME m. Paula L. Baillargeon **Gilman** of ME 7/25/1981

HATHAWAY,
Ronald Fred of Cambridge, MA m. Virginia True **Ripley** of Stockbridge, MA 6/15/1963; H - 26, teacher, b. WY, s/o Darrel M. Hathaway (WY) and Jane L. Crowther (MO); W - 24, at home, b. MA, d/o George Ripley (MA) and Ruth Bergeron (MA)

HAWKINS,
Carl R. of Gilmanton m. Debra L. **Wessely** of Gilmanton 12/8/1979
Carl R. of Gilmanton m. Diana L. **Wallace** of Belmont 9/12/1992
Charles Allan of Gilmanton m. Alyce M. **Deering** of Chichester 8/29/1943 in Pittsfield; H - 27, flight inst., b. Gilmanton, s/o Shurldin Hawkins (Boston, MA, farmer) and Amy Osborne (Gilmanton, housewife); W - 23, bookkeeper, b. Chichester, d/o Arthur Deering (Chichester, farmer) and Mildred Flanders (Wallingford, VT, housewife)
Garey Lee of Gilmanton m. Terri Ann **Swain** of Belmont 7/5/1996
Merton Everett of Center Harbor m. Mollie Dorothy **Margeson** of Gilmanton 12/27/1921; H - 18, laborer, b. Center Harbor, s/o Everett Hawkins (Center Harbor) and Lottie Edna Barker (Pensaukee, WI); W - 21, clerk, b. Grafton, NS, d/o J. LeBaron Margeson (Grafton, NS) and Sarah Loomes (Welsford, NS)
Rolland of Gilmanton m. Margaret **Gagnon** of Gilmanton 11/16/1956; H - 28, truck driver, b. NH, s/o Shurldin A. Hawkins (MA) and Amy D. Osborne (NH); W - 23, office worker, b. NH, d/o Eugene W. Gagnon (Canada) and Dorothy Hislop (ME)
Shurldin of Gilmanton m. Amy D. **Osborne** of Gilmanton 2/22/1914 in Loudon; H - 22, farmer, b. Boston, MA, s/o George Hawkins

(Boston, MA, merchant) and Nellie Hawkins (Boston, MA, housewife); W - 29, teacher, b. Gilmanton, d/o Charles F. Osborne (Gilmanton, farmer) and Grace A. True (Pittsfield, housewife)

HAYES,
Eben of Gilmanton m. Betsey **Tucker** of Canterbury 12/28/1907 in Canterbury; H - 66, farmer, 2nd, b. Barnstead, s/o Erans Hayes (Strafford, farmer) and Margaret Emerson (Farmington, housewife); W - 68, housekeeper, 2nd, b. Concord

Sean Patrick of Gilmanton m. Kim Marie **Conlin** of Gilmanton 4/26/1997

HAYNES,
Horace F. of Gilmanton m. Carrie B. **Howard** of Strafford 11/27/1895; H - 23, farmer, b. Loudon, s/o Samuel F. Haynes (Loudon, farmer) and Mary E. Doe (housewife); W - 20, housekeeper, b. Barrington, d/o John Howard (shoemaker)

HEALEY,
Charles E. of Chester m. Margaret H. **Warburton** of Gilmanton 3/24/1946; H - 25, barrel factory worker, b. Chester, s/o Everett Healey (Chester, millworker) and Florence Holland (Auburn, housewife); W - 22, stitcher, b. Gilmanton, d/o John H. Warburton (England, farmer) and Clara H. Elkins (Gilmanton, housewife)

HEATH,
Roger Eldon of Pittsfield m. Janet Leigh **Aycock** of Gilmanton 6/25/1966; H - 22, teacher, b. NH, s/o Eldon M. Heath (VT) and Elizabeth B. Duclos (NH); W - 21, teacher, b. MA, d/o Thomas W. Aycock (GA) and Shirley H. MacNeil (MA)

HEBERT,
Gregory Lionel of Laconia m. Dorothy Nora **Fleming** of Gilmanton 5/18/1974 in Laconia; H - b. 11/16/1953 in NH, s/o Armand Hebert (NH) and Beverly Bennett (NH); W - b. 11/15/1953 in NY, d/o Michael Fleming (Ireland) and Dorothy Cubbin (NY)

HEMLIN,
Theodore D. of Gilmanton m. Lori Ann **Dumais** of Belmont
9/12/1992

HEMPEL,
Paul J., III of Gilmanton m. Robin M. **White** of Gilford 8/20/1983

HENDERSON,
Philip Lee of Epsom m. Elin Denise **Nicholson** of Gilmanton
1/3/1998

HENDRICK,
Peter J. of Gilmanton m. Marjorie R. **Renno** of Gilmanton
2/20/1982

HENRY,
Willard G. of Gilmanton m. Patricia G. Tasseff **Miller** of Gilmanton 6/23/1973; H - b. 11/9/1920 in RI, s/o George F. Henry (CT) and Ella Mae Starkweather (RI); W - b. 11/25/1935 in NY, d/o William E. Miller (USA) and Grace M. Daniels (USA)

HERLIHY,
Robert P. of Gilmanton m. Enid B. **Werren** of Meredith 12/10/1977 in Meredith; H - b. 5/26/1947 in MA, s/o Francis Herlihy (MA) and Alice McCloud (MA); W - b. 7/14/1954 in NH, d/o Alfred Porter (NH) and Henrietta Biel (NH)

HERSOM,
Leon E. of Acton, ME m. Arletta H. **Munsey** of Gilmanton 3/22/1939; H - 22, farmer, b. Acton, ME, s/o Leon F. Hersom (Lebanon, ME, farmer) and Nellie A. Hayes (Limerick, ME, at home); W - 22, none, d/o John J. Munsey (Gilmanton, laborer) and Julia A. Bruce (Flosden, Canada, at home)

HEROUX,
Blaise Thomas of Concord m. Linda Ann **Mottola** of Gilmanton
9/6/1997

HEYMAN,
Casey J. of Yarmouth, ME m. Michelle L. **Smithers** of Yarmouth, ME 9/9/2000

HEYWOOD,
William C. of Pittsfield m. Una M. **Geddes** of Gilmanton 3/12/1932 in Antrim; H - 23, shoe worker, b. Pittsfield, s/o Fred Heywood (Barnstead, shoemaker) and Grace Jenkins (Pembroke, housekeeper); W - 23, nurse, b. Canada, d/o Duncan Geddes (Canada, farmer) and Ida Wilson (Canada, nurse)

HICKEY,
Robert Anthony, Jr. of Gilmanton m. Karen Jeanne **Gray** of Gilmanton 4/1/1989

HIGGINS,
Clifton E. of Laconia m. Jeanette P. **Page** of Gilmanton 11/22/1947 in Laconia; H - 20, mill operator, b. Northeast Harbor, ME, s/o Beverly Higgins (Bar Harbor, ME) and Cora L. Bracy (Brooklin, ME, mill inspector); W - 17, at home, b. Gilmanton, d/o Ray B. Page (Gilmanton, laborer) and Lorna L. Stockbridge (Gilmanton, housewife)

HILL,
Elwood H. of Gilmanton m. Ceda May **Dame** of New Durham 10/16/1898 in Farmington; H - 35, farmer, b. Gilmanton, s/o Joseph R. Hill (Alton, farmer) and Pluma E. Hill (Gilmanton, housewife); W - 17, housekeeper, b. Middleton, d/o Alonzo Dame (farmer) and Etta French (housewife)
Frank Arthur of Pittsfield m. Florence Ethel **Redman** of Gilmanton 7/22/1961 in Laconia; H - 42, machinist, b. NY, s/o Ray Hill and Iva Nellis; W - 47, assembler, b. NH, d/o Leslie Ford and Nellie Chase
Joseph P., Jr. of Gilmanton m. Patricia M. **Sirrell** of Gilmanton 4/15/1967 in Belmont; H - 21, self employed, b. NH, s/o Joseph P. Hill (NH) and Blanche E. Morse (NH); W - 24, at home, b. NH, d/o Verne H. Sirrell (NH) and Harriet M. Perkins (NH)
Leo Lawrence of Gilmanton m. Brenda Ann **White** of Laconia 4/12/1969 in Laconia; H - b. 9/20/1950 in NH, s/o Joseph P.

Hill (NH) and Blanche E. Morse (NH); W - b. 1/31/1951 in NH, d/o Rudolph White (NH) and Beverly Ulman (NH)

Leo Lawrence of Gilmanton m. Dorcas Lee **Judkins** of Berlin 7/4/1970 in Berlin; H - b. 9/20/1950 in NH, s/o Joseph Hill, Sr. (NH) and Blanche Morse (NH); W - b. 10/17/1951 in NH, d/o Kendrick Judkins (ME) and Dorothy Davidson (NH)

HILLIARD,

Alfred F. of Gilmanton m. Abbie B. **Stevens** of Gilmanton 6/27/1916; H - 29, farmer, b. Gilmanton, s/o Charles A. Hilliard (Gilmanton, farmer) and Hannah Davis (Sutton, housewife); W - 59, housework, 2nd, b. Manchester, d/o Frank Couch (Penacook, farmer) and Ella Davis (Warren, housework)

Leander A. of Gilmanton m. Lilla M. **Mastern** of New London 9/9/1894; H - 33, farmer, 2nd, b. Gilmanton, s/o Alfred S. Hilliard; W - 23, housekeeper, b. Sutton, d/o Henry Mastern (farmer)

HILLSGROVE,

Fred N. of Gilmanton m. Ella E. **Goodwin** of Alton 8/22/1942 in Pittsfield; H - 23, farmer, b. Dover, s/o Walter Hillsgrove (Wilmot, farmer) and Myrtie O. Day (Northwood, housewife); W - 22, social wkr., b. Alton, d/o Walter R. Goodwin (Alton, farmer) and Edna Bickford (Strafford, housewife)

George C. of Barnstead m. Sandra J. **Publicover** of Gilmanton 10/2/1965; H - 21, saw operator, b. NH, s/o Casper E. Hillsgrove (NH) and Doris K. Bixby (NH); W - 19, secretary, b. NH, d/o Robert G. Publicover (unknown) and Annie M. Shlaitas (NH)

Robert M. of Gilmanton m. Arzelia H. **Durgin** of Laconia 5/18/1957 in Laconia; H - 20, US Navy, b. NH, s/o Walter M. Hillsgrove (NH) and Louise E. Pike (NH); W - 16, at home, b. NH, d/o David W. Durgin, Sr. (NH) and Emma H. Back (IL)

Thomas Bruce of Alton m. Roseanna Eva **Perkins** of Gilmanton 10/9/1971 in Concord; H - b. 3/26/1950 in NH, s/o Fred N. Hillsgrove (NH) and Ella E. Goodwin (NH); W - b. 3/13/1951 in NH, d/o Harold C. Perkins (NH) and Rachel T. Goupil (NH)

Wayne H. of Gilmanton m. Nancy M. **Oliver** of Gilford 11/22/1975 in Laconia; H - b. 8/4/1955 in NH, s/o Joseph Hillsgrove (NH) and Lois Partridge (NH); W - b. 5/1/1959 in MA, d/o Edwin D. Oliver (MA) and Gladys A. McGrath (MA)

HILTZ,
Angus Blenum of Gilmanton m. Virginia Dawn **Banfill** of Belmont
    10/21/1967 in Belmont; H - 27, farmer, b. NH, s/o Fred Leslie
    Hiltz (MA) and Cynthia Irene Hiltz (NS); W - 23, teacher, b.
    NH, d/o Bertram Ira Grover Banfill (NH) and Vinie M.
    Dwinnells (NH)
Donald F. of Gilmanton m. Hilda Anne **Danforth** of Colebrook
    8/2/1969 in Colebrook; H - b. 1/27/1942 in NH, s/o Fred L. Hiltz
    (MA) and Cynthia Hiltz (Canada); W - b. 3/19/1944 in NH, d/o
    Benjamin Danforth (NH) and Blanche Leigh (Canada)

HINMAN,
Richard B. of Madison, CT m. Janice L. **Beckley** of Gilmanton
    10/29/1955; H - 23, Air Force, b. CT, s/o Burton L. Hinman
    (CT) and Christine Wismer (MA); W - 18, secretary, b. CT, d/o
    Lewis F. Beckley (CT) and Lillian F. Jameson (SD)

HIRST,
George W. of Sabattus, ME m. Carrie E. **Clark** of Gilmanton
    10/29/1911 in Alton; H - 50, farmer, b. Lisbon, ME, s/o James
    F. Hirst (Wakefield, England) and Ruth E. Linscott (Brownfield,
    ME); W - 64, housekeeper, 2nd, b. Gilmanton, d/o David Beede
    (Sandwich) and Elizabeth Varney (Dover)

HISLOP,
Donald, Jr. of Gilmanton m. Ruth I. **McAuley** of Berwick, ME
    9/16/1955; H - 22, machinist, b. NH, s/o Donald W. Hislop
    (NH) and Myrtle I. Hinds (MA); W - 18, messenger, b. ME, d/o
    John A. McAuley (Canada) and Clara A. Griffin (ME)
Donald W. of Gilmanton m. Myrtle I. **Hinds** of Framingham, MA
    7/30/1930; H - 18, farmer, b. Merrimac, MA, s/o R. Willis
    Hislop (Strafford, farmer) and Bertha M. Ellis (Gilmanton,
    housework); W - 22, attendant, b. Charlestown, MA, d/o Frank
    Hinds (Fitchburg, MA, foreman) and Florence Whitney (PEI,
    housework)
Richard W. of Gilmanton m. June R. E. **Manning** of Daytona
    Beach, FL 2/4/1947; H - 23, machinist, b. Gilmanton, s/o
    Robert W. Hislop (Rochester, farming) and Bertha M. Ellis
    (Gilmanton, housewife); W - 22, clerk, b. Miami, FL, d/o
    Joseph C. Manning (FL, saw mill owner) and Thelma L.
    Bankright (Hawthorn, FL, housewife)

Robert E. of Gilmanton m. Dorothy L. **Hinds** of Framingham, MA 4/13/1936 in Gilmanton I. W.; H - 27, laborer, Merrimac, MA, s/o R. Willis Hislop (Strafford, blacksmith) and Bertha Ellis (Gilmanton, at home); W - 21, at home, b. Allston, MA, d/o Frank C. Hinds (Waltham, MA, R. R. man) and Florence Whiteway (PEI, at home)

HOAG,
Lawrence C. of Gilmanton m. Margaret **Bordeau** of Gilmanton 4/9/1953 in Belmont; H - 21, Navy, b. NY, s/o Paul F. Hoag (NY) and Dorothy M. Smith (NY); W - 22, chief clerk, b. NH, d/o Jason J. Bordeau (VT) and Florence C. Edgerly (NH)

HODDER,
Robert J. of Gilmanton m. Candace S. **Weeks** of Belmont 5/19/2001

HOFFMAN,
Kenneth P. of Gilmanton m. Amy J. V. **Weglars** of Franklin 12/4/1982

HOLMAN,
Paul R. of Gilmanton m. Edna V. **Nelson** of Boston, MA 3/27/1936 in Gilmanton I. W.; H - 32, manufacturer, 3rd, b. Leominster, MA, s/o William E. Holman (Leominster, MA, manufacturer) and Alice Rockwell (Leominster, MA, at home); W - 27, at home, 2nd, d/o John F. Nelson (New Bedford, MA, manufacturer) and ----- (Hyde, England, at home)

HOOPER,
Steven R. of Gilmanton m. Janice S. **Sawyer** of Gilmanton 8/25/2001

HOPKINS,
James T., Sr. of Gilmanton m. Sonja N. **Mitchell** of Gilmanton 9/29/1990

HOPKINSON,
William P. of Gilmanton m. Grace A. **Casey** of Gilmanton 6/30/1956 in Gilford; H - 38, antique dealer, b. MA, s/o William

P. Hopkinson (MA) and Hazel B. Walton (NH); W - 39, antique dealer, b. MA, d/o Charles W. Barton (ME) and Minnie E. Russon (MA)

HORAN,
Arthur J. of Laconia m. Evelyn Nellie **Clifford** of Gilmanton 4/3/1948 in Franklin; H - 22, machinist, b. Greenfield, MA, s/o John J. Horan (Derry, paper hanger) and Laura Clifford (Concord, at home); W - 20, assembler, b. Gilmanton, d/o Earle Clifford (Belmont, road agent) and Nellie Ellsworth (Gilmanton, at home)

HORNIK,
Richard Henry of Washington, DC m. Susan **Barney** of Gilmanton 5/28/1972; H - b. 4/28/1948 in NY, s/o Henry W. Hornik (NY) and Dorothy E. Growvogel (NY); W - b. 7/4/1947 in NH, d/o Winston M. Barney (NH) and Linda R. Geiersgaard (ND)

HOTTLE,
John C. of Gilmanton m. Diana R. **Sumner** of Gilmanton 8/24/1969; H - b. 1/14/1946 in MD, s/o George A. Hottle (PA) and Caroline Keiper (PA); W - b. 7/11/1943 in NY, d/o Alfred M. Sumner (MD) and Margaret Lippincott (NJ)

HOWE,
Carl D. of Gilmanton m. Grace E. **Foss** of Gilmanton 12/24/1904 in Loudon; H - 31, sawyer, b. Grantham, s/o Henry P. Howe (Grantham, farmer) and Ellen Leavitt (Grantham); W - 20, housemaid, b. Gilmanton, d/o Charles W. Foss (Alton, farmer) and Lucy J. Marsh (Gilmanton)
Thomas Atkinson of Gilmanton m. Sarah Chase **Thorne** of Gilmanton 7/30/1988

HOWSON,
Richard G. of Jaffrey m. Doris M. **Riggs** of Jaffrey 6/30/1979

HUBBARD,
William L. of Concord m. June A. Haskell **Cota** of Gilmanton 6/10/1978 in Rochester; H - b. 7/17/1943 in NH, s/o Paul

Hubbard (NH) and Alberta Jackson (VT); W - b. 11/12/1946 in NH, d/o Ezra Cota (VT) and Marion Amadon (MA)

HUCKINS,
Lewis of Gilmanton m. Beverly **Champney** of Gilmanton 7/12/1980

HUEBER,
Jimmy of Gilmanton m. Heather L. **Morgan** of Gilford 7/17/1999

HUFSCHMID,
Erick of Gilmanton m. Maria **Hofpointer** of Lochmere 10/8/1971; H - b. 8/24/1928 in NY, s/o Anton Hufschmid (Germany) and Paula Geiger (Germany); W - b. 2/25/1937 in Austria, d/o Franz Hofpointer (Austria) and Kathy Dick (Austria)

HUGHES,
Wayne A. of Gilmanton m. Susan J. **Payne** of Gilmanton 7/4/1989

HUNKINS,
Dana W. of Gilmanton m. Arlene I. **Little** of Gilmanton 5/30/1977 in Belmont; H - b. 2/26/1923 in NH, s/o Clarence J. Hunkins (NH) and Ruth R. Churchwell (NY); W - b. 12/27/1923 in NH, d/o King Little (NH) and Iona Clough (NH)

Dana William of Laconia m. Arlene Iona **Little** of Gilmanton 5/29/1943 in Laconia; H - 20, chip collector, b. Laconia, s/o Clarence Hunkins (Laconia, electrician) and Ruth Churchwell (Patakurck, NY, Excello op.); W - 19, mail clerk, b. Laconia, d/o King R. Little (Gilmanton, farmer) and Iona M. Clough (Quincy, NH, mill oper.)

HURD,
Henry H. of Gilmanton m. Minnie E. **Jones** of Gilmanton 12/15/1897 in Contoocook; H - 67, carpenter, 2nd, b. Loudon, s/o Caleb Hurd (Tuftonboro, farmer) and Judith C. Hurd (Gilmanton, housewife); W - 44, housemaid, 2nd, b. Strafford, d/o William Sloper and Lucy Brown (Strafford)

HUTCHINS,
Mark R. of Laconia m. Tina M. **Davis** of Gilford 10/13/1979

HUTCHINSON,
Leonard of Gilmanton m. Annastasia W. **Wilbur** of Taunton, MA 1/21/1926; H - 27, chauffeur, 2nd, b. Taunton, MA, s/o Harry Hutchinson (England, boiler maker) and Elizabeth Wilmott (London, Eng., housewife); W - 26, bookkeeper, b. Taunton, MA, d/o Thomas Wilbur (Taunton, MA, lt. fireman) and Winnifred Carpenter (Taunton, MA, housework)

HYSLOP,
Frank E. of Gilmanton m. Lois L. **Lake** of Gilmanton 8/28/1965; H - 25, fixer, b. NH, s/o Donald W. Hyslop (MA) and Rachel A. Straw (NH); W - 18, mill worker, b. MA, d/o Robert W. Lake (NJ) and Ruby P. Head (MA)

Frank E. of CO m. Joyce E. Ellis **Armstrong** of CO 12/23/1977; H - b. 2/17/1940 in NH, s/o Donald Hyslop (NH) and Rachel Straw (NH); W - b. 6/27/1943 in NH, d/o Jack Armstrong (USA) and Lucille MacDonald (NH)

Glen G. of Gilmanton m. Frances Marie **Tilton** of Belmont 8/26/1970; H - b. 12/18/1949 in NH, s/o Donald Willis Hyslop (MA) and Rachel Anna Straw (NH); W - b. 8/9/1953 in NH, d/o Leslie James Tilton (MA) and Margueritte Truchon (NH)

John Thomas of Gilmanton m. Janet Ann **LaBonte** of Laconia 1/26/1968 in Belmont; H - b. 5/10/1945 in NH, s/o Donald W. Hyslop (MA) and Rachel Straw (NH); W - b. 12/25/1944 in VT, d/o Nelson W. LaBonte (MA) and Florence Stanford (NH)

Robert G. of Gilmanton m. Barbara J. **Dimock** of Gilmanton 9/25/1965; H - 25, printer's help., b. NH, s/o Robert E. Hyslop (MA) and Cecile C. Grant (Canada); W - 26, secretary, b. VA, d/o Ronald V. Dimock (MA) and Barbara L. Raddin (MA)

Willis E. of Gilmanton m. Sandra June **Moulton** of Concord 10/11/1969; H - b. 9/21/1946 in NH, s/o Donald Hyslop (MA) and Rachel Straw (NH); W - b. 6/29/1949 in NH, d/o Richard Moulton (NH) and Thelma Cookson (ME)

INGOLDSBY,
Karl Joseph of Gilmanton m. Judith Ann **Varney** of Gilmanton 10/28/1995

JACQUES,
Spencer L. of Gilmanton m. Lisa A. **Stanford** of Gilmanton 5/21/2001

JAHNLE,
Carl George of Gilmanton m. Virginia Mae **Carleton** of Woburn, MA 2/14/1952 in Moultonville; H - 42, storekeeper, b. MA, s/o Carl B. Jahnle (Germany) and Mary Jane Wray (MA); W - 39, nurse, b. NH, d/o Bartley Allen Carleton (VA) and Cora Isabel St. John (VT)

JAMES,
Eric M. of Gilford m. Laura **Moore** of Gilmanton 8/9/1980

JAWORSKI,
Anthony Michael of Gilmanton m. Julie-Anne Ruth **Lester** of Weare 5/27/1989

JEAN,
James C. of Gilmanton m. Arleen C. **Lowe** of Gilmanton 8/10/1981
Joseph A. of Litchfield m. Tina J. **Benney** of Gilmanton 11/23/1985

JEFFERSON,
Hilary of Gilmanton m. Beatrice B. **McCurdy** of Marblehead, MA 8/15/1964 in Littleton; H - 64, retired, b. NH, s/o Mark S. W. Jefferson (MA) and Theodora Bohnstedt (TX); W - 60, retired, b. MA, d/o Jesse Beatson (NY) and Julia M. Dutton (Canada)
Mark S. W. of Melrose, MA m. Thedora A. **Bohnstedt** of Gilmanton 8/17/1891; H - 28, school teacher, b. Melrose, MA, s/o Daniel Jefferson (London, Eng., bookseller) and Mary E. Mantz (London, Eng., housewife); W - 28, housekeeper, b. Independence, TX, d/o T. E. A. Bohnstedt

JENNESS,
Steven Michael of Meredith m. Beverly A. **Sanville** of Gilmanton 6/8/1968; H - b. 12/17/1946 in NH, s/o Roland K. Jenness (NH) and Bernice E. Thomas (NH); W - b. 5/28/1947 in NH, d/o William Henry Sanville (NH) and Florence W. Brassaw (NH)

JOHANSSON,
Michael S. of Laconia m. Jennifer L. **Hempel** of Gilmanton 7/11/1987

JOHNSON,
Charles A. of Strafford m. Mary E. **Young** of Gilmanton 7/3/1887; H - 27, fireman, b. Strafford, s/o Ivory Johnson (Strafford, farmer) and Martha A. Otis (Barnstead, housewife); W - 16, housewife, b. Gilmanton, d/o Alvin Young and Sarah E. Doe (Deerfield, housewife)
Eric E. of Burlington, VT m. Beth **Rizzon** of Burlington, VT 9/15/1985
James G., III of Gilmanton m. Julia **Capowski** of Verbank, NY 8/30/1986
Kristian Thane of Flagstaff, AZ m. Melissa Elizabeth **Oviatt** of Flagstaff, AZ 7/30/1994
Mark F. of Gilmanton m. Nance J. **Davidson** of Gilmanton 6/2/1984

JOHNSTON,
David Russell of Dover m. Mildred Virginia **Scovill** of Gilmanton 6/17/1966; H - 34, assist. principal, b. MA, s/o Joseph Matthew Johnston (MA) and Mary Arlene Smith (CT); W - 21, teacher, b. NH, d/o Lawrence Sorensen Scovill (MA) and Virginia A. Prescott (NH)

JONES,
Albert A. of Gilmanton m. Florence M. **Payson** of Concord 9/7/1894; H - 38, manufacturer, b. Gilmanton, s/o Richard H. Jones (Gilmanton, manufacturer) and Mertha A. Jones (Gilmanton, housekeeper); W - 27, housekeeper, b. Lawrence, MA, d/o Holland Payson (NS, merchant) and Mary F. Payson (E. Lebanon, ME, housekeeper)
Albert H. of Gilmanton m. Jennie M. **Flanders** of Gilmanton 2/17/1894 in Hopkinton; H - 24, lumber dealer, b. Gilmanton, s/o James A. Jones (Gilmanton, miller) and Mary E. Lock (housewife); W - 22, housekeeper, b. Gilmanton, d/o Asahel G. Flanders (carpenter) and Lizzie Flanders (housewife)
Allie C. of Gilmanton m. Lillian E. **Brown** of Belmont 1/2/1899; H - 33, farmer, b. Gilmanton, s/o Cyrus Jones (Gilmanton) and

Laura A. Maxfield (Gilmanton); W - 21, millhand, b. Belmont, d/o Frank A. Brown (Nashua, laborer) and Clara E. Clark (Sanbornton)

James Richard, Jr. of Phoenixville, PA m. Carletta **Eastmond** of Phoenixville, PA 11/26/1993

Karl E. of Gilmanton m. Mary E. **Canney** of Gilmanton 4/10/1926 in Loudon; H - 23, farmer, b. Gilmanton, s/o Allie C. Jones (Gilmanton, farmer) and Lillian Brown (Nashua, housework); W - 18, housework, b. E. Concord, d/o John W. Canney (Tuftonboro, carpenter) and Laura J. Smith (E. Concord, housework)

Lawrence Charles of Gilmanton m. Wilma Josephine **Foss** of Ellington, CT 11/17/1962 in Vernon, CT; H - 18, carpenter, b. CT, s/o Ernest M. Jones and Doris Price; W - 18, filer, b. ME, d/o George S. Foss and Georgie Everett

Morrill S. m. Mary **Going** 5/10/1922 in Belmont

Ralph Almond of Gilmanton m. Ruth M. **Thompson** of Gilmanton 8/3/1925; H - 21, farmer, b. Gilmanton, s/o Allie C. Jones (Gilmanton, farmer) and Lillian Brown (Belmont, housework); W - 18, housework, b. N. Wilmington, MA, d/o Andrew Thompson (Chelsea, MA, gold beater) and Minnie H. Wells (Chelsea, MA, housework)

JORDAN,
Jay E. of Alton m. Rebeecca A. **Lessard** of Gilmanton 5/3/1985

JOSLIN,
Edwin A. of Gilmanton m. Augusta M. **Foss** of Gilmanton 10/24/1903 in Pittsfield; H - 44, laborer, 2nd, b. Greenfield, s/o Oscar Joslin (farmer) and Berthia Swinerton (Lyndeboro); W - 17, housemaid, d/o John H. Foss (Greenfield, watchman) and Ethel M. Varney (Gilmanton)

JOY,
George Edwin m. Lila Mabel **Twombly** 6/15/1923

JOYCE,
Frank T. of Gilmanton m. Myrtle Pauline **Azotea** of Gilmanton 5/26/1962; H - 50, painter, b. NH, s/o Edward Tong (China)

and Ellen M. Langley (NH); W - 43, housework, b. NH, d/o Edward R. Cronan (VT) and Lidia Comes (NY)

JUDKINS,
Richard A. of Gilmanton m. Alice M. Ainsworth **Mansfield** of Gilmanton 11/29/1975; H - b. 11/1/1944 in NH, s/o Fenton Judkins (NH) and Geraldine Davidson (NH); W - b. 10/18/1950 in MA, d/o Lewis Mansfield (MA) and Claudia Chard (MA).

KARAGOZIAN,
Harold of Gilmanton m. Darin **Swanson** of Lochmere 4/27/1973 in Laconia; H - b. 12/14/1932 in MA, s/o Charles Karagozian (Turkey) and Mary Guleziam (Turkey); W - b. 4/1/1944 in IL, d/o Enar Swanson (IL) and Pauline Bailey (Ireland)

KEEFE,
Walter W. of Concord m. Elsie V. **Flanders** of Gilmanton 1/1/1934; H - 39, carpenter, b. PEI, s/o William H. Keefe (PEI, agent) and Margaret Robertson (PEI, homemaker); W - 28, at home, 3rd, b. Westford, MA, d/o Herman Purcell (Westford, MA, laborer) and Emma Randlett (Boston, MA, homemaker)

KEEGAN,
Arthur L. of Medford, MA m. Ena D. **Crandall** of Gilmanton 2/22/1987

KEENE,
Gregory Scott of Gilmanton m. Ann Morgyn **Morrell** of Gilmanton 9/30/1995

KEFFER,
David Brooks of New Haven, CT m. Barbara May **Finley** of Danvers, MA 7/14/1962; H - 25, stock broker, b. CT, s/o Harry B. Keffer (PA) and Benetta Smith (OH); W - 24, nurse, b. MA, d/o Harrison S. Finley (MA) and Mildred Withron (MA)

KEITH,
Robert Jackson of Northfield m. Marion M. **McClary** of Gilmanton 8/16/1947 in Belmont; H - 22, trucking, b. Sanbornton, s/o Frank M. Keith (Claremont, farmer) and Eva Deware (Pike,

housewife); W - 19, clock factory, b. Gilmanton, d/o Frank L. McClary (Gilmanton, farmer) and Leona Nutter (Maplewood, MA, housewife)

KELLEY,
Charles George of Gilmanton m. Hattie Belle **Page** of Gilmanton 10/22/1919; H - 33, farmer, b. Gilmanton, s/o George F. Kelley (Gilmanton) and Adelia C. Jones (Alton); W - 39, teacher, b. Utica, d/o C. Frank Page (Gilmanton) and Cora B. Gale (Gilmanton)

Donald Page of Gilmanton m. Phyllis Doris **Rogers** of Pittsfield 5/26/1951 in Pittsfield; H - 29, farmer, b. NH, s/o Charles G. Kelley (NH) and Hattie Page (NY); W - 27, nurse, b. NH, d/o George A. Rogers (NH) and Beatrice Coughlin (Ireland)

Edward W. of Gilmanton m. Nancy MacDonald **Kilton** of Gilmanton 11/17/1978; H - b. 4/11/1956 in NH, s/o Edward Kelley (NY) and Mary B. Shields (NY); W - b. 1/22/1949 in NH, d/o Robert L. Kilton (NH) and Janice E. Moulton (NH)

John David of Gilmanton m. Tina Marie **Hutchins** of Gilmanton 8/20/1988

John S. of Gilmanton m. Rita B. **Bradford** of Concord 7/1/1950 in Concord; H - 24, student, b. NH, s/o Charles G. Kelley (NH) and Hattie P. Page (NY); W - 23, R. N., b. ME, d/o Harold L. Bradford (ME) and Rena M. Fogg (ME)

Scott Michael of Gilmanton m. Melissa **Maltais** of Gilmanton 8/8/1999

KELLY,
Michael J. of Gilmanton m. Theresa D. **Hamel** of Manchester 9/11/1982

KENNEY,
John, Jr. of Gilmanton m. Barbara **Lempke** of Gilmanton 8/16/1976; H - b. 5/16/1933 in NH, s/o John Kenney, Sr. (NH) and Hagar Ross (NH); W - b. 5/31/1944 in Germany, d/o Stephen Kaciak (Poland) and Martha Kaciak (Poland)

John L. of Andover, MA m. Sandra A. Labranche **Dombrowski** of Andover, MA 8/26/1989

Warren Peter, Jr. of Westville m. Eunice **Hansen** of Gilmanton 11/11/1967 in Laconia; H - 34, foreman, b. MA, s/o Warren P.

Kenney, Sr. (MA) and Mary Rose Aucoin (MA); W - 29, at home, b. MA, d/o Louis S. Mansfield (MA) and Claudia E. Chard (MA)

KETCHUM,
Allen R. of Laconia m. Suzanne **Stevens** of Gilmanton 8/3/1974; H - b. 5/22/1951 in NH, s/o Robert R. Ketchum (NH) and Marie P. Allen (NH); W - b. 8/22/1952 in MA, d/o Richard H. Stevens (MA) and Nancy Wilson (MA)

KIMBALL,
David Wayne of Laconia m. Alberta Rae **Brown** of Gilmanton 5/3/1969; H - b. 5/21/1949 in NH, s/o Wesley J. Kimball, Sr. (NH) and Gladys M. Bresse (NH); W - b. 1.9.1951 in NH, d/o Raymond A. Brown (NH) and Bernice M. Willard (NH)
Edward C., II of Barnstead m. Debora S. **Daigle** of Gilmanton 11/6/1976; H - b. 10/19/1951 in NH, s/o Edward C. Kimball (NH) and Rita Canfield (NH); W - b. 5/23/1957 in MA, d/o Leo J. Daigle (MA) and Virginia M. Belcastro (MA)
John F. of Gilford m. Stacey A. **Coleman** of Gilmanton 6/10/1985
Scott A. of Belmont m. Myrtie B. **Smith** of Gilmanton 3/14/1900 in Laconia; H - 29, farmer, b. Belmont, s/o Jeremiah S. Kimball and Lavina F. Sanborn (Belmont, housewife); W - 24, housemaid, b. Gilmanton, d/o Edward E. Smith (Gilmanton, laborer) and Jane Evans (Gilmanton, housewife)

KINGHAM,
Ernest A. of Gilmanton m. Reba Dale **Harer** of Erwinna, IA 3/17/1937 in Laconia; H - 62, retired, 2nd, b. London, England, s/o George F. Kingham (Dublin, Ireland, importer) and Mary E. Spencer (London, at home); W - 48, vocalist and teacher, 4th, b. Watertown, NY, d/o Charles H. Harris (Orchow, NY, merchant) and Therza Amelia (Picton, Canada, at home)

KINSMAN,
John Manson of Gilmanton m. Cora A. **Russell** of Alton 12/24/1917 in Rochester; H - 49, blacksmith, b. Orono, ME, s/o Edward Kinsman (ME) and Elizabeth Brown (ME); W - 50, stitcher, b. Freeport, IL, d/o George A. Glidden (New Durham) and Mary E. Moulton (Framingham, MA)

KIRK,
Peter M. of Gilmanton I. W. m. Alicia **Ellingson** of Gilmanton I. W. 6/21/1975; H - b. 10/18/1951 in Canada, s/o John R. Kirk (Canada) and Jessie McPhail (Canada); W - b. 4/21/1952 in NH, d/o William Ellingson (WI) and Evelyn M. Bickford (NH)

KLEFOS,
Conrad E. S. of Hanover m. Joan **Biber** of Rumford 6/29/1976; H - b. 8/31/1953 in NH, s/o Brede Klefos (Norway) and Constance Snow (NH); W - b. 2/27/1953 in RI, d/o Raymond Biber (RI) and Catherine Morton (RI)
Kristofer Robin on Gilmanton m. Susan Marie **Good** of Concord 8/12/1978 in Wolfeboro; H - b. 4/5/1956 in NH, s/o Brede Klefos (Norway) and Constance Snow (NH); W - b. 3/28/1959 in CA, d/o Eldon E. Good (KS) and Elnora Morgan (OK)

KNOWLES,
Maitland Charles of Gilmanton m. Ola E. H. **Wright** of Gilmanton 2/19/1951 in Pittsfield; H - 47, mill operator, b. NH, s/o Harry C. Knowles (NH) and Alice Currier (NH); W - 42, at home, b. NH, d/o Walter J. Hillsgrove (NH) and Myrtie Day (NH)

KORDAS,
Richard Porter of Gilmanton m. Renee Wendy **Butler** of Gilmanton 7/18/1998

KRUEGER,
David William of Gilford m. Robin Sue **Adel** of Gilmanton 10/26/1974 in Laconia; H - b. 8/8/1945 in OH, s/o Carl Krueger (OH) and Mae R. Gring (PA); W - b. 10/22/1957 in NH, d/o Daniel J. Adel, Jr. (NH) and Carrol Ann Smith (NH)
Laurence Ray of W. Roxbury, MA m. Glenna Mae **Munsey** of Gilmanton 7/29/1950; H - 29, student, b. IA, s/o Henry J. Krueger (Sweden) and Theresa Stern (Germany); W - 21, at home, b. NH, d/o John J. Munsey (NH) and Julia Bruce (Canada)

LABRIE,
Alan Russell of Manchester m. Marie Malaine **Dube** of Gilmanton 6/24/1995

LACASSE,
Raymond Francis, Jr. of Gilmanton m. Sylvia Muriel **Dunn** of Gilmanton 7/3/1999

LACLAIR,
James M. of Gilmanton m. Kimberly A. **Jacob** of Gilmanton 4/21/2001

LAFAVE,
Edwin of Gilmanton m. Pauline M. **Fall** of Concord 6/26/1956 in Penacook; H - 29, farmer's helper, b. MI, s/o Edwin LaFave and Beatrice Perry; W - 23, at home, b. NH, d/o Otis Fall (NH) and Margaret Cheney (NH)

LAFLEUR,
Thomas Gordon of Gilmanton m. Diane **Marrion** of Gilmanton 5/24/1999

LAFOND,
Morris Daniel of Gilmanton m. Geraldine Susan **Robert** of Gilmanton 7/1/1995

LAGASSE,
Roger L. of Gilmanton m. Mary E. **Ferris** of Haverhill, MA 11/24/1992

LAMPREY,
Aldis J. of Gilmanton m. Ellen **Ricker** of Gilmanton 7/10/1907 in Belmont; H - 59, farmer, 2nd, b. Gilmanton, s/o Oliver Lamprey (Gilford, farmer) and Abigail Moulton (Tamworth, housewife); W - 50, housekeeper, 3rd, b. Dracut, MA, d/o Moses Ricker (farmer) and Uraury Manson (housewife)
Carlton A. of Belmont m. May A. **Lamprey** of Gilmanton 9/5/1899; H - 27, farmer, b. Belmont, s/o Arthur H. Lamprey (Belmont, farmer) and Emma O. James (Gilford); W - 22, school teacher, b. Gilmanton, d/o Madison C. Lamprey (Gilmanton, farmer) and Marilla Farrar (Belmont, housewife)
Herman F. of Gilmanton m. Susie **Colby** of Manchester 10/27/1915 in Belmont; H - 58, farmer, b. Gilmanton, s/o Cyrus Lamprey (Gilmanton, farmer) and Elsie Ellsworth (Gilmanton,

housewife); W - 55, housekeeper, 2nd, b. Manchester, d/o William Denby (Burlington, VT, machinist) and Belinda Kenniston (Island Pond, VT, housewife)

LANCE,
Mark Royce of Gilmanton m. Linda May Colby **Roy** of Gilmanton 9/2/1989

LANDRY,
Daniel Gary of Largo, FL m. Nannette Jean **Haywood** of Largo, FL 11/12/1994
Joshua R. of Gilmanton m. Min K. **Kang** of Gilmanton 6/30/2001
Robert Joseph of Dalton m. Judith Veronica **Orzolek** of Gilmanton 12/16/1967 in Lakeport; H - 21, Army, b. NH, s/o Philip Landry (NH) and Olivine E. Maurais (VT); W - 22, student, b. NH, d/o Chester N. Orzotek (sic) (MA) and Ella Leona Ross (MA)

LANE,
Myron W. of Gilmanton m. Hattie M. **Clough** of Gilmanton 10/7/1909; H - 37, farmer, b. Chichester, s/o Thomas B. Lane (Sanbornton, farmer) and Maria Williams (Gilmanton, housewife); W - 34, housemaid, b. Gilmanton, d/o M. S. Clough (Alton, farmer) and Elizabeth H. Prescott (Alton, housewife)
Steven J. of Gilmanton m. Lorie A. **Perrin** of Gilmanton 8/24/1996

LANGEVIN,
William O. of Pittsfield m. Evelyn D. **Hilt** of Pittsfield 4/17/1976; H - b. 2/1/1952 in Japan, s/o William P. Langevin (NH) and Mieko Hayashi (Japan); W - b. 3/28/1951 in ME, d/o Eugene W. Hilt (ME) and Inez L. Emerson (NH)

LANGLEY,
Bernard H. of Gilmanton m. Arline J. **Poirrier** of Laconia 7/20/1946; H - 27, civil engineer, b. Vineland, NJ, s/o Howard G. Langley (Gilmanton, t. official) and Laura Nelson (Perth Amboy, NJ, at home); W - 26, cost clerk, b. Laconia, d/o Henry A. Poirrier (England, machinist) and Carolyn Weber (Torrington, CT, at home)

Donald C. of Gilmanton m. Dorothy M. **Quinn** of Laconia 2/1/1947
in Belmont; H - 24, at home, b. Hopkinton, s/o Howard Langley
(Gilmanton, selectman) and Laura Newson (Vineland, NJ, at
home); W - 28, assembly, S & W, b. Winchester, MA, d/o
Everett L. Milne (Winchester, MA, retired) and Mabel G. Wells
(Woburn, MA, at home)

Henry N. of Gilmanton m. Grace A. **McClary** of Gilmanton
12/25/1942; H - 22, student, b. Metuchen, NJ, s/o Howard
Langley (Gilmanton, farmer) and Laura Nelson (Vineland, NJ,
housewife); W - 21, defense wkr., b. Gilmanton, d/o Horace
McClary (Gilmanton, caretaker) and Hattie A. Alberty
(Abington, CT, housewife)

Howard G. of Gilmanton m. Laura L. **Patten** of Belmont 1/13/1967
in Pittsfield; H - 19, machinist, b. ME, s/o Donald C. Langley
(NH) and Dorothy M. Milne (MA); W - 16, at home, b. NH, d/o
Frederick Patten (NH) and Andrea E. Hersey (NH)

Paul Nelson of Gilmanton m. Elaine M. **Thompson** of Gilmanton
12/29/1973; H - b. 5/10/1954 in ME, s/o Donald Langley (NH)
and Dorothy Milne (MA); W - b. 12/27/1951 in NH, d/o Edward
Thompson (MA) and Angela Delafano (MA)

Rufus Howard of Gilmanton m. Alice E. **Abbott** of Gilmanton
10/16/1892; H - 21, clerk, b. Cambridgeport, MA; W - 20,
teacher, b. Belmont, d/o George W. Abbott (Haverhill,
blacksmith) and Ellen C. Allen (Gilmanton, housewife)

LANGSTEN,
Mario L. of Gilford m. Susan A. **Berry** of Gilmanton 9/8/1979

LANK,
Clinton L. of Gilmanton m. Carolyn R. **Locke** of Barnstead
10/16/1954 in Chichester; H - 23, lineman, b. RI, s/o Clinton L.
Lank (NB) and Ruth O. Butman (RI); W - 18, secretary, b. NH,
d/o Elias W. Locke (NH) and Violet M. Gray (NH)

Howard J. of Barnstead m. Hazel I. **Parker** of Gilmanton 2/28/1947;
H - 20, plumbing, b. Providence, RI, s/o Clinton L. Lank
(Canada, lumberman) and Ruth O. Butman (Providence, RI,
housewife); W - 19, at home, b. Detroit, MI, d/o Leon D. Parker
(Fitchburg, MA, farmer) and Bella MacLeod (N. Whiton,
Canada, housewife)

LANNAN,
David Wayne of Gilmanton I.W. m. Irina Vladimirovna **Gorodilo** of Gilmanton I.W. 4/29/2000

LAROCHE,
Alfred E., Jr. of Laconia m. Melba Jean **Clifford** of Gilmanton 7/2/1949 in Laconia; H - 21, laborer, b. NH, s/o Alfred E. Laroche (NH) and Hazel M. Bagley (NH); W - 19, stenographer, b. NH, d/o Earle C. Clifford (NH) and Nellie M. Ellsworth (NH)
Stephen E. of Gilmanton m. Carol A. **Weeks** of Gilford 2/14/1987

LARSSON,
Hans R. of Gilmanton m. Nicole A. **Danforth** of Gilmanton 10/20/2001

LATHROP,
Elwin G. m. Alma L. **Smith** 10/24/1923
Harold E. of Gilmanton m. J. Teresa **Taylor** of Manchester 9/2/1933 in Manchester; H - 38, overseer, 2nd, b. Auburn, RI, s/o Elwyn G. Lathrop (Canaan Ctr., druggist) and Clara B. Hubbell (Binghamton, NY, housework); W - 36, stenographer, b. Granville, Can., d/o John T. Taylor (Granville, Can., farmer) and Flora I. Bagley (Canaan, VT, housework)

LAURENT,
Paul Eugene of Laconia m. Elizabeth Denise **Freeman** of Gilmanton 10/12/1974 in Laconia; H - b. 3/6/1947 in NH, s/o Oliver A. Laurent (NH) and Alice A. Drouin (Canada); W - b. 8/20/1949 in Canada, d/o Robert Freeman (Canada) and Grace Duncan (Scotland)

LAVALLEE,
Gary K. of Gilmanton m. Mary E. **Collins** of Gilmanton 9/9/1979

LAVINE,
Victor of Gilmanton m. Rosie **Ashcroft** of Gilmanton 7/16/1935 in Nottingham; H - 69, laborer, b. Canada, s/o Frederick Lavine (Canada) and Mary Pariseau (Canada); W - 38, at home, 2nd,

b. Canada, d/o Andrew DeSelle (Boston, MA) and ----- DeSelle (Canada, housework)

LEACH,
Henry Groves of Quincy, MA m. Jessie Elizabeth **Allan** of Wollaston, MA 7/4/1949 in Gilmanton I. W.; H - 46, telephone man, b. MA, s/o Harry R. Leach (MA) and Mabel J. Mann (NB); W - 35, physiotherapist, b. MA, d/o Chester E. Blackey (MA) and Mary J. Briggs (Wales)

LEAVER,
Robert M. of Hartford, CT m. Edith **Waters** of Canton, MA 6/30/1935; H - 28, salesman, b. Charlotte, NC, s/o Robert Leaver (Rochester, elec. engineer) and Anna T. Murray (Brookline, MA, housewife); W - 21, at home, 2nd, b. Canton, MA, d/o Oliver P. Wolfe (Weymouth, MA, dentist) and Nellie Belyes (St. John, NB, housewife)

LEAVITT,
George Wilbur of Gilmanton m. Nellie Etta **Rogers** of Gilmanton 4/29/1909 in Tilton; H - 30, fireman, b. Lynn, MA, s/o Charles A. Leavitt (Boston, MA, engineer) and Lura May Hurd (Sanford, ME, housewife); W - 34, housemaid, b. Dover, d/o Amasa S. Rogers (Brownfield, ME, farmer) and Annie O. Dame (Dover, housewife)

Henry Frank of Gilmanton m. Ethel May **Winch** of Gilmanton 6/30/1917 in Pittsfield; H - 50, farmer, b. Chichester, s/o George M. Leavitt (Pittsfield) and Rachel Hook (Chichester); W - 32, housekeeper, b. W. Hartland, ME, d/o Robert Scribner Smith (Brighton, ME) and Mary Anna Spencer (Medford, ME)

LECLAIR,
Thomas E. of Gilmanton m. Lorna R. **Corno** of Gilmanton 7/7/1990

LECOUR,
Ernest of Gilmanton m. Helen E. **Chase** of Loudon 10/3/1916; H - 24, works in wood, b. Lakeport, s/o Peter Lecour (St. Marie, Can., teamster) and Mary Foster (St. Marie, Can., housewife); W - 21, housework, b. Gilmanton, d/o Daniel Chase (Bristol, painter) and Adeline Fogg (Loudon, housewife)

LEITAO,
Edward A. of MA m. Mary M. **Defarrari** of MA 6/18/1982

LENNEBERG,
Eric H. of Ithaca, NY m. Elizabeth S. **Pfohl** of MA 5/17/1969; H - b. 9/19/1921 in Germany, s/o Robert Lenneberg (Germany) and Gertrude Stern (Germany); W - b. 11/6/1933 in MA, s/o Frederick Smith (CT) and Marion Smith (MA)

LEROUX,
Roger John of Gilmanton m. Louella M. **Guyer** of Gilmanton 8/31/1996

LEWIS,
Alan L. of Gilmanton I. W. m. Nancy A. **Kendall** of Gilmanton I. W. 6/24/1978; H - b. 7/9/1943 in CA, s/o Alex Appelbaum (NY) and Shirley Friedman (CA); W - b. 11/7/1953 in NH, d/o Philip Kendall (MA) and Mary Thompson (NH)

LINCOLN,
David C. of Tilton m. Barbara N. **Brawley** of Gilmanton 12/12/1976 in Laconia; H - b. 9/30/1949 in MA, s/o Charles Lincoln (MA) and Ernestine Briggs (MA); W - b. 9/16/1946 in NY, d/o Allen Barry (NY) and Nancy Collins (MA)

LINDBLOOM,
Donald K. of Gilmanton m. Nancy Carol **Ackerman** of Gilmanton 5/12/1991

LINDHOLM,
Michael H. of Gilmanton m. Anita D. **Haun** of Gilmanton 9/29/1980

LINDQUIST,
William E. of Gilmanton I. W. m. Bernice M. Cate **Dyment** of Concord 1/16/1975 in Concord; H - b. 10/25/1920 in MA, s/o John A. Lindquist (MA) and Helen Wassmouth (MA); W - b. 2/17/1912 in Canada, d/o Charles E. Dyment (Canada) and Anne Roy (Canada)

LINES,
Alan of Gilmanton m. Christine Ann **Ward** of Wollaston, MA 10/19/1962 in Belmont; H - 22, service, b. MA, s/o John William Lines (MA) and Iris Sylvia Austin (MA); W - 18, at home, b. NH, d/o Edward Leo Ward (MA) and Mildred Ruth Snow (MA)

Gary of Gilmanton m. Jane Louise **Schott** of Gilmanton 8/19/1967; H - 22, carpenter, b. MA, s/o John William Lines (MA) and Iris Silvia Austin (MA); W - 18, at home, b. MA, d/o Charles Kenneth Schott (Canada) and Thelma Suzanne Blackey (MA)

Gary of Gilmanton m. Betty **Graeme** of Pittsfield 9/15/1973; H - b. 11/20/1944 in MA, s/o John Lines (MA) and Iris Austin (MA); W - b. 3/25/1948 in NH, d/o Clarence Graeme (NH) and Rita Genest (NH)

Glen of Gilmanton m. Nancy Jane **Stockwell** of Gilmanton 7/27/1963; H - 20, mechanic, b. MA, s/o John W. Lines (MA) and Iris S. Austin (MA); W - 18, waitress, b. NH, d/o Leonard A. Stockwell (MA) and Ruth A. Clifford (NH)

John Alan of Gilmanton m. Jodi Lynn **Hilton** of Gilmanton 6/24/1989

Paul of Gilmanton m. Nancy E. **Strout** of Barnstead 4/21/1973 in Barnstead; H - b. 1/26/1955 in NH, s/o John Lines (MA) and Iris Austin (MA); W - b. 4/5/1956 in NY, d/o George Strout (ME) and Nadine Lindberg (ME)

Paul of Gilmanton m. Catherine E. **Colby** of Laconia 6/22/1985

LINSCOTT,
Ronald Hollis of Tenants Harbor, ME m. Ann Marguarite **Gledhill** of Tenants Harbor, ME 6/27/1964; H - 20, derrick op., b. ME, s/o Maynard R. Linscott, Jr. (ME) and Viletta M. Chadwick (ME); W - 19, at home, b. ME, d/o George H. Gledhill (NJ) and Marguarite L. Hall (ME)

LIQUE,
Ronald E. of Claremont m. Patricia **Hillsgrove** of Gilmanton 6/4/1955; H - 19, maint. work, b. VT, s/o Joseph A. Lique (VT) and Eva J. Taylor (VT); W - 20, secretary, b. NH, d/o Walter M. Hillsgrove (NH) and Louise E. Pike (NH)

LITTLE,
Joseph D. of Gilmanton m. Blanch E. **Gilman** of Belmont 5/9/1917;
 H - 23, farmer, b. Gilmanton, s/o Romie Little (Monstilo, MS) and Lola M. Barnum (Laconia); W - 23, at home, b. Belmont, d/o Edward O. Gilman (Woburn, MA) and Lizzie Q. Leavitt (Gilford)

King R. m. Iona M. **Clough** 11/28/1922 in Laconia

Philip Gilman of Gilmanton m. Evelyn **Hilliard** of Gilmanton 12/17/1939 in Gilford; H - 21, truck driver, b. Belmont, s/o Joseph D. Little (Gilmanton, machinist) and Blanche E. Gilman (Belmont, mill worker); W - 18, housework, b. Laconia, d/o Erving Hilliard (Laconia, teamster) and Marian Constant (Biddeford, ME, mill worker)

LITTLEFIELD,
George of Gilmanton m. Evelyn L. **Jones** of Gilmanton 2/12/1989

Wilmer L. of Ctr. Ossipee m. Dorothy W. **Byers** of Gilmanton 11/1/1986

LOCKE,
George Ozro of Gilmanton m. Edith May **Nutter** of Dover 11/19/1950 in Dover; H - 70, woodsman, b. NH, s/o Dexter Locke (NH) and Sarah Page; W - 64, stitcher, b. NH, d/o Elias Locke (MA) and Caroline Come (Canada)

Harold Ozro of Gilmanton m. Dorothy Merle **Farmar** of Plymouth 11/4/1951 in Chichester; H - 43, lumbering, b. NH, s/o George O. Locke (NH) and Edith L. Sargent (NH); W - 28, at home, b. NH, d/o Albert A. Farmar (VT) and Florence M. Mossy (VT)

James Nutter of Barnstead m. Natalie Jean **Price** of Gilmanton 11/14/1959; H - 21, student, b. NH, s/o Kent D. Locke (NH) and Margaret Johnston (MA); W - 20, bookkeeper, b. NH, d/o A. Richard Price, Jr. (NH) and Pauline M. Richards (MA)

Robert S. of Pittsfield m. Sylvia A. **Dudley** of Gilmanton 10/12/1958; H - 22, lumber, b. NH, s/o Harold O. Locke (NH) and Florence M. Coburn (MA); W - 19, photography, b. NH, d/o Irving D. Dudley (NH) and Dorothy A. Hurlbutt (NH)

LOCKWOOD,
Brian Arthur of Gilmanton m. Julie Dolores **Fifield** of Canterbury 9/23/1989

Earl E., Jr. of Northfield m. Christine A. **Provencal** of Gilmanton 2/12/1983

LONGLEY,
Alvah, Jr. of Concord m. Patricia J. **Bushnell** of Gilmanton 7/13/1957; H - 23, mover, b. NH, s/o Alvah T. Langley (NH) and Ina K. Kimball (NH); W - 17, typist, b. NH, d/o Richard B. Bushnell (VT) and C. Marie Barneetz (VT)

LORD,
Norman Junior of Belmont m. Bernice Laura **Greenwood** of Gilmanton 2/27/1960 in Belmont; H - 20, truck driver, b. NH, s/o Malvina Alice Parent (MA); W - 20, at home, b. NH, d/o Clifford A. Greenwood (NH) and Jeannette Mary Forest (VT)

LOUNSBURY,
Wilbur J., Jr. of Laconia m. Patricia A. **Bragg** of Gilmanton 6/5/1982

LUND,
Leon of Gilmanton m. Ina F. **Connell** of Gilmanton 4/25/1901; H - 22, laborer, b. Chicago, s/o Edward Lund (Wentworth) and Judith Lund (Wentworth); W - 23, housekeeper, b. Gilmanton, d/o John M. Connell (Strafford, merchant) and Emma Dean (Brooklyn, housewife)

LUTKUS,
David V. of Gilmanton m. Linda J. **Bjorkman** of Gilmanton 12/20/1986

LYNCH,
Jack D. of Gilmanton m. Susan M. **Hechler** of Gilmanton 7/16/1982
James Francis of Gilmanton m. Marian N. **Sagona** of Gilmanton 7/22/1994

LYSTER,
Herbert L. of Gilmanton m. Junie Belle **Lyster** of Waterford, VT 6/21/1899 in Waterford, VT; H - 27, butter maker, b. Durham, Que., s/o William H. Lyster (Kirkdale, Que., insurance) and Isabelle Leslie (Scotland, housewife); W - 20, housemaid, b.

Waterford, VT, d/o T. H. Lyster (Kirkdale, Que., farmer) and Ida Hall (Westmoreland, housewife)

MACASKILL,
Kenneth A. of Malden, MA m. Janie L. **Schott** of Gilmanton 8/24/1974; H - b. 5/13/1936 in MA, s/o George J. MacAskill (Canada) and Lena MacDonald (Canada); W - b. 2/1/1949 in MA, d/o C. Kenneth Schott (Canada) and Suzanne Blackey (MA)

MACDONALD,
Charles of Pittsfield m. Joy Leslie **Pennock** of Gilmanton 7/29/1962 in Alton; H - 21, machinist, b. NH, s/o Kenneth MacDonald (Canada) and Willyla Humphreys (Canada); W - 20, student, b. NH, d/o James G. Pennock (NH) and Florence V. Pennock (MA)

MACFAYDEN,
Donald E. of Portsmouth m. Laurose **Wilkens** of Gilmanton 4/10/1982

MACINNES,
Neil A. of Wayne, PA m. Gertrude **Robertson** of Gilmanton 9/5/1954; H - 30, elec. engineer, b. PA, s/o Alexander MacInnes (Scotland) and Viola Newbou (NJ); W - 25, at home, b. NH, d/o William T. Robertson (Scotland) and Eunice Whittemore (MA)

MACKENZIE,
James, II of Boston, MA m. Diane **Smith** of Gilmanton 12/22/1978; H - b. 12/1/1933 in NJ, s/o James MacKenzie (NJ) and Marie Thornton (GA); W - b. 8/11/1955 in NH, d/o Roger A. Smith (NH) and Yvette Daigle (NH)

MACKES,
Maurice M. of Kunkletown, PA m. Geraldine E. **Hawkins** of Gilmanton 8/6/1944; H - 28, crane operator, b. Kunkletown, PA, s/o Simon P. Mackes (Kunkletown, PA, farmer) and Elsie Christman (Kunkletown, PA, housewife); W - 23, at home, b.

Gilmanton, d/o Shurldin Hawkins (Chelsea, MA, farmer) and Amy O. Osborne (Gilmanton, housewife)

MAGOON,
Kenneth F. of Gilmanton m. Teresa R. **Diversi** of Concord 6/20/1936; H - 37, motor officer, 2nd, b. E. Rochester, s/o George Magoon (Guilford, ME, at home) and Helen Faunce (Lisbon Falls, ME, at home); W - 36, florist, 2nd, b. Concord, d/o Henry Diversi and Mary Diversi (Florence, Italy, at home)

MAHER,
Frederick H. of Gilmanton I.W. m. Jennifer L. **Ryan** of Gilmanton I.W. 12/2/2000

MAHONEY,
Brian F. of Gilmanton m. Karen J. **Lane** of Gilmanton 11/23/1990

MALLORY,
Bruce L. of Gilmanton m. Susan R. **Curtis** of Gilmanton 8/18/1979
John K., III of PA m. Joann L. **Baldwin** of PA 8/26/1978; H - b. 3/12/1946 in VA, s/o John K. Mallory (VA) and Suzanne Lippincott (PA); W - b. 6/9/1949 in CA, d/o Weldon A. Baldwin (OK) and Nancy Tingstrom (CA)
Mark L. of Gilmanton m. Nancy L. **Ball** of Gilmanton 8/14/1982

MALSBURY,
William A. of Gilmanton m. Minnie E. **Bickford** of Wolfeboro 8/6/1906; H - 22, laborer, b. Gilmanton, s/o Job G. Malsbury (barber) and Maud C. Heath (Dover, housewife); W - 16, weaver, b. Alton, d/o Alonzo Bickford (laborer)

MALTAIS,
Danny Roy of Gilmanton m. Linda Ruth **Davis** of Laconia 2/7/1970 in Laconia; H - b. 2/6/1950 in CT, s/o John E. Maltais (NH) and Irene E. LaPointe (NH); W - b. 2/23/1951 in NH, d/o Roger Davis (NH) and Rita Fortin (NH)
Danny Roy, Sr. of Gilmanton m. Anne E. **Drouin** of Laconia 12/13/1977 in Nashua; H - b. 2/6/1950 in CT, s/o John E. Maltais, Sr. (NH) and Irene LaPointe (NH); W - b. 3/24/1956 in

NH, d/o Benoit C. Drouin (Canada) and Elizabeth Corriveau (NH)

John E., Jr. of Gilmanton m. Holly C. **Chamberlain** of Gilmanton 7/24/1965 in Laconia; H - 20, molder, b. CT, s/o John E. Maltais (NH) and Irene LaPointe (NH); W - 19, presser, b. NH, d/o Robert W. Chamberlain (ME) and Marjorie M. Seavey (MA)

MANLEY,

Leroy A. of Gilmanton m. Virginia A. **Scovill** of Gilmanton 11/13/1954 in Porter, ME; H - 44, toolmaker, b. MA, s/o Elmer E. Manley (MA) and Edith M. Stonehouse (NS); W - 32, housework, b. NH, d/o Harold F. Prescott (NH) and Caroline H. Eastman (MA)

Leroy A. of Gilmanton m. Margaret **Prescott** of Weirs 7/3/1956 in Laconia; H - 45, grinder, b. MA, s/o Elmer E. Manley (MA) and Edith Stonehouse (NS); W - 41, inspector, b. NH, d/o Von Milton and Clara M. Saunders (ME)

MANN,

Brendan Michael of Gilmanton m. Melissa Sue **Defosses** of Franklin 9/12/1998

MANNING,

Harold George, Jr. of Gilmanton m. Virginia Nora **Morse** of Sanbornton 10/10/1964 in Sanbornton; H - 18, carp. helper, b. NH, s/o Harold G. Manning, Sr. (NH) and Rachel V. Poire (NH); W - 19, hairdresser, b. NH, d/o Harry A. Morse (VT) and Gladys M. Whitcher (NH)

John Wayne of Gilmanton m. Deborah Elaine **Rieck** of Gilmanton 7/27/1991

MANSFIELD,

Benjamin William of Gilmanton m. Mildred Hodgson **Grant** of Gilmanton 3/15/1921; H - 19, machinist, b. Gilmanton, s/o William I. Mansfield (Wells, ME) and Cora May Tilton (Gilmanton); W - 25, school teacher, b. Belmont, d/o Haven M. Grant (Berwick, ME) and Etta Belle Dow (Lakeport)

George E. of Gilmanton m. Martha I. **Corliss** of Laconia 5/31/1928; H - 21, chauffeur, b. Gilmanton, s/o William I. Mansfield (ME, farmer) and Cora Tilton (Gilmanton, housework); W - 18, housekeeper, b. Laconia, d/o Wesley Corliss (Laconia, shopkeeper) and Nellie Gray (Lakeport, housework)

Herbert L. of Gilmanton m. Laura Christina **Smith** of Pittsfield 9/19/1915 in Belmont; H - 19, farmer, b. Gilmanton, s/o William Ira Mansfield (Wells, ME, farmer) and Cora May Tilton (Gilmanton, housewife); W - 17, at home, b. Somerville, MA, d/o Frank A. Smith (Worcester, MA, machinist) and Christina A. Deal (Arlington, MA, housewife)

William Ira of Wells, ME m. Cora May **Tilton** of Gilmanton 3/24/1894; H - 21, farmer, b. Wells, ME, s/o Daniel Mansfield (Lynn, MA, merchant) and Lydia A. Mansfield; W - 18, housekeeper, b. Gilmanton, d/o William Tilton (farmer) and Ella J. Hilliard

MANSON,

Charles I. of Gilmanton m. Blanche L. **Rand** of Gilmanton 2/19/1928; H - 49, laborer, 3rd, b. Greenland, s/o Levi Manson (Greenland, farmer) and Martha Johnson (Portsmouth, housework); W - 42, housework, 4th, b. Gilmanton, d/o Horace J. Beck (Gilmanton, farmer) and Martha Leighton (Gilmanton, housework)

MARCOUX,

Dennis Edward of Gilmanton m. Nancy Lee **Wade** of Gilmanton 7/28/1995

MARDIN,

Robert of Boston, MA m. Esther **Epstein** of Yonkers, NY 8/20/1934 in Gilmanton I. W.; H - 25, pianist, b. Boston, MA, s/o Abram Mardin (Russia, tailor) and Fannie Liberman (Russia, housewife); W - 23, dressmaker, b. Brooklyn, NY, d/o Nathan Epstein (Russia, carpenter) and Lena Aronson (Russia, housewife)

Willard C. of Gilmanton m. Addie M. **Davis** of Gilmanton 1/12/1932 in Pittsfield; H - 42, farmer, 2nd, b. Littleton, s/o Willard Mardin (US) and Alva ----- (England); W - 26, housewife, 2nd, b. Northwood, d/o Mortie Davis (Pittsfield, housework)

MARGESON,

Austin H. of Gilmanton m. Harmony **Stockwell** of Gilmanton 9/4/1948; H - 19, student, b. Gilmanton, s/o Edward M. Margeson (Grafton, NS, farmer) and Edith E. Bruce (Flodden, PQ, housewife); W - 18, at home, b. Concord, d/o Harmon A. Stockwell (E. Corinth, ME, merchant) and Roxy E. Mitchell (NB, housewife)

Edward M. m. Edith M. **Bruce** 2/21/1923

Edward M., Jr. of Gilmanton m. Mildred Irene **Riggins** of Laconia 12/25/1944; H - 21, soldier, b. Gilmanton, s/o Edward M. Margeson (Halifax, NS, farmer) and Edith E. Bruce (Sherbrooke, Can., home); W - 20, clerk, b. Jennings, MO, d/o Cleo Riggins (OH, mechanic) and Estella Harman (Modesto, IL, at home)

Ramon W. of Gilmanton m. Junie L. **Waite** of Laconia 5/1/1948 in Laconia; H - 22, USA Air Force, b. Gilmanton, s/o Edward M. Margeson (NS, farmer) and Edith E. Bruce (Sherbrooke, Que., inspector, S & W); W - 17, store clerk, b. Laconia, d/o Harry Sterling (Lakeport, greenhouse worker) and Thelma I. Trumbull (Webster, housewife)

MARION,

Gerald Patrick of Hartford, CT m. Mary Ellen **Tracy** of Manchester, CT 4/30/1966; H - 49, ticket agent, b. CT, s/o Joseph Marion (Canada) and Delima Paquette (CT); W - 30, accountant, b. MA, d/o Stanley Howard Withrow (Canada) and Dora Lyle Martin (MA)

MARONI,

Gennaro of Dover m. Rinske Titia **Van Epen** of Gilmanton 12/17/1995

MARSH,

Erskine H. of Gilmanton m. Jennie B. **Davis** of Alton 11/8/1891 in Pittsfield; H - 29, shoemaker, b. Gilmanton, s/o Joseph W. Marsh (Gilmanton, blacksmith) and Adaline Barker (housewife); W - 27, housewife, b. Gilmanton, d/o Alfred Davis (farmer) and Elizabeth Davis (housewife)

Frank A. of Gilmanton m. Anna P. **Durgin** of Gilmanton 12/25/1892 in Middleton, MA; H - 41, farmer, b. Portsmouth, s/o Amos

Marsh and Comfort Cate (Gilmanton); W - 41, housewife, 2nd, b. Thornton, d/o Nathan B. Sanborn (Gilmanton, farmer) and Ruth Ann Cousens (Kennebunk, ME)

Herbert J. of Gilmanton m. Addie B. **Parsons** of Gilmanton 10/14/1895; H - 43, farmer, 2nd, b. Gilmanton, s/o Joseph Marsh and Hannah M. Page (Gilmanton, housekeeper); W - 28, housekeeper, b. Gilmanton, d/o George C. Parsons (Manchester, farmer) and Julia Swain (Gilmanton, housewife)

Irad H. of Gilmanton m. Mary **Savolainen** of Royalston, MA 10/18/1930 in Manchester; H - 21, fireman, USN, b. Gilmanton, s/o Joseph H. L. Marsh (Manchester, farmer) and Alice C. Page (E. Boston, MA, housework); W - 25, teacher, b. S. Ashburnham, MA, d/o John Savolainen (Finland, farmer) and Mary Nalli (Finland, housework)

James E. of Hampton m. Audrey K. **Roberts** of Gilmanton 6/19/1982

Joseph H. L. of Gilmanton m. Alice C. **Page** of Gilmanton 12/31/1903; H - 23, farmer, b. Manchester, s/o Herbert J. Marsh (Manchester, farmer) and Fannie Poore (Goffstown); W - 18, housemaid, b. S. Boston, MA, d/o Mary E. Austin

MARSHALL,

John of Gilmanton m. Marion Evelyn **Burbrick** of Middleton, MA 4/19/1952 in Gilmanton I. W.; H - 70, retired, b. Scotland, s/o John C. Marshall (Scotland) and Margaret Gibb (Scotland); W - 55, attendant, b. MA, d/o William E. Wylie (ME) and Lillian P. Peabody (MA)

MARSTON,

Rodney Lee of Gilmanton m. Holly Ann **Hughes** of Gilmanton 3/25/1989

MARTEL,

Glenn K. of Gilmanton m. Robin **Richardson** of Gilmanton 9/7/1999

Glenn Kenneth of Gilmanton m. Rebecca Lynn **Rowe** of Gilmanton 10/28/1989

MARTIN,
Francis C. of Boston, MA m. Harriet B. **Cogswell** of Gilmanton 1/25/1893; H - 34, physician, b. Boston, MA, s/o Henry A. Martin (London, England, physician) and Frances Crosby (Gilmanton, housewife); W - 26, housekeeper, b. Gilmanton, d/o James W. Cogswell (Gilmanton, farmer) and Abby F. Clifford (Loudon, housewife)
Paul Ronald of Gilmanton m. Frances May **Wells** of Gilmanton 7/21/1949 in Manchester; H - 20, lumbering, b. ME, s/o Adolph J. Martin (ME) and Mary A. Rollins (ME); W - 13, at home, b. NH, d/o Fred R. Wells (NH) and Dorothea B. Lucia (MA)
Paul Ronald of Laconia m. Anne Helen **King** of Gilmanton 4/16/1966 in Laconia; H - 37, maintenance man, b. ME, s/o Adolph Joseph Martin (NH) and Mary Ann Rollins (ME); W - 18, factory worker, b. MA, d/o Frank Edward King (NH) and Ruth Violet Downes (NH)
Ronald Wayne of Gilmanton m. Linda Lee **Smith** of Belmont 4/15/1969 in Laconia; H - b. 12/26/1949 in NH, s/o Paul Martin (ME) and Frances M. Wells (NH); W - b. 2/24/1950 in NH, d/o Warren E. Smith (MO) and May E. Hanson (MA)
William A. of Gilmanton m. Karen L. **Lang** of Gilmanton 11/7/1987
William C., Jr. of Tampa, FL m. Tammy M. **Kling** of Tampa, FL 8/18/1984

MASON,
John S. of Belmont m. Addie F. **Brown** of Gilmanton 12/20/1893; H - 27, railroad section foreman, 2nd, b. West Moore, VT, s/o Stephen N. Mason and Lavina Collie; W - 31, housekeeper, 2nd, b. Belmont, d/o Isaac A. Downs (Gilmanton, farmer) and Augusta Smith (Loudon, housewife)

MASONI,
Mark Curt of Gilroy, CA m. Lisa **Berlind** of Middletown, CT 6/29/1996

MATTHEWS,
Roy Ellsworth of Gilmanton m. Pearl Lillian **Clay** of Northfield 6/4/1918 in Franklin; H - 20, farmer, b. Canaan, VT, s/o Arthur Clinton Matthews (Canaan, VT) and Mary Matilda Brown (Wolfeboro Jct.); W - 16, works in hosiery, b. Somersville, CT,

d/o Charles Clay (Franklin) and Laura Evelin Hemming (Potan, Quebec)

MAXWELL,
Seth R. of Gilmanton m. Heather J. **Maser** of Gilmanton 9/9/1980

MAYHEW,
Eldon B. of Exeter m. Georgianna **Bickford** of Gilmanton 4/13/1941 in Exeter; H - 28, clerk, b. Exeter, s/o Paul M. Mayhew (Epping, shoe worker) and Lorana Buzzell (Newfield, housewife); W - 30, at home, b. Gilmanton, d/o Arthur Bickford (Franklin, farmer) and Ida M. Brewster (Barnstead, housewife)

MAYO,
Richard Dana of Gilmanton m. Sara Hodgins **McCarthy** of Pittsfield 7/14/1974 in Pittsfield; H - b. 4/7/1942 in MI, s/o William N. Mayo (MA) and Laverne Leonard (NY); W - b. 8/3/1944 in NH, d/o Elwin B. Hodgins (ME) and Pauline Morgan (VT)

McAVENIA,
Richard C., Jr. of Laconia m. Nancy Lynne **Clairmont** of Gilmanton 2/8/1986

McCAFFREY,
Brian Michael of Gilmanton m. Peggyann **Mallett** of Warwick, RI 8/30/1997

McCARTNEY,
John W. of Laconia m. Blanche M. **Weeks** of Gilmanton 2/28/1937 in Kingston; H - 65, merchant, 2nd, b. Laconia, s/o Charles McCartney (Boston, MA, farmer) and Jennie Weston (Manchester, at home); W - 54, retired teacher, b. Gilmanton, d/o Marcus Weeks (Alton, farmer) and Sylvia Kimball (Belmont, at home)

McCLARY,
Bertrude B. of Gilmanton m. Lois M. **Clifford** of Gilmanton 1/14/1934 in Gilmanton I. W.; H - 22, laborer, b. Pomfret, CT, s/o Horace McClary (Gilmanton, farmer) and Hattie A. Alberty (Charleston, MA, housework); W - 18, at home, b. Gilmanton,

d/o Earle Clifford (Gilmanton, laborer) and Nellie Ellsworth (Gilmanton, housework)

Curtis J. of Gilmanton m. Claire **Gallagher** of Belmont 8/23/1937; H - 23, laborer, b. Pomfret, CT, s/o Horace McClary (Gilmanton, laborer) and Hattie Alberty (Charlestown, MA, at home); W - 20, housework, b. Thornton Ferry, d/o William Gallagher (NS, laborer) and Hazel Smith (Campton, at home)

Curtis J. of Gilmanton m. Charlotte E. **McKay** of Barrington 4/9/1979

Frank J. of Gilmanton m. Christine A. **Leonard** of Gilmanton 11/27/1982

Frank L. of Gilmanton m. Betty M. **Deware** of Gilmanton 12/24/1957 in Chichester; H - 29, construction, b. NH, s/o Frank L. McClary (NH) and Leona M. Nutter (ME); W - 24, hosiery wkr., b. MA, d/o Robert W. Deware (NH) and Mary C. Brown (NH)

Frank Leslie of Gilmanton m. Leona Myrtle **Nutter** of Gilmanton 10/3/1921 in Loudon; H - 18, laborer, b. Gilmanton, s/o J. Frank McClary (Gilmanton) and Euphemia Battis (Pittsfield); W - 17, housekeeping, b. Parsonsfield, ME, d/o Fred A. Nutter (Parsonsfield, ME) and Carrie Marshall Dutch (Parsonsfield, ME)

George F. of Gilmanton m. Lura M. **Bunker** of Gilmanton 11/7/1945; H - 24, lumbering, b. Gilmanton, s/o Frank L. McClary (Gilmanton, bus driver) and Leona Nutter (Maplewood, ME, housewife); W - 24, at home, b. Gilmanton, d/o Daniel Bunker (Barnstead, farmer) and Florence L. Hilliard (Loudon, housewife)

Harold J. of Gilmanton m. Beatrice E. **Sibley** of Center Harbor 9/12/1946 in Belmont; H - 21, mechanic, b. Gilmanton, s/o Frank L. McClary (Gilmanton, farmer) and Leona Nutter (Parsonsfield, ME, housewife); W - 26, clock assembler, b. Sanbornville, d/o Ernest R. Sibley (Wakefield, farmer) and Ethel M. Richards (Wakefield, housewife)

Horace E. of Gilmanton m. Clara J. **Butcher** of Pittsfield 9/27/1899; H - 20, farmer, b. Gilmanton, s/o Joseph B. McClary (Sanbornton, farmer) and Frances Adams (Danbury, housewife); W - 17, mill hand, b. Dover, d/o Edward L. Butcher (Germantown, PA, carpenter) and Lydia Bardene (Providence, RI, housewife)

J. Frank of Gilmanton m. Euphanie A. **Battis** of Gilmanton 9/1/1895; H - 20, farmer, b. Gilmanton, s/o J. B. McClary (farmer) and Frances Adams (Bristol, housewife); W - 18, operative, b. Gilmanton, d/o Frank Battis

Willard G. of Gilmanton m. Dorothy **Butcher** of Pittsfield 11/28/1900; H - 34, teamster, b. Bristol, s/o Joseph B. McClary (farmer) and Frances A. Adams (housekeeper); W - 18, housekeeper, b. Dover, d/o Edward Butcher (Germanton, PA, carpenter) and Lydia Bardeen (housekeeper)

McCRADY,
Douglas B. of Gilmanton m. Doris L. **Dwyer** of Gilmanton 10/26/1985

McDONALD,
Arthur William, Jr. of Gilmanton m. Susan Hale **Crosby** of Gilmanton 7/16/1993

McELROY,
Garth J. of Gilmanton m. Megan J. **Libby** of Gilmanton 10/15/2000

McEWAN,
Frank W. of Dover m. Addie Nina **Weeks** of Gilmanton 6/19/1895 in Alton; H - 21, ex. messenger, b. Massena, NY; W - 18, housekeeper, b. Holderness

McINTYRE,
James P. of Gilmanton m. Martha L. **Kidder** of Gilmanton 8/19/2001

James Patrick of Gilmanton m. Anastasia **Forsyth** of Franklin 6/8/1991

McKENNA,
Robert Arthur of Gilmanton m. Johnna Marie **Furber** of Gilmanton 5/20/2000

McKINNA,
Robert J. of Gilmanton m. Mary E. Thomte **Ostendorff** of LA 6/20/1981

McLEOD,
Wilson C. of Gilmanton I. W. m. Mary A. Jardine **van Ogtrop** of Gilmanton I. W. 8/15/1978; H - b. 8/25/1938 in Canada, s/o Wilson C. McLeod (Canada) and Christine Ard (England); W - b. 6/4/1944 in Netherlands, d/o Frederik van Ogtrop (Amsterdam) and Heleen A. de Vries (Holland)

McQUADE,
Michael J. of Gilmanton m. Stephanie C. **Sardella** of Gilmanton 6/24/1990

McQUILLEN,
Michael Arthur of Gilmanton m. Deborah Christine **Miller** of Gilmanton 5/20/1994

McVEY,
Frederick G. of Gilmanton m. Jean Marion **Ermini** of Gilmanton 11/19/1988

McWHINNIE,
Andrew John of Gilmanton m. Gayle Ann **Bowman** of Gilmanton 6/10/1995
Robert C., Jr. of Gilmanton m. Teresa C. Scaff **Ross** of Gilmanton 6/20/1981
Stephen Paul of Gilmanton m. Gail Marie **Phippard** of Gilmanton 6/22/1996
Thomas J. of Gilmanton m. Denise M. **Lavoie** of Laconia 3/19/1983
Thomas John of Gilmanton m. Kathleen Mary **Bickford** of Gilmanton 6/10/1995

MERCIER,
Robert N., Jr. of Gilmanton m. Sally M. Smock **Bach** of Gilmanton 7/4/1981

MERRILL,
Charles E. of Gilmanton m. Amelia **Peaslee** of Gilmanton 1/14/1893; H - 46, farmer, b. Barnstead, s/o Aaron Merrill (Barnstead, farmer) and Elizabeth Caverly (Strafford, housewife); W - 43, housekeeper, b. Gilmanton, d/o Zaccheus

Peaslee (Gilmanton, farmer) and Betsy N. Parash (Gilmanton, housewife)

Charles L. of Gilmanton m. Mary E. **Weeks** of Gilmanton 9/17/1896; H - 27, barber, b. Gilmanton, s/o Jacob D. Merrill (Gilmanton, farmer) and Sarah Sanborn (Barnstead, housewife); W - 22, school teacher, b. Gilmanton, d/o Matthias Weeks (farmer) and Laurinda Hilliard (Colebrook, housekeeper)

Robert Mack, III of Gilmanton m. Beverly Joyce **Coursey** of Concord 9/26/1963 in Concord; H - 21, lithographer, b. NH, s/o Robert M. Merrill, Jr. and Lois E. Copp; W - 20, beautician, b. NH, d/o Charles Coursey and Joyce R. Cutting

MESERVE,
Steven Alan of Gilmanton m. Sarah Beth **Glidden** of Gilmanton 8/28/1999

MESSER,
Charles S. of New London m. Clara Maud **Yerxa** of Gilmanton 4/8/1914; H - 32, farmer, b. New London, s/o Edwin F. Messer (New London, farmer) and Sarah A. Perley (Springfield, housewife); W - 23, milliner, b. Somerville, MA, d/o Richard C. Yerxa (Kerwick, NB, farmer) and Esther Urquhart (Nashwalk, NB, housewife)

MICK,
Clarence S. of Newton Center, MA m. Caroline T. **Small** of Gilmanton 7/3/1948 in Laconia; H - 25, student, b. Newton, MA, s/o Wendell R. K. Mick (Newton, MA, retired) and Ruth M. Stetson (Newton, MA, housewife); W - 22, at home, b. New York, NY, d/o Richard L. Small (Braintree, MA, university professor) and Eleanor A. Taylor (New York, NY, housewife)

MINER,
Dennis Alan of Barnstead m. Lynn **Carey** of Gilmanton 9/9/1995

MITCHELL,
Clayton Paul of Pittsfield m. Maxine Lois **Riel** of Gilmanton 12/28/1960 in Pittsfield; H - 21, leather proc., b. NH, s/o Herbert I. Mitchell (MA) and Gladys M. Rogers (NH); W - 18,

student, b. NH, d/o Alden L. Riel (NH) and Martha P. French (NH)

Roderick E. of Gilmanton m. Marjorie A. **Shrake** of Gilmanton 10/9/1982

MOLBURG,

Donald J. of Laconia m. Lura F. **Riggs** of Gilmanton 6/15/1975; H - b. 1/5/1952 in NH, s/o Richard Molburg (NH) and Cynthia Decker (NH); W - b. 1/18/1955 in MA, d/o Lincoln Riggs (MA) and Esther Belcher (MA)

MONROE,

Norman Scott of Epsom m. Mary Hannah **Smith** of Gilmanton 12/22/1925; H - 30, poultryman, b. Epsom, s/o Norman H. Munroe (Annapolis, NS, farmer) and Helen G. Hardy (Epsom, housework); W - 27, domestic, 2nd, b. Gilmanton, d/o Alfred M. Brown (Epsom, farmer) and Edna M. Marsh (Gilmanton, housework)

MOODY,

Clarence N. of Loudon m. Nannie B. **Pease** of Gilmanton 8/19/1916 in Franklin; H - 20, fireman, b. Loudon, s/o Walter H. Moody (Loudon, farmer) and Mary M. Girard (VT); W - 19, at home, b. Gilmanton, d/o John L. Pease (Loudon, farmer) and Nancy Greenough (Concord, housewife)

Lyndon Grover of Wolfeboro m. Roberta Hayes **Gooch** of Gilmanton 6/30/1951 in Milton; H - 25, roller (mill), b. NH, s/o Grover T. Moody (NH) and Verna Brown (NH); W - 31, shoeworker, b. NH, d/o Colo E. Hayes (NH) and Bertha E. MacCarlie (ME)

Ona A. of Gilmanton m. Ethel L. **Jones** of Gilmanton 12/2/1916; H - 19, laborer, b. Loudon, s/o Walter H. Moody (Loudon, laborer) and Mary E. Gerard (Belmont, housewife); W - 17, housework, b. Gilmanton, d/o George A. Jones (Gilmanton, farmer) and Olive E. Moody (Canterbury, housewife)

MOONEY,

John J. of Laconia m. Elaine M. **Langley** of Gilmanton 4/14/1984

MOORE,
Hugh R. of Londonderry m. Irene M. **Moore** of Londonderry
   5/1/1983

MOOREHEAD,
Carl E. of Gilmanton m. Kimberly A. **Ouellette** of Gilmanton
   2/2/1985
Carl Ellison of Otsego, MI m. Jeanine Louise **Segale** of Gilmanton
   10/4/1952; H - 21, Navy, b. MI, s/o Ray E. Moorehead (MI) and
   Ellen Oland (MI); W - 19, receptionist, b. VT, d/o Louie J.
   Segale (NH) and Grace M. Astbury (Canada)
Rickey E. of Gilmanton m. Doreen D. **Thompson** of Gilmanton I.
   W. 6/28/1975; H - b. 3/22/1956 in NH, s/o Carl E. Moorehead
   (MI) and Jeanine Segole (VT); W - b. 3/16/1950 in NH, d/o
   Edward Thompson (MA) and Angela Delafano (MA)
Shane Alan of Gilmanton m. Kathleen **Langley** of Gilmanton
   5/18/1974; H - b. 9/23/1953 in NH, s/o Carl E. Moorehead (MI)
   and Jeanine Segalini (VT); W - b. 11/1/1950 in NH, d/o Donald
   Langley (NH) and Dorothy Milne (MA)

MORIN,
Leo Arthur of Gilmanton m. Sandra Lee **Gardner** of Gilmanton
   10/9/1962 in Belmont; H - 28, carpenter, b. NH, s/o Joseph A.
   Morin (NH) and Arlene E. Patten (NH); W - 18, at home, b.
   NH, d/o Louis J. Gardner (VT) and Evelyn E. Emmons (NH)
Steven F. of Gilmanton m. Patricia N. **Neal** of Gilmanton 10/3/1987

MORRILL,
Kerry Arthur of Meredith m. Terri Lynn **Gleeson** of Gilford
   10/23/1999

MORRISON,
William J. of Gilmanton m. Eileen A. **White** of Gilmanton 8/26/1983
William J. of Gilmanton m. Terry L. **Rogers** of Plainfield 5/24/1986

MORSE,
Gary Alan of Gilmanton m. Camille Lorraine **McKaig** of Gilmanton
   11/20/1999
Howard B. of Friendship, ME m. Mary F. **Geddes** of Gilmanton
   6/11/1955; H - 31, student, b. ME, s/o Frank M. Morse (ME)

and Villa B. Eugley (ME); W - 32, nurse, b. NH, d/o John A. Geddes (Canada) and Florence A. Edgerly (NH)

MOULTON,
Carl Leslie of Alton m. Linda Elizabeth **Riel** of Gilmanton 4/6/1963 in Alton; H - 20, barber, b. NH, s/o Herbert J. Moulton (NH) and Lillian Varney (NH); W - 19, secretary, b. NH, d/o Alden L. Riel (NH) and Pauline M. French (NH)

MOUNT,
Theodore E. of Laconia m. Shirley Ann **Sturgeon** of Gilmanton 3/27/1976 in Loudon; H - b. 10/9/1947 in NJ, s/o Edward N. Mount (NJ) and Rita B. Thibault (MA); W - b. 6/9/1957 in NH, d/o Albert Sturgeon (NH) and Rita Provencal (NH)

MOUSSA,
Fayez Hassan of Manchester m. Ferial Taher **Trabzony** of Manchester 11/21/1971; H - b. 2/22/1931 in Egypt, s/o Hassan Moussa (Egypt) and Nazli Hamdy (Egypt); W - b. 2/12/1944 in Arabia, d/o Taher Trazbony (Turkey) and Zakia Halaby (Arabia)

MUNDSCHENK,
Manuel Warren of Salem, MA m. June Marion **King** of Rockport, MA 2/24/1966; H - 44, supervisor, b. NY, s/o Manuel Mundschenk (NY) and Helen Lydia McComsey (NY); W - 38, at home, b. MA, d/o Eldor King (WI) and Doris Chandler (MA)

MUNSEY,
Herbert E. of Washington m. Karen M. Branon **Jared** of Washington 7/10/1981
Herbert Earl of NH m. Evelyn Elizabeth **Corson** of Pittsfield 12/23/1950 in Gilmanton I. W.; H - 30, weaver, b. NH, s/o John J. Munsey (NH) and Julia F. Bruce (Canada); W - 19, at home, b. NH, d/o Jesse S. Corson (ME) and Barbara I. McKay (NH)
James J. of Gilmanton m. Jean E. **Moreau** of Gilmanton 3/24/1984
James Jay of Gilmanton m. Audrey Mary **Woodward** of Gilmanton 2/13/1998
Thomas A. of Gilmanton m. Jean **Douphinett** of Gilmanton 10/15/1977; H - b. 3/21/1953 in NH, s/o Maurice Munsey (NH)

and Gloria Roberts (ME); W - b. 5/23/1954 in NH, d/o John
Douphinett (NH) and Gwendolyn Knowles (NH)

MUSE,
Matthew C. of Colebrook m. Jennifer N. **Adel** of Gilmanton
1/26/2001

NACLERIO,
Francis S. of NY m. Virginia C. Chamberlain **Dunn** of Gilmanton
9/17/1975; H - b. 8/14/1947 in NY, s/o Louis Naclerio (NY) and
Anna Y. Garguilo (NY); W - b. 12/13/1947 in NY, d/o Robert
Dunn (OH) and Virginia Vineyard (NY)

NEFF,
Ralph D. of Gilmanton m. Janet D. **Dodge** of Gilmanton 9/12/1987

NELSON,
Clarence of Pittsfield m. Dorothy V. **Bailey** of Chichester 6/9/1931;
H - 30, carpenter, b. Perth Amboy, NJ, s/o Henry Nelson
(Denmark, builder) and Louise Rasmussen (Denmark,
housework); W - 18, housework, b. Chichester, d/o Albert
Bailey (Pittsfield, carpenter) and Harriet Bullard (Wakefield,
MA, housework)
George M., II of Gilmanton m. Sharon A. **Fournier** of Manchester
6/18/1965 in Manchester; H - 23, teacher, b. NH, s/o George
M. Nelson (NH) and Eleanor Hyslop (NH); W - 21, teacher, b.
NY, d/o Dwight Fournier (ME) and Mary O'Halloran (ME)
Mark Ramsay of Hinsdale m. Nancy Elizabeth **Crosby** of
Gilmanton 12/28/1974; H - b. 12/11/1949 in VT, s/o James W.
Nelson, Jr. (NH) and Annabelle L. Nichols (VT); W - b.
5/27/1954 in NH, d/o Robert S. Crosby (NH) and Phyllis
Cutting (ME)
Timothy James of Gilmanton m. Jacqueline Ann **Christi** of
Winnisquam 10/1/1994
Wayne D. of Gilmanton m. Judith A. **Ehlen** of Gilmanton
12/26/1971; H - b. 10/8/1949 in NH, s/o George M. Nelson
(NH) and Eleanor Hyslop (NY); W - b. 11/29/1952 in NY, d/o
Henry A. Ehlen (NY) and Hattie Morris (NY)

NEWTON,
John J. of Gilmanton m. Deborah L. **Monier** of Gilmanton 9/9/1978 in Rindge; H - b. 6/17/1952 in MA, s/o John D. Newton (NH) and Patricia Collins (NH); W - b. 1/16/1951 in MA, d/o Edward A. Monier (MA) and Marjorie L. Stark (Canada)

NICHOLS,
Philip S., Jr. of Meredith Ctr. m. Carol **Trautwig** of Gilmanton 7/8/1961 in Laconia; H - 29, technician, b. MA, s/o Philip S. Nichols, Jr. (NH) and Beatrice L. Power (NH); W - 20, secretary, b. MA, d/o Gustav H. Trautwig (NH) and Della Bourgault (NH)

NIELSEN,
Thomas B. of Gilmanton m. Angie Marie **Macleod** of Gilmanton 6/3/1998

NILGES,
Sidney E. of Gilmanton m. Joymarie **Hoch** of Tilton 9/24/2000

NOLIN,
Lloyd D. of Stark m. Ronilee R. **Smith** of Gilmanton 7/1/1995

NORTON,
Mahlon R. of Manchester m. Edith A. Nelson **Jackson** of Gilmanton 9/12/1981

NOYES,
William A. of Lynn, MA m. Esther **Goodwin** of Gilmanton 4/8/1902; H - 27, shoemaker, b. Lyme, s/o Charles Noyes (laborer) and Dora V. Whitten (Canaan, housewife); W - 24, stitcher, b. Gilmanton, d/o Sylvester Goodwin (Gilmanton, farmer) and Sarah E. Doe (Deerfield, housewife)

NUGENT,
Earl C. of Sparks, NV m. Ruth M. **Little** of Gilmanton 3/8/1957 in Belmont; H - 34, clergyman, b. NH, s/o Winfield Nugent (NH) and Ethel K. Keach (NH); W - 21, clergyman, b. NH, d/o Charles P. Little (NH) and Rena F. Marsh (NH)

NUTTER,
Allen Roy of Gilmanton m. Marilyn Rene Dulie **Anderson** of Gilmanton 11/30/1974; H - b. 7/15/1948 in NH, s/o Joseph C. Nutter (NH) and Mary M. Hanson (NH); W - b. 8/11/1941 in MN, d/o Bertrum Anderson (Canada) and Audrey Shelrud (MN)

Clyde E. of Gilmanton m. Dorothy **Cate** of Loudon 2/14/1937 in Loudon; H - 34, mechanic, 2nd, b. Parsonsfield, ME, s/o Fred Nutter (Maplewood, ME, contractor) and Carrie Dutch (Parsonsfield, ME, at home); W - 23, nurse, b. Manchester, d/o Earl Cate (Loudon, farmer) and Ida Hill (Loudon, at home)

Debert Clayton of Gilmanton m. Carrie M. **Nutter** of Gilmanton 6/30/1925 in Tilton; H - 35, auto mechanic, b. Parsonsfield, ME, s/o Arthur Nutter (farmer) and Ella Hamden (Parsonsfield, ME, housework); W - 41, housekeeper, 2nd, b. Parsonsfield, ME, d/o Charles Dutch (Parsonsfield, ME, farmer) and Lucy Knox (Newfield, ME, housework)

Frank E. of Gilmanton m. Lizzie **Donnelly** of Boston, MA 12/6/1893; H - 26, farmer, b. Amesbury, MA, s/o Charles O. Nutter and Caroline Currier; W - 32, housekeeper, 2nd, b. Boston, MA, d/o Daniel Duffey

George W. of Gilmanton m. May S. **Joy** of Andover, MA 5/28/1902 in Haverhill, MA; H - 66, shoemaker, 3rd, b. Gilmanton, s/o John Nutter (Barnstead, farmer) and Sally W. Dudley (Gilmanton, housewife); W - 55, housemaid, 2nd, b. Sanbornton, d/o Isaac Bickford (Rochester, farmer) and Mehitable Henderson (Rochester, housewife)

Kenneth N. of Gilmanton m. Ethelyn G. **Rollins** of Laconia 8/15/1947 in Belmont; H - 22, lineman, b. Laconia, s/o Clyde E. Nutter (Maplewood, ME, auto mechanic) and Doris I. Springer (Lawrence, MA, post mistress); W - 23, time adjuster, b. Jefferson, ME, d/o Charles D. Jones (Walderboro, ME, farm manager) and Ruth E. Gatcomb (Marion, ME, housewife)

Madison P. of Gilmanton m. Josephine H. **Cook** of Gilmanton 11/11/1899; H - 40, miller, b. Gilmanton, s/o Samuel D. Nutter (Gilmanton) and Mary Allen (Epsom, housework); W - 29, storekeeper, b. Gilmanton, d/o Danford Cook (Plymouth) and Mary B. Dudley (Ashland, housework)

Malcolm H. of Tilton m. Phyllis Rae **Franzen** of Tilton 6/3/1972; H - b. 1/8/1915 in NH, s/o Addis Nutter (NH) and Marion G. Rand (NH); W - b. 5/3/1920 in NH, d/o Edward S. Webster (CO) and Lottie E. Marston (NH)

Robert C. of Gilmanton m. Kathleen A. **Langley** of Gilmanton 1/4/1969; H - b. 7/27/1943 in NH, s/o Kenneth N. Nutter (NH) and Ethelyn Jones (NH); W - b. 11/1/1950 in NH, d/o Donald C. Langley (NH) and Dorothy Milne (MA)

O'LEARY,
Bert of Gilmanton m. Elizabeth J. **Haskell** of Gilmanton 12/16/1905; H - 29, laborer, b. Gilmanton, s/o Arthur O'Leary (Milford, laborer) and Ida O'Leary; W - 17, housekeeper, b. Gilmanton, d/o George Haskell (Northwood, laborer) and Emma Haskell (Gilmanton, housewife)

O'SHEA,
John D., Jr. of Gilmanton m. Holly **Smith** of Gilmanton 2/1/1980

OCHS,
Neal L. of Malden, MA m. Jeanette **Hirschberg** of Malden, MA 5/24/1987

OLSON,
Steven C. of Laconia m. Jane E. **Mitchell** of Gilmanton 6/29/1975 in Gilford; H - b. 8/27/1952 in NY, s/o Edward Olson (NY) and Betty Heins (PA); W - b. 10/1/1950 in NH, d/o Leonidas Mitchell (NH) and Dorothy Carr (NH)

ONSAGER,
Hans Tanberg of Sanbornton m. Maryevelyn **Biggers** of Gilmanton 6/24/1972; H - b. 4/4/1942 in CT, s/o Lars Onsager (Norway) and Margarette Arledter (Austria); W - b. 3/29/1947 in MA, d/o James M. Biggers (NC) and Doris Childs (NH)

ORDWAY,
Charles W. of Gilmanton m. Hattie F. **Maxfield** of Gilmanton 4/21/1900; H - 29, teamster, b. Plymouth, s/o Willard Ordway and Sarah Locke; W - 29, shoemaker, b. Gilmanton, d/o John A. Maxfield (Gilmanton) and Aphia Page

OSBORNE,
Charles Roland of Gilmanton m. Sarah Purue **Garland** of Pittsfield 7/20/1920 in Pittsfield; H - 24, teacher, b. Gilmanton, s/o

Charles A. Osborne (Gilmanton) and Grace A. True (Pittsfield); W - 24, bookkeeper, b. Pittsfield, d/o Roscoe L. Garland (Wolfeboro) and Amy D. Knowlton (Charlestown, MA)

Charles Roland of Gilmanton m. Dorothy Hislop **Gagnon** of Gilmanton 9/25/1967 in Chichester; H - 71, farmer, b. NH, s/o Charles A. Osborne (NH) and Grace Ardena True (NH); W - 60, food service, b. ME, d/o Robert Willis Hislop (NH) and Bertha May Ellis (NH)

Paul A. of Loudon m. Marlene Lisa **Gagnon** of Gilmanton 9/3/1988

Thomas Cargill of Pittsfield m. Heather Mae **Lafrance** of Gilmanton 9/30/1995

True F. of Gilmanton m. Ada J. **Lamprey** of Belmont 3/21/1906 in Belmont; H - 45, farmer, b. Gilmanton, s/o Samuel Osborne (Gilmanton, farmer) and Julia A. Gilman (Gilmanton, housewife); W - 31, dressmaker, b. Belmont, d/o Albion C. Lamprey (Belmont, farmer) and Hattie A. Weymouth (Belmont, housewife)

OSLER,

Howard Benjamin of Gilmanton m. Mary Elizabeth **Douglass** of Laconia 6/25/1950; H - 49, salesman, b. NJ, s/o Benjamin F. Osler (NJ) and Alice Ann Tyler (NJ); W - 48, clerk, b. NY, d/o Buel G. Allen (NY) and Carrie M. Crannell (NY)

OSMER,

Steven D. of Gilmanton m. Sandra L. **Bresse** of Belmont 12/29/1979

OTT,

Melvin G. of Gilmanton m. Margaret E. **Van Riper** of Ridgewood, NJ 10/5/1980

PAGE,

Andrew T. of Gilmanton m. Mabel H. **Avery** of Gilmanton 8/1/1933; H - 32, farmer, b. Gilmanton, s/o Henry S. Page (Gilmanton, farmer) and Emma A. Tasker (Northwood, housework); W - 20, at home, b. Gilmanton, d/o George H. Avery (Strafford, farmer) and Carrie Paige (Laconia, housework)

David E. of Gilmanton m. Sarah **Brown** of Gilmanton 9/7/1889; H - 66, farmer, 3rd, b. Gilmanton, s/o William Page (Gilmanton, farmer) and Polly Cotton (Gilmanton, housewife); W - 50, housewife, 3rd, b. Sanbornton, d/o Alfred Hanford and Luida Hanford

Dudley N. of Gilmanton m. Martha **Goodwin** of Barnstead 6/15/1913 in Barnstead; H - 62, farmer, b. Gilmanton, s/o Jesse L. Page (Gilmanton, farmer) and Betsey Marsh (Loudon, housewife); W - 62, housemaid, 2nd, b. Barnstead, d/o Amasa Gilman (Gilmanton, farmer) and Mehitable Hill (Gilmanton, housewife)

Frank C. of Gilmanton m. Cora B. **Gale** of Gilmanton 6/15/1888; H - 30, laborer, 2nd, b. Gilmanton, s/o John S. Page (Gilmanton, farmer) and Sarah T. Smith (Gilmanton, housewife); W - 29, teacher, b. Gilmanton, d/o Sylvester J. Gale (Gilmanton, farmer) and Harriet S. Gilman (Gilmanton, housewife)

Frank H. of Gilmanton m. Ina E. **Battis** of Pittsfield 1/6/1905; H - 19, laborer, b. Laconia, s/o Clarence Page (Gilmanton, mill operator) and Louise Powell (Quebec, housewife); W - 17, housemaid, b. Pittsfield, d/o Frank L. Battis (Gilmanton, mason) and Lucy A. Moody (housewife)

Frank J. of Gilmanton m. Ethel M. **Merrill** of Gilmanton 3/23/1913 in Gilmanton I. W.; H - 26, farmer, b. Franklin, s/o George E. Page (Gilmanton, farmer) and Ella Jones (Loudon, housewife); W - 26, teacher, b. Gilmanton, d/o Frank Merrill (Stoneham, MA, farmer) and Clara Page (Barnstead, housewife)

Frank Josiah of Gilmanton m. Helen Otis **Wyatt** of Tilton 9/6/1919 in Tilton; H - 32, farmer, 2nd, b. Franklin, s/o George E. Page (Gilmanton) and Ella Jones (Loudon); W - 21, teacher, b. Tilton, d/o George C. Wyatt (Sanbornton) and Lucy E. Jackson (Melbourne, Que.)

Fred W. of Gilmanton m. Gertrude E. **Parsons** of Gilmanton 10/10/1897 in Loudon; H - 24, farmer, b. Gilmanton, s/o Dixi C. Page (Gilmanton, farmer) and Cyrena G. Page (Gilmanton, housewife); W - 25, housemaid, b. Gilmanton, d/o George C. Parsons (Manchester, farmer) and Julia Swain (Gilmanton, housewife)

Harold G. of Gilmanton m. Alfretta T. **Day** of Gilmanton 9/15/1925; H - 29, farmer, b. Plymouth, MA, s/o C. Frank Page (Gilmanton, farmer) and Cora B. Gale (Gilmanton, housework); W - 24, teacher, b. Plymouth

Herman A. of Gilmanton m. Anna B. **Page** of Gilmanton 12/26/1891; H - 21, carpenter, b. Gilmanton, s/o Albert R.

Page (Gilmanton, farmer) and Addie C. Clements (Alton, housewife); W - 27, housewife, b. Gilmanton, d/o Dixie C. Page (Gilmanton, farmer) and Serene Webster (Gilmanton, housewife)

Jesse F. of Alton m. Mary E. **Canney** of Gilmanton 11/16/1891 in Meredith; H - 42, farmer, b. Gilmanton, s/o Jesse L. Page (farmer) and Betsey Marsh (Loudon, housewife); W - 39, housewife, 2nd, b. Wolfeboro, d/o Thomas J. Tibbetts (Wolfeboro) and Sarah E. Lock (Wakefield)

John S. of Gilmanton m. Addie M. **Glidden** of Alton 4/26/1906; H - 22, box maker, b. Franklin Falls, s/o George E. Page (Gilmanton, farmer) and Ella Jones (Loudon, housewife); W - 21, housekeeper, b. Alton, d/o Orin Glidden (Alton, farmer) and Lizzie M. Burnham (Dover, housewife)

Joseph Leon of Gilmanton m. Sarah **Riggs** of Framingham, MA 6/27/1917 in Concord; H - 26, farmer, b. Franklin Falls, s/o George E. Page (Gilmanton) and Ella Jones (Gilmanton); W - 29, matron's assistant, b. Newfoundland, d/o Newman Riggs (Newfoundland) and Mary Barton (Newfoundland)

Luther E. of Gilmanton m. Mary L. **Preble** of Barnstead 12/31/1894; H - 62, farmer, 3rd, b. Gilmanton, s/o Henry Page (Gilmanton, farmer) and Hannah S. Sanborn (Gilmanton, housewife); W - 40, housekeeper, 2nd, b. Woolwich, ME, d/o Timothy W. Austin (Roxbury, MA, machinist) and Rebecca Preble (Woolwich, ME)

Ray B. of Gilmanton m. Lorna L. **Stockbridge** of Gilmanton 3/15/1930; H - 20, laborer, b. Gilmanton, s/o William A. Page (Gilmanton, farmer) and Sadie M. Buckman (Bridgewater, housework); W - 15, at home, b. Gilmanton, d/o George S. Stockbridge (Gilmanton, farmer) and Ina Roby (Pittsfield, housework)

Roger A. of Laconia m. Heidi J. **Freese** of Gilmanton 7/13/1985

Roy T. of Gilmanton m. Dora B. **Glidden** of Alton 1/26/1910 in Gilmanton I. W.; H - 21, farmer, b. Gilmanton, s/o Royal L. Page (Gilmanton, farmer) and Annie M. Osgood (Loudon, housewife); W - 22, housemaid, b. Alton, d/o Fred E. Glidden (Wolfeboro, farmer) and Mary L. Jones (Alton, housewife)

Walter H. of Gilmanton m. Fannie A. **Embree** of NS 11/2/1911 in Laconia; H - 41, carpenter, b. Gilmanton, s/o Dixi C. Page (Gilmanton, farmer) and Cyrena G. Webster (Gilmanton, housewife); W - 51, housemaid, b. NS, d/o Alexander Embree (NS, lumber) and Sarah M. Teed (NS, housewife)

Walter S. of Gilmanton m. Ida Belle **Baker** of Manchester 1/23/1918 in Manchester; H - 34, mechanic, b. Portsmouth, s/o Henry S. Page (Gilmanton) and Emma A. Tasker (Northwood); W - 38, physician, b. New Boston, d/o Benjamin F. Baker (New London) and Annie Ward (New London)

William A. of Gilmanton m. Sadie M. **Shattuck** of Gilmanton 6/30/1908 in Belmont; H - 36, merchant, b. Gilmanton, s/o Charles S. Page (Gilmanton, farmer) and Sarah J. Edgerly (Barnstead, housewife); W - 33, housekeeper, 2nd, b. N. Bridgewater, VT, d/o Ruel A. Buckman (Bridgewater, VT, farmer) and Julia Chamberlin (Plymouth, VT, housewife)

William S. of Gilmanton m. Cora **Couch** of Sutton 3/24/1887; H - 50, farmer, b. Gilmanton, s/o Jesse L. Page (Gilmanton, farmer) and Betsy L. Marsh (Loudon, housewife); W - 22, housewife, b. Sutton, d/o Daniel Couch (farmer) and Edna Austin (housewife)

PAIGE,

Carroll Monroe of Gilmanton m. Lynn Aaron **Sawyer** of Gilmanton 12/20/1996

PALMER,

George L. of Gilmanton m. Daisy **Smith** of Gilmanton 9/11/1896; H - 23, carpenter, b. Dover, s/o Aaron S. Palmer (painter) and Mira Goodwin (housewife); W - 17, housekeeper, b. Gilmanton, d/o Edward E. Smith (farmer) and Jane Perkins (housewife)

John Earl of Gilmanton m. Cynthia Lee **Boulanger** of Bethlehem 8/19/1995

Leon L. of Gilmanton m. Earline **Edgerly** of Farmington 10/12/1927 in Farmington; H - 24, farmer, b. Gilmanton, s/o George L. Palmer (Dover, farmer) and Daisy M. Smith (Gilmanton, housework); W - 18, housework, b. Farmington, d/o Earl Edgerly (Farmington, shoe worker) and Ethel M. Drew (Farmington, housework)

PANALEO,

Eugene J. of Gilford m. Suzanne R. **Boulanger** of Gilmanton 12/11/1984

PAPPAS,
Paul E. of Gilmanton m. Blanche L. **Boisvert** of MA 8/5/1967; H - 49, rereeler, b. MA, s/o Evangelos Pappas (Greece) and Sultana Katsogenos (Greece); W - 38, nurses aid, b. NH, d/o Walter L. Desjardins (USA) and Lillian Mae Dunbar (ME)

PARRINGTON,
Dennis J. of Gilmanton m. Cindy J. **Kelley** of Gilmanton 12/13/1980

PARSONS,
Frank W. of Gilmanton m. Gladys M. **Burres** of Gilmanton 12/18/1929; H - 51, teamster, b. Gilmanton, s/o Rufus Parsons (Quincy, MA, laborer) and Frances Hussey (Barnstead, housework); W - 17, at home, b. Gilmanton, d/o Orman Burres (Gilmanton, laborer) and Eva Jones (Gilmanton, housework)
Frank Waldo, Jr. of Gilmanton m. Priscilla Alice **Wells** of Gilmanton 10/14/1950 in Gilmanton I. W.; H - 20, lumbering, b. NH, s/o Frank W. Parsons (NH) and Gladys M. Burres (NH); W - 17, at home, b. MA, d/o Herbert A. Wells (ME) and Effie M. Noyes (VT)
Usher S. of Gilmanton m. Addie M. **Hill** of Gilmanton 12/24/1888; H - 23, farmer, b. Gilmanton, s/o George W. Parsons (Gilmanton, farmer) and Mary A. Hill (Alton, housewife); W - 23, housewife, b. Gilmanton, d/o Charles W. Hill (Gilmanton, farmer) and Lydia A. Berry (New Durham, housewife)

PARTRIDGE,
Ernest C. of Gilmanton m. Sheila E. **Horne** of ME 12/31/1981
Horace F. of Gilmanton m. Florence J. **Palmer** of Gilmanton 5/28/1924 in Laconia; H - 24, farmer, 2nd, b. Blackstone, MA, s/o Arthur C. Partridge (VT) and Lilla J. Woods (Nashua); W - 18, housework, b. Gilmanton, d/o George L. Palmer (Dover) and Daisy Smith (Gilmanton)
Leon E. of Gilmanton m. Viola G. **Robie** of Wolfeboro 2/23/1947 in Wolfeboro; H - 20, truck driver, b. Gilmanton, s/o Horace F. Partridge (Blackstone, MA, trucking) and Florence J. Palmer (Gilmanton, housewife); W - 17, at home, b. Wolfeboro, d/o Wilbur Robie (Salem, carpenter) and Winifred Nichols (Effingham, housewife)

Leon Everett of Gilmanton m. Lucille Jeanette **Tardy** of Alton 2/11/1949 in Alton; H - 22, miner, b. NH, s/o Horace F. Partridge (MA) and Florence J. Palmer (NH); W - 22, secretary, b. NH, d/o Roy A. Tardy (NH) and Helen Maud Beck (MA)

PATTEN,

Claude Burton of Gilford m. Florence Winnifred **Sanville** of Gilmanton 12/11/1971; H - b. 7/14/1899 in NH, s/o Joseph W. Patten (NH) and Georgia Powers (NH); W - b. 8/25/1920 in NH, d/o James Russell (NH) and Grace Wiggin (NH)

David Guy of Laconia m. Evelyn Jean **Mansfield** of Gilmanton 6/28/1969 in Laconia; H - b. 4/30/1952 in NH, s/o Frederick Patten (NH) and Andrea Hershey (NH); W - b. 5/22/1953 in MA, d/o Lewis Mansfield (MA) and Claudia Chard (MA)

PEARL,

John B. of Loudon m. Euola H. **Green** of Gilmanton 12/22/1915; H - 29, farmer, b. Loudon, s/o Leroy S. Pearl (Loudon, farmer) and Rhoda H. Peaslee (Loudon, housekeeper); W - 20, at home, b. Gilmanton, d/o Elmer L. Green (Gilmanton, farmer) and Antonia Kratzert (Germany, housewife)

PEARSON,

Edward W. of Norwich, VT m. Charlotte A. **Kelley** of Gilmanton 6/29/1948 in Pittsfield; H - 23, student, b. Concord, s/o John Pearson (Concord, managing trustee) and Margaret Withey (Salt Lake City, UT, housewife); W - 24, nurse, b. Gilmanton, d/o Charles G. Kelley (Gilmanton, farmer) and Hattie B. Page (Utica, NY, housewife)

PEASE,

Alna L. of Gilmanton m. Effie R. **Whitehouse** of Laconia 5/5/1897 in Laconia; H - 24, carpenter, b. Lakeport, s/o Leroy B. Pease (Loudon, carpenter) and Ellen S. Pease (Pittsfield, housewife); W - 19, housemaid, b. Canada, d/o Charles Whitehouse (Canada, stonemason) and Lucy J. Whitehouse (VT, housewife)

PEASLEE,
Charles H. of Gilmanton m. Lucinda A. B. **Patten** of Gilmanton 3/16/1907 in Belmont; H - 28, farmer, b. Gilmanton, s/o Caleb W. Peaslee (Gilmanton, farmer) and Luanna Abbot (Warner, housewife); W - 47, housekeeper, 2nd, d/o Daniel Bullard (Brookfield, MA) and Clarissa Bullard

PECK,
Robert John of W. Lebanon m. Beverly Pearl **Anair** of Gilmanton 11/22/1951; H - 32, truck driver, b. VT, s/o William J. Peck (VT) and Rosemary Callahan (VT); W - 21, at home, b. VT, d/o Leonard A. Anair (VT) and Grace M. Astbury (Canada)

PEMBROKE,
James Paul, Sr. of Gilmanton m. Judith Ina **Morley** of Gilmanton 7/17/1999

PENNOCK,
James Glynn of Gilmanton m. Doris Edna Bishop **Clark** of Gilmanton 6/12/1973; H - b. 6/27/1914 in NH, s/o James G. Pennock (NH) and Cynthia L. Douglas (NH); W - b. 2/16/1923 in NH, d/o Samuel Clark (NH) and Alice Daniels (Canada)

PERKINS,
Clarence L. of Gilmanton m. Louise P. **Hillsgrove** of Gilmanton 2/11/1943 in Laconia; H - 32, mill worker, b. Gilmanton, s/o Walter C. Perkins (Gilmanton, farmer) and Eva M. Glines (Gilmanton, housework); W - 30, housework, b. Milton, d/o Philip G. Pike (Lebanon, ME, meat cutter) and Rosamond E. Piper (Sanbornville, teacher)

Daniel W. of Gilmanton m. Sara L. **Stanley** of Gilmanton 10/22/1983

Fred G. of Gilmanton m. Bessie M. **Fairbanks** of Concord 6/11/1919 in Laconia; H - 50, millman, 3rd, b. Canada, s/o George Perkins (Canada) and Mary Leaner (Canada); W - 39, housekeeper, 2nd, b. Haverhill, MA, d/o Frank W. Wood (Haverhill, MA) and Alice L. Varney (N. Berwick, ME)

Harold Chester of Gilmanton m. Rachel Theresa **Goupil** of Laconia 9/2/1950 in Laconia; H - 20, lumbering, b. NH, s/o Walter C. Perkins (NH) and Eva M. Glines (NH); W - 18, housework, b.

NH, d/o Joseph P. Goupil (Canada) and Rose A. Remillard (NH)

Harold J. of Gilmanton m. Julie I. **Butman** of Gilmanton 8/23/1980

Lorenzo H. of Gilmanton m. Helen A. **Wyatt** of Farmington 8/18/1901; H - 28, farmer, b. Gilmanton, s/o Charles H. Perkins (Gilmanton, farmer) and Eliza Evans (housewife); W - 20, housekeeper, b. Farmington, d/o Asa Wyatt (farmer) and Belle Wyatt (farmer)

Lorenzo H. of Gilmanton m. Gertrude **Lincoln** of Cambridge, MA 1/5/1909 in Cambridge, MA; H - 36, 2nd, b. Gilmanton, s/o Charles H. Perkins (Meredith, farmer) and Eliza Evans (Moultonboro, housewife); W - 27, teacher, 2nd, b. Somerville, MA, d/o Charles A. Lincoln (Cambridge, MA) and Martha J. Avery (Cambridge, MA, housewife)

Walter C. of Gilmanton m. Eva M. **Glines** of Gilmanton 12/24/1908 in Alton; H - 23, carpenter, b. Gilmanton, s/o Charles H. Perkins (Meredith, farmer) and Eliza Evans (Moultonboro, housewife); W - 18, housemaid, b. Gilmanton, d/o Albert Glines (Boston, MA, painter) and Lucinda Jones (Loudon, housewife)

PERRIN,

Alexander M. of Gilmanton m. Mabelle E. **Rogers** of Alton 11/29/1945; H - 43, discharged, b. Scotland, s/o John F. Perrin (England, loomfixer) and Catherine Winning (Scotland, housewife); W - 26, shoeworker, b. Alton, d/o George E. Davis (Gilford, shoeworker) and Cora B. Jones (Alton, housewife)

PERRY,

Terence W. of Gilmanton m. Sarah Anne **Shaw** of Gilmanton 12/28/1986

PETRINI,

Edward Peter of Quincy m. Judith Helen **Thomson** of Malden 11/26/1972; H - b. 7/17/1943 in MA, s/o Francis D. Petrini (MA) and Primina M. Regis (NH); W - b. 10/5/1948 in MA, d/o Frederick Thomson (MA) and Martha Bell (MA)

PHILBRICK,
Timothy Cary of Gilmanton m. Dawna Jean **Lacroix** of Gilmanton 4/15/1989

William B. of Concord m. Virginia M. **Brown** of Gilmanton 1/17/1946 in Pittsfield; H - 23, refrigeration, b. Andover, MA, s/o Eugene L. Philbrick (Wakefield, MA, carpenter) and Emma Holden (Providence, RI, housewife); W - 23, stenographer, b. Gilmanton, d/o Morse E. Brown (Gilmanton, apple grower) and Rebecca Dollif (Biddeford, ME, housewife)

PHILIPPS,
Albert E. of Gilmanton m. Lucille R. **Larose** of Laconia 7/16/1987

PICARD,
Lynwood S. of Gilmanton m. Marilyn Jeanne **Hazleton** of Wakefield, MA 12/19/1992

PICKARD,
Oscar S. of Canterbury m. Dorothy I. **Stone** of Gilmanton 7/2/1938 in Canterbury; H - 31, laborer, b. Canterbury, s/o Charles H. Pickard (Canterbury, laborer) and Jennie O. Hodge (Salisbury, housewife); W - 25, housekeeper, b. Gilmanton, d/o Fred L. Stone (Franklin, fireman) and Mary L. Hilliard (Laconia, housewife)

PICKERING,
Fred C. of Gilmanton m. Emma F. **Trask** of Gilmanton 9/5/1893; H - 31, hotelkeeper, 2nd, b. Barnstead, s/o Hiram C. Pickering (farmer) and ----- Williams; W - 24, housekeeper, b. Dover, d/o John S. Trask and Cynthia Lougee (housewife)

PIDGEON,
Gilbert Liam of Gilmanton m. Maureen Susan **Ballester** of Gilmanton 7/16/1994

PINA,
Kenneth J. of Gilmanton m. Juanita A. **Lopes** of Gilmanton 6/15/1990

PINEAU,

Phillip E. of Gilmanton m. Lois A. **Trisfontaine** of Gilmanton
11/23/1985

PLACE,
Thomas D. of Gilmanton m. Linda L. **Ellsworth** of Gilmanton
7/25/1992

PLEETER,
Daniel of Gilmanton m. Wendy A. **Kidder** of Gilmanton 9/19/1987

PLOURDE,
Gary Wayne of Gilmanton m. Valerie Ann **Begin** of Laconia
2/13/1971 in Laconia; H - b. 5/31/1951 in NH, s/o Alphonse Plourde (NH) and Priscilla Browning (NH); W - b. 3/13/1953 in TX, d/o John R. Begin (NH) and Wanda Kilgore (TX)
Jason Michael of Gilmanton m. Angela Helen **Rowe** of Gilmanton
8/5/1994

PLUMMER,
Adam Robert of Gilmanton m. Dawn Marie **Hamilton** of Gilmanton
6/6/1998

POLITO,
Robert of Gilmanton m. Jacklyn Marie **Bilodeau** of Laconia
3/4/1989
William Joseph of Concord m. Joanne Laurose **Barns** of Gilmanton
11/21/1989

PONG,
Barry L. of Gilmanton m. Joan L. **Amirault** of Gilmanton 10/6/1979

PORTER,
Malcolm Hamlin of Laconia m. Rubietta M. **King** of Gilmanton
10/29/1988

POST,
Wilfred W. of Gilmanton m. Josephine M. **Byron** of Gilmanton
10/16/1932 in Tilton; H - 47, merchant, b. Boston, MA, s/o William E. Post (Lynn, MA, printer) and Ella M. Witham (Rockport, MA, housework); W - 35, domestic science, b.

Lawrence, MA, d/o Adilon Byron (Canada, carpenter) and Celina Landry (Canada, housework)

POTTER,
Charles F. of Gilmanton m. Ardena M. **Dimond** of Loudon 11/17/1888; H - 24, farmer, b. Gilmanton, s/o George H. Potter (Gilmanton, farmer) and Mary J. Foss (Gilmanton, housewife); W - 20, teacher, b. Loudon, d/o Jonathan R. Dimond (Loudon, farmer) and Maria Peaslee (Loudon, housewife)
George D. of Gilmanton m. Mildred E. **Page** of Gilmanton 9/12/1921 in Belmont; H - 31, farmer, b. Gilmanton, s/o C. Fred Potter (Gilmanton) and Ardena Dimond (Loudon); W - 27, housework, b. Dorchester, MA, d/o Herman A. Page (Gilmanton) and Anna B. Page (Gilmanton)
Robert Leo of Gilmanton m. Nancy Jane **Sanborn** of Laconia 6/10/1961; H - 30, farmer, b. NH, s/o George D. Potter (NH) and Mildred E. Page (NH); W - 19, receptionist, b. NH, d/o Frank Sanborn (NH) and Hazel McKay (NH)
Robert Leo, Jr. of Gilmanton m. Melissa Ann **Aikins** of Gilmanton 9/2/1989
Samuel Earle m. Julia Frances **Smith** 8/24/1923

POULIN,
Robert G. of Berlin m. Donna R. **Davis** of Gilmanton 8/21/1965 in Alton; H - 22, cook, b. NH, s/o Joseph G. Poulin (Canada) and Marie R. Gastongue (NH); W - 19, beautician, b. NH, d/o George E. Davis (NH) and Irene M. Page (NH)
Robert George, II of Laconia m. Kimberley Anne **Moore** of Gilmanton 6/12/1993
Robert J. of Gilmanton m. Susan J. **Weeks** of Gilmanton 6/10/1995

PRATT,
Ralph of Gilmanton m. Geneve May **Bolo** of Gilmanton 4/21/1896; H - 24, insurance agent, b. Bradford, England, s/o William Pratt (England, carpenter) and Susan Richards (England, housewife); W - 23, housekeeper, b. Dover, d/o Andrew Jackson Bolo (Dover, shoemaker) and Ella M. Trask (Farmington, housewife)

PRESCOTT,
George C. of Gilmanton m. Cora A. **Whitney** of Boston, MA 11/5/1896; H - 50, farmer, b. Gilmanton, s/o Jonathan Prescott (Chichester, farmer) and Miranda Clough (Canterbury, housekeeper); W - 33, housekeeper, b. Brockport, NY, d/o Samuel M. Robbins (MA, farmer) and Belinda Belknap (VT)

Leonard of Dover m. Olive **Canfield** of Gilmanton 4/6/1942 in Milton; H - 23, truck driver, b. Farmington, s/o George A. Prescott (Stratham, laborer) and Florence McDonald (Farmington, housewife); W - 23, at home, b. Gilmanton, d/o Armand Burres (Gilmanton, laborer) and Eva Jones (Gilmanton, housewife)

PRETZFELDER,
Millard, III of Stowe, VT m. Cleo Frances **Moody** of Chattanooga, TN 9/25/1993

PREVOST,
Richard F. of Gilmanton m. Gina Marie **McIntire** of Gilmanton 12/27/1996

PRICE,
Amos R. of Gilmanton m. Emma G. **Wight** of Gilmanton 10/5/1907; H - 23, farmer, b. Gilmanton, s/o Charles A. Price (Gilmanton, farmer) and Aura Emerson (Pittsfield, housewife); W - 23, housekeeper, b. Gilmanton, d/o Albert R. Wight (farmer) and Emma F. ----- (housewife)

Amos Richard of Gilmanton m. Paulene M. **Richards** of Alton 9/23/1938 in Alton; H - 17, farmer, b. Manchester, s/o Amos R. Price (Gilmanton, farming) and Emma Wight (Gilmanton, at home); W - 16, at home, b. Haverhill, MA, d/o Ernest Richards (Farmington, shoe cutter) and Pauline E. Wason (Bradford, MA, housewife)

Charles A. of Gilmanton I.W. m. Alice M. **Richardson** of Alton 7/28/2001

Charles Amos of Gilmanton m. Judith Beth **Hough** of Laconia 11/6/1971 in Lakeport; H - b. 1/28/1950 in NH, s/o Amos R. Price (NH) and Pauline Richards (NH); W - b. 8/18/1952 in NH, d/o Richard L. Hough (England) and Rena R. Valley (NH)

Jonathan Charles of Gilmanton m. Jolene Marie **Barton** of
   Gilmanton 6/10/1995
William R. of Gilmanton m. Ena M. **Stockwell** of Gilmanton
   10/21/1967; H - 20, farmer, b. NH, s/o A. Richard Price (NH)
   and Pauline M. Richardson (MA); W - 18, secretary, b. NH, d/o
   Leonard A. Stockwell (MA) and Ruth A. Clifford (NH)

PROULX,
Joseph of Gilmanton m. Myrtle E. **Fogg** of Belmont 2/15/1925 in
   Gilmanton I. W.; H - 47, woodsman, b. Bonarulurce, Que., s/o
   Joseph Proulx (St. Pie, Can., mason) and Phoebe Bean
   (Manchester, housework); W - 36, housework, 2nd, b.
   Gilmanton, d/o George Jones (Gilmanton, farmer) and Olin E.
   Moody (Gilmanton, housework)

PROVENCAL,
Frank John of Laconia m. Jane Arlene **Witham** of Gilmanton
   8/23/1962 in Belmont; H - 18, side last (mfg. shoes), b. NH, s/o
   Alfred George Provencal (VT) and Yvonne Mary Gagne (NH);
   W - 19, looper, b. MA, d/o Alden W. Witham (ME) and Dorothy
   I. Thomas (MA)
William J. of Gilmanton m. Barbara A. **McCoy** of Springfield, MO
   5/11/1990

PUBLICOVER,
Charles Jóseph of Gilmanton m. Phyllis Lynn Genest **Buatti** of
   Pittsfield 6/22/1973 in Pittsfield; H - b. 3/16/1949 in NH, s/o
   Robert W. Publicover (Canada) and Annie M. Shlaitas (NH);
   W - b. 10/12/1943 in NY, d/o Saverio Buatti (NY) and Anita M.
   Carcinelli (NY)
Robert William of Gilmanton m. Valerie Ann **Bennett** of Pittsfield
   7/22/1967 in Pittsfield; H - 19, US Marine, b. NH, s/o Robert
   George Publicover (Canada) and Annie Mary Shlaitas (NH); W
   - 18, student, b. NH, d/o Everett Bennett (NH) and Constance
   Clark (NH)

PUGH,
Charles Chapman of Needham, MA m. Elise Joanne **Wilkins** of
   Gilmanton 1/28/1961; H - 20, student, b. PA, s/o Thomas Pugh

(MA) and Helen Chapman (MA); W - 19, student, b. NY, d/o William Wilkins (NH) and Laurose Berge (NH)

PURTELL,
Stanley P. of Pittsfield m. Barbara J. **Parker** of Gilmanton 11/17/1956; H - 21, weaver, s/o Leonard M. Purtell (Canada) and Margaret E. Adams (NH); W - 18, stitcher, d/o Leon D. Parker (MA) and Bella McLeod (Canada)

RAFFERTY,
Bobby J. of Gilmanton m. Christy L. **Sanborn** of Gilmanton 2/14/1998

RAND,
Chester Franklin of Gilmanton m. Blanche L. **Small** of Gilmanton 5/9/1915 in New Durham Ridge; H - 21, laborer, b. Alton, s/o Charles F. Rand (Alton, farmer) and Ida Young (housewife); W - 27, housework, 3rd, b. Gilmanton, d/o James H. Beck (farmer) and Martha J. Piper (Gilmanton, housewife)

REDMAN,
Arthur E. of Gilmanton m. Florence E. **Ford** of Gilmanton 10/9/1931 in Meredith; H - 21, electrician, b. S. Brooksville, ME, s/o Everett J. Redman (Castine, ME, engineer) and Ida May Ladd (S. Brooksville, ME, housework); W - 18, housework, b. Warner, d/o Leslie W. Ford (Saranac, NY, farmer) and Nellie C. Chase (Soldier Valley, IA, housework)
Donald A. of Gilmanton m. Elizabeth **Maxfield** of Tilton 4/4/1953 in E. Tilton; H - 21, mill worker, b. NH, s/o Arthur E. Redman (ME) and Florence E. Ford (NH); W - 20, mill worker, b. NH, d/o Clinton T. Maxfield (NH) and Earleen Brown (NH)

REED,
Thomas R. of Gilmanton m. Charlotte A. **Monroe** of Laconia 8/3/1974 in Gilford; H - b. 10/20/1950 in NY, s/o Norman A. Reed (USA) and Margaret C. Robertson (NH); W - b. 7/28/1953 in NH, d/o Stanley Monroe (NH) and Cleora M. Watts (NH)

REINHOLZ,
Lance K. of Belmont m. Dianne S. **Hardwick** of Gilmanton 9/8/1979

RELF,
George D. of Gilmanton m. Lola M. Zinn **Kenney** of Gilmanton 5/18/1974 in Canterbury; H - b. 12/4/1937 in MA, s/o Thomas J. Relf (England) and Alitta Steeman (Holland); W - b. 5/26/1945 in ME, d/o John Kenney (NH) and Kathleen Brown (NH)

RHODES,
Edward E., Jr. of Walpole m. Margaret C. **Edgerly** of Gilmanton 6/28/1947; H - 38, poultryman, b. PEI, s/o E. Everett Rhodes (Norwood, MA, bookkeeper) and Etta Coffin (PEI, housewife); W - 26, teacher, b. Gilmanton, d/o Frank Edgerly (Nashville, TN, farmer) and Mary Morgan (Moss River, PQ, housewife)

RICE,
Herbert Edward, III of Gilmanton m. Patricia Ann **O'Connor** of Gilmanton 1/20/1996

RICHARDSON,
John C., III of Gilmanton m. Mary E. **Adel** of Gilmanton 7/5/1986
Leon H. of Gilmanton m. Anna M. **Charbonneau** of Gilmanton 10/9/1927 in Alton; H - 35, farmer, 2nd, b. Skowhegan, ME, s/o Albert Richardson (Skowhegan, ME, farmer) and Belle Ricker (Canaan, ME, housework); W - 35, housework, 2nd, b. Georgeville, RI, d/o Lewish H. Ange (night watch) and Mary Murray (housework)

RICHEY,
William S., Jr. of Gilmanton m. Diana M. Vanzanten **Hages** of Gilmanton 9/12/1989

RICKER,
Benjamin A. of Gilmanton m. Christehania B. **Flanders** of Gilmanton 11/25/1891; H - 65, farmer, 2nd, b. Wolfeboro, s/o Benjamin Ricker and Susan Fogg; W - 38, housewife, b.

Gilmanton, d/o Ira M. Flanders (Alton, farmer) and Susan H. Plummer (Gilford, housewife)

RIEL,
Timothy M. of Barnstead m. Joan B. **Potter** of Gilmanton 12/1/1984

RING,
Charles E. of Gilmanton m. Vinna E. **Sleeper** of Grafton 3/3/1909 in Grafton; H - 23, teamster, b. Loudon, s/o Frank E. Ring (Searsport, ME, shoemaker) and Martha A. Haines (Loudon, housewife); W - 21, housemaid, b. Grafton, d/o Frank Sleeper (farmer) and Frances Sleeper (Canaan, housewife)
Scott C. of Manchester m. Marcia Lou Georgia **Poitras** of Manchester 11/21/2000

RIOUX,
Frank of Gilmanton m. Melvina **Corbiel** of Concord 7/10/1903 in Loudon; H - 24, laborer, b. St. John, NB, s/o Paul Rioux (St. Johns, NB, farmer) and Mary Lavnis (St. Johns, NB); W - 21, b. Canada, d/o Adolord Corbiel (Canada, stonecutter) and Telde Glodu (Canada)

RITENOUR,
Richard O. of Lancaster, PA m. Robin L. **Penney** of Gilmanton 11/23/1985

ROBBINS,
Roscoe D. of Gilmanton m. Georgie E. **Bragg** of Gilmanton 8/9/1924; H - 26, chauffeur, b. Pittsfield, s/o Reginald Robbins (Pittsfield) and Ida Lyons (Saco, ME); W - 16, housework, b. Gilmanton, d/o George E. Bragg (Troy, ME) and Georgia E. Brown (Gilmanton)

ROBERTS,
Clive E. of Belmont m. Carlene A. **Hyslop** of Gilmanton 12/23/1970; H - b. 9/25/1950 in NH, s/o Leslie Roberts (NH) and Suzanne Sickmon (CA); W - b. 9/21/1951 in NH, d/o Donald W. Hyslop (MA) and Rachel Straw (NH)
Ernest W. of Gilmanton m. Louie F. **Baynham** of Gilmanton 10/30/1926 in Alton; H - 37, farmer, b. Birmingham, Eng., s/o

William Roberts (Stonebridge, Eng., salesman) and Elizabeth E. Swift (Bristol, Eng., housework); W - 32, housekeeper, b. Ross-on-Wye, Eng., d/o Joseph Baynham (Ross-on-Wye, Eng., plasterer) and Elizabeth L. Price (Upton Bishop, Eng., housework)

George Bernard, Jr. of Gilmanton m. Margaret Fay **Edmunds** of Concord 8/26/1967 in Concord; H - 28, insurance, b. MA, s/o George B. Roberts, Sr. (England) and Helene F. Eversen (NH); W - 26, teacher, b. NH, d/o Gerald C. Edmunds (NH) and Esther L. Ambrose (NH)

Neil Richard of Andover m. Susan Elizabeth **Munsey** of Gilmanton 2/12/1972; H - b. 10/3/1950 in NH, s/o Joseph A. S. Roberts (NH) and Marion Baxter (NH); W - b. 9/5/1951 in NH, d/o Maurice E. Munsey (NH) and Gloria Roberts (ME)

ROBINETTE,
Michael Joseph of Gilford m. Muriel Ann **Steenstra** of Gilmanton 8/10/1974 in Durham; H - b. 8/2/1952 in NH, s/o Robert Robinette (NE) and Joan LaRoche (NH); W - b. 4/13/1952 in NH, d/o Walter Steenstra (MA) and Ruth Miner (ME)

ROBINSON,
Eric Scott of Gilmanton m. Lisa Taryn **Fitzgerald** of Gilmanton 6/12/1988

Joseph of MA m. Linda J. **Orsi** of Brighton, MA 9/9/1978; H - b. 8/24/1956 in MA, s/o Robert E. Robinson (MA) and Cary L. Hayes (MA); W - b. 9/18/1956 in MA, d/o Reno J. Orsi (MA) and Virginia Maillett (MA)

ROBY,
Arthur E. of Gilmanton m. Annie M. **Hill** of Epsom 6/16/297 in Epsom; H - 37, farmer, b. Pittsfield, s/o Ernest J. Roby (Gilmanton, shoeworker) and Caroline L. Downs (Epsom, housework); W - 36, housework, b. Pittsfield, d/o John J. Hill (Barnstead, farmer) and Ellen M. Hall (Epsom, housework)

RODRIGUEZ,
Paul M. of Gilmanton m. Kristen L. **Woods** of Gilford 8/24/1987

ROLLINS,

Henry A. of Gilmanton m. Almyra **McMurphy** of Meredith 1/18/1931; H - 25, laborer, b. Lakeport, s/o Benjamin Rollins (Lakeport, painter) and Ida Bailey (Lakeport, housework); W - 18, housework, b. Meredith, d/o Robert McMurphy (Lakeport, laborer) and Ida Dolloff (Lakeport, housework)

Patrick A. of Gilmanton m. Patricia A. **Therrien** of Gilmanton 2/14/1998

Selden B. of Gilmanton m. Eva M. **Burres** of Gilmanton 8/19/1927 in Farmington; H - 51, laborer, 2nd, b. Gilmanton, s/o E. B. Rollins (Gilmanton, motorman) and Mary L. Sargent (Gilmanton, housework); W - 31, housework, 2nd, b. Gilmanton, d/o George Jones (Gilmanton, laborer) and Olive Moody (Gilmanton, housework)

Seldon B. of Gilmanton m. Alma L. **Ellis** of Gilmanton 6/6/1900 in Alton; H - 25, farmer, b. Gilmanton, s/o E. B. Rollins and Mary L. Sargent (housekeeper); W - 20, housekeeper, b. Alton, d/o Elbridge Ellis (farmer)

Victor E. of Lakeport m. Frances E. **Smith** of Tilton 10/10/1930; H - 22, roofer, b. Lakeport, s/o Benjamin F. Rollins (Lakeport, painter) and Ida A. Bailey (Richmond, Can., housework); W - 18, housework, b. New Hampton, d/o Victor R. W. Smith (N. Hampton, laborer) and Grace Hatch (Gilford, housework)

Walter E. of Gilmanton m. Marjorie A. **Hames** of Farmington 10/29/1955; H - 21, machinist, b. NH, s/o Selden B. Rollins (MA) and Eva M. Jones (NH); W - 23, at home, b. CT, d/o Robert Hames (CT) and Gladys Walters (CT)

ROSEWATER,

Joseph of Claremont m. Mary Augusta **Carlson** of Gilmanton 2/24/1951 in Pittsfield; H - 22, clerk, b. NH, s/o Joseph Rosewater (NY) and Alice L. Tipping (MA); W - 21, at home, b. NJ, d/o Fred H. Carlson (NJ) and Marion Brill (NY)

ROSS,

Dwayne C. of East Rochester m. Jennie L. **Moore** of Gilmanton 3/15/2000

ROTH,
Theodore F. of Gilmanton m. Cora B. **Whitehouse** of Plymouth 1/5/1947 in Boscawen; H - 40, cabinet maker, b. Boston, MA, s/o Frank C. Roth (Boston, MA, sheet metal worker) and Clarentine M. Demeritt (Boston, MA, housewife); W - 33, clerk, b. Peabody, MA, d/o Charles E. Whitehouse (ME, engineer) and Jane Stewart (Scotland, housewife)

ROWE,
Nicholas A. of Laconia m. Christina M. **Pickowicz** of Gilmanton 3/18/2000

RUMRILL,
Hamilton of Lynn, MA m. Barbara **Widger** of Swampscott, MA 6/27/1925; H - 28, electrical eng., b. Hillsboro, s/o Frank G. Rumrill (Hillsboro, barber) and Ella C. Marshall (Washington, housework); W - 27, secretary, b. Boston, MA, d/o Arthur C. Widger (Swampscott, MA, accountant) and Nellie M. Knowlton (Swampscott, MA, housework)

RUNNION,
Robert M. of Gilmanton m. Deborah J. **Cross** of Northfield 2/16/1980

RUSSELL,
Charles Sven of Gilmanton m. Beatrice Ann **Thompson** of Gilmanton 5/26/1951 in Gilford; H - 28, lumbering, b. CA, s/o Henry M. Russell (Ireland) and Madeline Stage (Russia); W - 23, at home, b. MA, d/o Maro P. Thompson (MA) and Cordelia L. Carpenter (MA)
Sven E. of Gilmanton m. Dawn M. **Henry** of Gilmanton 3/12/1977 in Laconia; H - b. 7/13/1954 in NH, s/o Sven C. Russell (USA) and Beatrice A. Thompson (NH); W - b. 4/22/1953 in CT, d/o John Henry (CT) and Dorothy Bunnell (CT)

ST. LAURENT,
Raymond E. of Pittsfield m. Pamela Louise **Emerson** of Gilmanton 6/1/1968 in Pittsfield; H - b. 6/9/1950 in NH, s/o Edgar St. Laurent (NH) and Betty Locke (NH); W - b. 1/4/1948 in NH, d/o Ralph A. Emerson (NH) and Ruth E. Emerson (NH)

SALGADO,
Carlos Reniery Diaz of Gilmanton m. C. L. **Lotz** of Gilmanton 9/11/1997

SANBORN,
Carl Jeremiah of Pittsfield m. Evelyn M. **Sanborn** of Melrose, MA 7/14/1914 in N. Springfield, VT; H - 26, farmer, b. Columbus, MO, s/o Jeremiah W. Sanborn (NH) and Belle G. Osborne (NH); W - 22, b. Pittsfield, d/o Frank E. Sanborn (Gilmanton) and Jennie Batchelder (Chichester)

Chad Patrick of Gilmanton m. Laurie Jane **Paquette** of Gilmanton 9/16/1995

Frank M. of Gilmanton m. Lilla M. **Hill** of Gilmanton 5/3/1904; H - 43, farmer, b. Thornton, s/o Nathan B. Sanborn (Gilmanton, farmer) and Ruth A. Cousens (Kennebunk, ME); W - 35, housemaid, b. Pittsfield, d/o Joseph R. Hill (Alton, farmer) and J. Pluma Hill (Canada)

Jeremiah W. of Gilmanton m. Myra E. **Wilson** of Nashua 10/23/1920 in Pittsfield; H - 73, farmer, 2nd, b. Gilmanton, s/o George W. Sanborn (Sandwich) and Mary N. Brown (Gilmanton); W - 61, housework, 3rd, b. NY State, d/o Chancy O. Pease and Arvilla Adams

Willie E. of Gilmanton m. Electa A. **Furber** of Alton 8/29/1891 in Alton; H - 24, blacksmith, b. Gilmanton, s/o Charles G. Sanborn (Gilmanton, farmer) and Amanda Stockbridge (Alton, housewife); W - 23, operative, b. Alton, d/o Samuel E. Furber (Alton, farmer) and Sarah Hodgdon (Barnstead, housewife)

SANDERSON,
William S. P. of Gilmanton m. Florence E. **Hoyt** of Gilmanton 7/29/1900; H - 37, druggist, b. Gilmanton, s/o C. S. P. Sanderson (druggist) and Anna J. Machk (Gilmanton, housewife); W - 33, housewife, b. Manchester, d/o George A. Hoyt (painter) and Letitia D. Hoyt (Loudon, dressmaker)

SANTERRE,
Gerard Joseph of Gilmanton m. Bernice Miriam **Hunkins** of Lakeport 12/24/1960 in Ashland; H - 38, carpenter, b. Canada, s/o Ademace Santerre (Canada) and Cimace Trimbal

(Canada); W - 44, Allen-Rogers, b. VT, d/o Ernest Kelley (VT) and Alice Andrews (VT)

SANVILLE,
Dennis W. of Gilmanton m. Deborah J. **Libby** of Laconia 7/24/1976 in Laconia; H - b. 5/16/1955 in NH, s/o William Sanville (NH) and Florence Bresse (NH); W - b. 9/9/1952 in WA, d/o Donald Libby (MA) and Leah Smith (ME)

Joseph L., 3rd of Gilmanton m. Sheryl A. **Lasheway** of Gilmanton 12/28/1984

Robert J. of Gilmanton m. Deborah J. **Hounsell** of Gilford 7/2/1977 in Gilford; H - b. 11/30/1957 in NH, s/o William Sanville (NH) and Florence Winifred (NH); W - b. 12/31/1955, d/o Thaddeus Malette (NY) and Barbara Harte (NY)

Thomas Henry of Gilmanton m. Evelyn Blanche **Jones** of Gilmanton 6/3/1967; H - 20, carpenter, b. NH, s/o William H. Sanville (NH) and Florence Bresse (NH); W - 20, secretary, b. NH, d/o Ralph A. Jones (NH) and Marjorie B. Stearns (NH)

Wilfred Lee of Gilmanton m. Brenda Gail **Glidden** of Farmington 11/6/1971; H - b. 10/9/1951 in NH, s/o William Sanville (NH) and Florence Bresse (NH); W - b. 5/13/1952 in NH, d/o Stanley Glidden (NH) and Dorothy Rollins (NY)

SARGENT,
Andrew A. of Gilmanton m. Carrie L. **Lapoint** of Gilmanton 8/18/2001

Charles P. of Gilmanton m. Alice A. **Dow** of Tilton 5/7/1894 in Loudon; H - 38, b. Gilmanton, s/o John L. Sargent (Loudon, farmer) and Mary McClure (Boscawen, housekeeper); W - 25, operative, b. Hill

Edwin W. of Concord m. Ruth M. **Jones** of Gilmanton 11/2/1929 in Gilmanton I. W.; H - 27, laborer, 2nd, b. Andover, s/o Leonard E. Sargent (VT, breakman) and Emily R. Young (Canada, housework); W - 23, at home, 2nd, b. Wilmington, MA, d/o Andrew Thompson (Chelsea, MA, gold beater) and Minnie H. Wells (Chelsea, MA, housewife)

Horace Daniel of Gilmanton m. Edna Estella **Palmer** of Gilmanton 4/11/1917 in Laconia; H - 22, farmer, b. Gilmanton, s/o Herbert Sargent (Gilmanton) and Carrie Belle Ellis (Alton); W - 18, housekeeper, b. Gilmanton, d/o George Ladd Palmer (Dover) and Daisy Mabel Smith (Gilmanton)

Jason H. of Burlington, VT m. Deanne C. **Beaudry** of Burlington, VT 6/4/1999

Prescott Nathan of Gilmanton m. Elizabeth Helen **Thompson** of Gilmanton 1/7/1961 in Laconia; H - 22, plastic supplies, b. NH, s/o Linwood Sargent (NH) and Frances Stone (NH); W - 17, stitcher, b. NH, d/o Henry S. Thompson (MA) and Beulah E. Horne (NH)

SAULNIER,
Robert Joseph, Jr. of Gilmanton m. Kimberly Jean **Downing** of Gilmanton 1/20/1997

SAWYER,
Bertram H. of Gilmanton m. Florence P. **Alden** of Boston, MA 5/25/1934 in Central Falls, RI; H - 39, dentist, 2nd, b. Melrose, MA, s/o Fred H. Sawyer (Portland, ME) and Elizabeth A. Hatch (Andover, MA); W - 30, reg. nurse, b. Boston, MA, d/o Richard C. Alden (Marlboro, MA, engineer) and Elsie A. Ellis (Natick, MA)

David of Gilmanton m. Betsey M. **Knowles** of Gilmanton 4/19/1908; H - 34, farmer, b. Gilmanton, s/o John R. Sawyer (Belmont, farmer) and Mary J. Marsh (Gilmanton, housewife); W - 22, teacher, b. Gilmanton, d/o Rufus A. Knowles (Belmont, farmer) and Arabella J. Moody (Gilmanton, housewife)

Duke of Gilmanton I. W. m. Virginia **Smith** of Gilmanton I. W. 11/12/1977 in Canterbury; H - b. 12/5/1953 in NH, s/o John W. Sawyer (NH) and Ruth Quimby (NH); W - b. 3/10/1957 in CT, d/o Reed W. Smith (CT) and Ruth B. Gates (CT)

Fred H. of Gilmanton m. Laura S. **Hanson** of Strafford 11/2/1924; H - 64, farmer, b. Lowell, MA, s/o John Sawyer (Hampstead) and Mary J. Sawyer (Henniker); W - 23, housework, b. Malden, MA, d/o Sidney Hanson (Barnstead) and Laura M. Nutter (Gilmanton)

Mark Aaron of Gilmanton m. Louise A. **Barnett** of Pittsfield 8/9/1969; H - b. 6/16/1940 in NH, s/o Harry B. Sawyer (VT) and Ruth Cody (NH); W - b. 8/6/1951 in NH, d/o Robert J. Barnett (NH) and Arlene Hoyt (NH)

Sewell B. of Farmington m. Gertrude **Mitchell** of Gilmanton 2/23/1916 in Farmington; H - 20, teamster, b. Lagrange, ME, s/o Horatio Sawyer (laborer) and Cora Sawyer; W - 25, housekeeper, 2nd, b. Gilmanton, d/o William Downes (farmer) and Mary Randall

SAYRE,
John B., Jr. of Canton, OH m. Janice **Gay** of Gilmanton 7/26/1958 in Gilmanton I. W.; H - 23, engineer, b. NJ, s/o John B. Sayre (NJ) and Frances Terhune (NJ); W - 23, teacher, b. IL, d/o Walter S. Gay (MA) and Doris Frost (NH)

Roger William of Pleasantville, NY m. Christy Ann **Herron** of Pleasantville, NY 6/20/1997

Scott Alan of Minneapolis, MN m. Kris Alice **Peick** of Minneapolis, MN 6/26/1993

SCHOTT,
Charles K. of Montclair, NJ m. Thelma S. **Blackey** of Wollaston, MA 8/23/1947; H - 27, salesman, b. Montreal, Canada, s/o Henry S. Schott (E. Orange, NJ) and Agnes Chisholm (NS, at home); W - 26, at home, b. Boston, MA, d/o Chester Blackey (Boston, MA, salesman) and Mary Briggs (England, housewife)

SCHUMACHER,
Loran Lee, Jr. of Gilmanton m. Linda K. **Rock** of Gilmanton 12/29/1982

SCOTT,
Joseph G. of Gilmanton m. Corella A. **Stevens** of Gilmanton 8/7/1985

SCOVILL,
Crosby Kent of Gilmanton m. Lois Ann **Leeper** of Needham, MA 10/7/1950 in Gilmanton I. W.; H - 27, m. seaman, b. MA, s/o Sorensen L. Scovill (NS) and Lenna Crosby (NS); W - 20, at home, b. MA, d/o George E. Leeper (MA) and Edna M. Phillips (CT)

Judson Lawrence of Gilmanton m. Elaine F. **Giuliano** of Milton, MA 8/6/1966 in Alton; H - 22, Navy, b. NH, s/o Lawrence S. Scovill (MA) and Virginia A. Prescott (NH); W - 21, secretary, b. MA, d/o Domenic Vasco Giuliano (MA) and Helen F. Crowder (MA)

Lawrence of Gilmanton m. Virginia A. **Scovill** of Alton 4/23/1955; H - 40, poultry farmer, b. MA, s/o Sorensen L. Scovill (NS) and

Lenna M. Crosby (NS); W - 32, housewife, b. NH, d/o Harold F. Prescott (NH) and Caroline H. Eastman (NH)
Lawrence S. of Gilmanton m. Virginia A. **Prescott** of Barnstead 12/10/1940 in Laconia; H - 25, farmer, b. Clinton, MA, s/o Sorensen Scovill (NS, farmer) and Lenna Crosby (NS, housewife); W - 18, at home, b. Barnstead, d/o Harold Prescott (Barnstead, farmer) and Caroline Eastman (Lynn, MA, housewife)
Paul M. of Gilmanton m. Karen E. **Wozmak** of Dover 12/5/1982

SEARS,
Robert Clifton of Brookline, MA m. Alice **Sanborn** of Brighton, MA 10/9/1918; H - 47, wool merchant, b. Medfield, MA, s/o Eben Thaxter Sears (Dennis, MA) and Susan Ella Leaman (Bristol, England); W - 39, stationery, b. Hanover, d/o J. W. Sanborn (Gilmanton) and Isabella G. Osborne (Loudon)

SECORD,
Harold Burton of Gilmanton m. Gertrude May **McNayr** of Alton 6/6/1917 in Alton; H - 18, farmer, b. Jamaica Plain, MA, s/o John Secord (St. Johns, NB) and Grace Evelyn Bemis; W - 19, clerk, b. Beverly, MA, d/o Richard McNayr (NS) and Sarah Nason (Salem, MA)

SEGALINI,
Recardo L. of Gilmanton m. Gloria J. **Hunkins** of Gilmanton 11/6/1965; H - 23, mechanic, b. NH, s/o Louie J. Segalini (NH) and Grace M. Astbury (Canada); W - 17, at home, b. NH, d/o Dana W. Hunkins (NH) and Arlene I. Little (NH)
Recardo L. of Gilmanton m. Elizabeth A. **Coulson** of Franklin 1/26/1980

SENIOR,
Ronald S. of Gilmanton m. Kristina F. **Hempel** of Gilmanton 4/28/1984

SEPULVEDA,
Guillermo of San Antonio, TX m. Suzanne Marie **Neal** of San Antonio, TX 10/15/1994

SERAVIA,
David Richard of Gilmanton m. Rose Marie **Hough** of Gilmanton 11/8/1972 in Laconia; H - b. 12/27/1953 in CA, s/o Dick Seravia (USA) and Marjorie A. Louison (USA); W - b. 12/20/1951 in NH, d/o Joseph A. Morin (NH) and Arlene E. Patten (NH)

SEVERANCE,
David S. of Gilmanton m. Kimberly J. **Brown** of Gilmanton 6/25/1983

SHAFTMAN,
David H. of IL m. Beatrice E. **Dudley** of Gilmanton 5/17/1975; H - b. 8/27/1924 in PA, s/o Nathan A. Shaftman (Russia) and Mollie Katz (Russia); W - b. 3/17/1953 in NH, d/o I. Dean Dudley (NH) and Dorothy Hurlbutt (NH)

SHANNON,
Carroll Calvin of Gilmanton m. Helen Teresa **Mahoney** of Gilmanton 1/4/1920 in Lakeport; H - 42, liveryman, b. Gilmanton, s/o Charles H. Shannon (Gilmanton) and Laura J. Lougee (Gilmanton); W - 30, telephone operator, b. Cork, Ireland, d/o Daniel J. Mahoney (Ireland) and Mary Coakley (Ireland)
Winfield S. of Gilmanton m. Bertha L. **Cook** of Gilmanton 12/2/1908; H - 35, clerk, b. Gilmanton, s/o George E. Shannon (Gilmanton, butcher) and Addie C. Smith (Gilmanton, housewife); W - 34, housemaid, b. Gilmanton, d/o Danford Cook (Plymouth, miller) and Mary B. Dudley (Ashland, housewife)

SHAPIRO,
Harold Elliot of Gilmanton m. Doris **Fisher** of Gilmanton 5/29/1994

SHATTUCK,
Steven J. of Concord m. Jo-Ann B. **McClary** of Gilmanton 1/29/1983

SHAW,
Clarence Ray of St. Johnsbury, VT m. Lillian **Dickens** of Worcester, MA 5/5/1917; H - 29, telegraph operator, b. St. Johnsbury, VT, s/o Albert H. Shaw (St. Johnsbury, VT) and Clara Holder (St. Johnsbury, VT); W - 30, stenographer, b. Yarmouth, NS, d/o James E. Dickens (NS) and Matilda Brown (Yarmouth, NS)

SHELLHORN,
Asa J. of Worcester, MA m. Anna D. **Peterson** of Groton, MA 10/5/1934 in Gilmanton I. W.; H - 29, dentist, b. Concordia, KS, s/o Bartlett Shellhorn (Pawnee City, NE, US Army) and Mary Barnes (Nemahaw City, NE, at home); W - 26, at home, b. Dorchester, MA, d/o Ewald T. Peterson (Helingborg, Sweden, cleaner) and Anna Anderson (Stockholm, Sweden, at home)

SHEPARD,
Wendell E. of Laconia m. Virginia H. **Twombly** of Gilmanton 7/3/1935 in Laconia; H - 23, laborer, b. Laconia, s/o Fred S. Shepard (Penacook, meat cutter) and Gertrude Sturtevant (Hartland, VT, at home); W - 18, at home, b. Exeter, d/o Clarence Twombly (Belmont, carpenter) and Hazel Pease (Salem, MA, at home)

SHIELDS,
James F. of Gilmanton m. Elsie L. **Steele** of Laconia 10/16/1945 in Northfield; H - 21, US Navy, b. Worthington, PA, s/o James F. Shields (Butler, PA, laborer) and Frances C. Martin (Roxbury, MA, at home); W - 18, chamber girl, b. Gilford, d/o Lester D. Steele (farmer) and Ernestine M. Willard (Belmont, at home)

SHORT,
John N. of Lowell, MA m. Mary F. **Folsom** of Gilmanton 2/4/1891; H - 49, clergyman, 2nd, b. Middlefield, MA, s/o Charles Short (Scotland, stone cutter) and Jane Short (Ireland, housewife); W - 45, housewife, b. Thornton, d/o Orrin Folsom (Gilmanton, farmer) and Lydia Ann Folsom (Gilmanton, housewife)

SHUMWAY,
Aaron of Gilmanton m. Shelli D. **Vendetti** of Gilmanton 8/19/1995

SHUNDA,
Gustave of Gilmanton m. Teresa A. **Flynn** of Gilmanton 10/7/2001

SIMINO,
Christopher William of Westmoreland m. Shiloh Sioux **Russell** of Westmoreland 10/16/1998

SIMONDS,
Frank E. of Alton m. Eleanor **Higgins** of Gilmanton 8/31/1934 in Laconia; H - 25, chauffeur, 2nd, b. Farmington, s/o E. F. Simonds (Sharon, VT, merchant) and Cynthia J. Davis (Alton, housewife); W - 18, at home, b. Meredith, d/o Frank Higgins (Elie Mines, VT, laborer) and Sadie Porter (Corinth, VT, housewife)

Richard of Alton m. Olive M. **Wells** of Gilmanton 11/30/1955 in Alton; H - 18, b. NH, s/o Frank E. Simonds (NH) and Eleanor Higgins (NH); W - 16, at home, b. NH, d/o Fred R. Wells (NH) and Dorothea B. Lucia (NH)

Richard Eugene of Alton m. Olive May Wells **Simonds** of Gilmanton 5/24/1963 in Alton; H - 26, laborer, b. NH, s/o Frank E. Simonds (NH) and Eleanor H. Higgins (NH); W - 24, housewife, b. NH, d/o Fred R. Wells (NH) and Dorothea B. Lucia (MA)

SIMONEAU,
Ulysses Charles of Laconia m. Julia **Covell** of Gilmanton 12/6/1952 in Laconia; H - 36, cook, b. NH, s/o Charles Simoneau (Canada) and Eva Bouley (NH); W - 37, coil winder, b. MA, d/o Konstant J. Shlaitas (Lithuania) and Mary A. Wasinoras (Lithuania)

SIMPSON,
Bruce W. of Laconia m. Gertrude L. **Wells** of Gilmanton 8/21/1965; H - 21, laborer, b. NH, s/o Curtis Simpson (unknown) and Barbara L. Sanborn (NH); W - 18, at home, b. NH, d/o Fred Wells (NH) and Dorothea Lucia (MA)

SIPES,
William Blaine of Gilmanton m. France Marie Frost **Leclerc** of Gilmanton 10/29/1989

SISTI,
Mark L. of Gilmanton m. Jane E. **Mitchell** of Gilmanton 9/5/1987

SKANTZE,
Donald E. of Gilmanton m. Kjersti **Aksnes** of Norway 6/26/1982
Walter H. of Alton m. Florence **Roberts** of Gilmanton 9/14/1957 in Gilmanton I. W.; H - 20, student, b. NJ, s/o Charles H. Skantze (NJ) and Catherine Russ (NJ); W - 20, student, b. MA, d/o George B. Roberts (MA) and Helene F. Emerson (NH)

SKIBA,
Russell J. of Gilmanton m. Cathy A. **Deschenes** of Gilmanton 9/27/1980

SLEEPER,
Jonathan of Gilmanton m. Emma A. **Bemis** of Gilmanton 1/2/1888; H - 69, farmer, 2nd, b. Alton, s/o Jonathan Sleeper (Brentwood, farmer) and Mary Woodman (Alton, housewife); W - 34, housewife, 2nd, b. Salem, d/o Timothy Wiggin

SLOCUM,
David P. of Gilmanton m. Marilyn M. **Strout** of Laconia 12/20/1968; H - b. 1/8/1936 in PA, s/o Roy A. Slocum (PA); W - b. 9/3/1942 in NH, d/o Harry A. Morse (NH) and Gladys Whitcher (NH)

SMITH,
Arthur Jason, Jr. of Gilmanton m. Kira Louise **Godbout** of Concord 10/12/1996
Brian William of Yakima, WA m. Becky Ann **Boyd** of Yakima, WA 10/14/1994
Charles H. of Gilmanton m. Lorraine R. **Cunningham** of Gilmanton 1/5/1979
Charles L. of Gilmanton m. Hattie M. **Stockbridge** of Gilmanton 7/24/1926; H - 20, chauffeur, b. Gilmanton, s/o J. Wilbur Smith (Gilmanton, laborer) and Edith Hannaford (housework); W -

19, housework, b. Gilmanton, d/o George S. Stockbridge (Gilmanton, farmer) and Ina Roby (Pittsfield, housework)

Edwin W. of Gilmanton m. Gladys E. **Plummer** of Gilmanton 3/15/1909 in Loudon; H - 39, laborer, b. Plymouth, s/o Frank J. Smith (Ossipee, blacksmith) and Hattie L. Gilman (Plymouth, housewife); W - 19, b. Rochester, d/o Lorenzo C. Plummer (Farmington, farmer) and Ella O. Osborne (Loudon, housewife)

George Lyndell of Gilmanton m. Ellen M. **Davis** of Gilmanton 11/27/1948; H - 21, lumbering, b. Gilmanton, s/o Charles L. Smith (Gilmanton, highway worker) and Hattie M. Stockbridge (Gilmanton, housewife); W - 20, at home, b. Gilmanton, d/o George E. Davis (Dover, lumbering) and Irene M. Page (Gilmanton, housewife)

Harold Thayer of Loudon m. Florene Louise **Dow** of Gilmanton 12/30/1951 in Chichester; H - 37, farmer, b. NH, s/o Reuben P. Smith (NH) and Flora M. Pitman (NH); W - 29, housework, b. NH, d/o James E. Hardy (NH) and Ruth M. Greene (NH)

J. Wilbur of Gilmanton m. Edith L. **Hannaford** of Gilmanton 12/14/1900; H - 32, farmer, 3rd, b. Gilmanton, s/o Charles T. Smith (Gilmanton, farmer) and Eva J. Foss (Gilmanton, housekeeper); W - 20, housekeeper, b. Manchester, d/o T. F. Hannaford (NY, broom mfg.) and Louise Landon (VT, housekeeper)

Joseph of Gilmanton m. Helen **McLain** of Manchester 4/25/1936 in Concord; H - 29, farmer, b. Philadelphia, PA, s/o William Smith (Spokane, WA, retired USA) and Mary Limpas (PA, at home); W - 32, housework, b. Groveton, d/o William McLain (Glasgow, Scotland) and Mary Gardner (Groveton, at home)

Kenneth James of Kittery, ME m. Martha Maria **Roche** of Kittery, ME 7/26/1997

Matthew M. of Gilmanton m. Sherri L. **Collins** of Gilmanton 10/1/1994

Oliver Cook of Washington, DC m. Barbara B. **Olmsted** of Gilmanton 7/31/1944; H - 46, 2nd Lieut. in USNR, b. Montpelier, ID, s/o Eugene D. Smith (Otisville, NY, engineer) and Emma Cook (England, housewife); W - 31, at home, b. Pleasantville, NY, d/o Herbert Olmsted (Boston, MA, retired) and Clara J. Wagner (Boston, MA, housewife)

Robert T. of Gilmanton m. Cheryl A. **Gibson** of Gilmanton 7/13/1990

Stephen R. of Gilmanton m. Debra A. **Streeter** of Gilmanton 12/20/1986

Warren M. of Gilmanton m. Ann M. **Haines** of Gilmanton 8/30/1897; H - 44, farmer, 3rd, b. Gilmanton, s/o Samuel A. Smith and Louisa Smith; W - 20, housemaid, b. Loudon, d/o Samuel T. Haines and Mary E. Haines

William A. of Gilmanton m. Iona B. **Knights** of Colebrook 12/6/1902; H - 19, teamster, 2nd, b. Alton, s/o Warren W. Smith (Gilmanton, farmer) and Mary E. Howard (Alton, housewife); W - 14, housemaid, b. Colebrook, d/o Albert Knights (farmer) and Lydia Knights (Colebrook, housewife)

SMITHERS,

Thomas W., IV of Gilmanton m. Dodie J. **Brown** of Gilmanton 8/29/1976; H - b. 6/20/1953 in MA, s/o Thomas W. Smithers, III (MA) and Elizabeth Belcastro (MA); W - b. 6/23/1956 in NH, d/o Harold Brown, Jr. (USA) and Alberta Watson (NH)

Thomas William, III of Gilmanton m. Margie Ruth **Robertson** of Gilmanton 12/7/1991

Timothy J. of Gilmanton m. Ronilee R. **Smith** of Gilmanton 7/21/1979

SNOW,

Craig T. of Gilmanton m. Deborah M. **Wonoski** of Gilmanton 6/30/1988

John C. of Alton m. Elizabeth Ann **Daigneau** of Gilmanton 6/7/1969; H - b. 10/14/1946 in NH, s/o William Snow (NH) and Ruth Sutton (NC); W - b. 11/27/1948 in NH, d/o Arthur Howard Daigneau (NH) and Daura Nena Cass (VT)

Steve R. of Gilmanton m. Roya R. **Reinholz** of Gilmanton 10/8/1988

SPARTOS,

Gary G. of Gilmanton I. W. m. Mary T. **Berry** of Gilmanton I. W. 10/16/1999

SPAULDING,

Frank A., Jr. of Gilmanton I. W. m. Ann M. **McGee** of Gilmanton I. W. 1/4/1975 in Tilton; H - b. 9/3/1939 in MA, s/o Frank A. Spaulding, Sr. (MA) and Florence Finamore (MA); W - b.

11/6/1946 in Ireland, d/o John McGee (Ireland) and Bridget McManus (Ireland)
Frank A., Jr. of Gilmanton m. Christine A. **Lines** of Gilmanton 6/2/1984

SPECK,
Joseph S., Jr. of Augusta, ME m. Mary A. **Bennett** of Gilmanton 9/6/1942; H - 18, clerk, b. Augusta, ME, s/o Joseph S. Speck (England, salesman) and Susan Peabody (Augusta, ME, housewife); W - 18, at home, b. Gilmanton, d/o Marvin S. Bennett (Clinton, NY, mail carrier) and Velina B. Vinal (Jefferson, ME, housewife)

SPENCER,
Adam D. of Gilmanton m. Rebecca L. **Rausch** of Gilmanton 10/5/1996

SPRINGER,
Harold L. of Gilmanton m. Evelyn **Wright** of Lyndonville, VT 4/18/1936 in Gilmanton I. W.; H - 28, truck driver, b. Nashua, s/o Sanford Springer (Providence, RI, salesman) and Edith Horsman (Bradford, England, postmaster); W - 26, at home, 2nd, b. Lancaster, d/o Beriah Wright (Lancaster, railroad) and Bessie Flynn (Lancaster, at home)
Harold Leslie of Gilmanton m. Dorothy Belle **Patch** of Franklin 12/10/1960; H - 53, carpenter, b. NH, s/o Sanford R. Springer (ME) and Edith Hosman (England); W - 53, presser, b. NH, d/o James Kelley (NH) and Jennie Emerson (NH)

STACEY,
Peter Martin of Marblehead, MA m. Dian Florence **Willard** of Gilmanton 6/18/1960; H - 22, electronic technician, b. MA, s/o Arthur M. Stacey (MA) and Katherine R. Thompson (MA); W - 17, student, b. NH, d/o Arthur E. Willard (NH) and Mary C. Heinis (MA)

STANCOMBE,
Arthur W. of Derry m. Judith C. **McIntire** of Gilmanton 8/14/1998

STANLEY,
Milton of Gilmanton m. Rebecca J. **Rosenblum** of Gilmanton 3/5/1977; H - b. 2/20/1917 in NY, s/o William Stanley (Russia) and Grace Goldfarb (Poland); W - b. 9/12/1940 in NY, d/o Walter Slifer (NY) and Ada Marshall (NY)
Norman G. of Gilmanton m. Denise V. **Boyce** of Gilmanton 5/19/1990
William D., III of Gilmanton m. Kara Lyn **Murray** of Gilmanton 4/25/1992

STANTON,
David F. of Gilmanton m. Carrie **Hunter** of Norwich, CT 2/14/1904; H - 30, engineer, b. Lancaster, s/o John Stanton (Whitefield, laborer) and Mary DeCato; W - 26, housemaid, d/o Hugh Hunter (gardener) and Mary -----

STANWOOD,
Christopher W. of Wellesley, MA m. Jeanne Sawyer **Faggi** of Concord, MA 7/29/1962; H - 52, insurance, b. MA, s/o William E. Stanwood (OH) and Mary Merrill (ME); W - 41, real estate, b. MA, d/o Howard M. Sawyer (MA) and Ruth Howes (MA)

STARRETT,
Edwin B. of Gilmanton m. Amy D. **Jelley** of Gilmanton 6/7/1904 in Laconia; H - 30, lumberman, b. New London, s/o Franklin B. Starrett (Francestown, farmer) and Roxey C. Hardy (Francestown); W - 17, housemaid, b. Nashua, d/o Cornelious Jelley (W. Shasey, NY, teamster) and Henniner Moren (Nashua)

STEELE,
Robert E. of Gilford m. Louise M. **Smith** of Gilmanton 1/18/1948 in Pittsfield; H - 21, laborer, b. Gilford, s/o D. Lester Smith (W. Thornton, laborer) and Mabel E. Willard (Belmont, mill worker); W - 17, at home, b. Gilmanton, d/o Charles L. Smith (Gilmanton, laborer) and Hattie M. Stockbridge (housewife)

STENDOR,
Jefferey J. of Gilmanton m. Debra L. **Brooks** of Laconia 1/16/1993

William F. of Gilmanton m. Brenda A. **White** of Laconia 4/11/1970 in Laconia; H - b. 2/1/1952 in IL, s/o Noel B. Stendor (MA) and Georgianna E. Gagnon (NH); W - b. 1/31/1951 in NH, d/o Rudolph White, Sr. (NH) and Beverly May Ulman (NH)

William F., II of Gilmanton m. Sheila L. **Thomas** of Gilmanton 7/21/1990

STEVENS,

Aaron D. of Gilmanton m. Ruby Florence **Willard** of Farmington 12/23/1916 in Farmington; H - 27, shoe shop, b. Beverly, MA, s/o J. Augustus Stevens (Beverly, MA, farmer) and Louise Spinney (NS, house wife); W - 21, box shop, b. Alton, d/o Smith Willard (Alton, shoemaker) and Sadie E. Lamper (Alton, housewife)

E. Kevin of Gilmanton m. Eileen M. **Walsh** of Tilton 7/8/1978 in Tilton; H - b. 1/4/1953 in NH, s/o Sherman Stevens (ME) and Mildred Ross (ME); W - b. 6/30/1958 in NH, d/o Thomas Walsh (NY) and Joan Foley (NY)

Richard H. of Gilmanton m. Eleanor J. **White** of Gilmanton 1/31/1983

William K. of N. Andover, MA m. Jo-Ann **La Spina** of N. Andover, MA 7/11/1992

STEWARTSON,

Carl L. of Concord m. Harriet E. **Sidebotham** of Concord 7/8/1933; H - 20, musician, b. Concord, s/o Frank E. Swartson (Somersworth, musician) and Clara E. Robinson (N. Pembroke, housework); W - 20, housework, b. Penacook, d/o John Sidebotham (Oldham, Eng., harn. maker) and Abbie M. Murray (Hooksett, housework)

STICKNEY,

Carl H. of Gilmanton m. Goldie L. **Guy** of Concord 12/8/1932; H - 22, mechanic, b. Lisbon, s/o Harold Stickney (Lyman, painter) and Salina Belware (Littleton, housework); W - 19, housework, b. Concord, d/o James Guy (Quebec, Can., stone cutter) and Mabel Webster (ME, housework)

STILES,
George L. of Gilmanton m. Frances M. **Green** of Gilmanton
11/7/1992

STITT,
Richard P. of Gilmanton m. Nancy O. **Lutters** of Gilmanton
10/24/1981

STOCKBRIDGE,
Carl L. of Gilmanton m. Eleanor **Patten** of Belmont 3/13/1941 in Berwick, ME; H - 19, farmer, b. Gilmanton, s/o George Stockbridge (Gilmanton, farmer) and Ina Roby (Pittsfield, housewife); W - 16, at home, b. Belmont, d/o Fred W. Patten (Alexandria, deceased) and Lura Gray (Canaan, housework)

Carl Lewis of Gilmanton m. Ruby Pamela **Lake** of Gilmanton 4/7/1962; H - 40, laborer, b. NH, s/o George S. Stockbridge (NH) and Ina M. Robie (NH); W - 35, housekeeper, b. MA, d/o Cyrus B. Head (KY) and Ruby H. Olsen (MA)

G. S. of Gilmanton m. Ida W. **Chase** of Lawrence, MA 11/9/1898; H - 25, farmer, b. Gilmanton, s/o Charles Stockbridge (Gilmanton) and Harriet N. Folsom (Gilmanton, housewife); W - 23, nurse, 2nd, b. N. Andover, MA, d/o Melvin T. Wadlin (Lyman, ME, machinist) and Sarah J. Cole (Boxford, MA, nurse)

George S. of Gilmanton m. Ina M. **Roby** of Gilmanton 1/6/1907 in Ctr. Barnstead; H - 33, farmer, 2nd, b. Gilmanton, s/o Charles Stockbridge (farmer) and Hattie Folsom (housewife); W - 20, housemaid, b. Pittsfield, d/o Ernest J. Roby (Gilmanton, shoemaker) and Carrie Dowst (Epsom, housewife)

Harry E. of Gilmanton m. Shirley B. **Osgood** of Alton Bay 9/18/1933; H - 22, laborer, b. Gilmanton, s/o George Stockbridge (Gilmanton, farmer) and Ina Roby (Pittsfield, housewife); W - 18, at home, b. E. Bridgewater, MA, d/o Perley Osgood (Holland, VT, salesman) and Laura A. Sweat (Ellinburgh, NY, housewife)

Harry Eugene of Gilmanton m. Carol Virginia **Higgins** of Laconia 4/23/1960 in Laconia; H - 49, mill worker, b. NH, s/o George S. Stockbridge (NH) and Ina M. Roby (NH); W - 25, shoe worker, b. ME, d/o Joseph B. Huggins (sic) (ME) and Cora J. Bracy (ME)

Joseph S. of Gilmanton m. Frances L. **Place** of Gilmanton
10/24/1928; H - 20, farmer, b. Gilmanton, s/o George S.
Stockbridge (Gilmanton, farmer) and Ina Robey (Barnstead,
housework); W - 15, at home, b. Alton, d/o Franklin S. Place
(Gilmanton, carpenter) and Luanna Hurd (Barnstead,
housework)

Joseph Samuel of Gilmanton m. Theresa Adeline **Boisvert** of
Pittsfield 7/30/1971 in Chichester; H - b. 9/12/1908 in NH, s/o
George Stockbridge (NH) and Ina Roby (NH); W - b. 3/8/1936
in NH, d/o Ernest Boisvert (NH) and Beulah Chagnon (NH)

Mark A. of Gilmanton m. Wendy L. **Trottier** of Gilmanton 8/29/1981

Michael J. of Gilmanton m. Crystal M. **McLeod** of Gilmanton
4/3/1982

STOCKWELL,

Andrew Donald of Gilmanton m. Arlene Theresa **Green** of Loudon
11/24/1989

Clifford H. of Gilmanton m. Jeannette T. **Hyslop** of Gilmanton
9/1/1979

Clifford Harmon of Gilmanton m. Frances Lorraine **Hyslop** of
Gilmanton 10/16/1960; H - 19, press operator, b. NH, s/o
Leonard A. Stockwell (MA) and Ruth A. Clifford (NH); W - 17,
student, b. NH, d/o Donald W. Hyslop (NH) and Rachel A.
Straw (NH)

Daniel C. of Gilmanton m. Katharine **Colby** of Gilmanton 9/18/1982

Daniel C. of Gilmanton m. Ginger R. **Willard** of Gilmanton 3/2/1985

John A. m. Janie N. **French** 10/17/1923

Leonard A. of Gilmanton m. Josephine G. **Hamel** of Gilmanton
11/27/1986

Leonard Alfred of Gilmanton m. Karen Elaine **Carlson** of
Gilmanton 8/31/1991

STONE,

Andrew William of Gilmanton m. Amanda Jane **Lindley** of
Gilmanton 10/6/1989

Charles L. of Gilmanton m. Hattie Ella **Rollins** of Lakeport
6/30/1930; H - 23, laborer, b. Gilmanton, s/o Fred L. Stone
(Franklin, fireman) and Mamie M. Hilliard (Weirs, housework);
W - 18, housework, b. Lakeport, d/o Benjamin Rollins

(Lakeport, painter) and Ida Anna Bailey (Richmond, Can., housework)

Charles W. of Gilmanton m. Mary L. **Nicholson** of Pittsfield 2/11/1935 in Manchester; H - 50, farmer, 2nd, b. Franklin, s/o Edmund Stone (NY, farmer) and Esther Montie (Canada, housewife); W - 41, waitress, 2nd, b. Pittsfield, d/o Frank Bouchard (Manchester, shoemaker) and ----- Byron (Manchester)

Edward G. of Gilmanton m. Elizabeth **Pickard** of Canterbury 10/12/1936 in Canterbury; H - 26, laborer, b. Gilmanton, s/o Fred L. Stone (Franklin, fireman) and Mamie Hilliard (The Weirs); W - 20, nursemaid, b. Northfield, d/o Walter Pickard (Canterbury, laborer) and Ida Shaw (Tilton, at home)

Fred L. of Gilmanton m. Mamie S. **Hilliard** of Laconia 7/10/1905; H - 27, farmer, b. Franklin Falls, s/o Edmund Stone (NY, farmer) and Mary Stone (Canada, housewife); W - 27, housemaid, 2nd, b. Laconia, d/o George H. Hilliard (Laconia, farmer) and Mary Swain (New Hampton, housewife)

STRATHERN,

Arthur of Laconia m. Vera **Edwards** of Gilmanton 6/26/1940 in Biddeford, ME; H - 21, truck driver, b. Laconia, s/o Harry Strathern (Island Pond, VT, janitor) and Edna Thyng; W - 21, waitress, b. NY, d/o Thomas Edwards (England, farmer) and Sadie Rossman (NY, housewife)

STRICKLAND,

Robert B. of Barnstead m. Sharon B. **Briscoe** of Gilmanton 8/9/1980

STUDLEY,

Edmund G. of Gilmanton m. Donna A. **Merkwan** of Gilford 7/12/1987

SULLIVAN,

Joel Marvin of Waltham, MA m. Claire Ellen **Tesorero** of Wellesley, MA 7/29/1961; H - 25, woodworker, b. PA, s/o William T. Sullivan (PA) and Mary E. Hodges (PA); W - 19, secretary, b. MA, d/o Philip E. Tesorero (MA) and Ruth F. Wilcox

SUMNER,
William L. of Atherton, CA m. Gail W. **Clement** of Rye, NY
   8/15/1965; H - 24, student, b. NY, s/o Alfred R. Sumner (MD)
   and Margaret S. Lippincott (NJ); W - 23, student, b. CA, d/o
   Robert E. Clement (CA) and Dorothy W. Deacon (IL)

SVENSON,
Carl J. of Gilmanton m. Phyllis C. **McMahon** of Gilmanton
   6/25/1994
Robert A. of Gilmanton m. Teri A. **Hemeon** of Gilmanton 9/10/1977
   in Laconia; H - b. 5/3/1948 in MA, s/o Elmo Svenson (NH) and
   Dorothy Flight (MA); W - b. 2/25/1959 in NH, d/o John
   Hemeon (NH) and Lorna Durgin (NH)

SWAIN,
John W. of Gilmanton m. Francis **Durrell** of Gilmanton 7/30/1900;
   H - 63, farmer, 2nd, b. Meredith, s/o John L. Swain and Olive
   Batchelder; W - 71, housewife, 3rd, b. Gilmanton, d/o Samuel
   Batchelder and Sally Clark

SWEENEY,
James Joseph, III of Gilmanton m. Wendy Leigh **Munroe** of
   Gilmanton 11/29/1989
Thomas George of Waltham, MA m. Patricia Ann **Dumais** of
   Waltham, MA 5/26/1962; H - 21, machinist, b. MA, s/o Joseph
   T. Sweeney (MA) and Dorothy I. Gross (MA); W - 20, clerk, b.
   NH, d/o Roger M. Dumais (NH) and Doris H. Rowe (NH)

SWETT,
Fred H. of Gilmanton m. Stella P. **Patten** of Belmont 10/7/1924; H -
   25, farmer, b. Gilmanton, s/o Herbert S. Swett (E. Kingston)
   and Carrie B. Page (Laconia); W - 18, housework, b. Bristol,
   d/o Fred M. Patten (Alexandria) and Lura M. Gray (Canaan)

SWIFT,
William of Dover m. Carolyn **Daigneau** of Gilmanton 6/15/1968; H
   - b. 6/6/1945 in ME, s/o Halbert Keith Swift (ME) and Margaret
   E. Quimby (MA); W - b. 9/28/1947 in NH, d/o Arthur Daigneau
   (NH) and Daura N. Cass (VT)

SWITZER,
Charles Wilbur of Gilmanton m. Theresa Elizabeth **Pickel** of Botsford, CT 10/8/1966 in Lebanon; H - 46, heat treater, b. NH, s/o Charles W. Switzer (VT) and Mae L. Adamson (ME); W - 42, typist, b. NH, d/o George W. Hall (Ireland) and Abigail Bunker (NH)

TADAKOWSKY,
John J., Jr. of Danbury m. Valerie J. **Eddy** of Gilmanton 7/24/1982

TALAMAS,
Glenn A. of Laconia m. Martha **Burgess** of Gilmanton 6/7/1975 in Franklin; H - b. 11/25/1951 in MA, s/o Andre T. Talamas (Haiti) and Loretta R. Zirpolo (MA); W - b. 4/18/1948 in MN, d/o Charles H. Burgess (WY) and Linda Cannon (MA)

TARANTINO,
Francis David of Lowell, MA m. Paula Ann **McVey** of Lowell, MA 10/10/1999

TARDY,
Michael E. of Laconia m. Barbara R. **Ehlen** of Gilmanton 8/10/1974; H - b. 2/19/1956 in NH, s/o Elwin Tardy (NH) and Gary Fournier (NH); W - b. 10/13/1955 in NY, d/o Henry Ehlen (NY) and Hattie Morris (NJ)

TASH,
Arthur of Gilmanton m. Mary Ella **Berry** of Gilmanton 11/21/1970; H - b. 7/12/1930 in MA, s/o Ernest Tash (NH) and Nettie F. Garland (NH); W - b. 8/27/1944 in MA, d/o Walter Berry (MA) and Mary Howard (MA)

TASKER,
Andrew F. of Gilmanton m. Elaine C. Frazio **Molignano** of Gilmanton 10/10/1981

TAYLOR,
Brian M. of Laconia m. Susan L. **Checkos** of Gilmanton 10/25/1990
James G. of Bemus Point, NY m. Caroline S. **Mick** of Gilmanton 5/9/1965; H - 55, CPA, b. NJ, s/o James G. Taylor (NY) and

Mary D. Campbell (Scotland); W - 39, teacher, b. NY, d/o
Richard L. Small (MA) and Eleanor A. Taylor (NY)

TEMPLE,
Bernard Edwin of Gilmanton m. Angelia Lee **Davies** of Gilmanton 5/13/1989

THOMPSON,
Andrew E. of MA m. Elizabeth D. MacKay **Reid** of Gilmanton 7/26/1975; H - b. 11/30/1918 in MA, s/o Robert Thompson (Ireland) and Isbella Cardwell (Ireland); W - b. 2/2/1910 in Canada, d/o Morton N. Ried (Canada) and Emma Gray (Canada)

Clement Andrew of Gilmanton m. Claire Simmone **Desmarais** of Manchester 10/5/1974 in Laconia; H - b. 6/10/1939 in NH, s/o Henry Thompson (MA) and Beulah Horn (NH); W - b. 1/19/1943 in NH, d/o Florant Desmarais (Canada) and Simmone Gauthier (NH)

Dayne F. of Gilmanton m. Mary B. **Hansen** of Gilmanton 4/24/1986

Dayne Frederick of Gilmanton m. Renee Kathryn **Pickard** of Gilmanton 11/5/1995

Edward C. of Gilmanton m. Angela D. **Delafano** of Revere, MA 10/12/1948 in Tilton; H - 24, lumbering, b. Fall River, MA, s/o Maro B. Thompson (Wilmington, MA, lumbering) and Cordelia L. Carpenter (Fall River, MA, housewife); W - 21, reader, b. Revere, MA, d/o John J. Delafano (Boston, MA, retired) and Matilda Caporale (Boston, MA, housewife)

Henry S. of Gilmanton m. Melvina A. **Fecteau** of Manchester 10/15/1925 in Gilmanton I. W.; H - 35, mechanic, 2nd, b. S. Ashburnham, MA, s/o Andrew Thompson (Chelsea, MA, gold beater) and Minnie H. Wells (Chelsea, MA, housework); W - 36, housework, 2nd, b. Martinsville, Que., d/o Orlo H. Rowell (Beecher Falls, VT, farmer) and Josephine M. Gilbert (Martinsville, Can., housework)

Herbert E. of Gilmanton m. Angie **Patten** of Belmont 3/9/1924; H - 20, shoeworker, b. Wilmington, MA, s/o Almon C. Thompson (Chelsea, MA) and Anna M. Wells (Chelsea, MA); W - 18, millworker, b. Bristol, d/o Fred Patten (Alexandria) and Lura M. Gray (Canaan)

Kenneth A. of Gilmanton m. Bernice **Davis** of Pittsfield 11/12/1932 in Gilmanton I. W.; H - 28, laborer, b. N. Wilmington, MA, s/o

Andrew J. Thompson (Chelsea, MA, goldbeater) and Minnie A. Wells (Chelsea, MA, housework); W - 28, housework, b. Bedford, d/o Clarence N. Davis (Ctr. Barnstead, shoe worker) and Mary J. Nanson (Portsmouth, housework)

Mark I. of Virginia Beach, TX m. Deborah A. **Osmer** of Virginia Beach, TX 12/5/1987

Maro B. of Gilmanton m. Cordelia L. **Carpenter** of Dighton, MA 11/21/1925 in Dighton, MA; H - 24, clerk, b. Wilmington, MA, s/o Andrew Thompson (Chelsea, MA, gold beater) and Minnie H. Wells (Chelsea, MA, housework); W - 28, housekeeper, b. Fall River, MA, d/o Joseph Carpenter (Canada, farmer) and Mariah Caron (Canada, housework)

Victor L., Jr. of Gilmanton m. Ethel G. **Adel** of Gilmanton 11/13/1965; H - 18, laborer, b. NH, s/o Victor L. Thompson, Sr. (Canada) and Alma Provenchal (unknown); W - 20, stitcher, b. NH, d/o Daniel J. A. Adel, Sr. (Germany) and Beatrice Willard (NH)

THOROUGHGOOD,

Richard J. of Ctr. Barnstead m. Diana **Purtell** of Gilmanton I. W. 11/17/1977 in Barnstead; H - b. 8/18/1957 in NH, s/o Ralph H. Thoroughgood (NH) and Phyllis Young (NH); W - b. 2/5/1961 in NH, d/o Stanley B. Purtell (NH) and Barbara J. Parker (NH)

THURBER,

John Spencer Tisdale of Alton m. Cheryl Fay **Wahlstrom** of Gilmanton 9/30/1995

TIBBETTS,

Henry A. of Alton m. Doris M. **Rollins** of Gilmanton 4/19/1924 in Laconia; H - 26, farmer, b. Alton, s/o Charles Tibbetts (Gilmanton) and Ida M. Perkins (Alton); W - 17, at home, b. Gilmanton, d/o Seldon B. Rollins (Gilmanton) and Elma L. Ellis (Alton)

Robert F. of Alton m. Olive B. **Partridge** of Gilmanton 2/23/1947 in Wolfeboro; H - 23, truck driver, b. Gilmanton, s/o Henry A. Tibbetts (Alton, farmer) and Doris M. Rollins (Gilmanton, housewife); W - 16, at home, b. Gilmanton, d/o Horace F. Partridge (Blackstone, MA, farmer) and Florence J. Palmer (Gilmanton, housewife)

Robert Oliver of Gilmanton m. Judith Lee **Wiggin** of Rochester 11/23/1968 in Rochester; H - b. 6/23/1947 in NH, s/o Robert F. Tibbetts (NH) and Olive Beatrice Partridge (NH); W - b. 2/15/1945 in NH, d/o Lester Arthur Wiggin, Jr. (ME) and Audrey Elizabeth Drew (NH)

TONG,
Frank Yue of Gilmanton m. Eileen G. **Sullivan** of Laconia 10/19/1938 in Laconia; H - 26, painter, b. Northfield, s/o Edward Tong (China, merchant) and Ellen Langley (Pittsfield, at home); W - 29, musician, b. Boston, MA, d/o Patrick J. Sullivan (Westerly, RI, compositor) and Jane F. Condon (Boston, MA, at home)

TRITES,
Donald Earl of Wellesley, MA m. Patricia Ann **Spellman** of Malden, MA 11/27/1960; H - 21, landscaper, b. MA, s/o Robert Earl Trites (Canada) and Katherine Benjamin (Canada); W - 18, waitress, b. MA, d/o Edward J. Spellman (MA) and Mary C. Baldasare (MA)

TRUMBULL,
James G. m. Eva A. **Thompson** 6/14/1922 in Lebanon

TRUMP,
Dennis H. of Gilmanton m. Katherine N. **Guptill** of Dover 9/26/1987

TUCKER,
Nathan B. of Gilmanton m. Frances W. **Shepard** of Gilmanton 7/18/1980

TURCOTTE,
David Daniel of Laconia m. Suzanne Lyn **Smith** of Gilmanton 12/9/1994

TURNER,
Russell E. of Franklin m. Joanne M. **Bradley** of Hill 7/12/1976; H - b. 12/10/1953 in MN, s/o Wallace Turner (IL) and Ruth Waugh (SD); W - b. 11/26/1957 in ME, d/o Joseph Bradley (ME) and Cynthia Alexander (ME)

TUTTLE,
Marcus M. of Gilmanton m. Sarah A. **Gunn** of Salisbury 10/11/1904; H - 61, shoemaker, 2nd, widower, b. Epping, s/o John Tuttle (Wolfeboro, shoemaker) and Martha E. Rollins (Lee); W - 60, housemaid, 3rd, widow, b. VT, d/o Ebenezar Sanborn and Ruth Sanborn

TWIGG,
George, IV of Bethesda, MD m. Sharon Angela **Maxfield** of Bethesda, MD 10/7/1995

TWOMBLY,
Benjamin K. m. Margaret E. **O'Brien** 9/27/1923

Charles A. of Gilmanton m. Edith G. **Smith** of Gilmanton 11/10/1956 in Chichester; H - 28, lumbering, b. NH, s/o Benjamin K. Twombly (NH) and Margaret E. O'Brien (NH); W - 23, stitcher, b. NH, d/o Charles L. Smith (NH) and Hattie M. Stockbridge (NH)

Clarence H. of Gilmanton m. Hazel A. **Pease** of Gilmanton 3/1/1915 in Pittsfield; H - 24, carpenter, b. Belmont, s/o Dixi C. Twombly (Lakeport, carpenter) and Emma Batchelder (Meredith, housewife); W - 20, housekeeper, b. Salem, MA, d/o Fred V. Pease (Loudon, carpenter) and Anna Pearse (Gilmanton, housewife)

Everett T. of Gilmanton m. Ona Faye **Emerson** of Chichester 8/3/1933; H - 24, laborer, b. Gilmanton, s/o Dixie C. Twombly (Laconia, carpenter) and Emma M. Batchelder (Meredith, housework); W - 18, at home, b. Pittsfield, d/o Clarence N. Emerson (Barnstead, plumber) and Inez P. Brock (Pittsfield, housewife)

Fred M. of Gilmanton m. Gertrude A. **Rollins** of Gilmanton 11/17/1929 in Gilmanton I. W.; H - 27, carpenter, b. Hampton, s/o Dixie Twombly (Gilmanton, carpenter) and Emma Batchelder (Meredith, housework); W - 25, shoe worker, b. Gilmanton, d/o Selden B. Rollins (Gilmanton, laborer) and Alma Ellis (Alton, housework)

James Richard of Gilmanton m. Maureen Rae **Munsey** of Chichester 6/8/1968 in Chichester; H - b. 10/29/1941 in NH, s/o Benjamin K. Twombly (NH) and Margaret E. O'Brien (NH); W - b. 2/10/1948 in NH, d/o Ray W. Munsey (NH) and Leola G. Smith (NH)

TWOMEY,
Brendan Francis of Gilmanton m. Crista Kendall **Spangler** of Gilmanton 9/25/1993

UHLENBERG,
Frank L. of Gilmanton m. Evelyn A. **Page** of Gilmanton 6/28/1947; H - 40, carpenter, b. Kenosha, WI, s/o Henry Uhlenberg (Germany, carpenter) and Levina Jensen (Denmark, housewife); W - 26, teacher, b. Gilmanton, d/o Frank J. Page (Franklin, road agent) and Helen Otis (Tilton, housewife)

Harvey of Gilmanton m. Muriel J. **Dutile** of Laconia 7/5/1954 in Laconia; H - 19, US Army, b. NH, s/o Frank L. Uhlenberg (WI) and Evelyn A. Page (NH); W - 20, telephone opr., b. NH, d/o Homer J. Dutile (NH) and Alice Bolduc (NH)

URQUHART,
Jeffrey Allen of Gilmanton m. Lynne Ellen **Balcom** of Wolfeboro 6/8/1991

VACHON,
Peter Joseph, III of Northfield m. Ricki Charlene **Russell** of Gilmanton 8/8/1998

VAILLANCOURT,
Tracy Alan of Gilmanton m. Angela C. **Colangeli** of Gilmanton 8/31/1996

VALAS,
Mark Randall of Gilmanton m. Christine Marie **Miller** of Gilmanton 11/26/1994

VERNON,
Arthur A. of Kingston, RI m. Hope **Jillson** of Gilmanton 8/18/1934; H - 31, teacher, b. Schenectady, NY, s/o Samuel Vernon (England, retired) and Minnie Chase (England, housewife); W - 32, at home, b. Providence, RI, d/o Girard E. Jillson (RI) and Harriet Forsyth (Bucksport, ME, teacher)

VIEN,
Alphia R. of Pittsfield m. Jeanette **Rollins** of Gilmanton 8/31/1946 in Chichester; H - 22, mill worker, b. Pittsfield, s/o Arthur Vien (Pittsfield, millworker) and Sophia Chagnon (Pittsfield, housewife); W - 18, stitcher (clothing), b. Gilmanton, d/o Seldon B. Rollins (Gilmanton, retired) and Eva M. Jones (Gilmanton, housewife)

VINCENT,
Rene C. of Gilmanton m. Mary E. **Fournier** of Concord 11/26/1983

VODA,
Dennis J. of Groton, CT m. Susan D. **Kincaid** of Gilmanton 7/12/1986

VOREL,
John A. of Gilmanton m. Bonnie G. **Link** of Gilmanton 11/5/1977 in Alton; H - b. 11/19/1949 in MA, s/o Herman Vorel (MA) and Margaret Lawless (MA); W - b. 12/9/1949 in NY, d/o Elmer Link (NY) and Elizabeth Sealander (NY)

VOUDREN,
Roger D. of Marlboro m. Irene L. **Morin** of Gilmanton 6/20/1953 in Marlboro; H - 20, US Army, b. NH, s/o Joseph H. Voudren (NY) and Doris M. Willet (MA); W - 17, operator, b. NH, d/o Joseph A. Morin (NH) and Alene E. Patten (NH)

VYCE,
Michael J. of Gilmanton m. Christine **Gerhardt** of Gilmanton 6/21/1985

WADE,
Edwin D. of Gilmanton m. Clara **Roy** of Gilmanton 1/22/1908; H - 35, farmer, b. Gilmanton, s/o Lyman Wade (Moultonboro, farmer) and Martha A. Wade (Center Harbor, housewife); W - 30, housekeeper, 2nd, b. France

WALDRON,
Brian Robert of Gilford m. Sheri Louise **West** of Gilmanton 1/31/1998

Jerry D. of Gilmanton m. Debra A. **Dodd** of Gilmanton 6/9/2001

WALKER,
Daniel Gary of Gilmanton m. Sandra Jean **Foote** of Gilmanton 9/20/1997
Gordon D. of Laconia m. Pauline **Twombly** of Gilmanton 8/8/1958 in Alton; H - 37, plumber, b. NH, s/o Bertram G. Walker (MA) and Marjorie M. Dame (MA); W - 21, at home, b. NH, s/o Benjamin K. Twombly (NH) and Margaret E. O'Brien (NH)
Stephen Arthur of Gilmanton m. Deborah Louise **Whitman** of Gilmanton 5/22/1999

WALLACE,
Charles Bert of Gilmanton m. Carrie Cutting **Caswell** of Laconia 12/3/1951 in Belmont; H - 26, US Navy, b. NH, s/o Bradley L. Wallace (NH) and Gladys M. Locke (NH); W - 31, bank teller, b. NH, d/o Elmer I. Cutting (NH) and Rose P. Hartley (NH)
David Allen of Plainville, MA m. Julie Ann **Binnall** of Plainville, MA 7/19/1998
Gary S. of Gilmanton m. Murdeen D. **Odman** of Gilmanton 6/6/1981

WALSH,
Jay of Concord m. Rebecca **Clairmont** of Gilmanton 4/23/1977 in Belmont; H - b. 7/5/1951 in RI, s/o William Walsh (RI) and Claire Sheridan (RI); W - b. 10/8/1952 in NH, d/o Joseph Clairmont (NH) and Katherine Bouchard (NH)

WALTON,
Jonathan Henry of Gilmanton m. Karne Dianne **Schricker** of Gilmanton 9/9/1995
Kenneth I., III of Gilmanton m. Linda L. **Rhodes** of Laconia 9/19/1981

WANAMAKER,
George of Litchfield m. Janice A. **McKiernan** of Gilmanton 6/15/1968 in Laconia; H - b. 5/10/1937 in MA, s/o Stephen Wanamaker (MA) and Helen R. Brown (MA); W - b. 1/26/1943 in MA, d/o Webster J. Boudreau (MA) and Olga Cranton

WANNE,
Allen Theodore of Philadelphia, PA m. Rachel Miriam **Wagner** of Philadelphia, PA 7/5/1997

WARBURTON,
John H. of Gilmanton m. Clara **Elkins** of Gilmanton 9/4/1912; H - 29, farmer, b. Liverpool, England, s/o Harry Warburton and Jane Warburton; W - 21, housemaid, b. Gilmanton, d/o John T. Elkins (Gilmanton, farmer) and Cora Ham (Gilmanton, housewife)

WARD,
Arthur Jay of Gilmanton m. Christine Ruth **Burgoyne** of Gilmanton 7/22/1972 in Concord; H - b. 6/19/1948 in NY, s/o Arthur E. Ward, Jr. (NY) and Laine Wanaselja (NY); W - b. 11/22/1950 in NY, d/o Francis O. Burgoyne (ME) and Florence Spafford (NH)

Raymond E. of Gilmanton m. Alma Mary **Gagnon** of Laconia 9/21/1929 in Laconia; H - 23, machinist, b. Worcester, MA, s/o Ellis A. Ward (Newton, MA, conductor) and Marion Varney (Wellesley, MA, at home); W - 22, maid, b. Laconia, d/o Octave Gagnon (St. Joseph, Que., carpenter) and Rosilla Blanchard (Canada, at home)

Raymond E. of Gilmanton m. Mary F. **Davis** of Northfield 7/9/1948 in Northwood Ridge; H - 42, machinist, b. Worcester, MA, s/o Ellis A. Ward (Newton, MA) and Marian M. Varney (Wellesley, MA, mill worker); W - 19, at home, b. Meredith, d/o Archie W. Davis (Hollis, chopper [lumber]) and Lillian A. Brown (Tilton, housewife)

WARREN,
Edgar W. of Haverhill, MA m. Abbie E. **Canney** of Dover 8/17/1910 in Gilmanton I. W.; H - 49, painter, b. Sandwich, s/o Joseph H. Warren (Newington) and Julia M. Warren (Strafford); W - 49, dressmaker, b. Dover, d/o Jerome B. Canney (Strafford) and Nancy P. Canney (Wakefield, MA)

WATSON,
Ernest, Jr. of Manchester m. Carol **Lank** of Gilmanton 4/2/1966 in Pittsfield; H - 20, student, b. NH, s/o Ernest Watson, Sr. (NH)

and Alice French (USA); W - 18, cook, b. NH, d/o Howard
John Lank (RI) and Hazel Isabel Parker (MI)
Jack D. of Gilmanton m. Loraine E. **Watson** of Gilmanton 2/6/2000
John D. of Gilmanton m. Mary B. **White** of Haverhill, MA
6/27/1887; H - 29, shoe cutter, 2nd, b. Gilmanton, s/o John
Watson (Alton, farmer) and Abbie B. Foss (Alton, housewife);
W - 31, dressmaker, b. New Castle, d/o Alexander White
(painter) and Sarah E. White (housewife)
Selwin A. of Gilmanton m. Lizzie B. **Sargent** of Gilmanton 9/5/1894
in Laconia; H - 30, shoemaker, 2nd, b. Gilmanton, s/o John
Watson (farmer) and Abbie Foss (housewife); W - 39,
housekeeper, 2nd, b. Gilmanton, d/o Moses Price (farmer)

WEALE,
Jason Chapman of Gilmanton m. Melissa Anne **Chapin** of
Gilmanton 6/28/1998

WEARE,
Charles D. of Gilmanton m. Nettie M. **Carpenter** of Marlow
4/5/1912 in Keene; H - 64, farmer, 2nd, b. Deerfield, s/o
Gardner Weare (Deerfield, farmer) and Abbie Young
(Gilmanton, housewife); W - 45, housemaid, 2nd, b. Reading,
MA, d/o Charles Beard (Bennett, VT, mechanic) and Laura
Dake (Bakerville, VT, housewife)

WEBSTER,
Daniel Warren of Gilmanton m. Barbara Arlene Andrew **Britton** of
Concord 8/26/1989
William C. of Gilmanton m. Marjorie E. **Pitman** of Nashua
6/6/1928; H - 37, machinist, b. Gilmanton, s/o Benjamin F.
Webster (Gilmanton, farmer) and Elizabeth Smith
(Frederickton, NB, housework); W - 38, teacher, b. Alexandria,
d/o Warren L. Pitman (Alexandria, farmer) and Julia A.
Tappan (Alexandria)

WEEKS,
Francis Marion of Gilmanton m. Candace Ann **Sargent** of
Rochester 4/24/1993
Frank M. of Alton m. Wini May **Scovill** of Gilmanton 11/29/1969; H
- b. 4/5/1945 in NY, s/o Frank M. Weeks, Sr. (NY) and

Veronica Marin (NY); W - b. 9/9/1949 in NH, d/o Lawrence Scovill (MA) and Virginia Prescott (NH)

Herbert N. of Gilmanton m. Cora I. **Rollins** of Gilmanton 8/1/1889; H - 29, farmer, b. Gilmanton, s/o Noah Weeks (Gilmanton, farmer) and Sarah A. McNeal (Gilmanton, housewife); W - 16, housewife, b. Rochester, d/o James A. Rollins (Gilmanton, farmer) and Julia Young (Gilmanton, housewife)

Herbert N. of Gilmanton m. Lilla M. **Benitez** of Gilmanton 8/8/1900; H - 40, farmer, 2nd, b. Gilmanton, s/o Noah Weeks (Alton, farmer) and Sarah A. McNeal (housewife); W - 27, housewife, 2nd, b. Gilmanton, d/o Agustus Durgin (Thornton, stage driver) and Anna P. Sanborn (Thornton, housewife)

Ivo F. of Gilmanton m. Addie A. **Flanders** of Belmont 7/2/1899 in Gilford; H - 22, farmer, b. Gilmanton, s/o Marcus S. Weeks (Alton, farmer) and Laura E. Foster (Belmont, housewife); W - 20, housemaid, b. Belmont, d/o Elwin S. Flanders (Gilmanton, farmer) and Jenny Thomley (Belmont)

John F. of Gilmanton m. Esther M. **Smith** of Gilford 6/24/1926 in Loudon; H - 23, farmer, b. Gilmanton, s/o Stephen L. Weeks (Gilmanton, farmer) and Bertha Batchelder (Loudon, housework); W - 22, teacher, b. Gilford, d/o Samuel W. Smith (Meredith, farmer) and Winnifred Page (Gilmanton, housework)

Lorrain E. of Gilmanton m. Charlotte E. **Mace** of Lynn, MA 9/5/1892 in Lynn, MA; H - 32, farmer, b. Gilmanton, s/o Matthias Weeks (farmer) and Laurinda Hillard (Colebrook, housewife); W - 28, housekeeper, b. Lynn, MA, d/o Andrew Mace and Abby Maria Silsbee

Maintland B. of Gilmanton m. Hazel B. **Moore** of Loudon 1/15/1924 in Loudon; H - 25, farmer, b. Gilmanton, s/o Stephen L. Weeks (Gilmanton) and Bertha Batchelder (Loudon); W - 26, teacher, b. Loudon, d/o Daniel Moore (Loudon) and Mary A. Sleeper (Loudon)

WELCH,

George E. of Gilmanton m. D. Emma **McGreger** of Manchester 9/10/1895; H - 55, farmer, 3rd, b. NS, s/o Richard Welch and Rosanna Pickett; W - 50, nurse, 3rd, b. Burlington, VT, d/o Lewis Leper and Mary Ann Greenough

Kenneth J. of Gilmanton m. Elizabeth A. **Ferguson** of Gilmanton 10/23/1982

WELCOME,
Gene Jay of Gilmanton m. Sarah M. **Baldwin** of Gilmanton 8/1/1992

WELLS,
E. Russell of Gilmanton m. Laura F. **Sawyer** of Gilmanton 6/16/1928; H - 25, farmer, b. Gilmanton, s/o Ernest L. Wells (Alton, laborer) and Laura G. Jones (Gilmanton, housekeeper); W - 26, housework, 2nd, b. Malden, MA, d/o Sidney Hanson (Barnstead, farmer) and Laura M. Nutter (Gilmanton, housework)

Ernest L. of Alton m. Laura G. **Jones** of Gilmanton 6/26/1904; H - 26, laborer, b. Alton, s/o Horace Wells (farmer) and Ida E. Hill (Alton); W - 22, housemaid, b. Gilmanton, d/o Joseph L. Jones (farmer) and Ida Glysson

Fred Harry of Gilmanton m. Helen Louise **Derusha** of Laconia 8/14/1971 in Laconia; H - b. 7/30/1941 in NH, s/o Fred R. Wells (NH) and Dorothea Lucier (MA); W - b. 4/11/1944 in NH, d/o Gordon Hibbard (ME) and Pearl Peavey (NH)

WENTWORTH,
Lawrence of Farmington m. Marguerite L. **Carty** of Gilmanton I. W. 8/26/1937 in Laconia; H - 20, shoe maker, b. Middleton, s/o Joseph Wentworth (Middleton, shoe worker) and Jennie Savoie (Dover, clerk); W - 21, hairdresser, b. New York, NY, d/o Edward Carty (NY, milkman) and Bernice Brown (Plymouth, at home)

WESCOTT,
Clarence S. of Gilmanton m. Lucy E. **Lafoe** of Laconia 11/2/1902 in Laconia; H - 29, farmer, 2nd, b. Meredith, s/o Joseph S. Wescott (Albany, NY, merchant) and Maria E. Bowles (Easton, housewife); W - 20, waitress, b. Compton, PQ, d/o Richard Lafoe (Campton, PQ, contractor) and Clara Fields (housewife)

WEST,
Corey B. of Gilmanton I.W. m. Karen L. **Quale** of Gilmanton I.W. 6/2/2000

WHELAN,
John Joseph, Jr. of Laconia m. Bonnie Kendra **Hartford** of
  Gilmanton 4/30/1966; H - 22, mechanic, b. MA, s/o John
  Joseph Whelan, Sr. (NS) and Donna May Oslo (AL); W - 21,
  secretary, b. NH, d/o Arlington Edward Hartford (NH) and Olive
  Dorothy Young (NS)

WHITE,
Francis Clifford of Laconia m. Donna Marie **Miller** of Gilmanton
  7/6/1962; H - 23, police officer, b. NH, s/o Franklin Edgar
  White (VT) and Lauretta Moussette (NH); W - 24, student
  nurse, b. NH, d/o John H. Gard, Jr. (NH) and Margaret Munsey
  (NH)
Stephen J., Jr. of Gilmanton m. Jennifer Lynn **Neylon** of Gilmanton
  8/23/1997

WHITEHOUSE,
Ralph of Gilmanton m. Muriel T. **Duchano** of Gilmanton 10/3/1953;
  H - 43, mill worker, b. NH, s/o Nicholas Whitehouse (NH) and
  Margaret Cassidy (MA); W - 32, housework, b. NH, d/o
  Jeremiah Wiggin (NH) and Laura Snow (MA)
Robert A. of Manchester m. Nellie C. **Page** of Gilmanton 12/3/1900
  in Goffstown; H - 21, farmer, b. Troy, VT, s/o E. B. Whitehouse
  (Middleton, carpenter) and M. E. Brown; W - 22, housekeeper,
  b. Gilmanton, d/o Dixi C. Page (Gilmanton, farmer) and
  Cyrena Webster (Gilmanton, housewife)

WICKS,
Walter Wayne of Gilmanton m. Sarah Leigh **Marquis** of Gilmanton
  9/11/1998

WIEGEL,
Terry J. of Mansfield, MA m. Lynn **Huston** of Mansfield, MA
  11/3/1984

WILKENS,
John Robert Paul of Gilmanton m. Janice Elizabeth **Beth** of
  Amherst, MA 7/5/1969; H - b. 6/6/1949 in NH, s/o William B.
  Wilkens (NY) and Laurose Schultz-Berge (NY); W - b.
  1/27/1949 in IL, d/o Loren Beth (IL) and Carol Koehler (IL)

John Robert Paul of Gilmanton m. Claire Marie **Pinard** of Gilmanton 11/26/1993

W. B., Jr. of Gilmanton m. Roberta A. **Aldrich** of Laconia 3/21/1958 in Laconia; H - 18, student, b, NY, s/o William B. Wilkins (NH) and Laurose S. Berge (NY); W - 17, student, b. NH, d/o Robert E. Aldrich (NH) and Rachel G. Roberts (NH)

WILLARD,

Arthur of Gilmanton m. Mary C. **Heinis** of Gilmanton 12/31/1936 in Pittsfield; H - 20, laborer, b. Belmont, s/o Israel Willard (Gilmanton, mechanic) and Georgie McClary (Gilmanton, at home); W - 18, nursery school asst., b. Cambridge, MA, d/o Louis Heinis (Jersey City, NJ, farmer) and Florence Smith (MA, housework)

Arthur, Jr. of Gilmanton m. Dorothy P. **Hiltz** of Gilmanton 11/23/1957; H - 20, woodworking, b. NH, s/o Arthur E. Willard (NH) and Mary C. Heinis (MA); W - 18, stitcher, b. NH, d/o Fred L. Hiltz (MA) and Cynthia I. Hiltz (Canada)

Edward L. of Gilmanton m. Rose M. **Hamel** of Belmont 1/15/1969; H - b. 8/12/1950 in NH, s/o Arthur Willard (NH) and Mary Heinis (MA); W - b. 12/22/1949 in NH, d/o William I. Hamel (NH) and Arlene Burke (NH)

Edward L. of Gilmanton m. Priscilla J. **Daigneau** of Gilmanton 8/14/1977; H - b. 8/12/1950 in NH, s/o Arthur Willard, Sr. (NH) and Mary Heinis (MA); W - b. 5/28/1957 in NH, d/o Arthur Daigneau (NH) and Daura Nena Cass (VT)

Israel Raymond of Gilmanton m. Candace Rae **Franzen** of Winnisquam 11/23/1963 in Belmont; H - 18, US Marine, b. NH, s/o Arthur E. Willard (NH) and Mary C. Heinis (MA); W - 18, at home, b. NH, d/o Elmer R. Franzen (NH) and Phyllis R. Webster (NH)

John Richard of Gilmanton m. Mary Rose **Connors** of Lowell, MA 7/4/1962; H - 23, mechanic, b. NH, s/o Arthur E. Willard (NH) and Mary C. Heinis (MA); W - 21, wirer, b. MA, d/o Harry C. Brown (England) and Anna May Dessetelle (MA)

Raymond C. of Gilmanton m. Hazel B. **Batchelder** of Gilmanton 10/14/1916 in Belmont; H - 24, farmer, b. Alton, s/o Smith A. Willard (Alton, shoemaker) and Sadie E. Lamper (Alton, housewife); W - 21, housework, b. Gilmanton, d/o C. M. Batchelder (Loudon, farmer) and Cora Staples (Williamstown, VT, housework)

WILLIAMS,
Gary L. of VA m. Helen C. **Dutton** of VA 12/27/1975; H - b. 8/10/1946 in FL, s/o Wesley Williams (GA) and Rosemary Schwebel (NY); W - b. 5/25/1943 in NH, d/o Dorothy Edgerly (NH)

Harry Elmore of Brookline, MA m. Ethel Louise **Stevens** of Gilmanton 10/6/1915 in Milton; H - 31, manager, b. Gloucester, MA, s/o John Williams (Sweden, fisherman) and Annie Williams (Gloucester, MA, housekeeper); W - 31, at home, b. Beverly, MA, d/o Joseph A. Stevens (Beverly, MA, farmer) and Louise Spinney (NS, housewife)

WILSON,
Charles E. of Gilmanton m. Alexandra **Hagstrom** of Cambridge, MA 9/3/1906; H - 31, farmer, b. Boston, MA, s/o George Wilson (Uddavalla, Sweden, seaman) and Selina Olsen (Gottoburg, Sweden, nurse); W - 21, dressmaker, b. Sweden, d/o Axel Hagstrom (Ulukehan, Sweden, custom officer) and Matilde Jacobsen (Tellbacka, Sweden, housewife)

John K. of Gilmanton m. Melinda S. **Pyne** of Gilmanton 10/20/2001

Woodrow S. of Gilford m. Judith **Prindle** of Gilmanton 8/25/1979

WINCH,
Russell P. of Gilmanton m. Ellen F. **Ross** of Hudson Falls, NY 6/21/1986

WINER,
Kalman A. of Gilmanton m. Linda **Tatelbaum** of Gilmanton 2/2/1975 in Ctr. Sandwich; H - b. 10/21/1942 in MA, s/o Harold Winer (NH) and Irene Brody (MA); W - b. 2/28/1947 in NY, d/o Milton Tatelbaum (NY) and Harriet Frank (NY)

WINSLOW,
William E. of Casco, ME m. Jobyna **Chapman** of Gilmanton 8/5/1946; H - 19, diesel mechanic, b. Taunton, MA, s/o George E. Winslow (Casco, ME, carpenter) and Hazel Kimball (Stowe, ME, housewife); W - 20, at home, b. Lynn, MA, d/o Job Chapman (Bath, ME, mechanic) and Ethel E. Cox (England, housewife)

WINSTANLEY,
James of Hudson m. Helen Elizabeth **Dudley** of Gilmanton 7/4/1970; H - b. 12/4/1949 in RI, s/o Ronald Winstanley (England) and Elizabeth Nickson (England); W - b. 10/28/1950 in NH, d/o I. Dean Dudley (NH) and Dorothy Hurlbutt (NH)

WITHAM,
Ezekiel E. of Gilmanton m. Jennie A. **Keyes** of Gilmanton 11/29/1914 in Barnstead; H - 74, laborer, 2nd, b. New Gloucester, ME,m s/o Jacob W. Witham (N. Gloucester, ME, farmer) and Mary Eveleth (Danville, ME, housewife); W - 57, housework, 3rd, b. Harmony, ME, d/o Jeremiah Blake (Paris, ME, farmer) and Abigail Rolfe (Harmony, ME, housewife)

George W. of Gilmanton m. Helen M. **Gilman** of Gilmanton 7/16/1938; H - 25, farm work, b. Cabot, VT, s/o Ralph E. Witham (Montpelier, VT, farmer) and Hattie Shuttle (Montpelier, VT, housework); W - 18, housework, b. Gilmanton, d/o Ira Gilman (Gilmanton, farmer) and Cora B. York (Pittsfield, at home)

John A. of Gilmanton m. Mary Lee **Geddes** of Gilmanton 11/3/1973; H - b. 1/20/1948 in NH, s/o Alden W. Witham (ME) and Dorothy Thomas (MA); W - b. 3/7/1954 in NH, d/o David W. Geddes (NH) and Anna Hogan (NH)

Peter T. of Gilmanton m. Margaret A. **Leonard** of Gilmanton 6/21/1986

WITHINGTON,
Timothy Mark of Gilmanton m. Tina Marie **Lebel** of Gilmanton 10/4/1997

WOOD,
Steven M. of Gilmanton m. Maureen K. **Hanlon** of Gilmanton 10/8/1988

WOODBURY,
Robert Charles of Gilmanton m. Frances Lorraine **Hyslop** of Gilmanton 10/11/1994

Steven Dennis of Gilmanton m. Susan Lynn **Doe** of Gilmanton 12/5/1993

WOODWARD,
Donald of Gilmanton m. Mary A. **Janas** of Nashua 4/24/1954 in Nashua; H - 20, farmer, b. NH, s/o Richard M. Woodward (NH) and Bernice I. Ford (NH); W - 19, at home, b. NH, d/o Jacob J. Janas (Poland) and Mary A. Los (Poland)

William of Gilmanton m. Barbara J. **Stock** of Ctr. Barnstead 9/13/1959 in Ctr. Barnstead; H - 22, lumber, b. NH, s/o Richard M. Woodward (NH) and Iris B. Ford (NH); W - 18, at home, b. NH, d/o Arthur H. Stock (MA) and Martha C. Henry (NH)

WYATT,
Douglas Colby of Laconia m. Dora Jean **Steele** of Gilmanton I. W. 5/5/1973 in Gilford; H - b. 1/29/1953 in NH, s/o Richard D. Wyatt (NH) and Edith Colby (NH); W - b. 4/19/1952 in NH, d/o Robert E. Steele (NH) and Louise Smith (NH)

YARNELL,
Glenn R. of E. Longmeadow, MA m. Kathleen Mary **Blanchette** of Gilmanton 9/20/1969 in Laconia; H - b. 6/1/1947 in MA, s/o Roy O. Yarnell (PA) and Marjorie Whittaker (MA); W - b. 11/28/1947 in NH, d/o Phillip J. Blanchette (NH) and Rena M. Brochu (NH)

YEARY,
Thomas J. of Mashpee, MA m. Judith G. **Lyman** of Mashpee, MA 6/26/1992

YEATON,
Harold B. of Deerfield m. Susan E. **Brown** of Gilmanton 12/17/1948 in Chichester; H - 62, farmer, b. Deerfield, s/o Edson F. Yeaton (Deerfield) and Hattie J. Noyes (Deerfield); W - 52, housework, b. Gilmanton, d/o Alfred M. Brown (Epsom, farmer) and Edna Marsh (Gilmanton, housewife)

YORK,
Fred A. of Gilmanton m. Martha A. **Smith** of Gilmanton 11/3/1927 in Gilmanton I. W.; H - 61, teamster, 2nd, b. Gilmanton, s/o Will C. York (Gilmanton, laborer) and Mary A. Smart (Durham, housework); W - 62, housework, 2nd, b. Medford, ME, d/o

William C. Spencer (Medford, ME, farmer) and Hanna L. Rogers (Oldtown, ME, housework)

Raymond S. of Gilmanton m. Caroline E. **Jones** of Gilmanton 2/1/1913 in Gilmanton I. W.; H - 23, farmer, b. Belmont, s/o Morrell York (Belmont, laborer) and Mary E. Clark (Belmont, housewife); W - 18, housemaid, b. Gilmanton, d/o George A. Jones (Gilmanton, laborer) and Olive E. Moody (Gilmanton, housewife)

YOUNG,

Brooks Elliott of Gilmanton m. Jayne Margret **Stanley** of Gilmanton 6/2/1989

Donald C. of Gilmanton m. Rachel F. **Gardner** of Manchester 4/23/1977 in Manchester; H - b. 9/26/1949 in NY, s/o Morton Young (NY) and Rose Marie Heim (NY); W - b. 5/16/1955 in NH, d/o Paul A. Gardner and Violet Veilleux (NH)

Frank D. of Gilmanton m. May A. **Temple** of Gilmanton 3/13/1910 in Laconia; H - 53, farmer, b. Gilmanton, s/o Jonathan Young (Gilmanton, farmer) and Martha A. Nelson (Gilmanton, housewife); W - 27, housemaid, 2nd, b. Island Pond, VT, d/o William Grady (Canada, farmer) and Mary Kane (Canada, housewife)

Fred B. of Gilmanton m. Addie F. **Aiken** of Barnstead 6/5/1887 in Alton; H - 20, shoemaker, b. Gilmanton, s/o Nathaniel Young (Gilmanton, farmer) and Lucy A. Prescott (Grafton, housewife); W - 16, operative, b. Barnstead, d/o David Aiken (Barnstead, farmer) and Annie Shaw (Concord, housewife)

Fred B. of Gilmanton m. Ida M. **Franks** of Calais, ME 10/4/1889; H - 23, shoemaker, 2nd, b. Gilmanton, s/o Nathaniel Young (Gilmanton, farmer) and Lucy A. Prescott (Grafton, housewife); W - 20, operative, b. Calais, ME, d/o Richard Franks (painter)

ZANES,

James E. of Gilmanton m. Johanna **deBruin** of Laconia 4/12/1953 in Laconia; H - 29, lumbering, b. NH, s/o Robert L. Zanes (NH) and Mina Edgerly (MS); W - 29, nurse, b. Indonesia, d/o Adrianus de Bruin (Holland) and Cornelia van Vugt (Holland)

Robert L., Jr. of Gilmanton m. Marlene Gloria **Paige** of Franklin 11/18/1950; H - 20, laborer, b. NH, s/o Robert L. Zanes (NH) and Mina Edgerly (NH); W - 19, at home, b. NH, d/o Fred J. Paige (NH) and Anne Marsh (NH)

Robert Lewes of Gilmanton m. Mina **Edgerly** of Gilmanton 11/27/1921; H - 32, lineman, b. Pittsfield, s/o Noah M. Zanes (Pembroke) and Nellie Blake (Gilmanton); W - 28, gov't clerk, 2nd, b. Wesson, MS, d/o Albert L. Edgerly (Sanbornton) and C. Elucina Keyes (Sycamore, IL)

William B. of Gilmanton m. Martha A. **Munsey** of Gilmanton 11/6/1910 in Laconia; H - 23, mechanic, b. Pittsfield, s/o Noah M. Zanes (Suncook, farmer) and Nellie E. Blake (Gilmanton, housewife); W - 23, teacher, b. Gilmanton, d/o Jay R. Munsey (Concord, farmer) and Josephine Osborne (Gilmanton, housewife)

ZELA,

Peter Mark of Gilmanton m. Barbara Jean **West** of Gilmanton 8/26/1989

ZVACS,

Joseph of Gilmanton m. Mabel **King** of Concord 9/14/1942 in Concord; H - 29, ski work, b. New York, NY, s/o Joseph Zvacs (Czechoslovakia, carpenter) and Paula Zilicophski (Czechoslovakia, housewife); W - 19, none, b. Malone, NY, d/o Charles King (Constable, NY, kennel keeper) and Rose Vermet (Belmont, NY, housewife)

BRIDES' NAMES

Abbott, Alice E. - Langley, Rufus Howard
Ackerman, Louella (Burbank) - Desrochers, Aleck
Ackerman, Nancy Carol - Lindbloom, Donald K.
Adams, Edith A. - Drew, David J.
Adel, Ethel G. - Thompson, Victor L., Jr.
Adel, Jennifer N. - Muse, Matthew C.
Adel, Mary E. - Richardson, John C., III
Adel, Robin Sue - Krueger, David William
Aiello, Susan M. - Dickinson, Thomas J.
Aiken, Addie F. - Young, Fred B.
Aikins, Melissa Ann - Potter, Robert Leo, Jr.
Aksnes, Kjersti - Skantze, Donald E.
Alden, Florence P. - Sawyer, Bertram H.
Alder, Sandra S. - Grady, James E.
Aldrich, Lucille - Dunn, Robert G.
Aldrich, Roberta A. - Wilkens, W. B., Jr.
Allan, Jessie Elizabeth (Blackey) - Leach, Henry Groves
Allen, Lucy J. - Beck, Smith C.
Alund, Coral Diane - Bishop, Wallace Putnam, Jr.
Amirault, Joan L. - Pong, Barry L.
Anair, Beverly Pearl - Peck, Robert John
Anders, Faye D. - Hartford, Anthony E.
Anderson, Ann-Marie - Beckley, Bruce Hallam
Anderson, Marion Rene Dulie - Nutter, Allen Roy
Anderson, Valerie S. - Blanchette, Gene R.
Anish, Elizabeth L. - Hackett, Wayne L. N.
Armstrong, Joyce E. Ellis - Hyslop, Frank E.
Ashcraft, Marie Ruth - Caprario, Ronald David
Ashcroft, Rosie (DeSelle) - Lavine, Victor
Aubut, Shari A. - Colby, Travis J.
Austin, Tammy Alberta - Aldrich, David Hartford
Avery, Mabel H. - Page, Andrew T.
Aycock, Gayle Taylor - Davis, Richard Poole
Aycock, Janet Leigh - Heath, Roger Eldon
Ayer, Helen F. - Batchelder, William N.
Azotea, Myrtle Pauline (Cronan) - Joyce, Frank T.

Bach, Sally M. Smock - Mercier, Robert N., Jr.
Bailey, Dorothy V. - Nelson, Clarence
Bailey, Lucy Charity - Blake, Jeremiah I.
Baker, Ida Belle - Page, Walter S.

Balcom, Lynne Ellen - Urquhart, Jeffrey Allen
Baldwin, Joann L. - Mallory, John K., III
Baldwin, Judith Helen - Gleason, Frederick E., Jr.
Baldwin, Sarah M. - Welcome, Gene Jay
Ball, Nancy L. - Mallory, Mark L.
Ballester, Maureen Susan - Pidgeon, Gilbert Liam
Ballinger, Jessica R. - Caldon, Brett M.
Banfill, Virginia Dawn - Hiltz, Angus Blenum
Baptistella, Victoria Ann - Gallant, Michael Paul
Barlow, Jane C. - Bacon, John M.
Barlow, Laurie Jeanne - Austin, Gerald Leonard, III
Barnard, Marcia L. (Eastman) - Dulude, Douglas D.
Barnett, Louise A. - Sawyer, Mark Aaron
Barney, Susan - Hornik, Richard Henry
Barns, Joanne Laurose - Polito, William Joseph
Barr, Suzann Joy - Caldon, Thomas W.
Barron, Mary A. - Baker, Sylvester E.
Bartholomew, Diana Eliot - Brown, Ralph Drisko
Barton, Jolene Marie - Price, Jonathan Charles
Bassemir, June T. - Gardner, Andrew H.
Batchelder, Hazel B. - Willard, Raymond C.
Battis, Euphanie A. - McClary, J. Frank
Battis, Ina E. - Page, Frank H.
Baynham, Louie F. - Roberts, Ernest W.
Bean, Sarah Lynn - Hamilton, Edward Anderson
Beaudry, Deanne C. - Sargent, Jason H.
Beaudry, Michelle C. - Aubut, Tracy E.
Beaver, Patrice M. - Emberley, Kevin T.
Beck, Blanche L. - Ellis, Herbert A.
Beck, Hulda A. - Beck, Charles W.
Beckley, Jancie L. - Hinman, Richard B.
Begin, Michele E. - Freeman, Francis R.
Begin, Valerie Ann - Plourde, Gary Wayne
Bemis, Emma A. (Wiggin) - Sleeper, Jonathan
Benitez, Lilla M. (Durgin) - Weeks, Herbert N.
Bennett, Mary A. - Speck, Joseph S., Jr.
Bennett, Valerie Ann - Publicover, Robert William
Benney, Tina J. - Jean, Joseph A.
Berlind, Lisa - Masoni, Mark Curt
Berry, Mary Ella - Tash, Arthur
Berry, Mary T. - Spartos, Gary G.

Berry, Susan A. - Langsten, Mario L.
Beth, Janice Elaine - Wilkens, John Robert Paul
Bibber, Beverly J. - Best, Barry C.
Biber, Joan - Klefos, Conrad E. S.
Bice, Sandra B. Twiford - Berry, Robert L.
Bickford, Evelyn Mabel - Fosie, Richard Elton
Bickford, Georgianna - Mayhew, Eldon B.
Bickford, Kathleen Mary - McWhinnie, Thomas John
Bickford, Minnie E. - Malsbury, William A.
Biggers, Maryevelyn - Onsager, Hans Tanberg
Bilodeau, Jacklyn Marie - Polito, Robert
Binnall, Julie Ann - Wallace, David Allen
Bjorkman, Linda J. - Lutkus, David V.
Blackey, Barbara Ann (Akerstrom) - Collier, Alfred Joseph
Blackey, Thelma S. - Schott, Charles K.
Blais, Charmein L. - Fanning, John R.
Blajda, Donna Lee - Dunbar, Raleigh E., Jr.
Blake, Linda - Austin, William C.
Blake, Linda Doris - Brown, Raymond Arthur
Blanchard, Carolyn - Brown, Robert A.
Blanchette, Kathleen Mary - Yarnell, Glenn R.
Blandini, Marcey Maria - Harriman, Paul Nathan
Blood, E. Hope - French, Clifton S.
Bloom, Marion - Demerit, Nelson L.
Bohnstedt, Thedora A. - Jefferson, Mark S. W.
Boisvert, Blanche L. (Dejardins) - Pappas, Paul E.
Boisvert, Jacqueline Muriel - Bosiak, Frank Charles
Boisvert, Theresa Adeline - Stockbridge, Joseph Samuel
Bolo, Geneve May - Pratt, Ralph
Bordeau, Margaret - Hoag, Lawrence C.
Boudreau, Sharyl Lee - Casale, John Dennis
Boulanger, Claire Lucille - Annetti, Anthony Domenick
Boulanger, Cynthia Lee - Palmer, John Earl
Boulanger, Suzanne R. - Panaleo, Eugene J.
Bousquet, G. Marie - Davis, Robert Bruce
Bowes, Carol M. - Allen, David W.
Bowes, Christine F. (Cloud) - Gilkes, Cooper A., Jr.
Bowman, Gayle Ann - McWhinnie, Andrew John
Bowman, Laura Anne - Baker, Donald Keeler
Boyce, Denise V. - Stanley, Norman G.
Boyd, Becky Ann - Smith, Brian William

Bradford, Rita B. - Kelley, John S.
Bradley, Joanne M. - Turner, Russell E.
Bragg, Georgie E. - Robbins, Roscoe D.
Bragg, Patricia A. - Lounsbury, Wilbur J., Jr.
Brake, Margaret Virginia (Joyce) - Bagley, Earl Everett
Brawley, Barbara N. - Lincoln, David C.
Bresse, Sandra L. - Osmer, Steven D.
Brewster, Ida M. - Bickford, Arthur R.
Briscoe, Sharon B. - Strickland, Robert B.
Britton, Barbara Arlene Andrew - Webster, Daniel Warren
Brock, Lois May - Brown, George Clinton
Broek, Belinda Joy - Aylward, Dana Alden
Brooks, Debra L. - Stendor, Jefferey J.
Brown, Addie F. (Downs) - Mason, John S.
Brown, Alberta Rae - Kimball, David Wayne
Brown, Carol E. - Austin, William C.
Brown, Dodie J. - Smithers, Thomas W., IV
Brown, Edith G. - Bragg, George E.
Brown, Florence P. (Day) - Clough, Irving A.
Brown, Kimberly J. - Severance, David S.
Brown, Leslie Ann - Forsyth, Ralph Gordon
Brown, Lillian E. - Jones, Allie C.
Brown, Sarah (Hanford) - Page, David E.
Brown, Susan E. - Yeaton, Harold B.
Brown, Virginia M. - Philbrick, William B.
Bruce, Edith M. - Margeson, Edward M.
Buatti, Phyllis Lynn Genest - Publicover, Charles Joseph
Buckley, Karen L. - Dudman, Gary S.
Bunker, Hazel G. (Carpenter) - Dimond, Chester L.
Bunker, Lura M. - McClary, George F.
Burbrick, Marion Evelyn (Wylie) - Marshall, John
Burdett, Carol L. - Downing, Ned W.
Burgess, Martha - Talamas, Glenn A.
Burgoyne, Christine Ruth - Ward, Arthur Jay
Burnham, Susan Jean - Grondin, Richard Paul
Burres, Eva M. (Sargent) - Rollins, Selden B.
Burres, Gladys M. - Parsons, Frank W.
Burres, Olive - Canfield, Stanley P.
Bushey, Barbara - Bordeau, Robert E.
Bushnell, Patricia J. - Longley, Alvah, Jr.
Butcher, Clara J. - McClary, Horace E.

Butcher, Dorothy - McClary, Willard G.
Butler, Renee Wendy - Kordas, Richard Porter
Butman, Julie I. - Perkins, Harold J.
Byers, Dorothy W. - Littlefield, Wilmer L.
Byron, Josephine M. - Post, Wilfred W.

Canfield, Olive (Burres) - Prescott, Leonard
Canney, Abbie E. - Warren, Edgar W.
Canney, Linda Sue - Clairmont, Kerry Joseph
Canney, Mary E. - Jones, Karl E.
Canney, Mary E. (Tibbetts) - Page, Jesse F.
Capowski, Julia - Johnson, James G., III
Carey, Lynn - Aylward, Dana A.
Carey, Lynn - Miner, Dennis Alan
Carignan, Marlene May - Chamberlain, Stephen Edward
Carleton, Virginia Mae - Jahnle, Carl George
Carlson, Karen Elaine - Stockwell, Leonard Alfred
Carlson, Mary Augusta - Rosewater, Joseph
Carpenter, Cordelia L. - Thompson, Maro B.
Carpenter, Nettie M. (Beard) - Weare, Charles D.
Carr, Annie M. - French, Will A.
Carter, Crystal A. - Gorman, Richard W.
Carty, Marguerite L. - Wentworth, Lawrence
Casey, Grace A. (Barton) - Hopkinson, William P.
Casey, JoAnn - Brown, Carl Strachan
Cassavaugh, Beatrice B. - Burgess, Paul M.
Caswell, Carrie (Cutting) - Wallace, Charles Bert
Cate, Dorothy - Nutter, Clyde E.
Chamberlain, Holly C. - Maltais, John E., Jr.
Chamberlain, Janis Louise - Decormier, Robert Armand
Champney, Beverly - Huckins, Lewis
Chapin, Melissa Anne - Weale, Jason Chapman
Chapman, Jobyna - Winslow, William E.
Charbonneau, Anna M. (Ange) - Richardson, Leon H.
Chase, Deborah Fowkes - Funk, Wilfred John
Chase, Donna Jene - Chamberlain, Dennis A.
Chase, Helen E. - Lecour, Ernest
Chase, Ida W. (Wadlin) - Stockbridge, G. S.
Checkos, Susan L. - Taylor, Brian M.
Cherry, Nancy A. - Fitzgerald, Robert C.
Childress, Nancy W. - Corriveau, Allan W.

Christi, Jacqueline Ann - Nelson, Timothy James
Clairmont, Cindy L. - Fillion, Jeffire S.
Clairmont, Nancy Lynne - McAvenia, Richard C., Jr.
Clairmont, Rebecca - Walsh, Jay
Clark, Carrie E. (Beede) - Hirst, George W.
Clark, Doris Edna Bishop - Pennock, James Glynn
Clark, Linda J. - Casazza, Joseph A.
Clarke, Lynn L. - Boyd, Robert O.
Clay, Pearl Lillian - Matthews, Roy Ellsworth
Clement, Gail W. - Sumner, William L.
Clement, Ida - Battis, Harry J.
Clifford, Evelyn Nellie - Horan, Arthur J.
Clifford, Lois M. - McClary, Bertrude B.
Clifford, Melba Jean - Laroche, Alfred E., Jr.
Clough, Hattie M. - Lane, Myron W.
Clough, Iona M. - Little, King R.
Cogswell, Anna M. - Edgerly, Walter J.
Cogswell, Harriet B. - Martin, Francis C.
Colangeli, Angela C. - Vaillancourt, Tracy Alan
Colburn, Kathleen M. - Blake, Alan J.
Colby, Catherine E. - Lines, Paul
Colby, Katharine - Stockwell, Daniel C.
Colby, Susie (Denby) - Lamprey, Herman F.
Cole, Brenda L. - Currier, Brett A.
Coleman, Stacey A. - Kimball, John F.
Collins, Mary E. - Lavallee, Gary K.
Collins, Sherri L. - Smith, Matthew M.
Conlin, Kim Marie - Hayes, Sean Patrick
Connell, Ina F. - Lund, Leon
Connors, Mary Rose (Brown) - Willard, John Richard
Conrad, Carol J. - Bryant, Clyde C., Jr.
Conrad, Sandra June - Burbank, George David
Converse, Alice G. - Flanders, Lewis Rufus
Cook, Bertha L. - Shannon, Winfield S.
Cook, Josephine H. - Nutter, Madison P.
Corbiel, Melvina - Rioux, Frank
Corliss, Martha I. - Mansfield, George E.
Corno, Lorna R. - Leclair, Thomas E.
Corson, Evelyn Elizabeth - Munsey, Herbert Earl
Cota, June A. Haskell - Hubbard, William L.
Couch, Cora - Page, William S.

Coulson, Elizabeth A. - Segalini, Recardo L.
Coursey, Beverly Joyce - Merrill, Robert Mack, III
Covell, Julia (Shlaitas) - Simoneau, Ulysses Charles
Crandall, Ena D. - Keegan, Arthur L.
Crosby, Nancy Elizabeth - Nelson, Mark Ramsay
Crosby, Susan Hale - McDonald, Arthur William, Jr.
Cross, Deborah J. - Runnion, Robert M.
Crowley, Mary A. - Boyd, Gregory R.
Cunningham, Lorraine R. - Smith, Charles H.
Currier, Cynthia - Gille, Paul
Curtis, Susan R. - Mallory, Bruce L.
Cutter, Vivian Eunice - Harper, David Graham

Daigle, Debora S. - Kimball, Edward C., II
Daigneau, Carolyn - Swift, William
Daigneau, Eliza Jane - Amadon, Roger William
Daigneau, Elizabeth Ann - Snow, John C.
Daigneau, Priscilla J. - Willard, Edward L.
Dame, Ceda May - Hill, Elwood H.
Dame, Ethel - Goodwin, Clifton
Danforth, Hilda Ann - Hiltz, Donald F.
Danforth, Nicole A. - Larsson, Hans R.
Danis, Tina M. - Hutchins, Mark R.
Dauphin, Pamela Lynn - Gentile, James Leonard, Jr.
Davidson, Nance J. - Johnson, Mark F.
Davies, Angelia Lee - Temple, Bernard Edwin
Davis, Addie M. - Mardin, Willard C.
Davis, Bernice - Thompson, Kenneth A.
Davis, Blanche I. - Bagley, Robert E.
Davis, Donna R. - Poulin, Robert G.
Davis, Elaine K. - Bussey, Robert D.
Davis, Elizabeth N. (Neville) - Foss, John Henry
Davis, Ellen M. - Smith, George Lyndell
Davis, Grace E. - Flanders, Robert J.
Davis, Jennie B. - Marsh, Erskine H.
Davis, Linda Ruth - Maltais, Danny Roy
Davis, Mary F. - Ward, Raymond E.
Day, Alfretta T. - Page, Harold G.
de Bruin, Johanna - Zanes, James E.
de la Garza, Ruth Ann - Davies, David Penchoen
Deering, Alyce M. - Hawkins, Charles Allan

Defarrari, Mary M. - Leitao, Edward A.
Defosses, Melissa Sue - Mann, Brendan Michael
Delafano, Angela D. - Thompson, Edward C.
Denault, Sandra Jean - Danis, Robert Edumond
Derusha, Helen Louise (Hibbard) - Wells, Fred Harry
Deschenes, Cathy A. - Skiba, Russell J.
Desmarais, Claire Simmone - Thompson, Clement Andrew
Desrosiers, Janet Susan - Fabian, Thomas Stephen
Devito, Barbara J. - Bourgoine, Bruce
Deware, Betty M. - McClary, Frank L.
Dickens, Lillian - Shaw, Clarence Ray
Diehl, Veronica Myrtle (McGee) - Briggs, Edward Herbert
Dimick, Anna Belle - Davis, Frank A.
Dimock, Barbara J. - Hyslop, Robert G.
Dimond, Ardena M. - Potter, Charles F.
Diversi, Teresa R. - Magoon, Kenneth F.
Dixey, Judith Ellen - Azotea, Beinvenido, Jr.
Dockham, Dorieann - Adel, Jack I.
Dockham, Kimberly A. - Fortuna, Steven E.
Dodd, Debra A. - Waldron, Jerry D.
Dodge, Janet D. - Neff, Ralph D.
Doe, Susan Lynn - Woodbury, Steven Dennis
Dolliff, Rebecca Roberts - Brown, Morse Everett
Dombrowski, Sandra A. Labranche - Kenney, John L.
Donnelly, Lizzie (Duffey) - Nutter, Frank E.
Dorwin, Denise D. Georgius - Georgius, Robert H.
Doucette, Roberta E. - Hammond, Anthony D.
Douglass, Mary Elizabeth (Allen) - Osler, Howard Benjamin
Douphinett, Jean - Munsey, Thomas A.
Dow, Alice A. - Sargent, Charles P.
Dow, Charity E. - Dutton, Douglas E.
Dow, Florene Louise (Hardy) - Smith, Harold Thayer
Downing, Carol L. - Aylward, Dana A.
Downing, Kimberly Jean - Saulnier, Robert Joseph, Jr.
Downing, Margaret L. - Couture, Lucien P.
Drouin, Anne E. - Maltais, Danny Roy, Sr.
Dube, Jaime M. - Cochrane, Ryan V.
Dube, Marie Malaine - Labrie, Alan Russell
Duchano, Muriel T. (Wiggin) - Whitehouse, Ralph
Dudley, Barbara J. - Austin, Bruce L.
Dudley, Beatrice E. - Shaftman, David H.

Dudley, Helen Elizabeth - Winstanley, James
Dudley, Sylvia A. - Locke, Robert S.
Dumais, Lori Ann - Hemlin, Theodore D.
Dumais, Patricia Ann - Sweeney, Thomas George
Dunn, Sylvia Muriel - Lacasse, Raymond Francis, Jr.
Dunn, Virginia C. - Chamberlain, Stanley R.
Dunn, Virginia C. Chamberlain - Naclerio, Francis S.
DuPont, Donna E. - Avery, Donald R.
Durette, Leona J. - Deware, Robert W., Jr.
Durette, Norma Jean - Boughton, Michael Grant
Durgin, Anna P. (Sanborn) - Marsh, Frank A.
Durgin, Arzelia H. - Hillsgrove, Robert M.
Durgin, Lilla M. - Benitez, Frank H.
Durrell, Francis (Batchelder) - Swain, John W.
Dutile, Muriel J. - Uhlenberg, Harvey
Dutton, Elizabeth Ann - French, Buzzie Bill
Dutton, Helen C. - Williams, Gary L.
Dwyer, Doris L. - McCrady, Douglas B.
Dwyer, Margaret T. - Curtin, Daniel J.
Dyer, Nellie R. - Fogg, Albion
Dyment, Bernice M. Cate - Lindquist, William E.

Eastmond, Carletta - Jones, James Richard, Jr.
Eddy, Catherine B. - Hahn, Thomas C.
Eddy, Valerie J. - Tadakowsky, John J., Jr.
Edgerly, Earline - Palmer, Leon L.
Edgerly, Esther Joyce - Burbank, Neil Stuart
Edgerly, Florence A. - Geddes, John A.
Edgerly, Florence C. - Bordeau, Jason
Edgerly, Margaret C. - Rhodes, Edward E., Jr.
Edgerly, Mina - Zanes, Robert Lewes
Edgerly, Mina Catherine - Adams, Edward Cass
Edmunds, Margaret Fay - Roberts, George Bernard, Jr.
Edson, Dorothy A. - Bowles, John R.
Edwards, Vera - Strathern, Arthur
Ehlen, Barbara R. - Tardy, Michael E.
Ehlen, Judith A. - Nelson, Wayne D.
Eisenhauer, Cynthia A. - Bedford, Daniel R.
Elkins, Bertha F. - Gooch, Wilbur A.
Elkins, Clara - Warburton, John H.
Ellingson, Alicia - Kirk, Peter M.

Elliott, Dawn Marie - Gill, Robert Allen
Elliott, Janice Ruth - Best, Barry C.
Ellis, Alma L. - Rollins, Seldon B.
Ellis, Gladys B. - Ellis, Oscar Alfred
Ellsworth, Cheryl Mae - Clairmont, David P.
Ellsworth, Hannah B. - Ellsworth, Alfred P.
Ellsworth, Lena M. - Davis, Elmer G.
Ellsworth, Linda L. - Place, Thomas D.
Ellsworth, Nellie M. - Clifford, Earl C.
Embree, Fannie A. - Page, Walter H.
Emerson, Ona Faye - Twombly, Everett T.
Emerson, Pamela Louise - St. Laurent, Raymond E.
Emond, Mary Louise - Boucher, Dennis Joseph
Epstein, Esther - Mardin, Robert
Ermini, Jean Marion - McVey, Frederick G.
Ervin, Heather L. - Boyajian, Bryan R.
Evans, Nicole Marie - Harvey, Brandon Thomas

Faggi, Jeanne (Sawyer) - Stanwood, Christopher W.
Fairbanks, Bessie M. (Wood) - Perkins, Fred G.
Fall, Pauline M. - LaFave, Edwin
Farmar, Dorothy Merle - Locke, Harold Ozro
Fatello, Audrey M. (Dowst) - Ellis, Horace D.
Fecteau, Melvina A. (Rowell) - Thompson, Henry S.
Ferguson, Elizabeth A. - Welch, Kenneth J.
Ferrara, Teresa - Amaral, Michael G.
Ferris, Mary E. - Lagasse, Roger L.
Fifield, Julie Dolores - Lockwood, Brian Arthur
Fillion, Elaine A. Monfette - Doucette, Robert G.
Finley, Barbara May - Keffer, David Brooks
Fish, Kimberly C. - Charcalis, Harry G.
Fisher, Doris - Shapiro, Harold Elliot
Fitzgerald, Beth S. - Gallien, Timothy N.
Fitzgerald, Lisa Taryn - Robinson, Eric Scott
Flanders, Addie A. - Weeks, Ivo F.
Flanders, Christehania B. - Ricker, Benjamin A.
Flanders, Elsie V. (Purcell) - Keefe, Walter W.
Flanders, Jennie M. - Jones, Albert H.
Fleming, Dorothy Nora - Hebert, Gregory Lionel
Flynn, Beulah A. - Dow, William E. L.
Flynn, Teresa A. - Shunda, Gustave

Fogg, Myrtie E. (Jones) - Proulx, Joseph
Foley, Tina Mae - Glass, Darrell Winston
Folsom, Mary F. - Short, John N.
Foote, Sandra Jean - Walker, Daniel Gary
Ford, Florence E. - Redman, Arthur E.
Forsyth, Anastasia - McIntyre, James Patrick
Fort, Nanette L. - Hamley, Thom M.
Fosburgh, Jody M. - Carmody, Walter J.
Fosie, Evelyn Mabel - Ellingson, William Roger
Foss, Augusta M. - Joslin, Edwin A.
Foss, Florence A. - Foss, Frank W.
Foss, Grace E. - Howe, Carl D.
Foss, Lulu M. - Berry, Lyman E.
Foss, Wilma Josephine - Jones, Lawrence Charles
Fournier, Gwendolyn A. - Freeman, Jerry R., Sr.
Fournier, Karen Ann - Baer, Richard Adolf
Fournier, Mary E. - Vincent, Rene C.
Fournier, Sharon A. - Nelson, George M., II
Franks, Ida M. - Young, Fred B.
Franzen, Candace Rae - Willard, Israel Raymond
Franzen, Phyllis Rae - Nutter, Malcolm H.
Frechette, Rachel Marie - Hatch, Michael James
Freeman, Elizabeth Denise - Laurent, Paul Eugene
Freese, Heidi J. - Page, Roger A.
French, Dereth W. - Dubuc, Russell T.
French, Janie N. - Stockwell, John A.
Fulton, Althea M. - French, Ivo P.
Furber, Electa A. - Sanborn, Willie E.
Furber, Johnna Marie - McKenna, Robert Arthur

Gagnon, Alma Mary - Ward, Raymond E.
Gagnon, Dorothy (Hislop) - Osborne, Charles Roland
Gagnon, Margaret - Hawkins, Rolland
Gagnon, Marlene Lisa - Osborne, Paul A.
Gale, Cora B. - Page, Frank C.
Gale, Joyce E. - Dimock, Roland V., Jr.
Gallagher, Claire - McClary, Curtis J.
Gallien, Carol - Darbyshire, Paul Michael
Gardner, Amy E. - Booth, William R.
Gardner, Chrystine - Arvanitis, James
Gardner, Rachel F. - Young, Donald C.

Gardner, Sandra Lee - Morin, Leo Arthur
Garland, Sarah Purue - Osborne, Charles Roland
Gaudet, Michelle R. - Caldon, Jeffrey S.
Gault, Bridget D. - Beane, Jason D.
Gault, Sadie L. - Burbank, Alonzo P.
Gay, Janice - Sayre, John B., Jr.
Geddes, Jacqueline - Gardner, Leslie A.
Geddes, Mary F. - Morse, Howard B.
Geddes, Mary Lee - Witham, John A.
Geddes, Una M. - Heywood, William C.
Georgopoulos, Denise Elaine - Ambelas, Gary George
Gerhardt, Christine - Vyce, Michael J.
Gershun, Ellen C. - Half, William H.
Gibbs, Orry R. Matulonis - Doster, Douglas S.
Gibson, Cheryl A. - Smith, Robert T.
Gilbert, Belinda A. - Cotton, Joseph H., III
Giles, Laurie J. - Belanger, Kenneth A.
Gilman, Alice May - Ellsworth, Lester H.
Gilman, Blanch E. - Little, Joseph D.
Gilman, Florence Bell - Dimond, Chester Lacy
Gilman, Helen M. - Witham, George W.
Gilman, Laura A. (Norton) - Cotton, Fred S.
Gilman, Maud E. - Ballard, Clarence P.
Gilman, Paula L. Baillargeon - Hatem, Thomas D.
Giuliano, Elaine F. - Scovill, Judson Lawrence
Giuliano, Ethel-Marie, Desmaris, Michael F.
Gledhill, Ann Marguarite - Linscott, Ronald Hollis
Gleeson, Terri Lynn - Morrill, Kerry Arthur
Glidden, Addie M. - Page, John S.
Glidden, Brenda Gail - Sanville, Wilfred Lee
Glidden, Dora B. - Page, Roy T.
Glidden, Elsie M. - Everett, Adelbert T.
Glidden, Florence M. (Tibbetts) - Fancy, Albert S.
Glidden, Sarah Beth - Meserve, Steven Alan
Glines, Eva M. - Perkins, Walter C.
Glum, Laurie Jean - Baldwin, Robert Henry
Glum, Mary E. - Gray, George H., Jr.
Gobis, Anna M. - Bunker, Merton E.
Godbout, Kira Louise - Smith, Arthur Jason, Jr.
Going, Mary - Jones, Morrill S.
Gooch, Lavinnia E. - Edgerly, George D.

Gooch, Nancy Carol - Beck, Wendell Ernest
Gooch, Roberta (Hayes) - Moody, Lyndon Grover
Good, Susan Marie - Klefos, Kristofer Robin
Goodall, Jennifer Ann - Foster, John Robert
Goodfield, Cliftine A. (Emerson) - Goodwin, Ralph Leslie
Goodreau, Kristen A. - Elliott, Anthony C.
Goodwin, Ella E. - Hillsgrove, Fred N.
Goodwin, Esther - Noyes, William A.
Goodwin, Martha (Gilman) - Page, Dudley N.
Goodwin, Rachel A. - Bryant, John A.
Gorodilo, Irina Vladimirovna - Lannan, David Wayne
Goupil, Anita B. - Eisenhauer, John D.
Goupil, Rachel Theresa - Perkins, Harold Chester
Graeme, Betty - Lines, Gary
Graeme, Mary Ann (Woodhouse) - Forsyth, Harvey A.
Graffam, Debra Ellen - Eastman, Gordon Merle
Grant, Mildred Hodgson - Mansfield, Benjamin William
Gray, Barbara C. - Clairmont, Lynn R.
Gray, Diane L. - Geddes, David W., Jr.
Gray, Jane E. - Gove, Charles R.
Gray, Karen Jeanne - Hickey, Robert Anthony, Jr.
Gray, Wendi L. - Adamson, Patrick E.
Green, Arlene Theresa - Stockwell, Andrew Donald
Green, Cora E. - Bloom, Edward D.
Green, Euola H. - Pearl, John B.
Green, Frances M. - Stiles, George L.
Greene, Mary A. - Baker, Fred L.
Greenfield, Briann Gail - Hanna, Morgan Randall
Greenleaf, Blanche E. (Pease) - Ellsworth, Earle M.
Greenwood, Bernice Laura - Lord, Norman Junior
Griffin, Lorraine - Foster, Robert B.
Groton, Athalee L. - Dyer, Joseph N.
Gullage, Jody Lee - Fanning, Michael James
Gunn, Sarah A. (Sanborn) - Tuttle, Marcus M.
Guptill, Katherine N. - Trump, Dennis H.
Guy, Goldie L. - Stickney, Carl H.
Guyer, Louella M. - Leroux, Roger John

Haas, Cynthia Ann - Bronson, James Paul
Hages, Diana M. Vanzanten - Richey, William S., Jr.
Hagstrom, Alexandra - Wilson, Charles E.

Haines, Ann M. - Smith, Warren M.
Haley, Diane L. - Camuso, Peter J.
Ham, Cora B. - Elkins, John T.
Ham, Marion Elizabeth - Clark, Eugene F.
Hamel, Josephine G. - Stockwell, Leonard A.
Hamel, Rose M. - Willard, Edward L.
Hamel, Theresa D. - Kelly, Michael J.
Hamelin, Yvette J. - Bennett, Adellman S.
Hames, Marjorie A. - Rollins, Walter E.
Hamilton, Dawn Marie - Plummer, Adam Robert
Hammond, Andrea S. - Elliott, Robert A.
Hanlon, Maureen K. - Wood, Steven M.
Hannaford, Edith L. - Smith, J. Wilbur
Hansen, Eunice (Mansfield) - Kenney, Warren Peter, Jr.
Hansen, Mary B. - Thompson, Dayne F.
Hanson, Laura S. - Sawyer, Fred H.
Hardwick, Dianne S. - Reinholz, Lance K.
Hardy, Catherine A. - Eddy, Dean E.
Harer, Reba Dale (Harris) - Kingham, Ernest A.
Harrison, Ellen J. - Barnett, Brian A.
Harrison, Teresa L. - Burlingame, Roger G.
Hartford, Bonnie Kendra - Whelan, John Joseph, Jr.
Hartford, Denise - Aldrich, Robert Bruce
Harty, Angelique N. - Guilmette, Randy C.
Haskell, Carol F. - Arsenault, George E.
Haskell, Elizabeth J. - O'Leary, Bert
Haun, Anita D. - Lindholm, Michael H.
Hawkes, Donna M. - Fitz, Spencer A.
Hawkins, Geraldine E. - Mackes, Maurice M.
Hawkins, Kimberly A. - Gould, Jeffrey C.
Hawkins, Lucile A. - Gilman, Paul E.
Hayes, Elizabeth D. - Bordeau, Philip P.
Hayes, Roberta T. - Goodwin, Ralph L.
Haywood, Nannette Jean - Landry, Daniel Gary
Hazleton, Marilyn Jeanne - Picard, Lynwood S.
Hechler, Susan M. - Lynch, Jack D.
Heinis, Mary C. - Willard, Arthur
Hemeon, Teri A. - Svenson, Robert A.
Hempel, Jennifer L. - Johansson, Michael S.
Hempel, Kristina F. - Senior, Ronald S.
Henchey, Judy (Stokes) - Cummings, Brian

Henderson, Jean - Glum, Edward F.
Henry, Dawn M. - Russell, Sven E.
Herron, Christy Ann - Sayre, Roger William
Herson, Arletta M. (Munsey) - Gale, Robert S.
Herzberger, Heidi - Halter, Daniel J.
Herzing, Mary Frances - Fortin, Paul Damase
Hickey, Joanne Elaine - Caprario, Ronald David
Higgins, Carol Virginia - Stockbridge, Harry Eugene
Higgins, Eleanor - Simonds, Frank E.
Higgins, Nina M - Foss, John Henry
Hight, Grace Gertrude (Blaisdell) - Clough, John Page
Hill, Addie M. - Parsons, Usher S.
Hill, Annie M. - Roby, Arthur E.
Hill, Blanche E. (Morse) - Batchelder, Albert W.
Hill, Charlotte B. (Dudley) - Gilman, Caleb K.
Hill, Lilla M. - Sanborn, Frank M.
Hill, Loleta E. - Giles, Oscar A.
Hill, Patricia L. Doe - Doe, Melvin B.
Hill, Patricia Louise - Doe, Frederick Earl
Hill, Vera - Bickford, Clarence H.
Hilliard, Evelyn - Little, Philip Gilman
Hilliard, Mamie S. - Stone, Fred L.
Hillsgrove, Louise P. - Perkins, Clarence L.
Hillsgrove, Patricia - Lique, Ronald E.
Hilt, Evelyn D. - Langevin, William O.
Hilton, Jodi Lynn - Lines, John Alan
Hiltz, Dorothy P. - Willard, Arthur, Jr.
Hinds, Dorothy L. - Hislop, Robert E.
Hinds, Myrtle I. - Hislop, Donald W.
Hirschberg, Jeanette - Ochs, Neal L.
Hislop, Dorothy - Gagnon, Eugene W.
Hoch, Joymarie - Nilges, Sidney E.
Hodge, Joyce L. - Chamberlain, Randy L.
Hoffman, Kristine - Flynn, David
Hofpointer, Maria - Hufschmid, Erick
Hogan, Anna Alice - Geddes, David Walter
Holt, Ruth M. - Bickford, George A.
Horne, Sheila E. - Partridge, Ernest C.
Hough, Judith Beth - Price, Charles Amos
Hough, Rose Marie (Morin) - Seravia, David Richard
Houle, Cleo Rachel - Greenwood, Clayton

Hounsell, Deborah J. - Sanville, Robert J.
Houston, Myra (Groton) - Dyer, Roland
Howard, Bertha - Haines, John H.
Howard, Carrie B. - Haynes, Horace F.
Howe, Flora - Giles, Fred S.
Hoyt, Florence E. - Sanderson, William S. P.
Hughes, Holly Ann - Marston, Rodney Lee
Hunkins, Bernice Miriam (Kelley) - Santerre, Gerard Joseph
Hunkins, Gloria J. - Segalini, Recardo L.
Hunt, Judy - Boddy, Christopher
Hunter, Carrie - Stanton, David F.
Hunter, Linda Lou Miller - Dore, Brian K.
Hurst, Devere D. - Groleau, James P.
Huston, Lynn - Wiegel, Terry J.
Hutchins, Tina Marie - Kelley, John David
Huxford, Annette - Brown, Arthur Robert
Hyslop, Carlene A. - Roberts, Clive E.
Hyslop, Darlene Lee - Clinton, Paul Douglas
Hyslop, Dianne Sue - Hardwick, Philip F.
Hyslop, Frances Lorraine - Stockwell, Clifford Harmon
Hyslop, Frances Lorraine - Woodbury, Robert Charles
Hyslop, Jeannette T. - Stockwell, Clifford H.
Hyslop, Rachel A. (Straw) - Goodwin, Ralph L.
Hyslop, Rachel R. - Divers, Andrew S.
Hyslop, Sally J. - Divers, David M.

Inman, Patricia A. - Amirault, Frank, Jr.

Jackson, Edith A. Nelson - Norton, Mahlon R.
Jackson, Susan - French, Buzzie Bill
Jacob, Kimberly A. - Laclair, James M.
Jacques, Renee - Ames, Michael E.
Janas, Mary A. - Woodward, Donald
Jared, Karen M. Branon - Munsey, Herbert E.
Javery, Betty A. (Riddinger) - Dion, Rodney Donat
Jelley, Amy D. - Starrett, Edwin B.
Jewell, Phyllis Louise - Clairmont, Lynn Robert
Jillson, Hope - Vernon, Arthur A.
Joki, Jill H. - Duca, William H., Jr.
Jones, Caroline E. - York, Raymond S.
Jones, Caroline M. - Cogswell, Thomas

Jones, Ella M. - Chamberlain, Harry I.
Jones, Ethel L. - Moody, Ona A.
Jones, Eva M. - Burroughs, Orman L.
Jones, Evelyn Blanche - Sanville, Thomas Henry
Jones, Evelyn L. - Littlefield, George
Jones, Harriet F. - Converse, Frank A.
Jones, Laura G. - Wells, Ernest L.
Jones, Laura May - Dymond, George Charles
Jones, Minnie E. (Sloper) - Hurd, Henry H.
Jones, Myra E. - Davis, Seldon J.
Jones, Ruth M. (Thompson) - Sargent, Edwin W.
Jordan, Marion L. - Forsyth, Harvey A.
Jordan, Syble O. - Forsyth, Harry G.
Joy, Helen May - Davis, Lester Charles
Joy, May S. (Bickford) - Nutter, George W.
Joyce, Linda A. - Eastman, Douglas R.
Joyce, Mabel Erdine - Greene, Horace Daniel
Joyce, Rosalie E. - Beauchesne, Donald H.
Joyce, Sandra (Denault) - Beck, Wendell E.
Judkins, Dorcas Lee - Hill, Leo Lawrence

Kamilis, Isidore - Drown, Bradford G.
Kang, Min K. - Landry, Joshua R.
Kaucher, Mary K. - Gardner, Andrew H.
Kelley, Charlotte A. - Pearson, Edward W.
Kelley, Cindy J. - Parrington, Dennis J.
Kelley, Donna Marie - Griffin, Shirley Edward
Kelley, Pamela Louise - Danby, Craig James
Kendall, Laura A. - Gilman, Haven F.
Kendall, Nancy A. - Lewis, Alan L.
Kenney, Lola M. Zinn - Relf, George D.
Key, Edna Lois - Andrews, Albert L.
Keyes, Jennie A. (Blake) - Witham, Ezekiel E.
Keyser, Holly Beth - Danby, Scott Raymond
Kidder, Martha L. - McIntire, James P.
Kidder, Wendy A. - Pleeter, Daniel
Kilton, Nancy MacDonald - Kelley, Edward W.
Kimball, Gertrude M. - Clough, Nahum O.
Kincaid, Susan D. - Voda, Dennis J.
King, Anne Helen - Martin, Paul Ronald
King, Debra Allyson - Baker, Lewis Vernon

King, June Marion - Mundschenk, Manuel Warren
King, Mabel - Zvacs, John
King, Rubietta M. - Porter, Malcolm Hamlin
Kling, Tammy M. - Martin, William C., Jr.
Knights, Iona B. - Smith, William A.
Knott, Kathryn E. - Garon, Richard K.
Knowles, Betsey M. - Sawyer, David
Kratzert, Antonia - Green, Elmer L.

LaBonte, Janet Ann - Hyslop, John Thomas
Labonte, Lucille Therese - Day, William F.
Lacroix, Dawna Jean - Philbrick, Timothy Cary
Lafoe, Lucy E. - Wescott, Clarence S.
Lafoe, Mary J. - Fogg, Albion
LaFrance, Heather Mae - Osborne, Thomas Cargill
Lake, Lois L. - Hyslop, Frank E.
Lake, Ruby Pamela (Head) - Stockbridge, Carl Lewis
Lamprey, Ada J. - Osborne, True F.
Lamprey, May A. - Lamprey, Carlton A.
Lane, Karen J. - Mahoney, Brian F.
Lane, Lizzie Batchelder - Brown, John Wheeler
Lang, Karen L. - Martin, William A.
Langley, Elaine M. - Mooney, John J.
Langley, Kathleen - Moorehead, Shane Alan
Langley, Kathleen A. - Nutter, Robert C.
Lank, Carol - Watson, Ernest, Jr.
Lapoint, Carrie L. - Sargent, Andrew A.
LaRoche, Candace J. - Daigle, Raymond M.
Larose, Lucille R. - Philipps, Albert E.
Lasheway, Sheryl A. - Sanville, Joseph L., 3rd
LaSpina, Jo-Ann - Stevens, William K.
Latouche, Mary - French, Fred S.
Lavoie, Denise M. - McWhinnie, Thomas J.
Lawrence, Gail M. - Brawley, Harry E., III
Leavitt, Ethel May - Downs, John E.
Lebel, Tina Marie - Withington, Timothy Mark
Leclerc, France Marie Frost - Sipes, William Blaine
Leeper, Lois Ann - Scovill, Crosby Kent
Lempke, Barbara (Kaciak) - Kenney, John, Jr.
Leonard, Christine A. - McClary, Frank J.
Leonard, Margaret A. - Witham, Peter T.

Lerner, Linda Joyce - Freeman, Murray Sumner
Leroux, Carol A. Bilodeau - Daigneau, Robert A.
Lessard, Rebeecca A. - Jordan, Jay E.
Lester, Julie-Anne Ruth - Jaworski, Anthony Michael
Lewis, Suzanne M. - Eastman, Albert N.
Libby, Deborah J. - Sanville, Dennis W.
Libby, Megan J. - McElroy, Garth J.
Lievens, Lucille L. Crews - Doucette, Robert G.
Lincoln, Gertrude - Perkins, Lorenzo H.
Lindley, Amanda Jane - Stone, Andrew William
Lines, Christine A. - Spaulding, Frank A., Jr.
Lines, Ronda - Connelly, Timothy S.
Link, Bonnie G. - Vorel, John A.
Linscott, Nina J. - Bruns, Frederick L.
Little, Arlene I. - Hunkins, Dana W.
Little, Arlene Iona - Hunkins, Dana William
Little, Ruth M. - Nugent, Earl C.
Littlefield, Linda Ann - Gassett, Ronald Kenneth
Littlefield, Nancy Lee - Briggs, Daniel George
Locke, Carolyn R. - Lank, Clinton L.
Locke, Linda Lea - Dore, Steven Brent
Lockhart, Barbara Ann - Guerrier, Kevin Kenneth
Lockwood, Christine Ann - Ellis, John Maurice
Longver, Kimberly A. - Berndt, David F.
Lopes, Juanita A. - Pina, Kenneth J.
Lotz, C. L. - Salgado, Carlos Reniery Diaz
Louis, Karen Lynn - Bishop, Dana A.
Lowe, Arleen C. - Jean, James C.
Lowrey, Janice M. - Belcastro, Jerome T.
Ludeman, Rebecca - Bryant, George H.
Lutters, Nancy O. - Stitt, Richard P.
Lynam, Judith G. - Yeary, Thomas J.
Lynch, Tamara Jane - Duane, Richard Daniel, Jr.
Lyster, Junie Belle - Lyster, Herbert L.

MacDonald, Mary A. - Green, Walter S.
Mace, Charlotte E. - Weeks, Lorrain E.
MacIn, Janet M. - Dandeneau, Joseph B.
Macleod, Angie Marie - Nielsen, Thomas B.
Maheux, Jane E. - Gray, William I.
Mahoney, Helen Teresa - Shannon, Carroll Calvin

Mailloux, Anne Marie Annis - Bartlett, Andrew John
Malcolm, Margaret S. - Cook, Jon D.
Malcolm, Silvia L. - Donaghy, Barry A.
Mallett, Peggyann - McCaffrey, Brian Michael
Maltais, Melissa - Kelley, Scott Michael
Manley, Elizabeth - Anderson, Arvid, Jr.
Mann, Carla M. - Archibald, Christopher S.
Manning, Frances Jane (Clancy) - Frary, Arthur Frederick
Manning, June R. E. - Hislop, Richard W.
Mansfield, Alice M. Ainsworth - Judkins, Richard A.
Mansfield, Evelyn Jean - Patten, David Guy
Manson, Blanche Lyle (Beck) - Avery, George Hawley
Marcoux, Candice J. - Dorley, Robert E.
Margeson, Mollie Dorothy - Hawkins, Merton Everett
Marquis, Sarah Leigh - Wicks, Walter Wayne
Marrion, Diane - Lafleur, Thomas Gordon
Marsh, Celia H. - Beede, Herbert
Marsh, Emma J. - Gilman, Arthur L.
Marshall, Nellie F. (Glidden) - Batchelder, Josiah A.
Martin, Adrienne G. - Dugal, Drew L.
Martin, Cynthia J. - Brunk, Michael D.
Maser, Heather J. - Maxwell, Seth R.
Mastern, Lilla M. - Hilliard, Leander A.
Matanis, Mabel D. (Moreau) - DeFlumero, Lawrence
Maxfield, Elizabeth - Redman, Donald A.
Maxfield, Hattie F. - Ordway, Charles W.
Maxfield, Sharon Angela - Twigg, George, IV
May, Lizzie M. - Eveleth, Clarence M.
McAuley, Ruth I. - Hislop, Donald, Jr.
McCarthy, Cynthia Susan - Clairmont, Omar Leo
McCarthy, Sandra Elaine - Cullen, John William, Jr.
McCarthy, Sarah (Hodgins) - Mayo, Richard Dana
McClary, Brenda L. - Cole, Daniel A.
McClary, Grace A. - Langley, Henry N.
McClary, Jean Louise - Frost, Maurice Arthur
McClary, Jessie B. - Harris, Ora Wendell
McClary, Jo-Ann B. - Shattuck, Steven J.
McClary, Marion M. - Keith, Robert Jackson
McClary, Sarah E. - Conner, Clarence A.
McClintock, Cynthia D. - Glum, Christopher E.
McCoy, Barbara A. - Provencal, William J.

McCulloch, Alyssa Todd - Feiges, Adam Joshua
McCurdy, Beatrice B. (Beatson) - Jefferson, Hilary
McDonough, Laurie Elizabeth - Forsyth, Michael Stanley
McGee, Ann M. - Spaulding, Frank A., Jr.
McGilbary, Charlotte (McNair) - Greenough, George H.
McGreger, D. Emma (Leper) - Welch, George E.
McIntire, Gina Marie - Prevost, Richard F.
McIntire, Judith C. - Stancombe, Arthur W.
McIntire, Judith Ellen (Cunliffe) - Baillie, Paul Sheldon
McIntyre, Susan R. - Adams, Brice R.
McKaig, Camille Lorraine - Morse, Gary Alan
McKay, Charlotte E. - McClary, Curtis J.
McKiernan, Janice A. (Boudreau) - Wanamaker, George
McLain, Helen - Smith, Joseph
McLean, Minnie F. - Edgerly, Roy C.
McLeod, Carol A. - Day, Larry V., Sr.
McLeod, Crystal M. - Stockbridge, Michael J.
McLeod, Margaret A. - Downing, Herbert W.
McMahon, Phyllis C. - Svenson, Carl J.
McMahon, Rena Grace (George) - Graves, William Alfred
McManus, Noreen A. - Gardner, William H.
McMurphy, Almyra - Rollins, Henry A.
McNayr, Gertrude May - Secord, Harold Burton
McVey, Paula Ann - Tarantino, Francis David
Meekins, Ruth May - Evans, Benjamin Isaac
Merkwan, Donna A. - Studley, Edmund G.
Merrill, Ethel M. - Page, Frank J.
Merrill, Florence Belle - Durgin, Arthur Leyland
Metalious, Marsha Joan - Dupuis, Edward Paul
Mick, Caroline S. (Small) - Taylor, James G.
Miller, Christine Marie - Valas, Mark Randall
Miller, Deborah Christine - McQuillen, Michael Arthur
Miller, Donna Marie (Gard) - White, Francis Clifford
Miller, Karen E. - Dean, John K.
Miller, Karen Elizabeth - Dean, John Kelly
Miller, Patricia G. Tasseff - Henry, Willard G.
Milmore, Margaret - Greenwood, Raymond
Mitchell, Darlene Marjorie - Blais, Clifford Edward
Mitchell, Gertrude (Downes) - Sawyer, Sewell B.
Mitchell, Jane E. - Olson, Steven C.
Mitchell, Jane E. - Sisti, Mark L.

Mitchell, Roxey E. - Carroll, Eugene E.
Mitchell, Sonja N. - Hopkins, James T., Sr.
Mitchell, Vera Elizabeth - Chamberlain, Eve. H.
Molignaro, Elaine C. Frazio - Tasker, Andrew F.
Monier, Deborah L. - Newton, John J.
Monier, Susan L. - Hansen, Richard A.
Monroe, Charlotte A. - Reed, Thomas R.
Moody, Cleo Frances - Pretzfelder, Millard, III
Moore, Elizabeth Kennedy - Haberstroh, Joseph Kevin
Moore, Hazel B. - Weeks, Maintland B.
Moore, Irene M. - Moore, Hugh R.
Moore, Jennie L. - Ross, Dwayne C.
Moore, Karen D. - Baker, Douglas A.
Moore, Karen E. - Fish, Stanley Allen
Moore, Kimberley Anne - Poulin, Robert George, II
Moore, Laura - James, Eric M.
Moore, Mary G. - Divers, John E.
Morancy, Arlene M. - Bucciarelli, Robert H.
Morgan, Donna L. - Blodgett, Thomas J.
Morgan, Heather L. - Hueber, Jimmy
Morgan, Mary R. - Edgerly, Frank A.
Moreau, Jean E. - Munsey, James J.
Morin, Betty Ann - Bryson, Jon Lindsay
Morin, Cecile R. - Clifford, Everett E.
Morin, Irene L. - Voudren, Roger D.
Morin, Rita Anne - Austin, Gerald, Jr.
Morley, Judith Ina - Pembroke, James Paul, Sr.
Morrell, Ann Morgyn - Keene, Gregory Scott
Morris, Lea M. (Lacour) - Gosselin, Frederick P.
Morse, Jane A. - Doe, Frederick E.
Morse, Virginia Nora - Manning, Harold George, Jr.
Mottola, Linda Ann - Heroux, Blaise Thomas
Moulton, Kathy J. - Burditt, Anthony D.
Moulton, Myra L. - Foss, Frank E.
Moulton, Sandra June - Hyslop, Willis E.
Mulhern, Helen L. - Carey, Jeremiah S.
Mullaney, Eleanor A.- Baron, Jay S.
Mullen, Cherylle Anne - Bussey, Charles Bernard
Mulroy, Patricia Mary - Beavers, Scott Allen
Munroe, Wendy Leigh - Sweeney, James Joseph, III
Munsey, Arletta H. - Hersom, Leon E.

Munsey, Glenna Mae - Krueger, Laurence Ray
Munsey, Marjorie Mae - Couture, Roger Arthur
Munsey, Martha A. - Zanes, William B.
Munsey, Maureen Rae - Twombly, James Richard
Munsey, Susan Elizabeth - Roberts, Neil Richard
Murphy, Helena G. - Barnes, William J.
Murray, Kara Lyn - Stanley, William D., III

Nadeau, Vicki L. - Braun, Carl L.
Nason, Gladys Ella - Bergevin, William J.
Neal, Patricia N. - Morin, Stephen F.
Neal, Suzanne Maria - Sepulveda, Guillermo
Needham, Carol A. - Bartlett, Andrew J.
Nelson, Carolyn E. - Bunnell, Robert E.
Nelson, Edna V. - Holman, Paul R.
Nelson, Elayne L. - Cole, Robert L.
Nelson, Marion G. - Bessey, Burton Marks
Ness, Nancy E. - Gibeau, Joseph L.
Nevins, Hazel - Bragg, Dellie
Newell, Maryann McKenna - Hatab, John Christopher
Neylon, Jennifer Lynn - White, Stephen, J., Jr.
Nicholson, Elin Denise - Henderson, Philip Lee
Nicholson, Mary L. (Bouchard) - Stone, Charles W.
Norell, Carol - Beck, James Nicholas, Jr.
Norton, Clara J. (Builard) - Gilman, Charles F.
Noyes, Charlene D. - Gordon, Harry W.
Nutter, Carrie M. (Dutch) - Nutter, Debert Clayton
Nutter, Cora F. - Hanscom, Herman F.
Nutter, Doris I. (Springer) - Bowdoin, Harry L.
Nutter, Edith May (Locke) - Locke, George Ozro
Nutter, Leona Myrtle - McClary, Frank Leslie
Nutter, Sarah E. - Hanson, Carl N.

O'Connor, Patricia Ann - Rice, Herbert Edward, III
Odman, Murdeen D. - Wallace, Gary S.
Oliver, Nancy M. - Hillsgrove, Wayne H.
Olmsted, Barbara B. - Smith, Oliver Cook
Orange, Lizzie H. - Brown, George H.
Orange, Mary G. - Glidden, Charles H.
Orsi, Linda J. - Robinson, Joseph
Orzolek, Judith Veronica - Landry, Robert Joseph

Osborne, Amy D. - Hawkins, Shurldin
Osborne, Eva G. - Griffin, Nathan D.
Osgood, Nancy Ann - Gard, Bruce Munsey
Osgood, Shirley B. - Stockbridge, Harry E.
Osmer, Deborah A. - Thompson, Mark I.
Ostendorff, Mary E. Thomte - McKinna, Robert J.
Ouellette, Kimberly A. - Moorehead, Carl E.
Ouellette, Lynne A. - Claremont, David A.
Oviatt, Melissa Elizabeth - Johnson, Kristian Thane

Page, Alice C. - Marsh, Joseph H. L.
Page, Alice J. - Emerson, Ansel
Page, Anna B. - Page, Herman A.
Page, Edna Austin - Green, Ronald Walter
Page, Ethel M. - Cushing, Russell W.
Page, Evelyn A. - Uhlenberg, Frank L.
Page, Hattie Belle - Kelley, Charles George
Page, Irene M. - Davis, George E.
Page, Jeanette P. - Higgins, Clifton E.
Page, Laura Ella - Clifford, Forrest H.
Page, Lizzie M. - Blake, Laural A.
Page, Mary E. - Duso, W. N.
Page, Mildred E. - Potter, George D.
Page, Nellie C. - Whitehouse, Robert A.
Paige, Marlene Gloria - Zanes, Robert L., Jr.
Paige, Michelle Leigh - Dion, Rudolphe Louis
Palladino, Kathy Susan - Fernandes, Peter David
Palmer, Edna Estella - Sargent, Horace Daniel
Palmer, Florence J. - Partridge, Horace F.
Paquette, Laurie Jane - Sanborn, Chad Patrick
Parker, Barbara J. - Purtell, Stanley P.
Parker, Hazel I. - Lank, Howard J.
Parsons, Addie B. - Marsh, Herbert J.
Parsons, Flora H. - Hall, Harold Chaperon
Parsons, Gertrude E. - Page, Fred W.
Partridge, Olive B. - Tibbetts, Robert F.
Patch, Dorothy Belle (Kelley) - Springer, Harold Leslie
Patscott, Sara E. - Baldwin, David G.
Patten, Angie - Thompson, Herbert E.
Patten, Eleanor - Stockbridge, Carl L.
Patten, Laura L. - Langley, Howard G.

Patten, Lucinda A. (Bullard) - Peaslee, Charles H.
Patten, Stella P. - Swett, Fred H.
Payne, Susan J. - Hughes, Wayne A.
Payson, Florence M. - Jones, Albert A.
Pearl, Mary L. - French, John S.
Pearl, Rhoda Ellen - Green, Archie Wyman
Pearson, Robin L. - Cheney, James M., Sr.
Pease, Hazel A. - Twombly, Clarence H.
Pease, Nanie B. - Moody, Clarence N.
Pease, Zilla N. - Dow, Oscar C.
Peaslee, Amelia - Merrill, Charles E.
Peaslee, Bessie - Foss, Carroll E.
Peaslee, Nettie R. - Foss, Frank W.
Peick, Kris Alice - Sayre, Scott Alan
Penney, Robin L. - Ritenour, Richard O.
Pennock, Cynthia L. (Nelson) - Brown, Earl D.
Pennock, Joy Leslie - MacDonald, Charles
Penta, Marie - Crandell, William E.
Perkins, Elizabeth F. Burleigh - Christofore, Richard W.
Perkins, Mariam - Bryans, Robert L.
Perkins, Patricia L. - Gates, Sidney C.
Perkins, Roseanna Eva - Hillsgrove, Thomas Bruce
Perrin, Lorie A. - Lane, Steven J.
Peters, Ardith A. - Bascuas, Joseph W.
Peterson, Anna D. - Shellhorn, Asa J.
Pfohl, Elizabeth (Stern) - Lenneberg, Eric
Phillips, Tina M. - DeBow, Ronald D.
Phippard, Gail Marie - McWhinnie, Stephen Paul
Pickard, Dorothy P. - Green, Elmer R.
Pickard, Elizabeth - Stone, Edward G.
Pickard, Renee Kathryn - Thompson, Dayne Frederick
Pickel, Theresa Elizabeth (Hall) - Switzer, Charles Wilbur
Pickowicz, Christina M. - Rowe, Nicholas A.
Pierce, Jessica Gertrude - Clough, James Allan
Pinard, Claire Marie - Wilkens, John Robert Paul
Pitman, Marjorie E. - Webster, William C.
Place, Frances L. - Stockbridge, Joseph S.
Place, Josephine Sybil - Davis, Frederick Alvah
Plummer, Gladys E. - Smith, Edwin W.
Poire, Trudy Lee - Brown, Daniel David
Poirrier, Arline J. - Langley, Bernard H.

Poitras, Marcia Lou Georgia - Ring, Scott C.
Polley, Bette (Cutting) - Gard, Bruce
Potter, Dorothy Winona - Byers, Robert Allen
Potter, Janet A. - Breton, Normand G.
Potter, Joan B. - Riel, Timothy M.
Potter, Ruth Eleanor - Batchelder, Isaac Walker
Potter, Virginia Mary - Geddes, Douglas M.
Pratt, Lura A. (Davis) - Canney, Forrest S.
Preble, Mary L. (Austin) - Page, Luther E.
Prendergast, Frieda (Dashner) - French, Guy Charles
Prescott, Margaret (Milton) - Manley, Leroy A.
Prescott, Muriel B. - Ford, William A.
Prescott, Virginia A. - Scovill, Lawrence S.
Price, Mary Ann - Forsyth, George Scott
Price, Natalie Jean - Locke, James Nutter
Price, Pauline Elizabeth - Downing, Gregory Michael
Price, Rebekah Elizabeth - Gilbert, Anthony Joseph
Prindle, Judith - Wilson, Woodrow S.
Prindle, Wendy Ann - Berlind, Allan
Provencal, Bethany L. - Columb, Ronald M.
Provencal, Christine A. - Lockwood, Earl E., Jr.
Prybylo, Carolyn A. - Bordeau, Paul C.
Publicover, Sandra J. - Hillsgrove, George C.
Purcell, Elsie V. - Flanders, Victor C.
Purtell, Diana - Thoroughgood, Richard J.
Pyne, Melinda S. - Wilson, Jon K.

Quale, Karen L. - West, Corey B.
Quimby, Cynthia Jane - Dore, Alan Michael
Quinn, Dorothy M. (Milne) - Langley, Donald C.

Raither, Christina M. - Beal, Stephen W.
Rand, Blanche L. (Beck) - Manson, Clarence I.
Rand, Wendy Orrie - Daigneau, Robert Arthur
Randlett, Daren J. - Gray, Wayne S.
Rankin, Nancy Elaine - Griffin, Robert Davis
Rausch, Rebecca L. - Spencer, Adam D.
Redman, Florence E. (Ford) - Chamberlain, LeRoy
Redman, Florence Ethel (Ford) - Hill, Frank Arthur
Reid, Elizabeth D. MacKay - Thompson, Andrew E.
Reid, Mabel M. - Dunn, Robert B.

Reinholz, Roya R. - Snow, Steve R.
Renno, Marjorie R. - Gardner, William H.
Reynolds, Charlene Elaine - Forcier, Kenneth Paul
Rhodes, Linda L. - Walton, Kenneth I., III
Richard, Evelyn M. (Reed) - Fontaine, Andrew J.
Richards, Paulene M. - Price, Amos Richard
Richardson, Alice M. - Price, Charles A.
Richardson, Robin - Martel, Glenn K.
Ricker, Ellen - Lamprey, Aldis J.
Rieck, Deborah Elaine - Manning, John Wayne
Riel, Janique A. - Fraser, William P.
Riel, Linda Elizabeth - Moulton, Carl Leslie
Riel, Maxine Lois - Mitchell, Clayton Paul
Riggins, Mildred Irene - Margeson, Edward M., Jr.
Riggs, Doris M. - Howson, Richard G.
Riggs, Lura F. - Molburg, Donald J.
Riggs, Sarah - Page, Joseph Leon
Riley, Lydia C. - Doyle, James F.
Ring, Annie M. (Haines) - Fogg, Orlando
Ripley, Virginia True - Hathaway, Ronald Fred
Rivard, Sheri A. - Chase, Gary A.
Rizzon, Beth - Johnson, Eric E.
Robert, Geraldine Susan - Lafond, Morris Daniel
Roberts, Audrey K. - Marsh, James E.
Roberts, Florence - Skantze, Walter H.
Robertson, Gertrude - MacInnes, Neil A.
Robertson, Margie Ruth - Smithers, Thomas William, III
Robie, Viola G. - Partridge, Leon E.
Roby, Carrie L. (Dowst) - Brock, Charles T.
Roby, Ina M. - Stockbridge, George S.
Roche, Martha Maria - Smith, Kenneth James
Rock, Linda K. - Schumacher, Loran Lee, Jr.
Rogers, Alice M. (Welsh) - French, Jeremiah S.
Rogers, Mabelle E. (Davis) - Perrin, Alexander M.
Rogers, Nellie Etta - Leavitt, George Wilbur
Rogers, Phyllis Doris - Kelley, Donald Page
Rogers, Terry L. - Morrison, William J.
Rollins, Alice E. - Beck, Ernest S.
Rollins, Cora I. - Weeks, Herbert N.
Rollins, Doris M. - Tibbetts, Henry A.
Rollins, Ethelyn G. (Jones) - Nutter, Kenneth N.

Rollins, Gertrude A. - Twombly, Fred M.
Rollins, Hattie Ella - Stone, Charles L.
Rollins, Jeanette - Vien, Alphia R.
Rollins, Thelma May - Golden, Alfred Kenneth
Rose, Carol A. - Bresse, John A., Jr.
Rosenblum, Rebecca J. (Slifer) - Stanley, Milton
Ross, Ellen F. - Winch, Russell P.
Ross, Sadie P. - Edgerly, Carlton J.
Ross, Teresa C. Scaff - McWhinnie, Robert C., Jr.
Rowe, Angela Helen - Plourde, Jason Michael
Rowe, Grace M. - Davis, Elwin W.
Rowe, Rebecca Lynn - Martel, Glenn Kenneth
Roy, Clara - Wade, Edwin D.
Roy, Linda May Colby - Lance, Mark Royce
Runnals, Bonnie Lee - Boisvert, James Garrett
Russell, Cora A. (Glidden) - Kinsman, John Mason
Russell, Erin D. - Goupil, Gary G.
Russell, Ricki Charlene - Vachon, Peter Joseph, III
Russell, Shiloh Sioux - Simino, Christopher William
Ryan, Jennifer L. - Maher, Frederick H.

Sagona, Marian N. - Lynch, James Francis
Salisbury, Jolene - Burdett, David
Salls, Susan E. - Daggett, Kenneth E.
Sanborn, Alice - Sears, Robert Clifton
Sanborn, Christy L. - Rafferty, Bobby J.
Sanborn, Evelyn M. - Sanborn, Carl Jeremiah
Sanborn, Nancy Jane - Potter, Robert Leo
Sansouci, Lois E. - Amell, Darrel L.
Sansouci, Lois E. Amell - Hardy, Forrest E.
Santin, Rita - Colin, Dennis P.
Sanville, Beverly A. - Jenness, Steven Michael
Sanville, Florence Winnifred (Russell) - Patten, Claude Burton
Sardella, Stephanie C. - McQuade, Michael J.
Sargent, Ada - Green, Walter S.
Sargent, Candace Ann - Weeks, Francis Marion
Sargent, Lizzie B. (Price) - Watson, Selwin A.
Savolainen, Mary - Marsh, Irad H.
Sawyer, Blanche L. - Ayer, Walter H.
Sawyer, Carol Ann - Golden, Patrick Michael
Sawyer, Janice S. - Hooper, Steven R.

Sawyer, Laura F. (Hanson) - Wells, E. Russell
Sawyer, Lynn Aaron - Paige, Carroll Monroe
Schott, Janie L. - MacAskill, Kenneth A.
Schott, Janie Louise - Lines, Gary
Schott, Suzanne B. - Derby, Wayne A.
Schricker, Karen Dianne - Walton, Jonathan Henry
Scovill, Mildred Virginia - Johnston, David Russell
Scovill, Virginia A. (Prescott) - Manley, Leroy A.
Scovill, Virginia A. (Prescott) - Scovill, Lawrence
Scovill, Wini May - Weeks, Frank M.
Seaman, Robin - Faulkner, William J.
Sears, Diana Carnegie (Steele) - Eklund, H. William
Seavey, Marjorie - Chamberlain, Robert W.
Seifert, Judith L. - Alley, Robert M.
Segale, Jeanine Louise - Moorehead, Carl Ellison
Sevene, Beverly A. - Greenwood, Leo M.
Shalek, Shawn Lee - Alton, Guy William
Shattuck, Sadie M. (Buckman) - Page, William A.
Shaw, Sarah Anne - Perry, Terence W.
Shepard, Frances W. - Tucker, Nathan B.
Sherwood, Francis - Dees, Jesse W.
Shrake, Marjorie A. - Mitchell, Roderick E.
Sibley, Beatrice E. - McClary, Harold J.
Sidebotham, Harriet E. - Stewartson, Carl L.
Simonds, Olive May (Wells) - Simonds, Richard Eugene
Sims, Sylvia A. - Chamberlain, Dennis A.
Sirrell, Patricia M. - Hill, Joseph P., Jr.
Slater, Suzanne - Everett, Allen T.
Sleeper, Vinna E. - Ring, Charles E.
Small, Blanche L. (Beck) - Rand, Chester Franklin
Small, Caroline T. - Mick, Clarence S.
Smith, Alma L. - Lathrop, Elwin G.
Smith, Daisy - Palmer, George L.
Smith, Diane - MacKenzie, James, II
Smith, Donna Marie - Forst, Brian Allen
Smith, Edith G. - Twombly, Charles A.
Smith, Esther M. - Weeks, John F.
Smith, Etta C. (McAlpine) - Ainsworth, Jason W.
Smith, Frances E. - Rollins, Victor E.
Smith, Holly - O'Shea, John D., Jr.
Smith, Julia Frances - Potter, Samuel Earle

Smith, Laura Christina - Mansfield, Herbert L.
Smith, Laura J. - Canney, John W.
Smith, Lillian M. - Bickford, Herbert S.
Smith, Linda Lee - Martin, Ronald Wayne
Smith, Louise M. - Steele, Robert E.
Smith, Martha A. (Spencer) - York, Fred A.
Smith, Mary Hannah (Brown) - Monroe, Norman Scott
Smith, Myrtie B. - Kimball, Scott A.
Smith, Ronilee R. - Smithers, Timothy J.
Smith, Ronilee R. - Nolin, Lloyd D.
Smith, Suzanne Lyn - Turcotte, David Daniel
Smith, Virginia - Sawyer, Duke
Smithers, Michelle L. - Heyman, Casey J.
Smithers, Tracy J. - Davis, Duane M.
Spangler, Crista Kendall - Twomey, Brendan Francis
Spellman, Patricia Ann - Trites, Donald Earl
Spiller, Carrie D. - Gray, Edwin M.
Springer, Arlene H. - Cox, Arthur A.
Stanford, Lisa A. - Jacques, Spencer L.
Stanley, Jayne Margret - Young, Brooks Elliott
Stanley, Rebecca - Boudreau, Michael
Stanley, Sara L. - Perkins, Daniel W.
Stanley, Virginia Minerva (White) - Grant, James Wallingford
Staples, Dora - Batchelder, Charles M.
Steele, Dora Jean - Wyatt, Douglas Colby
Steele, Elsie L. - Shields, James F.
Steenstra, Muriel Ann - Robinette, Michael Joseph
Steenstra, Nancy E. - Christie, John S.
Stevens, Abbie B. (Couch) - Hilliard, Alfred F.
Stevens, Cheryl - Ashton, Jonathan
Stevens, Corella A. - Scott, Joseph G.
Stevens, Dorothy - Goss, William H.
Stevens, Ethel Louise - Williams, Harry Elmore
Stevens, Melissa W. - Daigle, Robert J.
Stevens, Sandra - Guarino, Donald J.
Stevens, Stephanie - Fogg, Michael B.
Stevens, Suzanne - Ketchum, Allen R.
Stickney, Lucille M. - Ford, Herbert F.
Stock, Barbara J. - Woodward, William
Stockbridge, Hattie M. - Smith, Charles L.
Stockbridge, Lorna L. - Page, Ray B.

Stockbridge, Viola Muriel - Clark, Carroll Percy
Stockman, Ruth E. - Green, Laurence K.
Stockwell, Ena M. - Price, William R.
Stockwell, Harmony - Margeson, Austin H.
Stockwell, Mary Elizabeth - Adel, Jack Israel
Stockwell, Nancy Jane - Lines, Glen
Stone, Beverly - Baxter, William Frederick
Stone, Dorothy I. - Pickard, Oscar S.
Stone, Kim L. - Daigneau, Jason R.
Straw, Eva M. - Dame, Perley C.
Streeter, Debra A. - Smith, Stephen R.
Strout, Marilyn M. (Morse) - Slocum, David P.
Strout, Nancy E. - Lines, Paul
Sturgeon, Shirley Ann - Mount, Theodore E.
Sullivan, Eileen G. - Tong, Frank Yue
Sumner, Diana R. - Hottle, John C.
Swain, Terri Ann - Hawkins, Garey Lee
Swanson, Darin - Karagozian, Harold
Swift, Alice Moulton - Eveleth, Edwin Everett
Sylvain, Vycki M. - Harris, David G., Jr.

Tardy, Lena D. - Emerson, Loren H.
Tardy, Lucille Jeanette - Partridge, Leon Everett
Tarr, Ethel C. - Clough, Clarence F.
Tasker, Barbara A. - Geddes, Duncan John
Tatelbaum, Linda - Winer, Kalman A.
Taylor, J. Teresa - Lathrop, Harold E.
Taylor, Tammy Lee - Baiocchetti, Vincent Anthony, III
Tebbetts, Elizabeth A. - Connell, Daniel
Temple, May A. (Grady) - Young, Frank D.
Tenney, Dorrice T. Gardner - Bumpus, Charles H., Sr.
Tesorero, Claire Ellen - Sullivan, Joel Marvin
Therrien, Patricia A. - Rollins, Patrick A.
Thistle, Kathryn (Treat) - Brown, Morse E.
Thomas, Sheila L. - Stendor, William F., II
Thompson, Antoinette - Eastman, Clifford C.
Thompson, Beatrice Ann - Russell, Charles Sven
Thompson, Beulah Estelle (Horne) - Glidden, William Leslie
Thompson, Cheryl L. - Albert, Robert A.
Thompson, Doreen D. - Moorehead, Rickey E.
Thompson, Elaine M. - Langley, Paul Nelson

Thompson, Elizabeth Helen - Sargent, Prescott Nathan
Thompson, Ethel G. (Adel) - Carpenter, Al. S.
Thompson, Eva A. - Trumbull, James G.
Thompson, Harriett W. (Waller) - Coupal, Armand
Thompson, Janet L. - Donovan, Michael A.
Thompson, Ruth M. - Jones, Ralph Almond
Thomson, Judith Helen - Petrini, Edward Peter
Thorne, Olive May - Bosiak, Joseph
Thorne, Sarah Chase - Howe, Thomas Atkinson
Tilley, Hazel Maud - Anair, Lloyd Robert
Tilton, Cora May - Mansfield, William Ira
Tilton, Frances Marie - Hyslop, Glen G.
Timko, Margaret N. - Clow, Barry L.
Tippett, Beverly L. - Dodge, Paul T., Jr.
Todd, Diane I. - Eagles, Charles Malcolmson
Toth, Kristina Ann - Gamache, Christopher Joseph
Toutaint, Patricia Ann - French, Ivo Shepard
Towle, Lois R. - Foss, Richard C.
Tracy, Mary Ellen (Withrow) - Marion, Gerald Patrick
Trask, Emma F. - Pickering, Fred C.
Trautwig, Carol - Nichols, Philip S., Jr.
Trazbony, Ferial Taher - Moussa, Fayez Hassan
Trisfontaine, Lois A. - Pineau, Phillip E.
Trottier, Wendy L. - Stockbridge, Mark A.
Tucker, Betsey - Hayes, Eben
Twombly, Lila Mabel - Joy, George Edwin
Twombly, Lizzie E. - Bickford, David M.
Twombly, Pauline - Walker, Gordon D.
Twombly, Phyllis A. - Boudreau, Robert T.
Twombly, Sadie P. - Brown, Richard I.
Twombly, Sandra L. - Bean, Dennis E.
Twombly, Virginia H. - Shepard, Wendell E.

Vachon, Esther Ann (Bristow) - Azotea, Beinvenido, Jr.
Vallee, Jane Pauline - Cochran, Guy Eugene
Valpey, Mary Edith - Bishop, Lewis Marshall
Van Epen, Rinske Titia - Maroni, Gennaro
van Ogtrop, Mary A. Jardine - McLeod, Wilson C.
Van Riper, Margaret E. - Ott, Melvin G.
Varney, Ida L. - Gault, Charles W.
Varney, Judith Ann - Ingoldsby, Karl Joseph

Veasey, Sadie E. - Battis, John H.
Vendetti, Shelli D. - Shumway, Aaron
Verzier, Marie Agnes - Gowen, Frank B.
Vincent, Cindy J. - Clifton, Peter R.
Vorel, Shirley (MacNeil) - Barnes, Oliver Willard

Wade, Nancy Lee - Marcoux, Dennis Edward
Wagner, Rachel Miriam - Wanne, Allen Theodore
Wahlstrom, Cheryl Fay - Thurber, John Spencer Tisdale
Waite, Junie L. (Sterling) - Margeson, Ramon W.
Wallace, Diana L. - Hawkins, Carl R.
Wallace, Gladys (Locke) - Harris, James N.
Wallingford, Jennie - Emery, Alden Chester
Walsh, Eileen M. - Stevens, E. Kevin
Walsh, Etta E. - Ashcroft, Herbert W.
Walsh, Mary E. - Barron, Edwin S.
Warburton, Leanne - Downs, James A.
Warburton, Margaret H. - Healey, Charles E.
Ward, Christine Ann - Lines, Alan
Ward, Margaret Lynne - Dunham, Richard M., Jr.
Waters, Edith (Wolfe) - Leaver, Robert M.
Watson, Abbie I. - Geddes, Kenneth D.
Watson, Florence A. - Goodwin, Ernest H.
Watson, Loraine E. - Watson, Jack D.
Weatherbee, Sandra A. - Doherty, Brad S.
Weeks, Addie Nina - McEwan, Frank W.
Weeks, Blanche M. - McCartney, John W.
Weeks, Candace S. - Hodder, Robert J.
Weeks, Carol A. - Laroche, Stephen E.
Weeks, Mary E. - Merrill, Charles L.
Weeks, Susan J. - Poulin, Robert J.
Weglars, Amy J. V. - Hoffman, Kenneth P.
Weinmann, Daisy E. (Wood) - Chase, Arthur F.
Welch, Ellen F. (Flagg) - Garneau, John M.
Weller, Cynthia J. - Bartlett, Timothy E.
Wells, Frances May - Martin, Paul Ronald
Wells, Gertrude L. - Simpson, Bruce W.
Wells, Olive M. - Simonds, Richard
Wells, Priscilla Alice - Parsons, Frank Waldo, Jr.
Werren, Enid B. - Herlihy, Robert P.
Wessell, Donna L. - Guilbault, Robert C.

Wessely, Debra L. - Hawkins, Carl R.
West, Barbara Jean - Zela, Peter Mark
West, Rita E. - Britton, Jonathan D.
West, Sheri Louise - Waldron, Brian Robert
Wheet, Lee Edna - Dawson, Robert William
White, Brenda A. - Stendor, William F.
White, Brenda Ann - Hill, Leo Lawrence
White, Eileen A. - Morrison, William J.
White, Eleanor J. - Stevens, Richard H.
White, Mary B. - Watson, John D.
White, Robin M. - Hempel, Paul J. III
Whitehouse, Cora B. - Roth, Theodore F.
Whitehouse, Effie R. - Pease, Alna L.
Whitehouse, Nellie C. - Foss, Frank W.
Whitehouse, Tracy E. - Brennan, Casey B.
Whitman, Deborah Louise - Walker, Stephen Arthur
Whitney, Cora A. (Robbins) - Prescott, George C.
Whitney, Florence G. - Butt, Earl A.
Widger, Barbara - Rumrill, Hamilton
Wiggin, Judith Lee - Tibbetts, Robert Oliver
Wight, Emma F. - Price, Amos R.
Wight, Florence A. - French, Arthur W.
Wilbur, Annastasia W. - Hutchinson, Leonard
Wilkens, Laurose - MacFayden, Donald E.
Wilkins, Elise Joanne - Pugh, Charles Chapman
Wilkinson, Sally A. - Griffin, Robert D.
Willard, Bernice M. - Brown, Raymond A.
Willard, Beulah E. - Green, Jay H.
Willard, Dian Florence - Stacey, Peter Martin
Willard, Ginger R. - Stockwell, Daniel C.
Willard, Linda I. - Gullage, Dannie C.
Willard, Ruby Florence - Stevens, Aaron D.
Willette, Sharon J. - Boyden, Joy W.
Wilson, Dorothy E. - Bebo, Nelson W.
Wilson, Myra E. (Pease) - Sanborn, Jeremiah W.
Winch, Ethel May (Smith) - Leavitt, Henry Frank
Witham, Jane Arlene - Provencal, Frank John
Wonoski, Deborah M. - Snow, Craig T.
Woodard, Audrey Mary - Munsey, James Jay
Woods, Kristen L. - Rodriguez, Paul M.
Wozmak, Karen E. - Scovill, Paul M.

Wright, Evelyn - Springer, Harold L.
Wright, Ola E. H. (Hillsgrove) - Knowles, Maitland Charles
Wyatt, Edith L. - Eaton, Frank G.
Wyatt, Helen A. - Perkins, Lorenzo H.
Wyatt, Helen Otis - Page, Frank Josiah

Yerxa, Clara Maud - Messer, Charles S.
York, Cora B. - Gilman, Ira
Young, Joy Marie - Brough, Kelly Steven
Young, Mary E. - Johnson, Charles A.

Zela, Coreen K. - Desilets, Douglas H.
Zilichovsky, Bertha - Ellsworth, Leon E.

DEATHS

ABBOTT,
George W., d. 6/16/1894 at 43/11/18; consumption; blacksmith; married; b. Haverhill; Hazen Abbott and Margaret Cushman

ABERLE,
Philip S., d. 11/22/1981 in Gilmanton; George Aberle and Isabella Robinson; b. 2/2/1927**

ADAMS,
George W., d. 1/29/1904 at 75/6; farmer; widower; b. Gilmanton; George W. Adams (Gilmanton) and Lydia Willard (Loudon)
Jennie C., d. 2/1/1920 at 63/7/25 in Laconia; housework; widow; b. Brookline; ----- Brooks; Pittsfield
Mary Jane, d. 4/6/1888 at 61/4/11; housewife; married; b. Gilmanton; Samuel Parsons (Gilmanton) and Jemima Cass (Loudon)

ADEL,
Beatrice E., d. 7/16/1973 at 61 in Laconia*; shoe worker; married; b. NH; Israel Willard and Georgie McClary
Daniel J., Jr., d. 10/6/1978 at 47 in Laconia; welder; married; b. NH; Daniel J. Adel, Sr. and Beatrice E. Willard
Daniel J., Sr., d. 12/11/1979 in Laconia; b. 7/14/1907**

ADKINS,
Virginia P., d. 4/29/2000 in Laconia; Ernest Parkinson and Angelina Leone; b. 12/3/1919**

AFFLERBACH,
William Francis, d. 12/31/1997 in Laconia; William Afflerbach and Elizabeth Buck; b. 12/15/1918**

AIKEN,
Jacob, d. 5/15/1905 at 87/2/18; farmer; widower; b. Barnstead; John Aiken

ALBERTY,
Wilbur J., d. 8/19/1945 at 66/10/18; machinist; widower; b. Gilmanton; James R. Alberty (Prattsville, NY) and Amy Butler (Tyringham, MA)

ALLEN,
David G., d. 1/2/1888 at 56/0/20; farmer; single; b. Gilmanton; Dudley Allen (Gilmanton) and Polly E. Edgerly (Gilmanton)
Levi B., d. 1/24/1919 at 81/7 in Laconia; mason; single; b. Gilmanton; Joseph Allen and Priscilla Tuttle; Smith Meetinghouse
Louisa H., d. 1/25/1892 at 74/4; housewife; widow; John Hutchinson
Sedgwick W., d. 11/30/1920 at 91/5 in Gilmanton; contractor; widower; b. Shelburne, VT; Abbie Isham; Irasburg, VT

ALLEY,
Robert M., d. 3/27/2001 in Laconia; Charles Alley and Harriet Chase

AMELL,
Darrel L., Sr., d. 1/26/1982 in Laconia; Joseph Amell and Elizabeth LaFlower; b. 4/26/1932**

AMIRAULT,
Eleanor M., d. 5/29/1985 in Wolfeboro; Charles McCluskey and Virginia Hooten; b. 10/7/1916**

ANDERSEN,
George Henry, d. 5/23/1973 at 67 in Gilmanton; custodian; married; b. MA; Henry Albert Andersen and Anna Kristine Ruud

ARAGONA,
Bianca, d. 2/6/1967 at 82 in Laconia; housewife; married; b. Italy; Nicola Marcellini

ARLIN,
Harlan A., d. 9/28/1945 at 74/1/16; retired; b. Loudon; Augustus Arlin (Canterbury) and Abigail ----- (Loudon)

ARNOLD,
Guy M., d. 1/28/1992 in Lebanon; Frederick Arnold and Alberta Mather

ASHTON,
Jonathan A., d. 10/25/1996 in Lebanon; Richard V. Ashton and Helen Archer; b. 11/19/1950**

AUSTIN,
Dorothy L., d. 6/9/1991 in Hanover; William M. Austin and Sylvia E. Holford; b. 4/11/1925**
Peter F., d. 9/1/1990 in Laconia; Gerald L. Austin, Jr. and Rita Morin
Sarah D., d. 7/24/1902 at 66/9/5; housemaid; widow; b. Andover, MA; Hugh Truland and Sarah White
Walter Richard, d. 5/18/1961 at 58 in Hanover; none [occ.]; married; b. Arlington, MA; Charles Austin and Florence Peasley

AVERY,
Arthur, d. 12/24/1906 at 84; farmer; single; b. Alton; ----- (Alton) and ----- (Alton)
Bertha, d. 6/26/1912 at 14/0/6; single; b. Laconia; Chester Avery (Meredith) and Mary Hilliard (Laconia)
Blanche M., d. 12/19/1957 at 71 in Laconia*; housewife; widow; b. Gilmanton; James H. Beck and Martha J. Leighton
Carrie B., d. 1/30/1935 at 63/9/7 in Rochester; housewife; married; b. Laconia; Asa T. Page and Abbie Jackson; Gilmanton
George H., d. 2/8/1957 at 74 in Laconia*; teamster; married; b. Strafford; John Avery and Hannah -----
Stanton C., d. 10/15/1918 at 18/4/3; laborer; single; b. Barnstead; Chester Avery and Mamie Hilliard

AVISA,
Joseph, d. 11/7/1978 at 84 in Laconia; farmer; widower; b. Lithuania; Joseph Avisa and Caroline -----

AYER,
Blanche L., d. 1/6/1957 at 79 in Laconia*; housewife; widow; b. Gilmanton; John R. Sawyer and Mary Marsh
Daniel S., d. 9/13/1920 at 88/5/28 in Gilmanton; farmer; widower; b. Gilmanton; Francis Ayer and Susan Gale; Smith Meetinghouse
Frank, d. 3/8/1926 at 75/11/16 in Concord; farmer; single; Pine Grove
Walter H., d. 1/29/1956 at 83 in Laconia*; farmer; married; b. Gilmanton; Daniel S. Ayer and Nancy C. Canney

AYERS,
Ann E., d. 7/3/1917 at 83/1/7 in Laconia; widow; Joseph Plummer and Sally Lamprey
Joshua W., d. 3/3/1888 at 60/11/1; farmer; married; b. Barnstead; Samuel Ayers (Greenland) and Sarah S. Ayers (Greenland)
Mary J., d. 5/2/1905 at 75/10/19; housewife; widow; b. Barnstead; James Langley and Susan Drew

BABCOCK,
Helen Lucy, d. 6/3/1997 in Gilmanton; Constant Shlaitas and Mary Waishmoras; b. 6/23/1917**

BACHELDER,
Isabelle F., d. 7/2/1922 at 17

BADGER,
Frances A., d. 12/31/1927 at 59/8/26 in Boscawen; Smith Meetinghouse
Hannah E., d. 7/27/1904 at 70/7/12; housewife; widow; b. Gilmanton; Francis Ayer (Barnstead) and Susan Gale (Gilmanton)
Joseph, d. 12/20/1903 at 86/5/23; farmer; married; b. Belmont; William Badger (Gilmanton) and Hannah Cogswell (Atkinson)
Judith, d. 6/6/1928 at 18/8/13 in Laconia; Smith Meetinghouse
Mabel M., d. 8/6/1927 at 54/6/2 in Laconia; married; b. Belmont; Asa Morrison and Susan Maxfield; Smith Meetinghouse

BAGLEY,
Charles W., d. 4/16/1977 at 71 in Laconia; plumber; widower; b. NH; Erastus Bagley
Elizabeth G., d. 11/2/1976 at 74 in Wolfeboro; housewife; married; b. NH; Sceva Romprey and Gertrude Sawyer
Frank E., d. 7/17/1938 at 78/8/10 in Gilmanton; clerk; widower; b. Boston, MA; John J. Bagley (Ireland) and Rosiana McGee (Ireland)

BAKER,
Elsie L., d. 12/14/1903 at 5/11; b. Gilmanton; Fred L. Baker (NS) and Mary A. Greene (Gilmanton)
John C., d. 3/9/1896 at –; heart failure; farmer; married

BALCOM,
Laura A., d. 3/27/1926 at 82/5/22 in Alton; retired; widow; Smith Meeting House

BALL,
Ada Honorah, d. 5/14/1961 at 93 in Manchester*; ret. nurse; widow; b. ON; William F. Campbell and Anna Haight

BALLARD,
Clarence, d. 3/4/1941 at 64/0/23*; physician; widower; b. Concord; Charles Ballard and Cynthia Dunlap
Maude G., d. 9/30/1940 at 64/6/10*; housewife; married; b. Gilmanton; Horace T. Gilman (Gilmanton) and Hannah M. Edgerly (Gilmanton)

BANON,
Mary E., d. 7/13/1900 at 20/10/7; housewife; married; b. NS; A. S. Walsh (NS) and Sarah Fintsa (NS)

BAPTISTE,
Lillian K., d. 9/21/1943 at 84/2/10; widow; b. NY; ----- Roylance and Georgianna Gillette (NY)

BARR,
Otis D., d. 1/1/1983 in Concord; Otis Barr and Clara Alride; b. 2/3/1918**

BARRON,
George P., d. 2/14/1898 at 52/8/23; laborer; widower; b. Boston, MA; John C. Barron (England) and Elizabeth J. King (Boston, MA)

BARTHOLOMEW,
Carrie K., d. 12/25/1951 at 89/4/6 in Gilmanton; housewife; widow; b. Exeter; John H. Kimball and Mary F. Moulton

BARTLETT,
George W., d. 4/11/1924 at 67 in Gilmanton; lumbering; widower; b. Center Harbor; James Bartlett and Eliza Davis; Meredith

BASSETT,
Thomas Henry, Jr., d. 12/29/1997 in Laconia; Thomas Henry Bassett, Sr. and Eunice Caldwell; b. 12/11/1918**

BATCHELDER,
Albert Wesley, d. 4/15/1974 at 47 in Gilmanton; lumberman; married; b. NH; Wilky Batchelder and Florence Emerson
Edward V., d. 4/30/1916 at 3/2/16 in Gilmanton; C. Cresby (PA) and Edith G. Batchelder (Gilmanton)
John, d. 11/24/1952 at 89 in Center Harbor; laborer; widower; b. NH; George S. Batchelder and Sarah J. Bickford
Lucinda, d. 5/21/1939 at 80/0/2 in Gilmanton; housekeeper; married; b. W. Fairlee, VT; Daniel Bullard and Clara Batchelder (W. Fairlee, VT)
Myrtle, d. 11/10/1896 at 0/1/11; b. Gilmanton; C. M. Batchelder (Loudon) and Dora M. Staples
Nathan, d. 4/17/1900 at 74/10/28; farmer; married; b. Gilmanton
Susan A., d. 2/14/1920 at 80/4/18 in Laconia; housework; widow; b. Loudon; Loudon Center
Thomas C., d. 6/30/1944 at 83/7/24; lawyer; married; b. Gilmanton; Samuel Batchelder (Loudon) and Martha Cogswell (Gilmanton)
William N., d. 4/6/1918 at 69/7/14; wholesale prov. dlr.; married; b. Gilmanton; William B. Batchelder (Gilford) and Mary Sargent (Canterbury)

BATTIS,
Harry, d. 4/28/1899 at 22/2/22; laborer; married; b. Loudon; John Battis (Canterbury) and Lydia Bumans (Salisbury)
John F., d. 12/26/1912 at 82/3/26; black; farmer; b. Canterbury; Samuel Battis
Walter H., d. 9/10/1895 at 20; dropsy, heart failure; laborer; single; b. Gilmanton; John F. Battis

BEAN,
Clara F., d. 11/26/1923 at 65
Elizabeth, d. 1/15/1902 at 94/8/26; widow; b. Boston, MA; John King
Hannah E., d. 2/2/1920 at 73/0/19 in Laconia; teacher; single; b. Gilmanton; Josiah Bean and Harriet E. Beadley; Beech Grove
Harriet E., d. 4/22/1910 at 85/5/25; old age; widow; b. Dracut, MA; Benjamin Bradley (Dracut, MA) and Clarissa Fox (Dracut, MA)

Helen J., d. 6/14/1922 at 64
Hugh A., d. 2/5/1967 at 60 in Concord; mechanic; married; b. VT; David Bean and Sadie Kidder
Josiah J., d. 3/4/1903 at 82/1/20; farmer; married; b. Sandwich; Josiah Bean (Sandwich) and Olive Sanborn (Dracut, MA)
Rita S., d. 8/1/1991 in Laconia; Frank Santy and Irene Chase
Weymouth, d. 2/15/1892 at 86; farmer; married

BEARY,
William Aloysius, d. 4/14/1993 in Gilmanton; Thomas Beary and Mary Allen

BEAUCHEMIN,
Francis, d. 7/1/1940 at 66; laborer; single; b. Sherbrooke, PQ

BECK,
Alice E., d. 12/16/1975 at 74 in Laconia; nursing attend.; widow; b. NH; Selden Rollins and Alma Ellis
Charles William, d. 2/17/1952 at 72 in Farmington*; treer; widower; b. NH; Horace Beck and Marie Sanderson
Ernest Smith, d. 2/22/1951 at 51/5/26 in Alton; electrician; married; b. MA; Smith C. Beck and Lucy J. Allen
Harriet, d. 8/27/1908 at 85/11/15; widow
Hulda A., d. 1/4/1908 at 27/6/26; housewife; married; b. Dover; W. Beck (Effingham) and Amanda Ricker (Dover)
James H., d. 4/25/1941 at 84/11/10; farmer; widower; b. Gilmanton; Manasseh Beck (Barnstead) and Harriet Wentworth (Barnstead)
John S., d. 2/8/1923 at 79
Julia M., d. 10/18/1916 at 77/5/2 in Gilmanton; housewife; married; Nathaniel Hill (Haverhill) and Mary Corliss (Haverhill)
Mamie Margaret, d. 1/18/1949 at 68 in Laconia; needle maker; divorced; b. MA; Augustus Stetson and Mary Connors
Manasah, d. 12/27/1907 at 84/9/22; farmer; married; b. Farmington; Eben Beck (Barnstead) and Thirza Holmes (Barnstead)
Martha Jane, d. 4/14/1923 at 76

BECKLEY,
Lewis Frederick, d. 1/8/1964 at 55 in Laconia*; assembler; married; b. Derry; George H. Beckley and Lillian Williams

BEDFORD,
Doris Mildred, d. 4/16/1998 in Gilmanton; George Daigneault and Mildred Riel; b. 5/31/1924**

BEEDE,
Bessie Marion, d. 4/7/1993 in Gilmanton; James Wilkins and Elizabeth Irving
Celia M., d. 10/3/1935 at 86/6/27 in Laconia; at home; married; b. Gilmanton; Henry E. Marsh and Hannah Marsh; Beech Grove
David S., d. 5/20/1899 at 90/1/28; farmer; married; b. Sandwich; Moses Beede and Miriam Peaslee
Elizabeth V., d. 1/1/1901 at 86/10; housewife; widow
Herbert, d. 9/7/1948 at 92/4/12; carpenter (ret.); widower; b. Gilmanton; David Beede (Sandwich) and Elizabeth Varney (Dover)

BENNETT,
Alberto A., d. 4/7/1939 at 79/8/21 in Wolfeboro*; minister; widower; b. Bambridge, NY; Edwin L. Bennett (NY) and Mary McCall (NY)
Ella S., d. 1/16/1933 at 69/9/24 in Gilmanton; housework; married; b. Clinton, NY; Charles W. Stone and Electa Hull; Smith Meetinghouse
Ernest L., d. 1/23/1981 in Laconia; Samuel Bennett and Mary E. Hayes; b. 3/13/1913**
George T., d. 12/16/1925 at 53/7/10 in Gilmanton; laborer; single; b. Ireland; John Bennett and Jane Mullen; Ware, MA

BERG,
Sven Alban, d. 5/4/1970 at 91 in Epsom; engineer; married; b. Sweden; ----- and Anna Stegren

BERRY,
Ella A., d. 5/12/1899 at 41; housewife; married; b. Gilmanton; Reuben Page
George, d. 11/2/1894 at 74/8; asthma with heart trouble; mill hand; widower; b. Strafford; John Berry and Betsy Hall
Lulie, d. 11/12/1935 at 58/3/11 in Farmington; housekeeper; widow; b. Danvers, MA; John Foss and Ella Watson; Pine Grove
Mary L., d. 7/11/1979 in Gilmanton; Francis Howard and Mary E. Gallagher

Percy Nelson, Jr., d. 10/25/1999 in Gilmanton; Percy N. Berry, Sr. and Stella Hall

Walter C., d. 12/15/1971 at 71 in Gilmanton; contractor; married; b. MA; Fred S. Berry and Ella May Stevens

BERTRAND,
Jamie A., d. 7/20/1981 in Pittsfield; James M. Bertrand and Sandra A. Seaman

BICKFORD,
Arthur R., d. 2/5/1950 at 77/3/4 in Gilmanton; farm. & carp.; married; b. Franklin; David Bickford and Wealthy A. Smith

David, d. 1/5/1915 at 80/6/20 in Gilmanton I. W.; carpenter; widower; David Bickford (Rochester) and Elizabeth Jenness (Rochester)

David A., Jr., d. 10/10/1973 at 0/3 in Gilmanton; b. NH; David A. Bickford, Sr. and Linda Sanborn

David Frank, d. 6/21/1953 at 87 in Laconia; laborer; single; b. Dover; David Bickford and Weltha Smith

Edna, d. 1/14/1994 in Concord; Wayland Locke and Bertha Emerson; b. 2/17/1907**

Emily E., d. 4/14/1911 at 63/10; housekeeper; widow

Ida M., d. 1/30/1958 at 74 in Exeter*; housewife; widow; b. Barnstead; Mark Brewster and ----- Merrill

Myrtie E., d. 4/10/1900 at 30/1/18; housemaid; single; Riley M. Bickford

R. M., d. 8/16/1907 at 70/5/25; farmer; married

Ruth Mary, d. 10/4/1969 at 45 in Gilmanton; home; married; b. NH; Ernest W. Holt and Grace Hoyt

Weltha A., d. 8/11/1904 at 62/11/6; housewife; married; b. Loudon; Ransom J. Smith and Nancy G. Wells

BLACKEY,
Harold, d. 6/5/1966 at 72 in Gilmanton; hotel prop. retired; b. Brockton, MA; John W. Blackey and Roseina Brown

Mary J., d. 8/17/1990 in Laconia; Charles E. Briggs and Jessie L. Lintot

Rosiena B., d. 9/7/1943 at 82/6/28; hotel keeper; widow; b. Boston, MA; Edward Brown (Holland) and Elizabeth Thombiel (Ireland)

BLACKMAR,
Mortimer, d. 4/20/1942 at 74/9/17*; shoemaker; married; b. Gonic; Charles E. Mortimer (England)

BLACKSTONE,
Jennie B., d. 8/15/1894 at 0/1/14; cholera infantum; b. Laconia; Sumner Blackstone (Groton) and Lillian I. Welcome (Hill)
Winfield Lord, d. 6/16/1899 at 0/6; b. Gilmanton; Sumner E. Blackstone (Groton) and Lilla Wilcomb (Hill)

BLAISDELL,
Melissa H., d. 10/13/1978 at 85 in Epsom; school teacher, ret.; married; b. NH; Moses Jacobs and Mary Clark
Minnie, d. 5/20/1948 at 79/8/28; housewife; widow; b. Gilmanton; Albert F. Page (Gilmanton) and Mary J. Page (Barnstead)
Willis S., d. 5/24/1984 in Concord; William Blaisdell and Jennie -----

BLAKE,
Earl Henry, Jr., d. 6/27/1944 at 0/0/9*; b. Rochester; Earl H. Blake (Glencliffe) and Alice Dimond (Gilmanton)
George F., d. 10/2/1917 at 69/9/2 in Barnstead; carpenter; married; John Blake and Mary Buzzell
Jeremiah, d. 1/30/1890 at 89/10; physician; married; Enoch Blake (Hampton Falls) and Hannah Eastman (Kensington)
Joseph W., d. 4/3/1895 at 79/5/28; old age; married
Laural A., d. 8/14/1929 at 72/0/11 in Gilmanton; dairyman; widower; b. Peacham, VT; Daniel Blake and Marietta Conant; Smith Meetinghouse
Lucia D., d. 3/19/1905 at 95/7/16; housewife; widow; b. Sanbornton; Samuel C. Dudley
Mary A., d. 4/11/1903 at 86/0/9; widow; b. Barnstead; Abram Bunker (Barnstead) and Polly C. Sinclair (Barnstead)
Mary Elizabeth, d. 6/30/1914 at 51/10/8 in Whitman, MA; married

BLESH,
Rudolf P., d. 8/26/1985 in Gilmanton; Abraham L. Blesh and Belle Pickett

BLUNDEN,
Henry N., d. 8/29/1953 at 25 in Gilmanton; shoeworker; married; b. NH; Alvin J. Blunden and Mildred Cass

BOARDMAN,
Elliot Sheffeld, d. 1/7/1963 at 68 in Laconia; bank v. pres.; married; b. Bangor, ME; Samuel H. Boardman and Mary Sheffeld

BOISVERT,
Cade R., d. 4/26/2000 in Lebanon; Keith Lafoe and Ryann Livingston; b. 9/21/1999**

BONNIER,
Joseph Edmore, d. 5/3/2000 in Gilmanton; Edmore Bonnier and Florence -----; b. 7/18/1910**

BORDEAU,
Florence Cogswell, d. 7/5/1968 at 70 in Laconia*; housewife; widow; b. NH; Walter J. Edgerly and Anna Cogswell
Jason James, d. 9/4/1965 at 73 in Laconia*; laborer; married; b. St. Albans, VT; Frank Bordeau and Julia -----

BORIS,
Catherine, d. 2/12/1996 in Laconia; Martin Verbeck and Catherine -----; b. 11/26/1913**
Joseph Michael, d. 7/15/1997 in Laconia; Michael Boris and Antonia Shinkunas

BORJESON,
Frank Walter, d. 6/22/1993 in Gilmanton; William Borjeson and Caroline Larson

BOSIAK,
daughter, d. 1/27/1964 at – in Concord; b. Concord; Joseph Bosiak and Olive M. Thorne
Stephen, d. 10/17/1968 at 72 in Concord; farmer; married; b. Poland; Paul Bosiak and Jarocha -----

BOUCHARD,
Eliza M., d. 7/29/1979 in Laconia; Edward Geddis and Emma Plough

BOWEN,
Thomas R., d. 4/13/1941 at 68; laborer; widower

BOWERS,
Martha C., d. 4/30/1903 at 50/6/23; widow; Joseph B. Durrell (Gilmanton) and A. E. Shannon (Gilmanton)

BOWLES,
Rebecca, d. 5/9/1927 at 41/1/4 in Gilmanton; housework; married; b. Montpelier, VT; ----- Monette; Boscawen

BOYCE,
Kenneth G., d. 11/8/1988 in Laconia; George S. Boyce and Margaret E. Clark

BOYD,
Emma C., d. 11/23/1981 in Laconia; ----- and Violet Gray; b. 10/24/1931**
Mary Gertrude, d. 6/11/1953 at 68 in Rochester; cook; widow; b. Dover; Everett Emery and Ellen Welch

BRACKETT,
Ann M., d. 4/6/1911 at 82/11/22; housekeeper; divorced; b. Gilmanton; John French (Gilmanton) and Lucy T. Prescott (Gilmanton)

BRADLEY,
Charles, d. 7/14/1897 at 72; painter; married
Mary A., d. 2/14/1906 at 84; widow; David Cilley and Johanna Smith (Gilmanton)

BRAGG,
Edith, d. 8/1/1936 at 56/10/29 in Pittsfield; married
George E., d. 11/7/1912 at 31/5/23; laborer; married; b. ME; Wilbur Bragg

BRAKE,
Carol Ann, d. 12/14/1951 at 0/3/26 in Concord*; child; b. NH; [not stated] and Margaret Joyce Brake

BRETT,
Martha A., d. 9/18/1955 at 90 in Gilmanton; housewife; widow; b. Greenville, ME; Albion Tyler and Olive Hough

BREWSTER,
Elsie M., d. 2/1/1929 at 26/9/1 in Barnstead; Pine Grove
Mark W., d. 3/8/1918 at 57/8/14; farmer; married; b. Barnstead;
  Nathaniel Brewster (Strafford) and Sarah Babb (Strafford)

BRICKETT,
Gilbert, d. 3/17/1918 at 76/0/14; farmer; widower; b. Gilmanton;
  Abbott Brickett and Theodate Davis

BROADBENT,
Carrie L., d. 4/19/1929 at 77/1/10 in Gilmanton; housewife; married;
  b. Middleton, WI; Lynus Palmer and Jane Downing; Brockport,
  NY

BROCK,
daughter, d. 8/6/1903 at –; b. Gilmanton; Irving C. Brock (Pittsfield)
  and Caroline Dowst (Epsom)
daughter, d. 4/7/1907 at 0/0/7; b. Gilmanton; Irving C. Brock
  (Pittsfield) and Carrie L. Dowst (Epsom)
Caroline L., d. 12/21/1927 at 68/8/10 in Pittsfield; housework;
  married; b. Epsom; Ozen Dowst and Martha Griffin; Smith
  Meetinghouse
Irving C., d. 9/16/1944 at 75/2/29*; farmer; married; b. Pittsfield;
  John Brock (Pittsfield) and Rose Taylor (Pittsfield)
Vivian Izalee, d. 12/15/1909 at 0/2; b. Gilmanton; Irving C. Brock
  (Pittsfield) and Carrie L. Dowal (Epsom)

BROOKS,
Charles A., d. 4/25/1921 at 71/2/24 in Gilmanton; farmer; married;
  b. Pittsfield; Samuel Brooks and ----- Babb; Pittsfield
Lucy A., d. 3/17/1923 at 77

BROUGH,
Robert Arthur, d. 8/30/1996 in Manchester; Earl J. Brough and Eva
  C. Delisle; b. 10/29/1929**

BROWN,
Alfred M., d. 10/30/1950 at 77 in Gilmanton; farmer; married; b.
  NH; Robert C. Brown and Ann Babb
Arthur George, d. 8/19/1963 at 86 in Laconia; motorman; married;
  b. Gilford; John Brown and Elmina Bean

Beverly May, d. 8/30/1930 at 0/0/0 in Laconia; b. Laconia; George C. Brown and Lois M. Brech; Beech Grove

Carrie E., d. 7/20/1902 at 0/10/3; b. Pittsfield; Charlemagne Brown (Gilmanton) and Annie E. Griffin (Gilmanton)

Earl D., d. 2/22/1980 in Pittsfield; John P. Brown and Florence Day

Edna M., d. 1/25/1957 at 90 in Gilmanton; housewife; widow; b. Gilmanton; Richard W. Marsh and Hannah Peaslee

Edna Myrtle, d. 6/16/1970 at 70 in Epsom; housekeeper; single; b. NH; Alfred M. Brown and Edna Marsh

Frank J., d. 8/17/1921 at 62/8/9 in Gilmanton; farmer; widower; b. Gilmanton; Joseph Brown and Anna Rollins; Smith Meetinghouse

Fred M., d. 1/5/1943 at 71/11/27*; foreman; widower; b. Loudon; James Brown (Ireland)

George C., d. 7/26/1979 in Laconia; Dr. George H. Brown and Lizzie Orange; b. 7/6/1894**

George H., d. 12/5/1903 at 50/8/2; physician; married; b. Haverhill, MA; Horace Brown (Sanbornton) and Valeria Clark (Sanbornton)

Georgianna M., d. 4/28/1923 at 80

Grace Grapes, d. 1/11/1968 at 83 in Gilmanton; cook, ret.; married; b. NH; Albert Grapes

John J., d. 11/12/1918 at 61; married; b. Gilmanton; John Brown (Ellsworth) and Mary H. Downing (Ellsworth)

Jonathan, d. 3/26/1888 at 86/7; farmer; married; b. Chichester; James Brown (Hampton) and ----- (Hampton)

Joseph, d. 3/11/1901 at 63/5/7; farmer; married; b. Loudon; Jeremiah Brown (Loudon) and Betsy Arlin (Barrington)

Kathryn C., d. 4/8/1969 at 67 in FL; home; married; b. NJ; Eclariu Treat

Leonora, d. 10/23/1934 at 82/3/22 in Manchester; widow; b. Pittsfield; Simeon Jones and Lucy M. Dow; Smith Meetinghouse

Lois May, d. 6/23/1981 in Gilmanton; Joseph H. Breck and Nellie Jones; b. 1/19/1892**

Mary Ann, d. 2/5/1892 at 88/1; housewife; widow; b. Canterbury; Leavitt Clough (Canterbury) and Abigail Morrill (Canterbury)

Owen Jeddie, d. 7/16/1887 at 1/7/20; b. Gilmanton; Joseph Brown (Loudon) and Georgianna M. Rollins (Gilmanton)

Raymond A., d. 5/4/1982 in Concord; Percy Brown and Mildred Rogers; b. 2/15/1913**

Rebecca, d. 12/7/1955 at 60 in Concord; housewife; married; b. Biddeford, ME; Byron Dolloff and Ida Roberts
Richard I., d. 1/15/1980 in Concord; Alfred M. Brown and Edna Marsh; b. 6/18/1902**
Susan, d. 3/12/1918 at 77/1/19; married; b. Gilmanton; John Garrick (Scotland) and Mary Clucas (St. Johns, NB)
Valeria C., d. 6/12/1906 at 82/3/6; widow; b. Tilton; Archibald S. Clark (Tilton) and Priscilla Chase (Tilton)

BROWNING,
George, d. 3/8/1974 at 74 in Gilmanton; foreman, ret.; married; b. VT

BRUNELLE,
Elise Marie, d. 6/8/1990 in Hanover; Dale Brunelle and Lynne M. Rogalski

BUNKER,
Daniel, d. 11/25/1945 at 72/10/0; farmer; married; b. Barnstead; Daniel Bunker (Barnstead) and Hannah Tilton (Pittsfield)
Florence, d. 6/19/1967 at 85 in Concord; housewife; widow; b. Loudon; Hiram A. B. Hilliard and Virginia Osgood
Fred R., d. 9/5/1946 at 86/8/16 in Lancaster; minister; married; b. Prentissvale, PA; William H. Bunker (PA) and Sarah Kittridge (PA)
Hannah T., d. 12/27/1923 at 75
Hiram O., d. 6/10/1897 at 62/2/7; farmer; widower; b. Gilmanton; Silas Bunker (Gilmanton) and Sarah Merrow (Milton)
Mary A., d. 1/23/1914 at 80/8/27 in Gilmanton I. W.; widow; Hiram Lerthers (Lee) and Mary A. Elliott (Lee)
Melvin C., d. 7/7/1989 in Gilmanton; Daniel Bunker and Florence L. Hilliard

BURBANK,
Alonzo, d. 2/17/1905 at 66/9/15; laborer; married; b. Hopkinton
George, d. 6/16/1941 at 64/3/20*; laborer; single; b. Gilmanton; Alonzo Burbank (Contoocook) and Lucia Dustin (Haverhill)
Ida L., d. 10/26/1930 at 60/11/8 in New Durham; widow; b. Rochester; George W. Varney and Nancy -----; Smith Meetinghouse
Lucia A., d. 4/7/1907 at 56; cook; widow; b. Haverhill; Calvin Dustin

BURDETT,
Leonard D., d. 10/19/1983 in Gilmanton; Leonard F. Burdett and Mildred Munsey; b. 4/24/1917**

BURGESS,
Benjamin F., Jr., d. 3/17/1922 at 68

BURKE,
Thomas Hill, d. 11/2/1913 at 26/11/26; single; b. Lynn, MA; William J. Burke (Lynn, MA) and Carrie A. Roberts (Melvin Village)

BURNET,
Henry, d. 6/20/1937 at 63/8/28 in Gilmanton; gas sta. prop.; married; b. New York, NY; Henry Burnet and Matilda Lord; Union, Laconia

BURNS,
Thomas F., d. 8/11/1981 in Concord; Richard A. Burns and Mary Kelley; b. 2/20/1913**

BURRES,
Charles Floyd, d. 4/30/1967 at 81 in Gilmanton; caretaker; widower; b. Gilmanton; George Burres and Flora Marsh
Charlotte, d. 8/1/1942 at 59/2/15; housewife; married; b. St. John, NB; John Elliott (St. John, NB) and Mary ----- (St. John, NB)
Ed Leslie, d. 1/15/1921 at 1/0/18 in Gilmanton; b. Gilmanton; Orman Burres and Eva Jones; Smith Meetinghouse
Orman L., d. 4/1/1925 at 38/10/17 in Gilmanton; laborer; married; b. Gilmanton; George Burres and Flora Marsh; Smith Meetinghouse

BURROUGHS,
Flora, d. 4/22/1893 at 25; consumption; housewife; married; b. Gilmanton; Nehemiah Marsh
Frederick P., d. 1/14/1902 at 93/0/6; wheelwright; widower; b. Amesbury, MA; George Burroughs and Sukey Patten
Lois G., d. 4/23/1894 at 86; old age; housewife; married

BUTLER,
Annie, d. 5/17/1897 at 41/5/5; married; b. NY; James Johnson (Ireland) and Isabelle Renney (Ireland)

BUTMAN,
Doris A., d. 3/11/2001 in Laconia; Hy Bernson and Jennie -----; b. 9/20/1931**
Ralph Leonard, d. 8/22/1999 in Gilmanton I. W.; Roland Butman and Lucy -----; b. 8/23/1926**

BUZZELL,
Ann, d. 11/28/1901 at 56/0/12; housewife; married; b. Salem, MA; John Colvin (Salem, MA) and ----- (Salem, MA)
Rhoda, d. 4/16/1888 at 72; housewife; married

CABANA,
Gertrude, d. 9/11/1935 at 55/5/24 in Laconia; at home; married; b. Belmont; William Downs; Pine Grove

CALDON,
Joan Rachel, d. 3/7/1953 at 0/0/9 in Laconia; b. NH; Winston D. Caldon and Loise Gallagher

CAMPBELL,
Annie H., d. 10/27/1907 at 56/11/27; housekeeper; widow; b. Union, ON; James Haight (New York, NY) and Sarah G. Wright
Frank, d. 6/18/1907 at 67/6/19; insurance agent; married; b. Toronto, Canada; Alexander Campbell (Ireland) and Elizabeth Berry (Ireland)

CANNEY,
daughter, d. 4/1/1928 at – in Gilmanton; b. Gilmanton; Forrest S. Canney and Lura Davis; private cem.
Forrest A., d. 6/21/1904 at 26/10/7; clerk; single; b. Lynn, MA; Lafayette Canney (Tuftonboro) and Mary E. Tebbetts (Wolfeboro)
Helen A., d. 7/11/1948 at 80/0/20*; at home; widow; b. Plymouth; James Nelson (Plymouth) and Ellen Lynch (Louisville, KY)
Mina Belle, d. 12/9/1919 at 56/6/17 in Gilmanton; housewife; married; b. Strafford; Charles H. Perkins and Eliza Evans; Alton
William, d. 6/30/1906 at 92/5/22; wheelwright; widower; b. Tuftonboro; John Canney

CARLSON,
Charles K., d. 1/6/1954 at 6 in Gilmanton; b. Concord; Fred H. Carlson and Marion Brill

CARMAN,
Henry V., d. 11/17/1986 in Concord; Henry Carman and Ellen Crawford; b. 8/1/1915**

CARR,
John H., d. 9/16/1890 at 48; farmer; married; b. Gilmanton; ----- (Gilmanton) and Ruth Osgood (Gilmanton)

CARROLL,
William H., d. 12/10/1971 at 62 in Gilmanton; ret. banker; single; b. MA; John P. Carroll and Margaret McDonald

CARTER,
Frank A., d. 6/5/1888 at 41; railroadman; married; b. Concord; Abial Carter (Concord) and Nancy Morrill (Concord)
Grady Graham, d. 11/17/1932 at 22 in Gilmanton; U. S. Marines; single; b. Waterson, SC; R. M. Carter and ----- Carter; Green Pond, SC

CASEY,
Felix Anthony, d. 5/15/1998 in Gilmanton; John F. Casey and Mabel -----; b. 6/14/1923**

CASSERLY,
James J., d. 4/29/1957 at 64 in Concord; janitor; married; b. New York, NY; Richard J. Casserly and Mary Ann Gaffney
Sarah Ellie, d. 6/7/1962 at 63 in Concord; companion; widow; b. Martins Ferry, OH; Charles Stone and Mary Ellis

CASTALDO,
Frank, d. 10/23/1991 in Concord; Michael Castaldo and Elizabeth Castaldo

CASWELL,
George Edwin, d. 11/12/1939 at 60/11/20 in Dover*; belt maker; single; b. Strafford; George W. Caswell (Strafford) and Emma G. Ham (Barnstead)

CAVEN,
Alfred D., d. 8/13/2001 in Gilmanton; Donald Caven and Lilian White; b. 2/2/1917**

CAVERLY,
Abbie H., d. 4/16/1921 at 78/10/28 in Manchester; widow; b. Center Harbor; Uriah Hanscom and Mehitable Twombly
John Aaron, d. 5/8/1915 at 75/2/11 in Manchester; teamster; married; Stephen Caverly and Susan T. Hanscom
Mary, d. 9/23/1903 at 88/4/28; single; b. Strafford; John Caverly (Barrington) and Olive Jenness (Lee)

CHAFFEE,
Florence M., d. 3/10/1983 in Laconia; Daniel Dickey Mearns and Margaret Ann Crosier

CHAMBERLAIN,
Ada Bertha, d. 2/11/1959 at 93 in Laconia*; housewife; widow; b. Barnstead; David Emerson and Isabelle Frances Emerson
Charles Alva, d. 11/1/1998 in Gilmanton; Ora Alva Chamberlain and Dorothy Hamlin; b. 9/12/1918**
Charles H., d. 11/24/1921 at 75/7/26; farmer; married; b. Boston, MA; Moses Chamberlain and Annie Harper; Beech Grove
Harry Irving, d. 6/17/1973 at 86 in Rochester*; farmer; married; b. NH; Charles Chamberlain and Bertha A. Emerson
Robert W., d. 9/12/1985 in Gilmanton; Leroy Chamberlain and Josephine Jayne

CHAMBERS,
Emma M., d. 4/3/1945 at 68/7/3*; at home; widow; b. Gilmanton; Andrew Marsh (Gilmanton) and Martha ----- (Chelsea, MA)

CHAMPAGNE,
Herve G., Jr., d. 9/5/1990 in Laconia; Herve G. Champagne, Sr. and Yvonne Nault
John Rene, d. 9/1/1973 at 15 in Gilmanton; student; single; b. NH; Jean Champagne and Shirley Baker
Norman Rudolph, d. 9/1/1999 in Gilmanton; Harvey G. Champagne and Yvonne G. Nault

CHAPMAN,
son, d. 6/26/1945 at 0/0/0*; b. Laconia; Herbert D. Chapman (Westerly, RI) and Marie Deans (Phippsburg, ME)
Benjamin W., d. 1/19/1892 at 55/10; farmer; married
Herbert D., d. 6/28/1947 at 52/5/9; machinist; married; b. Westerly, RI; Herbert D. Chapman (Noank, CT) and Mabel Palmer (Stonington, CT)
Sarah Chase, d. 1/23/1892 at 65; housewife; widow
Sarah P., d. 9/6/1889 at 93/2/10; housewife; widow; b. Meredith; John Bryant (Meredith) and ----- Bickford
Walter H., d. 11/29/1907 at 0/3/10; b. Plymouth; Fred Chapman (Haverhill) and Harriett Hart (Corinth, VT)

CHASE,
Arthur F., d. 9/23/1971 at 89 in Rochester*; store owner; married; b. MA; Frank Chase and Mary Tappan
Bertha N., d. 8/11/1927 at 46/5/5 in Gilmanton; postmistress; married; b. Reading, MA; Henry Stock and Ada Beard; Reading, MA
Daisy, d. 5/27/1975 at 94 in Rochester; housewife; widow; b. MI; Frederick E. Wood and Margaret Hobbin
Edwin, d. 6/13/1938 at 76/10/13 in Gilmanton; retired; widower; b. Springfield; Romanzo Chase (New London) and Adeline Hardy (New London)
Elizabeth P., d. 9/17/1891 at –; housewife; widow
Frank A., d. 9/25/1940 at 86; retired laborer; widower; b. Douglas, MA; David Chase (Douglas, MA) and Bridget Quinn (Ireland)
Green, d. 9/15/1899 at 84/3; farmer; widower; b. Belmont; Zacharia Chase
John M., d. 10/18/1927 at 77/8/6 in Gilmanton; b. Deerfield; Nathan Chase and Eliza Chase; Northwood
Lena Emma, d. 9/15/1909 at 1/2; b. Gilmanton; Bernard L. Chase (Sheffield, VT) and Mabel E. Sargent (Sharon, VT)
Sarah Palmer, d. 2/12/1938 at 89/2/25 in Gilmanton; widow; b. Warner; Theodore Waldron (Warner) and Phoebe Palmer (Warner)

CHESLEY,
Mary Esther, d. 3/28/1938 at 85/0/12 in Barnstead*; retired; widow; b. Barnstead; John Blake (Barnstead) and Mary -----

William A., d. 2/13/1920 at 77/2/17 in Barnstead; farmer; married;
   b. Pittsfield; John M. Chesley and Sarah Jenkins; Pine Grove

CHILD,
Charles E., d. 5/12/1974 at 87 in Laconia; machinist; widower; b.
   NH; James Child and Ruth King

CHRISTIE,
David, d. 4/11/1927 at 58 in Gilmanton; teamster; b. Canada;
   Charles Christie and Lucy -----; Laconia

CLAIRMONT,
Joseph L., d. 2/17/1999 in FL; Levi Clairmont and Celina Robert; b.
   2/22/1921**
Olivine R., d. 10/27/1944 at 58/6/3; housewife; married; b.
   Rochester; Charles Corriveau (Canada) and Olive Lessard
   (Canada)

CLANCY,
Ivy A., d. 10/26/1966 at 63 in Laconia; housewife; married; b.
   Brighton, England; George C. Smart and Lillie Barber
William Joseph, d. 7/14/1974 at 82 in Manchester; fireman, ret.;
   widower; b. MA; Christopher Clancy and Nora Finnigan

CLARK,
Annie Jane, d. 12/8/1938 at 71/1/22 in Gilmanton; housewife;
   widow; b. Sydney, NB; Alexander J. Ball (London, England)
   and Jane Horne
John S., d. 6/20/1957 at 84 in Center Harbor; meat cutter; single; b.
   Roxbury, MA; John G. Clark and Mary Dean
Robert P., d. 4/9/1999 in Gilmanton; Edward Clark and Mary
   Degesus; b. 4/10/1933**
Rufus, d. 11/4/1894 at 64/2/12; cardiac apnoea; farmer; married

CLAY,
Violetta Louise, d. 8/23/1994 in Manchester; Wilfred Jalbert and
   Jennie Chrisman

CLEWLEY,
Harold Augustus, d. 11/2/1994 in Concord; Harold A. Clewley and
   Edna L. Coles; b. 2/16/1923**

CLIFFORD,
Earl Clinton, d. 11/27/1969 at 76 in Concord; road agent ret.; married; b. NH; John Clifford and Nancy Leavitt
Jennie N., d. 12/11/1933 at 79/0/16 in Concord; Buzzell Cem.
John L., d. 12/25/1922 at 69
Nellie M., d. 2/1/1975 at 85 in Concord; school teacher; widow; b. NH; Euraldo P. Ellsworth and Mary Allen

CLOUGH,
Betsey, d. 10/9/1895 at 82; dropsy; housekeeper; widow
Clara I., d. 6/5/1920 at 65/9/11 in Gilmanton; at home; divorced; b. Gilmanton; George Ross and Elizabeth Pillsbury; Hillside
Elbridge G., d. 3/5/1914 at 62/1/20 in Gilmanton; farmer; married; John P. Clough (Gilmanton) and Tamson H. Winkley (Alton)
Elizabeth H., d. 11/19/1907 at 65/4/22; housewife; married; b. Alton; Joseph Prescott and Harriet Place (Alton)
Emma S., d. 9/10/1919 at 67/6/20 in Gilmanton; at home; widow; b. Lowell, MA; Albert Sargeant; Pine Grove
George C., d. 8/9/1911 at 19; single; Oscar S. Clough and Clara I. Ross
Grace B., d. 5/19/1944 at 58/2/13; at home; married; b. Alton; Benjamin Blaisdell (Boston, NH) and Abbie Horne (Farmington)
Irving Augustus, d. 10/2/1952 at 92 in Laconia*; farmer (ret.); married; b. NH; Myrum S. Clough and Elizabeth Prescott
John P., d. 10/12/1893 at 69/11/25; cancer; farmer; married; b. Gilmanton; Nehemiah Clough (Alton) and Sally Rowe (Gilford)
John P., d. 4/8/1953 at 77 in Wolfeboro; ret. farmer; widower; b. Manchester; Elbridge Clough and Emma Sargent
Mirum S., d. 10/26/1922 at 89
Nahium O., d. 11/3/1912 at 58/7; farmer; married; b. Gilmanton; John P. Clough (Gilmanton) and ----- Winkley (Strafford)
Willie E., d. 1/10/1946 at 62/2/10 in Wolfeboro*; st. bee inspector; single; b. Gilmanton; Elbridge G. Clough (Gilmanton) and Emma Sargent (Lowell, MA)

COCHRAN,
Ralph E., d. 1/30/1971 at 57 in Laconia; machinist; married; b. MA; Ralph Cochran and Henrietta Redden

COFFIN,
Dorothy S., d. 11/4/1907 at 84/9/4; widow; b. Gilmanton; Abraham Coffin (Gilmanton) and Martha Moulton
Joseph M., d. 5/18/1887 at 64/5/7; farmer; married; b. Alton; Samuel Coffin (Alton) and Mary Mooney (Alton)

COGSWELL,
Abby, d. 3/30/1890 at 48; housewife; married; b. Loudon
Florence M., d. 2/15/1892 at 40/8; housewife; married; b. Manchester; Reuben D. Moores and Betsey Currier (Warner)
James W., d. 11/8/1892 at 54/8/22; farmer; married; b. Gilmanton; Thomas Cogswell (Atkinson) and ----- (Plaistow)
Thomas, d. 2/15/1904 at 63/0/7; lawyer; married; b. Gilmanton; Thomas Cogswell (Atkinson) and Mary Noyes (Plaistow)
Thomas, d. 6/2/1923 at 47

COLBATH,
Estella, d. 10/31/1924 at 53 in Rochester; housework; widow; b. Danvers, MA; John C. Foss and Ella M. Watson; Pine Grove

COLBY,
Joshua, d. 1/9/1898 at 71/2/9; farmer; married; b. Dunbarton; Jonathan Colby (Dunbarton) and Sarah A. Perkins (Dunbarton)

COLCORD,
Mary A., d. 11/15/1905 at 72; housewife; widow; b. Gilmanton
Richard R., d. 10/13/1903 at 71; shoemaker; married; b. Gilmanton; Edward Colcord (Gilmanton) and Mary Rogers (Gilmanton)

COLE,
Elayne L., d. 8/24/2000 in Lebanon; George Nelson and Eleanor Hislop; b. 10/8/1949**
Ella N., d. 10/20/1910 at 49/6/14 in Manchester; paralysis; married
Emily S., d. 7/18/1924 at 83 in Gilmanton; housework; widow; b. Gilmanton; William Swain and Hannah Moulton; Pittsfield

COLLINS,
Esther, d. 9/27/1902 at 68/1/11; housewife; married; ----- Burbank
Ezekiel A., d. 7/24/1924 at 73 in Gilmanton; farmer; widower; b. Gilford; Ezekiel Collins and Charlotte Crosby; Laconia

Kirsten, d. 10/1/1975 at 20 in Laconia; student; single; b. Germany; John J. Collins and Lucille Landry

Nellie M., d. 10/14/1909 at –; housework; single; b. Cambridge, MA; Patrick S. Collins (Ireland) and Annie A. Corrigan (Ireland)

Thomas T., d. 2/15/1890 at 70/2/26; farmer; married; b. Barnstead; John H. Collins and Phoebe H. Collins (Dover)

CONNELL,

Catherine H., d. 2/27/1908 at 88/4/24; widow; b. Strafford; Israel Caswell (Strafford)

Daniel, d. 4/5/1928 at 83/4/5 in Gilmanton; shoemaker; widower; b. Strafford; Eben G. Connell and Catherine Caswell; Pine Grove

Eben, d. 7/6/1897 at 77; farmer; married; b. Strafford

Elizabeth C., d. 4/8/1926 at 70/1/28 in Gilmanton; housework; married; b. Gilmanton; Reuben D. Tibbetts and Martha J. Gale; Pine Grove

Emma J., d. 3/30/1911 at 60/6/15; housewife; married; b. Brooklin, ME; Archibald Dean (ME) and Melinda Blake (ME)

John, d. 12/14/1896 at 69/10; heart and lung disease; merchant; single; b. Strafford

John M., d. 9/29/1934 at 86/9/17 in Gilmanton; ret'd merch.; widower; b. Strafford; Eben G. Connell and Katherine Caswell; Pine Grove

Laura, d. 1/27/1899 at 53/8; housewife; married; b. Somersworth

CONNER,

Elmer W., d. 12/23/1948 at 35/9/11; salesman; married; b. Northfield; Clarence A. Conner (Worcester, VT) and Jennie Chase (Springfield)

CONSTANT,

Joseph, d. 8/28/1905 at 0/2/14; b. Biddeford, ME; Almond Constant and Mary Ann Matthews

COOK,

Danford, d. 11/9/1898 at 77/4/23; miller; married; Jacob Cook and Relief Merrill

Frances G., d. 3/21/1988 in Laconia; Arthur Bicknell and Edith McKinnon; b. 9/9/1918**

Mary B., d. 6/11/1908 at 73/5/24; widow; b. Holderness; John Dudley and Sally Beede

Olga M., d. 1/30/1999 in Meredith; Peter Marchook and Tachana —; b. 4/7/1917**

Sarah C., d. 8/27/1895 at 26/10/21; pulmonary tuberculosis; single; b. Farmington; Thomas F. Cook (Farmington) and Cordelia A. Edgerly (Farmington)

COPELAND,
Tirzah C., d. 6/4/1940 at 71/1/27; housewife; married; b. Sanbornton; Prescott Howland (Sanbornton) and Lucinda Brown (Sanbornton)

CORBETT,
Richard Matthew, d. 9/1/1973 at 19 in Gilmanton; factory worker; single; b. MA; William B. Corbett and Mary E. O'Donnell

CORSON,
Jesse S., Jr., Corporal, d. 6/15/1952 at 25 in Gilmanton; U. S. Army and lumberjack; married; b. ME; Jesse S. Corson and Barbara I. Mackay

CORWINE,
Emma M., d. 6/24/1944 at 65/11/3; housewife; married; b. New York, NY; John Dietrich (Germany) and Pauline Rhein (Germany)

COTTON,
Fred S., d. 2/22/1947 at 72/2/18*; farmer; widower; b. Gilmanton; Joseph Cotton (Gilmanton) and Sarah Varney (Gilmanton)

Joel Fred, d. 5/28/1965 at 3 in Gilmanton; single; b. Concord; Joseph H. Cotton, Jr. and Virginia Cummings

Laura A., d. 6/9/1942 at 70/9/6; housewife; married; b. Strafford, VT; Steven E. Norton (Strafford, VT) and Clara J. Bullard (Strafford, VT)

Lydia A., d. 12/31/1897 at 80/4/4; housewife; widow; b. Gilmanton; John Cotton and Fannie Night

Sarah A., d. 2/10/1920 at 79/10/24 in Laconia; housework; widow; b. Gilmanton; Charles Varney and ----- Peaslee; Smith Meetinghouse

Virginia C., d. 9/20/1996 in Concord; ----- Cummings and Rena Stone

COUPAL,
Armand Eugene, d. 2/7/1993 in Laconia; Napoleon Coupal and Mary Derosier; b. 10/29/1910**

COUSINS,
William C., d. 1/26/1958 at 61 in Laconia*; laborer; married; b. Jersey City, NJ; William C. Cousins and Jean Donnelly

COX,
Blanche F., d. 7/21/1978 at 76 in Hanover; housewife; married; b. NH; Andrew J. French and Clara Tufts

CRANE,
Warren J., d. 6/20/1986 in Laconia; Charles W. Crane and Jennie Wadiak

CROSBY,
Edith M., d. 1/12/1981 in Epsom; William Feeny and Frances Tebbetts; b. 6/21/1887**
Harold D., d. 9/2/1912 at 29/6/17; single; b. Beverly, MA; Forman A. Crosby (NS) and Mary E. Swasey (Marblehead, MA)

CROSSLAND,
Sam, d. 3/23/1939 at 63 in Wolfeboro*; married; b. Bradford, England; John Crossland

CROWELL,
Constance W., d. 10/31/1973 at 42 in Hanover*; homemaker; married; b. CT; Leroy Wilson and Louice Couch

CROWLEY,
Robert E., d. 10/30/1983 in Laconia; John J. Crowley and Sarah Kelley
Sarah Eleanor, d. 1/1/1987 in Laconia; John J. Crowley and Sarah Kelley; b. 11/10/1905**

CUMMING,
Jane Scriven, d. 7/17/1998 in Gilmanton; William Scriven and Alice Davis; b. 1/16/1904**

CURRIER,
Pearl, d. 7/9/1990 in Gilmanton; Juan Munroe and ----- Griffen

CURTIN,
Daniel J., d. 1/10/1911 at 27/2/26; hatter; married; b. Troy, NY; Dennis Curtin (Boston, MA) and Catherine Allen (Troy, NY)

CUSHING,
Gelsey B., d. 9/28/1985 in Hanover; George B. Thomas and Catharine Cushing

CUTTING,
Marian A., d. 2/14/1997 in Laconia; Ralph Jones and Dora E. Dowe; b. 5/27/1907**

DAIGLE,
Leo J., d. 7/2/2001 in Gilmanton; Maxime Daigle and Caroline Cyr; b. 2/14/1932**

DAIGNEAU,
Arthur H., d. 5/1/1982 in Manchester; Thomas Daigneau and Valadie Auclair; b. 7/6/1911**

DAIGNEAULT,
Mildred M., d. 10/4/1975 at 83 in Laconia; knitter; widow; b. NH; Napoleon Riel and Rose Joyal

DALY,
Henry H., d. 8/16/1909 at 23/9/4; musician; single; b. NY; James J. Daly (Newfoundland) and Arabella C. Heart (Boston, MA)

DANFORTH,
Lorinda, d. 10/12/1898 at 82; spinster; single

DARROW,
Mary C., d. 4/15/1928 at 72/2/7 in Akron, OH; at home; widow; b. MA; ----- Burgess and Mary Cogswell; Smith Meetinghouse

DAVIES,
Frances Irene, d. 2/6/1997 in Gilmanton; Asher Buss and Flora Heller; b. 8/6/1902**

DAVIS,
son, d. 10/16/1948 at 0/0/0; b. Gilmanton; George L. Smith (Gilmanton) and Ellen M. Davis (Gilmanton)

Albert, d. 8/13/1908 at 62/7/10; farmer; married; b. Barnstead; David Davis (Barnstead) and Nancy Collins (Barnstead)

Arthur F., d. 7/8/1957 at 71 in Gilmanton; ret. mech. engr.; married; b. Turners Falls, MA; Charles S. Davis and Nellie F. Mason

Belle, d. 7/1/1948 at 75/7/0; cook (retired); widow; b. Enfield; John Dresser (Sutton) and Nancy Cheeney (Salisbury)

Charles C., d. 8/25/1917 at 68/4/17 in Gilmanton; retired; married; V. E. Davis and Mary W. Arrick

David E., d. 6/6/1947 at 20/1/5*; lumberman; single; b. Gilmanton; George E. Davis (Dover) and Irene M. Page (Gilmanton)

Edward A., d. 10/22/1942 at 83/7/15*; carpenter; widower; b. Webster, MA

Ellen C., d. 12/26/1898 at 49/6/15; housewife; widow; b. Canada

Elmer G., d. 3/4/1968 at 81 in Gilmanton; postman, ret.; widower; b. MA; Edward Davis and Celia -----

Fred E., d. 8/15/1926 at 69/11/3 in Alton; Pine Grove

George Ernest, d. 6/9/1951 at 62/0/9 in Laconia*; woodsman; married; b. NH; Reuben A. Davis and Flora Willey

Georgia M., d. 7/15/1962 at 88 in Boscawen*; housewife; widow; b. Gilmanton; Joseph Griffin

Hazen, d. 3/12/1982 in Gilmanton; Charles S. Davis and Nellie F. Mason

Helen May, d. 11/21/1962 at 29 in Concord*; housewife; married; b. Pittsfield; Calvin Joy and Gladys Fifield

Helene M., d. 8/15/1947 at 79/11/15*; housewife; married; b. Lydenham, England; William Twort (England) and Mary Huckstable (England)

Herbert J., d. 1/23/1934 at 74 in Gilmanton; laborer; single; b. Pittsfield; George W. Davis and Martha Fullerton; Pine Grove

Irene May, d. 4/28/1975 at 67 in Concord; housewife; widow; b. NH; William Boyd and Sadie Buckman

Lena Mildred, d. 12/28/1966 at 76 in Laconia; housewife; married; b. Gilmanton; Alfred Ellsworth and Hannah Birmingham

Nellie F., d. 7/9/1932 at 64/10/27 in Gilmanton; at home; married; b. Amesbury, MA; Davis Mason and Sara Drew; Melrose, MA

Orcelia I., d. 3/31/1934 at 76/6 in Gilmanton; housewife; married; b. Lowell, MA; Chauncey D. Gay and Mary Ellsworth; Beech Grove

William, d. 11/11/1974 at 63 in Gilmanton; lathe operator, ret.; married; b. MA; Michael Uzdavinis and Della Ladziata
William L., d. World War II in France*; single; b. Somerville, MA; William J. Davis and Beatrice M. Lowe (1949)

DAWSON,
Mary Celina, d. 4/26/1963 at 72 in Concord*; housewife; widow; b. Taunton, MA; George H. Fantom and Emma Varney

DAY,
Charles Howard, Jr., d. 5/17/1964 at 47 in Gilmanton; dyer; married; b. Manchester; Charles H. Day and Sadie B. Forbes
Lucille Therese, d. 2/13/1998 in Gilmanton; Andre J. Labonte and Theresa Jeanne D'Arc Hardy; b. 1/18/1954**

DEAN,
Malinda H., d. 2/26/1899 at 88/1/10; housewife; widow

DEARBORN,
Myrtie B., d. 4/2/1955 at 78 in Laconia; housewife; widow; b. NH; Edward E. Smith and Jane Evans
Thomas, d. 1/6/1946 at 0/3/27 in Laconia; b. Laconia; Frances M. Dearborn (Laconia)

DELANO,
Janet A., d. 6/29/1989; b. 5/23/1915**

DELSIE,
Mary Margaret, d. 7/13/1989 in Wolfeboro; Edward Cassidy and Margaret McGray; b. 5/12/1913**

DENAULT,
Eugene, d. 4/12/1967 at 59 in Concord; electrician; married; b. Holyoke, MA; Philip Denault and Alphonsine Clairmont

DENNETT,
Hannah, d. 10/8/1903 at 81/8/22; widow
Mark A., d. 4/4/1900 at –; farmer; married

DENNIS,
Rollin H., d. 11/2/1980 in Laconia; Harvey O. Dennis and Naomi E. Dailey

DERBY,
John Eveleth, Jr., d. 12/15/1993 in Gilmanton; John E. Derby, Sr. and Emily Priest

DESROCHERS,
Fred Alex, d. 4/19/1938 at 59/8 in Belmont*; painter; married; b. St. Agapit, Canada; Joseph Desrochers (Canada) and Sophia Desrochers (Canada)
Louella Stone, d. 2/11/1952 at 67 in Laconia*; housewife; widow; b. NH; Alonzo C. Burbank and Lucy A. Dustin

DEWARE,
Mary B., d. 4/21/1980 in Gilmanton; Dr. George H. Brown and Lizzie H. Orange; b. 5/7/1904**
Robert William, d. 7/12/1976 at 81 in Laconia; telephone worker; married; b. NH; Elwin Deware and Mary Christie

DEXTER,
Alfred, d. 6/5/1904 at –; b. Laconia; Caleb C. Dexter (NS) and Hattie Gault (Gilmanton)
Etta Florence, d. 8/4/1890 at 0/6; b. Gilmanton; Caleb Dexter (NS) and Hattie Gault (Gilmanton)

DICEY,
Mable, d. 8/24/1928 at 3/7/3 in Gilmanton; b. Gilmanton; Grover Dicey and Bessie Richardson; Pittsfield

DICKERSON,
daughter, d. 4/10/1921 at 0/0/1 in Gilmanton; b. Gilmanton; Paul Dickerson and Sarah E. McWilliams; South Road

DICKEY,
Guy Bradford, d. 9/28/1959 at 90 in Laconia; barber; single; b. Bennington; Nathaniel Dickey and Catherine Adams

DIMICK,
Anne Maria, d. 11/14/1918 at 76/9/5; none [occ.]; widow; b. New Hampton; Orrin Folsom and Julia A. Nelson

DIMOCK,
Arthur V., d. 8/2/1956 at 72 in Concord*; clergyman - ret.; married; b. Halifax, NS; Herbert Dimock and Littier Blackney
Barbara R., d. 1/28/1990 in Concord; Charles M. Raddin and Mary Ann Devine
Ronald V., d. 7/7/1990 in Gilmanton; Arthur V. Dimock and Winifred Crisp
Winifred Crisp, d. 4/24/1962 at 86 in Gilmanton; housewife; widow; b. Paradise, NS; William Crisp and Elizabeth Phinney

DIMOND,
Chester Lacy, d. 10/13/1973 at 66 in Gilmanton*; sawyer; widower; b. MI
Florence B., d. 2/16/1937 at 31/5/16 in Wolfeboro; housewife; married; b. Gilmanton; Ira Gilman and Cora York; Smith M. H., Gilmanton
Jonathan R., d. 2/10/1930 at 87/10/9 in Gilmanton; farmer; widower; b. Loudon; Gould Dimond and Sally Rollins; Loudon

DOAN,
Annie M., d. 5/5/1933 at 78/4/6 in Gilmanton; dressmaker; single; b. New York City; Henry Doan and Margaret Pasbach; Riverside, Alton
Charles L., d. 6/11/1928 at 63/1/16 in Gilmanton; widower; b. Portland, ME; Henry Doan and Margaret Pasbach; So. Portland, ME

DOCKHAM,
Mary E., d. 8/1/1986 in Laconia; Hubert Edgerly and Agnes Cutting; b. 3/14/1916**

DODGE,
Elizabeth, d. 1/10/1923 at 75
Herbert, d. 1/5/1915 at 32/9/24 in Gilmanton; chopper; married; Frank S. Dodge (New Durham) and Rosilla Pearl (Strafford)

DOE,
Claude A., d. 4/5/1983 in Laconia; Bert Doe and Venus -----
Florence A., d. 9/22/1983 in Laconia; Eugene E. Emerson and
   Sarah P. Barney

DOHERTY,
Edward, d. 8/10/1908 at 22; druggist; single; b. Boston, MA; Henry
   Doherty (Boston, MA)

DONAGHY,
Glenna Helena, d. 6/9/1965 at 40 in Gilmanton; housewife; married;
   b. Lubec, ME; Philip Gilmour and Thelma Myers

DONALDSON,
Carrie A., d. 2/23/1972 at 78 in Gilmanton; school teacher;
   divorced; b. NH; Herbert Donaldson and Henrietta Niles

DONOVAN,
Katherine, d. 7/1/1996 in Gilmanton; Edward Lancey and Liz Cook

DOUGLAS,
Clyde E., d. 3/14/1929 at 17/3/24 in Amesbury, MA; single; Pine
   Grove

DOW,
Abbie E., d. 2/26/1905 at 76/8; housewife; widow; John Allen and ---
   -- Sweatt
Arthur Louis, d. 9/17/1954 at 84 in Laconia; farmer, ret.; widower; b.
   NH; Daniel Dow and Olive Chase
Daniel, d. 1/24/1920 at 84/1/6 in Gilmanton; farmer; married; b.
   Gilmanton; Chalice Dow and Eliza Dow; Buswell Cem.
Eliza, d. 2/23/1905 at 97/5/23; housewife; widow; b. Gilmanton;
   John Dow and ----- Sweatt
Esther A., d. 3/13/1889 at 19/11/21; housewife; single; b.
   Gilmanton; Daniel Dow and Olive Chase
George L., d. 1/25/1892 at 49; mechanic; single
George W., d. 10/30/1912 at 80/7/28; laborer; widower; b. Epsom;
   Taylor Dow and Mary Emerson
George W., d. 8/11/1926 at 81/8/15 in Gilmanton; carpenter; b.
   Gilmanton; Challis Dow and Elizah Dow; Buzzell Cem.
Henry, d. 7/3/1899 at 61/9; veterinary surgeon

Lucy Ann, d. 3/28/1927 at 72/0/27 in Canterbury; Pine Grove
Mary L., d. 1/30/1910 at 80/5; heart disease; housewife; married; b. Gilmanton; William Sawyer (Gilmanton) and Betsy H. Connor (Gilmanton)
Nellie Ann, d. 6/23/1953 at 85 in Laconia; housewife; married; b. NH; Jarvis B. Rowe and Hanna McCarthy
Olive A., d. 1/29/1933 at 83/10/7 in Gilmanton; widow; b. Belmont; Green Chase and Caroline Tilton; Buswell
Oscar C., d. 12/12/1903 at 21/8/20; teacher; married; b. Gilmanton; Daniel Dow (Belmont) and Olive Chase (Belmont)
Willie T., d. 1/4/1937 at 75/5/28 in Laconia*; laborer; single; b. Gilmanton; George W. Dow and Mary L. -----; Pine Grove, Gilmanton I. W.

DOWNING,
Annie P., d. 3/2/1923 at 72
Deane, d. 12/17/1999 in Laconia; Antoine Williams and Minnie Bordelon; b. 10/23/1921**
Hazel Elizzabeth, d. 7/1/1967 at 68 in Laconia*; housewife; widow; b. Meredith; Mead Boynton and Alice M. Lawrence
Moses N., d. 6/10/1907 at 73/6/8; shoemaker; married; b. Ellsworth; David Downing (Ellsworth) and Betsey Parmer (Loudon)
Paul J., d. 1/12/1981 in Concord; Joseph P. Downing and Teresa Wirth; b. 3/22/1930**

DOWNS,
Augusta C., d. 11/8/1911 at 79/9/7; widow; b. Loudon
Charles H., d. 11/3/1906 at 48; farmer; single; b. Gilmanton; Isaac Downs (Gilmanton) and Augusta Smith
Ethel May, d. 1/15/1954 at 69 in Concord*; housewife; widow; b. ME; Robert Smith and Martha -----
Isaac A., d. 4/24/1907 at 77/6/12; farmer; married; b. Gilmanton; Daniel Downs (ME) and Phoebe Gilman (Gilmanton)

DOYLE,
James F., d. 10/8/1993 in Laconia; Charles W. Doyle and Gertrude M. Walsh; b. 10/20/1912**

DRAKE,
Amos G., d. 3/10/1888 at 69/6/18; farmer; married; b. Rye; Gilman Drake and Eliza Garland

DRAPEAU,
Joseph, d. 5/28/1990 in Wolfeboro; George Drapeau and Lucy Houde

DREW,
Edith, d. 3/8/1920 at 28/4/18 in Gilmanton; housewife; married; Henry Adams and Jennie Lund; Pittsfield

DRISCOLL,
John M., d. 12/30/1917 at 65/4/13 in Gilmanton; retired; married; William Driscoll (England) and Margaret Fitzgerald (England)

DUBE,
Peter, d. 2/17/1938 at 71/2/12 in Laconia*; farmer; single; Peter Dube (Canada) and Evelyn Garrett (Canada)

DUBIA,
Joseph O. L., d. 4/3/1906 at 0/0/1; b. Gilmanton; John Dubia (Newport, VT) and Josie Julia Claremont (Canada)
Naulbert John, d. 4/3/1906 at –; b. Gilmanton; John Dubia (Newport, VT) and Josie Julia Claremont (Canada)

DUBOIS,
Myra L., d. 8/27/1945 at 60/0/8; divorced; b. Penacook; Allen C. Beane (Fisherville) and Phoebe Crowther (Fisherville)

DUCHEMAULT,
Joseph, d. 3/1/1933 at 86/0/19 in Gilmanton; laborer; widower; b. Canada; Charles Duchemault and Esther Labadie; St. Lambert, Laconia

DUDLEY,
Betsy H., d. 5/17/1894 at 87/10/5; apoplexy; housewife; married; b. Gilmanton; Joseph Gilman (Newmarket) and Love D. Rowell (Nottingham)
Charles F., d. 2/9/1928 at 70/9/4 in Abington, MA; married; Smith Meetinghouse
Dorothy Hurlbutt, d. 9/12/1996 in Gilmanton; Clarence Hurlbutt and Carrie Donaldson; b. 10/31/1917**
Irving Dean, Jr., d. 3/24/1989 in Concord; Irving Dean Dudley, Sr. and Esther Clark; b. 7/19/1915**

John K., d. 12/10/1895 at 91/1/4; intestinal obstruction; farmer; widower; b. Gilmanton; Nathaniel Dudley (Gilmanton) and Mary Smith (Gilmanton)
Julia A., d. 11/29/1909 at 85/10/2; widow; b. Gilmanton
Mary P., d. 10/28/1913 at 45; widow; b. Gilmanton; Moses Peaslee (Gilmanton) and Betsy York (Barnstead)
Mercy, d. 1/27/1904 at 76/0/18; housemaid; single; b. Holderness; John Dudley (Sanbornton) and Sally Beede (Sandwich)
Titus S., d. 11/27/1889 at 68/11/1; farmer; married; b. Gilmanton; Nathaniel Dudley (Gilmanton) and Mary Smith (Gilmanton)

DUGGAN,
Patrick T., d. 5/25/2001 in Laconia; Robert Duggan and Mary Darone; b. 10/16/1958**
Robert Emmett, Jr., d. 10/22/1991 in Wolfeboro; Robert E. Duggan, Sr. and Marie Dunlea

DUNN,
Catherine A., d. 7/16/1981 in Laconia; Aden Newland and Grace Frank; b. 1/7/1908**
Dorothy E., d. 4/27/1975 at 42 in Laconia; secretary; married; b. NY; Harry P. Cubbin and Dorothy B. Mohr
William E., d. 11/20/1986 in Laconia; Edward Dunn and Clara Stump; b. 3/22/1906**

DUPLY,
Anna, d. 2/25/1928 at 71 in Gilmanton; Pine Grove

DURGIN,
Arthur Leland, d. 5/27/1953 at 72 in Wolfeboro; farmer; married; b. New Durham; Nehemiah Durgin and Ida B. McKeen
Florence M., d. 4/22/1977 at 92 in Gilmanton I. W.; teacher; widow; b. NH; Frank Merrill and Clara -----
Ida B., d. 3/12/1933 at 77/1/1 in Gilmanton; housewife; married; b. Fryeburg, ME; James McKeen and Mary Smith; Riverside, Alton
Nehemiah, d. 1/12/1936 at 86/9/22 in Gilmanton; farmer; widower; b. New Durham; James W. Durgin (NY State) and Hannah Varney (Alton)

DURRELL,
Bessie, d. 7/29/1912 at 48; widow
Edwin, d. 2/27/1919 at 77/4/23 in Laconia; Guinea Ridge
Fisk A., d. 8/9/1919 at 69/3/24 in Gilmanton; farmer; widower; b. Gilmanton; Joseph B. Durrell and Abigail Shannon; Guinea Ridge
Lewis E., d. 1/7/1889 at 54; farmer; married; b. Gilmanton; Thomas Durrell (Gilmanton) and ----- Hutchings (Gilmanton)

DUSTIN,
Moses N., d. 1/28/1895 at 64/10/1; black

EASTMAN,
Elsie H., d. 9/22/1966 at 51 in Laconia; housewife; married; b. S. Wolfeboro; Nelson Londo and Mildred Corson
Fern C., d. 9/15/1991 in Concord; Fred Beck and Bertha Jenkerson
Laurenia A., d. 7/29/1908 at 59/3/1; housewife; married; b. Gilmanton; Moses S. Gale (Gilmanton) and Sarah M. Weeks (Gilmanton)
Ralph W., d. 8/18/1982 in Hanover; R. Hiram Eastman and Caroline Schuman; b. 7/9/1906**
Robert W., d. 12/23/1985 in Wolfeboro; Hiram B. Eastman and Caroline Schumann; b. 12/29/1909**

EATON,
Catherine West, d. 5/22/1909 at 0/0/7; b. Gilmanton; Theodore Eaton (St. Louis, MO) and Theodora West (Holbrook, MA)

EDDY,
Harold M., Jr., d. 4/15/1986 in Gilmanton; Harold M. Eddy, Sr. and Ethel M. Rose

EDGERLY,
Albert T., d. 6/11/1909 at 57; married
Amy L., d. 10/8/1928 at 88/8/16 in Newmarket; Hillside
Angeline V., d. 9/4/1924 at 84 in Gilmanton; housework; widow; b. Gilmanton; Augustus Smith and Julia Robinson; Pine Grove
Anna Cogswell, d. 2/9/1951 at 76/4/22 in Laconia; housewife; married; b. NH; Col. Thomas Cogswell and Florence Moores
Catherine E., d. 5/17/1936 at 80/7/13 in Laconia; widow; b. Sycamore, IL; Ezra Keyes (NY) and Paulina Allen (NY)

Cynthia, d. 9/21/1900 at 64/10/13; housekeeper; single; b. Barnstead; Reuben Edgerly (Barnstead) and Sobrina McDaniels (Lee)

David G., d. 3/23/1905 at 69/3/27; farmer; married; b. Gilmanton; David Edgerly (Gilmanton) and Sally Tilton (Gilmanton)

Edwin K., d. 6/18/1895 at 33/10/29; Bright's disease; music teacher; single; b. Gilmanton; David G. Edgerly (Gilmanton) and Hannah Hussey (Barnstead)

Frank A., d. 3/23/1959 at 72 in Gilmanton; farmer; married; b. Nashville, TN; Albert J. Edgerly and Elmina C. Keyes

George David, d. 10/10/1949 at 35/0/15 in Laconia; dye mixer; divorced; b. Gilmanton; Roy C. Edgerly and Minnie F. McLean

Hannah D., d. 3/18/1898 at 71; housewife; widow

Hannah T., d. 4/9/1906 at 64/9/2; housewife; widow; b. Barnstead; John B. Hussey (Barnstead) and Betsey Aiken (Barnstead)

Horace, d. 12/14/1916 at 84/0/25 in Gilmanton; carpenter; married; Reuben Edgerly (Barnstead) and Sabrina McDaniels (Barnstead)

Julia A., d. 4/18/1929 at 88/9/19 in Gilmanton; retired; widow; b. Gilmanton; John Lougee and Rebecca Edgerly; Pine Grove

Laura F., d. 11/7/1910 at 79/8/15; bronchitis; single; b. Barnstead; Reuben Edgerly

Mary H., d. 6/26/1889 at 78; housewife; widow

Mary Rachel, d. 2/20/1969 at 85 in Laconia; home; widow; b. Canada; David M. Morgan and Alice A. Metcalf

Minnie Florence, d. 11/15/1962 at 80 in Wolfeboro*; town clerk; widow; b. Barre, VT; George B. McLean and Amy Lee

Myra L., d. 4/4/1946 at 91/1/11 in Laconia; housewife; widow; b. Gilmanton; Amos R. Price (Gilmanton) and Sarah Chesley

Owen J., d. 3/7/1904 at 79; farmer; married; b. Gilmanton; David Edgerly and Sally Tilton

Phyllis, d. 1/29/1920 at 3/9 in Laconia; b. Gilmanton; Florence Edgerly; Pine Grove

Reuben, d. 3/29/1888 at 84/7/26; farmer; widower; b. Barnstead; Ezekiel Edgerly (Salisbury, MA) and Molly Eastman (Salisbury, MA)

Roy C., d. 7/6/1939 at 61/8/9 in Gilmanton; farmer; married; b. Gilmanton; David G. Edgerly (Gilmanton) and Hannah Hussey (Barnstead)

Ruth Vernon, d. 4/19/1967 at 66 in Laconia*; finisher, ret.; single; b. Gilmanton; Walter J. Edgerly and Anna M. Cogswell

Sally, d. 1/17/1887 at 36/11/17; tailoress; widow; b. Gilmanton; Trueworthy Chesley (Gilmanton) and ----- Powers (Newtown)

Walter J., d. 3/17/1957 at 88 in Laconia*; salesman; widower; b. Gilmanton; Joseph Edgerly and Angelina Smith

EDSON,
Allen E., d. 6/6/1975 at 73 in Laconia; carpenter (ret.); married; b. VT; Willis Edson and Rena Rowell

EDWARDS,
Sadie Rosman, d. 4/3/1978 at 84 in Laconia; housewife; widow; b. NY

Thomas Sadler, Sr., d. 7/7/1966 at 84 in Concord*; feed broker; married; b. England

EHLEN,
Hattie, d. 8/30/1993 in Gilmanton; Frank Morris and Hattie Bachman

Henry Anthony, d. 5/16/1993 in Concord; Henry John Ehlen and Rose Moliz

EHRENSPERGER,
Harold Adam, d. 11/5/1973 at 76 in Gilmanton; professor ret.; single; b. IN; Charles Louis Ehrensperger and Louise Elvis

EISENHAUER,
Earl A., d. 7/19/1981 in Laconia; Charles E. Eisenhauer and Beatrice Tannar

ELKINS,
Belle D., d. 8/30/1893 at 39; chronic tubercular phthisis; teacher; single

Cora B., d. 2/5/1930 at 68/2/11 in Gilmanton; widow; John W. Ham and Abbey Y. Varney; Pine Grove

Daniel, d. 4/15/1897 at 92; farmer; widower; b. Rumney; Daniel Elkins and ----- Perkins

Daniel H., d. 10/8/1893 at 59; apoplexy; farmer; married; b. Thornton; Daniel Elkins (Thornton) and Mary F. Elkins (Gilmanton)

Helen Agusta, d. 8/30/1898 at 0/0/14; b. Gilmanton; Frank J. Elkins (Gilmanton) and Mary E. Dunbar (Quincy, MA)

John T., d. 6/18/1911 at 50/2/24; farmer; married; b. Gilmanton;
    Daniel Elkins (Gilmanton) and Liberty Ham (Alton)
Mary F., d. 1/3/1888 at 80/8/2
Sarah, d. 4/22/1896 at 69; heart disease; housekeeper; divorced; b.
    Gilmanton; Daniel Elkins (Rumney) and Mary F. Elkins
    (Gilmanton)

ELLIS,
Helen E., d. 2/27/1926 at 75/3/26 in Gilmanton; housework;
    married; b. Gilmanton; Reuben W. Page and Abagail T.
    Sanborn; Alton
Herbert A., d. 3/8/1930 at 66/5/5 in Gilmanton; farmer; divorced; b.
    Alton; Moses A. Ellis and Sally Lougee; Alton
Horace D., d. 3/18/1891 at 36; farmer; married; b. Alton; Alfred G.
    Ellis (Alton) and Mary A. Ellis (Alton)

ELLSWORTH,
daughter, d. 12/2/1900 at 0/0/1; b. Gilmanton; Lester H. Ellsworth
    (Gilmanton) and Alice A. Gilman (Lakeport)
Alden D., d. 3/9/1897 at –; laborer; married
Alfred P., d. 9/3/1932 at 74/5/29 in Gilmanton; farmer; widower; b.
    Gilmanton; John Ellsworth and Corlista Allen; Beech Grove
Artemas B., d. 2/15/1896 at 38; consumption; farmer; divorced; b.
    Gilmanton; John Ellsworth and Calista B. Ellsworth
Bertha A., d. 11/18/1972 at 94 in Laconia; housewife; widow; b.
    Austria; Johan Zillichovski and Susania Hurben
Blanche Estelle, d. 5/19/1961 at 75 in Belmont; ret. back seamer;
    married; b. Gilmanton; John Pease and Nancy Greenough
Clyde W., d. 1/15/1913 at 0/0/13; b. Gilmanton; Earle M. Ellsworth
    (Gilmanton) and Blanche Pease (Gilmanton)
Eunice, d. 2/23/1888 at 89; housewife; widow
Euraldo P., d. 10/1/1902 at 50/2/15; farmer; married; b. Gilmanton;
    James P. Ellsworth (Gilmanton) and Irea Lamprey (Gilmanton)
Hannah B., d. 11/28/1914 at 60 in Gilmanton; housewife; married;
    John Birmingham
James P., d. 4/28/1900 at 74/10/28; farmer; married; b. Gilmanton;
    David Ellsworth (Gilmanton) and Eunice Wolinsford
Jeremiah, d. 6/16/1887 at 66; farmer; married; b. Gilmanton; David
    Ellsworth
John W., d. 3/4/1893 at 32/11/18; consumption; farmer; single; b.
    Belmont; John Ellsworth and Calista B. Ellsworth

Mary E., d. 11/4/1919 at 59/11/24 in Gilmanton; widow; b. NY;
    Rufus Allen and ----- Sanborn; Laconia
Robert, d. 6/7/1933 at 37/10/3 in Concord; single; b. Gilmanton;
    Alfred P. Ellsworth and Hanna Burmingham; Beech Grove

EMERSON,
Albert H., d. 9/15/1895 at 78; old age, heart failure; farmer; widower
Alice J., d. 7/27/1930 at 61/9/25; in Barnstead; Pine Grove
Almena L., d. 3/20/1955 at 92 in Gilmanton; housewife; married; b.
    ME; Henry Doane and Margaret Munson
Ansel, d. 9/18/1953 at 84 in Rochester*; retired; widower; b.
    Barnstead; Charles Emerson and Emily Hall
Augustus Frederick, d. 4/11/1952 at 86 in Manchester*; lumber
    surveyor; married; b. NH; George H. Emerson and Mary E.
    Pickering
Eldora M., d. 5/13/1936 at 79/5/15 in Barnstead; housewife;
    married; b. Alton; David Lougee (Alton) and Laura Jones
    (Alton)
Emily J., d. 7/6/1935 at 96/9/12 in Rochester; retired; widow; b.
    Alton; William Hall and Jehoshebe Hussey; Pine Grove
Flora Belle, d. 10/28/1959 at 79 in Manchester*; housewife; widow;
    b. Dover; George W. Burd and Jennie Foss
Grace Bernice, d. 8/18/1893 at 0/5; heart disease; b. Gilmanton;
    Ansel Emerson (Barnstead) and Alice J. Page (Gilmanton)
Hulda D., d. 7/16/1894 at 75/6; heart failure; housewife; married;
    Thomas Currier (Weare) and Eunice Fox
Julian, d. 4/24/1955 at 92 in Laconia; fireman; widower; b. NH; Seth
    R. Emerson and Emily O. Gant
Mary E., d. 11/7/1918 at 73/1/4; home; married; b. Barnstead; John
    T. Pickering and Phebe C. Trefetherine (Kelley)
Simeon E., d. 1/29/1944 at 86/1/4*; farmer; widower; b. Barnstead;
    Simeon Emerson (Barnstead) and Mahala Adams (Barnstead)
William Clifford, d. 7/14/1996 in Gilmanton; Fred Emerson and Lora
    Berry

EMOND,
Joseph Arthur, d. 3/9/1963 at 96 in Gilmanton; provisioner; married;
    b. St. Jean, PQ; John B. Emond and Anathalie P. LaChance

EVANS,
Christina S., d. 1/9/1915 at 71/8/9 in Gilmanton; housewife; married; Thomas J. Rand (Rye) and Adeline Rand (Rye)
James Wong, d. 10/11/1934 at 0/1/21 in Pittsfield; b. Pittsfield; George W. Evans and Elsie Wong; Loudon Ridge
Theodore L., d. 2/2/1887 at 96/7/26; farmer; widower; b. Lyman, ME
William Y., d. 3/24/1915 at 73/0/22 in Gilmanton; farmer; widower; Leonard Evans (Portsmouth) and Elvira Young (Portsmouth)

EVELETH,
Alice M., d. 8/29/1956 at 77 in Laconia*; housewife; married; b. Taunton, MA
Edwin E., d. 12/9/1965 at 93 in Gilmanton*; liveryman; widower; b. Gilmanton; Samuel Eveleth and Hannah Brown
Hannah J., d. 7/28/1926 at 87/1/10 in Gilmanton; housework; widow; b. Concord; Jonathan Brown and Mary Clough; Smith Meeting House
John, d. 7/29/1888 at 87/6; farmer; widower; b. Ipswich, MA; Samuel Eveleth and Elizabeth Spiller
Samuel, d. 7/25/1905 at 69/3/21; farmer; married; b. Gilmanton; John Eveleth (Ipswich) and Mary R. Sanborn (Gilmanton)

EVERETT,
Matilda, d. 9/29/1911 at 79/4/21; widow; b. Plympton, NS; Joseph Thibbets (Clair, NS) and Unice Surrett (Clair, NS)

EVERSEN,
Martha K., d. 2/20/1971 at 89 in Laconia; pastry cook; widow; b. Sweden; William D. Wilhemson and Molly Svensen

FALAT,
Eugeniusz, d. 4/27/1984 in Laconia; b. 3/13/1920**

FALLON,
Dalton, d. 7/14/1916 at 69 in Gilmanton; retired; married; John Fallon (England) and Mary Evans

FANCY,
Albert S., d. 6/22/1929 at 56/7/3 in Laconia; truck driver; married; b. NS; Arthur Fancy and Bessie -----; Pine Grove

FARNSWORTH,
Frances, d. 9/6/1925 at 58 in Manchester; housekeeper; divorced; William F. Campbell and Annie Height; Pine Grove
Rexford, d. 1/19/1935 at 53/5/23 in Portland, ME; salesman; married; Roscoe Farnsworth and Octavia McKeen; Smith Meetinghouse
Rexford, d. 6/12/1977 at 58 in Laconia; laborer; single; b. MA; Rexford Farnsworth and Sadie Blake

FARRAR,
Ira, d. 2/7/1888 at 76/1/2; farmer; married; b. Gilmanton; Josiah Farrar and Dolly Dow
Sarah E., d. 7/31/1896 at 82; old age; housewife; widow; b. Gilmanton; Josiah Parsons

FARRELL,
Michael P., d. 6/10/1967 at 17 in Gilmanton; student; single; b. Concord; Edward J. Farrell and June Dodge

FAULKINGHAM,
Robert John, d. 9/13/1995 in Laconia; Lloyd L. Faulkingham and Margaret Gaffney

FELDMAN,
Thorlee L., d. 5/20/1975 at 26 in Gilmanton; school teacher; married; b. NY; Seymour Goldberg and Frances Schoenberg

FELLOWS,
Janet E., d. 2/18/1983 in Gilmanton; Elwin Edgerly and Emma Emerson; b. 10/30/1897**

FERLAND,
Pauline L., d. 3/31/2001 in Concord; C. L. Parker and Lucy Titus; b. 5/2/1925**

FERNANDEZ,
Violet M., d. 10/30/1999 in Gilmanton; Jesse Ferman and Grace Nolan; b. 7/2/1919**

FIFIELD,
John D., d. 3/29/1914 at 48/8/24 in Gilmanton; carpenter; married; Dana Fifield (Chelsea, VT) and Julia A. Pillsbury (Haverhill)

FILLION,
David A., d. 4/3/1986 in Gilmanton; William A. Fillion and Edith A. Kelley
Edith Amy, d. 10/21/1997 in Gilmanton; Ernest Kelley and Amy Andrews; b. 7/8/1907**
William A., d. 2/18/1975 at 65 in Gilmanton; machinist (ret.); married; b. Canada; Thomas Fillion and Celina Gilbert

FISHER,
Florence, d. 9/7/1947 at 82/0/28; ret. merchant; single; b. Wolverhampton, England; Henry Fisher (England) and Sarah Boocl (England)
Mabel G., d. 2/19/1982 in Laconia; George F. Wells and Sarah N. Hutchinson

FITZGERALD,
Ellen H., d. 3/3/1950 at 84/3/28; housewife; widow; b. Ireland; John Hughes and Bridget Irwin

FITZPATRICK,
Marie L., d. 11/12/1979 in Laconia; John Disanto and Louise Straub

FLANDERS,
Asahel G., d. 3/14/1928 at 80/11/14 in Gilmanton; carpenter; married; Rufus Flanders and Mary Hackett; Gilmanton Corner
Dyer, d. 8/4/1928 at 78/4/8 in Gilmanton; single; b. Gilmanton; Ira Flanders and Susan Plummer; Smith Meetinghouse
Elizabeth E., d. 4/6/1908 at 53/11/12; housewife; married; b. Rochester; James Locke (Barnstead) and Ellen Kimball (Barnstead)
Elizabeth E., d. 11/7/1931 at 80/9/21 in Gilmanton; Gilmanton Corner
Mary J., d. 12/7/1905 at 79/3/3; housewife; widow; b. Center Harbor; John Hackett (Ashland) and Mary Blanchard (Ashland)
Owen, d. 7/10/1936 at 74/11/15 in Gilmanton; laborer; single; b. Gilmanton; Ira Flanders (Gilford) and Susan Plummer (Gilmanton)

Susan H., d. 2/18/1899 at 75/7/17; housewife; widow; b. Gilford
Victor C., d. 10/28/1932 at 33/5/18 in Gilmanton; married; b.
    Gilmanton; Rufus Flanders and Almi Converse; Beech Grove

FLETCHER,
Howard Everett, d. 4/3/1973 at 53 in Gilmanton; leather curer;
    married; b. NH; Burton Fletcher and Judith Emma George

FOGG,
Albion, d. 4/23/1936 at 68/0/11 in Laconia; laborer
Arthur F., d. 2/20/1931 at 26/1/9 in Berwick, ME; teamster; single;
    b. Belmont; Jason Fogg and Myrtle Jones; Gilmanton
John, d. 1/7/1897 at 4; Orlando Fogg
Martha Ann, d. 6/22/1940 at 72/11/2*; housewife; widow; b. Loudon;
    ----- Haines (Loudon)
Mary J., d. 9/5/1905 at 22/4/12; housewife; married; b. Lakeport;
    Charles Lafoe
Orlando K., d. 1/2/1935 at 71/5/8 in Gilmanton; blacksmith;
    married; b. Gilmanton; David Fogg and Esther Smith; South
    Road

FOLAN,
Mary M., d. 6/25/1956 at 72 in Laconia; housewife; married; b.
    Ireland; Patrick Mogan

FOLEY,
Frank William, Jr., d. 10/29/1944 in Laconia; Frank William Foley,
    Sr. and Barbara Langley

FOLLANSBEE,
Marion Louise, d. 10/8/1993 in Laconia; Robert Grant and Anna
    Clem; b. 10/18/1923**

FOLSOM,
Eunice, d. 4/3/1889 at 79; housewife; widow; John Folsom
Lydia Ann, d. 4/17/1891 at 70/5; housewife; married; b. Gilmanton;
    Nathaniel Nelson (Gilmanton)
Orin, d. 4/21/1901 at 83; insurance agt.; widower; b. Gilmanton;
    Peter Folsom

FORD,
Fay Larkin, d. 6/1/1940 at 9/8/10*; student; single; b. Grafton; Royal
 A. Ford (Pittsfield) and Margaret B. Roby (Northfield)
Leslie W., d. 2/11/1937 at 66/4/24; farmer; married; b. Saranac,
 NY; Russell Ford and ----- Darrah; Ridge, Loudon Ridge
Margaret B., d. 9/22/1978 at 77 in Franklin; housewife; widow; b.
 NH; David Robie and Leona Liberty
Nellie Frances, d. 11/31/1946 (sic) at 75/4/29 in Gilmanton; at
 home; widow; b. Soldier Valley, IA; Hamilton P. Chase
 (Andover) and Sarah Waldron (Warner)
Royal Adams, d. 11/21/1969 at 67 in Franklin; railroad; married; b.
 NH; William McClary and Dorothy Butcher
Sarah Pearl, d. 3/30/1918 at 16/0/8; at home; single; b. Gilmanton;
 Leslie W. Ford (Saranac, NY) and Nellie F. Chase (Soldiers
 Valley, IA)

FORLER,
Gordon Frederick, d. 2/10/1962 at 67 in Laconia*; uphol.-furn. store;
 married; b. Hanover, ON; John Forler and Katherine
 Winneberg

FORSYTH[E],
son, d. 9/3/1957 at 20 mins. in Wolfeboro*; b. Wolfeboro; Harry G.
 Forsyth and Evelyn Rollins
daughter, d. 7/24/1961 at – in Wolfeboro*; b. Wolfeboro; Harry G.
 Forsyth and Evelyn Rollins
Florence E., d. 4/26/1928 at 39/5/25 in Gilmanton; housework;
 married; George Knatt and Alice M. Driver; Pine Grove
Harry Gordon, d. 3/25/1994 in Wolfeboro; Harvey Forsyth and
 Florence Knott; b. 3/22/1910**
Harvey, d. 10/14/1948 at 68/4/1; millman; widower; b. ON
Stevan H., d. 1/3/1957 at 0/1/26 in Wolfeboro*; b. Wolfeboro; Harry
 Forsyth and Evelyn Rollins
Syble O., d. 2/15/1941 at 26/3/23*; at home; married; b. Lancaster;
 Herman E. Jordan (Colebrook) and Jennie E. Smith
 (Groveton)

FORTUNE,
Alice C., d. 8/29/1974 at 63 in Laconia; clerk; single; b. MA; Daniel
 J. Fortune and Catherine McEachren

FOSBURGH,
Herman, d. 3/28/1985 in Concord; Edward Fosburgh and Helen Lyons; b. 1/22/1917**

FOSS,
Abbie F., d. 7/20/1930 at 65/0/11 in Cambridge, MA; cook; widow; b. Gilmanton; John A. Maxfield and Alphia Page; Smith Meetinghouse
Alvah, d. 9/19/1902 at 82/3; farmer; widower; b. Gilmanton; John Foss and Olive Clough (Gilmanton)
Bessie M., d. 11/14/1903 at 23; housewife; married; b. Gilmanton; Caleb W. J. Peaslee (Gilmanton) and Luanna M. Abbott (Warner)
Emily A., d. 10/26/1921 at 89/11/6; housewife; widow; b. Alton; Joseph Watson and Mary Foss; Pine Grove
Estella M., d. 8/19/1912 at 38/8/1; housewife; married; b. Goffstown; Jennie Blaisdell
Frank E., d. 9/28/1918 at 73/2/28; musician; widower; b. Pittsfield; Alvah Foss and Miriam Foss
Jerusha S., d. 1/21/1896 at 69/4/10; pneumonia; housewife; married; b. Enfield; John Pettingill and Mahale Kimball
John, d. 8/14/1918 at 88/4/1; carpenter; married; b. Gilmanton; Simon Foss
John Henry, d. 11/4/1938 at 77/9/7 in Gilmanton*; RR watchman; married; b. Haverhill, MA; John Henry Foss and Emily A. Watson
Mary, d. 6/20/1892 at 92/2/5; housewife; widow
Myra L., d. 4/26/1918 at 72; married; b. Gilmanton; Emrik Moulton (Pittsfield) and Mahala Chase (Belmont)
Nettie R., d. 4/19/1901 at 23; housewife; married; b. Gilmanton; Caleb Peaslee (Gilmanton) and Luanna M. Abbott (Warner)
Nina M., d. 6/4/1976 at 77 in Rochester; housewife; widow; b. VT; Frank Higgins and Sadie Porter
William J., d. 10/19/1899 at 80/10/16; farmer; widower

FOURNIER,
Dennis R., d. 2/7/1990 in Gilmanton; Medley Fournier and Marie Mazza
Leo Benjamin, d. 1/9/1995 in Laconia; Leon Fournier and Virginia Ramsey; b. 6/1/1925**

Rita Louise, d. 8/13/1994 in Gilmanton; Francis Metivier and Mary Louise Dubois; b. 9/15/1925**

FREDETTE,
James, d. 10/10/1957 at 73 in Hanover; ret. farmer; widower; b. Middlebury, VT; John Fredette and Theressa Ariel

FREEMAN,
Francis R., d. 11/23/2000 in Gilmanton; Robert Freeman and Georgianna Glines
George E., d. 2/2/1935 at 42/10/19 in Gilmanton; machinist; married; b. Warren; Laconia

FRENCH,
son, d. 2/2/1903 at –; b. Gilmanton; Fred S. French (Gilmanton) and Mary Latuche (Canada)
Albion H., d. 9/22/1922 at 73
Charles C., d. 5/18/1887 at 23; shoemaker; single; b. Gilmanton; George W. French (Gilmanton) and Martha A. Holmes (Strafford)
Charles H., d. 1/9/1913 at 73/5/6; farmer; married; b. Canterbury; Dearborn French (Canterbury) and Margaret Haynes (Canterbury)
Eliza O., d. 3/11/1892 at 29; housewife; widow; b. Gilmanton; Sylvester French (Gilmanton) and Mercy Hayes (Strafford)
Elizabeth, d. 7/26/1889 at 91/0/2; housewife; widow; b. Nottingham
Ella Mary, d. 4/2/1958 at 90 in Concord*; housewife; widow; b. Lemington, ME; Edwin Brown and Jennie Foss
Florence Wight, d. 12/29/1918 at 28/9/1; housewife; married; b. Gloucester, MA
Fred S., d. 12/4/1945 at 72/3/8*; farmer; divorced; b. Gilmanton; Charles H. French and Susanna Newton (Loudon)
Georgia C., d. 8/21/1910 at 51 in Concord; heart disease; domestic; single; b. Gilmanton; George French (Gilmanton) and Martha Holmes (Strafford)
John, d. 5/17/1921 at 50/6/15 in Goffstown; Buzzell Cem.
John L., d. 1/15/1905 at 0/0/1; b. Laconia; F. A. French (Concord) and Maud Haines (Concord)
John S., d. 4/10/1947 at 84/4/23; farmer; widower; b. Gilmanton; George S. French and Martha Holmes

Mary L., d. 3/13/1947 at 66/3/8; housewife; married; b. Loudon; Leroy Pearl (Loudon) and Rhoda Peaslee (Loudon)
Mercy E., d. 3/3/1913 at 80/3/7; housewife; married; b. Strafford; E. Hayes (Strafford) and M. Hayes (Strafford)
Merwin E., d. 5/11/1930 at 84/9/8 in Gilmanton; farmer; married; b. Gilmanton; Thomas French and Sarah Brown; Buzzell Cem.
Susan, d. 9/24/1925 at 78/8/26 in Belmont; widow; S. Newton; Smith Meetinghouse
Sylvester, d. 1/28/1914 at 80/11/8 in Gilmanton; farmer; widower; George W. French (Gilmanton) and Olive Shepherd (Gilmanton)
Warren B., d. 7/16/1911 at 73/6/28; farmer; divorced; b. Gilmanton; John French (Gilmanton) and Lucy T. Prescott (Gilmanton)
Wesley E., d. 5/22/1925 at 17/4/8 in Gilmanton; farmer; single; b. Gilmanton; William A. French and Annie M. Carr; Buzzell Cem.
William Clifton Shepard, Jr., d. 11/1/1999 in Gilmanton; William Clifton Shepard French, Sr. and Elizabeth Hope; b. 11/16/1932**

FRITZ,
Dorothy G., d. 4/29/2001 in Laconia; Fenton Moody and Daisie Edwards; b. 11/14/1913**

FROST,
Evelyn C., d. 5/4/1985 in Laconia; b. 2/16/1914**
Philip M., d. 3/2/1987 in Laconia; Harry M. Frost and Ida A. Cuthbertson; b. 8/17/1908**

GABLINSKE,
Harriett J., d. 9/5/1987 in Laconia; Albert E. Boutwell and Eva M. Rodgers; b. 2/9/1924**

GAGNON,
Eugene Wilfrid, d. 6/7/1965 at 63 in Laconia*; carpenter; married; b. Thetford Mines, Can.; Octave Gagnon and Rosetta Blanchette
Mederic, d. 5/5/1918 at 26/9/28; carpenter; single; b. Gilmanton; Octave Gagnon (Canada) and Rose Anna Blanchette (Canada)
Octave, d. 10/25/1941 at 76/3/24; carpenter; married; b. PQ; Alexis Gagnon (Canada)

GALE,
Abby B., d. 2/3/1908 at 37/7; single; b. Gilmanton; George A. Gale and Mary J. Ayers
Abraham S., d. 3/17/1890 at 69/5/25; blacksmith; widower; b. Gilmanton; Abraham Gale (Gilmanton) and Martha B. Moulton (Gilmanton)
George, d. 9/19/1919 at 83/6 in Gilmanton; veteran; married; b. Gilmanton; Robert S. Gale and Betsey Peasley; Smith Meetinghouse
George H., d. 6/19/1932 at 79/2/24 in Concord; wheelwright; married; b. Concord
Harriet S., d. 3/24/1919 at 84/11/8 in Laconia; at home; widow; b. Gilmanton; Rowell Gilman and Judith Edgerly; Smith Meetinghouse
Julia Katherina, d. 9/9/1966 at 56 in Laconia*; looper; married; b. Philadelphia, PA; Frank Korodin and Katherine -----
Robert S., d. 1/17/1894 at 89/8; old age; farmer; widower; b. Gilmanton; Daniel Gale (Gilmanton) and Dolly Smith (Gilmanton)
Robert S., d. 10/27/1980 in Rochester; Robert Gale and Anne Strum
Rufus, d. 1/1/1924 at 91 in Penacook; retired; widower; b. Gilmanton; Stephen Gale and Betsey Dudley; Smith Meetinghouse
Sarah M., d. 8/10/1897 at 76; housewife; married; b. Alton; Henry Weeks
Sarah P., d. 5/17/1932 at 82/7/6 in Penacook; at home; widow; b. Penacook; Luther Gage and Mary J. Cross; Smith Meetinghouse
Sylvester J., d. 6/15/1903 at 71/4/5; farmer; married; b. Gilmanton; Thomas J. Gale (Gilmanton) and Hannah Sanborn (Gilmanton)

GALLANT,
Edward A., d. 5/5/1995 in Lexington, KY

GALLETTA,
Corinne F., d. 9/26/1984 in Laconia; Axel Lilljequist and Anelia Sandstrom; b. 8/22/1896**

GALLIEN,
Joseph, d. 11/16/1957 at 78 in Laconia; store proprietor; widower;
b. Canada
Leonie, d. 10/14/1950 at 74/0/24 in Gilmanton; housewife; married;
b. PQ; Charles Blanchette and Malvina Blouin

GALVIN,
Charles A., d. 5/30/1979 in Gilmanton; Joseph L. Galvin and Mamie
A. Ferguson
Gladys E., d. 12/6/1980 in Gilmanton; Guy Farris and Violet Fales

GARD,
Annie Isabelle, d. 1/30/1969 at 94 in Gilmanton; home; widow; b.
OH; George Mitten and Elizabeth Fram

GARDNER,
Hervey Sawyer, d. 1/17/1968 at 68 in Laconia; engineer; married; b.
MA; Oliver Gardner and Helena Sawyer

GARLAND,
Gordon E., d. 11/4/1950 at 54 in Gilmanton; dentist; married; b. PQ;
Forrest A. Garland and Margaret Baxter

GASSETT,
Merle Edward, d. 4/28/1967 at 54 in Manchester*; road agent;
married; b. Windsor, VT; George Gassett and Lottie Babb

GAULT,
son, d. 3/7/1892 at –; b. Gilmanton; Charles W. Gault (Gilmanton)
and Ida L. Varney (Rochester)
Dorothy F., d. 5/5/1911 at 2/4/5; b. Gilmanton; John C. Gault
(Bridgewater) and Melvina Battis (Gilmanton)
Harvey, d. 12/5/1900 at –; b. Gilmanton; John C. Gault and Melvina
Battis
John C., d. 8/11/1911 at 45/8/6; carpenter; married; b. Bridgewater;
John Q. Gault and Emily Tropine
Roland William, d. 5/22/1961 at 57 in Gilmanton; lineman; married;
b. Bridgewater; John Gault

GEDDES,
Duncan, d. 1/30/1929 at 66/7/10 in Gilmanton; farmer; married; b.
   ON; Ebenezer Geddes and Katie Fergerson; Smith
   Meetinghouse
Florence A., d. 8/17/1983 in Gilmanton; Albert Edgerly and
   Catherine Keyes
Ida, d. 9/24/1950 at 76 in Concord*; housewife; widow; b. ON; Peter
   Wilson and Susan A. Savore
John Arnold, d. 8/17/1972 at 74 in Gilmanton*; farmer; married; b.
   Canada; Duncan Geddes and Ida Wilson
Kenneth D., d. 11/14/1970 at 63 in Rochester*; shoeworker;
   widower; b. Canada; Duncan Geddes and Ida Wilson
Ruth C., d. 7/2/1969 at 66 in Rochester*; home; married; b. MA;
   Edwin Pierson and Elizabeth Hookey
Walter R., d. 1/9/1979 in Pittsfield; Duncan Geddes and Ida Wilson

GEIGER,
John, d. 12/13/1967 at 72 in Cambridge, MA*; chef; married; b.
   Germany; Johann Geiger and Marie -----
Katharina, d. 5/16/1997 in Laconia; Thomas Gegger and Katharina
   -----; b. 2/25/1901**

GENEST,
Edith L., d. 10/25/1996 in Gilmanton; Alexander Meyers and Lillian
   Hazel

GEORGE,
James D., Jr., d. 11/8/1991 in Manchester; James D. George, Sr.
   and Annie Murray

GIFFORD,
Alva P., d. 9/18/1953 at 63 in Gilmanton; housewife; married; b.
   Beverly, MA; James A. Trask and Georgia Jacques

GILES,
Abbie A., d. 4/19/1921 at 79/8/7 in Gilmanton; none [occ.]; widow;
   b. Gilmanton; Dudley Staniels and Julia Hilliard; Pine Grove
Arthur E., d. 1/12/1905 at –; shoemaker; married; Reuben Giles
   (Sanbornton) and Abbie A. Staniels (Chichester)
Fred S., d. 1/21/1905 at 42/6/7; farmer; single; b. Laconia; Reuben
   Giles (Sanbornton) and Abbie A. Staniels (Chichester)

Oscar A., d. 7/14/1947 at 69/0/13; carpenter; divorced; b. Gilmanton; Reuben Giles (Chichester) and Abbie S. Daniels (Sanbornton)

GILL,
Clement John Joseph, Jr., d. 11/18/1978 at 50 in Gilmanton; mill worker; married; b. MA; Clement J. J. Gill, Sr. and Winifred Welsh

GILMAN,
son, d. 10/29/1957 at 5 mins. in Laconia*; b. Laconia; Paul E. Gilman and Lucille A. Hawkins

Abbie H., d. 4/4/1933 at 82/8/16 in Barnstead; housework; widow; b. Barnstead; Asa C. Hurd and Mary J. Goodwin; Pine Grove

Ada, d. 4/13/1891 at 20; student; single; b. Gilmanton; Cyrus Gilman (Gilmanton) and Ellen Clay

Caleb K., d. 9/8/1895 at 72; dropsy; farmer; married; b. Wentworth; Nathaniel Gilman and Eliza Haynes

Carrie E., d. 4/17/1908 at 58/10/4; housewife; married; b. Gilmanton; Cyrus Jones and Jane Osgood

Charles F., d. 6/19/1925 at 74/9/22 in Gilmanton; farmer; widower; b. Great Falls; Ira D. Gilman and Sarah J. French; Smith Meetinghouse

Charlotte, d. 5/4/1902 at 74/0/5; housewife; widow; Stephen Dudley

Clara J., d. 4/8/1915 at 62/9/12 in Strafford, VT; housewife; married; Daniel Bullard (US)

Clarance R., d. 10/23/1911 at 56

Cora, d. 12/28/1977 at 94 in Boscawen; housewife; widow; b. NH; Fred York and Ann Jones

Cyrus, d. 3/24/1892 at 83/5/5; farmer; widower; b. Gilmanton; Samuel Gilman (Gilmanton) and Sarah Jones (Gilmanton)

Enos T., d. 5/24/1908 at 84/0/16; farmer; widower; b. Gilmanton; Nicholas Gilman (Exeter) and Hannah True (Pittsfield)

Etta M., d. 10/13/1917 at 67/2/21 in Gilmanton; housewife; married; Asa T. Edgerly (Gilmanton) and Hannah D. Moulton (Gilmanton)

Haven F., d. 11/16/1911 at 42/10/21; farmer; married; b. Gilmanton; Enos T. Gilman (Gilmanton) and Anna Hancock

Horace T., d. 12/27/1929 at 82/11/0 in Penacook; farmer; widower; b. Gilmanton; James M. Gilman and Mary Ann Tilton; Smith Meetinghouse

Ira, d. 5/16/1938 at 71/9/9 in Gilmanton; farmer; married; b. Gilmanton; Ira D. Gilman (Gilmanton) and Martha French (Pittsfield)

John T., d. 5/4/1895 at 68/1; heart failure; farmer; widower; b. Gilmanton; Nicholas Gilman (Gilmanton) and Hannah True (Pittsfield)

Lewis M., d. 4/28/1903 at 0/2/18; b. Gilmanton; Ira Gilman (Gilmanton) and Cora B. York (Pittsfield)

Lucille, d. 10/29/1957 at 34 in Laconia*; housewife; married; b. Gilmanton; Shurldin A. Hawkins and Amy D. Osborne

Martha A., d. 2/26/1894 at 66/2/3; housewife; widow; b. Dover; Nathan French and Elizabeth Burman

Mary Ann, d. 2/8/1892 at 76; housewife; widow; b. Gilmanton; Richard Tilton

GIUDA,
Ann C., d. 5/20/1975 at 54 in Gilmanton; reg. nurse; divorced; b. NY; John B. Arado and Francesca DeVincenti

GIULIANO,
Helen Crowder, d. 11/17/1995 in Gilmanton; Frank Crowder and Nellie Wallace; b. 5/27/1913**

GLIDDEN,
Andrew Mooney, d. 1/1/1919 at 39/2/1 in Gilmanton; farmer; married; b. Alton; Benjamin C. Glidden and Melinda J. Page; Pine Grove

Beulah E., d. 5/2/1985 in Hanover; George Horne and Allie Meserve; b. 8/13/1910**

Sarah E., d. 11/28/1914 at 70 in Gilmanton I. W.; housework; divorced; Alonzo Heath (Canada) and Sarah E. Leathers (Alton)

William L., d. 1/11/1991 in Gilmanton; William L. Glidden and Mary H. Clough

GLINES,
Albert Henry, d. 5/2/1915 at 78 in Weymouth, MA

Lucinda, d. 2/9/1897 at 47; housewife; married; Josiah Jones and Mary Leavitt

GLUM,
Hope M., d. 1/3/1973 at 48 in Rochester*; nurse; married; b. CA; William Miller and Helen Garvey

GLYSSON,
Loren W., d. 5/2/1917 at 88/1/4 in Gilmanton; farmer; widower; Rufus Glysson (Williamstown, VT) and Hannah M. Waldbridge (Bruckfield, VT)
Rosina, d. 6/1/1896 at 57/2/21; cancer; housewife; married; b. Windsor, VT; Philander Thompson and Sarah Marsh

GOGUEN,
Ronald Lester, Sr., d. 1/16/1994 in Laconia; Delor Goguen and Eva Matthews; b. 10/16/1934**

GOLDEN,
Alfred Kenneth, d. 11/24/1998 in Laconia; John Golden and Blanche Locke; b. 8/11/1928**

GOMES,
Joseph R., d. 5/6/1983 in Laconia; Luther Gomes and Anna Andrew
Mary E., d. 1/16/1985 in Concord; John E. Hurtt and Emilie Taylor

GOOD,
Bernard Stafford, d. 10/28/1969 at 81 in Laconia; publishing; married; b. England; ----- Good and Susannah Moore

GOODWIN,
Byron C., d. 12/15/1925 at 3/2/5 in Barnstead; b. Barnstead; Clifton Goodwin and Ethel Dame; Pine Grove
Charles E., d. 8/26/1945 at 68/8/5; retired; single; b. Gilmanton; Charles H. Goodwin (Gilmanton) and Irene A. Dorr (Ossipee)
Charles H., d. 4/19/1924 at 80 in Gilmanton; retired; widower; b. Gilmanton; Gilman Goodwin and Esther Chesley; Pine Grove
Clifton, d. 12/5/1960 at 76 in Lakeport*; woodsman; widower; b. Gilmanton; Sylvester Goodwin and Sadie -----
David, d. 7/13/1904 at 76/10/13; blacksmith; widower; b. Gilmanton; Gilman Goodwin (Barnstead) and Estha Chesley (Barnstead)
Edwin D., d. 1/11/1902 at 24/11/12; none [occ.]; single; b. Pittsfield; David Goodwin

Edwin G., d. 12/12/1900 at 23/1/3; single; b. Pittsfield; Daniel Goodwin (Gilmanton) and Belinda Goodwin (Barnstead)

Eleanor F., d. 3/23/1907 at 46/5/12; single; b. Gilmanton; David Goodwin (Gilmanton) and Elizabeth Eaton (Barnstead)

Elizabeth E., d. 11/15/1930 at 79/7/6 in Farmington; Pine Grove

Ernest Henry, d. 11/4/1951 at 76/6/19 in Gilmanton; storkeeper (ret.); married; b. NH; Charles H. Goodwin and Irena A. Dorr

Ethel, d. 8/19/1956 at 66 in Wakefield*; housewife; married; b. New Durham; Alonzo Dame and Etta French

Florence Abbie, d. 5/13/1967 at 82 in Exeter*; postmaster; widow; b. Pittsfield; Daniel Watson and Nancy Wheeler

Fremont, d. 4/17/1903 at 46/10/28; farmer; married; b. Alton; Josiah S. Goodwin (Barnstead) and L. C. Langley (Alton)

Irena M., d. 10/22/1916 at 77/8/8 in Gilmanton; housewife; married; Henry Dow (Ossipee) and Betsy Young

James H., d. 9/4/1921 at 70/9/7 in Gilmanton; carpenter; married; b. Sanford, ME; Moses Goodwin and Tryphosa Reed; Reading, MA

Jennie L., d. 8/22/1917 at 79 in Gilmanton; retired; widow

Joseph B., d. 4/16/1917 at 81/1/17 in Gilmanton; farmer; married; David Goodwin and Abigail Babb

Josiah S., d. 4/15/1912 at 86/5/10; woodworker; married; b. Barnstead; David Goodwin (Barnstead) and Abigail Chesley (Barnstead)

Lizzie E., d. 2/20/1937 at 68/3/9 in Gilmanton; housekeeper; single; b. Gilmanton; David Goodwin and Elizabeth Eaton; Pine Grove, Gilmanton I. W.

Lovey C., d. 11/20/1919 at 89/11/7 in Gilmanton; housewife; widow; b. Alton; David Langley; Pine Grove

Rachel Anna, d. 10/20/1997 in Laconia; Frank A. Straw and Halie Brown; b. 12/18/1919**

Ralph L., Sr., d. 5/27/1989 in Gilmanton; Ernest H. Goodwin and Florence A. Watson; b. 2/11/1916**

Sarah R., d. 6/11/1928 at 86/9/24 in Rochester; widow; b. Deerfield; Joseph Doe and Mary Drew; Pine Grove

Sylvester, d. 5/6/1911 at 75/6/13; farmer; married; b. Gilmanton; Gilman Goodwin

Walter, d. 12/16/1918 at 3/0/6; b. Barnstead; Clifton Goodwin and Ethel Dame

Walter R., d. 9/6/1943 at 56/9/25*; farmer; married; b. Alton

GORDON,
Fannie, d. 1/10/1908 at 76/0/28; widow; Eben Beck (Barnstead) and Thirza Holmes (Farmington)
Jacob R., d. 5/11/1895 at 68; dropsy; shoemaker; married

GOSSELIN,
Lea, d. 11/17/1940 at 73/0/14; housewife; married; b. Canada; Charles Lecour (Canada) and Marie Veilleux (Canada)

GOVE,
Walter A., Sr., d. 3/14/1983 in Concord; Henry Gove and Mary Nugent

GRANT,
Anna E., d. 8/6/1906 at 60/3/10; housewife; widow; b. Gilmanton; Ira Farrar (Gilmanton) and Sarah Parsons
John O., d. 10/14/1901 at 65/3/12; stage driver; married; b. Gilmanton; Samuel Grant and Hannah Durrell
Sarah A., d. 12/15/1923 at 87

GRAVES,
Kathleen E., d. 12/29/2001 in Laconia; Lawrence Gemmell and Minnie Glidden

GRAY,
daughter, d. 3/28/1888 at 0/0/1; b. Gilmanton; Orrin W. Gray (Barrington) and Carrie O. Cater (Dover)
Edgar A., d. 5/9/1924 at 69 in Gilmanton; teamster; Grafton
Emanuel, d. 4/18/1888 at 0/0/21; b. Gilmanton; Orrin W. Gray (Barrington) and Carrie O. Cater (Dover)
Jane, d. 6/1/1925 at 88 in Gilmanton; none [occ.]; widow; Pine Grove
Jenness, d. 10/24/1912 at 79/11/17; laborer; married; Shem Gray (Strafford) and Hannah W. Doe (New Durham)
R. M., Dr., d. 6/6/1900 at 80; physician; married; b. Sheffield; George Gray (Sheffield) and Mary Miles

GREELEY,
Stephen S. N., d. 10/25/1892 at 79/9/2; clergyman; married; b. Gilmanton; Stephen L. Greeley (Gilmanton) and Nancy Norton (Newburyport, MA)

GREEN,
Ada E., d. 6/9/1898 at 15; housewife; married; b. Concord; Frank Sargent (Loudon) and Jennie Sanborn (Concord)
Alvah R., d. 9/25/1890 at 0/1/12; b. Gilmanton; Elmer L. Green (Gilmanton) and Antonio Kratzert (OH)
Arvilla H., d. 9/24/1898 at 68/9/28; housewife; married; b. Loudon; Smith Fogg and Betsey Hynes
Ernest Elkins, d. 9/16/1962 at 68 in Gilmanton; painter & paper.; married; b. Bow; Frank Green and Ada Elkins
Jay H., d. 9/9/1975 at 71 in Concord; log roller; married; b. NH; Elmer L. Green and Antonia Kratzert
Mary A., d. 7/4/1926 at 58/0/6 in Pittsfield; housework; widow; b. Sandwich; Royal McDonald and Mary A. Bickford; Smith Meeting House
Oliver L., d. 1/26/1906 at 73/10/4; farmer; widower; b. Loudon; David Green (Pittsfield) and Roxanna Sherbourne (Epsom)
Peter Paul, d. 4/9/1952 at 65 in Laconia; farming; married; b. Lithuania; Constantine Pocius and Veronica Markauskas
Peter Paul, d. 2/4/1954 at 26 in Gilmanton; mer. marine; divorced; b. Randolph, OH; Peter P. Green and Anastasia Yaki
Walter S., d. 12/23/1924 at 58 in Gilmanton; farmer; married; b. Gilmanton; Oliver Green and Arvilla Fogg; Smith Meetinghouse

GREENE,
Adrial H., d. 11/21/1904 at 74/4/19; farmer; married; b. Lynn, MA; James Greene and Mary Perkins
Archie W., d. 7/5/1956 at 58 in Loudon*; farmer; married; b. Gilmanton; Walter Green (sic) and Ada Sargent
Elmer L., d. 6/13/1933 at 69/0/1 in Gilmanton; farmer; married; b. Gilmanton; Oliver L. Greene and Arvilla Fogg; Smith Meetinghouse
Mary Frances, d. 8/18/1953 at 84 in Gilmanton; housewife; married; b. NH; Walter W. Carter and Emma J. Johnson
Norman David, d. 6/10/1931 at 0/0/8 in Gilmanton; b. Gilmanton; Roland W. Greene and Edna A. Page; Smith Meetinghouse
Roland W., d. 11/2/1939 at 47/6/16 in Gilmanton; retired; married; b. Gilmanton; Elmer L. Greene (Gilmanton) and Antonia Kratzer (Germany)

GREENLEAF,
Milton, d. 6/19/1941 at 82/11/20; shoemaker; married; b. Northwood; George Greenleaf and Elizabeth Winslow

GREENOUGH,
Nancy K., d. 9/2/1916 at 89/4/4 in Gilmanton; widow; ----- Morrill (Chichester) and Nancy Griffin
William C., d. 5/21/1903 at 81/3/29; farmer; married; b. Halifax, MA

GRIFFIN,
Etta E., d. 8/28/1957 at 93 in Pittsfield*; garment stitcher; single; b. Gilmanton; Joseph T. Griffin and Mary O. Brown
Eva G., d. 1/30/1934 at 54/1/20 in Gilmanton; housewife; married; b. Gilmanton; Charles A. Osborne and Grace A. True; Smith Meetinghouse
Linda, d. 10/29/1891 at 89/6; housewife; widow; b. Gilmanton
Mary Olavia, d. 8/28/1917 at 80/8/10 in Pittsfield; retired; widow; ---- Brown and ----- Bagley
Nathan D., d. 8/20/1943 at 76/4/25*; retired baker; widower; b. Gilmanton; Joseph T. Griffin (Gilmanton) and Mary O. Brown (Boston, MA)

GRITZ,
Lucy M., d. 11/7/1977 at 81 in Concord; housewife; married; b. Lithuania; Frank Martin and Martha Circius

GRONDIN,
Rosanna, d. 4/4/1905 at 2/7/28; b. NB; Ernest Grondin (Canada) and ----- Gallien (NB)

GROSJEAN,
Arthur Allen, d. 6/12/1967 at 83 in Rochester*; jeweler; married; b. Brooklyn, NY; Frederick Grosjean and Ida F. Allen

GROVER,
Cora A., d. 9/19/1912 at 33/6/7; b. N. Berwick, ME; Daniel Mansfield (Lynn, MA) and Lidia Ginn (N. Berwick, ME)
William J., d. 9/26/1904 at 0/0/3; b. Gilmanton; Joseph B. Grover (N. Berwick, ME) and Cora A. Mansfield (Malden, MA)

GRUBER,
Max. F., d. 4/7/1971 at 72 in Laconia; mech. engineer; married; b. Switzerland; Fritz Gruber and Martha Ritchard

GUY,
Walter J., d. 2/24/1965 at 80 in Laconia; unemployed; single; b. Gilmanton; Louis Guy and Sarah A. -----

HAINES,
Charles, d. 5/9/1918 at 48/3/29; laborer; single; b. Concord; Taylor Haines (Loudon) and Mary Doe
Clara P., d. 3/20/1913 at 66/8/10
Mary E., d. 5/24/1898 at 60/0/6; housekeeper; widow

HALE,
Elijah, d. 9/1/1888 at 47/9; black; farmer; married

HALL,
A. Parker, d. 4/9/1983 in Concord; Theron D. Hall and Annie D. Tibbetts
Ada, d. 3/27/1959 at 82 in Concord*; housewife; widow; b. Suncook; Edward Dudevoir and Josephine Strickford
Bertrand M., d. 6/27/1936 at 63/5/29 in Gilford
Charles Alfred, d. 3/6/1954 at 78 in Concord*; let. carrier; married; b. Concord; John S. Hall and Ella Willey
Harvey J., d. 10/22/1956 at 85 in Gilmanton; farmer; married; b. Gilmanton; Edgar F. Hall and Lydia Folsom
Julia, d. 10/24/1962 at 92 in Laconia*; housewife; widow; b. Wootin, PQ; ----- Chaperone
Theron E., d. 1/4/1971 at 81 in Laconia; farmer; single; b. MA; Theron D. Hall and Annie D. Tibbetts

HALLAHAN,
Thomas, d. 12/25/1933 at 68 in Gilmanton; caretaker; b. Chelsea, MA; Thomas Hallahan and Bridget Dowd; Holy Cross - MA

HAM,
Abbie Y., d. 2/16/1915 at 73/0/22 in Gilmanton; widow; James Varney and Matilda Otis (Strafford)
Edwin W., d. 4/1/1950 at 85 in Gilmanton; m'f'r (ret.); single; b. NH; James C. Ham and Mary E. Clark

Fred P., d. 8/18/1933 at 75/2/18 in Somerville, MA; literary work; married; Pine Grove
Henrietta J., d. 1/26/1910 at 81/2/7 in Somerville, MA; pneumonia; housewife; married; Abram S. Gale and Martha Moulton
John W., d. 4/7/1904 at 74/10/14; farmer; married; b. Gilmanton; John Ham (Epsom) and Mercy C. Brown (Epsom)
Lemuel M., d. 12/28/1911 at 83/8/29; retired; widower; b. Alton; Ezra Ham and Mary P. Hill
Nellie Elmer, d. 5/24/1887 at 20/1; housemaid; single; b. Barnstead; James Christie Ham (Gilmanton) and Mary Elizabeth Clark (Barnstead)

HAMB,
Joe Steven, d. 8/20-21/1982 in Gilmanton; Joe W. Hamb, Jr. and Lillian -----

HAMILTON,
Lydia S., d. 2/22/1896 at 85; heart disease; housekeeper; widow

HANSCOM,
Cora F., d. 3/12/1924 at 59 in Gilmanton; retired; divorced; b. Alton; Mirum Clough and Elizabeth Prescott; Pine Grove

HANSON,
Kennith C., d. 6/29/1922 at 14

HARDY,
Clarence N., d. 9/19/1911 at 62/0/10; musician; married; b. Peterborough; Samuel Hardy (Dublin) and Mary Foster (Roxbury)

HARRINGTON,
John, d. 9/25/1948 at 60/1/28; mach.-farmer; married; b. Chatham, NB; John E. Harrington (Chatham, NB) and Mary MacDougall (Blackville, NB)

HARRIS,
Donald Morrison, d. 6/19/1996 in Laconia; Myron Harris and Rachel -----; b. 3/28/1911**
Nelson L., d. 10/2/1926 at 76/2/26 in Gilmanton; farmer; married; b. Holdrum; Noah Harris and Mary J. Brown; Ashland, NH

HARTFORD,
Arlington E., d. 1/8/2000 in Laconia; Pierce Hartford and Addie Lyford; b. 6/24/1918**

HASKELL,
Bertha A., d. 8/21/1985 in Wolfeboro; Joseph Asselin and Azelia Caron; b. 1/18/1907**
Cedric, d. 2/23/1972 at 73 in Concord; broker; married; b. MA; Samuel C. L. Haskell and Mineola -----
Cedric William, d. 9/23/1991 in Gilmanton; Cedric L. Haskell and Bertha Asselin
Clara Augusta, d. 4/22/1893 at 0/0/24; colored; congestion of the lungs; b. Gilmanton; George F. Haskell (Canterbury) and Emma E. Battis (Northfield)
Emma E., d. 11/4/1910 at 43/11/24; uterine cancer; housewife; married; b. Northfield; John F. Battis (Northfield) and Lydia E. Burnham
Horace, d. 7/6/1981 in Gilmanton; Howard N. Haskell and Mabel B. Langdon; b. 1/11/1905**
Laura E., d. 9/24/1896 at 64/1/6; housewife; married; b. Contoocook; Eben Burbank and Amy Dow

HASTY,
Ada E., d. 12/4/1931 at 69/5/4 in Gilmanton; housework; married; b. St. Johns, NB; Richard T. Kingston and Jane Daly; Everett, MA
Gilbert M., d. 1/12/1940 at 75/5/3*; farmer; widower; b. Standish, ME; John Hasty (Standish, ME) and Emeline Dow (Standish, ME)

HAUSWIRTH,
Diane M., d. 6/30/2000 in Laconia; Damon Kilgore, Jr. and Effie Munroe; b. 9/22/1929**

HAWKINS,
Margaret Jean, d. 2/21/1964 at 31 in Gilmanton*; office worker; married; b. Gilmanton; Eugene Gagnon and Dorothy Hislop
Mollie D., d. 5/13/1958 at 58 in Laconia*; housewife; divorced; b. Grafton, NS; J. LeBaron Margeson and Sarah Jane -----
Shurldin Allen, d. 6/12/1964 at 73 in Laconia*; farmer; married; b. Boston, MA; ----- and Millie Hawkins

HAWTHORNE,
Carlos G., d. 3/9/1893 at 69; heart failure; lawyer; married; b. Hopkinton; Calvin Hawthorne (Henniker) and Rachel Jackman (Plaistow)

HAYES,
Eben H., d. 3/4/1920 at 78/3/25 in Gilmanton; farmer; widower; b. Barnstead; Evans Hayes and Mercy Hayes; Loudon
Leonard Ralph, Sr., d. 9/19/1965 at 62 in Gilmanton; mechanic; married; b. PQ; Edward Hayes and Sarah -----
Sarah M., d. 12/23/1902 at 67/10; housewife; married; b. Loudon; B. C. Merrill (Gilmanton) and Sarah Pickering (Barnstead)

HAYNES,
Carrie, d. 2/8/1896 at 68; pneumonia; housewife; married; David S. Young (Gilmanton) and Betsy Avery (Thornton)
Nancy S., d. 4/15/1905 at 76/6/23; housewife; widow; b. Gilmanton; Moses Flanders and Mary Page
Samuel T., d. 8/26/1889 at 82; farmer; widower
William, d. 1/22/1899 at 88/2; mechanic; widower

HAYWOOD,
Grace A., d. 9/24/1937 at 64/8/16 in Gilmanton; at home; widow; b. Pembroke; Wyatt Knowles and Elizabeth Jon; Parade, Barnstead

HEALEY,
John, d. 3/20/1980 in Laconia; Charles J. Healey and Glenna M. Munsey

HEILE,
Anna M., d. 2/19/1980 in Laconia; Theodore Epe and Anna Kulbertans; b. 7/24/1902**

HEMLIN,
David T., d. 10/7/2000 in Laconia; Theodore Hemlin and Miriam Koski; b. 3/22/1936**

HERLIHY,
Francis E., d. 11/22/1990 in Manchester; Patrick F. Herlihy and Mary F. Wilson

HETTLER,
Kathleen Taylor, d. 4/5/1992 in Gilmanton; Frederick R. Taylor and Winnifred Glennon; b. 11/22/1918**

HICKEY,
Bertha Marion, d. 11/7/1998 in Laconia; John Patenaude and Flora Bergeron

HIGGINS,
Lewis H., d. 8/10/1919 at 51/10/10 in hx; painter; married; b. NB; Dorchester, MA

HILL,
Albert W., d. 11/23/1920 at 53/0/29 in Laconia; farmer; single; b. Gilmanton; Charles Hill and Lydia Berry; Smith Meetinghouse
Eliza A., d. 10/31/1915 at 82 in Gilmanton; housewife; widow; John Leonard (Gilmanton)
Elizabeth A., d. 3/24/1898 at 73; housewife; widow; b. Tamworth; ----- Jackson (Tamworth) and ----- (Griffin)
Elwood H., d. 2/28/1925 at 62/3/9 in Pittsfield; farmer; married; b. Alton; Joseph R. Hill and Phemia -----; Pine Grove
Ezekiel, d. 9/6/1897 at 81/8; farmer; widower; b. Gilmanton; Jonathan Hill (Gilmanton) and Mehitable Flanders (Alton)
Florence Ethal, d. 11/4/1993 in Concord; Leslie W. Ford and Nellie F. Chase; b. 9/1/1913**
Frank Arthur, d. 1/10/1993 in Laconia; Ray Hill; b. 7/11/1919**
Jonathan P., d. 2/17/1893 at 83/11; farmer; widower; b. Alton; Andrew W. Hill
Joseph R., d. 11/15/1916 at 82/2/25 in Gilmanton; butcher; widower; Ezra Hill (Canada) and Hannah Howard (NH)
Lila, d. 5/13/1934 at 65 in Concord; divorced; b. Gilmanton; Joseph Hill and Paula -----; Pine Grove
Lydia, d. 7/18/1893 at 58/7/11; heart disease; housewife; widow; Eben B. Berry (New Durham) and Mercy R. Berry (Dover)
Lyford C., d. 8/30/1888 at 81/7; married
Mercedas May, d. 12/12/1967 at 86 in Concord*; housewife; widow; b. Middleton; Alonzo Dame and Etta French
Mercy C., d. 3/17/1889 at 75/3; housewife; married; b. Jackson; Asa Davis (Nottingham) and Hannah Elkins (Gilford)
Pluma E., d. 8/19/1908 at 70/2/26; housewife; married; b. Barnston, Can.; Nathaniel Hill (Canada) and Mary A. Corliss (Canada)

HILLIARD,
Alfred S., d. 4/18/1893 at 71/11; bronchitis and dropsy; farmer; widower; b. Pittsfield; Abraham Hilliard (Chichester) and ----- Tole (Chichester)
Leander A., d. 10/26/1941 at 81/1; laborer; married; b. Gilmanton; Alfred Hilliard (Gilmanton) and Emma Couch (Sutton)
Lillian E., d. 4/27/1943 at 72/2/19*; at home; widow; b. Sutton; Henry Mastine (Sutton) and Emma Couch (Sutton)

HILLS,
Esther L., d. 4/12/1990 in Gilmanton; Austin J. Lane and Marion Little

HILLSGROVE,
Joseph H., d. 9/8/1978 at 55 in Concord; store owner, oper.; married; b. NH; Walter J. Hillsgrove and Mytie Day

HILTZ,
Cynthia Irene, d. 12/15/1972 at 60 in Concord; housewife; married; b. NS; Angus Hiltz and Sadie Corkum
Fred L., d. 9/10/1991 in Laconia; Blenum Hiltz and Mabel Nass

HIPPERT,
Albina A., d. 2/12/1985 in Laconia; Frank Soukup and Elizabeth ----; b. 2/10/1893**
Ernest L., d. 12/24/1973 at 85 in Gilmanton*; inspector ret.; married; b. NY; Rheinhold Hippert and Rose -----

HISLOP,
Bertha May, d. 5/4/1960 at 78 in Rochester*; housewife; married; b. Gilmanton; Horace Ellis and Ella A. Page
Richard, d. 3/24/1948 at 0/0/5*; b. Laconia; Richard W. Hislop (Gilmanton) and June Manning (FL)
Robert Willis, d. 10/12/1960 at 79 in Concord*; blacksmith; widower; b. Rochester; Harry Hislop and Viennia Hussey

HOADLEY,
Betsey M., d. 3/16/1918 at 79/11; widow
Jasper H., d. 5/6/1902 at 59/0/1; farmer; married; b. Tunkhannock, PA; ----- and Sarah Macey

HOAG,
daughter, d. 9/24/1948 at 0/0/0*; b. Laconia; Paul Hoag (Brooklyn, NY) and Dorothy Smith (Long Island)

HOBBS,
Clayton Gerald, d. 1/21/1995 in Gilmanton; William Herbert Hobbs and Velma Luella Flint; b. 7/12/1896**

HODGDON,
Theodore W., d. 11/15/1956 at 69 in Gilmanton; farmer; b. Gilmanton; ----- and Emma Purcell

HOLBROOK,
Elizabeth, d. 1/3/1894 at 64; dropsy; housekeeper; single; b. Garland, ME
Eunice, d. 11/25/1891 at 89; housewife; widow; John Phipps (Sherburne, MA) and Hannah Colledge

HOMEN,
William R., d. 12/24/1973 at 31 in Gilmanton*; prop. grocery store; divorced; b. CA; William F. Homen and Lucy Medinas

HOOD,
Lurlene, d. 5/19/1976 at 78 in Laconia; none [occ.]; single; John E. Hood and Julia Longway

HORSMAN,
Ann Mary, d. 3/18/1938 at 82/10/1 in Gilmanton; housewife; married; b. Bradford, England; Richard Crossland (Bradford, England) and Ellen Walker (England)
John A., d. 8/2/1947 at 93/5/16; tailor; widower; b. Bradford, England; George Horsman (Bradford, England)

HOTTEL,
Diana, d. 2/11/1976 at 32 in Gilmanton; housewife; married; b. NY; Alfred A. Summer and Margaret Lippincott

HOULE,
Lionel, d. 12/28/1993 in Laconia; Albert Houle and Laura Labree; b. 1/29/1917**

HOWARD,
Charles, d. 1/2/1995 in Dover; Wilson Howard and Amanda Neal; b. 8/29/1917**
Sarah S., d. 1/14/1892 at 76/8; housewife; widow; b. Barnstead; Thomas Ayer (Barnstead) and Sally Gale (Gilmanton)

HOWE,
Carl D., d. 1/24/1912 at 38/5/1; sawyer; married; b. Grafton; Henry P. Howe and Clarisa Leavitt

HUFSCHMID,
Anton, d. 12/13/1968 at 77 in Gilmanton; architect; divorced; b. Germany; Anton Hufschmid and Maria Weberstetter
Erich, d. 6/25/1977 at 48 in Concord; provider; married; b. NY; Anton Hufschmid and Paula Geiger
Helen, d. 4/10/2001 in Concord; Harry Immohr and Anna Mohrnen; b. 2/27/1929**

HUGELMAN,
Allan H., d. 2/24/2000 in Concord; John Hugelman and Elizabeth Huetner; b. 2/14/1919**

HULL,
George H., Jr., d. 7/23/1894 at 45/10/21; pulmonary tuberculosis; married; b. Boston, MA; George H. Hull and Ann H. -----

HUNKINS,
Dana W., d. 1/15/1980 in Laconia; Clarence J. Hunkins and Ruth Churchwell; b. 2/6/1923**

HUNTLEY,
Kevin W., d. 6/19/2001 in Concord; John Huntley and Regina Stebbins

HURD,
Amy E., d. 5/29/1967 at 86 in Concord*; at home; widow; b. West Lebanon; Almon W. Walker and Elzina Thurston
Asa, d. 3/26/1918 at 95/5/19; stone mason; widower; b. Barnstead; Ebenezer Hurd and Nancy Whitehouse
Caleb, d. 12/23/1888 at 84/6; married

Clarence Edwin, d. 7/23/1933 at 52/8/13 in Kisbey, Canada; married; Pine Grove
Harriet L., d. 5/7/1908 at 78/1/7; single; b. Loudon; Caleb Hurd (Tuftonboro) and Judith C. Allen (Gilmanton)
Henry L., d. 7/13/1918 at 88/3/13; farmer; married; b. Gilmanton; Caleb Hurd (Cow Is., Lake Winnipesaukee) and Judith Allen
James A., d. 9/23/1914 at 77/9 in Gilmanton I. W.; barber; married; Caleb Hurd (Tuftonboro) and Judith Allen
Martha, d. 12/8/1914 at 82 in Gilmanton I. W.; widow; ----- Hodgdon
Minnie E., d. 1/28/1928 at 78/8/5 in Pittsfield; housework; widow; Pine Grove

HURST,
Ronald Rexford, d. 4/13/1993 in Concord; Albert W. Hurst and Norma J. Durette

HUSSEY,
Betsey, d. 12/22/1888 at 67/9
E. F., d. 2/7/1916 at 57/4/26 in Loudon; laborer; married; E. R. Hussey (Milton) and Bathsheba Goodwin (Milton)
John P., d. 12/19/1920 at 89/9/6 in Gilmanton; retired; widower; b. Gilmanton; Reuben Hussey and Alice Perkins; Pine Grove
Lydia A., d. 6/4/1905 at 80/0/7; single; b. Gilmanton; Reuben Hussey (Barrington) and Alice Perkins (Strafford)
Olive A., d. 2/19/1907 at 75/9/24; housewife; married; b. Gilmanton; John Foss and Olive Clough (Gilmanton)
S. Mittie, d. 9/15/1929 at 76/7/22 in Loudon; Buzzell Cem.

HUTCHINSON,
Clara E., d. 3/19/1938 at 85/11 in Gilmanton; retired; single; b. Gilmanton; George Hutchinson (Gilmanton) and Rosilla Watson (Alton)
Frank. d. 5/14/1924 at 72 in Gilmanton; laborer; single; b. Gilmanton; Frank Hutchinson and Eliza Downs; Pine Grove
George F., d. 11/24/1922 at 64
W'y C. H., d. 5/3/1896 at 84; old age; housewife; widow; b. Gilmanton; Stephen Eastman

HYDE,
Dorsey W., d. 4/30/1942 at 89/7/5*; music composer; widower; b. Hydetown, PA; Charles Hyde (Eagle, NY) and Abby Perley

Dorsey W., d. 1/31/1955 at 67 in Concord*; unemployed; married;
b. Plainfield, NJ; Dorsey W. Hyde and Katherine Clark
Edyth Medora, d. 10/11/1918 at 33/0/25; single; b. Gilmanton;
Dorsey W. Hyde (PA) and Catherine Clark (NY)
Katherine C., d. 4/6/1936 at 73/2/18 in Laconia; at home; married;
b. New York City; Frederick Clarke and Katherine Monteigh
Sybil M., d. 7/26/1956 at 74 in Laconia; housewife; widow; b.
England; Alfred Cox and Emily J. Wood

HYSLOP,
Donald W., d. 3/15/1966 at 54 in Gilmanton*; machinist; married; b.
Merrimack, MA; Robert W. Hyslop and Bertha M. Ellis
Frank T., d. 6/7/1944 at 0/4/6; b. Laconia; Robert E. Hyslop
(Merrimac, MA) and Cecile C. Grant (Montreal, PQ)

IMMOHR,
Anna J., d. 10/5/1974 at 74 in Laconia; housewife; divorced; b.
Germany; Henry Mohrmann and Anna Saghorne
Harry J., d. 2/9/1980 in Concord; Heinrich F. Immohr and Johanne
Lubben

INGALLS,
Charles J., d. 7/11/2001 in Laconia; Charles Ingalls and Irene Tyler;
b. 12/21/1926**

ISENBERG,
Bruce Allen, d. 3/12/1994 in Gilmanton; James A. Isenberg and
Nancy Peel

JACKSON,
Esther Mary, d. 12/27/1994 in Laconia; John Seymour McPhee and
Edith Chipmund; b. 3/27/1918**
James M., d. 1/7/1993 in Laconia; Walter L. Jackson and Eliza Ann
Percy; b. 3/5/1915**

JAHNLE,
Carl G., d. 10/1/1975 at 66 in Gilmanton; storekeeper (ret.);
married; b. MA; Carl B. Jahnle and Mary J. Wray Lattie
Helmtrude L., d. 12/7/1972 at 59 in Laconia; housewife; single; b.
MA; Carl B. Jahnle and Mary Jane Wray

JEFFERSON,
Olive Coffed, d. 4/29/1963 at 63 in Laconia; teacher (ret.); married;
    b. Toronto, Can.; John Coffed and Martha White

JEFFREY,
Eliza Mackintosh, d. 3/30/1960 at 77 in Laconia*; housewife; widow;
    b. Otley, England; Charles Mackintosh and Jane Hollings
Harry, d. 1/21/1956 at 75 in Gilmanton; farmer; married; b.
    England; John Jeffrey and Jane Perkins

JENDRAULT,
Fred D., d. 11/9/1926 at 68/10/15 in Alton; Pine Grove

JOHNSON,
Anna M., d. 10/30/1906 at 65/1/6; housekeeper; widow; b.
    Gilmanton; Enoch Moulton (Gilmanton) and Mahala Chase
    (Gilmanton)
Elaine G., d. 5/21/1987 in Gilmanton; John Govang and Agnes -----;
    b. 3/28/1945**
Elena E., d. 5/20/1937 at 83/5/5 in Gilmanton; housewife; widow; b.
    Limington, ME; Isiah Johnson; Franklin
George B., d. 6/27/1931 at 67/9/19 in Pittsfield; mail carrier;
    married; b. Detroit, MI; James M. Johnson and Elizabeth M.
    Morrill; Smith Meetinghouse
Henri R., d. 5/12/1932 at 43/2 in Gilmanton; colored; waiter; single;
    b. MS; Jackson, MS
Ida T., d. 5/17/1934 at 71/2/13 in Concord; widow; b. Gilmanton;
    Tyler G. Tilton and Jeanette Kerr; Smith Meetinghouse
Thoralf, d. 2/22/1974 at 70 in Concord; unknown [occ.]; married; b.
    Norway; Ole Johnson and Alma -----

JONES,
son, d. 12/23/1933 at 0/0/0 in Laconia; Karl Jones and Mary
    Canney; Smith Meetinghouse
Allie Cyrus, d. 3/22/1952 at 86 in Gilmanton; farmer; widower; b.
    NH; Cyrus Jones and Laura Maxfield
Annie M., d. 8/15/1903 at 59; housewife; married
Charles D., d. 1/17/1971 at 76 in Laconia; farm mgr. ret.; married;
    b. ME; Sandford Jones and ----- Lincoln
Cyrus, d. 4/26/1892 at 72; farmer; married; David Jones and Abigail
    Jones

Doris Mabel, d. 6/6/1918 at 4/0/6; b. Gilmanton; M. Willey (Boston, MA) and Ethel Louise Jones (Gilmanton)

Ernest, d. 12/11/1910 at 46/2/14; apoplexy; laborer; single; b. Gilmanton; James M. Jones and Nancy J. Bunker

Florence M., d. 7/15/1895 at 28/1; drowning; housewife; married; b. Lawrence, MA; Holland Payson (NS) and ----- (E. Lebanon)

George A., d. 5/28/1893 at 0/5; whooping cough; b. Gilmanton; George A. Jones (Gilmanton) and Olive Moody (Canterbury)

Ida Louisa, d. 2/23/1938 at 77/8/6; housewife; widow; b. Williamstown, VT; Loren Glysson (VT) and Rosina Thompson (Windsor, VT)

James Asa, d. 5/17/1901 at 77; miller; married; b. Gilmanton; James Jones (Gilmanton) and Ruth Hanson

Jessie N., d. 2/2/1895 at 19/11/4; phthisis pulmonalis; music teacher; single; b. Rochester; John Henry Jones (Rochester) and Jennie H. Evans (New Durham)

John Henry, d. 12/29/1892 at 50/1/14; merchant; widower; b. Rochester; Nathaniel B. Jones (Farmington) and Louisa A. Clements (Alton)

Joseph L., d. 1/29/1925 at 78/11/17 in Gilmanton; farmer; married; b. Loudon; Joseph B. Jones and Mary Leavett; Smith Meetinghouse

Lillian, d. 2/9/1933 at 53/3/21 in Gilmanton; at home; married; b. Belmont; Frank A. Brown and Clara E. Clark; Smith Meetinghouse

Louisa A., d. 8/6/1890 at 79/3/7; housewife; married; b. Alton; Enoch Clements (Dover) and Sally Swain (Rochester)

Marjorie B., d. 1/6/1978 at 67 in Concord; machine operator; married; b. NH; John Sterns and Blanche Whipple

Martha A., d. 9/27/1891 at 63/3; housewife; married; b. Belmont; Nathaniel Gale

Mary, d. 8/6/1905 at 84/3/22; housewife; widow; b. Grafton; Joseph Leavitt and Hannah Fifield

Mary C., d. 1/24/1934 at 25/1/24 in Laconia; housewife; married; b. East Concord; John W. Canney and Laura J. Smith; Smith Meetinghouse

Mary J., d. 1/4/1905 at 59/5; widow; b. Boston, MA; Edward Warner (Portsmouth) and Jane Townes (ME)

Morrill S., d. 9/30/1926 at 75 in Laconia; farmer; Smith Meeting House

Nathaniel B., d. 7/18/1904 at 91/3/7; carpenter; widower; b. Farmington; Samuel Jones (Farmington) and Mehitable Burnham (Rochester)

Ralph A., d. 1/16/1985 in Laconia; Allie C. Jones and Lillian Brown; b. 11/9/1903**

Richard H., d. 5/7/1894 at 79/11/18; widower; b. Gilmanton; James Jones and Ruth Hanson

Ruth Esther, d. 2/5/1976 at 78 in Laconia; housewife; widow; b. ME; Ernest Gatcomb and Marge Gardner

Walter Riddick, d. 10/15/1963 at 65 in Wolfeboro; contractor; married; b. Norfolk, VA; Noah Jones and Mary E. Williams

William, d. 5/28/1887 at 63; farmer; single; b. Gilmanton; James Jones (Gilmanton) and Ruth Hanson (Gilmanton)

JORDAN,

Harold V., d. 1/12/1984 in Laconia; James B. Jordan and Mary -----

Irene, d. 2/14/1984 in Gilmanton I. W.; Erling Wettre and Hilda Anderson

Jenet, d. 10/19/1939 at – in Wolfeboro*; b. Wolfeboro; Harold Jordan (MA) and Irene M. Wettre (Malden, MA)

JOSEPH,

Edith, d. 8/12/1927 at 17 in Gilmanton; negro; maid; single; b. Brighton, NS

JOY,

Lila M., d. 12/2/1967 at 71 in Concord; married; b. Belmont; D. C. Twombly and Emma Batchelder

JOYCE,

Frank T., d. 1/5/1985 in Laconia; Edward Tong and Ellen Langley; b. 2/4/1912**

Myrtle P., d. 2/20/1985 in Laconia; Edward Cronin and Lydia Coma; b. 6/10/1918**

KALWEIT,

Joseph, d. 2/24/1999 in Laconia; Joseph Kalweit and Anna Langsieb; b. 9/2/1916**

KARDINAL,
Herman H., Jr., d. 8/1/1994 in Rochester; Herman H. Kardinal, Sr. and Catherine E. Ferrick

KAWA,
Rusell J., d. 11/3/1965 at 45 in Hanover; agent - IRS; married; b. Woonsocket, RI; Joseph Kawa and Anna Humeniuk

KEAY,
Freda Emma, d. 10/13/1903 at 0/3/27; b. Lakeport; Gertie Keay

KEEFE,
William Francis, d. 10/3/1993 in Wolfeboro; Thomas Keefe and Rosa Dugdale; b. 6/14/1910**

KELLER,
William Wagenaar, d. 9/6/1995 in Laconia; Walter Keller and Alvira Wagenaar; b. 11/17/1928**

KELLEY,
Adelia C., d. 5/6/1947 at 86/0/1; housewife; widow; b. Alton; John Jones (Alton) and Lucinda Perkins (Alton)
Amy Alice, d. 11/12/1973 at 89 in Franklin; housewife; widow; b. VT; J. S. Andrews and Alice Sunbury
Anita Therese Marie, d. 2/26/1993 in Gilmanton; Arthur Twombly and Alexandrine Montambeault; b. 2/14/1929**
Charles G., d. 8/31/1965 at 79 in Concord*; farmer; married; b. Gilmanton; George F. Kelley and Adelia Jones
George F., d. 4/26/1915 at 63/9/20 in Gilmanton; farmer; married; Charles G. Kelley (Gilmanton) and Abby J. Sherburne (Northwood)
Hattie Belle, d. 1/1/1976 at 86 in Concord; housewife; widow; b. NY; C. Frank Paige and Cora B. Gale
Mary, d. 7/22/1989 in Laconia; Vernard Moulton and Bernice Allen Moulton; b. 8/24/1930**
Robert W., Sr., d. 6/4/1989 in Gilmanton; Ernest Kelley and Amy Andrews

KELLY,
Violet A., d. 2/3/1985 in Laconia; Peter H. Stevens and Annie B. Hudson; b. 4/8/1902**

KENDALL,
Mary Dow, d. 8/11/1887 at 84; housekeeper; married; b. Gilmanton; Ephraim Dow (Gilmanton) and Elizabeth French (New Hampton)
Prescott V. Z., d. 4/11/1889 at 95; mechanic; widower; b. Springfield, MA

KENNEDY,
Cora May, d. 1/20/1926 at 57/2/28 in Gilmanton; widow; b. Nashua; Joel D. Champion and Martha Abbott; Nashua

KENNEY,
Charles L., d. 8/2/2000 in Concord; Forrest Kenney and Emma Towle; b. 5/7/1916**

KENT,
Brian William, d. 10/17/1969 at 0/4 in Laconia*; b. NH; Robert Kent and Gloria Limburg

KERRIGAN,
Terence, d. 8/10/1889 at 17; farmer; single

KEYES,
William A., d. 6/22/1913 at 56/6/25; carpenter; married; b. Harrisburg, NY; Cyrus Keyes (Harrisburg, NY) and Pauline Smith (NY)

KIDDER,
Emerline, d. 10/31/1918 at 102/6; widow; b. Gilmanton; Isiah Green (Belmont) and Sally Dorr (Bow)

KIMBALL,
Jere. S., d. 3/11/1898 at 70/2; farmer; married; b. Belmont; Matthias Kimball (Belmont) and Eunice Buswell (Gilmanton)
Nathaniel T., d. 2/13/1968 at 72 in Wolfeboro; salesman; married; b. NH; Nathaniel Kimball and Elizabeth Trask
Sylvester W., d. 4/21/1896 at 45; angina pectoris; farmer; single; b. Gilmanton; Josiah Kimball (Gilmanton)

KING,
Frank Edward, d. 5/30/1992 in Laconia; George King and Grace French; b. 7/18/1902**

KITCHEN,
Marcus L. W., d. 8/28/1896 at 59; apoplexy; ret. merchant; married; Zeba H. Kitchen (NJ) and M. L. Ward (NJ)
Myra C., d. 12/15/1938 at 83/8/11 in Gilmanton; widow; b. New York, NY; Samuel S. Constant (Boston, MA) and Mary Tuttle (Boston, MA)

KNEE,
Charles W., d. 4/5/2001 in Epsom; William Knee and Ethel Littlefield; b. 12/7/1912**

KNIBBS,
James Robert, d. 7/20/1995 in Laconia; George Knibbs and Eva Reid; b. 12/7/1935**

KNOPF,
Mary F., d. 3/22/1981 in Laconia; Victor Oppel and Mary F. Wasner; b. 4/20/1916**

KNOTT,
John H., d. 10/26/1913 at 83/6/20; minister; married; Edward Knott and Ann Cowan

KNOWLES,
Arrabelle Z., d. 9/7/1942 at 91/10/20; widow; b. Gilmanton; George W. Moody (Tunbridge, VT) and Lucinda J. Moore (Loudon)
Charles Wallace, d. 7/19/1914 at 0/10/2 in Gilmanton; Charles W. Knowles (Gilmanton) and Trixy Grieves (Laconia)
George F. M., d. 12/23/1954 at 76 in Laconia*; farmer; single; b. NH; Rufus A. Knowles and Arrabella Z. Moody
Rufus Anderson, d. 4/3/1916 at 61/6/27 in Gilmanton; farmer; married; Leavitt Knowles (ME) and Betsy Manull (Boscawen)

KRAL,
Joseph, d. 5/2/1965 at 73 in Wolfeboro; tool & die mkr.; widower; b. Vienna, Austria; Joseph Kral and Katherine -----

KRUGER,
John J., d. 2/16/1982 in Gilmanton; Henry Kruger and Kathryn Bambrick

KYLE,
Esther Marie, d. 8/31/1964 at 78 in Gilmanton; housewife; married; b. Italy; Antonio P. Guerra and Jennie M. Isella

LABELLE,
Calixe, Mrs., d. 1/24/1912 at 80/1; housewife; married; b. Canada; Oliver Wyatt
Daric, d. 2/7/1920 at 87/11/6 in Gilmanton; laborer; widower; b. Canada; Antoine LaBelle; Tilton

LACROIX,
Alfred Edward, d. 12/18/1995 in Gilmanton; Harry J. Lacroix and Ludivine B. Jacob; b. 4/1/1924**

LAFRANCE,
son, d. 7/23/1922 at 0/0/1; Joseph LaFrance
Agnes Irene, d. 9/27/1918 at 7/11/2; b. Gilmanton; Joseph LaFrance (Canada) and Bertha Burbank (Gilmanton)
Bertha, d. 5/16/1960 at 82 in Hopkinton; widow; b. Gilmanton; Lonzo P. Burbank and Lucia Dustin
Hilda M., d. 1/6/1910 at 3/5/22; pneumonia; b. Gilmanton; Joseph Lafrance (Canada) and Bertha Burbank (Gilmanton)
Joseph H., d. 10/2/1954 at 77 in Laconia*; lumberman, ret.; married; b. Canada; Henry LaFrance
Josephine L., d. 10/8/1918 at 16/5/16; at home; single; b. Gilmanton; Joseph LaFrance (Canada) and Bertha Burbank (Gilmanton)
Lucian C., d. 9/29/1918 at 14/1/27; single; b. Gilmanton; Joseph LaFrance (Canada) and Bertha Burbank (Gilmanton)
Philip C., d. 1/2/1999 in Lebanon; Dr. A. Lafrance and Dorothy Lafarr

LAKIN,
Henrietta, d. 7/16/1949 at 76/9/26 in Gilmanton; housewife; widow; b. NH; Thomas Ring and Sarah Richardson

LAMBERT,
Bruce I., d. 5/29/1982 in Gilmanton; James Lambert and Lovanie Simpson

LAMOTTE,
Celina D., d. 12/3/1956 at 83 in Laconia; housewife; widow; b. Alburgh, VT; Martin Delaney and Mary Hemingway

LAMPREY,
son, d. 10/26/1888 at 0/0/1; b. Gilmanton; M. C. Lamprey (Laconia) and Etta M. Hodge (Salisbury)
Cyrus, d. 6/7/1894 at 74/1/7; farmer; married; b. Gilmanton; Richard Lamprey (Northwood) and Irene Cate
Ellen, d. 12/21/1927 at 73 in Gilmanton; housework; married; b. Dracut, MA; ----- Richardson; Laconia
Madison C., d. 6/27/1916 at 73/1/8 in Gilmanton; farmer; married; Oliver Lamprey (Gilmanton) and Abigail Moulton (Tamworth)
Oliver, d. 3/8/1890 at 76/5/5; farmer; widower; b. Gilford; Richard Lamprey and Irena Cate
Susie E., d. 7/1/1898 at 38/8/12; housewife; married; b. Belmont; Rufus L. Faust (Belmont) and Lucina Dickey (Orange, VT)

LANE,
Muria Williams, d. 10/15/1905 at 70/7/23; housewife; married; b. Gilmanton; Edmund Williams (Lee) and Fannie Osgood (Gilmanton)
Myra F., d. 12/20/1925 at 70/11/23 in Gilmanton; housework; married; b. Gilmanton; John W. Page and Sarah -----
Myron W., d. 9/13/1962 at 90 in Franklin*; farmer; widower; b. Chichester; Thomas Lane and Maria Williams
Thomas B., d. 4/23/1908 at 77/5; farmer; widower; b. Sanbornton; Joshua Lane (Meredith) and Abigail Berry (Chichester)
Walter John, d. 6/11/1976 at 89 in Concord; chemist; single; b. NH; Henry Lane and Myra Page

LANGLEY,
child, d. 11/5/1934 at – in Pittsfield; Howard G. Langley and Laura Nelson; Gilmanton
Dorothy M., d. 9/12/2000 in Gilmanton; Everett Milne and Mabel Wells; b. 10/9/1918**

LANSON,
Dennis Ezra, d. 8/3/1914 at 54/6/8 in Concord; farmer; widower; Calvin B. Lanson
Mary E., d. 7/10/1914 at 55/1/17 in Gilmanton; housewife; married; Horace Metcalf (Corinth, VT) and Eliza Oagthred (Cookshire, PQ)

LAROCHE,
Alfred E., d. 7/1/1984 in Tremont, ME; Alfred Laroche and Hazel Bagley; b. 7/22/1927**

LASHEWAY,
Arthur G., d. 4/8/1984 in Manchester; b. 6/27/1912**

LATHROP,
Alma S., d. 3/28/1956 at 87 in Gilmanton; housewife; widow; b. Gilmanton; Augustus Smith and Rosella Watson
Clara B., d. 10/30/1920 at 59/7 in Gilmanton; housewife; married; b. Sidney, NY; Canaan
Elwyn G., d. 5/7/1932 at 67/9/15 in Gilmanton; pharmacist; married; b. Canaan; George Lathrop; Canaan

LATTIC,
Mary Jane, d. 5/11/1970 at 78 in Gilmanton; nurse; widow; b. MA; Robert Wray and Jane Grant

LATTIE,
Albert Nelson, d. 1/10/1966 at 75 in Gilmanton; executive; married; b. Malden, MA; Albert Lattie and Phebe S. Smith

LAVINE,
Rose Ashcroft, d. 8/8/1972 at 74 in Laconia; none [occ.]; widow; b. Canada; Andrew Descelles and Margaret LaSalle

LAWSON,
Carl Herbert, d. 9/4/1966 at 65 in Wolfeboro; widower; b. Boston, MA; Emile Lawson and Sophie Peterson

LEAVITT,
Benson, d. 9/24/1919 at 62 in Laconia; laborer; single; b. Gilmanton; Joseph Leavitt and Betsey Sweat; Buswell Cem.

Eliza A., d. 9/26/1911 at 81/3/11; widow
Jeremiah, d. 5/6/1902 at 58/0/2; blacksmith; single; b. Gilmanton; Joseph Leavitt (Andover) and Betsey A. Sweatt (Gilmanton)
M. Augusta, d. 2/18/1888 at 48/1/22; housewife; single; b. Gilmanton; Joseph Leavitt (Acton, ME) and Betsey Sweatt (Gilmanton)

LEBELL,
Theresa Jeanne, d. 1/28/1999 in Gilmanton; Anthelm J. Ouellette and Rose Emelia Marquis

LEBLANC,
Alfred H., d. 1/23/1983 in Gilmanton; Avery LeBlanc and Anne Elizabeth Pothier; b. 9/11/1901**

LEE,
Emma W., d. 3/14/1936 at 74/11/11 in Gilmanton; single; b. Boston, MA; Joseph M. Lee (NY City) and Jane F. Kimball (Gilmanton)

LEIGHTON,
Katherin H., d. 5/25/1893 at 36/8; post partum hemorrhage; housewife; married; b. Lempster; Abram Bean and Agnes Richardson

LEKSON,
Erie B., d. 2/19/1898 at 18/10; clerk; single; b. Sweden; Andrew Lekson (Sweden) and Matilda Berg (Sweden)

LEONARD,
Caroline, d. 10/25/1986 in Manchester; Frederick Baugarten
John, d. 3/16/1892 at 52; single; b. Pembroke; John Leonard and Sarah Dow (Gilmanton)
Sarah, d. 10/2/1904 at 100/3/21; widow; b. Gilmanton; Ephraim Dow and Elizabeth French

LESTER,
Harold Benjamin, d. 11/28/1992 in Laconia; Orlando A. Lester and Mildred A. Meister; b. 2/13/1926**

LEWIS,
Mary J., d. 2/24/1913 at 77; housewife; widow; b. Pembroke;
    Prescott Kendall and Mary Dow

LEYLAND,
Carrie May, d. 4/13/1952 at 89 in Concord*; housewife; widow; b.
    NH; Asa Edgerly and Hannah Moulton
Joseph, d. 12/2/1941 at 79/5/17; farmer; married; b. England; John
    Leyland (England) and Elizabeth ----- (England)

LIBBY,
Francis, d. 2/9/1937 at 63 in Wolfeboro*; widower; Pine Grove,
    Gilmanton

LINDQUIST,
Margery M., d. 6/11/1971 at 47 in Gilmanton; secretary; married; b.
    ME; Bethel Whitten and Gladys Tucker

LINEHAN,
George T., d. 1/1/1988 in Gilmanton; Cornelius Linehan and Evelyn
    Lawler; b. 7/29/1937**

LINES,
Iris Sylvia, d. 5/29/1997 in Laconia; William Austin and Sylvia
    Holford
John W., d. 11/4/1985 in Hanover; William J. Lines and Elizabeth
    Buck; b. 11/3/1913**
Shaun Ryan, d. 11/30/1999 in Gilmanton I. W.; Paul Lines and
    Catherine E. Colby
William John, d. 1/5/1965 at 91 in Laconia; trans. fore.; widower; b.
    Aylesbury, England; Daniel Lines and Elizabeth England

LITTLE,
King R., d. 3/13/1976 at 79 in Laconia; ret. farmer; married; b. NH;
    Romie O. Little and Lola Bartum

LITTLEFIELD,
Marie E., d. 4/9/1954 at 0/0/87 in Laconia*; none [occ.]; single; b.
    NH; George E. Littlefield and Romona E. Bagley

LOCKWOOD,
Patricia A., d. 9/16/1997 in Gilmanton; John T. McDonald and Elizabeth Reinwald; b. 9/26/1934**

LODGE,
Alice Bean, d. 2/3/1914 at 64/6/10 in Gilmanton; widow; Josiah Jones Bean (Tamworth) and Harriet E. Bradley (Dracut, MA)

LORD,
Elmer J., d. 5/7/1922 at 59
Mary E., d. 6/20/1934 at 76 in Pittsfield; housework; widow; Gilmanton I. W.

LOUGEE,
Ann, d. 12/25/1889 at 68/8/23; housewife; widow; b. Alton; Samuel Woodman (Alton) and Betsy Woodman
Cecil R., d. 4/15/1928 at 40/7/15 in Rochester; laborer; married; b. Gilmanton; Reuben P. Lougee and Ella A. Watson; Pine Grove
Clara A., d. 11/3/1913 at 62/2/30; single
Cora Belle, d. 12/7/1929 at 69/9/3 in Newburyport, MA; Pine Grove
Ella M., d. 3/25/1902 at 54/10/29; housewife; married; b. Alton; Stephen S. Place and Abbie B. Foss
Ernest Boylston, d. 3/16/1952 at 74 in Center Harbor*; retired farmer; married; b. NH; Samuel S. Lougee and Hattie S. Sanderson
Eva Jane, d. 10/21/1949 at 94 in Laconia; housewife; widow; b. NH; Dixi C. Page and Cyrena G. Webster
John, d. 2/6/1893 at 86; old age; blacksmith; widower; b. Gilmanton; John Lougee and Betsey Marsh
Mary Alice, d. 3/4/1922 at 92
Mary R., d. 1/2/1894 at 91; old age; housewife; widow; b. Gilmanton
Rebecca, d. 2/18/1890 at 77/7; housewife; married; David Edgerly (Gilmanton) and Anna Lougee (Gilmanton)
Sally, d. 12/30/1891 at 96; housewife; widow; b. Gilmanton; Eliphet Kimball

LOVEJOY,
Mary Etta, d. 5/1/1993 in Gilmanton; Willis Prescott Lovejoy and Henrietta Downs

LOWERY,
Gertrude N., d. 5/24/1916 at 52/6/7 in Hooksett; housewife; married; Josiah Kimball and Anne Kimball
James, d. 8/17/1936 at 68 in Gilmanton; laborer; married; b. Hampton Falls; James Lowery (Albany, NY) and Mary A. Sexton (ME)

LUKSHA,
Nicholas M., d. 4/20/1977 at 57 in Gilmanton; teacher; married; b. MA; Nicholas M. Luksha, Sr. and Mary Ann Lis

LUND,
son, d. 8/3/1903 at –; b. Gilmanton; Leon C. Lund (Chicago, IL) and Ina F. Connell (Gilmanton)
Alice F., d. 10/5/1990 in Gilmanton; Harry Fox and Margaret -----
Ina C., d. 10/22/1941 at 63/10/3*; housewife; married; b. Gilmanton; John Connell (Strafford) and Emma Deane (ME)

LYNCH,
James F., d. 10/1/1994 in Lebanon; Francis C. Lynch and Beatrice Salamone

LYONS,
Mary Addie, d. 7/4/1943 at 80/0/3; widow; b. Thetford, VT; ----- Rowell

MACK,
Maria L., d. 11/26/1891 at 96/1/4; housewife; widow; b. Gilmanton; Thomas Burns (Milford) and Nancy Greeley (Gilmanton)

MACLEOD,
Malcolm C., d. 1/8/1944 at 81/4/13; married; b. Winslow, Canada; Murdo MacLeod (Canada) and Isabelle MacLeod (Canada)

MACMURPHY [see McMurphy],
Edson W., d. 12/7/1921 at 69/3/8 in Gilmanton; painter; married; b. Hooksett; N. B. MacMurphy and Jane Bean; Smith Meetinghouse
Nelson W., d. 11/23/1933 at 75/7/2 in Belmont; physician; b. Gilmanton; Rev. Nelson Burnham and Jane Bean; Smith Meetinghouse

MACNEIL,
Jessie B., d. 4/23/1980 in Laconia; Napoleon Benway and Hattie Caswell

MACPEEK,
Steven D., d. 4/15/1973 at 0/3 in Gilmanton*; b. NH; Douglas R. MacPeek and Stephanie A. Geddes

MAHEUX,
Ruth M., d. 8/26/1983 in Laconia; Israel Willard and Georgie McClary; b. 9/28/1922**

MAHEW,
Lorana L., d. 8/19/1971 at 78 in Exeter*; housewife; widow; b. NH; Arthur Bussell and Mabelle Burgess

MALSBURY,
Carrie M. B., d. 10/17/1945 at 78/2/9; at home; widow; b. Dover; Alonzo Heath (Oldtown, ME) and Elizabeth Leathers (Barrington)
Job G., d. 4/1/1941 at 75/1/10; barber; married; b. Prospertown, NJ; David Malsbury (Prospertown, NJ) and Matilda Warwick (Prospertown, NJ)

MALTAIS,
Annie, d. 8/26/1949 at 69/10/12 in Laconia; housewife; married; b. Pembroke; ----- Mahair and Mary Boudreau
John George, d. 8/25/1951 at 78/8/17 in Laconia; farmer (ret.); widower; b. NH; Eli Maltais

MANLEY,
Dorothy Edna, d. 12/8/1953 at 46 in Wolfeboro; at home; married; b. Freedom; Edward L. Huckins and Mary E. Harmon

MANNING,
Thomas H., Sr., d. 5/19/1964 at 77 in Concord; brick mason; married; b. Pittsfield, VT; Adolph Manning and Kathryn Hagen

MANSFIELD,
Archie, d. 8/17/1926 at 9 in Manchester; Buswell Cem.

Roswell, d. 12/17/1912 at 0/7/17; b. Gilmanton; William Mansfield (Wells, ME) and Cora Tilton (Wentworth)
William I., d. 4/5/1939 at 67/8/18 in Laconia*; farmer; married; b. Wells, ME; Daniel Mansfield (Wells, ME) and Lydia Green (Wells, ME)

MANSON,
Clarence I., d. 6/30/1949 at 70/4/29 in Gilmanton; hwy. ptlmn. (ret.); married; b. NH; Levi Manson and Martha Johnson

MARCHAND,
Francis H., d. 6/14/1986 in Gilmanton; Alva F. Marchand and Agnes Coughlin; b. 5/21/1922*
Joseph A., d. 9/19/1984 in Laconia; Albert Marchand and Matilda Fugere; b. 10/4/1898**

MARDEN,
Marie Martha, d. 6/11/1926 at 0/5/7 in Gilmanton; b. Gilmanton; George Marden and Mabel Hilliard; Laconia

MARDIN,
Barbara, d. 5/14/1944 at 12/2/24; single; b. Gilmanton; Willard Mardin (Littleton) and Addie Davis (Northwood)
Nancy A., d. 2/23/1930 at 64/11/9 in Gilmanton; housewife; married; b. Barnstead; Horace Davis and Martha Bridges; Barnstead
Willard C., d. 11/23/1962 at 74 in Gilmanton; farmer; divorced; b. Littleton; Willard C. Mardin

MARGESON,
E. Manning, d. 1/16/1984 in Laconia; J. Lebaron Margeson and Sarah J. Loomer; b. 2/12/1902**
J. LeBaron, d. 5/4/1930 at 69/11/2 in Gilmanton; farmer; married; b. NS; Edward Margeson and ----- Wilson; Beech Grove
Nelson, d. 11/30/1926 at 0/0/1 in Gilmanton; b. Gilmanton; Edward M. Margeson and Edith E. Bruce; Beech Grove
Norris, d. 11/30/1926 at 0/0/1 in Gilmanton; b. Gilmanton; Edward M. Margeson and Edith E. Bruce; Beech Grove
Sarah J., d. 9/10/1955 at 87 in Center Harbor*; housewife; widow; b. NS; Rueben Loomer and Mary S. Chase

MARSELL,
William H., d. 6/10/1985 in Burlington, MA; Joseph Marsell and Jennie Cole; b. 10/26/1900**

MARSH,
Charles T., d. 9/21/1942 at 80/0/10; penman; married; b. Loudon; Enoch P. Marsh (Dunbarton) and Hannah E. Brown (Canterbury)
Erskine H., d. 11/13/1939 at 77/7/7 in Pittsfield*; retired; widower; b. Gilmanton; Joseph Marsh (Gilmanton) and Frances A. Barker (Jamestown)
Frances A., d. 7/14/1895 at 68; Bright's disease; housewife; married; Gardner T. Barker
Frank A., d. 10/1/1895 at –; peritonitis; farmer; married
Gertrude M., d. 7/19/1900 at 16/5/19; school girl; single; b. Chelsea, MA; Andrew Marsh (Gilmanton) and Martha McCarthy (Boston, MA)
Hannah P., d. 3/30/1904 at 81/8/11; housewife; widow; b. Pittsfield; Samuel Peaslee
Hattie E., d. 6/14/1919 at 31/5/13 in Laconia; none [occ.]; single; b. Chelsea, MA; Andrew H. Marsh and Martha McArthur; Smith Meetinghouse
Henry E., d. 4/17/1891 at 67/2/17; farmer; married; b. Gilmanton; Edward Marsh (Gilmanton) and Elizabeth Page (Sidney, ME)
Herbert J., d. 4/13/1924 at 71 in Gilmanton; farmer; married; b. Gilmanton; Joseph Marsh and Hannah Page; Manchester
Joseph H. L., d. 5/27/1951 at 70/11/11 in Laconia*; school at. (ret.); married; b. NH; Herbert J. Marsh and Fannie Poor
Joseph L., d. 9/26/1916 at 62/0/6 in Gilmanton; laborer; married; Frank Marsh and Eliza A. Lamprey
Joseph W., d. 9/15/1909 at 85/6/27; blacksmith; widower; b. Gilmanton; Amos Marsh
Lucy J., d. 6/13/1912 at 58/2/29; housewife; married; b. Gilmanton; Nehemiah Marsh (Gilmanton) and Mary Dow (Gilmanton)
Maria H., d. 12/24/1934 at 78/4/22 in Pittsfield; housework; widow; Hiriam Pickering and Martha -----; Pine Grove
Mary E., d. 2/10/1908 at 74/1/2; widow; b. Gilmanton; Joseph Plummer (Gilmanton) and Sally Lamprey (Gilmanton)
Mary F., d. 1/18/1908 at 75/9/24; widow
Nehemiah L., d. 8/3/1896 at 67; heart failure; farmer

Ralph Davis, d. 3/29/1975 at 70 in Pittsfield; shoe worker; married;
b. NH; Erskine H. Marsh and Jennie Davis

Richard W., d. 9/10/1898 at 70; farmer; married; b. Gilmanton;
Isaac Marsh and Jemmima Sanborn

Willis B., d. 5/22/1930 at 84/9/8 in Gilmanton; blacksmith; divorced;
b. Gilmanton; Joseph Marsh and Adeline Barker; Pine Grove

MARSHALL,

Christiana, d. 6/8/1912 at 80/3/20; widow; b. Alton; Levi Allen
(Effingham) and Mary Clough (Alton)

Ina L., d. 5/27/1950 at 61/10/23 in Gilmanton; housewife; married;
b. Portland, ME; Albert Woodward and Caroline Ward

John, d. 1/18/1969 at 77 in Laconia*; mechanic; widower; b.
Scotland; John C. Marshall and Margaret Gibb

Marian, d. 1/23/1966 at 68 in Laconia*; practical nurse retired;
married; b. Middleton, MA; William Wylie and Lillian Peabody

Rainette A., d. 10/24/1993 in Laconia; Victor Belair and Ida
Gravison; b. 9/27/1924**

MARSTON,

Benjamin P., d. 4/12/1903 at 77/6/9; farmer; married; b.
Holderness; David L. Marston (Sandwich) and Sarah Piper
(Holderness)

MARTIN,

Edward G., d. 12/26/1990 in Wolfeboro; Edward S. Martin and
Edith Glover

Frank, d. 7/30/1920 at 52 in Gilmanton; farmer; married; b. Russia;
Alexander Martin; Pittsfield

Harriet C., d. 9/8/1945 at 78/10/15; at home; widow; b. Gilmanton;
James Cogswell (Gilmanton) and Abby Clifford (Loudon)

Mary A., d. 4/4/1966 at 68 in Laconia; housewife; married; b.
Berwick, ME; Almon Rollins and Mary Mayo

Paul R., d. 9/28/1990 in Laconia; Adolph Martin and Mary Rollins

MASON,

Ethel Pearl, d. 8/15/1939 at 41/2 in Gilmanton; housewife; married;
b. Saugus, MA; William England (England) and Etta Moody
(Lynn, MA)

George, d. 1/19/1941 at 73/7/13; laborer; widower; b. Conway;
Daniel Mason (Hiram, ME) and Susan Stanley (Conway)

MATTHEWS,
Marion Gertrude, d. 10/3/1963 at 65 in Laconia*; housewife; married; b. Gilmanton; Edwin Nelson and Helen Canney

MAXFIELD,
Bert A., d. 4/24/1936 at 64/2/23 in Gilmanton; farmer; single; b. Gilmanton; John Maxfield (Gilmanton) and Aphia Page (Wentworth)
Charles H., d. 4/27/1889 at 58; farmer; married; b. Gilmanton; Enoch Maxfield and Betsy Thompson
Edwin E., d. 8/12/1898 at 54; farmer; married; b. Gilmanton; Enox Maxfield
Herbert A., d. 6/16/1919 at 48/6/12 in Henniker; farmer; widower; b. Gilmanton; Charles H. Maxfield and Mariah Pierce; Smith Meetinghouse
Hiram B., d. 6/1/1894 at 60; blood poisoning; farmer; widower; b. Gilmanton; Enoch Maxfield and Sally Thompson
John A., d. 4/25/1902 at 62/3/14; farmer; widower; b. Gilmanton; Enoch Maxfield and Sally Thompson
Mrs. Walter, d. 9/12/1889 at 25/3 in Canterbury; housekeeper; married; b. Plymouth; Joseph Scales (Canterbury) and Nancy Gloves (Canterbury)

MAYHEW,
Paul Norton, d. 12/10/1954 at 64 in Exeter*; machinist; married; b. Epping; William Mayhew and Lillian White

McCALLION,
Margaret Mary, d. 10/14/1995 in Gilmanton; James McCallion and Amy Vera Stehlin

McCLARY,
Estella Ann, d. 2/5/1906 at 0/0/4; b. Gilmanton; William G. McClary (Bristol) and Dorothy Butcher (Dover)
Euphemia, d. 5/28/1954 at 76 in Laconia*; housewife; widow; b. NH; John Battis and Lucy Moody
Frances Ann, d. 1/5/1921 at 73/8/9 in Gilmanton; housewife; widow; b. Bristol; Joel Adams and Sarah Cross; Beech Grove
Frank, d. 5/30/1950 at 75/3/15 in Laconia*; mail car. (ret.); married; Joseph McClary and Francis Adams

Frank L., d. 5/30/1952 at 49 in Laconia*; truck driver; married; b.
NH; J. Frank McClary and Euphemia Battis
H. Amy, d. 8/29/1975 at 84 in Rochester; housewife; widow; b. MA;
Arthur Alberty and Harriet Johnson
Helen, d. 2/25/1940 at 36/7/16*; hosiery wkr.; single; b. Gilmanton;
Horace McClary (Gilmanton) and Clara Butcher (Dover)
Horace Elmer, d. 2/15/1963 at 83 in Rochester*; caretaker; married;
b. Gilmanton; Joseph McClary and Frances Adams
Joseph B., d. 12/21/1905 at 65/2/12; farmer; married; b.
Canterbury; Jonathan McClary
Stella May, d. 8/24/1905 at 0/6/23; b. Gilmanton; Horace McClary
(Gilmanton) and Clara Butcher (Dover)

McCLEAN,
Richard, d. 12/29/1992 in Concord; John McClean and Agnes
Curdie

McGINNIS,
Robert William, d. 7/20/1963 at 0/2/18 in Gilmanton*; b. Melrose,
MA; James A. McGinnis and Judith Luther

McGREGOR,
Bessie I., d. 10/3/1899 at 22/0/14; bookkeeper; single; b. Portland,
ME; Duncan McGregor (PEI) and E. Grace McDonald (PEI)

McGUIRE,
Kathleen, d. 3/17/1996 in Laconia; Martin Kneafsey and Winifred
Ruane; b. 2/21/1916**

McKINNA,
David D., d. 5/26/1983 in Gilmanton; David McKinna and Mary
Allan; b. 5/30/1925**
Mary, d. 6/26/1953 at 52 in Laconia; nurse; widow; b. Scotland

McLEOD,
Steven A., d. 2/2/1983 in Concord; Stanley W. McLeod and Carol
A. Rostrum

McMURPHY [see MacMurphy],
Nelson B., d. 8/31/1902 at 74/11/12; clergyman; married; b.
Hooksett; Samuel McMurphy

McNAYR,
son, d. 12/24/1902 at 0/0/3; b. Gilmanton; Richard McNayr (NS) and Sarah Nason (Salem, MA)

McSHARRY,
John A., d. 9/18/2001 in Gilmanton I.W.; John McSharry and Margaret O'Malley; b. 5/18/1928**
Virginia A., d. 4/26/2000 in Gilmanton I.W.; Leo Fraser and Rose Nicholson; b. 2/25/1932**

MEEKINS,
Betty A., d. 4/3/1950 at 0/8 in Gilmanton; b. Gilmanton; Ruth M. Meekins

MERRILL,
Alexander C., d. 12/18/1906 at 73/9/26; farm laborer; single; b. Gilmanton; Bela C. Merrill (Gilmanton) and Abbie M. Brown (Barnstead)
Amelia, d. 8/7/1933 at 83/11/27 in Gilmanton; Jacchais Peaslee and Betsy Parash; Smith Meetinghouse
Charles E., d. 9/3/1916 at 69/11/8 in Gilmanton; farmer; married; Aaron Merrill (Barnstead) and Elizabeth Caverly (Strafford)
Clara Page, d. 8/31/1922 at 70
Ezekiel E., d. 11/9/1891 at 78/7/11; farmer; married; b. Gilmanton
Florence Helen, d. 10/19/1968 at 84 in Concord*; teacher; widow; b. MA; Charles L. French and Jennie H. Benner
Frank N., d. 2/6/1921 at 68/3/13 in Gilmanton; farmer; married; b. Stoneham, MA; George M. Merrill and Mary Sleeper; Smith Meetinghouse
Jacob D., d. 5/24/1902 at 70/0/1; farmer; married; b. Gilmanton; John Merrill and Hannah Osborne
Joseph A., d. 4/4/1899 at 85/11/21; farmer; widower; b. Gilmanton; Paul Merrill
Joseph W., d. 12/5/1893 at 58; prostatitis; farmer; married; John Merrill (Gilmanton) and Hannah Osborne (Loudon)
Margaret O., d. 11/6/1890 at 75/5/15; housewife; married; b. Loudon; Elijah Osborn (Epping) and Margaret Green (Pittsfield)
Sidney A., d. 3/26/1906 at 57/0/11; physician; single; b. Barnstead; Aaron Merrill (Barnstead) and Elizabeth Coverly (Strafford)

METCALF,
Horace, d. 6/2/1913 at 95/11/15; farmer; widower; b. Corinth, VT; David Metcalf (Oakham, MA) and Candance Strattion (Rutland, MA)

MILLER,
Alice E., d. 10/18/1926 at 63/1/7 in Barnstead; housework; married; Pine Grove
Dorothy B., d. 2/25/1999 in Gilmanton; Edward Belanger and Marion Ackert; b. 11/12/1912**
Edmund H., d. 12/5/1927 at 65 in Boston, MA; widow; Pine Grove
Esther Shaw, d. 7/12/1954 at 50 in Laconia*; dancer, singer; married; b. HI; James E. Shaw and Ester Stevenson
Laura Geddes, d. 9/25/1977 at 95 in Meredith; housewife; widow; b. OH; Frederick L. Geddes and Kate Rosebrugh
Ruthe D., d. 6/20/1991 in Laconia; Arthur Davis and Louise Murray

MITCHELL,
John A., d. 4/18/1988 in Meredith; Arthur Mitchell and Hortence Orr
Minnie M., d. 6/22/1892 at 15; single; b. Loudon; Joseph Mitchell
William George, d. 3/16/1951 at 83/2/2 in Gilmanton; exper. engineer (ret.); single; b. MA; Richard Mitchell and Charlotte Stephenson

MONGEON,
Eva Marilyn, d. 4/1/1998 in Gilmanton; James H. Durant and Eliza Higgins; b. 8/27/1901**

MONTPLAISIR,
Louise M., d. 9/16/1988 in Laconia; Auguste Messier and Angeline Joyal; b. 10/28/1915**

MOODY,
Edson E., d. 7/18/1901 at 35; black; single
Katie I., d. 3/6/1894 at 16; miscarriage; housewife; married
Laura A., d. 4/17/1916 at 60 in Manchester; housekeeper; single; Stephen S. Moody (Gilmanton) and ----- Hoyt (Gilmanton)
Lucinda J., d. 3/7/1892 at 86/11/14; housewife; widow; b. Loudon
Willis, d. 7/6/1900 at 37/5; farmer; single; Walter Moody and Mary Moody

MOONEY,
Maude Marjorie, d. 2/10/1966 at 92 in Newport*; nurse (RN); single; b. Bolton, PQ; Amos Mooney and Ellen Moses

MOORE,
Richard, d. 8/29/1953 at 23 in Gilmanton; U. S. Navy; married; b. Laconia; Clifford G. Moore and Marion F. Helms

MORGAN,
Alice A., d. 3/7/1951 at 94/9/18 in Gilmanton; school teacher; widow; b. Cookshire, PQ; Horace Metcalf and Liza Oughtred
David M., d. 5/2/1908 at 62/6/12; farmer; married; b. Campton; Smith Morgan (Bradford) and Rachel Bagley (Bradford)

MORIN,
Arthur Joseph, d. 3/2/1951 at 11/1/9; student; single; b. NH; Joseph A. Morin and Irene E. Patten
Joseph A., d. 4/28/1979 in Laconia; John Morin and Maria -----

MORLEY,
Ruth F., d. 7/26/1979 in Laconia; Warren Fullerton

MORRILL,
Elizabeth P., d. 4/12/1904 at 60/10/7; housewife; widow; b. Gilmanton; Alfred Prescott (Gilmanton) and Octavia Beede (Sandwich)
Winifred Page, d. 9/7/1959 at 83 in Boscawen*; housewife; widow; b. Gilmanton; Dixie C. Page and Cyrena Webster

MORRISON,
Charles H., d. 5/31/1905 at 78/1/19; cabinetmaker; married; b. Sanbornton; Henry Morrison and Abigail -----
John S., d. 11/19/1925 at 83/6/29 in Laconia; farmer; married; b. Plymouth; Jacob Morrison and Sarah Stoddard; Smith Meetinghouse
Laura E., d. 3/11/1941 at 88/7/26; at home; widow; b. Gilmanton; Cyrus G. Allan (Gilmanton) and Laura Hutchinson (Gilmanton)
Rosetta, d. 11/29/1931 at 77/7/13 in Laconia; housework; widow; b. Gilmanton; Smith Meetinghouse

MORSE,
Clyde L., d. 8/10/1984 in Gilmanton; George E. Morse and Hattie B. Gibbs
Howard Bramhall, d. 3/25/1966 at 41 in Laconia*; plastic applicator; married; b. Friendship, ME; Frank Morse and Villa Eugleigh
John H., d. 5/7/1925 at 71/7/1 in Hillsborough; Pine Grove

MOULTON,
Caleb, d. 1/19/1892 at 85/10; farmer; married; b. Hampton
Daniel H., d. 11/2/1920 at 68/10/28 in Gilmanton; farmer; married; b. Ellsworth; Chase P. Moulton and Sarah M. Pillsbury; Thornton
Emma H., d. 6/17/1934 at 81/10/27 in Gilmanton; housewife; widow; b. Gilmanton; Reuben W. Page and Abigail T. Sanborn; Pine Grove, Thornton
John S., d. 12/31/1909 at 63/9/8; farmer; widower; b. Gilmanton; Caleb Moulton (Hampton) and Nancy Dow (Hampton)
Lena Agnes, d. 1/26/1954 at 77 in Wolfeboro; at home; single; b. Gilmanton; Daniel Moulton and Emma Page

MOYNIHAN,
John, d. 4/14/1939 at 80/4/19 in Concord*; stone cutter; single; b. Ireland; Daniel Moynihan (Ireland) and Hannah Mitchell (Ireland)

MUDGETT,
Ann C., d. 5/12/1905 at 75/5/4; housewife; widow; b. Gilmanton; Richard Jones (Gilmanton) and Susan Pulsifer (Gilmanton)
Belle, d. 6/11/1910 at 51/7/25; neuritis; housewife; married; b. Loudon; Frank Pettingill (Woodstock) and Betsy Stevens (Loudon)
Edward S., d. 6/10/1890 at 60/4; farmer; married; b. Belmont; Scribner Mudgett (Gilmanton) and Nancy Prescott (Gilmanton)
Eugene L., d. 12/11/1909 at 54/4; blacksmith; married; b. Gilmanton; Edward S. Mudgett (Gilmanton) and Cynthia Jones (Gilmanton)
George H., d. 5/18/1931 at 60/10/6 in Franklin; laborer; divorced; b. Gilmanton; Edward L. Mudgett and Cynthia Jones; Belmont
Levi H., d. 3/9/1911 at 83/3/26; widower

Samuel B., d. 2/10/1890 at 72; farmer; married; b. Gilmanton; Samuel Mudgett (Gilmanton) and Hannah French (So. Hampton)

Susie A., d. 4/15/1889 at 27/4/8; operative; single; b. Gilmanton; Edward S. Mudgett (Gilmanton) and Ann C. Jones (Littleton)

MUNDY,
Frederick L., d. 12/9/1981 in Gilmanton; Frederick Mundy and Frances Saylor

MUNSEY,
daughter, d. 10/10/1932 at 0/0/0 in Laconia; b. Laconia; John J. Munsey and Julia Bruce; Smith Meetinghouse

Amelia W., d. 9/9/1902 at 73/1/7; widow; b. Gilford; Enoch Hoyt (Gilford) and Lois Woodman (Sanbornton)

Amos P., d. 6/23/1890 at 70/1/20; farmer; married; b. Gilford; George W. Munsey and Hannah Barton

Charles W., d. 2/14/1893 at 44/2/2; drowning; farmer; married; Amos P. Munsey

Ellen, d. 1/30/1893 at 77; stomach and liver disease; housewife; married

Francis M., d. 11/14/1921 at 87/5/18 in Pittsfield; Pine Grove

Gary Earl, d. 12/14/1961 at 5 in Laconia*; b. Concord; Herbert E. Munsey and Evelyn E. Corson

George W., d. 3/13/1902 at 72/6/15; farmer; widower; b. Barnstead; John Munsey (Barnstead) and Sally Drew (Pittsfield)

Horatio, d. 7/5/1939 at 82/4; laborer; single; b. Roxbury, MA; George Munsey (Barnstead) and Sally Drew (Madbury)

Jay H., d. 10/9/1934 at 76/5/27 in Pittsfield; farmer; widower; b. Concord; Amos P. Munsey and Amelia Hoyt; Smith Meetinghouse

John Jay, d. 6/30/1964 at 71 in Gilmanton*; lineman; married; b. Gilmanton; Jay R. Munsey and Josephine Osborne

Josephine O., d. 3/12/1913 at 50/5/17; housewife; married

Julia Florence, d. 9/3/1965 at 72 in Laconia; coremaker; widow; b. Flodden, PQ; William Bruce and Margaret MacNaughton

MURPHY,
Jane Bean, d. 8/31/1905 at 78/4/28; housewife; widow; b. Gilmanton; Moses Bean (Gilmanton) and Polly Shepard (Gilmanton)

Jennie N., d. 11/1/1938 at 74/9/29 in Nashua*; housewife; widow; b. Epping; Thomas J. Norris and Abbie Fernald

Katherine V., d. 10/4/1993 in Manchester; Charles A. Dunne and Frances Smith; b. 11/7/1924**

Mary A., d. 2/2/1929 at 46 in Gilmanton; waitress; single; b. Boston, MA; James Murphy and Ann McFarland; Holyhood, MA

MUZZEY,

Harold Archer, d. 9/5/1966 at 74 in Gilmanton; machinist - retired; b. Croydon; George A. Muzzey and ----- Page

Mary Blanche, d. 3/8/1965 at 75 in Laconia; housewife; married; b. St. Pierrede, LA; Alfred P. Vezina and Arthemese Morel

NELSON,

Dorothy A., d. 7/3/1986 in Laconia; Charles W. Peabody and Eva T. Delano; b. 1/17/1910**

Edwin Sewell, d. 5/15/1938 at 95/11/27 in Gilmanton; farmer; widower; b. Gilmanton; John F. Nelson (Gilmanton) and Huldah Kimball (Gilmanton)

Hannah M. F., d. 4/14/1908 at 85/0/13; widow; b. Gilmanton; Henry Page (Gilmanton) and Sarah Page (Gilmanton)

Henry, d. 7/29/1949 at 86 in Laconia; carpenter (ret.); widower; b. Denmark; Rasmus Nelson and Laurine Henrickson

Hulda, d. 5/21/1902 at 91/11/10; widow

Josiah Dudley, d. 11/11/1922 at 89

Louise, d. 12/12/1940 at 81/3/19; at home; married; b. Demark; Rasmus Clausen (Denmark)

Martha F., d. 1/28/1906 at 73/11/3; housewife; married; b. Farmington; John W. Furber (Farmington) and Martha Nelson (Gilmanton)

Mary A., d. 7/24/1902 at 55/6/13; housewife; married; b. Barnstead; Jonathan Pickering and Elizabeth Foster

Maurice J., d. 8/24/1896 at 1/0/20; cholera infantum; b. Gilmanton; Edwin F. Nelson (Gilmanton) and Nellie A. Nelson (Warner)

NEWTON,

Lois C., d. 2/11/1908 at 85/9/15; widow; b. Loudon; George Wells and Sarah McArthur

NICHOLSON,
Marion M., d. 7/14/1967 at 62 in Gilmanton; dietician; married; b. Hodgdon, ME; Albert J. Murchie and Eva L. White

NIGHSWANDER,
Warren C., d. 5/11/1998 in Concord; Arthur Nighswander and Esther Richardson

NUTTER,
Arimenta B., d. 3/2/1898 at 53/10; housewife; married; b. Gilmanton; Levi Young and Sally Leavitt
Clyde E., d. 2/15/1941 at 38/8/12; garage prop.; married; b. Parsonsfield, ME; Fred Nutter and Carrie Dutch
Isaac, d. 5/28/1931 at 72/5/28 in Strafford; Pine Grove
Samuel D., d. 10/13/1888 at 64; stone-cutter; married; b. Gilmanton; Matthias Nutter (Barnstead) and Ruth Glidden (Alton)
Sarah, d. 12/12/1907 at 76; housewife; widow; b. Barnstead; ----- (Barnstead) and ----- (Barnstead)
Steven B., d. 3/23/1954 at 0/0/21 in Laconia*; b. NH; Kenneth N. Nutter and Ethelyn Jones
William, d. 8/14/1898 at 87/8/13; mechanic; married; b. Barnstead; Joseph Nutter (Barnstead) and Mary Clough
William E., d. 12/17/1912 at 46/2/15; single; b. Gilmanton; Samuel Nutter and Mary Allen

O'CONNOR,
Christine, d. 7/2/1971 at 0/4 in Gilmanton; b. MA; Paul O'Connor and Janice Hurley

O'GRADY,
Mary Ann, d. 1/21/1928 at 76/0/15 in Gilmanton; none [occ.]; widow; b. St. Bridgets, Can.; Peter Kane and Rose Thompson; Laconia
William Henry, d. 6/29/1927 at 79/1/17 in Gilmanton; retired; married; b. St. Bridgete, Can.; Timothy O'Grady and Elizabeth O'Mara; Laconia

O'LEARY,
Viola Elizabeth, d. 6/2/1906 at 0/2/14; Bert E. O'Leary (Franklin) and Elizabeth J. Haskell (Gilmanton)

O'SULLIVAN,
Jerome Patrick, Jr., d. 2/19/1977 at 29 in Gilmanton I. W.; laundromat oper.; single; b. Bridgeport, CT; Jerome P. O'Sullivan, Sr. and Ann Henry

OLIVER,
Mary H., d. 12/8/1999 in Concord; Robert Thorp and Alma Snyder

OLMSTED,
Clara W., d. 1/29/1957 at 80 in Laconia*; housewife; married; b. Boston, MA; Balthasar Wagner and Josephine Decker
Herbert W., d. 2/19/1974 at 92 in Concord; civil eng., ret.; widower; b. MA; William Olmsted and Katherine Royalance

ORANGE,
Elizabeth A., d. 3/3/1927 at 95 in Gilmanton; widow; b. Pembroke; Prescott Kendall and Mary Dow; Lowell, MA
Henry Smith, d. 10/26/1894 at 79/8/16; Brights disease; retired mer.; married; b. Milton; J. W. Orange (Milton) and Martha Runnels (Rochester)
Sadie H., d. 3/2/1927 at 62 in Gilmanton; housework; single; b. Lowell, MA; Henry S. Orange and Elizabeth Kendall; Lowell, MA

ORR,
Elinor B., d. 3/26/1970 at 86 in Canterbury; housewife; married; b. MA; Louis J. Barta and Mary S. -----

OSBORNE,
Abbie F., d. 4/8/1940 at 79/1/22*; at home; divorced; b. Barnstead; James C. Ham (Barnstead) and Mary Clark (Barnstead)
Ada J., d. 8/31/1927 at 53/3/4 in Pittsfield; married; b. Belmont; Albin Lampry and ----- Weymouth; Smith Meetinghouse
Charles O., d. 3/26/1935 at 80/8/23 in Pittsfield; retired; married; b. Gilmanton; Samuel Osborne and Julia A. Griffin; Smith Meetinghouse
Charles Roland, d. 12/29/1972 at 77 in Concord; farmer; married; b. NH; Charles A. Osborne and Grace A. True
Frank G., d. 6/12/1929 at 75/0/6 in Gilmanton; married; b. Gilmanton; John S. Osborne and Fannie Gilman; Smith Meetinghouse

Frank H., d. 9/18/1924 at 71 in Gilmanton; farmer; single; b.
    Barnstead; Joseph C. Osborne and Mary E. Griffin; Pittsfield
Grace A., d. 2/13/1956 at 97 in Loudon*; housewife; widow; b.
    Pittsfield; Charles True and Abbie Tilton
Hannah S., d. 2/11/1892 at 82/7; housewife; widow
Henry S., d. 5/25/1938 at 74/6/16 in Concord*; shoe cutter;
    widower; b. Salem, MA
John S., d. 12/23/1896 at 78/1/21; pneumonia; farmer; married; b.
    Gilmanton; Micajah Osborne (Gilmanton) and Mary Cogswell
    (Gilmanton)
Julia Griffin, d. 6/16/1911 at 86/3/29; housewife; widow; b.
    Gilmanton; Richard Griffin (Sandown) and Filinda Hutchinson
    (Gilmanton)
Sarah Purne, d. 12/11/1959 at 64 in Wolfeboro*; bookkeeper;
    married; b. Pittsfield; Roscoe L. Garland and Amy D. Knowlton
True F., d. 11/15/1939 at 79/3/10 in Pittsfield*; farmer; married; b.
    Gilmanton; Samuel Osborne (Gilmanton) and Julia Griffin
    (Gilmanton)
William Robert, d. 9/25/1965 at 74 in Concord*; antique dlr.;
    married; b. Worcester, MA; Archie Osborne and Frances Ham

OSGOOD,
Eben, d. 3/28/1887 at 72; married
Joseph E., d. 1/21/1892 at 72; farmer; married; b. Gilmanton;
    Daniel Osgood
Mrs., d. 4/20/1913 at --; housewife; married

OSLER,
Howard B., d. 5/2/1989 in Laconia; Benjamin F. Osler and Alice
    Tyler; b. 1/18/1901**

OSMER,
Steven D., Jr., d. 3/31/1980 in Concord; Steven D. Osmer and
    Sandra L. Bresse

OUELLETTE,
Lucy, d. 9/24/1974 at 77 in Laconia; housewife; widow; b. NH; Peter
    Greenwood and Victoria Dussiere

PAGE,
daughter, d. 10/19/1896 at 0/0/1; b. Gilmanton; Walter E. Page (Gilmanton) and Mabelle McClary (Gilmanton)

Abigail, d. 1/11/1892 at 72; housewife; married; b. Gilmanton

Addie C., d. 9/22/1922 at 71

Alice F., d. 5/10/1972 at 90 in Rochester*; housewife; widow; b. NH; Charles Foss and Emma Young

Alvin George, d. 2/3/1938 at 3/7/3 in Laconia*; b. Gilmanton; Andrew T. Page (Gilmanton) and Mabel Avery (Gilmanton)

Andrew Tasker, d. 3/18/1963 at 61 in Laconia*; carpenter; married; b. Gilmanton; Henry Page and Emma Tasker

Anna Bertha, d. 12/4/1944 at 80/4/10*; at home; widow; b. Gilmanton; Dixi C. Page (Gilmanton) and Cyrena G. Webster (Gilmanton)

Annie Glidden, d. 12/16/1958 at 74 in Gilmanton; housewife; married; b. Alton; Orrin D. Glidden and Elizabeth Burnham

Archie C., d. 12/26/1973 at 66 in Concord*; assistant road agent; married; b. NH; Dwight Page and Eva Foster

Asa F., d. 9/12/1906 at 90/6/27; farmer; widower; b. Gilmanton; Moses Page (Gilmanton) and Mary Tilton (Gilmanton)

Betsey F., d. 8/13/1895 at 83/7/5; embolism; housewife; widow; Joseph Marsh and Betsey Lougee

Charles A., d. 11/6/1914 at 62/8/11 in Gilmanton I. W.; retired; single; John Page

Charles Frank, d. 1/8/1953 at 95 in Gilmanton; farmer; widower; b. Gilmanton; John S. Page and Sarah T. Smith

Charles Lauren, d. 7/13/1949 at 80/7/23 in Gilmanton; farmer; single; b. Gilmanton; Charles S. Page and Sarah J. Edgerly

Charles S., d. 4/7/1908 at 79/0/22; farmer; married; b. Gilmanton; Moses F. Page (Sandown) and Dorothy Sanborn (Sandown)

Cora B., d. 11/14/1946 at 87/6/8 in Gilmanton; housewife; married; b. Gilmanton; Sylvester Gale (Gilmanton) and Harriet Gilman (Gilmanton)

Curtis H., d. 12/12/1946 at 76/8/8 in Laconia*; educator; single; b. Greenwood, MO; Benjamin G. Page and Martha T. Hidden

Cyrena G., d. 9/22/1910 at 76/0/21; heart failure; housewife; married; b. Gilmanton; Benjamin Webster and Sally Prescott

Dana S., d. 1/21/1935 at 76/4/16 in Boston, MA; jeweler; married; b. Gilmanton; Dixie Page and Cyrena Webster; Smith Meetinghouse

Dixi C., d. 8/4/1911 at 84/6/4; farmer; widower

Dwight R., d. 3/1/1928 at 49/6/23 in Alton; Pine Grove
Ella, d. 2/27/1943 at 83/10/4*; at home; widow; b. Loudon; Josiah B. Jones and Mary Leavitt
Emma A., d. 1/31/1921 at 62/6/3 in Laconia; housewife; married; b. Northwood; Vincent P. Tasker and Hannah Walker; Page Cem.
Ernest C., d. 7/18/1905 at 2/11; b. Gilmanton; Henry S. Page and Emma Tasker
Ethel M., d. 12/12/1915 at 29/5/12 in Gilmanton; housewife; married; Frank N. Merrill and Clara Page
Eva Foster, d. 2/15/1966 at 85 in Laconia*; housewife; widow; b. Belmont; Orrin William Foster and Mary Frances Johnson
Fanny A., d. 6/1/1943 at 83/3/22*; at home; widow; b. NS; Alexander Embree and Sarah Tweed
Frank Josiah, d. 6/25/1963 at 76 in Manchester*; road agent; married; b. Franklin; George Page and Ella Jones
Fred H., d. 11/7/1894 at 21/2/11; phthisis; single; b. Laconia; Asa F. Page (Gilmanton) and Abbie E. Jackson (Laconia)
George E., d. 1/5/1931 at 76/3/15 in Gilmanton; farmer; married; b. Gilmanton; John S. Page and Sarah Smith; Smith Meetinghouse
Hannah E., d. 2/3/1914 at 86/8/21 in Gilmanton; widow; Daniel Lougee and Sally Kimball
Helen Otis, d. 6/30/1966 at 68 in Laconia*; school teacher - housewife; widow; b. Tilton; George Wyatt and Lucy Jackson
Henry E., d. 7/10/1910 at 41/1/12; tuberculosis of liver; farmer; married; b. Gilmanton; Albert R. Page (Gilmanton) and Addie Clement (Alton)
Henry S., d. 4/18/1935 at 84/3/14 in Gilmanton; widower; b. Gilmanton; Samuel M. Page and Mary F. Page; Page Cem'y, Gilmanton
Herman A., d. 4/25/1930 at 59/4/26 in Gilmanton; farmer; married; b. Gilmanton; Albert R. Page and Adeline Clements; Smith Meetinghouse
Ida, d. 8/19/1892 at 0/6; b. Gilmanton; William S. Page (Gilmanton) and Cora E. Couch (Sutton)
Jesse F., d. 9/20/1924 at 75 in Barnstead; retired; Jesse L. Page and Betsey F. Marsh; Pine Grove
John S., d. 9/30/1891 at 66/5/11; farmer; married; b. Gilmanton; Moses Page and Dorothy Sanborn

John Sidney, d. 2/14/1925 at 0/0/7 in Gilmanton; b. Gilmanton; Frank J. Page and Helen Wyatt; Smith Meetinghouse

John Sidney, d. 11/16/1973 at 89 in Concord*; stationary eng.; widower; b. NH; George Page and Ella Jones

Laura A., d. 2/25/1920 at 78/1/19 in Barnstead; none [occ.]; single; b. Gilmanton; Joseph Page and Betsy Marsh; Smith Meetinghouse

Lorraine, d. 5/28/1921 at 78/2/8 in Boston, MA; farmer; widower; b. Gilmanton; Jesse L. Page and Betsy Marsh; Smith Meetinghouse

Lucretia R., d. 6/20/1893 at 75; marasmus; housewife; married

Lucy Mary, d. 11/3/1942 at 85/0/21*; at home; widow; b. Woolwich, ME; Timothy W. Austin (Roxbury, MA) and Rebecca Preble (Woolwich, ME)

Lucy T., d. 8/11/1895 at 66/11/13; heart failure; housewife; married; b. Gilmanton; Samuel Sanborn and Lucy Thurston

Luther E., d. 7/28/1908 at 75/11/7; farmer; married; b. Gilmanton; Henry Page and Hannah Sanborn

Mabel W., d. 7/17/1908 at –/6/25; dressmaker; single; b. Gilmanton; Albert R. Page (Gilmanton) and Addie C. Clement (Alton)

Mahala, d. 8/17/1891 at 73/8/29; housewife; widow; b. Sanbornton; Simon Tole (Hampton) and Molly Sanborn (Exeter)

Marion, d. 8/12/1907 at 44/8/6; finisher; single; b. Manchester; Samuel Page (Gilmanton) and Mary Page (Sandown)

Mary E., d. 7/2/1914 at 61/11/6 in Gilmanton I. W.; housewife; married; Thomas Tibbetts (E. Wolfeboro) and Sarah Locke (Wakefield)

Mary F., d. 1/21/1911 at 82/8/2; retired; single; b. Gilmanton; Benjamin Page (Gilmanton) and Sarah Page (Gilmanton)

Mary J., d. 6/13/1940 at 95/2/9; housewife; widow; b. Barnstead; Nathaniel Page (ME) and Polly Flanders (Alton)

Mary P., d. 5/12/1913 at 83/10/28; widow; Henry Page and Sarah Page

Minnie Frances, d. 11/13/1894 at 0/0/1; malformation of head; b. Gilmanton; Walter E. Page (Gilmanton) and Laura M. McClarey (Gilmanton)

Nathaniel, d. 5/8/1899 at 84/7; farmer; widower; True Page and Abigail Edgerly

Nelson C., d. 1/12/1919 at 33/6/8 in Laconia; farmer; married; b. Gilmanton; Royal L. Page and Annie M. Osgood; Pine Grove

Polly, d. 8/23/1897 at 85; housewife; widow

Ralph G., d. 4/14/1936 at 38/11/21 in Gilmanton; farmer; single; b. Gilmanton; George E. Page (Gilmanton) and Ella Jones (Loudon)

Rebecca M., d. 11/13/1893 at 57/4; edema of lungs; housewife; married; b. Gilford

Reuben W., d. 7/14/1893 at 76/5; cancer; farmer; widower; b. Sandown; Henry Page

Royal L., d. 4/7/1927 at 75/5/17 in Gilmanton; farmer; married; b. Gilmanton; Daniel L. Page and Mahala D. Towle; Pine Grove

Sarah Marie, d. 8/25/1951 at 76/5/6 in Laconia*; housewife; widow; b. VT; Ruel Buckman and Julia Chamberlain

Sarah T., d. 1/3/1893 at 65; cancer; housewife; widow; b. Gilmanton; Josiah Smith

Sylvester A., d. 2/10/1930 at 0/0/0 in Rochester; b. Rochester; Harold G. Page and Etta P. Day; Smith Meetinghouse

Vona H., d. 3/2/1907 at 48/5/13; housekeeper; widow; b. Gilmanton; John W. Ham (Gilmanton) and Lavonie Varney (Alton)

Walter D., d. 9/16/1952 at 78 in Wolfeboro*; farmer; married; b. NH; Albert R. Page and Adelaide C. Clements

Walter H., d. 11/9/1935 at 65/5/1 in Laconia; farmer; married; b. Gilmanton; Dixi C. Page and Cyrena Webster; Smith Meetinghouse

Walter S., d. 7/11/1946 at 63/1/13 in Manchester*; machine shop; widower; b. Portsmouth; Henry S. Page (NH) and Emma Tasker (NH)

Warren R., d. 3/26/1893 at 45; epilepsy; single; b. Gilmanton; Asa T. Page (Gilmanton) and Lucretia Page (Gilmanton)

William, d. 8/4/1899 at 63; farmer; married

William Albert, d. 1/25/1951 at 79/0/19 in Laconia*; farmer; married; b. Gilmanton; Charles Page and Jane Edgerly

PAIGE,

Abbie Ella, d. 4/30/1936 at 84 in Gilmanton; none [occ.]; widow; b. Laconia; John H. Jackson and Naomia Lewis

Albert Franklin, d. 1/28/1923 at 81

Asa F., d. 8/3/1925 at 81/7/20; painter; married; b. Gilmanton; Asa Paige and Eliza F. Edgerly; Pine Grove

Charles A., d. 8/5/1916 at 77/7/19 in Gilmanton; farmer; married; Jesse Paige and Betsy Marsh

Dudley N., d. 4/22/1933 at 81/10/24 in Rochester; married; b.
  Gilmanton; Jesse Paige and Betsy Marsh; Pine Grove
Edgar A., d. 7/17/1931 at 78/0/1 in Gilmanton; painter; divorced; b.
  Gilmanton; Asa Paige and Eliza Edgerly; Pine Grove
Ellen A., d. 4/17/1922 at 73
Eva Marie, d. 3/2/2000 in Gilmanton; Fritz Lehner and Maria
  Schroeder; b. 6/12/1933**
Fannie Belle, d. 4/21/1959 at 89 in Rochester*; secretary, ret.;
  single; b. Gilmanton; Harlan Paige and Lydia Sleeper
Harlan, d. 5/7/1921 at 82/8/28 in Gilmanton; retired; married; b.
  Gilmanton; Asa Paige and Eliza Edgerly; Pine Grove
John H., d. 6/23/1920 at 27/7/24 in Newport; b. Gilmanton; Charles
  F. Paige and Nona Ham; Pine Grove
Lydia E., d. 12/4/1924 at 86 in Gilmanton; housework; widow; b.
  Alton; Joseph Sleeper and Susannah Lougee; Pine Grove

PALMER,
Charles E., d. 11/6/1970 at 73 in Rochester*; hardware; married; b.
  NH; George L. Palmer and Daisy A. Smith
Daisy M., d. 3/23/1945 at 64/11/10*; housekeeper; widow; b.
  Gilmanton; Edward Smith (Lynn, MA) and Jane Evans
  (Ossipee)
George L., d. 12/22/1932 at 59/10/21 in Gilmanton; farmer;
  married; b. Dover; Aaron Palmer and Myra B. Goodwin; Pine
  Grove

PAPPAS,
Paul E., d. 8/13/1991 in Gilmanton; Evangelos Pappas and
  Soultana Catsogianos

PARKER,
Anna Belle, d. 2/10/1931 at 62/11/15 in Worcester, MA; at home;
  married; b. Gilmanton; William Dimick and Anna M. Folsom;
  Forest Hills, MA
Bella, d. 10/20/1950 at 54 in Concord*; housewife; married; b. PQ;
  Malcolm McLeod and Christie McLain
Leon Dwight, d. 3/27/1952 at 73 in Wolfeboro*; farmer; widower; b.
  MA; Irving D. Parker and Laura H. Green
Sarah J., d. 5/7/1929 at 79/4/26 in Worcester, MA; at home; single;
  b. Boston, MA; James Parker and Honora Granger; Boston,
  MA

William H., d. 1/27/1937 at 77/8/12 in Boston, MA*; widower; Smith
M. H., Gilmanton

PARSHLEY,
Clara E., d. 9/8/1920 at 65/4/1 in Gilmanton; widow; b. Laconia;
Hubbard Jackson and Naomi Lewis; Laconia
Levi Carroll, d. 8/12/1966 at 88 in Laconia*; laborer; widower; b.
Pittsfield; Frank P. Parshley and Evelyn Aiken

PARSONS,
Abbie J., d. 9/4/1950 at 76 in Concord*; single; b. Gilmanton;
George W. Parsons and Mary A. Hill
Addie Mercy, d. 10/24/1961 at 95 in Gilmanton; housewife; widow;
b. Gilmanton; Charles W. Hill and Lydia A. Bailey
Albert Hill, d. 9/29/1972 at 78 in Concord*; wood cutter; single; b.
NH; Usher S. Parsons and Addie M. Hill
Frances M., d. 8/2/1922 at 71
John T., d. 9/6/1918 at 67/10/14; farmer; married; b. Gilmanton
Lena R., d. 3/26/1933 at 59/4/10 in Gilmanton; at home; single; b.
Barnstead; Rufus B. Parsons and Fannie Hussey; Pine Grove
Rufus B., d. 5/26/1904 at 57/6/5; laborer; married; b. Quincy, MA;
Burleigh Parsons
Sarah J. R., d. 5/11/1916 at 94 in Concord; housework; single
Usher, d. 4/30/1935 at 69/0/10 in Gilmanton; farmer; married; b.
Gilmanton; George Parsons and Mary Hill; Smith
Meetinghouse
Zella, d. 2/14/1977 at 84 in Exeter; housewife; single; b. NH; Usher
S. Parsons and Addie M. Hill

PARTRIDGE,
Daisy M., d. 12/12/1963 at 29 in Hanover Ctr.*; tel. operator; single;
b. Gilmanton; Horace Partridge and Florence Palmer
Edwin A., d. 2/11/1987 in Laconia; Arthur C. Partridge and Lilla
Woods; b. 8/2/1902**
Horace W., d. 7/10/1930 at 4/6/16 in Gilmanton; b. Gilmanton;
Horace F. Partridge and Florence Palmer; Guinea Ridge
Jean V., d. 8/20/1983 in Hanover; George M. Nelson and Eleanor
Hyslop; b. 5/6/1938**
Leon E., d. 12/17/1985 in Gilmanton; Horace Partridge and
Florence Palmer; b. 12/7/1926**

PATTEN,
Lura May, d. 10/1/1967 at 86 in Laconia; housewife; widow; b. Canaan; Edgar Gray and Ellen Bliss
Ralph E., d. 9/30/1991 in Laconia; Fred W. Patten and Lura May Gray

PATTERSON,
Louise, d. 10/11/1989 in Hanover; Walter F. Smith and Katherine T. Morash; b. 6/19/1909**

PAYNE,
Dorothy, d. 10/12/1957 at 72 in Concord*; housewife; widow; b. Dover; Edward Butcher and Lydia Bardeen

PEABODY,
Earl M., d. 6/30/1934 at 36/9/10 in Gilmanton; manager; single; b. Swampscott, MA; J. D. Peabody and Carrie Montrose; Lynn, MA
Maynard, d. 12/7/1948 at 60/11/19; office worker; married; b. Union, ME; Elmer Peabody

PEARSON,
Mary J., d. 5/4/1927 at 83/10/6 in Fairfield, ME; housework; widow; b. Gilmanton; Andrew W. Woodman; Fairfield, ME

PEASE,
Addie L., d. 3/11/1914 at 68/6/12 in Gilmanton I. W.; housewife; married; Asa Page (Gilmanton) and Eliza Edgerly (Gilmanton)
Annie L., d. 2/8/1903 at 41/5/9; housewife; married; b. Gilmanton; Charles H. Pierce and Drizilla Batchelder
Ellen S., d. 6/12/1902 at 55/9/12; housewife; married; b. Pittsfield; Joseph Harvey and Emaline Tasker
John L., d. 2/6/1920 at 69/5/12 in Gilmanton; farmer; married; b. Loudon; Nathaniel Pease and Nancy French; Loudon Ridge
Lee V., d. 4/6/1899 at 19/5/20; farmer; single; b. Gilmanton; Fred V. Pease (Loudon) and Annie L. Pierce (Gilmanton)
Leroy B., d. 1/18/1923 at 79

PEASLEE,
Caleb W. J., d. 12/14/1899 at 49/0/24; farmer; married; b. Gilmanton; Moses H. Peaslee (Gilmanton) and Betsey York (Barnstead)
Cyrus, d. 9/14/1924 at 79 in Gilmanton; farmer; single; b. Loudon; Amos Peaslee and Rhoda Varney; Friends Cem.
Martha S., d. 8/30/1919 at 77 in Penacook; milliner; single; b. Gilmanton; Hazen Peaslee; Smith Meetinghouse
Zaccheus, d. 1/22/1892 at 80/0/11; farmer; widower; b. Gilmanton; Moses Peaslee and Betsey Gale

PELTIER,
Clarence Francis, d. 7/21/1991 in Laconia; John Peltier and Mary Conole; b. 8/24/1915**

PENDERGAST,
Eli E., d. 11/2/1904 at 64/8/17; shoemaker; single; b. Barnstead; Ezra Pendergast and ----- Elliott
Jane, d. 3/28/1900 at 73; housemaid; single; b. Barnstead; Thomas Pendergast (Barnstead) and Lucy Ayers (Barnstead)

PENDLETON,
Charles L., d. 12/29/1971 at 28 in Gilmanton; timekeeper; single; b. MA; Earle B. Pendleton and Evelyn Clark
Douglas J., d. 3/15/2001 in Gilmanton I. W.; Richard Pendleton and Audrey Anderson; b. 8/24/1964**
Earl B., d. 11/13/1978 at 72 in Laconia; machinist, ret.; married; b. ME; Herbert L. Pendleton and Esther Jenkins

PENNOCK,
Florence Verona, d. 10/1/1959 at 44 in Laconia*; housewife; married; b. Somerville, MA; George L. Pennock and Winnifred Canney
Helen B., d. 4/7/1974 at 58 in Gilmanton; stitcher; married; b. NH; George I. Grace and Alice Dorothy
Ira H., d. 11/7/1897 at 85; shoemaker; married
Nancy S., d. 6/10/1902 at 91/8; widow

PERKINS,
Betsy L., d. 12/22/1896 at 75; consumption; housekeeper; widow; b. Canada; Ezra Hill (Canada) and Hannah Howard (Strafford)

Charles H., d. 2/15/1915 at 74/9/16 in Gilmanton; farmer; widower; James Perkins (Alton) and Nancy Ricker (Gilford)
Clarence L., d. 5/23/1955 at 44 in Wolfeboro; board sawyer; married; b. Gilmanton; Walter C. Perkins and Eva Glines
Doris Eva, d. 1/15/1986 in Gilmanton; Walter C. Perkins and Eva M. Perkins; b. 12/18/1915**
Eliza L., d. 1/11/1910 at 67/8/13; heart disease; housewife; married; Theodore Evans (Lyman, ME) and Mary Knowles (Tuftonboro)
Ethel, d. 7/2/1902 at 0/0/27; b. Gilmanton; Lorenzo H. Perkins (Gilmanton) and Helen A. Wyatt (Farmington)
Eva Maude, d. 2/26/1975 at 84 in Gilmanton I. W.; housewife; widow; b. NH; Albert Flines and Lucinda -----
Leon Walter, d. 9/14/1967 at 49 in Concord; wood chopper; single; b. Gilmanton; Walter C. Perkins and Eva M. Glines
Lorenzo H., d. 4/26/1950 at 76 in Laconia*; farmer (ret.); married; b. NH; Charles Perkins and Eliza Evans
Nellie May, d. 3/11/1918 at 31/6/29; housewife; married; b. Gilmanton; John William Kirby (Canada) and Mary Isobel Ray (Canada)
Walter C., d. 1/16/1939 at 53/6/24 in Gilmanton; farmer; married; b. Gilmanton; Charles H. Perkins (Meredith) and Eliza Evans (Ossipee)

PERLEY,
Robert A., d. 8/5/2001 in Concord; Dr. John Perley and Melba Beagle; b. 2/29/1940**

PERRY,
son, d. 11/5/1938 at – in Laconia*; b. Laconia; Arthur Perry (Machias, ME) and Amy Chamberlain (Gilmanton)
Willis C., d. 6/30/1942 at 70/8/8; married; b. Winchendon, MA; Frank Perry and Cephila Lawrence

PHILLIPS,
Doris May, d. 7/8/1965 at 70 in Laconia; domestic; married; b. Rupert, VT; Judson Carpenter and Effie Guilder

PHINNEY,
Elisabeth W., d. 5/4/1998 in Gilmanton; Howard Ansel Willis and Lilla Avis Pike

Gordon, d. 1/18/1997 in Laconia; Gilbert Phinney and Ella J. Kay; b. 11/5/1907**

PICKARD,
Dorothy Irene, d. 3/31/1962 at 49 in Laconia; housewife; married; b. Gilmanton; Fred L. Stone and Mary Hilliard

PICKERING,
Fannie M., d. 1/19/1943 at 68/5/25*; housewife; widow; b. Dover; William Chadwick
Fred C., d. 12/5/1924 at 62 in Concord; lunch room; married; b. Barnstead; Hiram H. Pickering and Martha Williams; Pine Grove
James M., d. 3/8/1898 at 78; farmer; widower; Jacob Pickering

PIERCE,
Emma D., d. 3/1/1941 at 87/9/20; none [occ.]; widow; b. Wilmot Flats; Francis E. Chase (Wilmot Flats) and Harriet E. Busiel (Wilmot Flats)

PINKHAM,
Hannah T., d. 1/12/1914 at 76/5/10 in Gilmanton I. W.; widow; George Adams

PIPER,
Flora B., d. 5/8/1893 at 28; consumption; housemaid; single; b. Gilmanton; Dudley L. Piper (Gilmanton) and Martha J. Leighton (Gilmanton)

PIVIROTTO,
Jeannette, d. 10/24/1988 in Laconia; James A. Morin and Flora E. Barlow; b. 8/19/1927**

PLACE,
Alice R., d. 10/27/1923 at 56
Edwin J., d. 1/8/1950 at 89/3/22 in Brentwood*; laborer; widower; b. Gilmanton; George E. Place and Alice Smith
Ernest L., d. 2/15/1928 at 72/11/25 in Somerville, MA; blacksmith; married; b. Alton; Smith Place; Pine Grove
Franklin S., d. 2/17/1973 at 87 in Gilmanton; cabinet maker, ret.; widower; b. NH; Jesse Place and Grace Page

Grace W., d. 11/30/1950 at 85/11 in Amesbury, MA*; housewife; widow; b. Gilmanton; Asa F. Page and Eliza L. Edgerly

Jesse Franklin, d. 11/5/1937 at 56 in Gilmanton; millwright; married; b. Alton; Smith C. Place and Nancy J. Dicey; Pine Grove, Gilmanton I. W.

Luanna Mary, d. 11/7/1959 at 89 in Gilmanton; housewife; married; b. Barnstead; Asa Hurd and Mary Jane Goodwin

Nancy J., Mrs., d. 3/17/1888 at 67/3/16; married

Smith C., d. 3/5/1890 at 73/9; farmer; married; Jacob Place and Nancy Dicey

PLOURDE,
Valerie Ann, d. 8/10/1998 in Gilmanton; John Begin

PLUMMER,
Charles E., d. 7/27/1906 at 74/8/28; farmer; married; b. Gilmanton; Joseph Plummer (Gilmanton) and Sally Lamprey (Gilmanton)

Ella O., d. 8/25/1911 at 62/0/23; housewife; married; b. Loudon; John S. Osborne (Gilmanton) and Fanny L. Gilman (Gilmanton)

John W., d. 7/13/1906 at 73/5/20; watchmaker; married; b. Georgetown, MA; John S. Plummer (MA) and Sarah B. Hanson (MA)

POLITO,
Lillian May, d. 2/3/1994 in Laconia; Louis Pepper and Margaret Watson

PORCIELLO,
Mary, d. 9/18/1999 in Gilmanton I. W.; Alexander DaSilva and Aurora Dasigvn

POROSKY,
Roger B., d. 3/26/1999 in Laconia; Theodore Porosky and Marjorie Burg

PORTER,
Alfred J., d. 6/29/1979 in Laconia; Freddie Porter and Decla Begin

Harold F., d. 3/25/1992 in Gilmanton; Simon Porter and Florence Chetwynd; b. 4/15/1905**

Henrietta B., d. 7/7/1990 in Laconia; John Biel and Agnes Lasak

POTTER,
son, d. 1/23/1903 at 0/0/½; b. Gilmanton; Charles F. Potter (Gilmanton) and Ardena M. Dimond (Loudon)
Ardena M., d. 6/20/1946 at 77/11/25 in Loudon*; widow; b. Loudon; Jonathan Dimond (Loudon) and Maria Peaslee (Loudon)
C. Fred, d. 1/2/1931 at 66/11/6 in Gilmanton; farmer; married; b. Gilmanton; George H. Potter and Mary J. Foss; Smith Meetinghouse
Frank Proctor, d. 4/22/1995 in Laconia; Frank T. Potter and Gertrude Proctor; b. 1/18/1913**
George Dimond, d. 1/12/1952 at 61 in Gilmanton; farmer; married; b. NH; Charles F. Potter and Ardena M. Dimond
Mary Elizabeth, d. 9/5/1887 at 86/6/4; housekeeper; widow; b. Danville, VT; T. Ladd (Salisbury) and Elizabeth Jimpson (Salisbury, VT)
Mary J., d. 2/9/1911 at 70/1/6; housekeeper; widow; b. Gilmanton; Benjamin H. Foss (Gilmanton) and K. Whitten (Alfred, ME)
Mildred E., d. 8/19/1990 in Concord; Herman Page and Anna -----

POWER,
Harry Francis, d. 1/24/1978 at 76 in Laconia; maintenance; married; b. NS; Harry Power and Ellie Graham

PRESCOTT,
Alfred, d. 11/5/1889 at 77/6/8; printer; married; b. Gilmanton; Timothy Prescott (Kensington) and Anna Lock (Rye)
George R., d. 2/24/1940 at 78/3/20; carpenter; widower; b. Alton; Joseph Prescott (Epsom) and Harriet Place (Alton)
Harold F., d. 4/24/1954 at 56 in Paterson, NJ*; married; b. Barnstead
Harriet, d. 7/8/1902 at 1/6; b. Penacook; Leander Prescott (Penacook) and Minnie E. Nelson (Gilmanton)
Leander C., d. 8/1/1927 at 65/5/12 in Gilmanton; merchant; married; b. Epsom; William S. Prescott and Harriet Marden; Penacook
Meranda E., d. 9/24/1901 at 93/7/16; housewife; widow; b. Canterbury; Leavitt Clough (Canterbury) and Abigail Morrill (Canterbury)

PRICE,
Amos R., d. 12/22/1900 at 79/7; farmer; married; b. Gilmanton; William Price (Gilmanton) and ----- Rand (Gilmanton)
Amos Richard, d. 3/24/1967 at 82 in Wolfeboro*; farmer; widower; b. Gilmanton; Charles A. Price and Aura Emerson
Aura Emerson, d. 10/8/1954 at 91 in Laconia*; housewife; widow; b. NH; Simeon Price and Mahala Emerson
Charles Amos, d. 1/21/1932 at 75/5/30 in Gilmanton; farmer; married; b. Gilmanton; Amos R. Price and Sarah Sleeper; Pine Grove
Elizabeth M., d. 12/21/1906 at 14/2/14; single; b. Gilmanton; Charles A. Price (Gilmanton) and Aura E. Emerson (Barnstead)
Emma Wight, d. 4/8/1962 at 77 in Gilmanton; housewife; married; b. Gilmanton; Albert Wight and Emma Jones
Judith, d. 8/25/1892 at 85/0/19; housewife; widow
Lizzie, d. 5/8/1940 at 86/1/10*; housewife; divorced; b. Gilmanton; Moses Price (Gilmanton) and Sarah Goldthwaite (Peabody, MA)
Osborne W., d. 9/11/1942 at 81/6/15*; retired; married; b. Gilmanton; Amos Price (Gilmanton) and Sarah Sleeper (Alton)

PRINDLE,
Elizabeth R., d. 4/1/1949 at 0/2/6 in Gilmanton; b. Laconia; William E. Prindle and Myra Kitchen
Myra, d. 6/15/1976 at 55 in Gilmanton; housewife; married; b. NY; Victor Kitchen and Elsie Rodman

PROCTOR,
son, d. 4/11/1956 at 7 hrs. in Laconia; b. Laconia; Charles A. Proctor and B. Stephenson

PROULX,
Joseph C., d. 10/12/1926 at 49/9/3 in Gilmanton; laborer; b. Canada; Joseph Proulx and Phoebe Bean; Hillside

PUFFER,
Delora A., d. 8/21/1990 in Meredith; Charles R. Smith and Hadassah Goodwin

PULSIFER,
Lucinda, d. 11/7/1896 at 82; dropsy; housewife; married

PURDY,
Claude Henry, d. 11/19/1994 in Laconia; Henry Purdy and Celeste Brown; b. 9/8/1917**

PURTELL,
Stanley P., d. 8/31/1983 in Laconia; Leonard Purtell and Margaret Adams
Stanley P., Jr., d. 6/10/1986 in Hanover; Stanley P. Purtell, Sr. and Barbara Parker

QUIMBY,
Naomi, d. 2/22/1890 at 68; housewife; married

RANDALL,
Grace Leida, d. 11/3/1994 in Gilmanton; Ernest M. Kelley and Amy A. Andrews; b. 8/21/1909**

RANSOM,
Henry L., d. 6/10/1904 at 83; tinsmith; widower; b. Gilmanton
Mrs. Henry, d. 4/6/1896 at 70; cancer; housewife; married

READ,
Doris Alice, d. 2/5/1996 in Gilmanton; Francis St. Pierre and Elise Marceau
Walter Roy, d. 8/15/1997 in Laconia; Roy Read and Verna Ricker

RENHULT,
Frank K., d. 6/9/1972 at 74 in Rochester*; foreman; married; b. MA; Gustaf Renhult and Bertha Kattell

REYNOLDS,
Dennis Robert, d. 10/21/1973 at 17 in Gilmanton; student; single; b. MA; John Reynolds and Joan E. McCarthy

RHEAULT,
Norman G., d. 11/7/1972 at 36 in Gilmanton; accountant; single; b. NH; Lucien Rheault and Henrietta Messier

RHODES,
Jennie M., d. 2/28/1937 at 68/8/5 in Gilmanton; at home; widow; b. East Haverhill; William McLean and Irene Palmer; Riverside, Plymouth

RICHARDS,
Robert D., d. 8/21/1971 at 16 in Gilmanton; student; single; b. NH; Robert D. Richards and Marna Clements

RICHARDSON,
Romanto A., d. 9/25/1904 at 46; laborer; married; b. Gilmanton

RIEL,
Alden L., d. 4/26/1993 in Laconia; Jerry Riel and Evelyn Moulton

RILEY,
Olive, d. 1/24/1890 at 70; housewife; married

RINES,
Bernice, d. 6/27/1967 at 76 in Concord; telephone operator; widow; b. Gilmanton; Leslie Clarke and Minnie Howard

ROBBINS,
Norman, d. 12/31/1894 at 66; la grippe; miller; married; b. Hillsborough

ROBERGE,
Robert L., d. 3/8/1988 in Laconia; George Roberge and Lecia Holman; b. 6/6/1917**

ROBERTS,
Charles A., d. 11/26/1906 at 69/1/11; farmer; married; b. Ossipee; Charles A. Roberts (Ossipee) and Effie Beecham (Ossipee)
Frank H., d. 10/11/1989 in Hanover; Charles B. Roberts and Mary Mahoney; b. 6/16/1900**
George B., Sr., d. 5/6/1990 in Laconia; William C. Roberts and Elizabeth E. Swift
Helene Frieda Kristine, d. 7/17/1995 in Gilmanton; Olaf Martin Eversen and Martha K. Wilhelmson; b. 6/27/1904**

Margery A., d. 4/15/1938 at 40/5/2 in Pembroke*; housewife; married; b. England; William Porter (England) and Elizabeth Rudge (England)

Mary Ann, d. 2/23/1935 at 83/4/17 in Gilmanton; at home; widow; b. Gilmanton; Lewis Weed and Ann M. Knowles; Un'n Tomb, Laconia

Mary E., d. 4/2/1954 at 80 in Laconia; housewife; widow; b. NY; Patrick Mahony and Mary Nehill

Robert L. M., d. 8/24/1984 in Danbury, CT; Sylvester Roberts and Marjorie Porter

Sylvester M., d. 12/23/1946 at 51/3/5; seaman; widower; b. Birmingham, England; Swift Roberts (Birmingham, England)

ROBERTSON,

Eunice Whittemore, d. 9/23/1964 at 68 in Gilmanton*; housewife; married; b. Winchendon, MA; Henry J. Whittemore and Mary E. Derby

William Thomas, d. 8/7/1974 at 81 in Laconia; machinist, ret.; widower; b. Scotland; Christopher Robertson and Christina Black

ROBINSON,

David, d. 10/27/1926 at 32/4/27 in CA; steward; married; b. Huddersfield, England; J. F. Robinson; Smith Meeting House

Elizabeth Annie, d. 6/16/1951 at 91/9/25 in Center Harbor*; housewife; widow; b. NH; Wells Chase York and Mary Ann Smart

Marietta, d. 2/25/1895 at 15; neuralgia of heart; single; Nathaniel Robinson and Mary J. Twombly

Samuel W., d. 5/21/1933 at 67/9/25 in Boston, MA; b. Cambridge, MA; James R. Robinson and Dorothy Dudley; Smith Meetinghouse

ROBY,

Ervin, d. 10/13/1918 at 27; single; b. Edgewood, MD

ROGERS,

Almeda M., d. 8/15/1904 at 54/0/13; housewife; married; b. Gilmanton; Cyrus Lamprey (Gilmanton) and Eliza Ellsworth (Gilmanton)

Eva L., d. 8/15/1935 at 65/8/3 in Weymouth, MA; teacher; married; b. Belmont; Arthur Lamprey and Emma James; Gilmanton
Frederick, d. 8/18/1999 in East Derry; Silas Rogers and Rosalie Jones
Willis Artemus, d. 12/4/1996 in Gilmanton; William Leon Rogers and Lizzie Lovejoy; b. 6/21/1928**

ROLLINS,
[unnamed female, listed with Jacob], d. 9/–/1887 at 78; married
Alma L., d. 9/17/1922 at 42
Dorothy A., d. 7/25/1919 at 67/10/19 in Alton; housewife; married; b. Alton; Henry Young and Sarah Upton; Pine Grove
Eva M., d. 4/14/1955 at 59 in Wolfeboro*; housewife; widow; b. Gilmanton; George Jones and Olive Moody
Everett B., d. 4/24/1977 at 67 in Laconia; truck driver; divorced; b. NH; Seldon Rollins and Alma Ellis
Fred B., d. 1/14/1927 at 57/2/29 in Laconia; married; Guinea Ridge
Jacob, d. 9/–/1887 at 85; married
Lionel, d. 2/6/1956 at 34 in Gilmanton; laborer; divorced; b. Nottingham; Walter Rollins and Lucy Merrill
Mary L., d. 12/16/1917 at 69/10/17 in Gilmanton; housework; widow; Daniel Sargent (Gilmanton) and Louise ----- (Gilmanton)
Nathaniel G., d. 6/6/1953 at 71 in Laconia*; ret. shoemaker; single; b. NH; James A. Rollins and Juliette Young
Selden B., d. 11/24/1948 at 73/8/9*; pensioned; married; b. Gilmanton; Bartlett Rollins (Gilmanton) and Mary Sargent

ROSTRUM,
Blanche Valentine, d. 4/20/1992 in Gilmanton; ----- Bent and Eurice -----

ROWE,
Sarah, d. 10/9/1903 at 81; single

RUGGERI,
Peter, d. 11/29/1993 in Gilmanton; Neno Ruggeri and Virginia Cusinotta

RUOTSALA,
Herbert, d. 2/23/1997 in Manchester; Andrew Ruotsala and Helmi Hanninen

RUSK,
Isabella K., d. 9/30/1953 at 93 in Laconia; housewife; widow; b. Scotland; ----- Lawrence

RUSSELL,
Elvira O., d. 4/3/1899 at 70; housework; single; b. Wilton; Reuben Russell (Wilton) and Nancy Meson
Mark J., d. 11/14/1984 in Alton; ----- and Ricki Russell
Philip Arthur, d. 12/1/1962 at 60 in Gilmanton; farm supt.; divorced; b. Woodstock; Arthur Russell
Sven Charles, d. 8/13/1994 in Laconia; Mark Russell and Madeline Sage

ST. CLAIRE,
Ellen Margaret, d. 8/25/1972 at 78 in Laconia; housewife; widow; b. NH; Rufus Langley and Alice Abbot

SACKETT,
Alice H., d. 5/31/1948 at 86/4/0*; housewife; widow; b. Alton; Andrew Huckins (Madbury) and Maria Chamberlin (New Durham)
Austin H., d. 3/27/1904 at 19/2/29; shoemaker; single; b. Barnstead; George Sackett (Barnstead) and Alice Huckins (Alton)
David N., d. 11/7/1925 at 83 in Concord; widower; Pine Grove
George A., d. 7/26/1929 at 67/10/3 in Barnstead; Pine Grove
Sarah E., d. 10/22/1911 at 66/3/17; housewife; married; b. Laconia; Aaron G. Young (Barnstead) and Parmilva Gilman

SANBORN,
son, d. 7/14/1903 at 0/0/½; b. Gilmanton; James H. Sanborn (Sandwich) and Maria Shannon (Bethlehem)
Charles C., d. 5/14/1901 at 69/11/14; farmer; married; b. Gilmanton; Joseph Sanborn (Gilmanton) and Lydia Kelley (Gilmanton)
George W., d. 7/31/1903 at 81/2/21; farmer; widower; b. Sandwich; Jacob Sanborn (Unity) and Fannie Eastman (Landaff)

Isabelle G., d. 1/6/1919 at 67/11/13 in Gilmanton; housekeeper; married; b. Loudon; John S. Osborne and Rachel J. Brown; Family Cem.
Jeremiah W., d. 4/1/1933 at 86/1/27 in Gilmanton; farmer; married; b. Gilmanton; George Sanborn and Mary Brown; Sanborn's, at farm
Nathan M., d. 6/11/1903 at 62/11/10; painter; widower; b. Alexandria
Orin C., d. 5/8/1925 at 68/5/12 in Gilmanton; laborer; single; b. Thornton; Nathan B. Sanborn and Ruth Cousins; Beech Grove
Wayne Wilson, d. 2/15/1918 at 0/0/21; b. Melrose, MA; Carl J. Sanborn (Columbia, MO) and Evelyn M. Sanborn (Pittsfield)

SANDERSON,
Florence E., d. 1/8/1914 at 47/5/5 in Gilmanton; housewife; married; George Hoyt and Letitia Hoyt (Loudon)
William S. P., d. 9/13/1933 at 70/1/26 in Laconia; ret'd druggist; b. Gilmanton; Charles S. P. Sanderson and Anna Mack; Beech Grove

SANFORD,
Dorothy Eva, d. 10/31/1999 in Gilmanton; Ernest Blaisdell; b. 2/27/1927**
Viola Pearl, d. 9/14/1997 in Gilmanton; Charles E. Brackett and Mary E. Downing; b. 7/20/1907**

SANTERRE,
Bernice M., d. 4/26/1987 in Gilmanton; Ernest Kelley and Amy Andrews
Emile Gerard J., d. 10/11/1965 at 44 in Gilford; carpenter; married; b. Sutton, PQ; Ambroise Santerre

SANTIANO,
Madeline G., d. 12/31/1989 in Gilmanton; Andrew Nealon and Bridget R. Flaherty; b. 3/3/1902**
Michael, d. 10/13/1990 in Laconia; Luigi Santiano and Lena Dinubilia

SANVILLE,
William Henry, d. 1/13/1966 at 73 in Laconia; fireman, retired; b. Warner; Wilfred Sanville and Annie Moody

SARGEANT,
Horace Daniel, d. 9/28/1960 at 67 in Laconia*; farmer - ret.; married; b. Gilmanton; Herbert Sargeant and Carrie B. Ellis

SARGENT,
son, d. 6/16/1934 at – in Concord; b. Pittsfield; Erwin Sargent and Ruth Thompson; Gilmanton I. W.
son, d. 5/23/1964 at 28 min. in Laconia*; b. Laconia; Prescott N. Sargent and Elizabeth Thompson
Carrie M., d. 6/8/1939 at 78/2/27 in Gilmanton; none [occ.]; single; b. Gilmanton; Stephen W. Sargent (Alton) and Prudence Cardwell (MA)
Charles F., d. 9/11/1921 at 88/5/22 in Gilmanton; farmer; widower; b. Alton; Daniel Sargent and Louise Watson; Guinea Ridge
Charles L., d. 11/28/1940 at 79/8/6; farmer; widower; b. Gilmanton; Charles F. Sargent (Alton) and Susan E. Rollins (Alton)
Clarence L., d. 10/14/1938 at 22/0/25 in Laconia*; farmer; married; b. Laconia; Clarence Sargent (Gilmanton) and Rena Prescott (Alton)
Clarence Linwood, d. 9/5/1963 at 82 in Laconia*; salesman; married; b. Gilmanton; Charles L. Sargent and Viennia Ellis
Daniel, d. 2/2/1892 at 87; farmer; widower
Franklin D., d. 7/13/1913 at 74/2/14; farmer; widower; b. Gilmanton; Daniel Sargent (Chichester) and ----- Watson (Alton)
George A., d. 5/14/1897 at 45/1/4; farmer; single; John L. Sargent and Mary E. McClure
Herbert, d. 2/24/1926 at 61/11/23 in Gilmanton; farmer; married; b. Gilmanton; Charles F. Sargent and Susan E. Rollins; Guinea Ridge
Mary E., d. 3/12/1898 at 72/4; housewife; widow; b. Boscawen; John A. McClure (Exeter) and Sally Potter (Gilmanton)
Mary E., d. 7/–/1907 at –; married
Mrs. Daniel, d. 2/25/1888 at 77; housewife; married
Susan E., d. 2/3/1920 at 81/11/23 in Laconia; housewife; married; b. Alton; Guinea Ridge
Viennia, d. 4/22/1935 at 74/3/22 in Gilmanton; housewife; married; b. Alton; Alfred G. Ellis and Mary A. Ellis; Guinea Ridge
William Ives, d. 6/2/1958 at 89 in Concord*; grocery store; widower; b. Pittsfield; Ives C. Sargent and Annie Woodbury

SAVORY,
Belinda, d. 10/9/1899 at 87; housework; widow; b. Plymouth; ----- Ryan

SAWYER,
Betsy Moody, d. 4/6/1961 at 76 in Laconia*; housewife; widow; b. Gilmanton; Rufus Knowles and Arabelle Moody
David, d. 4/25/1956 at 82 in Laconia*; carpenter - ret.; married; b. Gilmanton; John Sawyer and Mary Marsh
Eliza J., d. 10/9/1918 at 76/4/2; housekeeper; widow; b. Gilmanton; George Chandler (MA) and Jane Bates (MA)
Elizabeth P., d. 4/29/1995 in Laconia; Lloyd Harrison and Mabel Goddard; b. 3/28/1910**
Fred, d. 4/18/1927 at 76/10/2 in Gilmanton; laborer; married; b. Lowell, MA; John Sawyer and Mary -----; Edgerly Cem.
Fred A., d. 2/7/1998 in Laconia; Otto Sawyer and Daisy Patten; b. 3/1/1919**
John R., d. 4/13/1909 at 68/3/4; farmer; married; b. Belmont; David Sawyer (Belmont) and Lucy C. Sleeper (Hebron)
Mary J., d. 4/26/1935 at 82/9 in Gilmanton; housewife; widow; b. Gilmanton; Richard Marsh and Hannah Peaslee; Smith Meetinghouse
Theodore Howard, d. 3/28/1909 at –; b. Gilmanton; David Sawyer (Gilmanton) and Betsey M. Knowles (Gilmanton)

SCANELLI,
Hennitta, d. 3/26/1979 in Concord; George Frederick and Selina ----

SCHILLINGER,
Joseph Anthony, d. 5/15/1997 in Gilmanton; John Henry Schillinger and Mary Frances Wenzel; b. 5/7/1920**

SCHMIDT,
Pauline, d. 1/2/1939 at 59/2/11; single; b. Hoboken, NJ; Frederick Schmidt (Germany)

SCHNEIDER,
August A., d. 7/11/1973 at 69 in Laconia*; alcoholic counselor; single; b. CT; Adam Schneider and Elizabeth Schneider

SCHOTT,
Suzanne B., d. 7/31/2001 in Gilmanton I.W.; Chester Blackey and Mary Briggs; b. 7/20/1921**

SCHREMPF,
Sharon M., d. 10/23/1981 in Laconia; Stephen Schrempf and Mary Ann White

SCHRICKER,
Earl, d. 3/7/1995 in Manchester; ----- and Mathilde Hambled; b. 10/26/1915**

SCHULTZ,
James Francis, d. 3/27/1990 in Manchester; George A. Schultz and Cecilia Farrell
Leon Walter, d. 3/19/1958 at 70 in Gilmanton; pharmacist - ret.; married; b. Antrim; Frank L. Schultz and Isadora Barrett

SCHWARTZBACH,
Pauline, d. 8/4/1933 at 74/0/7 in Gilmanton; at home; married; b. NY; Gustave Miller and Pauline Sherer; Brooklyn, NY

SCOVILL,
Lawrence S., d. 8/2/2000 in Laconia; Sorensen Scovill and Lenna Crosby; b. 4/13/1915**
Paul K., d. 9/23/1991 in Gilmanton; Lawrence S. Scovill and Virginia Prescott
Sorensen, d. 1/24/1948 at 71/7/8*; poultryman; married; b. Yarmouth, NS; Dennis Scovill (Yarmouth, NS) and Maria E. Crosby (Yarmouth, NS)

SCRANTON,
Elizabeth G., d. 3/26/1982 in Laconia; ----- Kane; b. 4/24/1908**

SEARLE,
Malcolm M., d. 1/6/1920 at 0/0/0 in Gilmanton; b. Gilmanton; Carl N. Searle and Martha Miller; Buffalo, NY

SEARS,
Carrie E., d. 4/20/1904 at 39/7; housewife; married; Reuben Giles (Sanbornton) and Abbie Staniels (Chichester)

SEAVEY,
Stuart Edward, d. 6/18/1960 at 74 in Laconia; cref-ret. (sic); married; b. Conway; Edward Charles Seavey and Edna Hayford

SEGALINI,
Grace A., d. 4/27/1990 in Gilmanton; Abijah Astbury and Jeanine Lowell
Louie J., d. 1/13/1977 at 62 in Laconia; test line oper.; married; b. NH; James Segalini and Maria -----

SEIBEL,
Charles G., d. 5/3/1984 in Laconia; Charles G. Seibel, Jr. and Grace Conant; b. 12/8/1913**

SELLIN,
Amy Joanna, d. 1/20/1973 at 77 in Gilmanton; housewife; married; b. MI; Eric Anderson
Thorsten, d. 9/17/1994 in Laconia; Jonas Sellin and Martha Westman; b. 10/26/1896**

SENIOR,
Keith Alan, d. 9/4/1963 at 19 in Concord; elec. helper; single; b. Plainfield, NJ; Walter M. Senior, Jr. and Mavis A. Keith

SEWELL,
Clara S., d. 9/11/1894 at 75/4/13; heart failure; housewife; widow; b. Gilmanton; Dudley Young (Gilmanton) and Sara Jacobs (Barnstead)

SHACKFORD,
Carrie P., d. 7/21/1925 at 66/6/21 in Gilmanton; housekeeper; widow; b. Sebago, ME; Joshua L. Usher and Harriet L. Bailey; Pine Grove

SHALAITAS,
Konstant J., d. 11/19/1971 at 84 in Concord*; ret. farmer; married; b. Lithuania

SHANNON,
Ann P., d. 2/26/1905 at 83/8/26; housewife; married; b. Gilmanton; John Kimball (Gilmanton) and Nancy Adams (Gilmanton)

Carroll, d. 12/19/1948 at 71/1/12; mail car. (ret.); married; b. Gilmanton; Charles Shannon (Gilmanton) and Laura Lougee (Gilmanton)

Charles, d. 2/11/1907 at 70/6/23; farmer; married; b. Gilmanton; Ira Shannon (Gilmanton) and Sally Ross (Gilmanton)

Emma M., d. 10/7/1937 at 81/8/17 in Whitman, MA*; Smith M. H., Gilmanton

Florence M., d. 4/16/1895 at 20/5; acute tuberculosis; school teacher; single; b. Gilmanton; Charles H. Shannon (Gilmanton) and Laura Lougee (Gilmanton)

Frank E., d. 2/15/1888 at 33/6; physician; married; b. Gilmanton; James C. Shannon (Gilmanton) and Judith W. Batchelder (Loudon)

George E., d. 12/23/1905 at 64/6/23; butcher; married; b. Gilmanton; Ira Shannon

Harry W., d. 12/1/1899 at 27/2/18; farmer; single; b. Gilmanton; James C. Shannon (Gilmanton) and Judith Batchelder (Loudon)

Ira, d. 11/22/1893 at 88/2; old age; farmer; widower; b. Gilmanton; George Shannon (Barnstead) and ----- Tebbetts (Alton)

James C., d. 2/1/1904 at 81/5/10; farmer; married; b. Gilmanton; George Shannon and Sally Tibbits

John C., d. 2/16/1910 at 85/11/22; old age; farmer; widower; b. Gilmanton; George Shannon (Barnstead) and Betsy Tebbetts

Judith W., d. 3/13/1904 at 68/8/22; housewife; widow; b. Loudon; Harry Batchelder and Soprona -----

Laura J. L., d. 11/15/1921 at 83/4/28 in Pittsfield; housework; widow; b. Gilmanton; John Lougee and Rebecca Edgerly; Pine Grove

Lorraine, d. 2/24/1905 at 66/4/19; farmer; single; b. Barnstead; Ephraim Shannon (Barnstead) and Mary A. Hurd (Cow Island)

Mabel, d. 4/12/1887 at 17/7; single; b. Gilmanton; Charles Shannon (Gilmanton) and Laura J. Lougee (Gilmanton)

May Belle, d. 2/15/1888 at 17/11; housewife; single; b. Gilmanton; James C. Shannon (Gilmanton) and Judith W. Batchelder (Loudon)

SHARKEY,
Adeline, d. 3/9/1963 at 67 in Laconia*; hairdresser; widow; b. New York, NY; Walter C. Miller and Anna Constock
John, d. 7/25/1975 at 73 in Laconia; painter (ret.); widower; b. PA

SHARP,
Orvis Wayne, d. 10/16/1984 in Manchester; John Sharp and Katherine Sanborn

SHATTUCK,
Harry, d. 8/27/1972 at 73 in Concord*; carpenter; married; b. VT; Willis Shattuck and Sara Buckman

SHAW,
Albert John, d. 11/20/1923 at 93
Edward K., d. 10/12/1965 at 70 in Concord; Hawaiian; entertainer; married; b. Honolulu, HI; James Shaw and Esther Stevenson

SHEARER,
Sophia, d. 4/1/1910 at 50/10/6; acute paralysis; housewife; married; b. Canada; Joseph Cusson (Canada) and Elizabeth Peck (Canada)

SHERWOOD,
Martha M., d. 9/23/1929 at 75/0/22 in Gilmanton; married; b. Philadelphia, PA; George B. Reed and Anna B. Gibbard; Cambridge, MA

SHIELDS,
Frances C., d. 3/12/1956 at 62 in Somerville, MA; married; b. Boston, MA; Henry C. Martin and Harriett Cogswell

SHLAITAS,
Mary A., d. 2/7/1979 in Gilmanton; John Waisnoras and Ursula Gricius

SHORT,
Mary L., d. 11/22/1900 at 85/5/13; housewife; widow; b. Newburyport, MA; Amos Pettingell (Newburyport, MA) and Joanna -----

SHORTRIDGE,
George A., d. 4/19/1937 at 64/7/2 in Alton; sawyer; single; b. Farmington; George F. Shortridge and Carrie Mason; Pine Grove, Farmington

SHUNK,
Helen, d. 5/14/1975 at 70 in Boscawen; bookkeeper; widow; b. MA; John Driscol and Nellie Cremin

SICHEL,
Muriel E., d. 6/24/1938 at 55/4/23 in Gilmanton; pvt. secretary; married; b. Reading, MA; Harold Windham (England) and Violet ----- (PA)

SIDLAUSKAS,
Joseph Anthony, d. 10/25/1966 at 78 in Laconia*; tool grinder retired; married; b. Lithuania; Joseph Sidlauskas and Anna Shukis
Petronella, d. 7/19/1979 in Laconia; John Celkiuti; b. 6/24/1896**

SIMMONS,
Abigail M., d. 9/14/1936 at 91/4 in Gilmanton; at home; widow; b. Loudon; Samuel Lovering (Loudon) and Mary Rogers (Loudon)

SIMONEAU,
Cecelia M., d. 2/3/1970 at 75 in Laconia*; housewife; married; b. NH; Joseph Bouley and Delia Houle
Charles J., d. 8/27/1972 at 81 in Laconia*; store clerk; widower; b. Canada; Joseph Simoneau and Marie Champagne

SIMPSON,
Bonnie Marie, d. 12/11/1993 in Gilmanton; Albert Moulton and Marion Drouin

SISSON,
Barbara J., d. 7/13/1988 in Laconia; Alfred Johnson and Amelia Everett; b. 11/19/1907**

SKANTZE,
Catherine Frances, d. 7/11/1992 in Gilmanton; Fred Nuss and Hannah Brown; b. 8/13/1911**

SLAUNWHITE,
Vernon, d. 8/2/1978 at 73 in Concord; chief mate; married; b. NS; William Slaunwhite and Rosella Linguard

SLEEPER,
Jonathan, d. 10/6/1893 at 74; heart disease; farmer; married; b. Alton; Jonathan Sleeper (Alton) and Mary Woodman (Alton)
Mary Jane, d. 3/2/1897 at 70; housekeeper; single

SMALL,
Richard L., d. 3/8/1980 in Laconia; Lewis F. Small and Harriet -----; b. 12/29/1894**

SMITH,
Arthur P., d. 1/8/1921 at 87/5/7 in Gilmanton; teacher; married; b. Waltham, MA; Nathan Smith and Elizabeth Wellington; Waltham, MA
Athol Everard, d. 7/19/1974 at 78 in Concord; engineer; married; b. ME; Norman A. Smith and Nellie F. Bragdon
Augustus W., d. 1/24/1894 at 79/3/12; pneumonia; shoemaker; married; b. Gilmanton; Timothy Smith
Bert M., d. 12/9/1929 at 52/4/27 in Gilmanton; fireman; divorced; b. Gilmanton; Edward E. Smith and Jane H. Evans; Pine Grove
Charles Lyndell, d. 5/22/1968 at 62 in Gilmanton; laborer; married; b. NH; John W. Smith and Edith Hannaford
Charles T., d. 3/8/1930 at 85/1/1 in Pittsfield; farmer; widower; b. Gilmanton; Augustus Smith and ----- Robinson; Pine Grove
Dolly J., d. 5/29/1901 at 7/4/4; school girl; b. Charlestown, MA; George E. Smith (Gilmanton) and Etta G. McAlpine (Warner)
Edith L., d. 4/26/1907 at 24/3/28; housewife; married; b. Manchester; Theodore F. Hannaford (NY) and Louise Landon (Manchester, VT)
Edward E., d. 11/25/1908 at 72/8/12; farmer; widower; b. MA; William Smith and Elizabeth Warburton
Ella A., d. 11/5/1916 at 65/3/15 in Gilmanton; house work; single; Samuel A. Smith and Louisa M. Nute
Emil L., d. 3/6/1917 at 50/9/8 in Alton; blacksmith; single; Edward E. Smith (MA) and Jane H. Evans (NH)
Eva J., d. 5/5/1914 at 66/9/22 in Gilmanton; married; Alvah Foss (Gilmanton) and Eva J. Foss

Frances Warren, d. 3/8/1949 at 62/11/5 in Gilmanton; housewife; married; b. Brooklyn, NY; Charles E. Short and Eleanor F. Tucker

George E., d. 4/30/1894 at 40/1; pneumonia; hotel keeper; married; b. Gilmanton; Augustus W. Smith (Gilmanton) and Julia A. Robinson (Gilmanton)

George K., d. 12/29/1902 at 76/9/26; shoemaker; widower

James, d. 5/24/1940 at 19/5/6*; single; b. Laconia; James Smith

Jane H., d. 9/20/1905 at 69/5/6; housewife; married; b. Moultonboro; Theodore Evans (Lyman, ME) and Mary Knowles (Sandwich)

John J., d. 7/27/1913 at 78/7/17; farmer; widower; b. Ipswich; William Smith

Kathleen C., d. 8/29/1957 at 41 in Gilmanton; housewife; married; b. Peabody, MA; ----- Reardon and Kathleen Lyons

Martha Jane, d. 6/18/1943 at 94/8/17; housewife; widow; b. Barnstead; Timothy Emerson (Barnstead) and Sarah E. Foster (Durham)

Mary, d. 1/8/1904 at 60; housekeeper; widow; b. Gilford; George Dockham (Meredith)

Mary G., d. 11/2/1897 at 84/11/4; single; b. Gilmanton; Timothy Smith (Gilmanton) and Betsy Smith (Gilmanton)

Offie M., d. 9/29/1907 at 90/6/6; widow; ----- Moody (Stowe, VT)

Pauline E., d. 4/2/1908 at 77/0/19; widow; b. Harrisburg, NY

Rebecca, d. 5/18/1903 at 65/10; housewife; married

Reed W., d. 6/21/1984 in Laconia; Irving E. Smith and Lila Johnson; b. 3/21/1927**

Robert S., d. 5/12/1926 at 70/3/28 in Gilmanton; farmer; married; b. Brighton, ME; Elezier Smith and Nancy Scriber; Pine Grove

Rosilla, d. 2/27/1910 at 78/9/9; housekeeper; widow; b. Alton; Joseph Watson and Mary Spencer

Roy Louis, Jr., d. 9/14/1993 in Laconia; b. 9/7/1925**

Sidney S., d. 5/4/1957 at 69 in Laconia*; cottages owner; married; b. Paterson, NJ; William Smith and Elizabeth Coulter

Warren M., d. 11/5/1932 at 79/4/15 in Gilmanton; farmer; b. Gilmanton; Samuel Smith; Smith Meetinghouse

William Evans, d. 12/9/1949 at 81 in Laconia; carpenter (ret.); widower; b. NH; Edward E. Smith and Jane H. Evans

SMITHERS,
Elizabeth R., d. 8/16/1999 in Concord; Bernard Belcastro and Veronica Ryan
Timothy John, d. 12/12/1992 in Laconia; Thomas W. Smithers, III and Elizabeth R. Belcastro

SNELL,
Raymond B., d. 12/15/1972 at 62 in Laconia; foreman; married; b. MA; Arthur B. Snell and Harriet South

SNOW,
Arline Sawyer, d. 5/17/1994 in Epsom; Berten Cabot Snow and Isabelle F. Coors (see following entry)
Arline Sawyer, d. 5/17/1995 in Epsom; Berten Cabot Snow and Isabelle F. Coors (see preceding entry)
Conrad E., d. 12/21/1975 at 86 in Gilmanton I. W.; lawyer (ret.); married; b. NH; Leslie P. Snow and Susan E. Currier
Katherine H., d. 1/7/1985 in Laconia; Frank S. Hartley and Laura E. Pulsifer

SORDELLINE,
George Salvatore, d. 2/26/1994 in Gilmanton; Erasmo Sordelline and Antonetta Castellano

SPEAR,
Electa Ann, d. 12/10/1909 at 66/10/27; housework; widow; Nathaniel Battis (Canterbury) and ----- Glover (Canterbury)
Joseph A., d. 4/17/1906 at 69/2/2; married; b. Ipswich; Joseph Spear (Ipswich) and Emily Pierce

SPEARE,
Jessie R., d. 10/20/1984 in Laconia; Morton Reid and Emma Gray; b. 3/19/1904**

SPRINGER,
Dorothy Belle, d. 4/17/1994 in Laconia; James Kelley and Jennie Emerson; b. 11/22/1907**
Edith, d. 11/20/1942 at 64/3/28; postmistress; widow; b. Bradford, England; John A. Horsman (Bradford, England) and Ann M. Crosland (Bradford, England)

Harold L., d. 5/2/1985 in Laconia; Sanford Springer and Edith Horsman; b. 5/11/1907**

Sanford R., d. 9/27/1914 at 40/2/29 in Gilmanton; store manager; married; Jefferson Springer (Trenton, ME) and Frances Hamor (Hills Cove, ME)

STANLEY,

Judie, d. 1/17/1989 in Laconia; Stanley Maciejewski and Theresa McCarthy

Milton, d. 12/14/1978 at 61 in Laconia; antique dealer; married; b. NY; William Rosenblum and Grace Goldfarb

STANTON,

M. W., d. 9/6/1913 at 65/0/21; day laborer; married; b. Alton; Hiram Leathers (Lee) and Ann Williams (Durham)

STAPLES,

Melvina B., d. 12/17/1894 at 64/1/25; disease of stomach and liver; housekeeper; married; b. Williamstown, VT; Hibbard Beckwith and Melvina Beckwith

STARRETT,

William L., d. 7/26/1920 at 57/3/28 in Gilmanton; farmer; married; b. China, ME; Samuel C. Starrett and Emily Mooher; Smith Meetinghouse

STEAD,

Florence, d. 8/6/1926 at 13/8/25 in Gilmanton; at school; single; b. England; James Stead and Annie Mackintosly; Saugus, MA

STEENSTRA,

Walter H., d. 6/28/1983 in Concord; Frederick H. Steenstra and Elisie V. Roberts; b. 12/10/1911**

STENDOR,

Noel B., d. 9/1/1978 at 57 in Gilmanton; trapper; married; b. MA; Frank Stendor and Agnes Letty

STEVENS,
Aaron D., d. 12/29/1940 at 53/10/3*; wood turner; divorced; b. Beverly, MA; Joseph A. Stevens (Beverly, MA) and Louise H. Spinney (Denmark)
Bonny Gale, d. 6/29/1969 at 14 in Gilmanton; student; single; b. NH; Sherman Stevens and Mildred A. Ross
Deborah Jean, d. 6/29/1969 at 7 in Gilmanton; student; single; b. NH; Sherman Stevens and Mildred A. Ross
George Luther, d. 2/8/1974 at 64 in Laconia; janitor, ret.; single; b. MA; Peter H. Stevens and Annie B. Hudson
Hope Anna, d. 6/29/1969 at 1 in Gilmanton; b. NH; Sherman Stevens and Mildred A. Ross
Joseph A., d. 10/6/1936 at 74/10/6 in Gilmanton; farmer; widower; b. Beverly, MA; Edward A. Stevens (Beverly, MA) and Abbie Shattuck
Louise H., d. 12/27/1931 at 72/0/6 in Gilmanton; housework; married; b. Argyle, NS; Edward Spinney; Pine Grove
Mahala M., d. 5/29/1889 at 87; housewife; widow; b. Loudon; Enoch Morse (Francestown) and Persis Ordway (Loudon)
Nancy Wilson, d. 6/7/1999 in Gilmanton; Harold Wilson and Claire Dunbrack; b. 2/7/1934**
Richard H., Sr., d. 6/28/1987 in Laconia; Peter Stevens and Angela Fitzpatrick
Vicki Marie, d. 6/29/1969 at 15 in Gilmanton; student; single; b. NH; Sherman Stevens and Mildred A. Ross
Wyatt M., d. 8/16/1912 at 59/1/3; mason; married; b. Belmont; Charles Stevens (Belmont) and Betsey E. Howe (New Hampton)

STEWART,
Warren E., d. 7/1/1920 at 80/7/6 in Laconia; widower; b. Providence, RI; Eric Stewart and Sallie Bailey; Smith Meetinghouse

STICKNEY,
Harold, d. 12/17/1948 at 61/10/14; int. decorator; married; b. Lyman; Sidney Stickney (Lyman) and Nellie Perkins (Guildhall, VT)

STOCK,
Henry, d. 8/11/1926 at 76/10/0 in Haverhill, MA; retired; married; b. Germany; John Stock and Mary -----; Reading, MA

STOCKBRIDGE,
Eugene, d. 1/21/1929 at 1/9/18 in Gilmanton; b. Gilmanton; George Stockbridge and Ina Roby; Smith Meetinghouse
George S., d. 12/14/1950 at 77 in Gilmanton; farmer; married; b. NH; Charles Stockbridge
Harry E., d. 11/9/1979 in Manchester; George Stockbridge and Ina Roby; b. 8/7/1911**
Ina Mildred, d. 12/8/1960 at 73 in Laconia*; housewife; widow; b. Pittsfield; Ernest Roby and Caroline Dowst
Izall M., d. 4/21/1910 at 0/0/4; heart weakness; b. Gilmanton; George Stockbridge (Gilmanton) and Ina M. Roby (Pittsfield)
Joseph S., d. 6/14/1999 in Gilmanton I. W.; George Stockbridge and Ina Roby; b. 9/12/1908**
Ruby P., d. 7/3/1986 in Concord; Cyrus B. Head and Ruby H. Olsen
Shirley B., d. 4/12/1953 at 37 in Wolfeboro*; housewife; married; b. MA; Perley P. Osgood and Laura Sweatt

STOCKWELL,
Harmon Alfred, d. 10/20/1967 at 70 in Gilmanton; store prop., ret.; married; b. Charleston, ME; Oridgen E. Stockwell and Flavella Tibbetts
Leonard A., Sr., d. 7/13/1988 in Gilmanton; Harmon A. Stockwell and Roxey E. Mitchell; b. 10/5/1922**
Roxey E., d. 2/1/1989 in Laconia; Walter Mitchell and Mary E. Heywood; b. 10/22/1900**
Ruth A., d. 7/31/1982 in Laconia; Earl Clifford and Nellie Ellsworth

STONE,
daughter, d. 10/23/1937 at 0/0/0 in Laconia*; b. Laconia; Edward Stone and Elizabeth Pickard; Pine Grove, Gilmanton I. W.
Earl L., d. 12/25/1917 at 3/7/23 in Gilmanton; Fred L. Stone (Franklin) and Mamie Hilliard (Weirs)
Edmund, d. 11/8/1924 at 84 in Concord; farmer; widower; b. Lake Champlain, NY; Joseph Stone and Esther Stone; Pine Grove
Edward, d. 7/8/1906 at 34/3/9; lawyer; married; b. Franklin; Edward Stone (Champlain, NY) and Esther Monte (Canada)

Edward George, d. 1/15/1973 at 62 in Center Harbor*; farmer ret.; divorced; b. NH; Fred L. Stone and Mamie Hilliard

Ester, d. 1/18/1915 at 71 in Gilmanton; married

Florence M., d. 7/14/1934 at 59/1/24 in Gilmanton; housewife; married; b. PEI; George Hubbard and Eliza Jary; Strafford Bow Lake

Fred Lougee, d. 9/21/1938 at 55/0/16 in Laconia*; fireman; widower; b. Franklin; Edmund Stone (NY) and ----- Gregory

George, d. 3/23/1906 at 28/6/14; shoe cutter; single; b. Franklin; Edward Stone (New York, NY) and Esther Monte (Canada)

Hattie E., d. 4/22/1937 at 23 in Gilmanton; housewife; married; b. Laconia; Benjamin F. Rollins; Bayside, Laconia

Kenneth R., d. 10/1/1975 at 63 in Gilmanton; odd jobs; single; b. NH; Fred L. Stone and Mary Hilliard

Mary Louise, d. 12/10/1936 at 43/11/12 in Gilmanton; housewife; married; b. Pittsfield; Frank Bouchard (Canada) and Olivine Biron (Manchester)

STRAW,

Alba Chase, d. 7/23/1940 at 80/2/22*; farmer; widower; b. Barnstead; Thomas S. Straw (Barnstead) and Louisa A. Hill (Barnstead)

Frank Allison, d. 5/20/1963 at 91 in Laconia; millhand; widower; b. Rumney; Luther M. Straw and Mabel M. Straw

STRID,

Folke W., d. 10/21/1962 at 52 in Laconia; painter; married; b. Sweden; Gustave Strid

STROPLE,

Ella Louise, d. 9/12/1964 at 54 in Taunton, MA; teacher; widow; b. Swampscott, MA; Clarence P. Delano and Agnes L. McNutt

George H., d. 1/9/1961 at 65 in Hartford, VT; salesman; married; b. Montreal, Can.; George H. Strople and Catherine A. Holmes

STURGEON,

Albert P., d. 1/3/1982 in Laconia; Joseph N. Sturgeon and Mary J. Fortier; b. 2/27/1921**

STYLES,
Gerald R., d. 10/18/1984 in Laconia; Raymond Styles and Irene Jones
Mary H., d. 8/11/1997 in Laconia; Edward J. Phillips and Doris Carpenter

SULLIVAN,
Dora B., d. 3/1/1971 at 87 in Concord; housewife; widow; b. England; Robert E. Bolton and Dorothy Foster

SUMNER,
Margaret Lippincott, d. 7/25/1995 in Gilmanton; Henry Lippincott and Lulu Lamont; b. 6/5/1915**

SWAIN,
Frances S., d. 3/29/1904 at 74/4/2; housewife; married; b. Gilmanton
George W., d. 6/3/1891 at 34; insurance agent; single; b. Gilmanton; William N. Swain and Mary Chamberlin
Hannah D., d. 8/19/1903 at 86/5/12; widow; b. Gilmanton; Joses Moulton and Hannah Dudley
Mary E., d. 9/8/1892 at 76/5; housewife; married; b. Gilmanton; Moses Bean (Gilmanton) and Mary Shepherd (Gilmanton)
William, d. 2/4/1887 at 76/5/29; farmer; married; b. Gilmanton; Stephen Swain (Hampton) and Nancy Sanborn (Gilmanton)

SWETT,
Herbert S., d. 1/28/1904 at 35/8/5; shoemaker; married
Stanley Fred, d. 9/20/1929 at 0/0/1 in Gilmanton; b. Gilmanton; Fred H. Swett and Stella Patten; Pine Grove

TAPPAN,
Ursule B., d. 5/27/1889 at 73/10/16; housewife; married; b. Sandwich; Josiah Bean (Sandwich) and Olive Sanborn

TASH,
Ernest L., d. 6/20/1975 at 85 in Concord; electrician; widower; b. NH; Frank Tash and Carrie Billings
Nettie F., d. 2/25/1964 at 78 in Wolfeboro; housewife; married; b. Rochester; Clarence Garland and Ada Horn

TAYLOR,
Geraldine B., d. 2/4/1981 in Laconia; Eli C. Bliss and Hannah Ham
James H., d. 12/8/1903 at 25/7/22; painter; married; b. E. Pepperal, MA
Sullivan A., d. 2/24/1902 at 63/1/5; physician; married; b. Strafford; Alfred Taylor

TEBBETTS,
George, d. 12/24/1935 at 81/10/23 in E. Concord; retired; widower; b. Farmington; Joshua Tebbetts and Mary Wentworth; Pine Grove
Martha J., d. 10/23/1890 at 65; housewife; widow; b. Gilmanton; Abraham Gale (Gilmanton) and Martha B. Moulton (Gilmanton)
Mary J., d. 3/5/1890 at 73/6/2; housekeeper; widow; b. Alton; Samuel Coffin (Alton) and Mary Mooney (Alton)

TEMPLE,
Howard I., d. 8/11/1922 at 20

TERRELL,
Fred H., d. 9/4/1923 at 66

TETER,
Martin L., d. 7/5/1919 at 78/10/3 in Gilmanton; farmer; widower; b. NY; Philip Teter and Jane M. Felter; Loudon Ridge
Olive E., d. 4/14/1908 at 70/10/16; housewife; married; b. NY; William Scott (NY) and Hannah ----- (NY)

THERIAULT,
Napoleon, d. 8/3/1924 at 48 in Gilmanton; shoe mfg.; married; b. Montreal, Can.; Napoleon Theriault and Lanzon -----; Haverhill, MA

THIES,
Frank Raymond, d. 6/26/1964 at 61 in Laconia; salesman; married; b. Everett, MA; ----- Thies and Mary Elderfield

THISTLE,
Robert W., d. 4/9/1962 at 72 in Bay Pines, FL; teller (retired); married; b. New York, NY; Robert Thistle and Mathilda Adams

THOMAS,
Alfred J., d. 10/15/1990 in Gilmanton; James Thomas and Laura Gallant

THOMPSON,
daughter, d. 3/12/1933 at 0/0/0 in Pittsfield; b. Pittsfield; Kenneth Thompson and Bernice L. Davis; Hillside
daughter, d. 9/12/1975 at 0/0/2 in Hanover; b. NH; Clement Thompson and Claire Desmarais
Albert W., d. 6/28/1934 at 73/1/23 in Lakewood, OH; janitor; married; b. Gilmanton; William B. Thompson and Luezer J. Asher; Pine Grove
Andrew J., d. 4/28/1953 at 87 in Gilmanton; gold beater; widower; b. Chelsea, MA; Henry F. Thompson and Sabra Kimball
Angela Deloris, d. 4/15/1993 in Manchester; John Delafano and Matilda Caporale
Clement A., d. 10/21/1986 in Wolfeboro; Henry S. Thompson and Beulah E. Horne; b. 6/10/1939**
Henry Stanley, d. 4/25/1959 at 69 in Wolfeboro*; insect & plant control - state forestry dept.; married; b. Ashburnham, MA; Andrew Thompson and Minnie H. Wells
L. Jane, d. 11/10/1900 at 68/4/6; housewife; widow; b. Oldtown, ME
Maro B., d. 10/21/1977 at 75 in Wolfeboro; farmer, ret.; widower; b. NH; Andrew J. Thompson and Minnie Wells
Mary A., d. 8/21/1982 in Hanover; Herman Dame and Edna Banks
Minnie H., d. 1/3/1926 at 56/6/20 in Gilmanton; housework; married; b. Chelsea, MA; Ivory Wells and Ruth S. Stanley; Pine Grove
William B., d. 4/1/1887 at 64/3/15; farmer; married; b. Gilford; William Thompson (Gilmanton) and Lydia Sanborn (Gilmanton)

TIBBETTS,
Edwin C., d. 9/26/1913 at 72/9/29; farmer; married; b. Gilmanton; Henry Tibbetts (Alton) and Mary Coffin (Alton)
Ida May, d. 5/17/1944 at 75/11/12*; at home; widow; b. Alton; Charles H. Perkins (Gilmanton) and Eliza Evans (Gilmanton)

TIERNEY,
George E., d. 5/8/1980 in Gilmanton; Peter Tierney and Annie Duval; b. 7/30/1906**

TILTON,
Lizzie, d. 10/18/1890 at 52; housekeeper; single; b. Gilmanton; Tyler Tilton
William, d. 1/24/1916 at 71/9/6 in Gilmanton; farmer; widower; Amos Tilton and Hannah Cotton

TOBY,
Helen B., d. 7/12/1915 at 73/11/20 in Cambridge, MA; retired; widow; Stephen Bowker and Lizzie S. Tinker

TOLENTI,
Mary Rose, d. 2/10/1963 at 47 in Concord; domestic; single; b. Milford, MA; Joseph Tolenti and Rose Marenghi

TORREY,
Beulah R., d. 9/5/1980 in Concord; Ernest Wells and Laura Jones; b. 5/12/1909**
Burleigh W., d. 12/1/1980 in Laconia; Walter L. Torrey and Alice Turcotte
Charles B., d. 5/3/1950 at 66 in Gilmanton; auctioneer; widower; b. NH; George F. Torrey and Elizabeth Thompson

TOWLE,
Jesse S., d. 9/24/1893 at 82; apoplexy; farmer; widower; b. Hampton; Simon Towle
Mary Ella, d. 5/28/1998 in Gilmanton; George Towle and Madeline -----; b. 4/23/1930**

TOWNE,
Arthur, d. 2/17/1912 at 82; widower

TOWNSEND,
Lydia A., d. 7/4/1904 at 62/10; housewife; married; b. Gilmanton; Samuel Grant (Gilmanton) and Hannah Durrell (Gilmanton)
Thomas, d. 12/16/1904 at 72; laborer; widower

TRAUTWIG,
Gustav H., d. 5/22/1981 in Gilmanton; William M. Trautwig and Lena C. Willrich; b. 6/8/1907**

TRUDELL,
Edith A., d. 5/9/1979 in Laconia; Eric Anderson and Anna Carlson; b. 6/3/1898**
Edmund Albert, d. 1/7/1994 in Laconia; Henry A. Trudell and Ida St. Cyr; b. 9/20/1904**

TUCKER,
Nathan, d. 8/31/1980 in Laconia; Charles Tucker; b. 5/19/1904**

TUTTLE,
George A., d. 4/22/1927 at 60 in Gilmanton; police offi.; married; b. Jefferson; Benjamin Tuttle and Betsy Hall; Jefferson, NH
Marion Etta, d. 4/26/1927 at 68 in Gilmanton; housework; married; b. Jefferson; Levi Stailbard and Mary Stanley; Jefferson, NH
Mary L., d. 1/19/1894 at 56/7/9; pneumonia; housewife; married; b. Gilmanton; Smith G. Dudley and Mary Pillsbury

TWOMBLY,
son, d. 12/26/1964 at – in Laconia*; b. Laconia; Charles A. Twombly and Edith G. Smith
Benjamin K., d. 5/6/1977 at 78 in Laconia; carpenter, ret.; married; b. NH; Dixie C. Twombly and Emma Batchelder
Brackett, d. 4/9/1892 at 71/2/29; shoemaker; single; b. Gilmanton; Paul Twombly (Falmouth, ME) and Sarah Weeks
Charles A., d. 3/5/1916 at 74 in Gilmanton; laborer; married; Benjamin B. Twombly (Gilmanton) and Sarah T. Bean (Gilmanton)
Dixie C., d. 2/25/1940 at 83/6/23; carpenter; married; b. Lakeport; Benjamin Twombly (Gilmanton) and Sarah T. Bean (Gilmanton)
Emma Mabel, d. 7/27/1952 at 85 in Concord; housewife; widow; b. NH; George H. Batchelder and Sarah J. Bickford
Fred W., d. 12/18/1971 at 79 in Concord*; contractor; married; b. NH; Dixie C. Twombly and Emma Batchelder
Gertrude A., d. 8/1/1994 in Wolfeboro; Seldon Rollins and Alma Ellis
Herbert A., d. 6/6/1942 at 77/0/13; carpenter; b. Gilmanton; Benjamin B. Twombly (Gilmanton) and Sarah Bean (Gilmanton)
Margaret E., d. 7/6/1977 at 70 in Laconia; housewife; widow; b. NH; James O'Brien and Cora Wentworth

Samuel M., d. 6/18/1887 at 65/3/12; laborer; married; b. Gilmanton; Ralph Twombly (Barnstead) and Nancy Morrison (Gilmanton)

ULMANIS,
Elmars, d. 1/28/1971 at 48 in Laconia; castings; divorced; b. Latvia; Karl Ulmanis

UNDERHILL,
Arden R., d. 2/26/1950 at 79/9/0 in Laconia; farm. & carp.; widower; b. Orange; Frank Underhill and Harriet Folsom

UPTON,
Henry W., d. 11/28/1906 at 23/9/12; clerk; widower; b. Everett, MA; Charles H. Upton and Abbie M. Brown

URQUHART,
Nelson A., d. 3/4/1992 in Laconia; Rodrick Urquhart and Katherine McCloud

VALAS,
Frank W., d. 9/17/1982 in Laconia; Alexander B. Vallasavich and Anelia Shuipes

VALLIERE,
Lazer Freeman, d. 8/28/1951 at 63/1/27 in Gilmanton; fireman (ret.); widower; b. Canada

VALPEY,
Nancy H., d. 12/25/1927 at 91/1/23 in Boston, MA; widow; b. Lynn, MA; Addison Newhall and Edith Guilford; Pine Grove

VAN BROCKLEN,
James W., d. 7/11/1972 at 74 in Concord; retired; single; b. NH; Warren Van Brocklen and Ella Stevens

VARNEY,
Adaline, d. 1/15/1892 at 66/9/10; housewife; married; Edmund Canney (Tuftonboro) and Betsey Brewster (Barrington)
Charles, d. 4/5/1889 at 87/3; farmer; widower; b. Dover; Nathaniel Varney (Dover) and Sarah Weymouth (Lee)

Charles C., d. 2/26/1901 at 66/6/4; farmer; widower; b. Gilmanton; Charles C. Varney (Dover) and Nancy Peaslee (Gilmanton)

Cynthia, d. 3/19/1929 at 77/6/10 in Gilmanton; single; b. Loudon; Richard D. Varney and Mary Peaslee; Pine Grove

Cyrus, d. 4/19/1907 at 83/8/28; blacksmith; widower; Othaniel Varney (Dover) and Anna Jones (Gilmanton)

Edwin, d. 8/1/1898 at 56/7; farmer; married; b. Gilmanton; Richard J. Varney and Mamni May

Frank R., d. 9/5/1975 at 91 in Laconia; land developer; single; b. NH; Edmund C. Varney and Laura E. Varney

George Brett, d. 2/14/1958 at 83 in Gilmanton; engineer - ret.; single; b. Gilmanton; Edwin Varney and Julia Brett

Georgie, d. 12/13/1891 at 46; housewife; married

Henry A., d. 4/10/1941 at 70/10/3; town engineer; widower; b. Gilmanton; Edwin Varney (Gilmanton) and Julia F. Brett (Bridgewater, MA)

Julia Franklin, d. 6/30/1925 at 80/3/19 in Gilmanton; widow; b. N. Bridgewater, MA; Zena F. Brett and Julia Tilden; Friends Cem.

Mary P., d. 2/13/1896 at 76/0/8; housewife; married; b. Pittsfield; Samuel Peaslee and Mary Jones

Naomi M., d. 4/9/1896 at 87/4/12; old age; housewife; married; b. Barton, VT; James May and Elizabeth Owen

Richard D., d. 9/26/1900 at 81; farmer; widower

Richard Frank, d. 6/12/1968 at 95 in Gilmanton; contractor, ret.; single; b. NH; Edwin Varney and Julia Brett

Richard J., d. 1/25/1899 at 86/2; farmer; widower; b. Gilmanton; Othaniel Varney

William, d. 11/1/1918 at 71; table decoration; single; b. Gilmanton

VEAZEY,
Julia A., d. 10/31/1922 at 65

VON BERNUTH,
Frederick A., d. 8/15/1917 at 82/10/1 in Gilmanton; retired merchant; married; Emil A. Von Bernuth (Prussia) and Louise Torpeck (Prussia)

Frederick A., d. 7/22/1947 at 82/4/18; pres. Cervon Inc.; married; b. Newark, NJ; Frederick Augustus von Bernuth Sr. (Germany) and Carrie Kitchen (Newark, NJ)

VOREL,
Herman, d. 1/31/1967 at 66 in Concord*; leather worker; married; b. Peabody, MA; Anthony Vorel and Mary Schope

WADE,
Henry E., d. 1/17/1908 at 9/2/17; b. Gilford; Edward D. Wade (Gilford) and Sadie Senter (Gilford)

WALDRON,
Herbert L., d. 8/16/1984 in Gilmanton; Charles O. Waldron and Clara Janvrin

WALKER,
Joseph J., d. 6/30/1972 at 63 in Laconia*; mechanic; single; b. PA; ----- and Edna M. Robinson

WALLER,
Helen K., d. 2/23/1970 at 77 in Laconia; housewife; widow; b. CT; Rueban Keeler and Hattie Isabelle

WALTERS,
Geraldine E., d. 4/5/1931 at 62/7/7 in Concord; retired; widow; b. Edinburgh; Gould C. McAlpine and Anna H. Osgood; Pine Grove

WANGER,
Michael John, d. 5/6/1970 at 0/1/28 in Meredith*; b. NH; ----- and Wandalee H. Wanger

WARBURTON,
Clara H., d. 4/24/1972 at 80 in Rochester*; housewife; widow; b. NH; John T. Elkins and Cora B. Ham
John Henry, d. 9/3/1963 at 81 in Gilmanton*; farmer; married; b. Liverpool, England; Henry Warburton and Mary J. Royle

WARD,
Mildred Ruth, d. 3/23/1993 in Laconia; James Snow and Winifred Carey; b. 6/9/1913**

WATERS,
Maude L., d. 6/19/1956 at 70 in Wolfeboro; housewife; widow; b. Barre, VT; George B. McLean and Amy H. Lee

WATSON,
John, d. 9/5/1901 at 76; farmer; widower; b. Alton; ----- and Mary Spencer (Strafford)
John D., d. 12/24/1927 at 69/9/4 in Concord; Pine Grove
Joseph, Jr., d. 5/20/1905 at 84/2/11; farmer; widower; b. Alton; Joseph Watson
Julius H., d. 4/2/1889 at 24; laborer; single
Martha S., d. 3/9/1976 at 91 in Bedford; housewife; widow; b. NH; William Parsons, M.D. and Marion Hosley
Maurice, d. 6/22/1936 at 62/1/20 in Gilmanton; physician; married; b. Haverhill; Henry P. Watson (Haverhill) and Evelyn Marshall (N. Stratford)
Mrs. John, d. 3/25/1900 at 75; housewife; married; b. Alton; Simon Foss (Strafford)
William H., d. 9/14/2000 in Laconia; Maurice Watson and Martha Parsons; b. 9/1/1917**

WATTS,
Zelma Griffin, d. 8/20/1978 at 74 in Plymouth; teacher; widow; b. Gilmanton; Nathan D. Griffin and Eva Osborne

WAUGH,
Mary Madline, d. 12/31/1963 at 58 in Concord*; school teacher; married; b. Peabody, MA; William Wrest and Annie Byrnes

WAYSHNOR,
John Joseph, d. 9/4/1960 at 69 in Gilmanton*; cook's helper; single; b. Lithuania; John Wayshnor and Ursula Gritz

WEARE,
Charles D., d. 6/2/1934 at 86 in Alton; farmer; married; b. Deerfield; Gardner Weare and Abigail Young; Pine Grove
Emma H., d. 5/14/1906 at 64/4/21; housewife; married
Nettie M., d. 9/2/1935 at 68/4/12 in Alton; housewife; widow; Pine Grove

WEBSTER,
Benjamin F., d. 1/6/1912 at 63/8/27; farmer; married; b. Gilmanton; Caleb P. Webster (Gilmanton) and Eliza Ann Lougee (Gilmanton)
Caleb, d. 1/18/1906 at 82; farmer; widower; b. Gilmanton
Elizabeth, d. 7/21/1932 at 73/0/4 in Gilmanton; widow; b. Fredericton, NB; Mares Smith and Elizabeth Cook; Smith Meetinghouse
Marjorie Ellen, d. 7/6/1967 at 77 in Gilmanton; housewife; married; b. Alexandria; Warren Pitman and Julia Tappan
Martha J., d. 4/1/1895 at 68; pneumonia; housewife; married; b. Gilmanton; Joseph Sanborn and Lydia Kelley (Gilmanton)
Martha J., d. 2/18/1937 at 83/0/3 in Concord*; retired; widow; b. Gilmanton; John Watson and Abbie B. Foss; Pine Grove, Gilmanton I. W.
Ruth H., d. 4/10/1978 at 66 in Laconia; office manager; married; b. MA; Harry Harris and Mildred Connors
William C., d. 1/26/1972 at 81 in Concord*; machinist; widower; b. NH; Benjamin F. Webster and Elizabeth Smith

WEED,
Albert H., d. 9/24/1929 at 74/2/7 in Gilmanton; farmer; single; b. Gilmanton; Lewis Weed and Ann M. Knowles; Beech Grove
Ann M., d. 1/20/1908 at 82/6/3; widow; b. Gilmanton; Joseph Knowles
Beverly W., d. 9/10/1941 at 28/4/10; housewife; married; b. San Antonio, TX; Edward A. Fitzgerald (Peoria, IL) and Winifred Woods (Amboy, IL)
Charles Henry, d. 5/3/1938 at 74/11/5 in Gilmanton; farmer; single; b. Gilmanton; Lewis Weed (Gilmanton) and Ann M. Knowles (Belmont)
Hannah Jane, d. 8/22/1936 at 75/11/12 in Gilmanton; at home; single; b. Gilmanton; Lewis Weed (Gilmanton) and Ann M. Knowles (Belmont)
Lewis, d. 8/9/1903 at 84/2/26; farmer; married; b. Gilmanton; Jesse Weed
Nellie M., d. 2/11/1941 at 71/1/21*; housework; single; b. Gilmanton; Louis Weed (Gilmanton) and Ann M. Knowles

WEEKS,
Alice B., d. 12/11/1933 at 39/3/6 in Laconia; housewife; married; b. Sanbornton; Joseph Bailey and Sarah Turcotte; Beech Grove
Bertha B., d. 6/6/1923 at 47
Charlotte Esther, d. 4/25/1917 at 53/7/25 in Gilmanton; housewife; married; Andrew Mace (ME) and Abbie M. Silsbee (Lynn, MA)
Elwin S., d. 10/24/1944 at 16/0/7; single; b. Belmont; Sumner I. Weeks (Gilmanton) and Elise M. Thompson (Belmont)
Herbert N., d. 9/28/1917 at 57/9/1 in Gilmanton; farmer; married; Noah J. Weeks and Sarah McNeil
Laurinda, d. 7/26/1905 at 73/6/26; widow; b. Colebrook; Barnes Hilliard (CT) and Judith Weeks (Gilmanton)
Leonard, d. 2/27/1887 at 52; farmer; married; b. Northwood
Lilla A., d. 9/2/1925 at 50/1/25 in Gilmanton; widow; Seward Durgin and Anna Sanborn; Beech Grove
Manley H. L., d. 3/10/1934 at 32/8/8 in Laconia; farmer; widower; b. Gilmanton; Herbert N. Weeks and Lilla Downing; Beech Grove
Marcus S., d. 3/28/1918 at 70/0/26; farmer; married; b. Gilmanton; Noah Weeks and Sarah McNeal
Mary L., d. 4/21/1898 at 62/6; housekeeper; single
Matthias, d. 9/3/1894 at 69/10/13; heart trouble; farmer; married; b. Gilmanton; Stephen Weeks (Gilmanton) and Betsy Weed
Noah, d. 1/12/1896 at 75/11; heart failure; farmer; widower; b. Alton; Henry M. Weeks
Sarah Ann, d. 6/4/1894 at 73/3; consumption; housewife; married; Jonathan McNeal
Stephen L., d. 11/28/1925 at 55/0/28 in Gilmanton; farmer; widower; b. Gilmanton; Mathias Weeks and Laurinda Hilliard; Loudon Ridge
Sylvia F., d. 4/14/1935 at 83/5/6 in Gilmanton; at home; widow; b. Belmont; Jeremiah Kimball and Lavina Sanborn; South Road
William H., d. 11/21/1926 at 79/2/22 in Loudon; farmer; single; b. Loudon; Stephen Weeks and Elizabeth Haynes; Buzzell Cem.

WELCH,
Marian, d. 1/29/1988 in Concord
Smith A., d. 12/19/1932 at 81/10/17 in Gilmanton; farmer; married; Larson Welch and Elizabeth Smith; Pittsfield

WELLS,
son, d. 2/3/1932 at 0/0/0 in Gilmanton; b. Gilmanton; E. Russell Wells and Laura Hanson; Smith Meetinghouse
Dorothea L., d. 4/23/1980 in Concord; Wilbur Lucia and Nell Ashcroft; b. 1/21/1910**
Fred Roscoe, d. 11/11/1958 at 53 in Hanover*; lumberman; divorced; b. Gilmanton; Ernest L. Wells and Laura Jones
Herbert, Sr., d. 11/11/1975 at 76 in Peterborough; retired elec.; widower; b. ME; Howard A. Wells and Justena A. Sadler
Laura, d. 2/21/1920 at 38/0/15 in Gilmanton; housewife; married; b. Gilmanton; Joseph Jones and ----- Gleason; Smith Meetinghouse
Laura F., d. 5/28/1966 at 64 in Concord*; housewife; married; b. Malden, MA; Sidney Hanson and Lura Nutter

WENTWORTH,
J. Frank, d. 10/10/1905 at 29/4/2; farmer; married; b. Gilmanton; John Wentworth and Sarah Hutchinson
John, d. 5/29/1887 at 80; farmer; married; b. Ossipee; John Wentworth
Sarah, d. 3/14/1892 at –; housewife; widow

WEST,
Herbert, d. 1/25/1974 at 73 in Laconia; printer; married; b. MA; Arthur West and Anna Brace

WHEELER,
Herbert A., d. 12/16/1967 at 67 in Concord; ass't. secretary; married; b. Parishville, NY; John Wheeler and Edna Latrace Wheeler

WHIPPLE,
Cecil L., d. 9/29/1898 at 2/7/6; b. Manchester; George E. Whipple (Kingston) and Frances M. Knight (Biddeford, ME)

WHITE,
Bertha M., d. 7/13/1986 in Laconia; John G. Pool and Margaret J. E. Cunningham

WHITEHOUSE,
Nellie C., d. 4/30/1929 at 50/8/20 in Laconia; housewife; married; b. Gilmanton; Dixie E. Page and Cyrena Webster; Smith Meetinghouse
Robert A., d. 2/22/1933 at 54/9/11 in Laconia; harness maker; widower; b. Troy, VT; Enos Whitehouse and Maria Brown; Smith Meetinghouse

WHITHED,
Mardis O., d. 5/17/1977 at 66 in Concord; agric. manager, ret.; married; b. MA; ----- Whithed and Myrtia L. Cook

WHITLEY,
George Q., d. 11/6/1971 at 64 in Laconia; seaman; single; b. MA; James I. Whitley and Anna Nilson
John Henry, d. 12/19/1968 at 66 in Laconia; cabinet maker; single; b. MA; James I. Whitley and Anna Nilson

WHITNEY,
David K., d. 8/15/1912 at 39/10/22; painter; married; b. Albany, NY; Chauncy Whitney (Albany, NY) and Estell W. Hagadron (Albany, NY)

WIGHT,
Albert R., d. 5/4/1915 at 72/8/5 in Gilmanton; farmer; married; Nahum Wight (Gilead, ME) and Mary A. Straw (Newfield, ME)
Emma F., d. 8/7/1922 at 71
Marion M., d. 11/15/1905 at 0/11/11; b. Gilmanton; Nahum Wight (Gilmanton) and Florence Leland (Ryegate, VT)
Mary Ann, d. 1/31/1970 at 89 in Gilmanton; teacher; single; b. NH; Albert R. Wight and Emma F. Jones
Nahum, d. 12/28/1905 at 30/3/27; butter maker; married; b. Gilmanton; Albert R. Wight (Gilmanton) and Emma F. Jones (Gilmanton)

WILKENS,
William B., Jr., d. 9/28/1959 at 20 in Laconia*; student; married; b. New York, NY; William B. Wilkens, Sr. and Laurose Schutz-Berge
William Bernard, d. 5/4/1997 in Gilmanton; Charles Wilkens and Elise Mayer; b. 10/9/1909**

WILKINSON,
   Sarah Jane, d. 3/19/1920 at 76/10/23 in Gilmanton; none [occ.];
      widow; b. Laconia; Hubbard Jackson and Naomi Lewis;
      Laconia

WILLARD,
   Arthur E., Sr., d. 7/4/1981 in Laconia; Israel R. Willard and Georgia
      McClary; b. 10/8/1916**
   Edward L., d. 4/20/1981 in Gilmanton; Arthur E. Willard, Sr. and
      Mary C. Heinis; b. 8/12/1950**
   Georgie Floremce, d. 5/5/1965 at 75 in Laconia*; housewife; widow;
      b. Gilmanton; Joseph McClary and Frances Adams
   Hazel B., d. 2/13/1920 at 24/9/3 in Laconia; housewife; married; b.
      Gilmanton; Charles Batchelder and ----- Staples; Alton
   Israel, d. 6/11/1954 at 65 in Gilmanton; sawyer, ret.; married; b.
      Gilmanton; Daniel Willard and Emmaritta Thomson
   Mary C., d. 4/21/1988 in Gilmanton; Louis Heinis, Sr. and Florence
      Smith; b. 2/6/1918**

WILLIAMS,
   son, d. 6/13/1887 at 0/0/2; b. Gilmanton; Henry Williams (Bellows
      Falls) and Nellie M. Burbank (Hopkinton)
   Flossie, d. 7/16/1894 at 1/2; cholera infantum; Henry Williams and
      Nellie Burbank
   Parke A., d. 1/9/1989 in Gilmanton; Albert Williams and Adeline
      Woodward

WILSON,
   Ada E., d. 2/24/1957 at 69 in Concord; housewife; married; b.
      Augusta, ME; James Chadbourne and Emma Roderick
   Benning, d. 2/19/1903 at 76/7; married; Benning Wilson and Nancy
      Gumerson
   Charles A., d. 2/19/1913 at 3/3/26; b. Gilmanton
   Mary, d. 7/8/1901 at 23/10/14; single; b. E. Boston, MA
   Selina M., d. 11/14/1909 at 56/7/6; laundress; widow; b.
      Gottenburg, Sweden; Samuel Olsen (Sweden)

WING,
   daughter, d. 2/24/1962 at – in Laconia; b. Laconia; Ormond Lee
      Wing and Honora Marie MacLellan

Douglas Stephen, d. 1/21/1964 at 0/0/5 in Laconia; b. Laconia; Ormond L. Wing and Honora M. MacLellan
Kimberly Jo, d. 12/22/1964 at 0/0/2 in Laconia; b. Laconia; Ormond L. Wing and Honora M. MacLellan

WITHAM,
Ezekiel, d. 2/6/1925 at 84/4/25 in Gilmanton; veteran ret.; married; b. New Gloucester, ME; Pine Grove

WOLFENDEN,
Leonard, d. 4/13/1974 at 65 in Laconia; textile worker; married; b. RI; Henry Wolfenden and Lily Buchanan

WONG,
Alice A., d. 8/18/1956 at 84 in Gilmanton; teacher - housewife; married; b. Belmont; George Abbott and Ellen Allen

WOOD,
Evelyn S., d. 10/22/1926 at 69/2/12; shoemaker; widow; b. Gilmanton; Levi Plummer and Elizabeth Rollins; Guinea Ridge
Fred E., d. 12/24/1932 at 75/10/28 in Gilmanton; retired; married; b. Sandown; Granville Wood and Electa Eastman; Detroit, MI
Margaret M., d. 1/24/1938 at 80/0/15 in Gilmanton; retired; widow; b. ON; Henry G. Habbin (England) and Elizabeth Belchambe (England)

WOODBURY,
Clarence E., d. 2/4/1981 in Concord; Joseph Woodbury and Mary –; b. 2/8/1905

WOODS,
May L., d. 2/12/1941 at 88/7/25; at home; widow; b. Danville, PQ; Samuel Doying and Mary Carlyle

WOODWARD,
Horace C., d. 3/8/1890 at 76/5/5

WORTHINGTON,
George, d. 5/31/1898 at 60/4/27; wheelwright; married; b. Oxford, CT; Thomas Worthington

WOZNY,
Joseph Anthony, d. 8/31/1973 at 60 in Gilmanton; maintenance sup. ret.; married; b. MA; Anthony Wozny

WRIGHT,
Harriet M., d. 8/16/1900 at 54/10/8; housewife; married; b. Barnet, VT; Hezekiah Cummings (Peacham, VT) and Harriet M. Bun (Williamston, VT)

WUDYKA,
Linda Ann, d. 7/5/1990 in Concord; Joseph Kalolsky and Anna Kieon; b. 8/22/1947**

WYSKIEL,
Barbara B., d. 10/20/1995 in Laconia; Leo Bertrand and Myrtle Burch

YELSKIE[S],
Anthony, d. 12/23/1978 at 93 in Laconia; janitor; single; b. Lithuania

YORK,
Fred Albert, d. 4/28/1952 at 89 in Alton; teamster; widower; b. NH; Wells C. York and Mary Parsons
Martha A., d. 11/11/1934 at 69/5/2 in Gilmanton; housewife; married; b. Medford, ME; William Spencer and Hannah Rogers; Pine Grove

YOST,
Laverna, d. 7/28/1976 at 78 in Laconia; housewife; married; b. OH; Grant Imes and Hattie Rose

YOUNG,
Cora Frances, d. 8/17/1943 at 80/3/5; housewife; married; b. Alton; Charles F. Lougee (Alton) and Eleanor Glidden (Alton)
Eben S., d. 8/25/1943 at 89/6/22; retired farmer; widower; b. Gilmanton; Johnathan Young (Gilmanton) and Martha Nelson (Gilmanton)
Frank D., d. 2/10/1939 at 82/8/9 in Gilmanton; farmer; single; b. Gilmanton; Jonathan Young (Gilmanton) and Martha Nelson (Gilmanton)

Frederick B., d. 2/15/1929 at 62/1/20 in Gilmanton; farmer; married; b. Rumney; Pine Grove

George E., d. 10/11/1948 at 33/11/24; truck driver's assistant; married; b. Roslindale, MA; Percy J. Young (Lakeport) and Anna M. Downing (Cambridge, MA)

Jessie E., d. 12/9/1978 at 84 in Peabody, MA; sales rec. ret.; widow; b. NY

Jonathan, d. 4/2/1900 at 82/1/17; farmer; widower; b. Gilmanton; David S. Young (Gilmanton) and Betsy Avery (Gilmanton)

Levi T., d. 1/14/1908 at 93/3/17; carpenter; widower; b. Gilmanton; Nathaniel Young and Martha Tuttle

Lucy A., d. 1/26/1916 at 83/11/16 in Gilmanton; widow; ----- Prescott

Mae Louise, d. 2/1/1965 at 68 in Laconia; housewife; married; b. Post Mills, VT; Fred Stone and Tirzah Howland

Nathaniel, d. 8/1/1892 at 68/4/24; farmer; married; b. Gilmanton; David S. Young (Gilmanton) and Betsey Avery (Thornton)

Nellie G., d. 1/25/1941 at 65/8/28*; housewife; widow; b. St. Bridget, PQ; William O. Grady (Canada) and Mary Ann Kane (Canada)

Samuel S., d. 2/18/1889 at 95/1; farmer; widower; b. Gilmanton

Sarah A., d. 7/2/1895 at 86/10; heart disease, dropsy; housekeeper; widow; b. Portland, ME; Abram Knight (Portland, ME) and Hannah Woodard

ZANES,

Noah M., d. 2/26/1929 at 75/11/13 in Gilmanton; stone mason; married; b. Pembroke; William Zanes and Abbie Marshall; Smith Meetinghouse

William B., d. 9/8/1948 at 61/5/23*; mechanic; married; b. Pittsfield; Noah Zanes and Nellie Blake

ZIMMERMAN,

Carle C., d. 2/7/1983 in Gilmanton; Charles P. Zimmerman and Lucinda Peyton

Madeleine A., d. 2/27/1989 in Laconia; Charles Andrist and Emily Miller

ZVACHS,
Joseph, d. 10/10/1939 at 57/9/9 in Gilmanton; carpenter; married;
    b. Austria; John Zvachs (Austria) and Paula Zilichovsky
    (Austria)
Paula Maria, d. 2/23/1958 at 73 in Laconia; housewife; widow; b.
    Austria; ----- Zilichousky

Other Heritage Books by Richard P. Roberts:

Alton, New Hampshire Vital Records, 1890–1997

Barnstead, New Hampshire Vital Records, 1887–2000

Barrington, New Hampshire Vital Records

Dover, New Hampshire Death Records, 1887–1937

Gilmanton, New Hampshire Vital Records, 1887–2001

Marriage Records of Dover, New Hampshire, 1835–1909

Marriage Records of Dover, New Hampshire, 1910–1937

Milton, New Hampshire Vital Records, 1888–1999

Moultonborough, New Hampshire Vital Records

New Castle, New Hampshire Vital Records, 1891–1997

New Hampshire Name Changes, 1768–1923

New Hampshire Name Changes, 1923–1947

Ossipee, New Hampshire Vital Records, 1887–2001

Rochester, New Hampshire Death Records, 1887–1951

Vital Records of Durham, New Hampshire, 1887–2002

Vital Records of Effingham and Freedom, New Hampshire, 1888–2001

Vital Records of Farmington, New Hampshire, 1887–1938

Vital Records of Lyme and Dorchester, New Hampshire, 1887–2004

Vital Records of New Durham and Middleton, New Hampshire, 1887–1998

Vital Records of North Berwick, Maine, 1892–2002

Vital Records of Orford and Piermont, New Hampshire, 1887–2004

Vital Records of Pittsburg, New Hampshire, 1904–2008

Vital Records of Sandwich, New Hampshire, 1887–2007

Vital Records of Tamworth and Albany, New Hampshire, 1887–2003

Vital Records of Tuftonboro and Brookfield, New Hampshire, 1888–2005

Vital Records of Wakefield, New Hampshire, 1887–1998

Vital Records of Warren, New Hampshire, 1887–2005

Wolfeboro, New Hampshire Vital Records, 1887–1999

www.ingramcontent.com/pod-product-compliance
Lightning Source LLC
Chambersburg PA
CBHW071932240426
43668CB00038B/1247